THE DOCTRINE

OF THE

GREEK ARTICLE

APPLIED TO

THE CRITICISM AND ILLUSTRATION

OF THE

NEW TESTAMENT.

BY THE LATE RIGHT REV.
THOMAS FANSHAW MIDDLETON, D.D.
LORD BISHOP OF CALCUTTA.

Articuli certe naturæ cognitio sat est necessaria, quamvis cum publico malo Ecclesiæ hæc soleant, non sine suspicione pudendæ ignorantiæ, rideri.
BOHLIUS IN THESAURO THEOL. PHILOL.

WITH PREFATORY OBSERVATIONS AND NOTES BY
HUGH JAMES ROSE, B.D.
LATE JOINT-DEAN OF BOCKING.

NEW EDITION.

Wipf & Stock
PUBLISHERS
Eugene, Oregon

Wipf and Stock Publishers
199 W 8th Ave, Suite 3
Eugene, OR 97401

The Doctrine of the Greek Article
Applied to the Criticism and Illustration of the New Testament
By Middleton, Thomas Fanshaw
ISBN: 1-59752-223-6
Publication date 5/25/2005
Previously published by J. G. F. & J. Rivington, 1841

TO

MRS. MIDDLETON,

WHO, IN THE WORDS OF HER HUSBAND, WAS

" THE COMPANION OF ALL HIS TRAVELS,

" THE DEPOSITORY OF ALL WHICH HE THOUGHT,

" AND THE TRANSCRIBER OF ALMOST EVERY THING HE WROTE,"

THIS NEW EDITION

OF HIS CHIEF WORK IS INSCRIBED,

WITH EVERY FEELING OF RESPECT AND SYMPATHY.

PRELIMINARY OBSERVATIONS.

BY THE EDITOR.

THE last edition of Bishop Middleton's work on the Greek Article (published in 1828) being exhausted, application has been made to me to superintend a new edition, with such additions as I should judge advisable. Having long felt the highest veneration for Bishop Middleton's character and abilities, I heartily rejoice at finding any opportunity of testifying my feelings towards him, and regret only that my powers second my inclinations so ill, that any thing which I can add to a work of his must be unworthy of it and of him.

I wish to say a few words on the work itself, and then to state what I have endeavoured to do in the present edition.

The inquiry into the Greek Article is a work to which sufficient justice has not been done in this country. I have been surprised to find how many men to whom I am accustomed to look with the highest respect, have not even read the volume [1],

---

[1] The rapid sale of the last edition is rather owing, I think, to the value justly set upon Bishop Middleton's notes on the New Testament, than to any interest in the theory of which he intended them only as the illustration. I may perhaps add here, that, as I have found no *formal* objections made to Bishop Middleton's theory, I have thought that Mr. Le Bas's call for a full discussion of the question, would, on the whole, be best complied with by noticing such observations of modern critics as *appear* to be inconsistent with the Bishop's rules, leaving his powerful reasoning in defence of them to speak for itself. See Mr. Le Bas's admirable Life of Bishop Middleton, vol. i. p. 11.

and how little its real doctrines and real value are known. One reason probably is, that as it does not consist of detached and unconnected rules, but is, in point of fact, a very refined and ingenious theory, professing, at least, to account for all the usages of the Article on one principle, it cannot be examined in parts, but must be considered as a whole. As a whole, it appears to me to be a very remarkable specimen of metaphysical acuteness and subtilty; such, indeed, as to require very close and very patient attention, that a due estimate of the theory on which they are employed may be formed. Such attention, I must think, would not be ill bestowed. Even they who have collected only such partial and detached rules for the use of the Article as the observations of various Critics supply, have learnt from them the extreme importance of the Article, and would readily confess, that a principle which would account for its use universally, (i. e. with such few exceptions as must obtain in every language, in the case of a part of speech used at every instant,) would be a matter of very great consequence indeed. Nor would they who are most skilled in the habits and history of languages, be the slowest to believe in the existence of such a rule, notwithstanding the exceptions to which I have alluded. Now Bishop Middleton's inquiry, at all events, *professes* to point out such a principle. They who knew the man, or who know any thing of his critical powers from his remarks on the N. T., might believe, without difficulty, that he was no framer or encourager of wild theories; and that though, like all men, he may have been deceived, his powerful, severe, and thoughtful mind would never have laid before the public any thoughts which had not been long weighed, and rigorously brought to every test which his powers and learning would supply. A *prima facie* case for the fair examination of the Inquiry is thus, I think, made out; and the importance of the matter is such, that it is very much to be wished that they who have the means and time, would confute Bishop Middleton, if he be

PRELIMINARY OBSERVATIONS.

wrong, or would add their testimony to his theory, if they find it correct. Nothing of this sort, however, has appeared, with the exception of Professor Scholefield's testimony, in the Preface to the last edition. I have heard it, indeed, said of one or two great scholars, now dead, that they did not believe in Bishop Middleton's theory; but I have never heard any thing more definite as to their objections, than that one of them stated that Bishop Middleton always chose his MS. This applies, of course, only to the illustrations of the theory from the N. T.; but, when Bishop Middleton's notes on the N. T. are examined, I do not think that the objection can have any weight. If rules are laid down for the use of any word, and, where those rules are broken in a received text, MSS. either good or many, supply various readings *which support the rules*, surely not only can there be no objection to the appeal to such MSS., but the rules themselves are almost as much confirmed as by their being observed in the text. I may safely appeal to the reader of Bishop Middleton's notes, to say whether he is in the habit of calling in the assistance of one MS. against the authority of many, or of bad MSS. against good ones.

As far as my own observation has gone, I must say, unhesitatingly, that I have found the violations of Bishop Middleton's rules very rare: but I am sensible that my own reading for critical purposes has latterly been so much interrupted by bad health and other occupations, that my testimony is of little moment.

There are now a few observations which appear to me not unworthy of the attention of those who are inclined to consider Bishop Middleton's theory.

First, I would observe that one of his rules, *not connected with his theory*, is proved *fully* by instances, viz. that *definite* Nouns used κατ' ἐξοχήν, and requiring the Article on that account, nevertheless lose it very often when occurring after a Preposition [1]. Now this fact, as Bishop Middleton mentions, has not been observed by Philologers [2], and consequently a very large class of instances which they are perpetually bringing to prove the existence of anomalies of a different kind, must go for nothing. Thus Schäfer (on Plutarch, vol. ii. p. 286, v. 35, Anim. vol. v. p. 126,) says on εἰς πόλιν ἀπὸ στρατοπέδου, ' In his *similibusque τοπικοῖς nihil interest addatur articulus an omittatur ;*' and he quotes from the same page, εἰς τὸ στρατόπεδον, ἐν τῇ πόλει and ἐκ τῆς πόλεως. Unless other instances can be brought, his remark is not valid [3]. Again, Stallbaum (on Plat. de Rep. ii. p. 378, D.) says that the Article is often omitted before υἱὸς and πατήρ; but the only instances which he brings there are after ὑπό. Heindorf (ad Gorg. p. 523.) gives seven instances of omission of the Article with γῆ, but they are all after Prepositions.

[1] This is as remarkable in English as in Greek. *From beginning to end, from top to bottom, from East to West ; by coach, by ship ; by sea, by land ; by day, by night ; up town, about house ; in shade, at church.*

The first three instances are cases of Correlatives ; in the next two, there is a tacit reference, I think, to a Correlative ; the next four are cases of words where the same liberty is taken occasionally without a Preposition ; the two next cases are common Provincialisms.

[2] See, however, my quotation in p. 98. I see too that Poppo in his Index to Xenophon's Anabasis, voce θάλαττα, notices the occasional omission of the Article with this word *after some Prepositions.* It is difficult to say on which side the following remark of Krüger (on Dion. Hal. Hist. p. 95.) ought to be cited : 'Articulus in tritis his μετὰ Ἰλίου, μετὰ Εὐβοίας ἅλωσιν non adscisci solet.' Heindorf (on Plat. Theætet. p. 20. A. Ἐν δὲ κιθαριστοῦ) observes the omission of the Article in such expressions. This arises, of course, from the writer knowing that he might not improperly omit it in the Correlative governed by the Preposition.

[3] In his Meletemata, p. 116. Schäfer's instances are still worse. Soph. Trach. 256. σὺν παισὶ καὶ γυναικί. Soph. Fr. ap. Schol. ad Aj. 190. μητρὸς φθορεύς, where φθορεὺς is the Predicate, and thus μητρὸς loses the Article rightly. Xen. An. vii. 8, 9. and 22. are both cases of enumeration. Eustath. ad Iliad. p. 405. 31. and 307. 25. ἁμὰ παισί. And then, strange to say, Schäfer goes on to give instances where the Article *is* used with γυνή, &c. &c.

PRELIMINARY OBSERVATIONS.

It may not be worth while to multiply instances under this head, (they are indeed too numerous to admit of citation,) but the Student must not neglect, when he finds Critics asserting that such and such words are used without the Article, and inferences are thence drawn, that there is no regularity as to its use, &c., &c., to examine the instances, and see whether very many of them are not attributable to this fact respecting the Preposition¹. I have observed below that a large portion of Winer's examples are of the kind alluded to.

The same remark applies to another anomaly pointed out by Bishop Middleton, viz. the omission of the Article in *Enumerations*². Thus we have in Plat. de Rep. p. 574, Ἀντεχομένων δὴ καὶ μαχομένων γέροντός τε καὶ γραός, where, these words being used in the sense of *father* and *mother*, Stallbaum adduces the instances to show that in such cases of relationship the Article is omitted. So in Plat. Crito, p. 51. A. (μητρός τε καὶ πατρὸς καὶ τῶν ἄλλων προγόνων ἁπάντων τιμιώτερόν ἐστι πατρίς,) where Stallbaum remarks that the Article is omitted before πατήρ³, μήτηρ, παῖς, ἀδελφός, γῆ, πόλις, ἀγρός, when used *de genere in universum*, the two first words of the quotation supply no instance. Matthiæ again (268. obs. 2.) quotes Xen. Cyrop. vi. 3. 8. Συνεκάλεσε καὶ ἱππέων καὶ πέζων καὶ ἁρμάτων τοὺς ἡγεμόνας, as an exception to the rule (noticed by Heindorf ad Plat. Phæd. p. 64. E.) that the Article should stand with one Correlative if it does with the other; whereas the peculiarity arises from the source now under consideration.

It will be found that these two anomalies do away with a

---

¹ Stallbaum's correction of Plat. Phæd. 64. E. in compliance with Heindorf's rule, noticed just below, is, on this ground, unnecessary.

² This again is an English peculiarity. '*Sun, moon, and stars.*'

³ It is a favourite notion among modern critics that words signifying *relationship* lose the Article. See Schäf. on Plutarch, Anim. vol. iv. p. 409. App. ad Demosth. p. 329. Melett. p. 45. ad Soph. Œd. T. 630. Buttman ad Men. § 7. and many others. It is quite certain that such words are very frequently used in enumerations.

large class of the irregularities as to *particular words* alleged by critics. It must be added, that the words in which critics allege the existence of such irregularities are very few in number, and are words perpetually used as designating either objects of great importance or the common relations of life. The very fact that such irregularity is noticed, and that it exists in so few cases, is a strong proof of the correctness of the rules from which the deviation is said to take place. And the words referred to are precisely those where irregularity might be expected, and where in other languages it actually takes place. Looking to the example from the Crito, where the Article, if used with πατρός, would be used nearly as a Possessive, we might say in English " Country is dearer than father and mother, and every other ancestor together;" or even " Men esteem country before father, and mother, and every relation." Here, doubtless, we might also say, " *One's* country," and " Their country," &c. In other languages, liberties are beyond all question taken with words designating relations of such extreme importance as to be perpetually in the thoughts or on the tongue. I shall examine the words in question a little farther on.

It must be observed farther, that in every language, while the same thought may be expressed with very great difference of forms and words jointly, it may also be expressed in words approaching very nearly to one another, while the forms, whatever may be their resemblance to a careless eye, are clearly distinct. Thus, in our own language, in speaking of an army under severe distress, we might say, " they felt very great dejection," or " their dejection was very great"—two forms differing widely. But we might also say, " the dejection was very great," which approaches much nearer to the last: or, again, " there was great dejection." So in Greek (Xen. Anab. iv. 8. 21.) we have (in Bornemann's edition) Ἔκειντο δὲ οὕτω πολλοί, ὥσπερ τροπῆς γεγενημένης, καὶ πολλὴ ἦν ἡ ἀθυμία. Now, in this very place, many MSS. omit ἡ before ἀθυμία; and we have in the same book, 37, πολλὴ ἀθυμία ἦν τοῖς Ἕλλησιν. A careless reader might hence infer that there was no rule at all for the Article; and that in expressing (what is undoubtedly) the same thought, it might be either used or omitted, whereas the forms of expression are as different in the Greek as in the two *last* English cases above. *With the Article*, we must construe " The dejection (viz. that felt by the troops) was great"—*without it*, " There was great dejection." It is true, indeed, that in the former case, no dejection had been previously *spoken of*, but in many cases we may refer to what has not been *actually* mentioned, when its existence is quite obvious, and, so to speak, necessary. Under severe sufferings, it is clear that among a large body of men there will be some dejected; so clear, indeed, that it would be unnecessary for an historian to notice it. He therefore *assumes*, if he pleases, the existence of such dejection, and then uses the Article with it when stating *to what degree* it existed. At the very end of the same book, we have καὶ καλὴ θέα ἐγένετο, where some MSS. read ἡ θέα. The forms differ; but either is correct.

It is not easy to say how far this extends; yet nothing can be more certain, than that it does not at all make the use of the Article irregular or undecided. Let us look at another case. Bishop Middleton has observed, that in cases of *enumeration*, the Article is frequently omitted. But it is not *necessarily* omitted. The fact is, that two forms of expression may be used. In a note on Xen. An. vii. 8. 9. (Λαβεῖν ἂν καὶ αὐτὸν καὶ γυναῖκα καὶ παῖδας καὶ τὰ χρήματα) Bornemann cites many similar instances, as vii. 1. 28. Cyrop. vii. 1. 33. and 2. 26. De Rep. Ath. ii. 17. Hipparch. i. 1. Thucyd. vi. 12. Plat. Gorg. § 61. Lucian. Piscat. 33. Among these a very good one is Cyrop. vii. i. 33. ἐπλεονέκτουν μέντοι οἱ Αἰγύπτιοι καὶ πλήθει καὶ τοῖς ὅπλοις. " In number and in their arms." We might also say, " In their number and their arms;" or " In number and arms." That is, (1.) both words might have, or (2.) both might omit the Article, or (3.) the first might omit and the second take it, with equal correctness, and without the slightest laxity in the use of the Article. It is only that we may express the same idea in several forms; not that, when we *have* chosen *one* of these forms, it is any longer indifferent whether we use the Article or not.

The extreme laxity of translation which we allow ourselves in cases where the idea is not altered by it (and we have just seen in how many ways the same idea may be expressed), leads us very often to think that there is laxity in the *usage* of the Article.

To these remarks must be added another, viz. that it is reasonable to suppose beforehand, and that critics have actually often observed how frequently MSS. vary as to the omission and insertion of the Article; and that, consequently, some exceptions to any rules laid down for its use, must be fairly expected on that score. Again, it is quite certain, that with words which are occurring every moment, liberties will be taken which will not be offered to those of rare occurrence. Of course, if it were supposed that these liberties were constant or universal, they would do away all notion of applying rules to the words to which they relate. But that is not the case. Such liberties are occasional, partial, and often mere vulgarisms, used by those who disregard all philosophical accuracy in their language.

I must now proceed to state, that Bishop Middleton's other canons embrace and explain many of the cases where the use of the Article has been considered as extremely anomalous. I do not say that this proves the truth of the canons, but it certainly entitles them to fair consideration. Thus ἡγεῖσθαι θεοὺς is brought forward as a flagrant case of irregularity in the Article. Bishop Middleton himself has fully shown that (if his canons be allowed) the word could not have the Article here.

At the same time I must add, that many of the cases alleged by critics as irregularities, are not so; and that more exact attention will show that they are either strictly regular, even according to rules allowed on all hands to be true, or that the irregularity itself falls under certain well-defined limits. Thus Siebelis (on Pausan. i. 3. 5.) gives several instances of Correlatives where the Genitive has *not* the Article, although the other word has. But then every one of these instances is the name of *a country*. See the same Critic on Pausan. v. 14. 5.

It will now be necessary to consider those words which are said by various critics to permit an irregular use of the Article.

Words in which the Article is said to be omitted.

Bishop Middleton observes (Chap. iii. Sect. i. § 3—5.) that Nouns, existing singly, take the Article; and that, consequently, the great elements of nature usually have it. But it is unquestionably true, that in many languages there are great liberties taken with the names of these elements. For example, in English, we not only say *by sea* and *by land*[1], and "*we got to land*," but we find constantly such phrases as "*Land* was out of sight," "We saw *land*," "We had *sea* on the right hand, and *land* on the left," and so on.

In English we may observe that similar liberties are often taken with words the one of which is used as a representative of the other. Thus, although we cannot in English take the liberties with *sun* which are taken in Greek with ἥλιος, yet we shall find that in many cases *day* is with us the representative of ἥλιος, and that then it is exposed to the same licence.

---

[1] Language is so delicate a thing, that it is very dangerous to speculate on it without long and full observation. I am not very sure that *Sea* and *Land*, *Day* and *Night*, &c., are not a species of *Correlatives*; and that, if the Article is omitted with one, it is so with the other; and that this will hold even where both are not expressed. Thus we say *by sea*, even when land is not *mentioned*, there being a reference to it.

Thus the Greeks said ἅμα ἡλίῳ ἀνίσχοντι, or ἡλίου ἀνατέλλοντος, &c. &c. And we say *day broke, day came at last.* It is rather curious to remark, that we only use *sun* in composition for such purposes, and that then the compound word, when used to denote *time*, hardly admits the Article. Thus, sun-rise, sun-set, take the Article only when they denote *the act*, not *the time* of the day.

I have just observed that *sun* is not treated in English as ἥλιος is in Greek. The same applies to *moon* and σελήνη, *heaven* and οὐρανός. The words so used in English seem to me principally what denote the great periods of the year, *Spring, Winter*, &c.; or again, *harvest*, or the times of the day, *morning, noon*, &c.; or again, sun-rise, &c.; or the names of *meals*; and *sea* and *land*, &c., in all of which the word *time* is suppressed.

Ἀρχή. This word is a good specimen of the way in which Winer's list is made up. He does not bring a single instance of omission of the Article with this word, except after Prepositions. Nor does an instance of irregular use occur in the N. T. Wherever the Article is omitted, it is in enumeration, &c.; in those cases, in short, where it is occasionally omitted, according to known principles, with every word. The only apparent case is in Mark i. 1; but there the usage is strictly correct, τοῦτό ἐστιν being understood as in xiii. 9. ἀρχαὶ ὠδίνων ταῦτα.

βασιλεύς. See Heindorf ad Plat. Euthyd. p. 309. Heindorf says that the Article is more usual, but cites Aristoph. Plut. 173; Plat. Charmid. § 12. In both of these cases μέγας is used. Schäf. Mel. p. 4. Engelb. ad Plat. Menex. p. 291. Gottleb. ad Menex. p. 47. Aristoph. Eq. 478. Zeun. ad Xen. Cyr. i. 512. I find in Isoc. Archid. ad finem, ἡγουμένου βασιλέως ἐκ τῆς οἰκίας τῆς ἡμετέρας. But here the omission is right; " When *a* king of our race led them." In the Evag. p. 79. ed. Battie, we have βασιλεῖ τῷ μεγάλῳ, and again p. 102.

γῆ. Poppo, ad Xen. Anab. vi. 2. 1. and in his Index, cites no case of omission except after a Preposition; nor do I find any other in Krüger or Bornemann. Heindorf on Plat. Gorg. cites seven cases of omission, *all* after Prepositions. See Dorvill. on Chariton. p. 166. In the N. T. there is one good instance, viz. 2 Pet. iii. 10. καὶ γῆ καὶ τὰ ἐν αὐτῇ ἔργα κατακαήσεται. Acts xvii. 24. is a case of enumeration. In Mark xiii. 27. Luke ii. 14. Heb. viii. 4. there is a Preposition; and 2 Pet. iii. 5. is a doubtful case. See Heind. ad Plat. Gorg. p. 265. In the phrase γῆς ἄνακτα, in Soph. Œd. Col. 1630, the Article is omitted with γῆς, because it is omitted with ἄνακτα.

Γυνή. I do not find any instances given by the critics except such as are explicable by one or other of Bishop Middleton's rules—(*enumeration*, coming after a *Preposition*, &c.). In 1 Cor. v. 1. ὥστε γυναῖκά τινα τοῦ πατρὸς ἔχειν, I do not see the reason for the omission, if the reading is correct. In 1 Cor. vii. 10. and 11. γυνὴ and ἀνὴρ are without the Article, but this is an exclusive proposition.

γνώμη. Krüger ad Xen. An. i. 6. 9. gives instances of the omission of the Article before this word in formulæ, like ἀπόφηναι γνώμην (as ibid. v. 5. 3. and 6, 7. Thuc. ii. 86; iv. 125; vii. 72; viii. 67. Arrian. Exp. iii. 21. 8.); and he conceives that it is omitted elsewhere also, as in Thuc. i. 53. (where the phrase is εἰ δ᾽ ὑμῖν γνώμη ἐστίν, ii. 12. ἦν γὰρ Περικλέους γνώμη πρότερον νενικηκυῖα. This opinion has not been mentioned before, (indeed Thucydides goes on to explain it,) and therefore, even if the construction were quite certain as to this point, the Article is not necessary,) vi. 47.

I need only observe, that in the first instance of the latter class, and in all those of the first, the omission of the Article is proper and necessary, on a principle which Bishop Middleton has laid down in speaking of the omission with *Verbs Substantive*, &c., but which even he has not perhaps carried quite far enough. It seems to me at least, that wherever, in the case of a Noun following a Verb, the action of the Verb *in any way* expresses or implies the *producing, calling into existence* or *action*, the thing expressed by the Noun, there the Article ought, on Bishop Middleton's principle, to be omitted. Thus Plat. Protag. p. 325. E. πολὺ μᾶλλον ἐντέλλονται ἐπιμελεῖσθαι εὐκοσμίας τῶν παίδων, ἢ γραμμάτων τε καὶ κιθαρίσεως. Here εὐκοσμία is a quality not yet existing in the children, but to be infused by the master's care; and so of the other words. So, again, id. ib. p. 327. A. ἀναγκάζουσα ἀρετῆς ἐπιμελεῖσθαι. Crito, p. 45. D [1]. In Crito, p. 51. A. we have ὁ τῇ ἀληθείᾳ τῆς ἀρετῆς ἐπιμελόμενος, (where there is a sneer at Socrates,) he is spoken of, not as attending to virtue so as to produce it where it did not exist before; but supposing it to exist, to attend to it. Perhaps the usage in the Crito, p. 52. A. ἀλλ' ἤρου, ὡς ἐφῆσθα πρὸ τῆς φυγῆς, θάνατον, is to be referred to the principles here laid down.

Ἐκκλησία. Winer puts this in the list; but out of 115 instances, I find only 1 Cor. xiv. 4. ἐκκλησίαν οἰκοδομεῖ, where the word is not used with the strictest regularity. In this case, therefore, I conceive that either there is a false reading, or that we may take the word indefinitely, *a church;* " edifies not himself, but a *whole assembly*."

Εὖρος. Xen. An. iv. 3. 1. ποταμὸν εὖρος ὡς δίπλεθρον, *et al.*, although in other cases the Article is added. So of πλῆθος, μῆκος, σταθμός, &c. (as in Æsch. Soc. ii. 24.) The

---

[1] Some may, perhaps, refer these two cases to the remark in p. 95. Γνώμη, however, does not belong to the class there noticed.

PRELIMINARY OBSERVATIONS.   xvii

fact is, that two different forms of expression are used; just as in English we might say, "A wall which in its thickness was two feet;" or, "A wall which in thickness was two feet." The Article, if used, is used here as a Possessive; and it is obvious that all these qualities may be spoken of as *belonging* to the thing to which they refer, in which case the Article is right; or as *abstract* qualities, in which case it is not required. In English we might say, "The river in *its* widest part was, &c.;" or, "The river in *the* widest part was, &c." Besides which, it must be observed, that a Preposition is understood in all these cases; which would certainly, if expressed, justify the omission of the Article; and it is not easy to say how far this may affect the question.

ἥλιος. Bishop Middleton has himself noticed that this word may be considered almost as a proper name; and Poppo (ad Xen. An. v. 7. 6.) makes almost the same remark. Krüger (ad Xen. An. i. 10. 16.) observes only that the Article is omitted when ἥλιος is joined with δύεσθαι. But this is not so. In the place whence I cite Poppo's remark, we have ὅθεν ἥλιος ἀνίσχει. And I find ἅμα τῷ ἡλίῳ δυομένῳ in ii. 2. 16. while we have ἅμα ἡλίῳ ἀνίσχοντι, ii. 1. 3. (and so Lucian Ver. Hist. i. p. 642. ed. Var.) ἀνατέλλοντι, ii. 3. 1. περὶ ἡλίου δυσμάς, vi. 3. 32. (See Jacobs ad Luc. Tox. p. 99.) It is worth observing, that in the N. T. out of thirty-two instances, the Article is omitted only eight times; twice in the phrase ἡλίου ἀνατείλαντος, Matt. xiii. 6. Mark iv. 6. in which it occurs, Mark xvi. 2. twice in an enumeration, Luke xxi. 25. Acts xxvii. 20. (and 1 Cor. xii. 40. is nearly the same); twice after ἀπὸ ἀνατολῆς or -ῶν, Rev. vii. 2; xvi. 12. In Rev. xxii. 5. we have χρείαν οὐκ ἔχουσι φωτὸς ἡλίου, where it could not be otherwise any more than in the five preceding cases.

ἡμέρα. We have ἡμέρα ἐγένετο in Xen. An. ii. 2. 13. and

a

so in classical writers constantly. Luke iv. 42. and Acts xvi. 35; xxiii. 12. γενομένης δὲ ἡμέρας. vi. 13. ὅτε ἐγένετο ἡμέρα. xxii. 66. Acts xxvii. 29. 33. 39. John ix. 4. ἕως ἡμέρα ἐστίν. Acts xii. 3. ἦσαν δὲ ἡμέραι τῶν ἀζύμων. 2 Pet. i. 19. ἕως οὗ ἡμέρα διαυγάσῃ.

It will be observed, that if Bishop Middleton be right, even in these cases the Article would be *improper*, the Verb being *Substantive*, (the last case, in fact, comes under the same head,) and in all the other numberless places in the N. T. where this word is used, it is used with the strictest attention to the regular rules for the Article; the Article being omitted only after Prepositions, in Enumerations, or after Substantive Verbs, (as 1 Thess. v. 4. and 8 [1]). As I do not see the word ever alleged by the Critics to be irregular in this point, except in such cases as the above, it ought not to be in the list. We have ὀψίας γενομένης in the same way, Matt. xvi. 2.

ἥμισυ. In Xen. Hell. iv. 3. 15. we have Σὺν Ἀγησιλάῳ (ἦν)—ἥμισυ μόρας τῆς ἐξ Ὀρχομένου. But this, I apprehend, is to be construed: "There was with Agesilaus half a mora, *viz.* that which came from Orchomenus." This construction is very common. With Pausanias it is perpetual. Thus καὶ νῆσον Ὠκεανὸς ἔχει τὴν Βρεταννῶν, i. 33. 4. Siebenkees, on i. 3. 5, indicates i. 27. 9; iv. 31. 9. (λόγῳ τῷ Μεσσηνίων,) ix. 40. 4. and 32. 6; and Herod. v. 50 [2]. In Xen. An. v. 10. 10. 1 Thuc. viii. 61. the omission is after a Preposition. In Mark vi. 23. the Article is omitted after ἕως. In Luke xix. 8. we have τὰ ἡμίση τῶν ὑπαρχόντων; and elsewhere, viz.

---

[1] The only case which appears to me *doubtful* is Acts xxvii. 33. Τεσσέραν καὶ δεκάτην ἡμέραν προσδοκῶντες.

[2] In Pausanias, however, this usage is pushed to extremities. Thus iv. 11. 9. ὅτι ἔργου τοῦ πρὸς Ἰλίῳ καὶ τούτοις μέτεστι, the Article ought certainly to occur. This is a peculiarity of the writer.

Rev. xi. 9. 11; xii. 14. it is used indefinitely. This word, therefore, must be taken out of the list.

θάλαττα. That the Article is omitted before this word there is no doubt. Thus Xen. An. iv. 7. 20. ὄψονται θάλατταν. v. 1, 2. ἐπεὶ θάλατταν ἔχομεν.

I have already noticed the use of this word in English. I am inclined to think, that in the celebrated exclamation in Xen. An. iv. 7. 24. our English cry would have been, *Sea, Sea*, without the Article. (So Θεοῦ φωνή, in Acts xii. 22.)

In the N. T. it is very remarkable how almost constantly the word takes the Article. Out of ninety-two cases, I only find, though the greater part of these are cases *after* a Preposition, four where it is omitted on that account, viz. Acts vii. 36; x. 6. and 32; 2 Cor. xi. 26. In Luke xxi. 25. it is omitted from *Enumeration*; in James i. 6. Jude 13. the Correlative word is indefinite. In Rev. iv. 6. the word is used indefinitely. In xiv. 7. I presume it is omitted on the ground of Enumeration—θάλασσαν καὶ πηγὰς ὑδάτων. But it is remarkable, that οὐρανὸς and γῆ preceding have the Article. Matt. iv. 15. is an obscure place, but I see not why ὁδὸς should not be indefinite there.

θύρα. Krüger, in his Grammatical Index to Xenophon's Anabasis, cites Lucian. Dial. Mort. ix. 3. for omission of the Article with θύρα, (which does not occur, by the way, in the place of Xenophon, ii. 5. 31. to which he refers,) but the expression is ἐπὶ θύρας ἐφοίτων. Winer cites Matt. xxiv. 33. Mark xiii. 29; but these are both with ἐπί. The word is strictly used through the N. T. with the Article indeed usually and the Preposition. This word, then, must go out of the list.

κόσμος. Winer alleges only such phrases as ἀπὸ καταβολῆς κόσμου, ἀπ᾽ ἀρχῆς κόσμου, ἐν κόσμῳ. This word, then, must also go out of the list.

μεσημβρία. The Article is only omitted after Prepositions. Winer cites πρὸς νότον, πρὸς ἑσπέραν, &c. This word must go out of the list.

νεκροί. This word, when used for *dead bodies*, is occasionally used by the Greeks without an Article; as by Lucian. Ver. Hist. i. p. 663. ed. Var.; and Winer quotes Thuc. iv. 14; v. 10. I find it without the Article in Æl. V. H. xii. 27. D. N. A. xiv. 27. It has the Article in Xen. An. iv. 2. 18. and 23. Æl. N. A. iv. 7; i. 16; xiii. 3. In the N. T. it is used quite regularly.

πρόσωπον. Winer cites only cases after a Preposition as usual; and the fact is, that the word is strictly regular. In the phrase λαμβάνειν πρόσωπον, the Article could not be used.

In 1 Pet. iii. 12. there is an Enumeration; ὦτα before is without the Article [1].

φώς (a man). Soph. Aj. 807. ἔγνωκα γὰρ δὴ φωτὸς ἠπατημένη. Is there any instance in prose?

ψυχή. In Plato the Article is often omitted. Thus, Phæd. p. 83. C. ψυχὴ παντὸς ἀνθρώπου, x. 16. D. καταδεῖται ψυχὴ ὑπὸ σώματος [2]; (though such omission, in both Correlatives, seems common in other words and languages). De Rep. p. 398. C. ψυχή ἐστιν ἁρμονία.

---

[1] I may observe here, that in some cases of Enumeration we find the *first* word with the Article, and the others not; as in this case, and Æsch. Socr. Dial. ii. 2. τὰ ἀνδράποδα, καὶ ἵπποι, καὶ χρυσός, καὶ ἄργυρος.

[2] Schäfer on Plutarch, t. iv. p. 409. notes that the Article is omitted in words expressing *parts* of the body. But I want proof of this.

PRELIMINARY OBSERVATIONS.

With respect to the Abstract Nouns mentioned by Winer, nothing can be more curious than his list.

Ἀγάπη occurs 116 times in the N. T., and is *always* regular, unless 2 Cor. ii. 8. κυρῶσαι εἰς αὐτὸν ἀγάπην be thought an exception, which I do not take it to be, on the grounds stated under γνώμη. Κακία is always regular; πλεονεξία the same. (It is so in 2 Cor. ix. 5.) Πίστις, in all the numerous instances in which it occurs, is quite regular, except in Heb. xi. 1. Ἁμαρτία is always regular, for such phrases as ἁμ. τίκτειν (James i. 15.) or ἐργάζεσθαι (Id. ii. 9.) belong to the same class as those noticed under γνώμη. And in the expression ἀφιέναι ἁμαρτίας, the Article would be improper; for the expression is evidently not intended to express 'the forgiveness of *all* sins,' but 'the forgiveness of any sin.' Thus, in the phrase 'Who can forgive sins but God alone?' the question is not, 'who can forgive *every* sin?' but 'who can compass such a work as the forgiveness of sin?'

In the case of ἀρετή, I am not yet convinced that there is not a law for the use of the Article, although I have failed to ascertain it. Stallbaum ad Protag. p. 320. B. and 361. A. says that it is used *without* the Article for *virtue in general;* but the MSS. vary in both these places, and ἡ ἀρετὴ occurs in p. 320. C. I see no variation, however, noted in p. 324. A. and C. and p. 328. C.

There are a few other words on which it may be right to add an observation or two. I have already spoken of the names of *arts* as being apparently irregular, and explained why. (See note in p. 50.) I may add here a few more instances, to show that the words are used in both ways.

Plat. Sympos. 186. E. has ἥ τε οὖν ἰατρική, ὥσπερ λέγω, πᾶσα διὰ τοῦ Θεοῦ τούτου κυβερνᾶται· ὡσαύτως δὲ καὶ γυμναστική, καὶ γεωργία. Μουσικὴ δὲ καὶ παντὶ κατάδηλος.

Aristotle, through his Rhetoric, uses, I think, quite constantly ἡ Ῥητορικὴ and ἡ Διαλεκτική; and we may, perhaps, in every instance construe it, *The Art of Rhetoric*. In i. 1. 2.

xxii PRELIMINARY OBSERVATIONS.

we have it contrasted with other arts which have no Article, ἰατρική, γεωμετρία, ἀριθμητική; and so elsewhere. This seems to me easily explicable. He would naturally mention with more form and emphasis the art which was the particular object of his treatise, as well as Logic, with which he is perpetually considering its connexion and difference as an art, (see p. 50.) while others which are only casually mentioned would be treated less ceremoniously, and called medicine, arithmetic, &c.; not The art of medicine, &c.

In Æsch. Socr. ii. 27. we have ἔστιν ἄρα ἡ ἰατρικὴ τῶν ἐπιστημῶν ἡ πρὸς τοῦτο χρησίμη. Here, being mentioned distinctly as *an art*, it has the Article [1]. In § 36. however, we have εἴπερ ἡ ἰατ. οἷά τε ἐστὶ τὸν νοσοῦντα παύειν, φαίνοιτο ἂν ἡμῖν ἐνίοτε καὶ ἰατρικὴ τῶν χρησίμων οὖσα πρὸς τὴν ἀρετὴν εἴπερ διὰ τῆς ἰατρικῆς τὸ ἀκούειν πορισθείη.

We now come to the words ἄνθρωπος and ἀνήρ. Of the first I would remark, that the following passage from the Protagoras of Plato (p. 321. C. D.) seems to settle definitively that in the Singular there is great laxity of usage:

Προμηθεὺς—ὁρᾷ τὰ μὲν ἄλλα ζῶα ἐμμελῶς πάντων ἔχοντα, τὸν δὲ ἄνθρωπον γυμνόν τε καὶ ἀνυπόδητον καὶ ἄστρωτον καὶ ἄοπλον· ἤδη δὲ καὶ ἡ εἱμαρμένη ἡμέρα παρῆν, ἐν ᾗ ἔδει καὶ ἄνθρωπον ἐξιέναι ἐκ γῆς εἰς φῶς. Ἀπορίᾳ οὖν ἐχόμενος ὁ Προμηθεύς, ἥντινα σωτηρίαν τῷ ἀνθρώπῳ εὕροι, κλέπτει Ἡφαίστου καὶ Ἀθηνᾶς τὴν ἔντεχνον σοφίαν σὺν πυρί—ἀμήχανον γὰρ ἦν ἄνευ πυρὸς αὐτὴν κτητήν τῳ ἢ χρησίμην γενέσθαι,—καὶ οὕτω δὴ δωρεῖται ἀνθρώπῳ· τὴν μὲν οὖν περὶ τὸν βίον σοφίαν ἄνθρωπος ταύτῃ ἔσχε.

Now in one or two of these instances explanations might, I

---

[1] Care must be taken in examining passages. Thus in Plato Protag. p. 322. B. we have (in speaking of the primitive condition of man) πολιτικὴν γὰρ τέχνην οὔπω εἶχον—ὅτ' οὖν ἀθροισθεῖεν ἠδίκουν ἀλλήλους ἅτε οὐκ ἔχοντες τὴν πολιτικὴν τέχνην. In the first case, the Article is omitted because the Proposition is *Negative;* and in the second, it would be inserted (even if not necessary on other grounds) on the score of *Renewed Mention.*

think, be devised, which would account for the use of the Article; but then they would be fatal to the explanations of other cases. Thus, it might be said that in the first case the Article is used because the genus was intended, and omitted in the second because an individual was meant. But then, what is to be said of the omission in the last case? In the Singular then, ἄνθρωπος and ὁ ἄνθρωπος appear to denote *the genus;* but even here it appears that where the genus is to be *emphatically* brought under notice, the Article is used.

With respect to the opinion of Critics, I can hardly attach much weight to it. Stallbaum (on Plat. Pol. p. 619. B.) says, that when used *de genere universo,* ἄνθρωπος sometimes has, and sometimes has not, the Article. He refers to his notes on the Crito, p. 51. A. and Protag. p. 355. A. See, on ἄνθρωπος, Bornemann. de gem. Cyrop. recens. p. 65. N. Thuc. i. 41; vi. seq.; vii. 47. Xen. Œc. vi. 8. Aristot. Pol. vii. 12. 4. Athenag. Leg. 10. Rechenb.

With respect to ἄνθρωποι, I would wish accurate inquiry to be made whether it is not used without the Article, as we use *men,* i. e. not so decidedly for a *generic* description as *man,* or *mankind,* or ὁ ἄνθρωπος, or οἱ ἄνθρωποι; as, for example, 'The man passed *among men* for an old man.' This does not, of course, mean *all mankind* on the one hand, nor *any particular persons* on the other, but generally such men as knew him. It *seems* to me, at least, that when the most generic description is meant to be given, the Article is added; but it wants very long and careful observation to decide this [1].

As to ἀνήρ, I must be contented with giving what I find in the Critics. Heindorf (on Plat. Theætet. p. 162. A. φίλος ἀνήρ) refers to a Note on Phædr. p. 267. A. where he inserts the Article in the sentence, σοφὸς γὰρ ἀνήρ. So De Rep. i. p. 331. E. He refers too to Brunck, (on Soph. Œd. C. 1486,)

---

[1] In Thuc. i. 41. one must translate, 'In a time when *men,* attacking their enemies, think little of any thing in comparison with victory.'

xxiv PRELIMINARY OBSERVATIONS.

and wishes to insert the Article. Also in Euthyd. p. 283. B. and Theætet. p. 162. H. All these are *Nominatives*; and Matthiæ (264. 262. 5.) says, that in the *oblique* cases the omission is not found, *except* in the Tragedians. But in the note on this latter place (of the Theætetus) Heindorf says, that on longer observation he would *not* now *insert* the Article *against* MSS. He refers, in confirmation of this, to Plat. Phæd. p. 98. B. where Stallbaum, after Wyttenbach and others, thinks that irrision is denoted by the omission of the Article. And again, on Pol. ix. p. 595. C. ἀλλ' οὐ γὰρ πρό γε τῆς ἀληθείας τιμητέος ἀνήρ, Stallbaum attributes the omission to contempt. This, however, is still a Nominative, where the reading must be very uncertain.

Stallbaum also (on Plat. Phæd. p. 98. B.) says, that the omission of the Article denotes *irrision*. He quotes Soph. Aj. 1162. 1170. Aristoph. Ach. 1128. Herm. ad Soph. Œd. C. 32. But in the places of the Ajax, the expression is simply, 'I have seen a man bold, &c.' It is not the omission of the Article in what is meant to be a *definite* description, but that the speaker in Greek, and in every language, speaking in indignation or scorn, describes his adversary *indefinitely*, and leaves the application to be made by that adversary, or others.

Herman (on Soph. Phil. 40.) observes, that in the Tragedians *some* words take or omit the Article, even though *definitely* used; but some have it always in a given *definite* sense. Thus ἀνὴρ always has it when it means a particular man, (not a husband,) as is clear (1.) from our finding the Article with it always in the oblique cases, where a *certain* man is spoken of; and (2.) from this, that in the *Attic* parts the first syllable never can be long, except where the Article is joined with it; and that it never requires the Article where the first syllable is short.

But in the Attic Dramatic writers we cannot doubt about the usage. Thus, in Soph. Aj. 59.

Ἐγὼ δὲ φοιτῶντ' ἄνδρα μανιάσιν νόσοις
Ὤτρυνον.

See too Aristoph. Lysist. 152.

I have just noted a few references to various Critics who deliver some of Bishop Middleton's more familiar rules.

Chap. iii. Sect. i. § 1. *Renewed mention.* See Krüger on Xen. Anab. i. 4. 2. and 7; iv. 5. 16; v. 9. 13; vii. 6. 5. and 8. 6 [1].

§ 2 and 3. Κατ' ἐξοχὴν and Monadic Nouns. Bornemann (ad Xen. Anab. iii. 2. 13.) mentions the use of the Article of any celebrated thing. So Krüger, on the same book, iii. 5. 11. on τὸν προδότην, *the well-known traitor.* See his note on v. 1. 4. 7. On v. 9. 5. he says that it is necessary '*ad rem de more factam significandam,*' and in his Index says that it signified '*rem in vulgus notam,*' giving as instances Xen. An. i. 1. 6. τὴν Ἑλληνικὴν δύναμιν, *the (well-known) Greek army*; v. 9. 5. αἱ σπονδαί, *the (usual) libations (after supper)*; vii. 1. 19. ταῖς ἀξίναις, those which the soldiers were in the habit of carrying. See Poppo's observation on Schneider's note on iv. 7. 27. τοὺς δακτυλίους. (The δακτύλιοι are so noticed also in Lucian's Dialogues of the Dead, in that between Alexander, Hannibal, and Scipio [2].)

§ 4. *Possessive.* See Krüger on Anab. i. 10. 5. and v. 7. 5. Poppo on vi. 5. 7.

§ 7. *Correlatives.* In Soph. Œd. C. 1348. where we have τῆσδε δημοῦχος χθονός, we find Brunck wishing to read τῆσδ' ὁ. It is curious to find that Schäfer, who opposes him, brings as similar instances, (1.) v. 1476. ἄνακτα χώρας τῆσδε, and (2.)

---

[1] Krüger refers to his Index as a supplement to his notes, and it contains some valuable observations.

[2] The quotation from Pericles's λόγος ἐπιτάφιος, in Aristot. Rhet. i. 7. contains some good examples: τὴν νεότητα ἐκ τῆς πόλεως ἀνῃρῆσθαι ὥσπερ τὸ ἔαρ ἐκ τοῦ ἐνιαυτοῦ εἰ ἐξαιρεθείη.

v. 1630. γῆς ἄνακτα. Nor does Elmsley make any remark in citing this from Schäfer. Without impropriety, I hope I may observe, that there is very frequently to be found in Critics a want of this nice discrimination of the uses of the Article, which we find in Bishop Middleton.

Siebelis, on Pausan. i. 3. 5. gives instances of Relation where the Genitive has not the Article; but they are *all* names of countries, which follow nearly the laws of Proper Names. See him again on v. 14. 5.

Herman, on Soph. Philoc. 888. ἡ δυσχέρεια τοῦ νοσήματος, says that this is *Definite, id quod in hoc morbo molestum est;* and that if ἡ be omitted, it is *Infinite, si quid in eo molestum est,* as in German, *Es hat dich doch nicht Lästigkeit der Krankheit vermocht.*

On v. 81. he says, that as τῆς νίκης means *victory in general,* κτῆμα ought to have the Article, to signify ' *non aliquam sed omnem victoriæ adeptionem.*'

I add an instance where the apparent irregularity can be explained. Plat. Protag. p. 325. C. τῶν οἴκων ἀνατροπαί. Here ἀνατροπαί is anarthrous, because it is the Predicate where ἡ ζημία was Subject. But then, why τῶν οἴκων? Because without the Article, the sense would be wholly different. The sentence is, "But in the case where death to their children, and exile, and confiscation of property, and, to say all in a word, destruction of their families." Without the Article we must construe " destruction of families." If this had been predicated as the consequence, another evil might have seemed to be in the writer's mind. Just before, in speaking of confiscation of property, the Article is not wanted, and is not used.

On the matter of *Predicate and Subject,* it may be well to observe, that Matthiæ says that the Subject has not the Article, if it is a *general* idea. Two of his three instances are, Isoc. ad Demonic. p. 8. B. καλὸς θησαυρὸς παρ' ἀνδρὶ σπουδαίῳ χάρις ὀφειλομένη. Nicocl. p. 28. A. λόγος ἀληθὴς καὶ νομικὸς καὶ δίκαιος ψυχῆς ἀγαθῆς καὶ πιστῆς εἴδωλόν ἐστι. The third is, ἄνθρωπος (in the Protagoras) πάντων χρημάτων μέτρον ἄνθρωπος.

Again, he says that the Predicate has the Article, if it is a definite object, in which it is affirmed that it belongs to the general idea in the subject, as Eur. El. 381.

τίς δὲ πρὸς λόγχην βλέπων
Μάρτυς γένοιτ' ἂν ὅστις ἐστιν ἀγαθός;

Plat. Phæd. p. 78. C. ταῦτα μάλιστα εἶναι τὰ ἀξύνθετα. (This case is especially explained by Bishop Middleton.) Philemon ap. Stobæum, Floril. Grot. p. 211. εἰρήνη ἐστὶ τἀγαθόν. (This is a singular instance indeed.) Lucian. Dial. Mort. 17. 1. τοῦτ' αὐτὸ ἡ κόλασίς ἐστιν, where a *particular* punishment is spoken of.

I will now proceed to give the additional instances which I have lately collected, which bear upon Mr. Granville Sharp's rule.

Plat. de Rep. p. 398. C. τὴν ἁρμονίαν καὶ ῥυθμόν.

Id. Pol. iv. p. 586. E. τῇ ἐπιστήμῃ καὶ λόγῳ.

Id. ibid. viii. p. 557. C. οἱ παῖδές τε καὶ γυναῖκες.

Id. Legg. vi. p. 784. C. ὁ σωφρονῶν καὶ σωφρονοῦσα.

Id. ibid. v. p. 771. E. τῇ παρούσῃ φήμῃ καὶ λόγῳ

Id. Protag. p. 327. B. ἡ ἀλλήλων δικαιοσύνη καὶ ἀρετή.

} Cited by Krüger on Dion. de Thucyd. p. 140.

Id. Pol. vi. p. 516. B. τῶν ἄστρων τε καὶ σελήνης.

Aristot. Rhet. i. 1. 1. ὁ δ' ἐκκλησιαστὴς καὶ δικαστὴς ἤδη περὶ παρόντων καὶ ἀφωρισμένων κρίνουσι.

Id. ibid. 2. 7. τὸ γὰρ τέκμαρ καὶ πέρας ταὐτόν ἐστι, κατὰ τὴν ἀρχαίαν γλῶτταν.

Id. ibid. 3. τῆς διαλεκτικῆς καὶ ῥητορικῆς. But in i. 1. 3. ἡ διαλεκτικὴ καὶ ἡ ῥητορική.

Id. ibid. 3. 1. τοῦ μᾶλλον καὶ ἧττον.

Id. ibid. 4. τὸ σύμφερον καὶ βλαβερόν; and again, τοῖς ἐπαινοῦσι καὶ ψέγουσι.

Id. ibid. 9. 1. τῷ ἐπαινοῦντι καὶ ψέγοντι.
Id. ibid. 10. 1. περὶ δὲ τῆς κατηγορίας καὶ ἀπολογίας.
Id. ibid. τὸ δίκαιον καὶ ἄδικον.
Id. ibid. 11. 2. τοῖς εἰθισμένοις τε καὶ δυναμένοις.
Id. ibid. ἐν τῷ μεμνῆσθαί τε καὶ ὁρᾶν.
Id. ibid. τὰς μαχητικὰς καὶ τὰς αὐλητικὰς καὶ ἐριστικάς.
Id. ibid. τοῖς πένθεσι καὶ θρήνοις.
Pausanias vi. 6. 2. τὴν Λοκρίδα καὶ Ῥηγίνην.
Thucydides i. 54. ὑπὸ τοῦ ῥοῦ καὶ ἀνέμου.
Ibid. 140. τὴν βεβαίωσιν καὶ πεῖραν τῆς γνώμης.
Ibid. 141. ἥ τε μεγίστη καὶ ἐλαχίστη δικαίωσις.
Ibid. 143. τὴν μὲν γῆν καὶ οἰκίας ἀφεῖναι, τῆς δὲ θαλάσσης καὶ πόλεως φυλακὴν ἔχειν.
Ibid. ii. 50. τὰ γὰρ ὄρνεα καὶ τετράποδα.
Ibid. iv. 34. ὑπὸ τῶν τοξευμάτων καὶ λίθων.
Xen. Mem. i. 1. 19. τά τε λεγόμενα καὶ πραττόμενα καὶ τὰ σιγῇ βουλευόμενα.
Id. Cyrop. i. 6. 17. δοκεῖ ἥ τε ὑγίεια μᾶλλον παραμένειν καὶ ἰσχὺς προσγενέσθαι. But this is no instance; health *existed before;* strength is a new acquirement.
Id. Anab. ii. 1. 7. τὰς τάξεις τε καὶ ὁπλομαχίαν.
Id. ibid. ii. 2. 5. οἱ στρατηγοὶ καὶ λοχαγοί [1].
Isocrates Archid. p. 58. ἢ τοῦ διάγεσθαι καὶ περιποιῆσαι σφᾶς αὐτούς.
Id. Evag. p. 83. τὸ δι' ἑτέρων ζητεῖν τὴν κάθοδον καὶ θεραπεύειν τοὺς αὑτοῦ χείρους ὑπερεῖδε.
Id. ibid. p. 89. ἐν τῷ ζητεῖν καὶ φροντίζειν καὶ βουλεύεσθαι.
Id. ibid. p. 102. τῶν Ἡμιθέων τοὺς πλείστους καὶ ὀνομαστοτάτους. This is of the same person.
Id. Busir. p. 163. τὴν Λακεδαιμονίων ἀργίαν καὶ πλεονεξίαν.

[1] I may mention that Xenophon's practice about these words differs. We have στρατηγοὶ καὶ λοχαγοὶ without any Article very often, as Anab. iii. 5. 7; iv. 3. 26. 6. 12. 7. 25; vi. 3. 12. 4. 30. Cyrop. iii. 3. 11. *Both* have the Article in ii. 5. 25; v. 2. 13; vii. 1. 13. and elsewhere. See iv. 4. 21; v. 4. 23; vi. 5. 4.

PRELIMINARY OBSERVATIONS. xxix

Id. ibid. p. 177. τῶν πλεῖστα εἰδότων καὶ βουλομένων ὠφελεῖν, of the same people.

Herodian i. 17. 25. τοῦ φαρμάκου καὶ μέθης.

Id. i. 17. 3. τοὺς πρεσβυτέρους καὶ λοιποὺς πατρῴους φίλους.

Id. i. 16. 7. τὴν ἔνδοξον καὶ ἐνιαύσιον πορφύραν. (See too i. 16. 10.)

Id. ii. 4. 12. τήν τε Ἰταλίαν καὶ ἐν τοῖς λοιποῖς ἔθνεσι ἀγεώργητόν τε καὶ παντάπασιν οὖσαν ἀργόν.

Krüger's observations on this point are worth quoting. On Xen. An. vii. 2. 16. he says, that properly the Article is not added to the second word, when ' *utrumque vocabulum in unam notionem conjunctum cogitandum est*,' but that as it is usually of very little consequence whether this is signified or not, the Article is often inserted where it would not be expected. On vii. 7. 36. τὸ πολὺ καὶ τὸ ὀλίγον he inserts the Article on the authority of *one* MS., because ' *sine eo voces π. et ὀ. conjungi posse diceretur, cum ut oppositæ cogitandæ sint.*' In the same sentence he edits ἡ δύναμις τοῦ ἀποδίδοντος καὶ τοῦ λαμβάνοντος, but seven MSS. omit the second Article.

On this subject it may be sufficient to observe, that of all these instances, none goes against Mr. Sharp's rule as explained by Bishop Middleton, with the exception of the two first from Aristotle's Rhetoric. That they should have been so long overlooked, standing where they do, is a proof how little interest is excited by the subject. On these instances I hardly know what to say, except that the fact, that the sentence is explaining how the Ecclesiast and Dicast *differ*, prevents any possibility of the two words being referred to the same person; and that in the same way, in the second case, the obvious fact, that the writer is treating of and explaining two different terms, and showing that they come to the same thing, would prevent any misunderstanding. If these explanations are not thought sufficient, it must be allowed that Mr. Sharp's rule is not *universal*, but its *general truth* cannot be shaken.

In connexion with this subject, it deserves attention, that

the Greek writers not only, as Bishop Middleton remarks, omit the Article altogether in an *enumeration of particulars*, but that they occasionally insert the necessary Article or Articles with the first clause or clauses of a sentence, and omit it before the others, where other particulars are enumerated in clauses of a form exactly like the first. Thus, Thuc. iii. 2. τῶν λιμένων τὴν χῶσιν καὶ τειχῶν οἰκοδόμησιν καὶ νεῶν ποίησιν. Here *both* Articles are omitted in the second and third clauses.

Plat. Pol. viii. p. 533, seq. ἀρέσκει τὴν μὲν πρώτην μοῖραν ἐπιστήμην καλεῖν, δευτέραν δὲ διάνοιαν, τρίτην δὲ πίστιν, καὶ εἰκασίαν τετάρτην.

Xen. Œc. ix. 7. ἄλλη (φυλὴ) τῶν ἀμφὶ λοῦτρον, ἄλλη ἀμφὶ μάκτρας, ἄλλη ἀμφὶ τραπέζας.

Plat. Protag. p. 329. C. μόρια δ' αὐτῆς ἐστιν ἡ δικαιοσύνη καὶ σωφροσύνη καὶ ὁσιότης.

There are some few instances which I have observed, for which I cannot satisfactorily account, and I think it right to add them. A very few exceptions, however, do not at all go to shake rules, which of course can only be *general*, and very possibly observers of greater sagacity than myself will see the reasons for these exceptions, or show that they fall within Bishop Middleton's rules.

Plat. Gorg. p. 497. E. Ἀγαθοὺς ἄνδρας καλεῖς ἄφρονας καὶ δειλούς. Why not τοὺς ἄφρονας?

Id. Theætet. p. 151. E. Αἴσθησις, φῆς, ἐπιστήμη.

Id. Charmidas, p. 161. A. οὐκ ἄρα σωφροσύνη ἂν εἴη αἰδώς. As the two last are not *reciprocating* Propositions, I do not see why the Article is omitted.

Id. Protag. p. 329. D. ὥσπερ προσώπου τὰ μόρια, μόριά ἐστι στόμα τε καὶ ῥὶς καὶ ὀφθαλμὸς καὶ ὦτα ἢ ὥσπερ τὰ τοῦ χρυσοῦ μόρια οὐδὲν διαφέρει τὰ ἕτερα τῶν ἑτέρων. Why is the Article omitted before προσώπου? Just below we have ὥσπερ τὰ τοῦ προσώπου μόρια[1].

---

[1] It may be well finally to subjoin instances which I have observed, where

It only remains that I should state what has been done in this edition. In the first place, Mr. Winstanley's book against Mr. Sharp, which was the most considerable of all published on the subject, has, I believe, been fully examined in all its material parts. Mr. Winstanley shows much reading and great attention to the question, but does not, as I trust I have shown, at all shake Mr. Sharp's positions, as explained and confirmed by Bishop Middleton. As the rule has been much canvassed in speaking of certain titles and names given to our Lord, I have, with considerable labour, given in my Appendix a full view of *every* instance of each of the most remarkable titles applied to Him. I have likewise examined Winer's book, which is one of the most celebrated of modern books on the New Testament, and have given from him, and also from Gersdorf's work on the Characteristics of the Style of the Writers of the New Testament, whatever seemed most important on the Article. Besides this, I have used all the diligence I could in collecting the *dicta* of modern foreign Critics on this subject. I cannot in truth say that I think they amount to very much, except to this, that they show that most Critics have paid very little attention to the subject. Still it was only right, that in a new Edition of the only great work on the Greek Article, whatever had been said by eminent Scholars should be added; and this, to the best of my ability, I have done, besides adding such other instances of the use of the Article as my own reading chanced to supply.

Critics have given explanations of particular passages where the Article occurs in a way which, to a Student, might be embarrassing.

Soph. El. ὁ σὺν γυναιξὶ τὰς μάχας ποιούμενος.

His battles, whatever battles he fight.

Id. ibid. 554. τὰ πολλὰ πνεύματ', those many winds which are accustomed to blow, (the Euripus being very stormy,) or the many winds which detained the Greek fleet.

TO

THE REVEREND

JOHN PRETYMAN, D.D.,

ARCHDEACON AND RESIDENTIARY OF LINCOLN,
PREBENDARY OF NORWICH, &c. &c.

My dear Sir,

The satisfaction which usually attends the termination of a literary labour, is, in the present instance, greatly increased by the opportunity afforded me of publicly stating the obligations which I owe to a Patron and Friend. The day which first recommended me to your notice, is distinguished in the annals of my life. Your nice and inflexible regard to integrity, your accurate estimate of mental powers, and your almost intuitive knowledge of character, confer honour on those who, in any, even the lowest degree, possess your favourable opinion: but when I reflect that, endowed with these qualities, you selected me to discharge a trust, the most momentous which man can delegate, allowing largely, as I ought to do in such a case, for the fallibility of human judgment, I cannot but feel the value of your preference; I cannot repress emotions of self-complacency and pride.

But not merely for the gratification of my vanity am I indebted to your kindness; I have to acknowledge substantial benefits. You have smoothed the path of my future life; you have supplied incitements to diligence; you have facilitated my exertions, whatever be the end to which they may hereafter be directed; you have placed me in a situation in which indolence might sink into repose, and in which, if activity fail of its reward, defeat may find consolation.

And yet, Sir, the retrospect cannot be contemplated without deep regret. Of the two excellent young men whose minds it became my duty to cultivate, one is now no more[1]: the wound inflicted

---

[1] HENRY GEORGE PRETYMAN died of a decline on the 16th October, 1807, having just completed his 17th year: his remains are deposited in Bristol Cathedral, on the North side of the Altar: in the ensuing autumn he would have proceeded to the University. I cannot but be solicitous to record some memorial of his mind: to those, therefore, who have the candour to excuse the defects of a juvenile trifle, I offer the following inscription, supposed to be intended for a statue of our immortal statesman, Mr. PITT. I might have selected a more favourable specimen of my lamented Pupil's talents: but the present is recommended by its brevity, by the interest of its subject, and by its being his last attempt in Greek composition. It was written in December, 1806; and it is printed exactly as it was found among his papers.

by his departure, is yet unhealed; and the chasm which he has left in our affections, will not soon be closed. I mean not to wrong Parental anguish by pretending to share it; Nature has given it a character of its own; it is a Sacred Sorrow, which is profaned by the intrusion of affected sympathy. You will concede, however, that mine is a case of no common disappointment, and you will allow me to indulge in expressions of grief, which well may be sincere. Your second Son, from the completion of his sixth year, had been committed to my sole tuition: and with daily opportunities of observing his character, and of witnessing his conduct, not to have loved him, would have evinced an insensibility which I hope does not exist. While the

---

ΕΙΣ ΤΟ ΠΙΤΤΟΥ ΑΓΑΛΜΑ.

Μῶν, ὦ 'γάθ', αὐχεῖς Ἀγγλικὸς πεφυκέναι;
βαιόν γ' ἐπισχὼν Ἀγγλίας σωτῆρ' ὅρα.
βροντὴ γὰρ ὡς ἤστραπτεν ἧς γλώσσης σθένος,
ὀργάς τ' ἔθελξεν αἱμύλος μύθων χάρις·
πυκναῖς δὲ βουλαῖς τοῦδε, γῆς Εὐρωπίας
ἔπτηξ' ἀλάστωρ, ἠδ' ἄγρας ἡμάρτανεν·
οὐ γὰρ δόλοισι ΠΙΤΤΟΣ ἐσφάλη ποτέ,
ἀλλ' ἄκρον ὡς πύργωμα τῆς μοναρχίας
ἔστη, θρόνους τ' ὤρθωσε τοὺς ἐρειψίμους·
ψυχῆς δὲ μᾶλλον ἠγάπησε πατρίδα,
πάντων τ' ἄναξ (ὦ θαῦμα) τέθνηκεν πένης.
θρήνων ἀπλήστων λήγετ', ὦ ΠΙΤΤΟΥ φίλοι,
γοώμενοι μάταια· κάλλιστον γέρας
οἱ πρόσθεν ἐχθροὶ προσφέρουσ' ἀκουσίως,
θανόντος ἔργα καὶ λόγους μιμούμενοι.

qualities of his heart engaged my esteem, the endowments of his mind commanded my admiration. To simplicity ever unsuspicious, to warmth and generosity of feeling, to a temper the most docile and affectionate, to the habitual yet unconscious exercise of native benevolence, and to firm faith in the truths of our Religion, he added a quick and clear apprehension, a lively and creative fancy, much acuteness of discrimination, and a power which is rarely possessed in youth, that of directing all the energies to a given subject. Of his attainments I should not speak without great hesitation, if less partial judges had not inferred from them the certainty of his future distinction: I was encouraged to hope that *Cambridge* would number him among her illustrious sons; and I anticipated the grateful and repeated tidings,

> ὅτι οἱ νέαν
> κόλποισι παρ' εὐδόξοιο Πίσας
> ἐστεφάνωσε κυδίμων ἀέθλων
> πτεροῖσι χαίταν.

Thus prematurely is dissolved a connexion of more than thirteen years' continuance. At a crisis so interesting, I have solicited permission to prefix your name to the following Volume. The merits of the performance may not entitle it to your zealous patronage; but its design, and the circumstances in which it has been produced, lead me to hope that you will not regard it with total indifference. It is, I trust, strictly within the line of our Profession; it was written in intervals of relaxation from duties originating in your partiality; and I cannot suppose that here Association will suspend its wonted influence on the feelings, though it may not bias your judgment.

I have now, Sir, to take my leave of you, with fervent prayers for your own happiness, and for that of your Family. I am shortly to withdraw from polished and literary society, from friendships endeared to me by similarity of pursuits, and by uninterrupted habits of kindness and confidence, to exercise the obscure, but important function of a Village Pastor: I am to seek other companions, to form new connexions, to engage in fresh projects: but whatever be my destiny, I cherish the belief that your good wishes will attend me, and that if ever your good opinion can avail to my welfare, you will not withhold it.

I am,
My dear Sir,
With sentiments of unfeigned
Gratitude and respect,
Your obedient and faithful Servant,
THOMAS FANSHAW MIDDLETON.

Norwich, 1st *Jan.* 1808.

PREFACE.

THE Student in Theology cannot fail to have remarked, that the exposition of various passages of the New Testament is by Commentators made to depend on the presence or the absence of the Article in the Greek original. He has observed, that on this ground frequently they have attempted to correct mistranslation, to strengthen what they thought too weak, or to qualify what was deemed too strong. Criticisms of this kind he probably regarded as being at least plausible, till he perceived that they sometimes degenerated into refinements not having any visible foundation in truth ; that distinctions were made, which were not warranted by the general tenor of Scripture ; that the examples by which it was sought to establish the proposed exposition, were not always strictly parallel ; and that Critics, instead of accurately investigating the laws of the Greek idiom, were not unfrequently content to argue from the practice in their own.

These charges, however, even if we admit them in their full extent, detract nothing from the general value of Grammatical Interpretation as applied to the Sacred Volume : they tend only to show that a particular philological question has not hitherto been sufficiently examined. To the Grammatical interpretation of the N. T. every sensible and unbiassed Christian will give his strenuous support. When, indeed, we consider how many there are who seek to warp the Scriptures to their own views and prepossessions, it seems to be the only barrier which can be opposed successfully against heresy and corruption. Partial Versions may be framed, and false Expositions sent forth into the world : but these cannot, if the friends of religion accurately study the original of the Scriptures, long mislead mankind. It was the judicious admonition of one of the Fathers, and the lapse of centuries has not abated its force or propriety, ἡμεῖς οἱ πιστοὶ παρ' ἑαυτοῖς ἐξετάσωμεν καὶ βασανίσωμεν τῶν ῥημάτων τὴν ἀκρίβειαν.

That the uses of the Greek Article should not have been more correctly ascertained, may excite surprise, when we perceive that hints tending to prove the importance of the subject may be traced even in the writings of the Fathers. In Justin, in Irenæus, in Clement of Alexandria, in Origen, in Athanasius, in Epiphanius, in Chrysostom, and in Theophylact, we find that stress is sometimes laid on the Article as prefixed to particular words, though no principles are generally inculcated: and a Latin Father, *Jerome*, remarking on Galat. v. 18. that πνεύματι is there anarthrous, adds, *quæ quidem minutiæ magis in Græcâ quàm in nostrâ linguâ observatæ, qui ἄρθρα penitus non habemus, videntur aliquid habere momenti*. Indeed, if we regard the subject as a question merely of Profane Philology, it possesses a degree of interest which might have more strongly recommended it to notice. In the course of the last century almost every topic connected with Greek Criticism has been minutely and profoundly discussed: we have seen disquisitions on the Homeric Digamma, on the Greek Accents, on Dialects, on the quantity of the Comparatives in ΙΩΝ [1], on the licence allowed in Tragic Iambics and on their Cæsura, on the Greek Particles, and on Metres, especially those of Pindar. I will not deny that these inquiries are all of them of the highest importance to the cause of Classical Literature: yet the present, considered in the same point of view, may claim at least a secondary rank, whilst in its connexion with Theology, and, perhaps, I may add, with the Philosophy of Grammar, it admits them not to any competition [2].

[1] See the masterly critique in the Monthly Review, New Series, vol. xxix. p. 427, *et seqq.*

[2] It is true that a work intitled "*Vindiciæ Articuli ὁ, ἡ, τό, in N. T.*" was published by *Adrian Kluit*, and, if I mistake not, in the Dutch language, about forty years ago. When I commenced my undertaking, I was not aware that such

This subject, however, has of late acquired additional interest from the Controversy occasioned by a work of Mr. *Granville Sharp's*. This gentleman contends that such phrases in the N. T. as τοῦ Χριστοῦ καὶ Θεοῦ ought to be interpreted of one individual, so as to afford evidence of our Saviour's Divinity, and that such had been the rendering of many of our older English Versions: Beza had also strenuously supported the same opinion; as did many other Critics. The interpretation maintained by Mr. Sharp became the more probable from being sanctioned by the excellent Editor of *Dawes's Miscellanea Critica*, the present *Bishop of St. David's* [Dr. Burgess]. The same interpretation was also powerfully confirmed by the elaborate researches of Mr. *Wordsworth*, who has proved that most of the disputed texts were so understood by the Fathers. If any thing under this head remained to be done, it was to show that the same form of expression in the Classical Writers required a similar explanation, and also to investigate the principle of the Canon, and to ascertain its limitations: this I have attempted in some of the following pages.

But the Criticism, as well as the Illustration, of the N. T. is involved in the present inquiry. *Michaelis* (Introd. vol. i. p. 267.) has well observed, that "the difference even of an Article must not be neglected in collating a MS.:" and yet in this respect the MSS. are frequently at variance. It is, then, much to be desired, that even in this particular, the text should be restored as nearly as possible to the reading of the Autographs: and I perceive not how this can be effected with any tolerable ground of security, unless we first ascertain what reading the idiom requires, or at least prefers: for the mere majority of MSS. will hardly satisfy the Critic: in many instances it will be seen that "*major pars meliorem vicit.*"

a book existed; and that it exists, is all which I know of it now, when my work is nearly printed off. Our agreement, therefore, if we ever agree, must be regarded as independent evidence of the same truth. I suspect, however, that we have proceeded on different principles, because *Schleusner*, in his Lexicon, though he appeals to Kluit, has in many important passages explained the Article in a manner from which, as will be seen, I entirely dissent.

In this investigation, however, and indeed in tracing the most obvious uses of the Greek Article, I found it impossible to proceed with any thing like certainty, unless the Article itself were first clearly defined, and its nature well understood. It has therefore been my endeavour, in the former Part of my volume, to resolve the question, *What is the Greek Article?* and to show that the solution offered will explain its principal uses in the Greek Writers: examples of these several uses are, of course, subjoined. In the Second Part I have applied to the Greek Text of the New Testament the doctrine laid down in the Part preceding. In each of them, if I have, in any considerable degree, attained the ends proposed, I shall not have occasion to regret the time and the labour which it has cost me : the former Part will not then be uninteresting as a Grammatical speculation ; it may assist the young men who, in our Schools and Universities, exercise themselves in Greek composition ; and, judging from the errors in respect of the Article, which still deform many editions of the Classics, it may not be wholly useless to Editors, who have not particularly attended to the subject. On the same supposition, the Second Part will be found, in some instances, to have corrected faulty translation ; in others, where different interpretations have their advocates, to give to one side the preponderance ; in some, to vindicate the integrity of the Text from wanton conjecture ; in others, to restore its purity by the adoption of rejected readings: in a word, to be subservient both to the Illustration and to the Criticism of the N. T. I am aware, however, that to plan and to execute are very different things ; that the imagination readily conceives what the hand cannot pourtray ; and that the best performances of the strongest minds bear but a faint resemblance to the archetype. I am, therefore, to expect that I shall need the Reader's indulgence ; on which, however, I cannot produce any very unusual claims. To him who urges the difficulty of his subject, it is fair to retort, that he ought to have measured his own strength. I might, indeed, allege, that a more ready access to libraries (for my own is not large, ὀλίγον τε φίλον τε) would certainly have enriched my work, and might possibly have prevented some mistakes: even this, however, would be of little avail; and every thing, perhaps, which is usually adduced on such occasions, may be comprised in the brief declaration, ὃ γέγραφα, γέγραφα.

But though I cannot assert extraordinary pretensions to the *lenity* of the Reader, I shall be justified in the attempt to counteract the effect of prejudice. An opinion prevails, that practical inferences deduced from inquiries of this kind are unsafe and futile: there are persons who appear to believe that the usages of language are rarely reducible to fixed rules; that their agreement is merely coincidence, and that Idiom is to be attributed solely to custom. I do not hold such reasoning to be at all philosophical; *custom* in language bears a close analogy to *chance* in physics; each of them is a name for the operation of unerring causes, which we want either the ability or the inclination to apprehend. Qualified by such a confession, each of these terms may be tolerated; but neither of them is to be employed as the appellation of a power which disdains to act harmoniously and consistently with itself, and is impelled only by caprice. In the formation of language every thing indicates design tending to discoverable ends: and in its actual application, though there are some anomalies, they bear no proportion to the instances in which the strictest regularity, the most undeviating uniformity, prevails. Of the Greek language these remarks are true in an especial degree: and there is some colour for the singular notion of *Lord Monboddo*, that this tongue was formed by grammarians and philosophers according to the rules of art. That some licence, indeed, in the use of the Article takes place in certain cases, it will be seen that I have readily admitted: but even for this we shall frequently be able to account, nor is it ever such as to invalidate the general truth of my theory. With respect to those canons which I have considered as most certain, I ought to state that they are confirmed not merely by the examples adduced, but by multitudes which, for several years past, have occurred to my observation: yet if a few untoward instances from unquestionable authorities can be cited against me, (and they have not been studiously suppressed,) I must seek refuge in the remark of a distinguished Critic, that "when a rule has been established by ninety-nine examples out of a hundred, an exception in the hundredth will not overturn it [1]."

There are also Readers who turn with disgust from every thing which has the appearance of subtilty. I cannot deny that the reasoning of my First Part may occasionally require a somewhat close attention: but the subject, if we would really understand it, seems not to admit the superficial treatment which the taste of our day would unhappily introduce into science of almost every kind. To throw a veil of mystery over that which in itself is plain and obvious, is indeed culpable: but more injury, I believe, arises to the human mind from the attempt to make all knowledge popular: it is better that the frivolous should remain in ignorance, than that the thinking and inquisitive should not have their faculties duly exerted. If the subject which I have undertaken to discuss has derived from my method of considering it an obscurity which does not really belong to it, I regret the waste of my own labour, as well as that of the Reader's; but I am much more apprehensive of having failed in that acuteness of distinction, that logical precision, and that depth of research, without which inquiries of this nature cannot be prosecuted to their full extent.

The Second Part, accompanied throughout by the Greek Text, would have assumed the form of a new edition of the Greek Testament: I thought it better, however, to trust to the hope, that they who were interested in the subject, would have the Greek Testament lying open before them, than to increase the bulk of the work by an appendage which might justly be condemned as of no real use.

---

[1] Mr. Marsh's Letters to Mr. Travis, p. 257.

TABLE OF CONTENTS.

PART I.

		PAGE
CHAP. I.	Opinions of Grammarians respecting the Greek Article	1—5

CHAP. II. Article defined.
- Sect. I. On the Article in Homer 6
- —— II. Object of its relation 14
- —— III. Obscure reference 18
- —— IV. Anticipated reference vindicated 21
- —— V. Participle of Existence understood 25

CHAP. III. Appellatives.

Sect. I. Insertions in Reference.
- § 1. Renewed mention 32
- § 2. κατ' ἐξοχήν 33
- § 3. Monadic Nouns 34
- § 4. Article in sense of Possessive Pronoun .... ib.
- § 5. Objects of Nature............ ib.
- § 6. Neuter Adjectives............. 35
- § 7. Correlatives 36
- § 8. Partitives 38
- § 9. μὲν and δὲ. .... ib.

Sect. II. Insertions in Hypothesis.
- § 1. Hypothetic Use 39
- § 2. Classes 40

Sect. III. Omissions.
- § 1. Propositions of Existence 42
- § 2. After Verbs Substantive, &c. ... 43
- § 3. After Verbs of appointing, &c. .. 45
- § 4. Apposition .... ib.
- § 5. Exclusive Propositions 46
- § 6. Governing Nouns before Indefinite governed 48
- § 7. Governed after Indefinite governing 49

Sect. IV. Insertions and Omissions combined.
- § 1. Subject and Predicate 50
- § 2. Attributes connected by Copulatives....................... 56

CHAP. IV. Proper Names.
- On what occasions the Article is placed before Proper Names .... 71—88

TABLE OF CONTENTS.

			PAGE
Chap. V. Abstract Nouns.	Sect. I. Insertions.	§ 1. Most Abstract sense	91
		§ 2. Personification	92
		§ 3. Possessive Pronoun	93
		§ 4. Reference	ib.
	Sect. II. Omissions.	§ 1. Sundry causes of omission	94
		§ 2. Adverbially	95
Chap. VI. Anomalies.		§ 1. After Prepositions	98
		§ 2. Enumeration	99
		§ 3. Ordinals	100
		§ 4. Superlatives	101
Chap. VII. With certain words.		§ 1. πᾶς in the Singular	102
		§ 2. — in the Plural	103
		§ 3. — with Abstract Nouns	105
		§ 4. ὅλος	ib.
		§ 5. οὗτος	106
		§ 6. ὅδε	107
		§ 7. ἐκεῖνος	ib.
Chap. VIII. Position in Concord.		§ 1. With one Article	110
		§ 2. With two Articles	111
Chap. IX.		How far Classical Rules respecting the Article apply to the N. T.	115—130

PART II.

Notes on the NEW TESTAMENT .... 123—470
Appendix I.—On the *Codex Bezæ* .... 471—485
———— II. (By the present Editor.)—The Usage of the various
        Appellations of our Blessed Lord .... 486—496
INDEX 497

PART THE FIRST.

PART I.

INQUIRY INTO THE NATURE AND USES
OF THE
GREEK ARTICLE.

CHAPTER I.

OPINIONS OF GRAMMARIANS RESPECTING THE GREEK ARTICLE.

WE learn from Glass, in his *Philologia Sacra*, that Julius Cæsar Scaliger called the Greek Article *loquacissimæ gentis flabellum*; and that Budæus represents the Attic writers as at one time inserting the Article by a Pleonasm, and at others omitting it by an Ellipsis. This doctrine, while it seems to command assent from the authority of those who have propounded it, is nevertheless so abhorrent from the genius of a philosophical language, like that of the ancient Greeks, that no fallible authority is of sufficient force to rescue it from the consequences of its inherent improbability. If in any language there could be a Part of Speech which, without offence to Syntax, might thus be employed or discarded at the pleasure of the speaker, that language might with more reason be supposed to be the French; which has not, like the Greek, the appearance of having been contrived by a synod of philosophers, but might rather be thought to owe its peculiarities to the fashion of the court and the habits of the gay and frivolous. In French, however, the laws respecting their Articles are rigorously observed; and an Englishman, who has not attended to the rules, will probably find, that of the faults which he commits in translating into that language a page of English, those which regard the Articles are not the least considerable part. The nation, therefore, to which in modern times all others are accustomed to impute loquacity, does not employ its Articles as mere *flabella* ; and there is at least a presumption, that among the Greeks the Article was subservient to some graver purpose.

He, however, who pretends to determine the uses of the Greek Article, should first endeavour to investigate its nature and origin. Without such an inquiry he may, indeed, collect from Greek writers something like rules for its insertion or omission ; but he will not be able to give them probability and consistency: they will not be of general application ; he will be driven to the unsatisfactory solution of Pleonasm and Ellipsis ; and he will be compelled to admit, as is done continually, that though the Article is by its nature a *Definitive*, it is sometimes used to mark *indefiniteness*, or is wholly without meaning : a doctrine which is countenanced in the excellent Lexicon to the New Testament by Schleusner. *Quodcunque ostendis mihi sic, incredulus odi*. There must be some common principle, by attending to which these opposite uses of the Article may be reconciled to each other and to common sense ; there must be, to use the words of Plato [1], τὸ νοούμενον ἓν εἶναι, ἀεὶ ὂν τὸ αὐτὸ ἐπὶ πᾶσιν· and it is worth our while to inquire for it. But first it may be right briefly to examine the principal opinions on the subject.

I have often thought, that if *Aristotle* had left us a treatise on Grammar, it would have ranked with the most valuable remains of antiquity; and yet the little which he has said respecting the Article in his *Poetics* is so obscure, that Mr. Twining, his very learned translator, confesses his inability to understand it. Aristotle says that an Article is " a sound without signification, which marks the beginning or the end of a sentence, or distinguishes, as when we say, THE word φημὶ, THE word περί [2]."

[1] Vol. X. Ed. Bipont. p. 83.
[2] Ἄρθρον δέ ἐστι φωνὴ ἄσημος, ἢ λόγου ἀρχὴν ἢ τέλος ἢ διορισμὸν δηλοῖ, οἷον τὸ φημὶ καὶ τὸ περί, καὶ τὰ ἄλλα. Mr. Twining observes, "the commentators all tell us that this means the prepositive and the subjunctive Article ; but none of them have clearly and fairly shown us how the one, because it is

Whatever be the true interpretation of this passage, I despair of discovering in it any thing to my present purpose.

A great deal of curious matter on the subject of the Article, and indeed on almost every part of the science of Grammar, may be found in *Apollonius Dyscolus*, a very acute writer, who flourished about the middle of the second century. Of many of his remarks I shall make use hereafter. I do not perceive that he has any where defined the Article, and consequently he has no theory; though he has many facts, for the most part corroborating the theory, which I suspect to be the true one. He makes Articles and Pronouns to be different things, yet he allows a relation between them, and says that if the Article lose its Substantive, it then becomes a Pronoun. This writer makes frequent mention of *Trypho*, who had composed a Treatise expressly on the subject of the Article: the work is unfortunately lost.

Theodore Gaza, who lived in the fifteenth century, gives us in his Grammar[1] the following account: " The Article is a declinable Part of Speech prefixed to Nouns. It is, indeed, divided into the Prepositive and the Subjunctive: but, properly speaking, the Prepositive only is the Article; and it serves to recall that which had previously been known in the discourse." This Grammarian, therefore, seems to understand the Article to be a distinct Part of Speech, as was observed of Apollonius: nor is it true that it is always employed to recall that which had previously been known in the discourse.

Mr. Harris has devoted to the Article a large portion of his

---

placed before a word, marks the beginning of a sentence or discourse, or how the other marks the end of it, because it follows the word to which it belongs. In the sentence before us, for example, in what sense does the subjunctive Article ἥ mark the end of the sentence, τέλος λόγου ?" I am not sure that Aristotle and his commentators may not mean that the Nominative of ὁ, as in ὁ ἄνθρωπος for example, must, in the natural order of speaking, precede every thing which can be affirmed of ὁ ἄνθρωπος, and that in the same natural order the affirmation will be completed, before ὁ ἄνθρωπος can be referred to by ὅς in a clause subjoined: in this sense ὁ might be said to mark the beginning of a sentence, as ὅς will mark the end of it. I know not whether this conjecture deserve any notice: I offer it for the want of something more satisfactory.

[1] Ed. Basil. 1523. p. 155. Τὸ δὲ ἄρθρον ἐστὶ μὲν λόγου πτωτικὸν μέρος προτασσόμενον τοῖς ὀνόμασι· διαιρεῖται δὲ εἰς προτακτικόν τε καὶ ὑποτακτικόν· κυρίως γε μὴν ἄρθρον τὸ προτακτικόν· ποιεῖ δ' ἀναπόλησιν προεγνωσμένου τοῦ ἐν τῇ συντάξει.

Hermes: he has, however, so closely followed Apollonius, that he is liable to the same objection. He makes the Article to be *nearly allied* to the Pronoun, and infers from Apollonius, that they may be best distinguished by the circumstance, that "the genuine Pronoun always stands by itself, while the genuine Article requires a Noun for its support." This is so vague, that it may be applied with nearly equal propriety to mark the difference between Substantives and Adjectives; and yet between the Article and the Adjective there is not any analogy.

But the author from whom most was to be expected on this subject is *Lord Monboddo*, who has written very largely on the Origin and Progress of Language, and was deeply versed in the remains of the Greek philosophers and metaphysicians. He observes, vol. ii. p. 53, "This Part of Speech (the Article) very well deserves a chapter by itself; for, if I mistake not, it is of as subtle speculation as perhaps any thing belonging to language, particularly as it is used in Greek." He attempts to show that "its office is different from that of a Pronoun of any kind, and that it deserves to be ranked by itself among the Parts of Speech." After many remarks distinguished by ingenuity and acuteness, he gives the following definition: "It is the prefix of a Noun, denoting simply that the Noun to which it is prefixed is the same with that which was before mentioned, or is otherwise well known." In such instances as ὁ σοφὸς ἐπαινεῖται, Lord Monboddo would say that ὁ σοφὸς, though not previously mentioned, is yet well known, because it represents a species which must be better known than any individual of it. My principal objection to this definition is, that it makes the Article a distinct Part of Speech, the contrary of which will be shown, and also that it is not consistent with what Apollonius had remarked, that the Article, in losing its Noun, becomes a Pronoun. It is not conceivable that Parts of Speech originally distinct should be liable to such a transformation.

Mr. *Horne Tooke*, in the two parts of the *Diversions of Purley* already published, has not given us any explicit account of the Greek Article: all which I can collect is, that he is dissatisfied with that of Mr. Harris. Our English THE, which, we are so frequently told, is very similar to the Article of the

Greeks, Mr. Tooke makes to be the Imperative of a Saxon Verb, signifying to *take* or to *see*. In this case, I apprehend the Greek and English Articles in their nature and origin have very little resemblance: and, perhaps, in no respect do languages differ more widely, than in the several contrivances which they have adopted on this occasion.

The opinions of other Grammarians might have been detailed, so as to extend this chapter to a considerable length. I am not, however, aware that they would furnish us with any view of the subject different from all those which have been already given. My own idea of the Greek Article shall be reserved for another chapter.

CHAPTER II.

ARTICLE DEFINED.

The Greek Prepositive Article is the Pronoun Relative Ὁ, so employed that its relation is supposed to be more or less obscure; which relation, therefore, is explained in some Adjunct annexed to the Article by the Participle of Existence expressed or understood [1].

Hence the Article may be considered as the *Subject*, and its Adjunct as the *Predicate*, of a Proposition, differing from ordinary Propositions only as *Assumption* differs from *Assertion*: for this is the only difference between the Verb and the Participle, between ἐστὶν and ὤν.—The Adjunct annexed to the Article will hereafter be called its *Predicate*.

But before the reader can be expected to acquiesce in this account, it will be necessary to offer its vindication at some length.

SECTION I.

ON THE ARTICLE IN HOMER.

The inquirer into the nature of the Greek Article will first turn his attention to Homer, as being the earliest Greek

---

[1] It might by some be expected, that I should rather have called the Article a Pronoun Demonstrative; since Pronouns Relative are, according to grammarians, those which have relation to persons or things already mentioned; whilst those which are Demonstrative, now for the first time point out the person or thing in question. It will be shown, however, that the Article was originally used as a Pronoun Relative, in the usual acceptation of that term, and that subsequently, when it ceased to be so used, there was still an implied reference to some object which had occupied the mind of the speaker, though perhaps not previously declared. Apollonius de Syntaxi, p. 104. Ed. 1590, has on a similar occasion a similar distinction. He says that οὗτος and ἐκεῖνος, though strictly speaking they are Demonstrative Pronouns, sometimes become Pronouns Relative: in which case δεῖ νοεῖν, ὅτι ἡ ἐκ τούτων δεῖξις ἐπὶ ΤΟΝ ΝΟΥΝ φέρεται, ὡς τὰς μὲν τῆς ὄψεως εἶναι δείξεις, τὰς δὲ ΤΟΥ ΝΟΥ.

writer, whose works have descended to the present time: but Homer's use of the Article is, if we adopt the belief of some critics, a subject of much perplexity. We are indeed told, that what we call the Article, was the invention of later times. Heyne[1] has words to this effect: "That Homer knew nothing of the Article, and that ὁ is with him equivalent to αὐτὸς or ἐκεῖνος, has been repeatedly remarked, and the remark has been confirmed by the inquiries of many learned men, especially of Wolf[2] and Koeppen."—Now, that what the Grammarians denominate the Article is thus employed by Homer, I readily admit: the difficulty is to understand, on what solid ground *Homer's* use of the Article is wholly distinguished from that of subsequent writers; and if any thing excites my wonder, it is, that what has been acknowledged to hold true partially, should not be perceived to be true universally: for though the later usage of the Article may afford instances, the exact parallels of which are not to be found in Homer, yet these variations are so few, and so evidently deducible from a common origin, that we shall hardly be justified in considering the Article of Homer as being different in its *nature* from that of Pindar, Xenophon, or Lucian: as well might we assert, that the language of Homer is radically distinct from that of succeeding Greek writers, because some of his words gradually fell into disuse, or were afterwards employed in a somewhat different acceptation. But let us attend to Homer's use of the Article, and observe whether the supposed difference really exist: in other words, whether if, as is admitted, the Article of Homer be a Pronoun, the Article of other Greek writers must not be allowed to be the same Pronoun.

The first occurrence of the Article in the Iliad is A. v. 6. τὰ πρῶτα, in which there is nothing peculiar: κατὰ τὰ ὄντα πρῶτα πράγματα will complete the Ellipsis. In v. 9. we have Ὁ γὰρ βασιλῆϊ χολωθείς· in which sense, indeed, subsequent writers generally used αὐτὸς or ἐκεῖνος. In v. 11. we meet with ΤΟΝ Χρύσην, i. e. with the Article prefixed to a proper name, than which nothing is more common in the Greek prose

[1] Excurs. II. ad Iliad. P.
[2] *Wolf*, however, revokes his decision on this subject. See note on *Reiz. de Prosod.* p. 74. He there says, " PINGUIUS *quædam scripsi de Homerico usu Articuli,*" &c.

writers: but of this more will be said in the sequel. V. 12. Ὁ γὰρ ἦλθε resembles v. 9.—In v. 19. ΤΑ δ᾽ ἄποινα (unless it be τάδ᾽ ἄποινα, as Heyne suspects, I think without cause) is the proffered ransom of Chryseis.—V. 33. ἔδδεισεν δ᾽ Ὁ γέρων· Chryses had been called γέρον above, v. 26.—In v. 35. Ὁ γεραιὸς differs from ὁ γέρων only in having the Article prefixed to an *Adjective*.—In v. 47. Ὁ δ᾽ ἤϊε, &c. is similar to v. 9.—In v. 54. we have ΤΗι δεκάτῃ scil. ἡμέρᾳ.—In v. 55. ΤΩι used with reference to Achilles just mentioned.—In addition to these examples, which are not *selected*, but taken without any omission, I will notice Z. 467. ὁ πάϊς, the child spoken of before.—Λ. 847. τὸ ἕλκος the wound of Eurypylus. —Π. 358. Αἴας ὁ μέγας by way of distinction.—Α. 576. τὰ χερείονα νικᾷ.—Κ. 11. ἐς πεδίον τὸ Τρωϊκόν.—Β. 278. ἡ πληθύς.—Ι. 342. τὴν αὐτοῦ φιλέει καὶ κήδεται. scil. γυναῖκα.— Δ. 399. τὸν υἱὸν his son.—Ε. 146. τὸν δ᾽ ἕτερον.—Ε. 414. τὸν ἄριστον Ἀχαιῶν.—Ζ. 41. οἱ ἄλλοι.—Α. 198. τῶν ἄλλων.—Ξ. 31. τὰς πρώτας. Many other examples might easily be collected. Now the question is, with respect at least to the latter class, in what do they differ from the examples, which occur in the writers of succeeding ages? Would the reader, supposing them to have been taken from Thucydides or Demosthenes, have doubted for a moment in what light they should be considered? And if he were told, that in all such instances, what he took for an Article was in truth a Pronoun, would he not immediately ask, wherein then lay the difference? for assuredly, if he were not acquainted with the dispute respecting the usage in Homer, he would never suspect the slightest peculiarity in the nature or use of the Article (or Pronoun) in any one at least of the examples last adduced; and if he were convinced with the critics, that Homer's Article was every where a Pronoun, equivalent to αὐτὸς or ἐκεῖνος, he would be compelled to acquiesce in the conclusion, that the same might be affirmed of the Article universally. But would this conviction immediately ensue? Certainly, an apparent difference between the latter class of examples and some of the former ones, such as ὁ γὰρ ἦλθε, &c. might induce him to adhere to the commonly received opinion, that Articles and Pronouns are distinct things; especially if that opinion had been derived from any of the high authorities, which may be found in its favour. "That there is," says Harris[1], "*a near relation* between Pronouns and Articles, the old Grammarians have all acknowledged; and some words it has been doubtful to which class to refer. The best rule to distinguish them is this: the genuine Pronoun always stands by itself, assuming the power of a Noun, and supplying its place. The genuine Article never stands by itself, but appears at all times associated to something else, requiring a noun for its support, as much as Attributes or Adjectives." The Grammarians, however, of whom Harris speaks, are not *all* those of antiquity, since the Stoic School, of whom Grammar and Dialectics were the favourite studies, did, according to *Priscian*, consider the Pronoun and the Article as the same thing, making only this distinction, that they called the Pronoun the *defined*, and the Article itself the *undefined Article*[2]. There is, therefore, no great presumption in proceeding to inquire, whether the former opinion, not indeed as it is limited to Homer, but asserted generally, be not founded in truth.

It is obvious, that in such phrases as ὁ γὰρ ἦλθε, ὁ δ' ἤιε, τὴν μὲν ἐγώ, &c. A. 183. ὁ and τὴν must be considered as Pronouns. The pronominal nature of ὁ is, therefore, in *some* instances, established beyond contradiction; and we have only to ascertan whether this pronominal nature be ever lost. Thus we read Iliad I. 341.

ὅστις ἀγαθὸς καὶ ἐχέφρων,
ΤΗΝ αὐτοῦ φιλέει καὶ κήδεται, ὡς καὶ ἐγὼ ΤΗΝ
Ἐκ θυμοῦ φίλεον,

where the latter τὴν is a *Pronoun* relating to *Briseis*, and the former, if we attend to the common distinction, is no other than the Article to γυναῖκα understood: but is not the one as much the representative of γυναῖκα, as the other is of Briseis? Here, indeed, γυναῖκα is so evidently implied, that no obscurity arises from its being omitted. But suppose the case otherwise; and that, though the context would afford a tolerable clue to the sense, some little obscurity were still to

---

[1] Herm. p. 73.
[2] This passage is quoted by *Harris*. "Articulis autem pronomina connumerantes, *finitos* ea *articulos* appellabant: ipsos autem articulos, quibus nos caremus, *infinitos articulos* dicebant." Herm. p. 74.

remain. For instance, if A. 33. we had read ὡς ἔφατ'· ὁ δ' ἔδδεισεν[1], the sense could hardly have been mistaken, but yet would not have been absolutely certain: ὁ ΓΕΡΩΝ makes every thing clear; for though independently of the context ὁ might refer to any male already mentioned, yet ὁ γέρων must refer to the only *old man* hitherto spoken of: but does ὁ on this account lose its nature? In the former instance it is admitted on all hands to be strictly a Pronoun: and how does the addition of γέρων v. 33. or γεραιὸς v. 35. destroy its essence? As well might we say that the *ille* of the Latin ceases to be a Pronoun, as often as it is associated with a Substantive, Adjective, or Particle, with all of which it is so frequently found.

But there are instances by which it may be clearly proved, that Homer himself entertained no idea of the difference between the Pronoun and the Article; for that it was an even chance, supposing a difference, which of the two he had used: which could not consistently happen, were the difference essential. Thus in narrating the conflict between Hector and Patroclus, Π. 793. he says,

ΤΟΥ δ' ἀπὸ μὲν κρατὸς ΚΥΝΕΗΝ βάλε Φοῖβος Ἀπόλλων,
Ἡ δὲ κυλινδομένη καναχὴν ἔχε ποσσὶν ὑφ' ἵππων.

Supposing the sentence to conclude thus, which unquestionably it might do, Ἡ would according to the vulgar distinction be a *Pronoun* referring to κυνέην, exactly as τοῦ refers to Patroclus: but so it happens, that the writer has added in the next verse Αὐλῶπις τρυφάλεια. The common doctrine will teach us, that this makes a prodigious difference, and that though we had determined, as might the writer also, to regard Ἡ as a Pronoun, it is at once degraded on the appearance of τρυφάλεια, and sinks into a mere *Article;* and yet the only alteration which takes place, is, that instead of relating to κυνέην, as was supposed, it is made to relate to the synonymous word τρυφάλεια. It is plain, therefore, in this example, that the difference between the Article and the Pronoun is not *essential*, but *accidental;* and consequently, when we are speaking of the *nature* of the Article, that there is no differ-

---

[1] As in ὁ γὰρ ἦλθε, &c.

ence at all. Now if we recollect that there is no conceivable instance, in which the very same thing may not happen without the least violation of the author's meaning, that is, in which to the Article, used confessedly as a Pronoun, we may not subjoin the noun, &c. of which it is intended to be significant, as A. v. 9. ὁ γὰρ, &c. is ὁ γὰρ ΘΕΟΣ or ὁ γὰρ ΑΠΟΛΛΩΝ, it becomes evident that there is no ground whatever for making a distinction between the *nature* of the Article ὁ and the Pronoun ὁ, and that the "near relation" is in truth no other than perfect identity. They differ no more than he, who should announce his name to me, would differ from the same man, if he concluded that his name were known to me already. And what is here said with respect to examples taken from Homer, is true universally. Hence the remark of Heyne and others, that Homer knew nothing of the Article, might have been made with equal reason of any subsequent Greek writer. Homer's Article, it is admitted, is a Pronoun: but so is the Article universally; and Homer's usage of the Article, as the reader must be convinced, from the instances adduced, has nothing in it peculiar, but accords strictly, so far as it goes, with the practice of succeeding ages. The German Critic appears, indeed, to have been alarmed by some untractable examples; and therefore he proceeds to call in question the *authenticity* of the Article, wherever it is found in Homer [1]; or, where it cannot be omitted without injury to the verse, he insinuates that the *verse itself* is spurious. Thus may any theory, however extravagant, be supported: but this is trivial in comparison with the hardihood which could deny that the *Iliad* was the production of one mind [2].

[1] Thus on Iliad P. 635. Ἠμὲν ὅπως ΤΟΝ νεκρὸν ἐρύσσομεν, he adopts the correction of Bentley, Ἠμὲν ὅπως νεκρόν τε ἐρύσσομεν. But what is to be done with v. 509. of the same book, Ἤτοι μὲν ΤΟΝ νεκρὸν ἐπιτράπεθ᾽?

[2] See Heyne's Homer, Vol. VIII. Excurs. iii. ad Lib. xxiv. For an ingenious, and, I think, a satisfactory account of the origin of the Hymns attributed to Homer, the reader may consult the *Epistola Editoris* prefixed to Hermann's valuable edition of those Poems. If the incongruities which occur in the Hymns, were found also in the Iliad, I should readily accede to Heyne's opinion: the Hymns, however, are, comparatively speaking, short Poems, in each of which the plan, such as it is, is perpetually interrupted by the introduction of extraneous matter: the plan of the Iliad, the most perfect, perhaps, which any Epic Poem can boast, is continued without interruption or deviation through the Twenty-four Books.

As connected with the subject of the Article in Homer, I will briefly notice two passages from eminent Greek writers, *Plutarch* and *Eustathius*. The passage from Plutarch is generally referred to by Philologists, and it has not been overlooked by Heyne, nor indeed by his forerunner, Clarke. It is in the *Platonicæ Quæstiones*[1], though I cannot but wonder that Heyne should advert to it at the very time when he asserts, that Homer knew nothing of the Article. Plutarch says, that " even Homer, who excels in beauty of diction, prefixes Articles to few of his Nouns, as to cups wanting handles, or helmets needing crests: hence some verses, in which he has done so, have been marked as spurious; for example:

Αἴαντι δὲ μάλιστα δαΐφρονι θυμὸν ὄρινε
ΤΩι Τελαμωνιάδῃ· and
———— ὄφρα ΤΟ κῆτος ὑπεκπροφυγὼν ἀλέοιτο·

and a few others: and yet the multitude of verses, in which the Article does not appear, suffer nothing in point of beauty or perspicuity." If this be Plutarch's meaning, so far from proving that Homer never used the Article, it proves incontestably that he sometimes *did* use it, though rarely; and it ought to be remembered, that Plutarch in this place was not likely to admit the use to be more frequent than it really is, since the main object of his argument was to prove, that only Nouns and Verbs are essential to language.

The passage from *Eustathius* is of a different cast: I have it on the authority of *Reizius de Prosodia Græca*. It asserts only, that "when the Articles throw away their Nouns, and thus become Pronouns, they are pronounced with a greater vehemence of tone: thus, if in ὁ γὰρ ('Ἀπόλλων) βασιλῆϊ χολωθείς, we omit Ἀπόλλων, ὁ is there uttered more audibly[2]." At first this may appear to indicate a real distinction between the Article and the Pronoun, marked by a difference of pronunciation: but when considered, it affirms only what we should expect to happen; that when the object, of which the

---

[1] P. 412. Edit. Bas. 1574. ὅπου καὶ ″Ομηρος ἐπέων κόσμῳ περιγενόμενος ὀλίγοις τῶν ὀνομάτων ἄρθρα, ὥσπερ λαβὰς ἐκπώμασι δεομένοις, ἢ λόφους κράνεσιν, ἐπιτίθησι.

[2] Eustath. p. 22. σφοδρότερον ἐκφωνοῦται κατὰ τοὺς τόνους .... ἐξακούστερον ἐκφωνεῖται.

ARTICLE DEFINED.

Article is meant to be significant, is not added, the mind of the hearer is forcibly to be directed to the Article itself, as the sole and unassisted representative of the speaker's meaning. The writer admits, that ὁ Ἀπόλλων and ὁ alone in the verse alluded to are perfectly equivalent: whence it is obvious, that in the judgment of Eustathius ὁ has in both cases the very same nature, viz. that of a Pronoun; but that in the one the person, whom it designates, is not easily mistaken, while in the other the addition of *Apollo* removes all ambiguity. Heyne, indeed, remarks on οἱ δὲ θεοὶ, Δ. 1. (a most legitimate example of the Article, in a verse too, which from its situation is completely proof against the *exterminating process*) that θεοὶ "*accipiendum est per interpretationem*," as if it were thus pointed, οἱ δέ, θεοί, πὰρ Ζηνί, &c. But is not this uniformly true of the acknowledged Article in *all* Greek writers? Does not the Noun subjoined in all cases equally answer the purpose of explanation? Or is explanation in this instance more necessary or more allowable than in thousands of others? The gods, it is true, had not recently been mentioned; and, therefore, οἱ by itself, however well understood by the writer, would have conveyed no clear idea to the reader: but neither in cases, in which the acknowledged Article is found, is the object of relation in general at all more clear, though known of course to the speaker: in both, therefore, something explanatory is subjoined. The Argument, then, which Heyne has employed to show that Homer, in this place, Δ. 1. has not used the Article, proves demonstratively that he has used it, by showing that he has placed the Pronoun οἱ (as Heyne would justly call it) in the very situation, in which, though it changes not its nature, it assumes the name of an Article, and exercises a function, by which alone the Article is distinguished.

The Article ὁ and the Pronoun ὁ are, then, essentially the same thing, differing only in having or not having an Adjunct: and the Pronoun in both these ways is repeatedly employed by Homer. Hence it appears that the opinion of the Stoics (see page 9.) was not incorrect: ὁ is always a Pronoun, though it usually retains that name only when it is a *defined Article*, i.e. when the object of its relation is so plainly marked, that no mistake can arise, and when, consequently, no Adjunct is requisite; they called it an *undefined Article*, when such addition became necessary to the perspicuity of its meaning. But of this addition, more in the following heads of inquiry. Under the present it may be observed, that of the Pronominal or *defined* use of the Article, that I mean in which it is used without an Adjunct, we find numerous remains, of a date much later than the time of Homer. The Ionic writers, as Herodotus for example, whose language so nearly resembles that of Homer, use the Article in this manner in all its cases beginning with T. The same thing has been observed of the Dorians [1]. By the Attic writers also it is so employed under certain restrictions, as after Prepositions [2]; in joining together persons or things, the names of which are suppressed; in partition and opposition; and where it is followed by the subjunctive Article ὅς [3].

SECTION II.

OBJECT OF ITS RELATION.

The second question which will occur, supposing it to have been shown that the Article, as used originally, and even by later writers, was no other than the Pronoun, respects the *object* of its *relation*.

In solving this question, which has indeed been already touched upon, it may be of use to attend to the Gender of the Article; and this, as every one knows, is invariably the same with that of the Predicate annexed or understood: insomuch that certain ancient Grammarians were hence of opinion, that the Article was invented to *mark the Gender* [4]. This opinion Apollonius has very clearly refuted; and he humourously observes, that as well might we suppose Nouns invented to show the Gender of the Article [5]; but when he adds, that the Article

---

[1] Reiz. de Prosod. Gr. p. 7.   [2] Reiz. p. 11.

[3] As Aristot. Top. vi. 13. § 14. ἐὰν μὴ καθ' αὑτὰ ᾖ ΤΑ, ἐξ ΩΝ σύγκειται, ἀγαθά. Here is another instance, and that not from Homer, in which the Article and Pronoun are demonstrated to be essentially the same: τά is τὰ πράγματα, but how is its nature affected, whether πράγματα be expressed or understood? Similar examples may be found in Lysias, Plato, &c.

[4] Οὐ μετρίως δέ τινες ἐσφάλησαν ὑπολαβόντες τὴν παράθεσιν τῶν ἄρθρων εἰς γένους διάκρισιν παρατίθεσθαι τοῖς ὀνόμασι. Apoll. p. 28.

[5] Ὡς τὰ ὀνόματα ἐπενοήθη εἰς διάκρισιν τῶν ἐν τοῖς ἄρθροις γενῶν. p. 30.

removes the ambiguity of Gender merely ἐκ παρεπομένου, he seems to go too far, and to ascribe to mere coincidence that which arises out of the nature of the case ; and this is the point now to be examined.

Apollonius, who every where distinguishes between the Pronoun and the Article [1], ascribes relation to both; though in tracing this relation through certain uses of the Article, he is compelled to admit that the relation is sometimes different from what is generally understood by the term. His words are, " Sometimes the relation is to some person whom we *anticipate* [2], where the Article appears to be *indefinite;* as when we say, Let him who has slain a tyrant be honoured : for here the Article refers to a *future* person." Here, no doubt, the fact can thus only be explained : but this is not the only case, in which we are compelled to have recourse to such a solution. We sometimes find the Article prefixed to Nouns, with which it has no generical agreement, as τὸ Ἀριστάρχοι, ἡ σήμερον, &c. where Apollonius acknowledges, what is beyond dispute, that the Article refers to the thing understood, i. e. to ὄνομα, ἡμέρα, &c. as the case may require. There are also instances, in which, by the confession of the speaker, the Article cannot refer to any thing preceding, as in what the Scholiast on Aristophanes calls " swearing elliptically," of which we have an example in an Epigram of Strato, from an inedited Anthology referred to by *Köen* ad *Greg. Cor.* p. 65.

Εἰ μὴ νῦν Κλεόνικος ἐλεύσεται, οὐκ ἔτ' ἐκεῖνον
Δέξομ' ἐγὼ μελάθροις, οὐ μὰ ΤΟΝ———οὐκ ὀμόσω.

In this and all similar instances it is plain, that the speaker considers himself as not having at all developed his meaning, inasmuch as the object of the relation is not expressed.

It is evident, then, that the reference is *sometimes* proleptical or anticipative ; and this circumstance added to the generical agreement, induces a suspicion, that it will always bear,

---

[1] Πῶς οὖν τοσαύτης διαφορᾶς οὔσης παραδέξεταί τις τὸ ὑφ' ἓν μέρος λόγου ὑπάγειν τὰ ἄρθρα καὶ τὰς ἀντωνυμίας ; p. 94.

[2] Ἔσθ' ὅτε καὶ προληπτικώτερον πρόσωπον ἀναφέρει· ὅτε δὴ καὶ ἀοριστῶδες φαίνεται· ὁ τυραννοκτονήσας τιμάσθω· τὸ γὰρ ὡς ἐσόμενον πρόσωπον ἀνεπόλησεν. p. 32.

if not always require, to be so explained: but let us observe. On opening the *Anabasis* of *Xenophon* at hazard, I find (Book III. not far from the beginning) the following passage: Ὁ μέντοι Ξενοφῶν, ἀναγνοὺς τὴν ἐπιστολήν, ἀνακοινοῦται Σωκράτει τῷ Ἀθηναίῳ περὶ τῆς πορείας. Καὶ ὁ Σωκράτης, ὑποπτεύσας, μή τι πρὸς τῆς πόλεώς οἱ ὑπαίτιον εἴη, Κύρῳ φίλον γενέσθαι, ὅτι ἐδόκει ὁ Κῦρος προθύμως τοῖς Λακεδαιμονίοις, κ. τ. λ. Throughout this passage, let us attend to the reference of the Article as often as it is used. Ὁ μέντοι. Who? the reference must not here be considered as retrospective; for since Xenophon was last mentioned, mention had been made both of Cyrus and of Proxenus: if, therefore, the reference be to Xenophon, it is distinguishable only by the addition of his name. To what does ΤΗΝ refer in ἀναγνοὺς τὴν ἐπιστολήν? The last feminine Substantive is πατρίδος, and ἐπιστολὴ has not yet occurred; the reference is to ἐπιστολὴν subjoined, which alone the writer could have in view. Σωκράτει τῷ Ἀθηναίῳ· here the reference is not to Σωκράτει generally and absolutely, because such a reference would be useless; but it is to that distinguishing attribute of Socrates, which is annexed, viz. his being an Athenian. Τῆς πορείας is similar to τὴν ἐπιστολήν.—Καὶ ὁ Σωκράτης· here it may be said that the Article may refer to Σωκράτης just mentioned. Certainly it may; but the writer did not think this reference sufficiently marked, or he needed not have attempted to make it plainer by repeating the name. Τῆς πόλεως· similar to τὴν ἐπιστολήν. Ὁ Κῦρος is similar to ὁ Σωκράτης. Τοῖς Λακεδαιμονίοις· no plural Substantive has yet occurred; τοῖς is evidently an anticipation of Λακεδαιμονίοις. In the same manner we might proceed, and with the same result, to the end of the volume.

In these instances, then, no doubt can arise as to the object of the relation: at least, it will be admitted to be *anticipative*, wherever the Noun, &c. annexed to the article is allowed to be absolutely necessary to the perspicuity of the sense. Cases, indeed, will occur, of which two are found in the passage above cited, where the reference *may* be understood *retrospectively*: but then it is obvious in all such instances, that exactly in proportion as is the evidence that the reference is retrospective, so will it be also evident that the Noun annexed is superfluous. Thus, if in ὁ Σωκράτης above it be said, that ὁ will naturally refer to Σωκράτης in the preceding period, it must also be granted, that Σωκράτης annexed is needlessly introduced, and is absolutely without meaning: but this, surely, is more than the thinking reader will affirm or believe; and he will probably rather adopt the solution, that though the object of the relation might be conjectured without assistance, yet the writer judged it to be safer to afford that assistance by immediately subjoining the name of the person, to whom the Article was intended to refer. It is not consonant with the nature of language, nor with the practice of good writers, to suppose that words are ever wholly devoid of use. It is better to say in all such cases, that the caution of the writer was extreme [1].

If the doctrine here maintained be true, we see the reason why the Article in all good writers is placed immediately, or almost immediately, before its *Predicate;* for the reference being anticipative, the mind of the hearer will not bear long suspense: till the object of reference be known, every thing intervening will be disregarded. In *retrospective* reference, like that of ὃς or *qui*, the case is altogether different; for there no suspense can take place: it is not known by the hearer, when an object is mentioned, that it will afterwards be referred to, nor till the reference is actually made.—The principal breach of this rule respecting the juxta-position of the Article and its *Predicate* is observable in the case of proper names. Thus we read in Homer Il. xviii. v. 202. Ἡ μὲν

---

[1] Of this *extreme caution* there are some remarkable instances in *Ælian:* I will adduce one of these, in which the Predicate of the Article assumes an unusual form, while it strongly supports the doctrine that such Predicate is the object of a relation supposed to be obscure. The passage will be found *Var. Hist.* lib. i. cap. 30. Ὁ μὲν ἵππευε σὺν τῷ βασιλεῖ ΤΟ ΜΕΙΡΑΚΙΟΝ. Now only two persons, the King and the Youth, had been mentioned : and the King seems by the context to be excluded from answering to ὁ, which of course will therefore relate to the Youth. The writer, however, has subjoined τὸ μειράκιον; a convincing proof that he considered such an addition as explanatory of the relation intended in the Pronoun, for else it has *no* meaning at all. Had the sentence begun with ὁ νεανίας, or some other masculine Noun synonymous with μειράκιον, the usual form would have been observed. He has, however, violated the practice; but in so doing he has very remarkably confirmed the principle: for ὁ νεανίας would have afforded no new ground of argument. The same author has other similar examples.

ἄρ' ὣς εἰποῦσ' ἀπέβη πόδας ὠκέα Ἶρις· but the reader is not here kept in much suspense, since if Iris had not been named *at all*, the sense would have been tolerably clear, and the reference would have been made to *Iris*, whose arrival and address are the principal subjects of the preceding verses. But more of this when we come to speak particularly of PROPER NAMES.

SECTION III.

OBSCURE REFERENCE.

But the reader may still entertain some doubt respecting the existence of a relation admitted to be obscure: it will therefore be expedient to show, that the reference here described is not without its parallel, and that there is in it no obscurity, which does not arise out of the nature of the case.

In truth, the reference of Pronouns, even of those, I mean, which are acknowledged to be such, is at best obscure. Apollonius has remarked this fact in the following words : " Pronouns are of no use, when deprived of the person indicating and the person indicated: for, when written, they are of all things the most indefinite, because then they are detached from their proper subject-matter. Hence we see the reason why perfect writing requires the addition of the Nouns themselves[1]." He goes on afterwards, indeed, to show that this remark applies only to Pronouns of the third person : a limitation, however, which does not affect the point now in question. It is, doubtless, on a principle analogous to that laid down by Apollonius, that the Latin writers sometimes explain the reference contained in their Pronoun Relative *qui*, in which, however, the reference is perhaps as strongly marked as in any Pronoun of any language. Thus we find such expressions as the following : " Bellum tantum, *quo bello* omnes premebantur, Pompeius confecit." *Cic.* " Ultra eum locum, *quo* in *loco* Ger-

---

[1] "Ἕνεκεν τούτου καὶ πρὸς οὐδὲν χρειώδεις εἰσιν αἱ ἀντωνυμίαι, στερούμεναι τοῦ τε δεικνύντος προσώπου καὶ τοῦ δεικνυμένου· εἴγε καὶ αἱ ἐγγραφόμεναι πάνυ ἀοριστότατοί εἰσιν, ὅτι καὶ τῆς ἰδίας ὕλης ἀπεώσθησαν· ἔνθεν δοκεῖ πάνυ εὐλόγως κατὰ τὰς ἐντελικὰς γραφὰς χωρὶς τῶν προστεθειμένων ὀνομάτων τὰ τοῦ λόγου μὴ καθίστασθαι. P. 118.

mani consederant." *Cæs.* " Diem instare, *quo die* frumentum militibus metiri oporteret." *Cæs.* [1] And so in a multitude of instances. In all these we have a confession of *obscure reference*, though the object of that reference has immediately preceded the Pronoun, without the intervention of any other Noun to create extraordinary ambiguity.

In the passage cited in Chapter I. from Theodore Gaza, it was affirmed that there are two Articles, the Prepositive ὁ and the Subjunctive ὅς; though according to that Grammarian, the Prepositive only, strictly speaking, deserves the appellation. This seems to be the proper place to attempt solutions of the two questions, Why ὅς was ever denominated an Article, and why that denomination was deemed unsuitable? We have just seen in what manner the Latins sometimes used their *qui:* if the Greek ὅς had been constantly so explained, it would, on the principles advanced in this Essay, deserve to be considered as an Article, no less than does ὁ ; for we should then have a Pronoun Relative, the confessedly obscure reference of which was explained by an Adjunct. In such a sentence as ἡ κώμη, εἰς ἣν (κώμην) ἀφίκοντο, μεγάλη ἦν, I should regard εἰς ἣν κώμην to be a legitimate example of the case, in which the Article, with its Predicate, conjointly referred to something preceding, though the insertion of the Predicate marked *extreme caution*. This, however, is not the exact passage, as it stands in Xenophon; nor do I know where one precisely of the same form is to be found. In Xenophon's Anab. iv. 4. it is εἰς ἣν ἀφίκοντο κώμην, μεγάλη ἦν. This case differs from the former, inasmuch as κώμην is not here added from extreme caution, but from absolute necessity, because the object of reference had not yet been mentioned, and could not be conjectured. The analogy, however, between ὅς and ὁ may be traced in the following authentic example: in the Iliad Δ. 306. ῝ΟΣ δέ κ' ᾽ΑΝΗΡ ἀπὸ ὧν ὀχέων ἕτερ' ἅρμαθ' ἵκηται, κ. τ. λ. we have a close resemblance of the manner in which the Article is subservient to *Hypothesis*. See below, Chap. III. Sect. 2. But as this hypothetic use of ὅς is not very common, and as the other is scarcely, if at all, to be found, it was a natural consequence, that ὁ, in which both these uses are so frequent,

---

[1] Vid. Sanctii Minervam, lib. ii. cap. 9.

should come to be considered as the only legitimate Article; the Pronoun ὅς not having connection with any Noun, except that to which it was *subjoined*. They were called ἄρθρα, as we learn from the Grammatical Treatise published with St. Basil, but ascribed to Johannes Moschopulus, διὰ τὸ συναρτᾷσθαι τοῖς ὀνόμασιν· though, perhaps, this etymology may be doubted.

There is not, then, any thing in the idea of *obscure relation* which should lead us to question its existence; since we find it recognized both in theory and in practice, and that too in cases in which the obscurity is least liable to create confusion, viz. in those in which the reference may be understood retrospectively; which in the case of the Article does not always happen. But what will be the consequence, should a Pronoun, in the arrangement of a sentence, precede the Substantive, to which it is intended to refer? What, for example, in the following lines of Horace?

> At neque dedecorant tua de *se* judicia, atque
> Munera, quæ multa dantis cum laude tulerunt
> Dilecti tibi *Virgilius Variusque Poetæ*.

Here we have an instance of relation to the full as obscure as that for which I contend; nor could the hero of these verses ever conjecture to whom the Pronoun was intended to refer, till the names of Virgil and Varius were actually pronounced. To the writer or speaker, indeed, they exhibit nothing of obscurity; but neither does the anticipative reference of the Article, and for the same reason in each case: the object of reference is to him previously known.

There is, moreover, nothing more natural than this kind of anticipation. We easily suppose, till we have taken time to reflect, that what we ourselves understand must be understood by others; and in the ardour of speaking we are apt to adopt symbols recommended by their obviousness, and to us sufficiently significant of our meaning, even where we are conscious that to others that meaning is not without ambiguity. This propensity finds the readier excuse, whenever the subject not only is uppermost in our own minds, but is supposed to be so also in the mind of the hearer, which will happen whenever we refer to something recently mentioned; and this practice must be the more habitual to a people so rapid in thought and in expression, as were the ancient Greeks.

It may, then, be affirmed, that in the reference of the Article there is no other obscurity than that which arises out of the *nature* of that reference; which has been shown generally to be anticipative; for that even where it is not necessary so to understand it, that is, where the Article may be made to refer to something preceding, still a strict regard to perspicuity prefers a repetition of the object to the risk of ambiguity and confusion.

SECTION IV.

ANTICIPATIVE REFERENCE VINDICATED.

Further, it may be questioned, how far this doctrine of the anticipative reference of the Article accords with well known facts. The Grammarians have asserted, and every one must have observed, that the Article is apparently subservient to the purpose of *relation* in the more usual sense of that term. Indeed its relative and its *definitive* powers seem to some writers to comprehend every thing which properly belongs to it, and to constitute its very essence. Thus it will be said, in the passage adduced (p. 16.) from Xenophon, τὴν ἐπιστολήν, though no letter has been directly mentioned, recalls the idea of one *implied* in μετεπέμψατο. So τῆς πορείας relates to the expedition *proposed*. So also τῆς πόλεως will be understood of Athens, κατ' ἐξοχήν. All this, and much more of the same kind, may be admitted without any danger to the hypothesis, unless the reference of the Article and its Predicate *conjointly* be confounded with that of the Article *alone*; than which no two things are more distinct. Indeed, it could not be affirmed in the instances here adduced, that the respective Articles have *by themselves* any such reference, because till the several Substantives, ἐπιστολήν, &c. were pronounced, the hearer could not possibly know what the speaker intended to add; nor would the reference in these instances be at all more plain, if, instead of the obsolete Pronouns τήν, &c. any of the more usual ones had been employed. It is evident, therefore, even where a *retrospective* reference is admitted to exist, that this reference is not declared by the Article considered *independently* of its Predicate. The Article in these instances produces the effect not directly, but circuitously; it refers us to its Noun annexed; which Noun may possibly be the same with one already mentioned, and which, therefore, it recalls, or at least, as in the instances before us, with one already implied, and standing so prominent to the mind of the hearer, that he can hardly fail to make the application. And this is all which is meant by Apollonius, when he says, that the Article recalls the *third person*[1], and that the *Article with a Noun* is equivalent to the Pronoun Relative[2]. So much for the only cases in which the anticipative reference of the Article is liable to be called in question.

But the same Apollonius admits that there are instances in which the Article is used without any such retrospective reference. He tells us that it is sometimes employed *indefinitely*, as in ὁ τυραννοκτονήσας τιμάσθω[3]· and further on he adds, that the Article is applied not only to *defined* persons, but also to that, which in its nature is most *undefined*, as in ὁ περιπατῶν κινεῖται, which, as he observes, is the same with εἴ τις περιπατεῖ, &c. Some other examples of an use equally indefinite will be noticed hereafter.—Now these instances and this admission of the great Grammarian are alone sufficient to excite a surmise, that the reference of the Article is very different from that which is commonly supposed; for surely nothing can be more improbable, than that any thing, in its nature one and the same, should be subservient to purposes diametrically opposite. Either the Article marking *definiteness* must be essentially different from that used to signify *indefiniteness*, (which, however, is not pretended,) or else its reference must be of such a nature, as, properly understood, to combine and unite in one form these contradictory appearances. Sound philosophy offers us only these alternatives. The kind of reference, then, here maintained, seems adapted to reconcile these differences: for if the Article, strictly so called, in itself be always anticipative, and if the retrospection observable in the Article and its Predicate conjointly cannot subsist without the Predicate (for

---

[1] P. 54.
[2] Ἀντὶ τῶν ὀνομάτων τῶν μετ' ἄρθρων. P. 103.
[3] P. 76.

else no Predicate is employed; see above), it is just as intelligible why ὁ περιπατῶν should be spoken of *any* person whatever, as why ὁ ῥήτωρ should mean the *particular* orator, of whom mention has recently been made: for in strictness the meaning of the article will be the same in each case; and the difference in the result will be merely accidental. Ὁ περιπατῶν is equivalent to *ille, qui circumambulat*, whether any person has been affirmed to walk about, or not: and so ὁ ῥήτωρ is no more in itself than *ille, qui est orator;* though possibly the very recent mention of some ῥήτωρ may lead the hearer to identify the persons respectively implied. But this is by no means always the case. Examples of the contrary are abundant. Thus in *Demosth.* de Cor. § 68. ὁ ΤΟΝ ῥήτορα βουλόμενος δικαίως ἐξετάζειν καὶ μή, &c.; τὸν ῥήτορα no more refers to any definite or particular person, than does ὁ βουλόμενος; but is applicable to every individual of whom *Orator* can be predicated.

The reference, therefore, of the Article itself is in strictness always *anticipative*, and its power of recalling persons and things already mentioned is not of the *essence* of the Article, however, by the aid of its *Predicate*, this power may indirectly be exerted. I conclude that I am here understood to speak of the Article usually so called: for when it has no Predicate, that is, when, as the Grammarians tell us, it passes into a Pronoun, it is plain that the reference is supposed to be marked with sufficient clearness, and that such reference cannot be other than retrospective.

But here it becomes important to ascertain the *limits* of this anticipation: is the speaker always at liberty to anticipate an Adjunct? Assuredly not; for then the Article might be used without necessity or meaning. The limits, however, are plainly deducible from the principles already laid down. We have seen that the Article and its Predicate together constitute what I have denominated an assumptive proposition: the question, therefore, is only what are the cases in which an assumptive proposition may be employed? Evidently it can be employed only where the assumption contained in it is admissible, from its being the assumption of that which will immediately be recognized in consequence of something which had preceded; or else, where it is only conditional, the subsequent assertion not being intended to apply in any greater extent, than is conceded to the assumption. Now the legitimacy of the former kind of assumption will be manifest, if we consider, that in making it we do nothing more, than assume of a Pronoun those attributes or properties which, either from previous mention or from some other implied cause, are immediately understood to belong to the person or thing which the Pronoun represents. Thus, if I have been speaking of a horse, or of any thing in which the presence of a horse is implied, ἑώρακα τὸν ἵππον will be a legitimate assumption: otherwise it will not; for the assumption will not be admitted, not being intelligible. As often, however, as assumptions are made of that, which is implied in something preceding, it will happen, as in ἑώρακα τὸν ἵππον, that the same person or thing is meant, which had already engaged our notice: and hence, as these cases occur so frequently, some Grammarians have made the Article to be merely a *Definitive*. In objecting to this doctrine, I do not deny that the Greeks, whenever they wish to speak of any thing *definitely*, do employ the Article: and this end could not by any other means be attained more fully. A Pronoun more or less obscurely recalling the Antecedent so intended, and having its obscure relation explained by the addition of the peculiar attributes of that Antecedent, must evidently form as complete a repetition of the intended object, as the mind can conceive. The Pronoun alone may be insufficient, of which we have had examples: and in the repetition merely of the Noun, the individual spoken of would not be identified with that which had preceded; but the conjunction of both the Pronoun and its Adjunct leaves no ambiguity. Still, however, the Article is not in its nature a Definitive; for then what is usually called its *indefinite* sense could not have existence: it answers the purpose of a Definitive merely κατὰ συμβεβηκός: in strict truth, its Adjunct has a better claim to the title, being, as we have seen, added to the Pronoun to ascertain its relation.—Of the other kind of assumption the case is somewhat different: it has no retrospective reference or effect; and in order to render it legitimate, nothing more is necessary than that the assertion connected with it should be bounded in its extent by the limits of the assumption. Thus in ὁ περιπατῶν κινεῖται, κινεῖται is asserted of every one who *walks about*, and of no other, whether such persons be infinite in number, or finite, or none at all. So Aristotle (de Mor. Nicom. lib. iv. cap, 2.) ἀγαπῶσι τὰ αὑτῶν ἔργα ΟΙ γονεῖς καὶ ΟΙ ποιηταί· here we find two sets of persons assumed, the one comprehending a very large proportion of the human race, and the other only a few individuals; yet since the extent of the assertion is in each case exactly commensurate with that of the assumption, the assumption is perfectly allowable: so also (ibid.) Aristotle has said, πλουτεῖν οὐ ῥᾴδιον ΤΟΝ ἐλευθέριον· this assumption also is legitimate, whatever be the degree of liberality existing among mankind: the proposition is only, that *supposing* a man to be liberal, it is difficult for such an one to grow rich; of him who is not admitted to be liberal no such difficulty is affirmed.

It seems, therefore, that the remark made above (p. 20.) of the Article's being the symbol of that which is uppermost in the speaker's mind, is applicable not only to the case of reference to something already mentioned, but also to the person or thing which is about to become the subject of an assertion: for such must at the time be the object most familiar to our own minds, though perhaps most foreign from that of our hearer.

Hence it may briefly be observed, that the obscurity of reference in the former use of the Article is often great, but in the latter it is always total; since it is there impossible for the hearer to anticipate the Predicate.

On the whole, it appears that the Article may be used, either when, conjointly with its Predicate, it recalls some former idea, or when it is intended to serve as the subject of an hypothesis. All the various uses of the Article will come under one of these two divisions. The cases of *Proper Names*, and that of the names of *Abstract Ideas*, will be considered apart.

SECTION V.

PARTICIPLE OF EXISTENCE UNDERSTOOD.

The only remaining question, to which the definition attempted is likely to give rise, respects the subintellection of the Participle of Existence, as a *Copula* between the Article and its Predicate. It is worthy of remark, that *Lennep*, speaking of the Article, has these words: "*Articulus* Ὁ *vicinitatem habere propriè videtur cum Participio Verbi* εἰμι *vel* ἐω *sum*[1]." His precise meaning I pretend not to ascertain; nor are *vicinitatem* and *videtur* words capable of very close restriction. It is probable, however, that he had some vague notion of the truth which I would establish: possibly he meant, that the Article in some places appeared to indicate an ellipsis of the Participle, and to convey the same meaning as if the Participle had been expressed; and this is not partially, but universally, the case. If, indeed, it be admitted, on the proofs already given, that the Article is no other than a Pronoun, the subintellection of the Participle becomes a necessary consequence; for else between the Pronoun and its Predicate there will be no more connection than if they occurred in different propositions. Ὁ ἀνὴρ must signify He, or the Male, *being* or *assumed to be* a man; or else the Pronoun and the Substantive have no common medium, no principle of union, by which they can be brought to act together in developing the ideas of the speaker. The conclusion will be the same, though the reasoning will be somewhat different, if we suppose the Predicate of the Article to be an *Adjective*. Thus in the proposition, ὁ ἀγαθὸς Σωκράτης φιλοσοφεῖ, ὁ ἀγαθὸς is equivalent to ὁ ᾽ΩΝ ἀγαθός, as *Gaza* indeed admits. He says that the latter phrase, τὸ ἐντελὲς ἦν[2], i. e. that the former one is an ellipsis: the same is evident of ἠρᾶθ᾽ ὁ γεραιὸς in Homer, and of all similar instances[3]. Frequently, indeed, we find the Participle of Existence *expressed:* thus Aristotle (de Mor. loc. laud.) οἱ μάλιστα ἄξιοι ΟΝΤΕΣ ἥκιστα πλουτοῦσι· where the author's meaning would have been equally certain, had the Participle been omitted.

In order to perceive that the conclusion will not be different where the Predicate of the Article is a *Participle*, it is necessary to attend a little to the nature of Propositions, and to the distinction between the Participle and the Verb. Logicians teach us that every Proposition contains a *Subject* and a *Predi-*

[1] Etymol. vol. ii. p. 632. Edit. Scheidii.
[2] Gramm. lib. iv. p. 131.
[3] Compare the use of the Article in such expressions as the following: ἅπανθ᾽ ἕτερα τοῦ ἑνός, καὶ τὸ ἓν τῶν μὴ ἕν. Plato. *Parmen.* 40. J. S.

cate connected by a *Copula*; and that where this *Copula* is not marked by a distinct word, it is implied in the Verb. Thus in *Homo EST animal*, the Copula is manifestly *est*: in *Homo ambulat*, we find it not, indeed, distinctly expressed, but we are sure that it exists in *ambulat*, for *ambulat* is equivalent to *EST ambulans* [1], *ambulabit* to *ERIT ambulans*, &c. Now if this happen invariably in the Verb, what will take place in the Participle? This differs from the Verb, says *Harris* [2], in losing the *assertion:* I think he would have done still better in adding, " In place of which it takes an *assumption* [3];" for if in Σωκράτης γράφει there be an *assertion* that Socrates writeth, in Σωκράτης γράφων, there is an *assumption* of the same truth; so much so, that if the fact of his writing be disallowed, the assertion depending on it will amount to nothing: thus in Σωκράτης γράφων ἥδεται, the assertion of his being *delighted* has no foundation, if Socrates never write.—It is plain, then, that the Participle differs from the Verb in being connected with its subject by ὤν, instead of ἐστὶ in the Present Tense, and by the corresponding Participle of Existence in others; and this will hold equally, whether that subject be a Noun or a Pronoun, which latter the Article has been shown to be. We are, therefore, authorized to conclude, that the Participle of Existence is virtually employed as an *assumptive Copula* between the Article and its Predicate, even when that Predicate is a Participle: which, unless it *contain within itself* the assumptive Copula, must require the subintellection of such a Copula just as much as does the Adjective, (see p. 26.) since the difference between the Participle and the Adjective is, as *Harris* and others have observed, that the former, besides an attribute,

---

[1] Arist. Met. lib. iv. 6. Οὐδὲν γὰρ διαφέρει τὸ ἄνθρωπος ὑγιαίνων ἐστὶν ἢ τὸ ἄνθρωπος ὑγιαίνει· ἢ τὸ ἄνθρωπος βαδίζων ἐστὶν ἢ τέμνων τοῦ ἄνθρωπον βαδίζειν ἢ τέμνειν.

[2] Herm. p. 184. " Every complete Verb is expressive of an attribute of time and of an assertion. Now if we take away the assertion, and thus destroy the Verb, there will remain the attribute and the time, which will make the essence of a Participle."

[3] It is true, indeed, that if an assumption (as will be shown) exist in the Participle, it must also have existed in the Verb, of which the Participle is a component part. In the Verb, however, the assumption was quiescent, being absorbed in the assertion: in the Participle it exercises a function as important, as did the assertion in the Verb.

expresses *time*[1]: but time is not a Copula: consequently the Participle will require the assumptive Copula just as much as does the Adjective.

[1] *Mr. H. Tooke,* vol. ii. p. 470, denies, after Sanctius, that there is in the Participle of the *Present Tense* any adsignification of *Time:* and his proofs consist in instances so chosen, that this Participle is associated either with a Verb of the Past or Future Tense, or else with the words *always, at all times,* &c. Of the former kind is " *accessit* amans pretium *pollicens:*" now in this example I really should have thought that the adsignification of time was plainly marked, and was necessary to the sense. It is true that the *present time* therein expressed is not the moment of my writing these remarks: but at that rate, present time cannot be made the subject of discussion: *dum loquimur, fugerit:* but surely in *pollicens* there is an adsignification of time, and that too *present* time, in respect of the act implied in *accessit:* that act, indeed, is spoken of as being past; yet as having once been present; and the meaning is, that the two acts, viz. *accedendi* and *pollicendi,* were simultaneous. Mr. Tooke allows that the Participles of the other Tenses *do* express time: and yet his argument will serve just as well to show that this too is a mistake: thus when Dido asks, " Quem *metui moritura?*" it may be objected that *moritura* cannot have a *future* tense, because of *metui:* yet the answer is plain: Dido was *moritura, quum metueret:* in all such cases we are to refer the time of the Participle to the time of the act, &c. implied in the Verb: for past, present, and future, cannot be meant otherwise than in respect of that act. Thus I may say, *lapsus* clamavi, *labens* clamavi, *lapsurus* clamavi; and all of them with an adsignification of relative time.

Mr. Tooke's own examples are, " The *rising* sun *always* gladdens the earth," and " Do justice, justice *being at all times* mercy." Now of the former of these I think it may be affirmed, that if we be permitted to attend to the *meaning* of the proposition, (and Mr. Tooke is a zealous advocate for common sense,) it is only that the Sun gladdens the Earth, so often as its rising is a present act: to say *always,* is not very correct. The difficulty proposed in the latter example is to make out, how time present can be signified, where any thing happens *continually:* and yet even this involves no absurdity, unless it be absurd to say, that all time consists of an indefinite number of moments, in each of which, as it is present, the proposition is true. And this is a natural, because a compendious method (Mr. Tooke would call it an *abbreviation*) of expressing truths of this kind, instead of saying it always was so, and now is so, and ever will be so. Accordingly, Mr. Tooke with the Participle *being* has associated *at all times:* I observe, that he has not given any instance, in which it may be connected with Adverbs either of *past* or of *future* time: he has not joined *being* with *anciently* or *hereafter:* with which, however, if that word have no adsignification of time present, it is not easy to discover, why it will not endure to be associated. It will hardly be said, that *at all times* comprises *time past* and *time future:* this would be, to use Mr. Tooke's own phrase on this very subject, but " a shabby evasion:" at any rate, if the term be thus comprehensive, let it be resolved into the three times, of which it is composed, and the experiment be made separately on each: an example is wanted similar to the following: " this building, *being anciently* a Chapel, is now a Barn." If I mistake not, a more specious instance, than any of those adduced by Mr. Tooke, is Homer's

Ὅς ἤδη τά τ' ἰόντα τά τ' ἐσσόμενα ΠΡΟ τ' ἘΟΝΤΑ.

This

But I have said, unless the Participle *contain within itself* the assumptive Copula; for some Grammarians have thought that they discovered in the formation of Participles the very Copula in question. Scaliger says (see Hermes, p. 370.) that though the Romans rejected from their language the simple word *ens*, they used it in the composition of their active Participles; so that *audi*ENS is ἀκούων ὤν. This is true, no doubt; but how happens it that ἀκούων 'ΩΝ is foreign from the Greek idiom? Evidently because the Greeks have made the very same use of 'ΩΝ, which the Latins made of *ens*: they have incorporated it with their Participles of the Present Tense in each of their six Conjugations. The assumptive Copula, therefore, in ὁ ἀκούων does not require to be *distinctly* expressed, being already contained within the Participle.

Under this head it may be observed, that in the Greek Idiotisms, οἱ ἀμφί, &c. ὁ τότε, &c. ὁ Φιλίππου, and many others of the same sort, every reader supplies ὄντες or ὤν, as the case may require, without hesitation.

The Article, then, always indicates the subintellection of

This example, however, tends to confirm the opinion of those Grammarians who make ἐών to have been originally a Participle of a Past Tense, though even so early as in Homer's time this acceptation seems not to have been sufficiently intelligible without the aid of πρό: that τά τ' ἐόντα *by itself* would be understood of things present is evident from this very passage, and from many others of Homer. So also, in the 25th of the Hymns ascribed to Orpheus,

ἐπιστάμενος ΤΑ τ' 'ΕΟΝΤΑ,
"Οσσα τε πρόσθεν ἔην, ὅσα τ' ἔσσεται ὕστερον αὖτις.

We have also in Plutarch de Isid. et Osir. this ancient inscription, ἐγώ εἰμι πᾶν τὸ γεγονὸς καὶ 'ΟΝ καὶ ἐσόμενον. In like manner in Xenoph. Conviv. Xantippe is said to be ΤΩΝ ΟΥΣΩΝ καὶ τῶν γεγενημένων καὶ τῶν ἐσομένων χαλεπωτάτη. In all such passages, he who denies that ὤν has an adsignification of present time, must possess a degree of scepticism with which it would be folly to contend.

But, after all, my hypothesis will not be affected, unless that *something more* which, according to Mr. Tooke, the Participle contains over and above the attribute, be both distinct from and incompatible with the assumptive Copula.

The dispute respecting ὤν is not confined to Grammarians; it has found its way into Theology. Socinus thought that this Participle, having no adsignification of present time, might as well be confined to the *Past*; and that thus an important passage, John iii. 13, ὁ ὢν ἐν οὐρανῷ, might be softened by being rendered *qui* ERAT *in cœlo*. See Glass, *Philol. Sacr.* p. 434. ed. 1711.

the Participle of Existence, where that Participle is not expressed, or otherwise implied.

I do not find that *Apollonius* has directly treated of this subintellection; but in some of his remarks we perceive plainly, that he recognised the principle, though he has not, if I remember rightly, positively adverted to the fact.

I will add only, in confirmation of this part of my theory, that it explains the reason, why the Article is prefixed only to Nouns, Adjectives, and Participles[1]: for if the word annexed to the Article be in all cases the *Predicate* of an assumptive Proposition, of which the Article is the *Subject*, and the Participle of Existence expressed or implied the *Copula*, it is plain that the word so associated must be something, which in its nature is capable of being predicated, but which has not, where the insertion of ὢν is admissible, a Copula *within itself;* for then there would be two *Copulæ* of the same kind, which no proposition admits. Thus if in an assertive proposition I say, *He is* ———, leaving the place of the Predicate vacant, I can fill up this vacancy only by adding, *a Philosopher, wise,* or *walking*, &c, I cannot add *walks* any more than in Greek to ὁ ἐστὶν I could add ΠΕΡΙΠΑΤΕΙ, because *walks* and ΠΕΡΙΠΑΤΕΙ contain each an assertive *Copula*, the place of which in the proposition in question is already occupied: and the same is true, if instead of the *assertive Proposition He is*, we take the *assumptive* one, *He being:* we can, therefore, say only ὁ φιλόσοφος, ὁ σοφός, ὁ περιπατῶν.

---

[1] Verbs of the Infinitive Mood. *Author's MS.*

CHAPTER III.

APPELLATIVES.

In the last Chapter it was my endeavour to produce evidence in favour of each distinct head of the Hypothesis: I am next to show that, if it be admitted, it is capable (if I may use the expression) of solving the principal *phænomena:* in other words, that it will account for the most remarkable peculiarities in the usage of the Article, and that what may to some appear to be *arbitrary custom*, is in truth, supposing the principles laid down to be sufficiently established, a natural, if not a necessary consequence. Should this point be made out to the satisfaction of the reader, it is obvious that some weight will accompany the decisions, to which this inquiry may lead. If the prevailing *usage* in its principal varieties be such, as would arise out of the supposed *nature* of the Article, that *nature*, it will be concluded, has been accurately ascertained. I shall, therefore, on the evidence already adduced, suppose the Article to be such as it has been described to be, and shall now proceed to apply what has been said, to the explanation of the most remarkable *insertions* of the Article; to its most remarkable *omissions;* and to some cases of insertion and omission *combined*.

SECTION I.

INSERTIONS IN REFERENCE.

It has been shown, that all the insertions of the Article are reducible to two kinds, arising out of one property, viz. its anticipative reference: for the anticipation must be either of that which is known, or of that which is unknown: in the former case the Article with its Predicate is subservient to the purpose of retrospective reference, in the latter to that of hypothesis. Under the former of these heads we may class the cases which are the subject of the present Section.

§ 1. *Renewed mention*. When a person or thing recently mentioned is spoken of again, the Article, as is well known, is inserted when the mention is renewed; and this happens, not only when the *same* Noun is *repeated*, but also when a *synonymous* one is used expressive of the same person or thing, and even when *no* such Noun has preceded, but the existence of such person or thing may be inferred from what has been said; for then also the name of the person or thing, of which the existence is so inferred, has the Article prefixed.

EXAMPLES.

Xen. Mem. lib. III. cap. 13. Κολάσαντος δέ τινος ἰσχυρῶς ᾽ΑΚΟΛΟΥΘΟΝ, ἤρετο τί χαλεπαίνοι ΤΩι θεράποντι.

Æschin. cont. Ctes. § 56. οὗτος ΠΡΟΔΟΥΣ τοῖς πολεμίοις Νύμφαιον φυγὰς ἐγένετο, ΤΗΝ κρίσιν οὐχ ὑπομείνας.

Ibid. § 34. ὅταν τι ΨΕΥΔΩΝΤΑΙ, ἀόριστα καὶ ἀσαφῆ πειρῶνται λέγειν, φοβούμενοι ΤΟΝ ἔλεγχον.

These examples present very different degrees of obscurity in the relation of the Article, though in each the reference is made equally clear by the subjoined explanation or Predicate. In the first we almost anticipate ἀκολούθῳ; and on finding the synonymous word θεράποντι, we of course have no difficulty in perceiving that the Article and its Predicate form a renewed mention of ἀκόλουθος above. In the second, τήν, though anticipating an idea as much the object of the *speaker's* attention as was that introduced by τῷ in the former, presents a relation which to the mind of the hearer is involved in total obscurity, yet by the addition of κρίσιν the relation of the whole is just as evident as it was in the first example. It was not at all more certain that τῷ θεράποντι indicated the same person who had just been denominated ἀκόλουθος, than that τὴν κρίσιν is the *trial* to which the *traitor* would have been subjected.—It is superfluous to produce instances in which the very *same* Noun is repeated, since they so frequently occur.

But it will often happen, that even with the aid of the Predicate, the reference will not appear to have been made to any person or thing, which has been actually mentioned, nor even to that, the existence of which (as in Exam. 2. above) may be inferred from something already said: there lie dormant in the mind of every hearer a multitude of ideas, which are perfectly familiar to it, though not constantly the subjects of its contemplation, and to which, therefore, a reference may be made with the same certainty that the relation will be perceived, as if it were to something recently spoken of, or actually present to the mind. Of this reference there are various kinds, so closely allied to each other, that sometimes they are scarcely distinguishable.

Thus the Article is said to be used

§ 2. ΚΑΤ' ΕΞΟΧΗΝ, when it refers to some object, of which there are many, but no one of which is so familiar to the mind of the hearer, as that which is made the Predicate of the Article.

EXAMPLES.

Thucyd. lib. ii. § 59. Ἡ νόσος ἐπέκειτο ἅμα καὶ Ὁ πόλεμος, i.e. the *celebrated plague*, and the *Peloponnesian War*.

Demosth. de Cor. § 30. ΤΟ μέρος τῶν ψήφων οὐ λαβὼν, i.e. the well known fifth part: where some MSS. insert πεμπτόν, a manifest gloss.

Æsch. cont. Ctes. § 13. Ὁ ῥήτωρ γέγραφε, &c. meaning *Ctesiphon*.

In the last example it will immediately be seen, that excellence does not necessarily enter into the idea, which this use of the Article is intended to convey: Æschines did not mean to compliment the friend of his great enemy; but in both instances the reference of the Article and the Predicate is at once perceived, as being made to objects which are familiar to the mind of him who is addressed. This remark is important, because the opinion is very prevalent, at least among the commentators on the New Testament, (as will be seen hereafter,) that this use of the Article *always* indicates *pre-eminent worth* or *dignity;* than which no opinion can be more unfounded. Pre-eminent dignity will, it is true, frequently be found expressed by Nouns with the Article prefixed; and for the obvious reason, that such dignity forms in every mind one of those ideas, which it has probably at some time or other entertained,

D

and to which, therefore, a reference may consistently be made. Thus, ancient writers sometimes speak of *Homer* under the appellation of Ὁ ποιητής. Considering his acknowledged preeminence, such a phrase must have been, in most cases, of obvious application: yet even this phrase, as *Harris* admits, was not exclusively so understood, being used by *Plato* to signify *Hesiod*, and by *Aristotle* to mean *Euripides*. On the whole it is not safe to infer universally, from this use of the Article, any thing more, than that the person or thing spoken of is from some cause or other *well known*: the *particular* cause may be a subject of further consideration.

§ 3. Very nearly allied to the use last mentioned, is that of the Article prefixed to *Monadic Nouns;* i. e. Nouns indicating persons or things, which exist singly, or of which, if there be several, only one, from the nature of the case, can be the subject of discourse.

EXAMPLES.

Lysias, Orat. Gr. vol. v. p. 139. Ἐκκόψας ΤΑΣ θύρας εἰσῆλθεν εἰς ΤΗΝ γυναικωνῖτιν.
Demosth. de Cor. § 53. ΟΙ μὲν Πρυτάνεις ΤΗΝ Βουλὴν ἐκάλουν εἰς ΤΟ Βουλευτήριον· ὑμεῖς δ᾽ εἰς ΤΗΝ Ἐκκλησίαν ἐπορεύεσθε.
Plato Theæt. vol. ii. p. 50. ἡμῖν Ὁ παῖς ἀναγνώσεται.

§ 4. Under the same division may be classed the numerous examples, in which the Article has the sense of a *Possessive Pronoun*.

EXAMPLES.

Demosth. de Cor. § 59. οὐχὶ ΤΩι πατρὶ καὶ ΤΗι μητρὶ μόνον γεγενῆσθαι, ἀλλὰ καὶ ΤΗι πατρίδι· where *his* may be supplied.
Theocr. Idyll. iii. 52. ἀλγέω ΤΑΝ κεφαλάν· *my*, &c.
Plato Theæt. vol. ii. p. 169. πρόσχες ΤΟΝ νοῦν· *your*, &c.
Arist. de Mor. Nic. lib. iv. c. 3. πέντε ΤΟΝ ἀριθμόν· *their*, &c.[1]

---

[1] Matt. xi. 29. ἀνάπαυσιν ταῖς ψυχαῖς. H. J. R.

§ 5. The same kind of reference will serve also to explain the Article, as we usually find it prefixed to the names of the great *objects of nature*.

EXAMPLES.

Arist. de Cœlo, ii. 4. Σχῆμα δ' ἀνάγκη σφαιροειδὲς ἔχειν ΤΟΝ οὐρανόν.
Demosth. de Fals. Leg. vol. i. 426. οὔτε ΤΟΝ ἥλιον ᾐσχύνοντο οἱ ταῦτα ποιοῦντες, οὔτε ΤΗΝ γῆν, &c.[1]

§ 6. Moreover, the Article is frequently prefixed to Adjectives of the Neuter Gender, when they are used to indicate some attribute or quality in its general and abstract idea[2].

EXAMPLES.

Eurip. Hippol. 431. ΤΟ σῶφρον ὡς ἀπανταχοῦ καλόν.
Plato, vol. i. p. 11. λέγε δὴ τί φῂς εἶναι ΤΟ ὅσιον καὶ ΤΟ ἀνόσιον.
Than such ideas, none are more familiar to the mind.

In all these cases the reference of the Article is more *obscure* than in the case of *renewed mention*, strictly so called; but yet is explicable on the same principle: for in all of them it is to something which is easily recognized, though not hitherto particularly mentioned.

The next *insertions* of the Article, which this part of the

---

[1] There are, however, instances in which ἥλιος especially rejects the Article, having become in some degree a Proper Name [*].

[2] Hence Aristot. (Anal. Pr. cap. 40.) has noticed the difference between ἡ ἡδονὴ ἀγαθόν and ΤΟ ἀγαθόν. The former proposition is true; the latter false. Yet as Lord Monboddo has remarked, (on Lang. vol. ii. p. 72,) Philoponus seems to have mistaken the meaning of ἡ ἡδονή ἐστι τὸ ἀγαθόν, having confounded it with ἀγαθόν. They who would be convinced how much more is contained in the former than in the latter, may find the difference exemplified with respect to τὸ καλὸν and καλόν, in the *Hippias Major* of Plato, as lively a dialogue, and as refined a satire, as exists perhaps in any language.

---

[*] The learned Author, as has been noticed in a periodical publication, has here fallen into a slight mistake; γῆν, in this place, is not an example to his purpose, but has the Article for an obviously different reason: τὴν γῆν, πατρίδα οὖσαν, ἐφ' ἧς ἔστασαν. The passage will be found in Vol. i. p. 477. of Bekker's admirable edition.—J. S.

inquiry leads me to notice, are those which respect *Correlatives* and *Partitives:* the insertion, in these cases also, will be found to arise out of the nature of the Article and its Predicate, as already explained.

§ 7. *Correlatives* are words in *regimen*[1], having a *mutual* reference; and consequently so circumstanced, that if the first relate to the second, the second must relate to the first. The Greek writers, it is observable, mark the relation in the *second* wherever it is necessary to mark it in the first[2]: in other words, where the first has the Article, the second has it likewise.

EXAMPLES.

Plat. Theæt. vol. ii. p. 126. ἡ ΤΟΥ γεωργοῦ δόξα, ἀλλ' οὐχὶ ΤΟΥ κιθαριστοῦ, κυρία.

Id. ibid. p. 182. ὁ ΤΟΥ πλέθρου ἀριθμὸς καὶ πλέθρον, ταυτόν.

Id. ibid. p. 71. ἡ ΤΩΝ σωμάτων ἕξις.

It is plain that ΤΟΥ γεωργοῦ and ΤΟΥ πλέθρου are not spoken of as indicating in themselves any *particular* husbandman, &c.: they become particular only by their connection with their respective Correlatives. A particular opinion (ἡ δόξα) is supposed to imply a particular person, to whom that opinion belongs. In such cases, therefore, the relation expressed by each Article and its Predicate conjointly is abundantly authorized. Apollonius has adverted to this usage. He says that Nouns in regimen must have Articles prefixed to *both* of them, or to *neither:* and that we must say either λέοντος σκυμνίον, or ΤΟ ΤΟΥ λέοντος σκυμνίον. He excepts *Proper Names* in the Genitive, and also Βασιλεύς, from its affinity with them. De Synt. p. 90. There are, however, very many instances in which the Article of the first Noun is, from causes hereafter to be noticed, omitted: in those instances, the second Noun also, as will be seen, sometimes loses its Article.

---

[1] By *regimen* I understand the condition both of the governing and governed Noun: by the term *first* I mean the governing Noun, whatever be its position in the sentence; and by the *second*, the Noun governed.

[2] The practice in our own tongue is wholly different: we can say, "*the* mast of *a* ship," &c.: and this, consequently, is another of the cases in which the Greek Article is supposed to be without meaning. I need hardly suggest, that the Greek practice has more of philosophical correctness.

But besides the case of Proper Names and that of Βασιλεύς, I have noticed a few examples in which the rule has not been observed: they are not, however, such as to justify the expression, τὸ λέοντος σκυμνίον· for there no other usage would interfere with the ordinary idiom of the language; a circumstance which, I think, invariably happens where there is any deviation from the rule. Thus,

Plato, vol. ii. p. 64. διὰ ΤΗΝ ἄδικόν τε καὶ ἄτεχνον συναγωγὴν 'ΑΝΔΡΟΣ καὶ ΓΥΝΑΙΚΟΣ.

Ibid. p. 185. μὴ Ἡ θέσις σε ταράττῃ ΛΕΓΟΜΕΝΩΝ τε καὶ ΓΡΑΦΟΜΕΝΩΝ.

Dion. Hal. vol. i. edit. Reiske, p. 5. ἐπὶ ΤΑΣ παραδεδομένας ΠΟΛΕΩΝ τε καὶ 'ΕΘΝΩΝ ἡγεμονίας.

Plutarch de Isid. p. 279. ΤΟ δὲ ΚΑΝΘΑΡΩΝ γένος.

Xenoph. Cyrop. p. 140. καὶ 'ΑΝΘΡΩΠΩΝ ΤΟ πᾶν γένος αἰδεῖσθε.

Plato, vol. ii. p. 190. οἰηθέντες ἔχειν ΤΟΝ ἀληθέστατον 'ΕΠΙΣΤΗΜΗΣ λόγον[1].

Now in all these instances we may observe something extraneous interfering with the ordinary practice. In the three first examples, the Nouns governed come under the head *Enumeration*, (see Chap. vi. § 2,) which may cause them to be anarthrous. In the fourth and fifth instances, the governing Noun is γένος: I think it not improbable, if we consider that ΟΙ κάνθαροι and ΟΙ ἄνθρωποι will signify the respective γένος of each, (see next Section of this Chapter,) that this circumstance may have rendered ΤΩΝ superfluous: though, at the same time, from conformity with the practice in other cases, we commonly find, even after γένος, that the Article is inserted. In the last example, we might have expected ΤΗΣ ἐπιστήμης. This, however, is what I have called an Abstract Noun, and such (as will be seen, Chap. v.) frequently reject the Article, however definite in their sense.

The only Greek prose writer[2], so far as I know, who, with-

---

[1] Genitives used in an adjective sense, and placed before the governing Noun, omit the Article: thus τὰ πολέμων (Socr. Eccl. Hist. p. 118.) is equivalent to τὰ πολέμων πράγματα, i. e. τὰ πολεμικὰ πράγματα. Origen. c. Cels. p. 116. τὴν ἀνθρώπων φύσιν. Philo, p. 92. ὁ Θεοῦ λόγος. *Author's MS.*

[2] This limitation of the learned Author must be borne in mind, as the poets furnish us with such examples as τὸ γὰρ πόλεως ὄνειδος. Æsch. Theb. 534. J. S.

out these or similar reasons, appears to disregard the usage, is *Philo Judæus*. His style is, indeed, florid and oratorical, but at the same time by no means correct. Josephus, another Jew, and the contemporary of Philo, is not liable to the same censure.

§ 8. The reasoning is similar in the case of *Partitives*, between which and their respective *Wholes*, the same mutual relation subsists[1]. Indeed many of them fall in immediately with the preceding division: thus Æsch. cont. Ctes. § 20. τὰ μέγιστα ΤΩΝ αἰσχρῶν. The only difference is, that many Partitives are of such a nature as not to admit the Article before them, as τίς, ὅσος, or else admit it only in particular cases, as πολλοί, εἷς. The following examples will serve as illustrations in general.

EXAMPLES.

Isoc. Paneg. § 14. διαφέρουσιν αἱ μείζους ΤΩΝ συμμαχιῶν πρὸς τὴν ἀσφάλειαν.
Ibid. § 16. εἰ δεῖ τὸν ἀκριβέστατον ΤΩΝ λόγων εἰπεῖν.
Æsch. cont. Ctes. § 3. συνεργοῦντές τισι ΤΩΝ ῥητόρων.
Demosth. de Cor. § 5. μηδενὸς ΤΩΝ μετρίων.
Ibid. § 58. μόνῳ ΤΩΝ ἄλλων.
Ibid. §. 61. ἔστιν ἃ ΤΩΝ ψηφισμάτων.
Aristot. Metaph. lib. x. c. 1. αἱ μαθηματικαὶ ΤΩΝ ἐπιστημῶν.
Plat. Theæt. vol. ii. p. 178. πολλοὶ ΤΩΝ σοφῶν.
Ibid. p. 118. ἕνα ΤΩΝ νομέων.
Ibid. p. 92. ἕκαστος ΤΩΝ ἀνθρώπων.
Demosth. de Cor. § 12. ὅσα προσετίθετο ΤΩΝ πολισμάτων.
Plat. Theæt. vol. ii. 127. ΤΩΝ ἰδιωτῶν ὁστισοῦν.
Arist. Top. lib. i. c. 11. ἔνια ΤΩΝ προβλημάτων.

This rule, however, is sometimes violated, especially in the case of ἀνθρώπων.

§ 9. On the same principle we may explain the two Articles which are employed when two things are *opposed* to each other

---

[1] This usage also is noticed by Apollonius; and the cause assigned by him agrees with what is here advanced: he says, τὸ μέρος τῶν πρός τι καθέστηκε, καὶ ἔχει πρὸς τὸ ὅλον τὴν ἀπότασιν. P 41.

by μὲν and δέ: for in them also a species of *mutual relation* subsists. In the Pronominal sense (as it is called) of the Article, the usage is extremely common: thus Isoc. ad Demon. ΤΟ μὲν ἀνόητον· ΤΟ δὲ μανικόν· but we trace it also in cases in which the Article has its *Predicate*, and that too, sometimes, where the *opposition* is not the most natural, as between *persons and things*. Thus Demosth. de Cor. § 2. φύσει πᾶσιν ἀνθρώποις ὑπάρχει ΤΩΝ μὲν λοιδοριῶν ἀκούειν ἡδέως, ΤΟΙΣ δ' ἐπαινοῦσι, &c.

SECTION II.

INSERTIONS IN HYPOTHESIS.

§ 1. The following use of the Article differs from the preceding ones, in which the Article and Predicate together recall some familiar idea, being here subservient to the purpose of *Hypothesis*. In both cases the Predicate explains the obscure relation of the Article; but in the latter, the Article, even with the aid of its Predicate, does not carry back the mind to any object with which it has been recently, or is frequently, conversant. It is merely the representative of something, of which, whether known or unknown, an assumption is to be made.

EXAMPLES.

Demosth. de Cor. § 71. πονηρὸν Ὁ συκοφάντης ἀεί.
Ibid. § 94. Τί χρῆν ΤΟΝ εὔνουν πολίτην ποιεῖν;
Xen. Mem. lib. iii. c. 1. ἃ δεῖ ΤΟΝ εὖ στρατηγήσοντα ἔχειν.
Arist. de Mor. Nic. lib. iii. c. 6. Ὁ σπουδαῖος γὰρ ἕκαστα κρίνει ὀρθῶς.
Idem. Prob. § 18. ΤΟ μὲν οὖν ἓν ὥρισται· ΤΑ δὲ πολλὰ ΤΟΥ ἀπείρου μετέχει.

In these instances the Article is used, according to the Grammarians, *indefinitely*: and this circumstance, combined with the general notion of the *defining* power of the Article, is one of the causes which have led to the opinion, that its uses can never be determined with certainty. If, however, the Article be a Pronoun, the subject of a proposition, of which the Adjunct is the assumptive Predicate, it is evident that the pretended ambiguity has no existence; for the object of the Article's relation is equally defined, whether that object (as in the case of *renewed mention*) be the person who has been spoken of in the preceding sentence, or whether it be some person or character now introduced for the first time. In both cases the Article is clearly explained by its Predicate: that *Predicate* may indeed require to be understood with greater or less latitude, the degree of which the context and the general tenor of the argument will decide with sufficient exactness: thus in the example from Demosthenes, if συκοφάντης had recently been mentioned, we should immediately infer that ὁ συκοφάντης was the *renewed mention* of the same person: as the context stands, we clearly perceive, that ὁ συκοφάντης must mean every person[1] of whom συκοφάντης can be predicated. The error has arisen from confounding the relation of the Article and its Predicate *conjointly*, with that of the Article *alone:* between which I have endeavoured to establish the true distinction.

§ 2. In the same manner the Article is employed *plurally*, to denote whole *classes* and *descriptions* of *persons* or *things*.

EXAMPLES.

Xen. Mem. lib. iii. c. 1. διαγιγνώσκειν σε ΤΟΥΣ ἀγαθοὺς καὶ ΤΟΥΣ κακοὺς ἐδίδαξεν, i. e. the two classes.

Plut. de Isid. p. 264. λεγόμενον ΤΟΥΣ θεοὺς φρουρεῖν, ὥσπερ ΟΙ κύνες ΤΟΥΣ ἀνθρώπους.

Æschines cont. Ctes. § 2. καταδουλούμενοι ΤΟΥΣ ἰδιώτας.

Ibid. § 90. δεινὸν, ὦ 'Αθηναῖοι, εἰ ΤΑ μὲν ξύλα καὶ ΤΟΥΣ λίθους καὶ ΤΟΝ σίδηρον[2], τὰ ἄφωνα ὑπερορίζομεν, &c.

Demosth. de Cor. § 58. ΤΑ ῥήγματα καὶ ΤΑ σπάσματα, ὅταν τι κακὸν τὸ σῶμα λάβῃ, τότε κινεῖται.

[1] It is only due to Mr. Winstanley to observe, that he clearly saw this property of the Article. After explaining that it includes every thing to which the term to which it is affixed can apply, he says that it must be defined " to be the symbol of universality or totality." He then goes on to observe, that if prefixed to an Appellative, it denotes the whole genus: thus ὁ ἄνθρωπος means *all mankind*. And if the Appellative be limited by any form of distinction, then the words include as much as they can: thus ὁ ἀγαθὸς ἄνθρωπος is *every good man*. H. J. R.

[2] This word, not being used in the plural, must be considered as in the *singular*, denoting the *genus*.

III.]   APPELLATIVES.   41

This usage is so prevalent, that, as far as I have observed, the Attic writers prefix the Article to plural Nouns almost universally, so often as an affirmative is true alike of ALL the persons or things in question. The reason of this will be evident, if we admit the principle laid down in the last paragraph: for then τὰ ῥήγματα must signify every thing, of which ῥῆγμα can be affirmed. This remark will serve to explain the true meaning of the Article in very many passages, in which it is usually supposed to be a mere *verbum otiosum*[1]. I would call this the *inclusive* sense of the Article, the force of which will be better understood from what will be said of Exclusive Propositions.

It is worthy of notice that the *hypothetical*, as well as the other use of the Article, was known to Homer: thus ΤΟΥ κακοῦ and ΤΟΥ ἀγαθοῦ. Iliad xiii. vv. 279, 284.

To some one of these heads we may, I believe, refer every *insertion* of the Article, of which the Greek writers supply examples: and every such insertion will be explicable in one of the two ways proposed: either that the Article with its Predicate denotes a *relation* immediately recognized by the hearer, or else, where no such relation can be recognized, they serve conjointly to indicate an *hypothesis*. The Article *itself* is in each case the same, the object of its relation being known to the speaker, though unknown to the hearer, till it is explained in the Predicate[2].

SECTION III.

OMISSIONS.

From the most remarkable *insertions* of the Article, it will be right to proceed to its most remarkable *omissions*, and to show that they too may be accounted for on the principles laid

---

[1] Thus Plat. Theæt. vol. ii. p. 159. τὰ ἐν ΤΟΙΣ κατόπτροις τῆς ὄψεως πάθη· in *all* mirrors *whatever*.

[2] There are cases in which the Article is properly expressed in Greek, though omitted in English, and which the Author has not particularly specified under any of his divisions. They may perhaps both be classed under Monadic Nouns, (p. 34.) To receive a drachma *a day*—δραχμὴν τῆς ἡμέρας λαβεῖν. *A* second Geryon—Γηρυὼν ὁ δεύτερος. (Æsch. Agam. 843.) See Chap. vi. § 3.—J. S.

down. To this end nothing more will be requisite at present, than to remind the reader of what was said above respecting the *Copula*. This was shown to be, in all cases, the *Participle of Existence*: whence it will follow, that the existence of the person or thing, to the name of which the Article is prefixed, is always supposed: nor, indeed, is it possible to indicate a *mode* of existence (as is done in the Predicate) without assuming the existence itself.

§ 1. Hence in propositions which merely *affirm* or *deny existence*, the name of the person or thing, of which existence is affirmed or denied, is without the Article. In each case the reason of the omission is, *mutatis mutandis*, the same: for to *affirm* the existence of that, of which the existence is already assumed, would be superfluous; and to *deny* it, would be contradictory and absurd.

EXAMPLES.

Arist. Categ. c. vii. § 19. ἘΠΙΣΤΗΤΟΥ μὲν γὰρ μὴ ὈΝΤΟΣ, οὐκ ἘΣΤΙΝ ἘΠΙΣΤΗΜΗ.

Æsch. cont. Ctes. § 58. ΕΙΣΙ γὰρ καὶ δειλίας ΓΡΑΦΑΙ.

Ibid. § 26. ἘΣΤΑΙ μὲν ΕΙΡΗΝΗ.

Demosth. de Cor. § 48. οὐκ ἩΝ τοῦ πρὸς ὑμᾶς πολέμου ΠΕΡΑΣ.

Ibid. § 99. τῶν κολακεύειν ἑτέρους βουλομένων ἘΞΕΤΑΣΙΣ ἩΝ.

Plat. Theæt. vol. ii. p. 173. τῶν ἐπιστημῶν ΕΙΣΙΝ αὖ ΕΠΙΣΤΗΜΑΙ.

LXX. Ps. lii. 1. οὐκ ἘΣΤΙ ΘΕΟΣ [1].

In all these instances the several Nouns would have had the Article prefixed, had the propositions affirmed or denied of them any thing besides existence: for then the assumption of the existence of the things represented by the Nouns would have been necessary [2].

---

[1] The same words occur, Isaiah xlv. 14. where, however, Breitinger's edition has Ὁ Θεός. The Vatican MS. as referred to by him in the V. R. has properly omitted the Article. There is a difference between this and the preceding clause in the same verse: in ἘΝ ΣΟΙ ὁ Θεός ἐστι the existence of God is *assumed*.

[2] In Gersdorf's Beiträge zur Sprach-charakteristik der Schriftsteller des N. T. p. 325—327, and again, p. 330, 331, is a large collection of similar

III.] APPELLATIVES. 43

§ 2. Another *omission*, which arises out of the nature of the *Copula*, is that which is observable in all Nouns preceded by Verbs or *Participles, Substantive* or *Nuncupative*[1]. In such cases the Noun is always *anarthrous*.

EXAMPLES.

Demosth. de Cor. § 23. ΑΙΤΙΟΣ ΕΙΜΙ τοῦ πολέμου.
Æsch. cont. Ctes. § 20. τοὺς κονδύλους, οὓς ἔλαβεν ἐν τῇ ὀρχήστρᾳ ΧΟΡΗΓΟΣ ΏΝ.
Ibid. § 43. ὁ τολμῶν ἐν ταῖς ἐπιστολαῖς γράφειν ὅτι ΔΕΣΠΟΤΗΣ ΈΣΤΙΝ ἁπάντων ἀνθρώπων.
Ibid. § 61. Ἀριστείδης ὁ ΔΙΚΑΙΟΣ ΈΠΙΚΑΛΟΥΜΕΝΟΣ.
Demosth. de Cor. § 52. ὃν οὐκ ἂν ὀκνήσαιμι ἔγωγε ΚΟΙΝΟΝ ΑΛΙΤΗΡΙΟΝ ΕΙΠΕΙΝ.
Æsch. con. Ctes. § 47. ΠΡΟΔΟΤΑΣ τῶν Ἑλλήνων τοὺς Βοιωτάρχας ΈΚΑΛΕΣΕ.
LXX. Ps. xlvi. 8. ὅτι ΒΑΣΙΛΕΥΣ (scil. ΈΣΤΙ) πάσης τῆς γῆς ὁ Θεός.
Esai. ix. 6. καὶ ΚΑΛΕΙΤΑΙ τὸ ὄνομα αὐτοῦ μεγάλης Βουλῆς ΑΓΓΕΛΟΣ, ΘΑΥΜΑΣΤΟΣ, ΣΥΜΒΟΥΛΟΣ, ΙΣΧΥΡΟΣ, &c. &c.

The reader, who has attended to the sections on the principal insertions of the Article, will perceive that in all these examples the Nouns and Adjectives, which are printed in capitals, are used in senses which might seem to require the Article. In general they express some attribute or dignity possessed exclusively, and might therefore be expected to take the Article κατ᾽ ἐξοχήν: but this is forbidden by the Verb or Participle preceding; which is used to indicate, as hitherto unknown, the very truth which the presence of the Article would imply to be known or supposed already: for such, as we have seen, is the force of the assumptive Copula understood. Hence, if in the passage above quoted from Æschines, the

---

passages from the New Testament. Gersdorf, not having the key to these passages, of course considers them as anomalous. A collection of this kind is a strong confirmation of Bishop Middleton's rule. H. J. R.

[1] Εἰ μέντοι ἐπιφέροιτο τὸ ΓΕΝΕΣΘΑΙ, τὸ ΚΑΛΕΙΣΘΑΙ, τὰ τούτοις σύζυγα, ἀποστήσεται τὸ ἄρθρον. Apoll. p. 70.

Persian monarch had written ὅτι Ὁ δεσπότης ἐστίν, &c. the sense would have been, that he was the person *recognized* (for here hypothesis has no place) to be the lord of mankind: in which capacity, however, as he well knew, he was not recognized by the Greeks, and if he had been so recognized, the whole declaration would have been gratuitous. And similar reasoning will be applicable to the remaining examples, as well as to others which may present themselves to observation. It is true, indeed, that propositions may be found resembling that in question, supposing the reading to have been Ὁ δεσπότης: and they deserve to be considered. Thus we read LXX. 1 Kings xviii. 36. Κύριος αὐτός ἐστιν Ὁ Θεός· in which words the people of Israel, convinced by a miracle, declare their faith in Jehovah. But how does this proposition differ from that in Æschines? The difference is exactly such as, admitting the principles laid down, we should expect. The Greeks did not recognize any person as the universal sovereign: but the people of Israel *did* admit the existence of a Supreme Being; and the only question had been, whether Jehovah or Baal were he. Their declaration, therefore, amounts to this: that the God of Elijah, and not Baal, was the proper object of adoration, or that God and Jehovah were the same: and thus the case refers to that above, supposing Ὁ δεσπότης had been the reading. Had the Persian prince and some other been contending for the sovereignty of the world, and had the Greeks been accustomed to obey one of these, then might Xerxes have been represented as having styled himself Ὁ δεσπότης πάσης τῆς γῆς. Such propositions are called *reciprocating*: they will be further noticed. For a similar reason we sometimes find that the Predicate after εἰμὶ has the Article, where the subject is a Pronoun Personal or Demonstrative, ἐγώ, σύ, οὗτος, &c.[1] In such instances the existence is assumed, the purport of the proposition being to identify the Predicate with the subject: so in Plato, vol. x. p. 89. εἰ εἰσὶν ΑΥΤΑΙ ΑΙ ἰδέαι τῶν ὄντων, where that there are ἰδέαι τῶν ὄντων is the basis of the inquiry; and the only doubt is, whether these be they.

---

[1] Thus Matt. xvi. 16. σὺ εἶ ὁ υἱὸς τοῦ Θεοῦ· xxvii. 11. σὺ εἶ ὁ βασιλεὺς τῶν Ἰουδαίων. H. J. R.

§ 3. From the omission caused by Verbs Substantive and Nuncupative we pass by an easy transition to that, which is observable after Verbs of *appointing, choosing, creating,* &c. where the Noun expressive of *appointment, choice,* &c. is always anarthrous.

EXAMPLES.

Demosth. de Cor. § 59. ἩΓΕΜΩΝ καὶ ΚΥΡΙΟΣ ἩιΡΕΘΗ Φίλιππος ἁπάντων.

Æsch. cont. Ctes. § 41. καὶ ΣΤΡΑΤΗΓΟΝ ΕἹΛΟΝΤΟ Κόττυφον τὸν Φαρσάλιον.

Ibid. § 17. ΜΑΡΤΥΡΑΣ τῆς ἀπελευθερίας τοὺς Ἕλληνας ποιούμενοι.

Plat. Theæt. vol. ii. p. 81. τῷ τὴν αἴσθησιν ἘΠΙΣΤΗΜΗΝ ΤΙΘΕΜΕΝΩι.

Ibid. p. 97. οὔκ, εἰ τὸ ὁρᾶν γε ἘΠΙΣΤΑΣΘΑΙ ΘΗΣΕΙΣ.

LXX. Esai. v. 20. οἱ ΤΙΘΕΝΤΕΣ τὸ σκότος ΦΩΣ καὶ τὸ φῶς ΣΚΟΤΟΣ.

Idem, Exod. ii. 14. τίς σε ΚΑΤΕΣΤΗΣΕΝ ἌΡΧΟΝΤΑ καὶ ΔΙΚΑΣΤΗΝ ἐφ᾽ ἡμῶν;

The reason of the omission in all such examples is very plain.

The Article could not be prefixed to any of these Nouns, because the *existence* of the *appointment*, &c. is not of a nature to be *recognized*, being now first declared: and hypothesis, as before, is out of the question. This case, indeed, is immediately resolvable into the former by means of εἶναι or γενέσθαι everywhere understood; of which we find frequent traces:

Thus LXX. Deut. xxvi. 17, 18. τὸν Θεὸν εἵλου σήμερον ΕΙΝΑΙ σου θεόν, καὶ Κύριος εἵλετό σε ΓΕΝΕΣΘΑΙ λαόν.

The omission, then, in these several cases, however different they may appear, is one and the same, being a necessary consequence of the subintellection of the Participle of existence.

§ 4. It seems to be from the same cause that Nouns in *apposition*, not explanatory of the essence of the preceding Noun, but of the end or object, to which the person or thing implied in it is affirmed to be subservient, are always anarthrous [1].

[1] Where the Noun is explanatory of the essence, it usually has the Article. Winer, in Part i. says, *always;* but in Part ii. he gives us examples of the

EXAMPLES.

Demosth. de Cor. § 69. ΔΥΝΑΜΙΝ εἶχεν ἡ πόλις τοὺς νησιώτας.
Ibid. § 15. τῷ προδότῃ ΣΥΜΒΟΥΛΩι χρῆται.
Æsch. cont. Ctes. § 56. λαμβάνει ΔΩΡΕΑΝ τοὺς ὠνομασμένους Κήπους. In such examples, some case of ὤν, or else εἶναι or ὥστε εἶναι, may always be supplied.

§ 5. Another remarkable omission, which I purpose to notice, depends on a principle somewhat, though not altogether, different from that, by which the former ones are explained: I allude to the practice observable in *exclusive Propositions*. I mean those which are not merely *negative*, but in which the negation is meant to extend to every individual or to the whole species in question, so as to *exclude universally*. The following are

EXAMPLES.

Demosth. de Cor. § 28. οὐ ΝΑΥΣ, οὐ ΤΕΙΧΗ τῆς πόλεως τότε κεκτημένης.
Ibid. § 31. οὐχ ἹΚΕΤΗΡΙΑΝ ἔθηκε Τριήραρχος οὐδείς, οὐ ΤΡΙΗΡΗΣ ἔξω καταληφθεῖσα ἀπώλετο τῇ πόλει.
Æsch. cont. Ctes. § 36. μήτε ΓΗΝ καρποὺς φέρειν, μήτε ΓΥΝΑΙΚΑΣ τέκνα τίκτειν, μήτε ΒΟΣΚΗΜΑΤΑ γονὰς ποιεῖσθαι.
Ibid. § 17. ἀπαγορεύει μήτε ΟΙΚΕΤΗΝ ἀπελευθεροῦν, μήτε ἀναγορεύεσθαι ΣΤΕΦΑΝΟΥΜΕΝΟΝ.
Ibid. § 15. οὐδὲν ἦν ἂν εὐδαιμονέστερον ΠΡΟΔΟΤΟΥ.
Plat. Theæt. vol. ii. p. 62. ΣΤΕΡΙΦΑΙΣ μὲν οὖν ἄρα οὐκ ἔδωκε μαιεύεσθαι.

contrary, Acts x. 32. Σίμων βυρσεύς. Luke ii. 36. Ἄννα προφῆτις. Acts xx. 4. Γάϊος Δερβαῖος, vii. 10. But in all these places, the word is not used as *a description* or *definition* by which every one will recognize the person; and should not be so translated. It is not *Simon the Tanner*, in opposition to *Simon the Miller*, but, as our version has it, *one Simon a tanner; i. e. who is a tanner*. So Luke, as writing for persons who would not know Anna, states the fact that she was a prophetess, and does not *describe* her as *the* prophetess whom all knew. H. J. R.

Joseph. de Bell. Jud. lib. i. 18. ἐπειδὴ μήτε ἹΠΠΟΙΣ μήτε ἈΝΔΡΑΣΙΝ ὑπελέλειπτο ΤΡΟΦΗ[1].

The reader will observe, that in these examples the force of the negation will not be duly estimated, unless it be taken to *exclude universally* the several objects spoken of. Thus, in the first example, the orator wishes to be understood to deny that the city had *any* ships, or *any* walls whatever; and something similar may be remarked of those which remain. In all of them the word *any* may in English be supplied before the several Nouns, or (which is the same thing) the negative must be rendered by *no*, in order adequately to give the sense.—This omission, I have said, depends in some measure on the same principle, from which the former ones result: for if the city possessed *no* ships, &c. the orator could not consistently have said ΤΑΣ ναῦς, ΤΑ τείχη, the Article by means of its Copula implying, as has been shown, an existence either recognized or conditionally admitted: both which are inconsistent with the nature of the proposition. But this is not all. There is in the Article, as has been remarked above (p. 14.), an *inclusive* or *generic* sense, which renders it wholly unfit to appear in propositions like the present: because a negation of a whole considered as a whole is not co-extensive with a negation of all the parts. Thus, in the passage from Æschines, an imprecation that ΤΗΝ γῆν, ΤΑΣ γυναῖκας, ΤΑ βοσκήματα might not yield their respective produce, would apply only to the earth, to women, and to cattle in *general:* and, therefore, the fulfilment to such a curse would be found in the *partial failure* of each kind of produce: inasmuch as the *whole* earth, *all* women, &c. could not be said to yield their produce, if there existed a single instance of failure. But the imprecation, as it stands in Æschines, will not be accomplished, if there be a single instance of *produce*; i. e. it *will* be accomplished, if there be no single instance: it is, therefore, in the anarthrous form far more strong, since the force of it *then* is, that no *portion* of earth, no *individual* woman, no *single* beast, may produce, &c. It is as if the

---

[1] Q. Whether this does not extend to interrogations, where an exclusion is conveyed, though not in a direct form? Thus τίς μερὶς πιστῷ μετὰ ἀπίστου; This in a different form would be—There is no portion for *any* believer. And, consequently, πιστῷ is anarthrous. If it had been τῷ πιστῷ, it would have been —There is no portion for *believers generally*, &c. H. J. R.

writer had said, μήτε (εἶναι) γῆν, οἵαν κ. φ. μήτε (εἶναι) γυναῖκας, &c. in which view of the subject the Article would be omitted according to what is said above respecting propositions affirming or denying existence. In this example, it is obvious that the Articles, if they were employed, would require to be considered, not as marking, with the aid of their Predicates, a *relation* which must be recognized, but an *assumption* which may be *admitted*, according to the distinction already laid down: but in the proposition from Demosthenes, reading it ΤΑΣ ναῦς and ΤΑ τείχη, the Articles, if they were used, would evidently serve to indicate *known relations*. In that instance, therefore, the objection to the Articles would assume a somewhat different form, arising from their different use, though it would ultimately terminate in the same result as in the former case: for to say that the city did not possess its *wonted* or *well-known* ships and walls, would have fallen as far short of the speaker's meaning, as would the imprecation, that the earth and women, *generally speaking*, might not yield produce. His argument requires him to deny that it possessed *any* ships or *any* walls *whatever*. And since in all propositions of this sort the object is to *exclude altogether*, the Article, to whichever of its two ends it might be subservient, would frustrate the purpose of the speaker.

§ 6. Another omission respects Nouns in *regimen*. It was remarked, that, according to Apollonius, the Article is prefixed to both the governing and the governed Nouns, or else it is omitted before both. An omission will, therefore, frequently be observable, where the governing Noun might seem to require the definite form. The laxity of some modern tongues may appear to justify such a phrase as ΤΟ σκυμνίον λέοντος· but the accuracy of a philosophical language denies, that of λέοντος, which is indefinite, there can be any definite σκυμνίον. Exactly as the insertion of the Article before the governed Noun (see above, p. 36.) is made necessary by its insertion before the Noun which governs, so the indefiniteness of the governed will cause the governing Noun to assume the indefinite form. And this is true of the governing Nouns, if there be more than one: in a series of Nouns in regimen, all will be anarthrous, if the last be indefinite.

EXAMPLES.

Herod. lib. iv. p. 153. ΔΕΡΜΑ δὲ ἀνθρώπου καὶ παχὺ καὶ λαμπρόν.
Thucyd. lib. v. § 111. τὸ αἰσχρὸν καλούμενον ὀνόματος ἐπαγωγοῦ ΔΥΝΑΜΕΙ ἐπεσπάσατο, &c.
Æsch. cont. Ctes. § 80. πέντε νεῶν ταχυναυτουσῶν ΤΡΙΗΡΑΡΧΟΥΣ ὑφῃρημένος.
Demosth. de Cor. § 79. οἰκέτου ΤΑΞΙΝ, οὐκ ἐλευθέρου παιδὸς ἔχων.
Plat. vol. iv. p. 43. λόγου τινὸς ΑΡΧΗΝ λέγεις.
Ibid. vol. ii. p. 57. μή τι ἄλλο φράζεις ἢ ΕΠΙΣΤΗΜΗΝ ὑποδημάτων ΕΡΓΑΣΙΑΣ;
Demosth. c. Timoc. vol. i. p. 739. πονηρῶν καὶ ἀχαρίστων οἰκετῶν ΤΡΟΠΟΥΣ.

Nor is it merely where the governed Noun is indefinite in *meaning* that this usage takes place: even where it is from its nature definite in sense, as in the case of proper names, &c., if it be indefinite in *form*, i. e. if it be anarthrous, the governing Noun is not unfrequently anarthrous also.

Plut. Conviv. p. 99. Αἰσώπου ΛΟΓΟΝ.
Ibid. τὰ κάλλιστα περαίνεται θεοῦ ΓΝΩΜΗι.
Plut. de Isid. p. 277. τὸν ὠνούμενον ΒΙΒΛΙΑ Πλάτωνος [1].

§ 7. The same principle of correlation will explain why, when the Noun governing is indefinite, the governed becomes anarthrous [2].

---

[1] Thus, 1 Cor. ii. 16. τίς ἔγνω νοῦν Κυρίου; H. J. R.

[2] Many examples will occur which seem repugnant to this canon: the principle, however, requires that the governing Noun should be not merely anarthrous, but also indefinite in sense: for it may, though definite, have become anarthrous in conformity with some rule, which yet may not require that the governed Noun should become anarthrous also: and yet the governed Noun does not unfrequently lose its Article, and thus fall into the form which Apollonius (see above, Sect. i. § 7.) has inadvertently asserted to be necessary: so Thucyd. lib. i. § 2. διὰ γὰρ ἀρετὴν ΓΗΣ, where ἀρετὴν loses its Article by Chap. vi. § 1. of this Essay.—[The reader will find in Gersdorf's work, above cited, a large number of examples from the New Testament, scattered through pages 314—334, where there is an anarthrous word after a Preposition, followed by a Genitive with the Article. There is a collection of examples also in Winer ii. 3. 7. b. p. 39. See 1 Cor. ii. 16. 1 Pet. iii. 12. 20. Luke i. 5; xiii. 19. 1 Cor. x. 21. H. J. R.]

EXAMPLES.

Plut. Conviv. p. 99.   ΨΥΧΗΣ γὰρ ὄργανον τὸ σῶμα.
Plat. Lach. vol. v. p. 164.   διδάσκαλον ΜΟΥΣΙΚΗΣ.
Lys. c. Andoc. vol. v. p. 206.   δίκην 'ΑΣΕΒΕΙΑΣ.
Xen. Œcon. p. 480.   τις ἐπιστήμη ΟΙΚΟΝΟΜΙΑΣ[1].

SECTION IV.

INSERTIONS AND OMISSIONS COMBINED.

Having now considered the principal *insertions* and the principal *omissions* of the Article, occurring separately, I proceed, as was proposed, to notice one or two cases of insertion and omission *combined*.

§ 1. One case is that of the *Subject* and *Predicate* of pro-

[1] The only case of *omission* of the Article on which I cannot entirely satisfy myself, is that before the names of *Arts*, as ἱππική, μουσική, which has been remarked by Pors. ad Hec. 788. Elmsl. ad Aristoph. Ach. 499. Heindorf ad Plat. Soph. 442. Ast. ad Plat. Prot. p. 19. Schaefer. Melett. Critt. p. 4. and others. I find that the usage is any thing but uniform. Thus the Article is always used with μουσική in Isocrates, (viz. 74. b. 199. a. 486. 286. in the two last cases after περί,) except in 189. a. which is a case of enumeration. So he uses ἱππική, p. 148. c. and μαντική, p. 385. c. with the Article even after Prepositions. In Æschines again I find μουσική, p. 86. 19. and p. 89. 1. and in Demosthenes, p. 1391. 9. with the Article. Schaefer *seems* to think that the addition of the Article is not Greek, as he says (Melett. p. 4.), " omnino haud exiguus est numerus nominum articulo fere carentium : velut μουσική, quod statim sequitur, ubi si quis scribendum censeret τῆς μουσικῆς εὑρετής hellenismi parum se callidum proderet." This might be true, doubtless, on a ground stated already by Bishop Middleton ; but Schaefer, I conceive, makes the omission of the Article before μουσική independent on its omission before εὑρετής. Just below he says, in speaking of Xen. Cyr. viii. 1. 34. " Ex vera linguæ Græcæ ratione, καὶ ἱππικῆς δὲ ἀληθεστάτην." If I am right in my view of what he says, the instances already produced from the Greek orators overturn his assertion. But undoubtedly the Article is very often omitted before these words. The inconstancy of the usage makes the difficulty of the case. These words are, in fact, Adjectives used substantively by an ellipsis. If they are considered exclusively in this light, they appear to require the Article, and its omission is remarkable. If, on the other hand, they are considered as having become, in fact, substantives, they must follow the law of other substantives. Thus in Xen. Mem. prope init. we have μαντικῇ χρώμενος, which is what one would expect, if μαντική be a mere Substantive; and there is then nothing to notice. But neither use of these words seems wholly established.

Elmsley (ubi suprà) considers τραγῳδίαν ποιῶν as coming under this head. But the omission of the Article there belongs to § 3. of this section. H. J. R.

III.]   APPELLATIVES.   51

positions, in which, as has been often remarked, the subject is generally found *with* the Article, and the Predicate *without* it. Before we examine the cause of this usage, it may be right to give

EXAMPLES.

Aristot. Anal. Post. ii. 3.   οὐ γάρ ἐστι ΤΟ ἐπίπεδον ΣΧΗΜΑ, οὐδὲ ΤΟ σχῆμα ᾿ΕΠΙΠΕΔΟΝ.

Ibid. de Interp. c. 11.   ῾Ο ἄνθρωπός ἐστιν ἴσως καὶ ΖΩΟΝ καὶ ΔΙΠΟΥΝ καὶ ῞ΗΜΕΡΟΝ.

Plut. de Aud. Poet. p. 11.   ΖΩΓΡΑΦΙΑΝ μὲν εἶναι φθεγγομένην ΤΗΝ ποίησιν, ΠΟΙΗΣΙΝ δὲ σιγῶσαν ΤΗΝ ζωγραφίαν.

Eurip. Fragm.
    Τίς οἶδεν, εἰ ΤΟ ζῆν μέν ἐστι ΚΑΤΘΑΝΕΙΝ,
    ΤΟ κατθανεῖν δὲ ΖΗιΝ κάτω νομίζεται;

Plat. Theæt. vol. ii. p. 157.   οὐκ ἄν ποτε δοξάσειεν, ὡς ῾Ο Θεαίτητός ἐστι ΘΕΟΔΩΡΟΣ.

LXX. Job xxviii. 28.   ἰδοὺ ῾Η Θεοσέβειά ἐστι ΣΟΦΙΑ.

Plat. vol. xi. p. 39.   οὔτε ῾Ο πατὴρ ῾ΥΙΟΣ ἐστιν, οὔτε ῾Ο υἱὸς ΠΑΤΗΡ.

In these examples, the Noun having the Article is the *Subject* of the proposition, and that without it the *Predicate*. The ground of this usage, the reader, who has admitted the truth of the preceding observations, will probably in great measure anticipate: since propositions of this kind are in reality no other than combinations of the two cases of insertion for the sake of hypothesis, and omission after Verbs Substantive. The point to be examined is, how comes it that this insertion and this omission should be necessary to the propositions themselves. Now it is to be considered, that these are conversant, not about *particular*, but about *universal* truths. But universal truths can be declared only by making the subject of the declaration universal; and this, as we have seen, is effected by means of the Article in its *hypothetical* and inclusive use. Thus, in the first example from Aristotle, τὸ ἐπίπεδον signifies the thing (being) surface, i. e. every thing of which surface can be predicated, or surface universally: so also τὸ σχῆμα, in the second clause, is figure in its most comprehensive and extended acceptation. But let us attend to σχῆμα without the Article, as it is found in the *first* clause. Is it *there* true, that the writer speaks of figure universally? Certainly not: for, to

E 2

say that *surface*, in its most comprehensive sense, was not *figure* in its most comprehensive sense, would indeed be true, but it would fall very far short of the meaning of the proposition. Aristotle plainly intends to say, that what is surface (τὸ ἐπίπεδον) is not figure *at all*; which is saying much more: for that which is not figure generally and abstractedly may yet be figure particularly. Thus a triangle is a figure; but the definition of figure comprehends much more than the definition of triangle [1]: consequently the proposition, that surface universally is not figure universally, would comprehend much less than that which says, surface is not figure *at all*. The same reasoning will apply to the other part of the second clause: and something similar will explain the remaining examples. Thus ὁ ἄνθρωπος is man, the species: i. e. according to the account of the Article given above, He (being, or who is) Man; or every male, of whom man can be predicated. But suppose we had read TO ζῶον? It would mean either an animal standing in a relation which might be recognized, or else that which may be assumed to be an animal, i. e. animal universally, in which form the proposition would assert, the former use of the Article being here inadmissible, that the species man and the genus animal are the same: which is absurd. In the next example, poetry in general is not asserted to be painting generally,. but only *speaking* painting, a particular kind; and *vice versâ* in the second clause. In the fragment of Euripides (first clause), TO ζῆν is life in the general acceptation: but κατθανεῖν is more limited, being used to signify, not death in the extended acceptation (which in the next clause is called TO κατθανεῖν), but something of which death is now for the first time predicated: to have said that life and death, each understood in the most general sense, were one and the same thing, would have been evidently false.—In the passage from Plato, Socrates means to say, that he could never imagine that the person *assumed* and admitted to be Theætetus was Theodorus. The proposition from the LXX.

---

[1] A very competent judge assures me that this is liable to misconstruction; for that the definition of figure contains *less*. The reader, then, will be pleased to understand me, as speaking not of the *terms* and *restrictions* of the definition, but of the things which it comprehends and to which it is applicable: and these are evidently more in figure than they are in triangle.

asserts, that piety, however comprehensively understood and in all its forms, is wisdom: not wisdom, indeed, understood in the same latitude, because benevolence also is wisdom, so is temperance: but a species of wisdom, so that he is wise, in a certain way, but not he alone, who is pious.

It is evident, then, that the usage, which has here been explained, is not arbitrary in its origin, but has its foundation in reason and in truth. Unless, however, we advert to the principle, we shall sometimes conclude that the rule is violated, where in reality it is strictly observed. Thus *Fischer*, in his Remarks on *Weller*[1], has adduced as an *exception* Pind. Pyth. vii. 18. τὸ δ' ἄχνυμαι, φθόνον ἀμειβόμενον ΤΑ καλὰ ἔργα. The Article is here used in its *hypothetical* or assumptive sense, and the meaning of the proposition is, that "actions *admitted* to be honourable are followed by envy[2]." This example, therefore, is a *confirmation* of the principle, on which the rule depends; but writers who advert not to the reason, but only to the appearance of things, frequently fall into such mistakes. It may be of use to add, that where propositions are not in their simplest form, i.e. where the Subject and Predicate are not joined by the Verb Substantive as a Copula, it will be necessary to resolve them, before any thing can be determined respecting the observance or violation of this usage; because the *reason* of the rule is applicable only to such propositions. With respect to φθόνον, in the passage adduced, I doubt not but that ΤΟΝ φθόνον, would have been equally good Greek.

But let us next consider what will happen, supposing the Predicate, as well as the Subject, of such propositions to have the Article. The consequence, indeed, has been shown with respect to the propositions before us; excepting only that from Plato. Let us, therefore, suppose the reading to have been Ὁ Θεόδωρος. Shall we say, that it would not have been Greek, and also good sense? This would, I think, be more than the case would justify. The meaning would then have been, "Socrates could never imagine Theætetus and Theodorus to be the same person." But how will this meaning be deduced? It will be evident, if we consider that the proposition

---

[1] Vol. i. p. 320.
[2] Similar to this is οὐ ῥᾴδιον ΤΑ καλὰ πράττειν ἀχορήγητον ὄντα. Arist. de Mor. Nic. i. 9.

ὅτι Ὁ Θεαίτητός ἐστιν Ὁ Θεόδωρος is the substance condensed of the two propositions ὅτι ὁ Θεαίτητός ἐστι Θεόδωρος, ἢ (in an affirmative proposition καὶ) ὅτι ὁ Θεόδωρός ἐστι Θεαίτητος· for to say that one would not take Theætetus to be Theodorus nor Theodorus to be Theætetus, amounts plainly to this, that one would not take either for the other: which is exactly the same thing as to say, that one would not take them to be the same person. But this is more than the proposition asserts, as it stands in Plato, though not more than Socrates might have said with truth, had his purpose required him to introduce both propositions, to which that having the two Articles would be equivalent. It was enough, however, to say, that Theætetus could not be taken for Theodorus. But suppose the case otherwise, and that his argument had been incomplete, unless he had maintained the *converse* also: he would then, if he consulted brevity, have employed the single proposition ὅτι ὁ Θεαίτητός ἐστιν ὁ Θεόδωρος, because it contains the substance of the two; for whichever of the two be chosen, it comprehends not only that, but its *converse*.

Hence we see the origin of *convertible* or *reciprocating* propositions[1], which are such, that of either term taken as the Subject the other may be affirmed as a Predicate. Such propositions, therefore, will have the Article prefixed to both terms alike, neither of them being the *Subject* more than the other. The reader, who reflects on the nature of these propositions, will not expect to meet with many examples; since the things or attributes, which may thus be predicated either of the other, are in their nature few, and, even of these the identity may be affirmed, as we have seen, in two distinct propositions, such that the Subject of the first is made the Predicate of the second. However, of the convertible form I have noticed the following

EXAMPLES.

Arist. Mor. Nicom. lib. ii. c. 9. ἐστὶν Ἡ ἀρετὴ Ἡ ἠθικὴ μεσότης[2].

---

[1] On those cases where the proposition is composed of a pronoun personal or demonstrative, the Copula and a Predicate with the Article, see above, iii. 3. 2. p. 44.—H. J. R.

[2] Ibid. lib. ii. c. 6. we find μεσότης ἐστιν ἡ ἀρετή· to have said Ἡ μεσότης would not have been true.

Ibid. lib. iii. c. 6. τοῖς ΤΟ βουλητὸν Τ' ἀγαθὸν λέγουσιν.
Plutarch de Plac. Philos. lib. i. c. 3. ἔστι δὲ Ὁ Θεὸς Ὁ νοῦς[1].

But even where, as in the preceding instances, *one* proposition is used, this is by no means the only form. Thus we find convertible propositions, in which the article is *wanting* to both Subject and Predicate.

EXAMPLE.

Arist. de Interp. c. 6. ΚΑΤΑΦΑΣΙΣ ἐστιν ἈΠΑΦΑΝΣΙΣ τινὸς κατά τινος.

The only difference is, that the affirmation thus made in one instance is obviously true universally; and, therefore, the method of *induction* being employed by the hearer, the sense will be exactly the same.

But there is a third form, in which convertible propositions may be expressed: it is to join the two convertible Nouns by a Copulative, and to make them the Subject of a proposition of which the Predicate is ταυτό: for, to affirm identity of two things, is the same as to affirm that either may be predicated

---

[1] Winer, in considering propositions of this kind, contents himself with saying, that the Predicate also has the Article when it is *thought of as something definite*. This explanation is neither so comprehensive as Bishop Middleton's, nor so clear, when the Bishop's is rightly understood. And in consequence, Winer, in both his first and second parts, has fallen into constant confusion. He seems to have no notion of, or no belief in, the hypothetic use of the Article, or its use in universal propositions. (See, however, his first part, 14. 3.) Consequently, he puts together, as similar, such propositions as ἡ δὲ πέτρα ἦν ὁ Χριστός (1 Cor. x. 4.) and ἡ ἁμαρτία ἐστὶν ἡ ἀνομία (1 John iii. 4.) although in the first case the first Article arises from *renewed mention*, and the second indicates the *one* Messiah; while, in the second, each shows the universality of the proposition. (See this place below.) Again, he confounds οὐχ οὗτός ἐστιν ὁ τέκτων; (Mark vi. 3.) with ἐκεῖνά ἐστι τὰ κοινοῦντα, vii. 15; whereas, in the first case, the Article indicates a *well known* person; and in the second is hypothetical, the basis of the proposition being, as Bishop Middleton observes of another instance of the same case above, that there are things which defile a man; and the object of it being to identify them with certain things under consideration. In all cases the learner must take care to observe the difference which Winer has confounded, and to remember, that in the case both of Pronouns and Nouns generally, the fact that the Predicate has the Article, does not necessarily prove a reciprocating proposition, as it may serve the purpose of renewed mention, &c. &c. &c. Wherever Winer's remarks seemed sound I have used them.—H. J. R.

of the other; and the result will be the same, according to what has just now been observed, whether both the Nouns have the Article or both be without it.

EXAMPLES.

Arist. Top. lib. i. c. 5. ταυτόν ἐστιν ΑΙΣΘΗΣΙΣ καὶ 'ΕΠΙΣΤΗΜΗ.

Plat. Theæt. vol. ii. p. 69. ΦΑΝΤΑΣΙΑ καὶ ΑΙΣΘΗΣΙΣ ταυτόν.

Ibid. p. 55. ταυτὸν ἄρα ΣΟΦΙΑ καὶ 'ΕΠΙΣΤΗΜΗ.

Arist. Eth. ad Eudem. lib. i. c. 1. πολλοὶ γὰρ ταυτό φασιν εἶναι τὴν ΕΥΔΑΙΜΟΝΙΑΝ καὶ τὴν ΕΥΤΥΧΙΑΝ.

From this digression on the nature of reciprocating propositions, into which, however, the doctrine of the Subject and Predicate has unavoidably led me, it will be right to proceed to the consideration of another remarkable insertion and omission of the Article; to the investigation of which the hypothesis proposed appears to afford a proper clue: I allude to the usage, which has given birth to a theological controversy, and to which the public attention has recently been called by Mr. Sharp and Mr. Wordsworth.

§ 2. When two or more Attributives [1] joined by a Copulative or Copulatives are *assumed* of the *same* person or thing,

---

[1] By Attributives Mr. Harris means *Adjectives, Verbs,* and *Participles:* (see Hermes, p. 87.) These, however, are not alike capable of being assumed, and are not, therefore, alike objects of the present canon. The Adjective is *assumible*: thus ὁ ἀγαθὸς is ὁ 'ΩΝ ἀγαθός. The Participle also, as we have seen, is assumible; it even contains within itself the assumptive Copula. But the Verb is not assumible; it can only be *asserted*: the Verb, therefore, is not such an Attributive as the canon supposes. But though the Verb must be excluded from our present consideration, there is, on the other hand, a large class of Nouns (so at least they are denominated) which are as truly assumible Attributives as is the Adjective: I mean all those significant of *character, relation,* or *dignity*: these we find interchanged and associated both with Adjectives and with Participles: they are interchanged, as when ὁ βουλεύων is put for ὁ βουλευτής, and they are associated, as in ὁ περίεργος καὶ ΣΥΚΟΦΑΝΤΗΣ, τὸν ΓΟΗΤΑ καὶ περιτετμηκότα. To these, therefore, the canon may be expected to apply.—The reader will recollect, that assumption is the basis of the whole: otherwise the article could not be employed. Thus in Plato, vol. xi. p. 4. ἡγουμένη (scil. ἐμὲ) ΔΙΚΑΣΤΗΝ 'ΑΓΓΕΛΟΝ εἶναι, κ. τ. λ. though one person only is spoken of, the attributes are not assumed of him, but are *asserted*: to have written, therefore, ΤΟΝ δικαστὴν would have involved an impropriety.

before the first Attributive the Article is *inserted;* before the remaining ones it is *omitted*[1].

[1] It will perhaps surprise some persons to find, that Winer, in his first part, coolly enounces *his* rule on the subject thus :—If *two* or *three* definite Nouns in the same number and gender stand together, only the first of them has usually the Article. The instances which he subjoins are as remarkable as his thus setting aside, without notice, what is here said by Bishop Middleton. The instances are, Acts ix. 31. ὅλης τῆς Ἰουδαίας καὶ Γαλιλαίας καὶ Σαμαρείας. Matt. xxi. 12. πάντας τοὺς πωλοῦντας καὶ ἀγοράζοντας. Jude 4. τὸν μόνον δεσπότην καὶ κύριον. The two first of these examples belong obviously to the classes noticed by Bishop Middleton at the end of this chapter : the first of them being of the same description as Proper Names, (see p. 63) ; the second belonging to that class in which no mistake can arise (see p. 69), because the attributives in them cannot be predicated of the same subject without the most evident contradiction. The last is one in which Mr. Sharp's rule is observed.

But what follows is still more remarkable. " Compare, however," says Winer, " in contradiction to this, the following places." John ii. 22. τῇ γραφῇ καὶ τῷ λόγῳ. Here Winer's rule is not contradicted, as the words are *not* in the same gender. Matt. vii. 12. ὁ νόμος καὶ οἱ προφῆται. Here they are not in the same number. 1 Cor. xi. 3. ὁ θεὸς καὶ πατήρ. Here the two relate to the same person. Tit. i. 4. Here there is no example at all. Rom. xii. 2. τὸ ἀγαθὸν καὶ εὐάρεστον καὶ τέλειον. Here all the words relate to the same thing. Luke xxii. 2. οἱ ἀρχιερεῖς καὶ οἱ γραμματεῖς. Ib. 4. τοῖς ἀρχιερεῦσι καὶ τοῖς στρατηγοῖς. In these two last examples Winer's own rule is violated, and that which he so quietly sets aside confirmed.

In his second part, he observes, that when the Nouns are of a different gender, the Article is repeated, as Acts xiii. 50. Col. ii. 13 ; iv. 1. Rom. viii. 2. with many other places, except Col. ii. 22. Luke i. 6. 23. 49 ; xiv. 23. Rev. v. 12. Compare Plato, Pol. viii. p. 557 ; ix. p. 586. But he adds, that if the Nouns are of the *same* gender, the Article is omitted, where they can be considered as forming part of one whole, as Mark xv. 1. where the Elders and Scribes are considered as forming only one class. Col. ii. 8. 19. 2 Thess. iii. 2. 1 Pet. ii. 25 ; iii. 4. Rom. i. 20. Phil. ii. 17. 25. Eph. ii. 20. Tit. i. 15. 1 Tim. iv. 3. 7. Heb. iii. 1. Luke xiv. 3. 21. Now among these examples, the 5th, 6th, 9th, 11th, 12th, 13th, and 14th, are cases where the *same* person is referred to ! The 1st, 3d, 4th, 10th, 15th, and 16th, are plurals ! and of the remainder, examples 2d and 7th are cases of abstract Nouns, and the only one left, viz. the 8th, is nearly the same ! Next Winer says the Article is omitted, when, by καί, a clearer description is added. Col. iii. 17. 1 Pet. i. 3. 2 Pet. i. 11 ; ii. 20. Phil. iv. 20. Every one of these is a case of Mr. Sharp's rule. Then the Article is omitted, says Winer, when between the first Substantive and its Article, a genitive, or other defining word, is added, which also applies to the second, as 1 Thess. ii. 12. τὴν ἑαυτοῦ βασιλείαν καὶ δόξαν ; iii. 7. Phil. i. 19. 25. Eph. iii. 5. Acts i. 25. (Winer is so careless, that he has given here three examples where the defining word is not between the Substantive and Article) Of these examples, Eph. iii. 5. is a plural, and the others are cases of *incompatible* or *abstract* Nouns. Thus δέησις and ἐπιχορηγία could never be mistaken. I know not, however, whether these may not be referred to another consideration

EXAMPLES.

Plut. Vit. Cic. Ed. Bast. p. 68. 'Ρώσκιος 'Ο υἱὸς ΚΑΙ κληρονόμος τοῦ τεθνηκότος ἠγανάκτει.
Demosth. de Cor. § 27. τίς 'Ο τῇ πόλει λέγων ΚΑΙ γράφων ΚΑΙ πράττων ΚΑΙ ἑαυτὸν δούς, &c.
Ibid. § 61. 'Ο σύμβουλος ΚΑΙ ῥήτωρ ἐγώ.
Plato, vol. ii. p. 91. ΤΩι νεωτέρῳ τε ΚΑΙ ὑγροτέρῳ 'ΟΝΤΙ προσπαλαίειν.
Ibid. p. 192. ΤΟΝ σιμόν τε ΚΑΙ ἐξόφθαλμον.
Æsch. cont. Ctes. § 56. 'Ο περίεργος ΚΑΙ συκοφάντης Δημοσθένης.
Ibid. § 71. ΤΟΝ γόητα ΚΑΙ βαλαντιοτόμον ΚΑΙ διατετμηκότα τὴν πολιτείαν.
Ibid. § 90. ΤΟΝ γράψαντα μὲν πανυστάτην ἔξοδον, προδόντα ΔΕ τούς, &c.
Herod. lib. iii. p. 133. 'Ατόσσῃ ΤΗι Κύρου μὲν θυγατρὶ, Δαρείου ΔΕ γυναικί.
Aristoph. Equit. 247.
παῖε, παῖε ΤΟΝ πανοῦργον ΚΑΙ ταραξιππόστρατον
ΚΑΙ τελώνην ΚΑΙ φάραγγα ΚΑΙ Χάρυβδιν ἁρπαγῆς
ΚΑΙ πανοῦργον ΚΑΙ πανοῦργον· πολλάκις γὰρ αὖτ' ἐρῶ.
Plut. de Is. et Osir. p. 263. ΤΟΝ γὰρ βασιλέα ΚΑΙ Κύριον Ὄσιριν γράφουσιν.
Philo Jud. p. 309. Ed. 1640. 'Ο Κύριος ΚΑΙ θεὸς εὐεργέτης ἐστίν.
Ibid. p. 658. ἐξέπεμπε πρὸς ΤΟΝ τῆς 'Ιουδαίας ἀρχιερέα ΚΑΙ βασιλέα· 'Ο γὰρ ΑΥΤΟΣ ἦν.
Suidas (voce Χριστὸς) Χριστὸς, 'Ο Κύριος ΚΑΙ θεὸς ἡμῶν[1].

---

entirely; whether, I mean, this is the case of the simple Article at all. Fourthly, the Article is omitted, says Winer, when the words connected are Adjectives and Participles which are predicated of the same subject. See Acts iii. 14; ii. 20. Mark ix. 25. John xxi. 24. Luke vi. 49. Phil. iii. 3. It will be observed, how nearly Winer approaches finally to Mr. Sharp's rule. What is yet more singular, he goes on to notice the cases where the Article is added, which he describes as cases where Nouns are to be considered as independent, i. e. in short, cases falling under Mr. Sharp's rule, that the Article is added, when the Nouns relate to different things.—H. J. R.

[1] Mr. Winstanley has produced some quotations which he conceives to be violations of this rule. Let us look at them. The first is a passage from Plato,

APPELLATIVES.

In all these instances it will immediately be seen, that the several Attributives connected by Copulatives are meant to be

(Ep. vi. T. iii. p. 323. D. ed. Serran. 1578,) quoted by Clemens Alexandrinus, p. 598. C. ed. Sylb. 1641, or T. ii. p. 710. ed. Potter, 1715.
Τὸν πάντων θεὸν αἴτιον καὶ τοῦ ἡγεμόνος καὶ αἰτίου πατέρα κύριον ἐπομνύντας. Here, says Mr. Winstanley, τοῦ ἡγ. κ. αἰ. is an agreement with the rule, but τὸν πάντων θεὸν—καὶ πατέρα κύριον is in direct opposition to it. He goes on, however, to quote the same passage from Origen (c. Cels. vi. 8. T. i. p. 636. B. ed. Paris, 1733, or p. 288. ed. Hœsch. 1605, or p. 280. ed. Spenc. 1677), who gives it thus:—καὶ τὸν τῶν πάντων θεόν, ἡγεμόνα τῶν τε ὄντων καὶ τῶν μελλόντων, τοῦ τε ἡγεμόνος καὶ αἰτίου πατέρα καὶ κύριον ἐπομνύντας. Where the differences of reading are so very considerable, I would put it to the candid reader, whether any appeal can be made to the passage. We may observe, that both an Article and a Copulative are omitted in one quotation and inserted in the other.

The next passage is: τῷ θεῷ τῶν ὅλων προσέχετε καὶ διδασκάλῳ τῶν περὶ αὐτοῦ μαθημάτων τῷ Ἰησοῦ. Orig. c. Cels. iii. p. 75. (T. i. p. 497. D. or p. 172. ed. Hœsch. or p. 157. ed. Spencer.)

The third is: τῷ δὲ θεῷ πατρί, καὶ υἱῷ τῷ κυρίῳ ἡμῶν Ἰησοῦ Χριστῷ σὺν τῷ ἁγίῳ πνεύματι δόξα—a passage for which Mr. Winstanley refers to Burgh's Inquiry, p. 359.

Mr. Winstanley seems aware that the same objection may be taken to both of these passages, viz. that the article is *repeated*. But he contends that, repeated as it is in these passages, it is a mark of the *identity* of object of the Noun to which it is prefixed with the one immediately preceding it, and not of difference from the foregoing one.

To speak particularly of the last of these passages, I am at a loss to see how Mr. Winstanley can see any confirmation of his views in it. The corresponding words are θεὸς and κύριος, and these have each of them the Article. Πατρὶ in the first clause, and υἱῷ in the second, are *not* the leading words, but adjuncts to the leading word. Mr. Winstanley's criticism, I confess, I cannot understand. In speaking of this passage, he says, that if the Article be reckoned any thing more than a mark of identity with the Noun immediately preceding, Mr. Sharp must give up one of his passages, viz. τοῦ θεοῦ καὶ κυρίου Ἰ. Χ. τοῦ μέλλοντος κ. τ. λ. What similarity exists between these passages, I cannot see. The first has two clauses, in each of which there is a leading word and an adjunct; the other, if it *has* two clauses, has *no* adjunct to the leading word in the first; and in the second, the Article is affixed to the adjunct, whereas it is affixed to the leading word in the first passage. Two passages less alike it would be difficult to find.

Of the other three passages adduced by Mr. Winstanley, two are noticed elsewhere. The third is μεθ' οὗ δόξα τῷ θεῷ καὶ πατρὶ καὶ ἁγίῳ πνεύματι. (Ep. Eccl. Smyrn. de Martyr. Polyc. § 22.) Here there is no difficulty. The expression, ὁ θεὸς καὶ πατὴρ, for the Father, is familiar to every reader of the Fathers; and the distinction between the persons of the Trinity was, of course, deemed too clear for any confusion to arise. In short, the case is one of those which Bishop Middleton notices below, where the two Nouns cannot be predicated of the same *person* without contradiction.—H. J. R.

understood of the person or thing signified in the Article preceding. The reason of this usage, if the nature of the Article has been rightly explained, it will not be difficult to discover In the first example Ὁ is the subject of an assumptive proposition, of which υἱὸς καὶ κληρονόμος is the Predicate, ὢν being, as usual, understood; and the meaning is, that "He (Roscius) being both son and heir of the deceased," &c. But what will happen, supposing the Article prefixed to κληρονόμος also? We shall then have *two* assumptive propositions and *two* subjects coupled together by καί: i. e. υἱὸς and κληρονόμος will then be assumed respectively of two *distinct persons;* they cannot be assumed of one and the same, if the Article be a Pronoun, because two Articles coupled together, and yet having reference to the same person, involve the absurdity of joining an individual to himself. So in the sixth instance, ὁ περίεργος καὶ συκοφάντης. But where two distinct persons are *intended*, we actually find the Article repeated. Thus in Demosth. de Cor. § 56, we read ὁ γὰρ σύμβουλος καὶ Ὁ συκοφάντης .... διαφέρουσι[1]. Here the second Article could not have been omitted; because σύμβουλος and συκοφάντης would then both have been predicated of ὁ, and of course of one person: nor will the change of διαφέρουσι into διαφέρει restore the sense: the proposition will then be, that "he who is at once an adviser and a sycophant differs" from some other character not mentioned. These remarks explain the *principle* of Mr. Granville Sharp's First Rule[2], as the examples above adduced are proofs, that the rule accords with the usage of the best Greek writers.

But though the principle of the rule admit a very obvious solution, when the nature of the Article is once properly understood, its *limitations* may still require to be considered.

We find the rule applicable only to the case of the words, which I have denominated assumible Attributives. Hence many Nouns are not subject to its operation, all being excluded, except those which are significant of character. We are, therefore, to inquire what there is inherent in the ex-

---

[1] So also Æsch. c. Ctes. § 58. ἐν τοῖς αὐτοῖς ἐπιτιμίοις ᾤετο δεῖν ἐνέχεσθαι ΤΟΝ ἀστράτευτον, καὶ ΤΟΝ λελοιπότα τὴν τάξιν, καὶ ΤΟΝ δειλόν.

[2] "Remarks on the Greek Article in the New Testament," &c. 2d edit. p. 3.

cluded Nouns to cause so remarkable a difference. Now these Nouns must be either names of substances *considered as substances*, proper names, or names of abstract ideas: and the *exceptions* from the rule will be such as

1. Ὁ λίθος ΚΑΙ χρυσός.
2. ΤΟΝ Ἀλέξανδρον ΚΑΙ Φίλιππον. Æsch. cont. Ctes. § 81.
3. ΤΗΝ ἀπειρίαν ΚΑΙ ἀπαιδευσίαν. Plato, vol. xi. p. 31[1].

The first sort of Nouns are names of substances *considered as substances:* for names of substances may be considered otherwise; and the distinction is important. They are otherwise considered so often as the name *supposes* the substance, and *expresses* some attribute: so υἱός, ῥήτωρ, ἡγεμών, δοῦλος, δεσπότης, &c. are indeed so far names of substances, that they *pre-suppose* a substance, but their immediate use is to mark some *attribute* of the substance ἄνθρωπος, which is in all of them understood: for to be υἱός, ῥήτωρ, ἡγεμών, &c. is no more of the *essence* of ἄνθρωπος than it is to be *wise, happy, rich,* &c. Such Nouns, therefore, as was before hinted, differ little in their nature from Adjectives: they are *Adjectives of invariable application,* being constantly used of ἄνθρωπος; whereas common Adjectives, ἀγαθός, μέλας, ὠκύς, &c. are applicable to substances of various kinds, and are not applied to any one in particular. It was, then, to be expected of attributive Substantives, that any number of them coupled together might be predicated of an individual represented by a Pronoun; for it is to be remembered, that in such phrases as ὁ σύμβουλος καὶ ῥήτωρ, ὁ is no otherwise connected with σύμβουλος, than in τὸν σιμὸν καὶ ἐξόφθαλμον, τὸν is connected with σιμόν: in all cases, to which the rule applies, the Article is a Pronoun representing some substance, of which the Attributives, whether Nouns, Adjectives, or Participles, are predicated, and, consequently, is not the Article of the *first* Attributive, but of all collectively. This is sufficiently plain where the Attributives are Adjectives or Participles, and will be equally plain in the remaining case, if the reader will advert to the *nature* of attributive Sub-

---

[1] ἡ ὄψις τε καὶ ἀκοή. Plat. Phæd. p. 65. B. xv. 12. Wyttenb. This is cited by Dobree, Adv. p. 117. Of course all this applies still more strongly to the Plurals of such Nouns where they admit them; as Plat. Phæd. 94. D. 61. fin. Wyttenb. ταῖς ἐπιθυμίαις καὶ ὀργαῖς καὶ φόβοις.—H. J. R.

stantives rather than to their form. But suppose that, instead of these attributive Nouns, we introduce others, which express mere *substances:* this consequence will follow, (if we attempt to apply the rule,) that substances in their nature distinct and incompatible will be predicated of one individual: e. g. λίθος καὶ χρυσὸς will both be assumed of ὁ, the representative of some Noun understood: but this is evidently absurd; distinct *real* essences cannot be conceived to belong to the same thing; nor can distinct *nominal* essences, without manifest contradiction, be affirmed of it. *Essence* is single, peculiar, and incommunicable; whereas the same *attribute* may belong to many objects, and the same object may possess divers attributes.

We are, however, to be cautious in determining that any Noun is expressive simply of substance. There are many, which, though properly significant of substance, are yet frequently used to indicate the attribute or attributes by which that substance is principally distinguished. Thus when Homer says, Il. N. 131. ἀσπὶς ἄρ' ἀσπίδ' ἔρειδε, κόρυς κόρυν, 'ΑΝΕΡΑ δ' 'ΑΝΗΡ, there can be no doubt that ἀνὴρ is as truly the name of a substance considered independently of all its attributes, as is ἀσπὶς or κόρυς : but when we read, Il. Z. 112.

'ΑΝΕΡΕΣ ἐστέ, φίλοι, μνήσασθε δὲ θούριδος ἀλκῆς,

the same word ἀνὴρ is evidently used, not as a Noun significant merely of substance, but as an Attributive; and an Adjective, the purest species of Attributive, would have answered the speaker's purpose: 'ΑΝΔΡΕΙΟΙ ἐστέ, φίλοι, &c. though less figurative and poetical, certainly conveys the idea. In this instance, therefore, ἀνέρες *supposes* the substance, and *expresses* a distinguishing attribute, viz. *valour*. Now since things animated have almost always some prominent character, some attribute, the operation of which unavoidably attracts notice, it will follow, that almost every Noun expressive of an *animated* substance, may be employed as an Attributive, and consequently that two or more of such, when the attributes referred to are not in their nature incompatible and contradictory, may be made subservient to the principle of the rule [1].

---

[1] Nouns expressive of *inanimate* substances seem to have this difference, that though they have attributes (and we have no idea of any thing which has not)

The reason why *proper names* are excepted is evident at once: for it is impossible that *John* and *Thomas*, the names of two distinct persons, should be predicated of an individual. It is obvious, therefore, that in the phrase τὸν 'Αλέξανδρον καὶ Φίλιππον, τὸν is the Article of 'Αλέξανδρον only, and not of *both* names; as would happen, were the principle of the rule intended to apply.

Nouns, which are the names of *abstract ideas*, are also excluded, and from a cause not wholly dissimilar: for, as *Locke* has well observed, " Every distinct abstract idea is a distinct essence ; and the *names*, that stand for such distinct ideas, are the names of things essentially different [1]." It would, therefore, be as contradictory to assume that any quality represented by Ἡ were at once ἀπειρία and ἀπαιδευσία, as that the same person were both Alexander and Philip: whence it is immediately evident, that such an assumption could not be intended [2]. Under this head we may class Verbs in the Infinitive Mood, which differ not in their nature from the names of the corresponding abstract ideas. Thus we read in Plato, vol. xi. p. 43. ΤΩι ἰδεῖν τε ΚΑΙ ἀκοῦσαι· in the next page we have ΤΗι ὄψει τε ΚΑΙ ἀκοῇ. The two cases evidently require the same explanation. Infinitive Moods so coupled together are extremely common.

Thus far it appears, then, that the limitations of the rule are not arbitrary, but necessary, and that the several kinds of excluded Nouns have one disqualifying property belonging to them all; which is, that no two of any class are in their nature predicable of the same individual; whilst *attributive*

---

yet those attributes, from their inertness and quiescence, make so little impression on the observer, that he does not commonly abstract them from his idea of the substance, and still less does he lose sight of the substance, and use its name as expressive of the attribute. Add to this, that to characterize *persons* by the names of *things* would be violent and unnatural, especially when two or more things wholly different in their natures are to be associated for the purpose : and to characterize any *thing* by the names of other things would be "confusion worse confounded."

[1] Essay, Book iii. chap. iii. § 14.
[2] Several of Mr. Winstanley's exceptions belong to this class ;
ἡ—ἀγαπητικὴ ἡμῶν διδασκαλία τε καὶ πολιτεία. Clem. Alex.
τῆς τούτου θρασύτητος καὶ τόλμης. Lys.
τῆς ἐκείνου γνώμης καὶ κακοδαιμονίας. Demosth.
ἡ Μακεδονικὴ ἀρχὴ καὶ δύναμις. Demosth.—H. J. R.

Nouns are such, that several of them *may* be assumed of the same person without any contradiction or falsehood.

But though, when attributives coupled together are assumed of the same subject, the first only has the Article prefixed, will it be true *conversely*, that when the Article is prefixed to the first only of such Attributives, they are always assumed of the same subject? This is a very necessary inquiry. That the Subject is the same in the examples above adduced, is sufficiently evident; and there is not, I am persuaded, any ancient writer of Greek prose from whom a multitude of similar passages might not be collected: still, however, if a sufficient number of unquestionable authorities could be produced, from which, the circumstances being precisely the same, a different conclusion might be drawn, that is, if in forms of expression *exactly agreeing* with Ὁ υἱος ΚΑΙ κληρονόμος the Attributives could be shown to be intended of *different* persons, then the rule, whatever may be said respecting its *principle*, would not be of safe application.

Mr. Sharp, whose attention, however, appears to have been confined to the New Testament, has remarked that the rule is not *always* applicable to *Plurals*; and yet, if the ground of the usage has been properly explained, it will certainly be supposed that in Plurals also the rule should uniformly hold. If υἱὸς ΚΑΙ κληρονόμος must be understood of ὁ, then υἱοὶ ΚΑΙ κληρονόμοι should, for any thing that appears, be also both understood of οἱ, supposing οἱ referring to *two Roscii* to precede; nor have I in *such* instances observed that the rule is ever infringed. Of its application to Plurals, the following are a few

EXAMPLES.

Herod. lib. ii. § 35. ΤΑ μὲν αἰσχρὰ ἀναγκαῖα ΔΕ ἐν ἀποκρύφῳ ἐστὶ ποιέειν χρεών.

Isocr. Paneg. § 16. ΟΙ πρόγονοι τῶν νῦν ἐν Λακεδαίμονι βασιλευόντων ἔκγονοι Δ' Ἡρακλέους κατῆλθον, &c.

Ibid. § 32. ἐτίμων ΤΟΥΣ αὐτόχειρας ΚΑΙ φονέας τῶν πολιτῶν.

Plutarch de discrim. Amici, &c. p. 35. οἱ ζωγράφοι ΤΑ φωτεινὰ ΚΑΙ λαμπρὰ ΤΟΙΣ σκιεροῖς ΚΑΙ σκοτεινοῖς, &c.

Xen. Mem. lib. ii. c. 1. ΟΙ ἀνδρεῖοι ΚΑΙ δυνατοὶ ΤΟΥΣ ἀνάνδρους ΚΑΙ ἀδυνάτους, &c.

From these instances it is plain that in *Plurals* as well as in Singulars the rule is frequently observed: but the question is, does this *always* happen? Are there no cases in which, though the Article be wanting before the second Attributive, we are compelled to understand that Attributive of persons or things different from the Subjects of the first? In the course of a somewhat extensive examination, I have met with a very few instances like the following: Herod. lib. i. p. 51. αἱ εὔμορφοι ΤΑΣ ἀμόρφους ΚΑΙ ἐμπήρους ἐξεδίδοσαν· where it may be said, that the ἔμπηροι must be supposed to be in general distinct from the ἄμορφοι, the one indicating an adventitious, and the other a natural, defect; and that the author, though he has not prefixed the Article to the second Attributive, meant so to distinguish them. Granting, then, this to be the case, and that other less questionable instances may be found tending to corroborate the exception, what reason can be alleged, why the practice in Plural Attributives should differ from that in Singular ones? The circumstances are evidently dissimilar. A *single* individual may stand in various relations and act in divers capacities; and, consequently, if two relations or characters be connected by a Copulative, and the first be preceded by a Pronoun, the reader will reasonably understand them both of the person represented by that Pronoun, because such is the general usage, and the compliance with it will not involve any contradiction. But this does not happen in the same degree with respect to Plurals. Though *one* individual may act, and frequently does act, in several capacities, it is not likely that a *multitude* of individuals should all of them act in the *same* several capacities, and by the extreme improbability, that they should be represented as so acting, we may be forbidden to understand the second Plural Attributive of the persons designed in the Article prefixed to the first, however the usage in the Singular might seem to countenance the construction. My meaning may be illustrated by a familiar example. An individual is at once a Member of Parliament and the Colonel of a Regiment. Speaking of such an one, and having occasion to advert to these two characters, we might say in Greek, Ὁ βουλευτὴς ΚΑΙ λοχαγός, and if by such a phrase we meant to indicate two *different* persons, we should speak in a manner not authorized by the Greek idiom. But suppose we should say, speaking of several persons, ΟΙ βουλευταὶ ΚΑΙ λοχαγοί· the inference would be, either that the persons sitting in parliament and those commanding regiments are usually the same, or else, knowing them not to be the same, we should understand the words as expressive of two distinct classes: and what is the alternative? If they be the same, the rule is strictly observed: if notoriously they are distinct, the rule, indeed, is violated, but in such a manner that no ambiguity can ensue; for though ΟΙ λοχαγοὶ would have been more accurate, our previous knowledge on the subject prevents the possibility of mistake. So in the passage from Herodotus our observation having taught us that the ἄμορφοι are not usually ἔμπηροι, and *vice versâ*, we are not liable to understand these epithets of the same individuals, any more than if the second of them had the Article prefixed. It is obvious that in the Singular Number confusion might arise: that *one* person should be ἄμορφος and ἔμπηρος has nothing in it remarkable: and, consequently, if the second Article be omitted, the principle of the general rule will prevail. Ὁ ἄμορφος καὶ ἔμπηρος would inevitably be understood of the same individual [1].

[1] I have noticed one passage, which, as it presents a difficulty, it would be disingenuous to suppress. Herod. ed. Steph. lib. iv. p. 154. has these words: τῶν παλλακέων τε μίην ἀποπνίξαντες θάπτουσι, καὶ τὸν οἰνοχόον, καὶ μάγειρον, καὶ ἱπποκόμον, καὶ διήκονον, καὶ ἀγγελιηφόρον, καὶ ἵππους, καί, κ. τ. λ. Not having *Wesseling* at hand, I cannot ascertain whether this be the reading of the MSS. It is impossible, however, that *all* these various offices should have been united in the same person; and this obvious impossibility may be the reason, that the writer has expressed himself so negligently. I once thought that μάγειρον, ἱπποκόμον, &c. might signify *one* of every kind: but then we should expect ἕνα τῶν μαγείρων, as in μίην τῶν παλλακέων. I do not recollect any similar example.

It has subsequently occurred to me, that the several Nouns, μάγειρον, ἱπποκόμον, &c. may be anarthrous by part I. chap. vi. § 2*.

---

* In the conclusion of his note, the learned Author refers the example in question to the case of Enumeration: it may, however, be reduced under the class of examples in which the Article has the force of the Possessive Pronoun. Taking τὸν οἰνοχόον as equivalent to τὸν οἰνοχόον αὐτοῦ, we should not have expected αὐτοῦ, if expressed with the first Substantive, to be repeated with all or

APPELLATIVES.

Nor is this reasoning entirely hypothetical; since we find in very many instances, not only in the Plural, but even in the *Singular* Number, that where Attributives are in their nature *absolutely incompatible*, which is not the case in ἄμορφοι καὶ ἔμπηροι, i. e. where the application of the rule would involve a contradiction in terms, there the first Attributive only has the Article, the perspicuity of the passage not requiring the rule to be accurately observed [1]. In the following examples, the second Attributive cannot be understood of the persons or things referred to in the first.

---

[1] Mr. Winstanley has collected a list of five exceptions to the rule, of which four are comprised by this remark of Bp. Middleton.
1. The case of national appellations.
2. When *one* of the nouns is a plural.
3. When one is impersonal, as τὸν ἐπίσκοπον καὶ πρεσβυτέριον.
4. When the signification renders farther personal distinction unnecessary, as ὁ ἀγαθὸς καὶ κακός.

The other is when *one* is a proper name, and on this Mr. W. brings two instances from Ignatius: (1.) τοῦ θεοῦ—καὶ Ἰησοῦ Χριστοῦ, and (2.) τοῦ πατρός, καὶ Ἰησοῦ Χριστοῦ. He thus tries to defeat the effect of Mr. Sharp's rule, in one case, by a side blow. But these instances are not in point. That a Proper Name often drops the Article contrary to rule, as τὸν ἄνδρα Μαρίας, (Matt. i. 16.) we know; but the question is, supposing Χριστὸς to be a mere proper name (as Mr. W. says), to stand *first*, and *have* the Article, whether a word following, joined to it by the Copulative, and *not* having the Article, can be understood of a different person. This, at least, is *one* question to which Mr. W.'s cases do not apply. It remains afterwards for consideration, whether ὁ Χριστὸς can be considered entirely as a Proper Name. H. J. R.

---

any of the subsequent ones: and on a similar principle we may dispense with the repetition of the Article.

Having made this remark, however, I think it right to add, that I do not consider it necessary to the character of the Author, and the soundness of his hypothesis, that every single example should be clearly reducible to one or other of his rules. Those rules are grounded on the general practice of the best Greek authors; and if in their writings a very few cases be found which seem at first to be inconsistent with them, these may be left as matter of further investigation, or may be considered as unusual forms of expression, which the best writers are not always careful to avoid: at any rate, they must be much more numerous than at present they appear to be, and we must be very certain that they admit of no consistent solution, before we allow them to have much weight against the mass of evidence adduced on the other side. J. S.

EXAMPLES.

Thucyd. lib. i. in init. τὸν πόλεμον τῶν ΠΕΛΟΠΟΝΝΗΣΙΩΝ καὶ 'ΑΘΗΝΑΙΩΝ.

Ibid. i. § 10. τὰς (scil. ναῦς) ΜΕΓΙΣΤΑΣ καὶ 'ΕΛΑΧΙΣΤΑΣ.

Isocr. Paneg. § 42. τῶν μύθων τοῖς ΤΡΩΙΚΟΙΣ καὶ ΠΕΡΣΙΚΟΙΣ.

Demosthenes c. Lept. vol. i. p. 476. τοῖς ΘΑΣΙΟΙΣ καὶ ΒΥΖΑΝΤΙΟΙΣ ἐγράφη.

Xen. Œcon. p. 481. τοὺς ΤΡΑΓΩιΔΟΥΣ τε καὶ ΚΩΜΩιΔΟΥΣ [1].

We frequently find the same thing happening in *Singular* Attributives; but it is only in those which cannot be predicated of the same subject, without the most evident and direct contradiction.

EXAMPLES.

Aristot. Eth. ad Eudem. lib. i. c. 8. ἐν ὅσοις ὑπάρχει τὸ ΠΡΟΤΕΡΟΝ καὶ ῾ΥΣΤΕΡΟΝ [2].

---

[1] So Dion. Hal. iv. p. 2246, 9. τὰς αὐτῶν γυναῖκας καὶ θυγατέρας. Professor Dobree (Advers. p. 116.) has given several examples of plurals from Thucydides, as i. 26. 45. τούς τε οἰκήτορας καὶ φρουρούς· ii. 50. med. τὰ ὄρνεα καὶ τετράποδα· iv. 11. τοὺς τριηράρχους καὶ κυβερνήτας· from Aristophanes, as Ran. 784. Eq. 320. Eccl. 198. 699. 8. Pac. 555. Plut. 89. (though the last, and fourth and fifth, he marks as doubtful); from Plato, as Gorg. 498. C.—176.12. Heind. οἱ ἀγαθοί τε καὶ κακοί, where, too, as Professor Scholefield observes, Bekker reads, οἱ κακοί. Alcib. i. p. 117. A.—22. Stallb. περὶ τῶν δικαίων καὶ ἀδίκων καὶ καλῶν καὶ αἰσχρῶν καὶ κακῶν καὶ ἀγαθῶν, καὶ συμφερόντων καὶ μή. H. J. R.

[2] Thuc. v. 47. τῷ μὲν ὁπλίτῃ καὶ ψιλῷ καὶ τοξότῃ.

Soph. El. 265. λαβεῖν θ' ὁμοίως καὶ τὸ τητᾶσθαι.

Thuc. ii. 49. τό τε πλέον καὶ ἔλασσον ποτόν.

Mr. Winstanley has collected many instances from Aristotle's Ethics, in p. 17. ὁ ἐγκρατὴς καὶ ἀκρατής.—ὁ ἀγαθὸς καὶ κακός. And to this class belong others which he adduces as exceptions to Mr. S.'s rule (p. 40.) τοῖς σφετέροις τέκνοις καὶ φίλοις. Arist. τοῦ βελτίονος ἀεὶ καὶ μορίου ϝαὶ ἀνθρώπου. Professor Dobree *(ubi supra)* quotes the two places of Thucydides above, and iv. 63. τὸν εὖ καὶ κακῶς δρῶντα, and Plat. Phæd. 75. C.=31. Antep. Wytt. τοῦ ἀγαθοῦ καὶ δικαίου καὶ ὁσίου. But it is only due to that great scholar to observe, that Mr. Kidd mentions, from remembrance of a conversation, that he had afterwards withdrawn the instance from Thucydides, τό τε πλέον καὶ ἔλασσον, and also one from Plato Gorg. p. 259. D.=43. 13. Heindorf. καὶ τὸ αἰσχρὸν καὶ τὸ καλὸν καὶ ἀγαθὸν καὶ κακόν, which, in truth, hardly seems to afford an instance of exception. Professor Dobree notices also the example from the Gorgias which Bishop

Aristot. de Interp. cap. 12. περὶ τοῦ 'ΑΔΥΝΑΤΟΥ τε καὶ 'ΑΝΑΓΚΑΙΟΥ.
Plato, Theæt. vol. ii. p. 134. μεταξὺ τοῦ ΠΟΙΟΥΝΤΟΣ τε καὶ ΠΑΣΧΟΝΤΟΣ.
Ibid. p. 142. τὸ ΤΑΥΤΟΝ καὶ 'ΕΤΕΡΟΝ.
Idem, Gorg. vol. iv. p. 32. τοῦ 'ΑΡΤΙΟΥ καὶ ΠΕΡΙΤΤΟΥ, τοῦ ΔΙΚΑΙΟΥ καὶ 'ΑΔΙΚΟΥ [1].

The Attributives here coupled together are in their nature plainly incompatible; and we cannot wonder, if, in such instances, the principle of the rule has been sacrificed to negligence, or even to studied brevity, where misconception was impossible. The second Article should, in strictness, have been expressed: but in such cases the writers knew that it might safely be understood.

Having thus investigated the canon, and having explained the ground of its limitations and exceptions, I may be permitted to add, that *Mr. Sharp's* application of it to the New Testament is in strict conformity with the usage of Greek writers, and with the Syntax of the Greek Tongue; and that few of the passages which he has corrected in our common version can be defended without doing violence to the obvious and undisputed meaning of the plainest sentences which profane writers supply. If, for example, Eph. v. 5, we are with our common version to translate ἐν τῇ βασιλείᾳ ΤΟΥ Χριστοῦ ΚΑΙ Θεοῦ, " in the kingdom of Christ and of God;" or Tit. ii. 13. ΤΟΥ μεγάλου Θεοῦ ΚΑΙ Σωτῆρος ἡμῶν 'Ιησοῦ Χριστοῦ, " of the great God and (of) our Saviour Jesus Christ," we

---

M. cites last, and again, Gorg. 488. C. 7.—140. Antep. Heind. ὡς τὸ κρεῖττον καὶ ἰσχυρότερον καὶ βέλτιον ταυτὸν ὄν, which is an excellent example. It ought to be added, that, except for Mr. Kidd's observation, there would be no reason to suppose that Professor Dobree cited these examples as exceptions to Mr. Sharp's rule. He makes no remark on the rule, either in its favour or against it. He had observed these examples in the course of his reading, and noted them as bearing on the matter. H. J. R.

[1] To these may be added two of Mr. Winstanley's favourite instances (p. 20. and 21). Clement of Alexandria (p. 76. ed. Sylburg. Paris, 1641), speaking of the relation of a pious Christian to God, says, γίνεται τὰ πάντα τοῦ ἀνθρώπου, ὅτι τὰ πάντα τοῦ Θεοῦ· καὶ κοινὰ ἀμφοῖν τοῖν φίλοιν τὰ πάντα, τοῦ Θεοῦ καὶ ἀνθρώπου. No confusion could arise from such an omission of the Article, just as in the cases above cited. And the same remark applies to the next instance from Proverbs xxiv. 21.

φοβοῦ τὸν Θεόν, υἱέ, καὶ βασιλέα. H. J. R.

must in consistency translate also from *Plutarch*[1], "Roscius the son, and *another person* heir to the deceased;" though a Singular Verb follows: from *Demosthenes*, "the adviser and I an orator:" and so on in an endless series of absurdities: for Θεός, σωτήρ, &c., the Nouns in question, are as truly what I have denominated Attributive Nouns, as any which can be found; and they are so far from being in their nature *incompatible*, that some of them are even of kindred import. We are, therefore, in the instances from the New Testament, to complete the ellipsis according to the principles already established; viz. τοῦ (ὄντος) Χριστοῦ καὶ Θεοῦ, of him being, or who is, &c. τοῦ (ὄντος) μεγάλου Θεοῦ καὶ Σωτῆρος ἡμῶν· and so in *most* of the disputed texts: why I do not affirm in *all* of them, will appear hereafter. That the Fathers understood such passages in the manner in which Mr. Sharp would translate them, and as, without doubt, they will be translated at some future period, has been fully ascertained by the researches of Mr. Wordsworth: and whatever may be thought of the Fathers in some other respects, it may surely be presumed that they knew the use of one of the commonest forms of expression in their native tongue. But more of this in the SECOND PART.

---

[1] See above, p. 58.

CHAPTER IV.

PROPER NAMES.

Though much has been said respecting the insertions and omissions of the Article, it will have been perceived, and, indeed, it was hinted, that *Proper Names*, and the *Names of Abstract Ideas*, are not always subject to these general laws. The case of Proper Names shall be first considered.

On what occasions the Greeks prefixed the Article to Proper Names, is among the most curious inquiries connected with Greek literature: the observations which I have been able to make on this subject, if they do not present an undeviating uniformity of practice, at least bear evidence to the truth of the principles on which the doctrine of this Essay is founded.

Apollonius has said, that " Proper Names, on account of their inherent peculiarity, require not the Article so much as do Nouns, which express only common ideas [1] :" and, indeed, if they had originally taken the Article to define and limit their meaning, it might well be urged, that they needed not such assistance. *Harris* appears to have felt the force of this objection ; which could not but occur to him, since he supposes the Article to be something distinct from the Pronoun, and that its use is only to *define*. " Upon these principles," (says Harris [2]) " we see the reason why it is absurd to say ὁ ἐγώ, ὁ σύ, because nothing can make these Pronouns more definite than they are [3]: the same may be asserted of *Proper Names*; and though the Greeks say ὁ Σωκράτης, ἡ Ξανθίππη, and the

---

[1] Τὰ κύρια διὰ τὴν ἐν αὑτοῖς ἰδιότητα οὐχ οὕτως προσδεῖται τοῦ ἄρθρου, καθάπερ τὰ κοινὴν ἔννοιαν ἔχοντα. P. 75.

[2] Hermes, p. 225.

[3] The reason why such expressions do not occur, is rather because ὁ is a Pronoun of the *third person,* and of course cannot have a Predicate either of the *first* or *second,* without manifest contradiction. *He* cannot be *I* nor *you.*

like, yet the Article is a mere pleonasm, unless perhaps it serve to *distinguish sexes*." This conjecture, to which, however, the writer was driven by his notion that the Article is naturally a definitive, is surely altogether unfounded [1]. Generally speaking, the *termination* of names in the Greek language clearly marks the Gender: or, if this were insufficient, and to remedy the defect the Article were required, it would be prefixed, if not always to each name, at least to each on its *first occurrence;* the very contrary of which, as we shall see hereafter, is the prevailing usage. But to understand how the Article came to be associated so frequently with Proper Names, we shall do well to go back as far as we can to the origin of the practice, by attending to what is observable in *Homer*. This inquiry has, indeed, been in part anticipated: we are now to enter into it more particularly.

That there is no essential difference between the Pronoun ὁ of Homer and the Article ὁ of later writers, has, I think, been abundantly demonstrated: I shall, therefore, consider them as being one and the same thing. Now it is a common practice with Homer, when he has occasion to attribute any act to his gods or heroes, to defer the mention of their names to the conclusion of the sentence, and first to ascribe such act to persons *obscurely referred to* in the corresponding Article placed at the *beginning*. Thus Iliad, A. 488.

---

[1] It reminds us of the scene in Aristophanes, Nub. 677.

ΣΩΚ.
εἶτ' ἔτι γε περὶ τῶν 'ΟΝΟΜΑΤΩΝ μαθεῖν σε δεῖ,
ἅττ' "ΑΡΡΕΝ' ἐστίν, ἅττα δ' αὐτῶν ΘΗΛΕΑ.

ΣΤΡΕΨ.
ἀλλ' οἶδ' ἔγωγ', ἃ θήλε' ἐστίν.

ΣΩΚ.
εἰπὲ δή.

ΣΤΡΕΨ.
Λύσιλλα, Φίλιννα, Κλειταγόρα, Δημητρία.

ΣΩΚ.
ἄῤῥενα δὲ ποῖα τῶν ὀνομάτων;

ΣΤΡΕΨ.
μυρία·
Φιλόξενος, Μελησίας, Ἀμυνίας.

Αὐτὰρ Ὁ μήνιε (νηυσὶ παρήμενος ὠκυπόροισι)
Διογενὴς Πηλέως υἱὸς πόδας ὠκὺς Ἀχιλλεύς.

E. 759.   ΟΙ δὲ (ἔκηλοι
Τέρπονται) Κύπρις τε καὶ ἀργυρότοξος Ἀπόλλων[1].

Δ. 20. ΑΙ δ' (ἐπέμυξαν) Ἀθηναίη τε καὶ Ἥρη.

If the reader would see more examples, he may turn to B. 402. Γ. 81. 118. E. 17. 449. 508. 655. &c. In all these it is observable that the writer is in no haste to declare the *name* of the person, whom he has in view, but that his mind is intent rather on the *act* to be attributed to him, of whom the Article at the beginning of the sentence is the temporary representative. It is the *sullen anger* of Achilles, the *secret delight* of Venus and Apollo, and the *stifled murmurs* of Minerva and Juno, which the speaker, having pronounced the Article by which these persons are obscurely designated, is most eager to notice. Their names, indeed, in many cases scarcely need to be added: the acts attributed and the context of the narration leave little doubt respecting the persons meant. Those, however, of whom we are about to affirm or deny an action, are of necessity uppermost in our minds: and, therefore, however the speaker may defer the explanation, which a strict regard to perspicuity may in the end require, it is highly natural at the outset of the proposition to employ some symbol significant of the person, about whom the thoughts are occupied: accordingly, I have remarked that in all such instances the Article is placed at the *beginning* of the sentence, or as nearly so as the circumstances will allow.

Such examples seem to illustrate the *origin* of the practice in question: but let us try, whether Homer's writings will not assist us in tracing it downwards nearer to the usage of succeeding writers. In the class of instances adduced above, some *act* is attributed to the person signified by the Article, before the name is announced; but examples occur, in which the Article and the Proper Name are brought nearer to each

---

[1] In this example the Article, which refers to Κύπρις and Ἀπόλλων, is in the worthier Gender; and the meaning is Ἡ Κύπρις καὶ Ὁ Ἀπόλλων, as is plain from the instance subjoined, where αἱ is equivalent to Ἡ καὶ Ἡ.

other, being separated only by some word of inferior import: thus, Iliad, B. 105, 6, 7.

Αὐτὰρ Ὁ (αὖτε) Πέλοψ δῶκ' Ἀτρέϊ, ποιμένι λαῶν·
Ἀτρεὺς δὲ θνήσκων ἔλιπε πολύαρνι Θυέστῃ·
Αὐτὰρ Ὁ (αὖτε) Θυέστ' Ἀγαμέμνονι λεῖπε φορῆναι.

In these instances we find the writer using the Article with less appearance of utility than in the former examples; because here we have merely a Particle [1], by which the mind is kept in little or no suspense: and, unquestionably, if he had written simply Πέλοψ, as in the next line he has written Ἀτρεύς, the sense would have been sufficiently clear, though that the Pelops here spoken of was the same with the one just mentioned, would not have been marked with equal distinctness. Or if the Pronoun *be* employed, the Proper Name might be more safely omitted than in most of the preceding examples, since ὁ would be supposed to refer to Πέλοπι in the foregoing verse, and the addition of the name is an exercise of that *extreme caution*, instances of which have been already noticed. Here, therefore, we are getting nearer to the usage of succeeding times. But it may be asked, does Homer ever place the Article *immediately* before a Proper Name; and in this case, what are the circumstances? On the celebrated passage, Il. A. 11. οὕνεκα ΤΟΝ Χρύσην ἠτίμησ' ἀρητῆρα, *Heyne* [2], after observing that the Article, especially as prefixed to Proper Names, was confessedly unknown to Homer, and after giving some conjectural emendations of preceding critics, concludes, "*nihil expediri potest:*" whilst *Wolf* [3] declares, "*nihil dubito quin* τὸν Χρύσην *Poeta dixerit, ut personam famâ celebrem et auditoribus jam tum, quum primum ejus nomen audirent, notissimam.*" It is certainly a difficulty,

---

[1] *Valckenaër* ad Phœnissas, v. 147, has said that the Tragic Poets *never* prefix the Article to Proper Names; but *Professor Porson*, with that nice discrimination to which Greek literature is so deeply indebted, corrects the assertion of Valckenaër: his words are "rarò, nisi propter emphasin quandam, aut *initio sententiæ, ubi particula inseritur*." In the two instances, which he adduces in proof of the last mentioned usage, *Thebes* and *Argos* strongly interest the feelings of the respective speakers. See Eurip. *Phœn.* 522. and *Suppl.* 129.

[2] Hom. Il. vol. iv. p. 13.

[3] Ad Reizium de Prosod. Gr. p. 74.

that Chryses is now for the first time mentioned; but whether this difficulty be so great, that we must introduce δὴ or τοὶ[1] into the place of τὸν without any authority from Editt. or MSS., deserves, not merely for the sake of this passage, to be carefully considered. Between prefixing the Article to the name of a person then first mentioned, and making it the temporary representative of one, who, though already mentioned, has not been spoken of for some time past, the difference appears not to be great; and yet of the latter usage unquestionable instances abound. In Il. N. 765, 6. we have

ΤΟΝ δὲ τάχ' εὗρε μάχης ἐπ' ἀριστερὰ δακρυοέσσης
Δῖον 'Αλέξανδρον·

where, till 'Αλέξανδρον is pronounced, the hearer can form no tolerable conjecture who is the person meant: for the last mention of *Paris* is in v. 660, and even there no circumstance is alluded to, which could in this place assist the hearer's apprehension. That τὸν has reference to Χρύσην, might as easily be inferred in the one case, as that it related to 'Αλέξανδρον in the other: in neither, however, would such an inference be drawn. It is plain, therefore, that we are to consider what passes in the mind of the *speaker;* and the hearer is to be satisfied, if, when the sentence is completed, he can then account for the introduction of the Article, however obscure till then its reference might be. Now we have seen that in the eagerness to attribute an act, it is not unusual to employ a *symbol* of the person intended, and to defer the actual mention of his name: but if the person, though not hitherto mentioned, be already well known, and therefore of easy recognition, it seems scarcely less allowable that the speaker should first *allude* to him, even though the *allusion* may require to be explained immediately afterwards: it is as if the speaker should say, "you know whom I mean;" not, indeed, that we do or can know so much with certainty, till the name has been declared; but that we shall then perceive the reason of the anticipation. In the case before us, the speaker felt that Chryses was known by all who had heard of the pestilence just

---

[1] See Heyne *ad loc.* If conjecture were the only resource, I should prefer τοῦ depending on ἀρητῆρα, to any of the emendations proposed.

described, to have been the author of it; and though it be necessary to mention his name, yet the circumstance of his notoriety might at the same time be noticed. That Homer has a method of marking the notoriety of *facts* which, however, require to be mentioned, is known to all who have attended to the uses of the Particle ῥα. In such passages as Il. B. 76, 77.

τοῖσι δ᾽ ἀνέστη
Νέστωρ, ὃς 'ΡΑ Πύλοιο ἄναξ ἦν ἠμαθόεντος,

and B. 36.

Τὰ φρονέοντ᾽ ἀνὰ θυμόν, ἃ 'Ρ' οὐ τελέεσθαι ἔμελλεν,

it is evident that this expletive, as some hastily denominate it, has the force of the words, *as is well known*, or *as the reader is aware;* and in the disputed passage, had the reading been οὕνεκα 'ΡΑ Χρύσην, &c., the Particle would have required to be so explained, and conjecture would not have been attempted: with the Article, as the verse now stands, the only difference seems to be, that the notoriety of the *person* principally concerned, and not of the *fact* with which he is concerned, is the subject of indirect notice. At the same time, the act and the actor are so closely connected, that of whichever of the two the recognition is presupposed, the result will be much the same.

I am inclined, then, to regard this as an instance in which Homer has placed the Article immediately before a Proper Name, and that too of a person who had not hitherto been mentioned: and the solution given by Wolf will be the true one, if understood with some modifications. That Homer meant to intimate that Chryses was well known, is of itself too vague an assertion: Chryses was not, independently of the circumstances which precede the mention of his name, better known than most of the persons spoken of in the poem: but as having caused the pestilence just mentioned, he must have occupied the thoughts of the speaker, and his notoriety in that particular view the hearer would readily recognize. There is another passage, Θ. 532, which in some measure confirms this reasoning. In his address to the Trojans, Hector says, Εἴσομαι αἴκε μ᾽ 'Ο Τυδείδης, &c. Though Diomede had frequently been mentioned in the course of the poem, his name now occurs for the *first time in the speech*, which is the thing to be considered: and the force of the Article seems to be explicable, not so much on the ground that Diomede was a well-known personage, as that he was well known in the character of the antagonist of Hector: it was, therefore, not unnatural that Hector should, when speaking of an approaching battle, have the idea of Diomede uppermost in his mind; and the hearers, though they could not previously conjecture to whom the Article would refer, would afterwards, connecting it with the Proper Name, perceive its force and propriety. Ο Τυδείδης occurs again, Λ. 659, where the presence of the Article may be accounted for in a similar manner.

On the whole, I am disposed to think that the practice of introducing Proper Names by means of the Article, merely on the ground of *notoriety*, was of later date than the period under review: else we should have found in the Iliad many and unquestionable examples of this usage, since the heroes of Homer were all of them traditional personages, whose names and exploits must have been familiarly known to his readers from their earliest childhood.

From this examination, then, of the usage in Homer, we may at least deduce the *origin* of the practice of placing the Article before Proper Names, though it does not furnish us with any thing like a general rule on the subject. Nothing can be more certain than that the Article, so far from ever being intended to define the name, as most writers take for granted, is rather defined *by the Name*. All the perplexity, in which the question has been enveloped, has arisen from not considering that the Article is a genuine Pronoun; and that Pronouns of the third person, being applicable to a multitude of individuals, frequently require the speaker, if he would avoid ambiguity, to add the *Name* of the individual meant. In the first and second persons no such obscurity can exist; but in passing to the third we sometimes experience, even in our own language, a species of difficulty analogous to that, which, if I mistake not, first occasioned (not the Article to be placed before the Proper Name, but) the Proper Name to be added to the Article. In writing a letter I speak of myself in the first person, and address my correspondent in the second: here no ambiguity can occur: but in the very same letter let every *I* and *you* be turned into *he*, by some person, who narrates the contents: or, to quit hypothesis, let any one turn to a newspaper containing Parliamentary Debates; in the report of speeches he will meet with *He* (Mr. A.), *Him* (Mr. B.) continually. Every such instance illustrates the practice in question. In both cases we first *obscurely* intimate the person whom we *have in mind*, and declare his name afterwards, in order to prevent mistake.

It is, however, admitted, that Homer's writings do not enable us to lay down rules, by which we can know universally, when the Articles should be inserted or omitted before Proper Names. Nor can this create surprise. It is of the character and essence of poetry to disregard minute relations and dependencies; and in proportion as it departs from the style of narration and indulges in lofty flights, it is negligent of perspicuity: for which reason, in Pindar and in the Chorusses of the Tragedians, the Article more rarely occurs [1]. Homer's style, it is true, is less artificial, and approaches nearer to the narrative kind; but even in Homer it was not to be expected that the Article should be regularly employed on every occasion, in which writers of prose would deem it necessary. To omit the Article, where in strictness it should be inserted, is an admissible poetic licence [2]: to insert it, where it should be omitted, is not so; the reason of which is plain: in the one case perspicuity is not promoted so far as it might be; but in the other the reader is positively misled: the difference is that of withholding information, which would be true, and of giving that which is false. It will happen, therefore, that though Homer never uses the Article before a proper Name without reason, he commonly omits it without scruple: and, consequently, the instances, in which it immediately precedes the name, being so very few, nothing like a rule on the subject can be deducible from his practice.

It might seem, then, that we should look to the prose

---

[1] *Heyne*, I recollect, has remarked this of Pindar: and *Porson* ad Medeam, v. 984. says, "*Articulos vitandos in choricis censeo.*"

[2] Apollonius (p. 79.) observes, that the very first word of the Iliad would in a *Prose* writer have taken the Article; which is, probably, true.

writers, if we would detect the laws by which the Article, as it respects Proper Names, is inserted or omitted; since in general their style is not of the elevated kind, which disdains minutiæ, nor were they subject to the restraint, which metre in some degree imposes on the poet. If, indeed, we could be certain that the copies, which we possess, of Xenophon and Demosthenes were absolutely correct, and that in no instances had Articles been added or omitted through the carelessness of transcribers or the ignorance of editors and critics, to the prose writers alone we should at once appeal for the decision of the question: but this is by no means the case. On consulting different MSS. of the same Greek prose writer, we find on this very subject of the Article, especially where Proper Names and the Names of Attributes occur, more disagreement than on any other point whatever. Exactly in proportion as the writer of prose is free from restraint, so also is his transcriber and editor: and where the principle had been little examined, or at least where no principle had been generally admitted, it was to be expected that critics would sometimes venture on readings, the legitimacy of which it was not easy to controvert. It is even supposed, that the Article was not unfrequently written over Proper names by the teachers of Greek, in order to assist the learner, and thus improperly gained admittance into the text [1]. On the whole, therefore, though the usage of the prose writers be ultimately the object of our inquiry, we cannot with safety consult them on this head, unless we carry with us some previous knowledge on the subject. The writer, then, from whom such knowledge will be best obtained, will be, if such exist, one who having written in verse is little exposed to wanton interpolations, and whose style and matter are at the same time little or not at all re-

---

[1] *Valckenaër* ad Phœn. v. 147. has said, that this sometimes has happened even to the poets. "Articulus scilicet a poetis neglectus, ubi videbatur in usu communi requiri, versibus poetarum in puerorum commodum a literatoribus superscribi solebat, atque hinc sæpenumero sedem non suam occupat." And *Rudolph* (Comm. Soc. Phil. Lips. vol. iv. Part I. p. 80.) remarks, "Homerum certe sexcentis Articulis auctiorem haberemus, nisi metrum obstitisset, quominus in textum reciperetur, ubi Grammatici eum addendum in scholiis putarunt: ac in ipso Platone tanta est etiam in Articulis addendis inconstantia ac passim in omittendis constantia, ut sæpius mihi a Grammaticis additus quam a Librariis omissus videatur."

moved from those of ordinary discourse. Just such a writer is *Aristophanes*. Except in his Chorusses, his language is most simple and unaffected; whilst his metres have generally protected him from the critics, and his indelicacy has completely excluded him from schools. We may, therefore, regard Aristophanes as the author, from whom, if we learn not all which we want, much may be learned well.

In this writer, then, we may observe, that the Proper Names of men never have the Article, except,

1. When the same person has been *recently mentioned*: or,
2. When the person is, from some cause or other, of such *notoriety*, that even without previous mention he may be recognized by the hearer.

Of the former kind we may instance

Lysist. 796. ΤΟΥ Μελανίωνος, and 807. ΤΩι Μελανίωνι· this person had been spoken of, v. 785. ἦν νεανίσκος Μελανίων τις.—Nub. 30. μετὰ ΤΟΝ Πασίαν· he is the person, whom Strepsiades had mentioned, v. 21. δώδεκα μνᾶς Πασίᾳ.—Ibid. 146, 147. we have ΤΟΥ Χαιρεφῶντος . . . ΤΟΥ Σωκράτους· but in v. 144. we find ἀνήρετ᾽ ἄρτι Χαιρεφῶντα Σωκράτης.— Av. 970. we read ἠνίξαθ᾽ Ὁ Βάκις τοῦτο πρὸς τὸν ἀέρα· but the same Bacis had, v. 962. been mentioned by the speaker. More examples might easily be found.

Under the second head, i. e. of Names not hitherto mentioned, we may produce Acharn. 10. and Av. 807. κατὰ ΤΟΝ Αἰσχύλον.—Av. 910. κατὰ ΤΟΝ Ὅμηρον.—Nub. 1188. Ὁ Σόλων.— Ibid. 1055. ΤΟΝ Νέστορα.—These must immediately be recognized from their pre-eminence. But we find also very many examples, in which the notoriety is that proceeding from vice or folly. In this case we may observe that Aristophanes uses the Article more constantly than he does in the former; thus presuming of those, whom he would satirize, that they are already objects of general indignation. In the Plutus, 174, 175. we have the first mention of Pamphilus and Belonopoles :

Ὁ Πάμφιλος δ᾽ οὐχί, κ. τ. λ.

Ὁ Βελονοπώλης, κ. τ. λ. the one a peculator and the other his parasite.—So also Av. 513. ΤΟΝ Λυσικράτη, a corrupt General.—Ibid. 168. Ὁ Τελέας, who, as the Scholiast informs us, was a common subject of ridicule.—Ranæ, 422. ΤΟΝ

Κλεισθένη, well known on account of his effeminacy.—We find also, Acharn. 243. Ὁ Ξανθίας, recognized by the hearers as the servant employed for the purpose in question.—These, so far as I recollect, are the only occasions, on which the *Names of Men* have the Article prefixed by Aristophanes, unless indeed when the person is called to, in which use the Article is not confined to Proper Names; as

Ranæ, 608. Ὁ Διτύλας, Χ'Ω Σκεβλίας, Χ'Ω Παρδόκας,
    Χωρεῖτε δευρί.
Ibid. 521.   Ὁ παῖς ἀκολουθεῖ δεῦρο.

or when not the person himself is meant, but the Drama, which is named from him: as, Ran. 863.

——————— ΤΟΝ Πηλέα τε καὶ ΤΟΝ Αἴολον
καὶ ΤΟΝ Μελέαγρον, κάτι μάλα ΤΟΝ Τήλεφον.

All these are plays of Euripides; and in such instances the Article is never omitted.

The names of *Deities* and *Heroes* have also very frequently the Article prefixed: thus, Ran. 671. Ἡ Περσέφαττα.—Ibid. 1045. ΤΗΣ Ἀφροδίτης.—Plut. 727. ΤΩι Πλούτωνι.—Nub. 1067. ΤΗΝ Θέτιν . . . . Ὁ Πηλεύς.—Ibid. 257. ΤΟΝ Ἀθάμανθ'.—After μὰ and νή, the name of the deity or person invoked takes the Article, as, Ran. 42. μὰ ΤΗΝ Δήμητρα.—Ibid. 51. νὴ ΤΟΝ Ἀπόλλω.—Ibid. 183. νὴ ΤΟΝ Ποσειδῶ.—Vesp. 1438. ναὶ ΤΑΝ Κόραν.—Acharn. 867. ναὶ ΤΟΝ Ἰόλαον.—Nub. 814. μὰ ΤΗΝ Ὁμίχλην.—And Av. 521. we have "Ὀμνυσιν ΤΟΝ χῆνα.—Ran. 1374. we find the Article even where the name is suppressed, μὰ ΤΟΝ ἐγώ, &c. The only exception, which I have noticed, is in the name of *Jupiter*. It might have been expected, that in swearing by the chief of the Gods more than usual solemnity would have been observed: the frequent and colloquial use of this oath seems, however, to have rendered it less solemn than the others; and we find τὸν Δία and Δία indiscriminately. Thus, Ran. 305.

——————— ΔΙΟΝΥΣ.κ ατόμοσον.
            ΞΑΝΘ. νὴ τὸν Δία.
ΔΙΟΝΥΣ. καῦθις κατόμοσον.
            ΞΑΝΘ. νὴ Δί'.
        ΔΙΟΝΥΣ. ὄμοσον.
            ΞΑΝΘ. νὴ Δία.

Lastly, the Proper Names of *Places*, whether countries, cities, mountains, &c. commonly, but not always, take the Article, as Acharn. 653. ΤΗΝ Αἴγιναν.—Av. 710. ἐς ΤΗΝ Λιβύην.—Ibid. 191. ΤΟΝ Λεπρεόν.—Nub. 72. ἐς ΤΟΥ Φελλέως.—Ibid. 193. ΤΟΝ Τάρταρον.—Ibid. 320. πρὸς ΤΗΝ Πάρνηθ', &c. In all these instances, and many more which the reader may collect, the Article is found prefixed to a name, of which there had been no previous mention [1].

[1] Winer observes, that in the New Testament the names of countries and rivers are seldom without the Article, (except Αἴγυπτος, and sometimes Μακεδονία,) those of cities occasionally. But he says afterwards, that these latter want it usually when following Prepositions. I find that Ἔφεσος has the Article when not following a Preposition, (viz. Acts xix. 17; xx. 16.) except in Acts xix. 26. and there some MSS. insert ἕως. So Δαμασκός, Acts ix. 3; xxii. 6. has the Article. In every other case it follows a Preposition; and although Winer may refer the Article to *renewed mention* in *both* these cases, yet he has then no instance to rely on. Ἱεροσόλυμα occurs only thrice, except after a Preposition. In Matt. ii. 3. (on which see Bishop Middleton) and iii. 5. there is doubt as to the reading; and in iv. 25. the omission is to be referred to enumeration. In St. John it has the Article thrice after the Preposition, v. 2. (which may be called renewed mention); x. 22; xi. 13. With Ἱερουσαλήμ [*] we find the Article omitted from enumeration in Luke v. 17. and vi. 17; from its being in regimen in Luke xxiii. 28. The Article is omitted without cause in Luke xxi. 24. and thrice after κατοικέω in Acts i. 19; ii. 14; iv. 16; again, Acts xxi. 31. (See Bishop Middleton on Matt. ii. 3.) Twice the word occurs in the Vocative, viz. Matt. xxiii. 3. 7. Luke xiii. 34. In Luke xxi. 20. Acts v. 28. Heb. xii. 22. Rev. iii. 12; xxi. 2. 10. it has the Article. In *every other case* it follows a Preposition. Καπερναούμ never occurs but after a Preposition, except twice in the Vocative. Τάρσος never, except after a Preposition. Ἀντιόχεια never, except after a Preposition. One of the cases is remarkable, viz. Acts xiv. 21. εἰς τὴν Λύστραν, καὶ Ἰκόνιον, καὶ Ἀντιόχειαν, which reminds us of τὸν Ἀλέξανδρον καὶ Φίλιππον. See p. 63. above. These are the places mentioned by Winer; and this examination will show how far his remark is true. He observes, finally, that when a place has once been mentioned, (and without the Article,) on its *renewed* mention the Article is added. Thus ἕως Ἀθηνῶν, in Acts xvii. 15; then xvii. 16. and xviii. 1. with Article; εἰς Βέροιαν, Acts xvii. 10; with Article in verse 13; εἰς Μακεδονίαν, Acts xvi. 9; and then six times with the Article, (which is, however, omitted in xx. 3.); εἰς Μίλητον, Acts xx. 15. and with Article in verse 17.—H. J. R.

---

[*] I might have noticed this word (in commenting on Schleiermacher's theory) as another peculiarity in St. Luke. It occurs only once in St. Matthew and St. Mark, not at all in St. John; twenty-seven times in St. Luke, (of which five are in chapter ii.) forty-one times in the Acts; seven or eight times in St. Paul; three times in Revelations, and no where else.—H. J. R.

It is obvious that the Proper Names of deities, &c. and of places, have the Article, on the ground of notoriety; and this case is similar to that of the names of pre-eminent men, such as *Homer*, *Æschylus*, &c.: consequently, there are but two occasions, on which, if we may rely on Aristophanes, who wrote in the best æra of the language, Proper Names of any kind can have the Article prefixed: indeed, even these two are in strictness reducible to one, the only difference lying in the *origin* of the notoriety, which is common to both. In the one case it is the result of previous mention, whilst in the other such mention is superfluous.

Having thus considered the practice of Aristophanes, it may be right to turn to one or two of the writers of prose, and to inquire how far their usage and his correspond. Herodotus, on various accounts, deserves at least a brief notice. Without having examined the whole of his work with a view to the present subject, I may be allowed to state the result of a careful perusal of the fourth Book, confirmed as it is by a cursory inspection of several other parts of his History. In the case of *previous and recent mention*, the instances, in which he prefixes the Article to the Proper Names of men, are almost innumerable[1]. Thus, p. 140. Δαρείου . . . . Ὁ Δαρεῖος.— P. 142. Ἀγάθυρσον . . . . . Γελωνόν . . . ΤΟΝ τε Ἀγάθυρσον καὶ ΤΟΝ Γελωνόν.—P. 148. Σατάσπης . . . . ΤΟΥ Σατάσπεος.—P. 155. Ἀνάχαρσις . . . . Ὁ Ἀνάχαρσις. —P. 156. Ὀκταμασάδην . . . . Ὁ Ὀκταμασάδης.—P. 159. Ζάμολξιν . . . . ΤΟΝ Ζάμολξιν, &c. &c. Sometimes he adds οὗτος . . . . thus, p. 159. τὸν Ζάμολξιν τοῦτον.—P. 3. οὗτος ὁ Κανδαύλης.—Ibid. τούτῳ τῷ Γύγῃ, &c. which form abundantly explains the Article in all cases of renewed mention, where the Article alone is employed. Without previous mention he does not, so far as I have observed, ever prefix the Article to the name of any person[2], however illustrious and

---

[1] I use the Edition of H. Stephens, Paris, 1570.

[2] I have, indeed, met with instances both in Herodotus and Demosthenes, which are exceptions from the *letter*, though not, I think, from the *spirit* of this remark. Thus Herod. lib. iv. p. 147. φασὶ δὲ οἱ αὐτοὶ καὶ ΤΗΝ Ἄργιν τε καὶ ΤΗΝ Ὦπιν, &c.—Lib. vii. p. 283. λέγεται λόγος ὡς Ἀθηναῖοι ΤΟΝ Βορῆν, &c. —Demosth. vol. ii. p. 1050. πρότερον ἀγῶνες ἐγένοντο ἡμῖν . . . περὶ τοῦ κλήρου ΤΟΥ Ἁγνίου.—P. 1311. καὶ γὰρ ἃ περὶ ΤΟΝ Κλεινίαν αἰτιᾶται.—Now all

well known. Thus we find the names of *Homer, Hesiod, Pythagoras, Ajax, Jason, Cadmus, Europa, Œdipus,* &c. all introduced without that intimation of notoriety, by which in after times they were generally accompanied. In this respect, therefore, as well as in the dialect and diction, we may observe some resemblance between Homer and Herodotus.—In the name of deities the case is somewhat different: they are often, but by no means so often as was afterwards the practice, first mentioned with the Article prefixed: thus, B. iv. p. 178. τῇ Ἀθηναίῃ . . . . τῷ Τρίτωνι . . . . τῷ Ποσειδέωνι. More frequently, however, is it omitted.—The names of places seem in this writer to take the Article very much in the same manner, as in succeeding ages. The same latitude appears already to have been authorized; and if there were any limitations, they are such that I am unable to detect them.

From Herodotus we will pass to Demosthenes. The Oration against Leptines furnishes not a single instance of a Proper Name of a man having the Article prefixed on the *first mention*, excepting those only of *Solon* (vol. i. p. 484.) and *Draco*, p. 505, names familiar to an Athenian audience [1]. Instances in which the Article is used, when the name is *repeated*, are very common: thus, p. 466. Ὁ Λεύκων.—P. 470. Ὁ Ἐπικέρδης.—P. 476. ΤΩι Φιλίππῳ.—P. 478. ΤΩι Κόνωνι.—P. 497. Ὁ Λυκίδας; all of whom had first been introduced without the Article: and the same thing is obvious in the other Orations. The names of deities in Demosthenes commonly have the Article.—Vol. i. p. 437. Ὁ Ζεύς.—Ibid. Ἡ Διώνη.—Vol. ii. p. 949. ΤΗΣ Ἀθηνᾶς.—P. 1068. ΤΗι Ἥρᾳ.—P. 1313. ΤΩι Ἡρακλεῖ.—P. 1369. ΤΩι Διονύσῳ.—The Proper Names of places, those at least of great celebrity, take or reject the

---

these instances have one common character; which is, that though the persons be in themselves obscure and had not previously been mentioned, yet it is evident from the context that they might be *recognized;* those spoken of by Herodotus being represented to have been the subjects of *rumour* or *tradition,* and those mentioned by Demosthenes, either of *lawsuits* or of *accusation.* They were, therefore, *liable to recognition,* which is all that the *spirit* of the rule requires.—With respect to Ὁ Μοιριάδης (vol. ii. p. 822.) I have no doubt that his name had occurred in the *Testimony,* which had just been read.

[1] At p. 457. we find τοῦ Χαβρίου, first mentioned ; but I take τοῦ to be an ellipsis of τοῦ παιδός· though, if it be otherwise, there will be no difficulty, considering how eminent was the person in question.

Article, without any other apparent reason than the pleasure of the writer. National appellations, as Ἀθηναῖοι, Θηβαῖοι, &c. partake of the same uncertainty.—I need not trouble the reader with the particulars of my researches into other prose authors, the general result being the same. From all of them it is plain, that the Article, as applied to Proper Names, as well as to Appellatives, is a Pronoun of *obscure reference*, and that conjointly with its Predicate it recalls an idea, which has already had a place in the hearer's mind[1]. Its *hypothetical* use (see above, p. 39) is evidently, by the nature of the case, excluded.

But though the Article cannot be inserted before Proper Names, unless they have been previously mentioned, or at least are previously known, how happens it, that before such names the Article is so frequently omitted? In the answer to this question the reader will be reminded of what was said above respecting the almost constant omission of the Article in poetry, even before Appellatives in strictness requiring its insertion. To say Ὁ Καλλίας, Ὁ Λύκων, when Callias and Lycon are now for the first time heard of, would involve both falsehood and absurdity; for it would amount to a declaration, that the hearer knows, or ought to know, whom I mean. But in the other case, i. e. if Lycon or Callias being already known be spoken of without the Article, the same inconvenience will not ensue: the hearer, indeed, will not be assisted so far as he might be, in perceiving that the *same* Lycon, or the *well-known* Lycon, is meant; but he will conclude, with the strongest probability, that no other is intended, since few individuals are called by that name, and still fewer to whom the particular circumstances will apply. The difference, therefore, between the two cases, is that of asserting what is false, and of neglect-

---

[1] Instances, indeed, will now and then occur, which appear to contradict the conclusion here laid down: but where various readings have been collected, some one, by which the rule is supported, will generally be found; and even where no such reading is preserved, unless the number of collated MSS. be very great, and some of them, at least, of very high authority, it is surely more reasonable to trust to a rule, of which the principle can be shown, and which is almost invariably observed, than implicitly to believe in the infallibility of copyists: and we may adopt the opinion, if not the very words, of Professor *Porson*, expressed on some other occasion (I cannot find the passage), "hujusmodi exempla aut emendata aut *emendanda* sunt."

ing to assert what is true; and the omission is a venial licence, because it can hardly lead to error. This, notwithstanding the poetic practice, is more than can be affirmed of the omission before Appellatives. Poetry, indeed, for the reason before alleged, may be expected to be anarthrous; and the reader becomes habituated to its peculiar style; but if in prose we should meet with ἵππος, meaning the same horse[1] who had just before been mentioned, mistake would be almost inevitable; and the reason is plain: an Appellative is a name common to every individual of a whole species; and consequently, if there be nothing which identifies *this* horse with that before spoken of, it may reasonably be concluded that a different one is meant: but Proper Names are in their nature very much, though not entirely, restricted to given individuals; and therefore, on the renewed mention of Callias, or Lycon, we shall infer the identity, even though it be not expressed.— On the same ground, the names of deities and places may, or may not, have the Article. Their notoriety, even when not asserted, will occur to the hearer's mind.

And now we perceive why such phrases exist as τὸν Ἀλέξανδρον καὶ Φίλιππον, above noticed (p. 63). The writer prefixes the Article to the first name, for one of the two reasons already alleged, and omits it before the second, either because it is not admissible, or because, though admissible, it may, not only by the general licence, but equally, I think, from the particular circumstances, fairly be neglected. In the instance ΤΟΝ Ἀλέξανδρον καὶ Φίλιππον, the latter name certainly admits, and even requires, the Article, as much as does the former; but the mention of the *well-known* Alexander determines Philip to be no other than Alexander's father.— Again we have in Herodotus, B. iv. p. 147. ΤΗΣ Ὠπιός τε καὶ Ἄργιος. The females had recently been mentioned together: Ἄργιος, therefore, though admitting the Article as much as Ὠπιος, will be understood as having it.—In Demosth. vol. ii. p. 1048. we meet with ΤΟΥ Αἰαντίδου καὶ Θεοτελοῦς· the latter had not been mentioned; and therefore here no licence is used. —Vol. i. p. 476. ΤΗΝ Πύδναν καὶ Ποτίδαιαν· cities which are

---

[1] It must at the same time be observed, that a case so strong as that here supposed, is rarely found, even in poetry.

PROPER NAMES. 87

generally spoken of together, from their having shared, about the same period, the same fate.

Further, as the Article cannot in ordinary cases be placed before Proper Names *ad libitum,* so, *à fortiori,* it is not inserted where particular rules, arising out of its nature, require its omission. Of these rules, as will be evident on turning to them, two only are applicable to the present question: I mean that respecting Verbs Substantive and Nuncupative, and that which relates to propositions asserting or denying existence. So in Herod. B. iv. p. 142. σφι οὐνόματα θέσθαι, τῷ μὲν ᾽ΑΓΑΘΥΡΣΟΝ αὐτέων, τῷ δ᾽ ἑπομένῳ ΓΕΛΩΝΟΝ.—P. 165. οὐνόματα κέεται τάδε ΛΥΚΟΣ, ᾽ΟΑΡΟΣ, ΤΑΝΑΪΣ, ΣΥΡΓΙΣ.— P. 144. τὸ καλέεται ΚΡΗΜΝΟΙ.— Demosth. vol. i. p. 666. ΘΕΡΣΑΓΟΡΑΣ ὄνομα αὐτῶν θατέρῳ, τῷ δ᾽ ᾽ΕΞΗΚΕΣΤΟΣ.— That the Article cannot be inserted before Proper Names in Propositions affirming or denying *existence,* may, I think, be collected from some passages in the Clouds of Aristophanes. In v. 365. (edit. *Hermann,* 1799,) Strepsiades says,

῾Ο ΖΕΥΣ δ᾽ ἡμῖν, φέρε, πρὸς τῆς γῆς, ᾽οὐλύμπιος οὐ θεός ἐστιν;

To which Socrates replies,

Ποῖος Ζεύς; οὐ μὴ ληρήσεις· ΟΥΔ᾽ ᾽ΕΣΤΙ ΖΕΥΣ.

And afterwards, when Strepsiades has become a thorough convert to the same doctrine, he also adopts the same form of expression: v. 824. ΟΥΚ ᾽ΕΣΤΙΝ, ὦ Φειδιππίδη, ΖΕΥΣ. I say, however, *when he is entirely converted;* for in v. 379. while he is yet wavering in his faith, he says, τουτί μ᾽ ἐλελήθη ῾Ο ΖΕΥΣ οὐκ ὤν[1]· which may appear to be an objection to the rule, but is not so, when considered as coming from a *half convert:* there is, indeed, a contradiction in the terms, but then a contradiction is intended; as if we should say in English, "that Jupiter is not ▇▇▇▇r, is more than I suspected." He who should so express hi▇▇▇lf, would evidently betray that his mind fluctuated between the two opinions[2].

[1] Hermann reads this sentence interrogatively: I follow Brunck.
[2] There is another passage which may require vindication: v. 815. we have τῆς μωρίας! ΤΟΝ ΔΙΑ νομίζειν, spoken by Strepsiades. *Ernesti* felt some doubt respecting ΤΟΝ in this place, and *Hermann* has substituted τό, contending that

On the whole, the irregularity observable with respect to *Proper Names* does not in the least affect the general doctrine of the Article; and it was partly with a view to this conclusion, that I have entered so fully into the subject.

the Greeks said νομίζειν, ἡγεῖσθαι ΘΕΟΥΣ, never ΤΟΥΣ Θεούς· the former is, unquestionably, the prevailing usage, but the latter form sometimes occurs, as Hermann (ad Eurip. Hec. 781.) has since admitted. The reason of this variation, however, seems to be somewhat different from that which he adduces. The original expression is evidently νομίζειν Θεοὺς ΕΙΝΑΙ, where the Article would be superfluous. So Herod. B. iv. p. 159, ἄλλον θεὸν νομίζοντες ΕΙΝΑΙ· but in after times the *origin* of the phrase was gradually disregarded, and εἶναι no longer being expressed, νομίζειν Θεούς, came to be used in a looser signification, meaning, not so much to believe in the existence of gods, as to *reverence* the gods, supposing them to exist; and in this sense of the phrase the Article was not improperly admitted. The passage which Hermann quotes in illustration, Soph. Antig. 190.

———————τοὺς φίλους ποιούμεθα,

is not entirely apposite, though it has an apparent difficulty, which deserves to be noticed: for if τοὺς φίλους mean friends, whose existence is assumed, how can we be said, ποιεῖσθαι, to make them? The meaning is, "the friends whom we make, we make in the manner specified." So Homer, Il. Δ. 399. (which *Heyne*, after objecting to the Article, thinks similar to Il. A. 11.)

————ἀλλὰ ΤΟΝ υἱὸν
Γείνατο εἷο χέρεια μάχῃ,

the son whom Tydeus begat, he begat inferior to himself, &c.—Aristoph. Av. 820. καλὸν σύ γ' ἀτεχνῶς καὶ μέγ' εὗρες Τ'ΟΥΝΟΜΑ· the name which you have invented, you have invented (or is) fine and sounding. See also Acharn. 1095. ΤΗΝ Γοργόνα. In like manner, Plat. Gorg. vol. iv. p. 87. εἰ χρυσῆν ἔχων ἐτύγχανον ΤΗΝ ψυχήν, &c. Similar instances abound.

CHAPTER V.

ABSTRACT NOUNS.

SECTION I.

INSERTIONS.

I come now to the consideration of the use of the Article before *Abstract Nouns*, or the *Names* of *Attributes* and *Qualities;* a subject of greater difficulty than any other which belongs to this Preliminary Inquiry. On its first appearance, indeed, it presents a degree of perplexity which seems to defy arrangement; but on a nearer view we shall discover, that certain laws are for the most part observed, though some licence be allowed; and that those laws are explicable from the nature of the Article, as it has already been illustrated.

It is to be premised, that Nouns of this class are capable of being employed in two different ways: though they always express abstract ideas, they may be used either in a more or in a less abstract sense. Ἀδικία, for example, will signify injustice *generally*, whatever be its kind or degree: but it will also express every *particular act* of injustice, by the contemplation of which we form the more abstract idea: and in this latter use these Nouns in Greek admit the Plural Number, or, which is equivalent, they are in the Singular capable of being joined with words indicating their possible plurality. Thus in Aristot. de Mor. Nic. lib. v. c. 10. we have ἙΚΑΣΤΗΝ ἀδικίαν· and plurally in the same work, lib. vi. c. 7. πολλαὶ ἔσονται ΣΟΦΙΑΙ. Demosth. vol. ii. p. 1099. ΚΟΛΑΚΕΙΑΙΣ. Ibid. p. 1452. ἈΝΔΡΙΑΙ καὶ ΘΡΑΣΥΤΗΤΕΣ, &c. Ibid.

p. 875. 'ΑΛΗΘΕΙΑΙΣ. It is true that instances of this kind do not very frequently occur: but their occurrence, however rare, sufficiently proves, that the *Names of Attributes* and *Qualities* may be of *particular*, as well as of *general* application; and consequently that an expedient, by which they may be known to be employed in their most general meaning, is not without its use. This, if I mistake not, is the force of the Article in very many passages, in which a superficial observer might regard it as being merely an expletive: and we shall further perceive, that where the sense of these Nouns is meant to be *limited*, the Article is invariably omitted. This remark may be of use to the reader, before we proceed to deduce rules from the practice of the best writers.

It will be expected that we begin, as in former instances, with Homer: but the assistance to be derived from this quarter is here of little or no value. It is a remarkable fact, that Homer rarely makes use of abstract terms, and still more rarely, if ever, does he employ them in their most abstract and general sense. Some persons, perhaps, who have read the Iliad, will be surprised to learn, that ὀργή, αἰσχύνη, φύσις, ἐλευθερία, παιδεία, εὐδαιμονία, δικαιοσύνη, ὑγίεια, ἐπιστήμη, and many others of the same kind, are words which do not once occur in the whole Poem [1]. Σιγῇ, σιωπῇ, τύχῃ, δίκῃ, τέχνῃ, &c. are found only in the Dative, indicating merely the *manner* in which some act is performed: this may be denominated the *adverbial* use of Abstract Nouns; and in this use of them, they are always, as we shall afterwards have occasion to remark, *anarthrous*. In the passage, Z. 339. (which, indeed, is elsewhere repeated, and was probably a proverbial saying at the time) νίκη δ' ἐπαμείβεται ἄνδρας, I think we may consider νίκη as a personification: but whether we so understand it, or choose to regard it as used in the most abstract sense, it is without the Article, and so are these Nouns elsewhere in Homer, whatever be the manner in which they are employed [2].

---

[1] I have observed that Nouns of this description are more common in the Odyssey than in the Iliad.

[2] We find, indeed, in the Odyssey, B. 206. Εἵνεκα τῆς ἀρετῆς ἐριδαίνομεν, which *Damm*, the excellent Lexicographer, renders by "propter *talem* præstantiam," explaining τῆς by ταύτης or τοίης. Yet Apollonius, p. 112. classes this example with ὣς ἡ ῥίμφα θέουσα· his interpretation, therefore, supposes τῆς to

Since, then, the Article is often found in later writers prefixed to the Names of Attributes, it is in these writers only that we can investigate the rules of its insertion; and these rules are reducible to four: the Article is inserted,

1. When the Noun is used in its most abstract sense.
2. When the Attribute, &c. is personified.
3. When the Article is employed in the sense of a Possessive Pronoun.
4. When there is reference either retrospective or anticipative.

§ 1. Of the first rule the following may serve as

EXAMPLES.

Plat. vol. iv. p. 68. Ἡ ἀδικία καὶ Ἡ ἀκολασία μέγιστον τῶν ὄντων κακόν ἐστι.
Ibid. p. 70. ἰατρικὴ γίγνεται πονηρίας Ἡ δίκη.
Aristot. de Mor. Nic. lib. i. c. 13. ἔστιν Ἡ εὐδαιμονία ψυχῆς ἐνέργειά τις.
Ibid. lib. v. c. 10. ἀλλότριον εἶναί φασιν ἀγαθὸν ΤΗΝ δικαιοσύνην.
Ibid. lib. vi. c. 6. ἐπεὶ δ' Ἡ ἐπιστήμη περὶ τῶν καθόλου ἐστὶν ὑπόληψις, κ. τ. λ.
Ibid. lib. vi. c. 10. ἔστι δὲ εὐστοχία τις Ἡ ἀγχίνοια.
Demosth. vol. i. p. 796. Ἡ νεότης ΤΩι γήρᾳ, κ. τ. λ.
Ibid. p. 777. Ἡ εὐταξία τῶν αἰσχρῶν περίεστι, κ. τ. λ.

It will immediately be seen, that there is a close analogy between this use of the Article when prefixed to abstract Nouns, and the hypothetical use of it already mentioned in the case of Appellatives. In the same manner as ΟΙ ἄδικοι will signify all who are unjust, so Ἡ ἀδικία will mean every act of which injustice can be assumed. We may also remark, that in Appellatives both the uses of the Article are of frequent occurrence; whilst in Proper Names it is almost exclusively employed to recall some former idea; and in abstract Nouns, it

be, not in concord with ἀρετῆς, but dependent on it: and this is conformable with the context. On τῆς ἀρετῆς in the Iliad, Λ. 762. *Bentley* has conjectured ἧς with the Digamma.

is, on the contrary, chiefly, though not entirely, subservient to Hypothesis.

§ 2. The Article, however, is frequently used before these Nouns, where they are *personified*.

EXAMPLES.

Aristoph. Av. 1536.

Καὶ ΤΗΝ Βασιλείαν σοι γυναῖκ' ἔχειν διδῷ.
Τίς ἐστιν Ἡ Βασιλεία ;

Ranæ 95. ἅπαξ προσουρήσαντα ΤΗι Τραγῳδίᾳ.
Xenoph. Mem. lib. ii. c. 1. Ἡ Κακία ὑπολαβοῦσα εἶπεν.
Id. ibid. καὶ Ἡ Ἀρετὴ εἶπεν.
Demosth. vol. i. p. 378. οἱ τὰ ἀκρωτήρια ΤΗΣ Νίκης περικόψαντες ἀπώλοντο.
Plat. vol. iv. p. 77. ἀλλὰ ΤΗΝ Φιλοσοφίαν, τὰ ἐμὰ παιδικά, παῦσον ταῦτα λέγουσαν.

The reason of this practice seems to be founded in the *notoriety* (see above on PROPER NAMES) of these imaginary persons; and it may further be explained from the *perfect abstractedness*, with which Attributes must be regarded, before they admit personification. The mind cannot form the idea of Ἡ Ἀρετή, *a person*, till it has learnt to comprise under one general notion all the various acts which can be denominated virtuous. At the same time it must be confessed, that the usage here is not constant: but in this irregularity there is nothing which the nature of the case might not lead us to expect. As in Proper Names neither notoriety, nor even recent mention, absolutely enforces the insertion of the Article, so in Abstract Nouns personified, which are analogous to Proper Names, the Article is sometimes omitted. Thus in Plat. vol. iv. p. 76. we read Ἀλκιβιάδου τε τοῦ Κλεινίου καὶ ΦΙΛΟΣΟΦΙΑΣ. Here *Alcibiades* and *Philosophy* must be regarded as two persons: Φιλοσοφίας does not need the Article more than Ἀλκιβιάδου: accordingly, before both it is omitted. It will, however, be remembered, that there is a wide difference between omitting the Article where it might have been inserted, and inserting it where it would have no meaning: this distinction is of primary importance, and it is therefore here repeated.

§ 3. A third case, in which the names of Attributes take the Article, is when that Article has the meaning of a Possessive Pronoun.

EXAMPLES.

Aristoph. Ran. 45. ἀλλ' οὐχ οἷός τ' εἴμ' ἀποσοβῆσαι ΤΟΝ γέλων, *my* laughter.
Ibid. Equit. 837. ζηλῶ σε ΤΗΣ εὐγλωττίας, *your*, &c.
Demosth. vol. i. p. 74. ΤΗΝ ὀργὴν ἀφιέντας, *their*, &c.

§ 4. Lastly, these Nouns take the Article where they have reference of any kind.

EXAMPLES.

Demosth. vol. i. p. 17. Ἡ τῶν πραγμάτων αἰσχύνη [1].
Plat. vol. iv. p. 31. ἐὰν μὴ προειδῇ περὶ τούτων ΤΗΝ ἀλήθειαν.
Ibid. p. 34. ΤΗΝ μακρολογίαν, ᾗ τοπρῶτον ἐπεχείρησας χρῆσθαι.

It will hardly be necessary to remind the reader, that in the two last cases these Nouns follow the common rules for Appellatives.

---

[1] The whole passage in Reiske's *Oratores Græci* stands thus : καὶ πρόσεσθ' ἡ ὕβρις, καὶ ἔτι ἡ τῶν πραγμάτων αἰσχύνη· but these are various readings : " ἡ *primum abest a Parisinis primo et octavo: item ab Harley: et Aug. primi supplemento: posterioris* ἡ *loco dant Ald. et Taylor.* γε :" See Reiske's Note. Now unless πραγμάτων depend on ὕβρις as well as on αἰσχύνη, which does not appear to be the case, the second Article is absolutely necessary : Reiske, indeed, as is evident from the comma placed after ὕβρις, supposes it to have no connexion with πραγμάτων, but then he has done wrong in writing Ἡ ὕβρις, which is altogether without meaning. The Article, in such cases, cannot be inserted, and the MSS. which reject it, are right. Somewhat similar to πρόσεσθ' ὕβρις is Plat. vol. i. p. 45. χάριν προσειδέναι· where ΤΗΝ χ. π. would be unexampled. It has already been observed, that the MSS. frequently vary with respect to the insertion or omission of the Article before Proper Names, and still more before abstract Nouns. The MSS. of Demosthenes abundantly confirm this remark ; and his editor, in several instances, has adopted a wrong reading with respect to the Article, where MSS. supply the right one.

SECTION II.

OMISSIONS.

Thus much for the *Insertion* of the Article before Abstract Nouns: respecting the *Omission* little will be said, because for the most part, it is observable only in cases which have already been considered and explained.

§ 1. Thus, where Abstract Nouns are the Predicates of Propositions not intended to be reciprocating, the Article is omitted. Arist. Mor. Nic. lib. vi. c. 5. οὐκ ἂν εἴη ἡ φρόνησις ἘΠΙΣΤΗΜΗ οὐδὲ ΤΕΧΝΗ. In Propositions which merely assert or deny existence: Arist. Mor. Nic. lib. v. c. 10. ἐν οἷς τὸ ἀδικεῖν, οὐ πᾶσιν ἈΔΙΚΙΑ. Ibid. lib. vii. c. 1. τρία ἐστὶν εἴδη, ΚΑΚΙΑ, ἈΚΡΑΣΙΑ, ΘΗΡΙΟΤΗΣ· which will explain many cases of Nouns in Apposition. Demosth. vol. i. p. 97. ἔστω ΠΑΡΡΗΣΙΑ. Arist. de Mor. ad Nic. lib. vii. c. 3. δεινὸν γάρ, ἘΠΙΣΤΗΜΗΣ ἐνούσης.—After Verbs Nuncupative, where the Noun in question is the Name by which any thing is said to be called: Plat. iv. p. 37. καλῶ δὲ τὸ κεφάλαιον ΚΟΛΑΚΕΙΑΝ. In Exclusive Propositions: Demosth. vol. i. p. 529. οὐδὲν ὝΒΡΕΩΣ ἀφορητότερον, i. e. than *any kind* of insult. Had the Article been used in this place, the meaning would have been, that nothing is more intolerable than *all* insult. See above on Appellatives.—And in general, as was before intimated, these Nouns are without the Article whenever they are used in a limited sense, that is to say, in any manner in which they cannot be taken in the most abstract acceptation. This will easily account for the anarthrous use after Verbs of *having, obtaining, fulness,* &c. and the Adjectives allied to the last: for it would be absurd to affirm that any one *has, obtains, is full of,* &c. any attribute or quality so exclusively, that the attribute cannot be ascribed to any other: and in this respect attributes differ from things which may in their nature belong solely to certain individuals. Hence we read,

Plat. vol. iv. p. 70. ὁ μὴ ἔχων ΚΑΚΙΑΝ.

Ibid. ὁ ἔχων ἈΔΙΚΙΑΝ.

Ibid. p. 57. ἆρ' ἂν τυγχάνῃ ΔΙΚΗΣ τε καὶ ΤΙΜΩΡΙΑΣ;

Demosth. vol. i. p. 142. ταῦτ' 'ΑΠΙΣΤΙΑΝ, ταῦτ᾽ 'ΟΡΓΗΝ ἔχει.

Ibid. vol. ii. p. 1232. ἂν δὲ ληφθῶσι, ΣΥΓΓΝΩΜΗΣ τυχεῖν.

Plut. Conviv. p. 93. ἀνεπλήσθη τὸ πρόσωπον 'ΕΡΥΘΗΜΑΤΟΣ.

Demosth. vol. i. p. 151. ΚΟΛΑΚΕΙΑΣ καὶ ΒΛΑΒΗΣ καὶ 'ΑΠΑΤΗΣ λόγος μεστός.

The same usage prevails where the Nouns are names of substances.

Verbs of *partaking* do also, for the most part, though not invariably, follow the same rule: the reason of the uncertainty seems to be, that usually they are employed merely in the sense of *having*, though if they were used strictly in the sense of having or dividing *with others*, the Abstract Nouns subjoined to them might take the Article; for though attributes and qualities are wholes which no single individual can claim to the exclusion of every other, yet of these wholes he may be a *partaker*, and in truth is so of every attribute which can be ascribed to him even in the smallest degree: however, it was to be expected, for the reason alleged, that the anarthrous use would be by far the more common.

On the same principle it is, that in the common phrases, ἄνοιαν, αἰσχύνην, &c. ὀφλισκάνειν, δίκην διδόναι, ἡσυχίαν ἄγειν, and many more, the Article is invariably omitted[1]. Since in many of these phrases two words are employed to convey the meaning of one, and in all of them a single Verb may be imagined, which would express the meaning, I shall consider this as a *Hendiadys*, and shall hereafter refer to what is here said of all such phrases under that appellation.

§ 2. In the same manner we may account for the anarthrous use of Abstract Nouns, when they are employed in the Dative Case *adverbially*. In this sense they are of very common occurrence, and are sometimes so joined with real Adverbs, that their import cannot be mistaken: thus in the first and fourth of the following

---

[1] Yet we find ΤΗΝ εἰρήνην, ΤΗΝ σύμβασιν, ΤΑΣ ἀνοχὰς ποιεῖσθαι. In such phrases, however, there is, probably, a reference to the *war*, the termination or suspension of which is in question.

EXAMPLES.

Eurip. Orest. p. 191. ΔΙΚΑι μέν, καλῶς δ' οὔ.
Arist. de Mor. Nic. lib. vi. c. 3. ὙΠΟΛΗΨΕΙ καὶ ΔΟΞΗι ἐνδέχεται διαψεύδεσθαι.
Demosth. vol. i. p. 41. ΦΥΣΕΙ δ' ὑπάρχει τοῖς παροῦσι τὰ τῶν ἀπόντων.
Thucyd. lib. v. § 70. ἐντόνως καὶ 'ΟΡΓΗι χωροῦντες.
Plato, vol. iv. p. 89. οὔτε ΣΟΦΙΑΣ 'ΕΝΔΕΙΑι οὔτ' ΑΙΣΧΥΝΗΣ ΠΕΡΙΟΥΣΙΑι.

In these Examples, it is to be observed, that the manner in which any thing is said to happen or be done, is not spoken of with reference to any particular subject to which such manner is more especially attributable. But the case *may* be otherwise: the manner may be adverted to as being the attribute more especially of the subject in question: and then the Article will be prefixed, and will, as in the instances already mentioned, have the force of a Possessive Pronoun.

EXAMPLES.

Arist. Rhet. lib. ii. cap. 15. ζῶσι ΤΗι μνήμῃ μᾶλλον ἢ ΤΗι ἐλπίδι.
Thucyd. lib. v. § 72. ΤΗι ἐμπειρίᾳ Λακεδαιμόνιοι ἐλασσωθέντες τότε, ΤΗι ἀνδρείᾳ ἔδειξαν οὐχ ἧσσον περιγενόμενοι[1].

On the whole, it appears that Abstract Nouns, for the most part, refuse the Article, never taking it, excepting in the four cases before exemplified. The only caution requisite respects the more or less abstract sense in which these Nouns may be used. Many instances will occur in which they are anarthrous, where, had they been used in the more abstract sense, the proposition would still have been true. Such passages are not to

---

[1] In this passage, it may be supposed that both ἐμπειρίᾳ and ἀνδρείᾳ should, according to what has been advanced above, be anarthrous. *Baver*, however, in his excellent edition of Thucydides, Lips. 1790, has shown, that τῇ ἐμπειρίᾳ must be rendered *per artem* HOSTIUM: and by τῇ ἀνδρείᾳ we must plainly understand "by the bravery of the Spartans." The Articles, therefore, are necessary, the Nouns not being employed in the adverbial sense, but with reference to particular subjects.

be subjected to the rashness of conjectural emendation. It was sufficient for the writer, if his assertion were likely to gain assent in its limited form; and it was better to affirm in part, without the danger of contradiction, even where the proposition might have been couched in the most general and unlimited terms, than to risk an extreme latitude of assertion where it was not needed. This remark may contribute to account for the frequent absence of the Article where, unquestionably, it might have been employed by the first of the four canons.

CHAPTER VI.

ANOMALIES.

It has thus far been my endeavour to investigate the nature of the Article, and to show that its principal insertions and omissions before the several classes of Nouns are explicable on the proposed hypothesis. It was not, however, to be expected, in a case of this sort, that we should meet with no *anomalies;* and it will not be deemed injurious to that hypothesis, if certain usages occasionally prevail, of which it pretends not to assign the cause. It is sufficient, if they furnish no evidence of its futility: and it is to be observed, that they are omissions of the Article where it might have been inserted, not insertions irreconcileable with its alleged nature.

§ 1. It has been shown that the Article is commonly prefixed to Nouns, which are employed κατ' ἐξοχήν, and in some similar cases noticed above: but I am not aware that any philologist [1] has remarked how frequently such Nouns become anarthrous after *Prepositions*.

EXAMPLES.

Plat. Theæt. sub init. κατὰ ΠΟΛΙΝ, the city (Athens).
Ibid. κατ' 'ΑΓΟΡΑΝ, the Forum.

---

[1] Locella (ad Xen. Eph. p. 223. 242.) observes, that in the case of names of countries and towns, the Article is more frequently omitted than inserted after a Preposition; and Winer says that this applies to the New Testament. But Winer, when he occasionally alludes to the omission of the Article after the Preposition, has no idea of the *extent* of this irregularity. We find him not only mentioning Matt. v. 10. and Acts x. 35. as similar instances of an *abstract* Noun used without an Article, though the one is after a Preposition, and the other not; but in a long list of such words, and of another class, like ἥλιος, γῆ, οὐρανός, &c. we find exactly the same want of discrimination of cases. (Pt. ii. pp. 35—38.) —H. J. R.

ANOMALIES.

Ibid. εἰς ΛΙΜΕΝΑ, the Piræus.
Ibid. μέχρι ᾽ΕΡΙΝΕΟΥ Θεαίτητον προΰπεμψα, to the well-known wild fig-tree.
Aristot. Hist. An. lib. vi. c. 15. ἃ ἐξηραίνετο ὑπὸ ΚΥΝΑ, the dog-star.
Aristot. Anal. Post. lib. ii. c. 2. στέρησις φωτὸς ἀπὸ ΣΕΛΗΝΗΣ.
Xen. Cyrop. lib. vii. p. 106. πλησίον ΘΑΛΑΣΣΗΣ.
Thucyd. lib. v. § 75. τοὺς ἔξω ᾽ΙΣΘΜΟΥ ξυμμάχους ἀπέτριψαν.
Herod. lib. ix. p. 327. πρὸς ῾ΗΛΙΟΥ δύνοντος.
Dion. Hal. vol. iv. p. 2003. ἐντὸς ΤΕΙΧΟΥΣ.

Hence it is evident, that the absence of the Article in such instances affords no presumption, that the Nouns are used indefinitely. Their definiteness or indefiniteness, when they are governed by Prepositions, must be determined on other grounds.

§ 2. Another irregularity may be observed, where several Nouns are coupled together by Conjunctions, or where (which is equivalent) the Conjunctions are omitted by the figure *Asyndeton*. Though the Nouns would, if they stood singly, require the Article, yet when thus brought together, they very frequently reject it. This anomaly I shall hereafter speak of by the name of *Enumeration*; since it is only in the detail of particulars, that it seems to take place.

EXAMPLES.

Æsch. c. Ctes. § 38. καὶ ΧΕΙΡΙ καὶ ΠΟΔΙ καὶ ΦΩΝΗι καὶ πᾶσιν οἷς δύναμαι.
Ibid. § 43. καὶ γὰρ ΝΑΥΤΙΚΗ καὶ ΠΕΖΗ ΣΤΡΑΤΕΙΑ καὶ ΠΟΛΕΙΣ ἄρδην εἰσὶν ἀνηρπασμέναι.
Demosth. de Cor. § 34. τῆς δὲ ἀναγορεύσεως ἐπιμεληθῆναι ΘΕΣΜΟΘΕΤΑΣ, ΠΡΥΤΑΝΕΙΣ, ᾽ΑΓΩΝΟΘΕΤΑΣ.
Arist. Eth. Eudem. lib. i. c. 2. θέσθαι τινὰ σκόπον τοῦ καλῶς ζῆν, ἤτοι ΤΙΜΗΝ, ἢ ΔΟΞΑΝ, ἢ ΠΛΟΥΤΟΝ, ἢ ΠΑΙΔΕΙΑΝ.
Plat. vol. iv. p. 46. οὐκοῦν λέγεις εἶναι ἀγαθὸν μέν, ΣΟΦΙΑΝ τε καὶ ῾ΥΓΙΕΙΑΝ καὶ ΠΛΟΥΤΟΝ καὶ τἄλλα.

But the most striking instance, which I remember to have met with, is in the Cratylus of Plato, vol. iii. p. 281. et seqq.

περὶ δὲ τῶν τοιῶνδε τί σε κωλύει διελθεῖν, οἷον ʽΗΛΙΟΥ τε καὶ ΣΕΛΗΝΗΣ καὶ ΑΣΤΡΩΝ καὶ ΓΗΣ καὶ ΑΙΘΕΡΟΣ καὶ ΑΕΡΟΣ καὶ ΠΥΡΟΣ καὶ ΥΔΑΤΟΣ καὶ ʽΩΡΩΝ καὶ ΕΝΙΑΥΤΟΥ; where it is observable, that each of these, when spoken of *separately* in the course of the discussion, is found *with* the Article; as in the answer given by Socrates, Τί δὲ οὖν βούλει πρῶτον; ἤ, ὥσπερ εἶπες, ΤΟΝ ἥλιον διέλθωμεν; and so of the rest.

Nor is it merely, where three or more Nouns are so connected, that this usage prevails: where there are only *two*, it is not uncommon.

Demosth. de Cor. § 34. γνώμῃ ΒΟΥΛΗΣ καὶ ΔΗΜΟΥ.

Xen. Hiero. p. 533. οὕτως καὶ ΝΥΚΤΑ καὶ ΗΜΕΡΑΝ διάγει.

Plato, vol. ii. p. 143. ΑΝΘΡΩΠΟΙΣ τε καὶ ΘΗΡΙΟΙΣ.

Thucyd. lib. i. § 103. ἐξῆλθον δὲ αὐτοί, καὶ ΠΑΙΔΕΣ καὶ ΓΥΝΑΙΚΕΣ.

§ 3. It might be supposed, that Ordinals would uniformly be preceded by the Article, inasmuch as the Nouns, with which they are joined, do, from this very circumstance, become *Monadic*. In a series of things of the same class only one can be *first*, one *second*, &c. Ordinals, however, for the most part, whether the Nouns, with which they agree, be expressed or understood, are anarthrous [1].

EXAMPLES.

Thucyd. lib. v. § 19. Ἀρτεμισίου μηνὸς ΤΕΤΑΡΤΗι φθίνοντος.

Ibid. § 39. καὶ ΕΝΔΕΚΑΤΟΝ ἔτος τῷ πολέμῳ ἐτελεύτα.

Demosth. de Cor. § 17. Ἐλαφηβολιῶνος ΕΚΤΗι ἱσταμένου.

Æsch. c. Ctes. § 29. ΕΒΔΟΜΗΝ δ' ἡμέραν τῆς θυγατρὸς αὐτῷ τετελευτηκυίας.

---

[1] It is not meant, that this practice, any more than the preceding, is without exception: Ordinals not unfrequently take the Article. The reason of the irregularity seems to be, that while their natural definiteness gives them a right to the Article, it at the same time renders the Article unnecessary.

Plut. de Is. et Osir. p. 262. ΠΡΩΤΟΥ δὲ μηνὸς 'ΕΝΝΑΤΗι.
Thucyd. lib. vii. § 2. μιᾷ νηὶ ΤΕΛΕΥΤΑΙΟΣ ὁρμηθείς.

§ 4. Superlatives have so close an affinity to the Ordinals signifying *first* and *last*, that they also sometimes reject the Article.

EXAMPLES.

Dion. Hal. vol. i. p. 5. τις αὐτῶν ἀρχήν τε ΜΕΓΙΣΤΗΝ ἐκτήσατο.

Xen. Hell. lib. ii. p. 278. τῶν πάντων ΑΙΣΧΙΣΤΟΝ τε καὶ χαλεπώτατον καὶ ἀνοσιώτατον πόλεμον.

CHAPTER VII.

THE USE OF THE ARTICLE WITH CERTAIN WORDS.

It may be right to notice the construction of the Article with ΠΑΣ, ΟΛΟΣ, ΟΥΤΟΣ, &c. At the same time it should be remarked, that the usages, to which I here allude, cannot be considered as anomalous, because in given circumstances they are found to be invariable, and because they admit explanation.

ΠΑΣ.

§ 1. When πᾶς or ἅπας in the Singular Number is used to signify that *the whole* of the thing implied by the Substantive, with which it is joined, is intended, the Substantive has the Article; but when it is employed to denote that *every individual* of that species is spoken of, then the Substantive is anarthrous [1].

Of the former use we may instance,

Æsch. c. Timarch. vol. iii. p. 84. εἰς πᾶσαν ΤΗΝ πόλιν.

Herod. lib. ix. p. 328. Ἡ ἵππος ἅπασα.

Xen. Hell. lib. iii. p. 292. ἅπαν ΤΟ στράτευμα.

Thucyd. lib. ii. § 57. ΤΗΝ γῆν πᾶσαν ἕτεμον.

Demosth. de Cor. § 59. πάντα ΤΟΝ αἰῶνα διατετέλεκε, *his whole life*.

Isocr. Pan. § 48. ὑπὲρ παντὸς ΤΟΥ πολέμου.

Sometimes, indeed, we find the Article prefixed to πᾶς, and not to the Substantive; thus,

Herod. lib. ix. p. 336. τῷ ἅπαντι στρατοπέδῳ νικᾶν.

Id. ibid. p. 340. ὁ πᾶς ὅμιλος.

Demosth. c. Timoc. vol. i. p. 763. ἡ πᾶσα ἐξουσία. For the anarthrous usage we may adduce

---

[1] That these are the two meanings of πᾶς, is plain from *Hesychius*, though he says nothing about the Article: πᾶς· ὅλος, ἕκαστος.

Xen. de Rep. Ath. p. 403. ἔστιν ἐν πάσῃ γῇ τὸ βέλτιστον ἐναντίον τῇ δημοκρατίᾳ.
Xen. Cyrop. lib. vii. p. 108. εἰς πάντα κίνδυνον ἦλθον.
—— Anab. lib. iii. p. 178. διὰ παντὸς πολέμου αὐτοῖς ἰέναι.
Plut. Conviv. p. 94. πάσης τέχνης καὶ δυνάμεως ἀνθρωπίνης.
Demosth. c. Timoc. vol. i. p. 721. δοκεῖ πᾶν ἂν ἑτοίμως ἔργον ποιῆσαι.
Plat. Lach. vol. v. p. 198. οὐκ ἂν πᾶσα ὗς γνοίη.

The reason why in the one case the Article is used, whilst in the other it is omitted, is obvious: when we speak of the *whole* of any thing, that thing must be assumed to be known; but in the other sense of πᾶς no particular individual can by the nature of the case be meant.

To settle the usage with respect to πᾶς in the Plural is not so easy: for though it may seem that where the Substantive is without reference, the Article should be omitted, yet since Plurals, where they are not limited in number or extent, represent whole classes of things, it will often happen, where there is no reference, that the Article will be used hypothetically. In such cases, indeed, it would always be inserted, were it not that πάντες, πᾶσαι, &c. do of themselves, when joined with a Substantive, indicate that the whole class is meant.

§ 2. Hence, where there is not reference, the usage is variable: where there is reference, the Article is, of course, inserted[1].

---

[1] In the New Testament, Gersdorf and Winer observe, that the Article is always used; that the exceptions, at least, are very few, and almost all doubtful on critical grounds. The only ones which appear sufficiently established are, Luke xiii. 4. Acts xvii. 21; xix. 17; xxii. 15. Rom. v. 12. 18. 1 Thess. ii. 15. 1 Tim. ii. 4. Tit. iii. 2.—The reader will observe, that in all these cases, except Acts xvii. 21. and xix. 17. the word without the Article is ἄνθρωποι. Bishop Middleton's watchful eye had already observed the irregularity of a similar kind, with this word, in the case of Partitives. See above, Chap. II. Sect. i. 8.

The additional instances which I have observed relate also, almost all, to the same word. See Acts iii. 21. Rom. xii. 18. 1 Cor. vii. 7; x. 1. (πατέρες); xv. 19. 2 Cor. iii. 2. 1 Thess. v. 26. (ἀδελφοί). 1 Tim. iv. 10. Tit. ii. 11. Heb. i. 6. (ἄγγελοι). 1 Pet. ii. 1. (καταλαλιάς). All these instances, except where I have cited the words, apply to ἄνθρωποι; and I may observe, that 1 Tim. iv. 10. and 1 Pet. ii. 10. are doubtful cases, some MSS. omitting ἀνθρώπων in the first, and πάσας in the second. In Acts iii. 21. the Article is omitted in consequence of its omission before στόματος. (iii. 3. 7.) In two cases, Rom. xii. 18.

Of the former kind we have

Demosth. c. Timoc. vol. i. p. 741. ὥστε πάντας ἀνθρώπους εἰδέναι.

Ibid. p. 760. κατὰ πάσας τὰς πόλεις.

Plat. Lach. vol. v. p. 199. τὰ παιδία πάντα.

Xen. Anab. lib. vi. p. 224. καὶ ὄσπρια πάντα.

Id. Œcon. p. 482. πασῶν τῶν τεχνῶν.

Arist. Rhet. lib. ii. c. 6. οὐ γὰρ πάντα τὰ κακὰ φοβεῖται.

Of the second may be instanced,

Arist. Rhet. lib. ii. c. 9. καὶ περὶ ἁπάσας ΤΑΣ κατηγορίας σκεπτέον, the well-known *ten*.

Demosth. c. Timoc. vol. i. p. 706. παρὰ πάντας ΤΟΥΣ νόμους.

Ibid. p. 759. ἐπὶ πᾶσι ΤΟΙΣ πολίταις.

In the Plural also of πᾶς, as well as in the Singular, we sometimes find the Article prefixed to it, and not to the Substantive: the Substantive, indeed, is frequently understood.

EXAMPLES.

Lys. c. Agorat. vol. v. p. 514. τοῖς πᾶσιν ἀνθρώποις δόξετε δίκαια ψηφίσασθαι.

Xen. Cyrop. lib. vii. p. 111. οὐδ' ἂν οἱ πάντες σφενδονῆται μείνειαν πάνυ ὀλίγους.

Arist. Rhet. lib. ii. cap. 2. τοῖς πᾶσιν ὀργίζεται.

Xen. Cyrop. lib. viii. p. 132. σωφροσύνην τοῖς πᾶσιν ἐμποιεῖ.

---

and 2 Cor. iii. 2. the omission is after a Preposition ; and Heb. i. 6. is a quotation from the LXX. See the Bishop's observation on this point, at the end of chap. ix.

It may, perhaps, be useful to notice the following cases where the position of πᾶς, in the plural, is *after* the Article and Substantive, viz. Matt. xxv. 29. John xvii. 10. Acts vi. 26 ; viii. 40. 1 Cor. vii. 17 ; xiii. 2 ; xv. 7. 2 Cor. i. 1 ; xiii. 2. 12. Phil. i. 13. 2 Tim. iv. 21. Rev. viii. 3. In ninety-nine cases out of one hundred, the position of πᾶς (plural) is *before* the Article and Substantive. I have not *observed*, in the New Testament, this word between the Article and Substantive in the plural, except in Acts xix. 7. In the Singular, I have only observed this position in Acts xx. 18. and 1 Tim. i. 16.

In conclusion I must observe, how rarely the Article is added to πᾶς (plural) when that word stands by itself. The instances which I have collected are, 1 Cor. x. 17 ; xi. 12 ; xii. 19 ; xv. 27, 28. 2 Cor. v. 15. 17, 18. Gal. iii. 22. Eph. i. 10. Phil. iii. 8. 21. Col. i. 16, 17. 20 ; iii. 11. 1 Tim. vi. 13. Heb. ii. 8. (twice) 10.—H. J. R.

I do not perceive that this position of the Article implies any difference in the sense, or that any could be expected.

§ 3. Lastly, Abstract Nouns joined with πᾶς want the Article where there is not reference, and have it where there is reference. Thus,

Æsch. c. Timarch. vol. iii. p. 89. ὀλιγώρως ἔχοντας πρὸς ἅπασαν αἰσχύνην.

Id. c. Ctes. vol. iii. p. 449. ἐπὶ πάσῃ ἀεργίᾳ.

Plat. Lach. vol. v. p. 182. λόγων καλῶν καὶ πάσης παρρησίας.

Ibid. p. 189. οὐ πᾶσά γε καρτερία ἀνδρία σοι φαίνεται.

Arist. Rhet. lib. ii. cap. 2. πάσῃ ὀργῇ ἔπεσθαι.

Plut. Conviv. p. 96. ἡδονῆς πάσης ἀπέχεσθαι ἀλόγιστόν ἐστιν.

Demosth. vol. i. p. 151. ἐν ἀδοξίᾳ πάσῃ καθεστάναι.

Xen. Hell. lib. vi. p. 343. ἐν πάσῃ δὴ ἀθυμίᾳ ἦσαν[1].

Where there is reference, the Article is inserted.

Æsch. c. Ctes. vol. iii. p. 551. πάσῃ τῇ δυνάμει Δαρεῖος κατεβεβήκει, with all *his* force.

Plat. Apol. vol. i. p. 40. ὑμεῖς δέ μου ἀκούσεσθε πᾶσαν τὴν ἀλήθειαν, of the matter before the court.

Demosth. c. Bœot. vol. ii. p. 995. πᾶσα εἰρήσεται ἡ ἀλήθεια, similar to the preceding instance.

Sometimes the Article is placed before πᾶς.

Æsch. de fals. leg. vol. iii. p. 224. τῆς πάσης κακοηθείας.

Demosth. c. Timoc. vol. i. p. 763. ἡ πᾶσα ἐξουσία.

This word has been examined the more minutely from its being of some importance in the New Testament[2].

ΌΛΟΣ.

§ 4. The construction of ὅλος resembles that of πᾶς. The Substantive being without reference, wants the Article; and the contrary.

---

[1] This is the true reading, and is given in H. Stephens's edit. of 1581: some subsequent editors have admitted τῇ for δή.

[2] Ἕκαστος, says Winer, after Orelli ad Isoc. Antid. p. 255. sq. does not admit the Article. See Luke vi. 44. John xix. 23. Heb. iii. 13. It is, indeed, not frequently used as an Adjective in the New Testament.—H. J. R.

EXAMPLES.

Demosth. c. Timoc. vol. i. p. 762. ἐνιαυτὸν ὅλον.
Id. ibid. p. 709. ὅλην ΤΗΝ πόλιν.
Aristot. Rhet. lib. ii. cap. 4. περὶ ὅλον ΤΟΝ βίον, their, &c.
Æsch. de fals. leg. vol. iii. p. 199. κατέτριψε ΤΗΝ ἡμέραν ὅλην.
Xen. Cyrop. lib. ii. p. 26. ὅλαις ΤΑΙΣ τάξεσι.

When ὅλος is used in the sense of *wholly* or *altogether*, its Substantive is anarthrous. Thus,

Xen. Hell. lib. v. p. 328. μὴ γνώμῃ προσφέρεσθαι ὅλον ἁμάρτημα.
Demosth. c. Steph. vol. ii. p. 1110. πλάσμα ὅλον ἐστὶν ἡ διαθήκη.
Aristoph. Av. 430. τρίμμα, παιπάλημ' ὅλον.

ΟΥΤΟΣ.

§ 5. The Noun which is joined with the Pronoun οὗτος, always has the Article prefixed [1].

EXAMPLES.

Herod. lib. ix. p. 327. ΤΟΝ πόνον τοῦτον.
Ibid. p. 339. αὕτη Ἡ μάχη.
Thucyd. lib. v. § 20. αὗται ΑΙ σπονδαί.
Plat. Lach. vol. v. p. 199. ταῦτα ΤΑ θηρία.
Lysias, c. Andoc. vol. v. p. 199. ἕνεκα ταύτης ΤΗΣ ἑορτῆς.
Demosth. c. Timoc. vol. i. p. 744. τοῦτον ΤΟΝ ἕνα.

This usage, though it be uniform in the best prose writers, was unknown to Homer; in both of whose poems οὗτος ἀνήρ, and similar phrases, are sufficiently common [2]. The Article,

---

[1] Gersdorf observes, that in St. Matthew, St. Mark, St. Luke, and St. Paul, οὗτος comes *before*, and in St. John *after*, the Substantive. The exceptions are few and doubtful. (P. 434.) Ἐκεῖνος, on the other hand, is usually after the Substantive, and before it only where a Preposition occurs.—H. J. R.

[2] In Pindar also the same form is common.—Even Sophocles, an Attic writer, has, Œd. Tyr. 831. Ed. Brunck. ταύτην ἡμέραν. So also Æschylus.

therefore, in this instance, as in some others, was not originally deemed necessary. It is, however, not difficult to account for its insertion at a period when all Nouns employed definitely came to have the Article prefixed to them: for they are never more restricted in sense than they unavoidably must be, whenever they are joined with οὗτος.

Proper Names, though for the most part they take the Article with οὗτος, are yet subject to uncertainty, on the principle already stated. See on PROPER NAMES.

It is only, however, where the identity of the Pronoun and Noun is *assumed*, that the foregoing usage takes place: where it is *asserted*, the Noun (unless there be some reason to the contrary unconnected with the present consideration) is anarthrous. Hence, if the Proposition be, " He is a man," οὗτος ἀνήρ (ἐστι) will be the true form. In the subjoined passage of Xen. Œcon. p. 490, the two cases are clearly distinguished: ἔστι μὲν γὰρ ΠΕΝΙΑ αὕτη σαφής, τὸ δεόμενόν τινος μὴ ἔχειν χρῆσθαι· ἀλυποτέρα δὲ αὕτη Ἡ ἔνδεια τὸ μή, &c. In the former clause, πενία σαφὴς is intended, not to be taken with αὕτη, but to follow ἐστί.

ὉΔΕ.

§ 6. What has been said respecting οὗτος will, for the most part, apply to ὅδε. Thus,

Plat. vol. v. p. 166. τῆσδε ΤΗΣ ἡμέρας.
Demosth. c. Timoc. vol. i. p. 714. ΤΟΝ νόμον τόνδε.

There are, however, instances, in which the Article is omitted, when the Noun precedes, especially if it be a Proper Name.

Herod. lib. v. p. 192. ἔχεται δὲ τούτων γῆ ἥδε.
Plato, vol. v. p. 172. Σωκράτη τόνδε.
Id. vol. x. p. 90. Ἀριστοτέλει τῷδε.

ἘΚΕΙΝΟΣ.

§ 7. Nouns joined with this word have the Article in both Numbers, for the reason alleged in οὗτος.

EXAMPLES.

Herod. lib. ix. p. 336. κείνην ΤΗΝ ἡμέρην.
Plat. vol. v. p. 182. ἐκείνης ΤΗΣ ἡμέρας.
Demosth. c. Timoc. vol. i. p. 705. ἐκείνοις ΤΟΙΣ χρόνοις.
Lysias, c. Agorat. vol. v. p. 512. ἐκεῖνοι ΟΙ ἄνδρες ἐτελεύτησαν.

When this word is associated with a Proper Name, we sometimes find that the Article, at least where the Proper Name precedes, is omitted[1].

EXAMPLES.

Demosth. vol. i. p. 731. ἐκείνου ΤΟΥ Θρασυβούλου.
Ibid. p. 301. Καλλίστρατος ἐκεῖνος.

---

[1] But see Thucyd. iii. 59. *Author's MS.* The passage referred to is, ἡμέρας τε ἀναμιμνήσκομεν ἐκείνης. The object of the reference is to intimate, that with other Nouns, as well as Proper Names, when they precede ἐκεῖνος, the Article is omitted.—J. S.

CHAPTER VIII.

POSITION IN CONCORD.

To this account of the uses of the Article I will subjoin a few remarks on its *position* in the *concord of the Substantive and the Adjective*.

The Article, as every one knows, is found very commonly prefixed to Adjectives; but Adjectives are not, strictly speaking, the Predicates of the Assumptive Propositions, of which the Articles are the subjects. In ὁ δίκαιος ἀνὴρ the construction is ὁ (ὢν) δίκαιος ἀνήρ· and in ὁ δίκαιος alone, there is no other difference than that ἀνὴρ is understood. This is sufficiently evident from what has been already shown. The Predicate, therefore, in such cases, is always the Substantive (expressed or understood) conjointly with its Adjective, the two together being considered as forming one whole. Of these two, however, the Substantive is the more important; since it may alone be the Predicate of the Article, which the Adjective cannot. In the Adjective, some Substantive, if not expressed, will be understood: and what is here said respecting Adjectives, will apply equally to Participles. On these grounds we may account for the *position* which the Greek usage has prescribed to the Article in immediate concord, where one Article only is employed, and also for the *order* of the Substantive and the Adjective, where the Article is repeated.

Apollonius (p. 86) has remarked, that ἐμὸς ὁ πατήρ is not equivalent to ὁ ἐμὸς πατήρ· the difference is, that in the former position of the Article, the Verb ἐστὶ is to be supplied between ἐμὸς and ὁ πατήρ, and the sense is, "mine is the father;" whilst in the latter, something is to be affirmed or denied of one who is already *assumed* to be my father : e. g. ὁ ἐμὸς πατὴρ 'ΑΠΕ-ΘΑΝΕ. Care, therefore, must be taken to distinguish the two kinds of Concord which Substantives and Adjectives admit : for they may agree, as in the former case, though an assertive

Copula intervene; and they may agree, as in the latter, where they are not so separated. The second kind of concord is that with which alone we are here concerned.

§ 1. In Concord, then, where the attribute is assumed of the substance, supposing one Article only to be employed, it must be placed immediately before the Adjective.

EXAMPLES.

Herod. lib. ix. p. 324. δουρυαλώτου ἐούσης ΤΗΣ ᾿ΑΤΤΙΚΗΣ χώρης.

Xen. de Redit. p. 537. εἰ δὲ πρὸς ΤΟΙΣ ΑΥΤΟΦΥΕΣΙΝ ἀγαθοῖς πρῶτον μέν, &c.

Ibid. p. 266. ἐβουλεύσαντο περὶ ΤΩΝ ᾿ΕΝΕΣΤΗΚΟΤΩΝ πραγμάτων.

Isocr. Pan. § 24. περὶ ΤΗΣ ΚΟΙΝΗΣ σωτηρίας ὁμονοοῦντες.

Plat. vol. ix. p. 236. ΤΗΝ ᾿ΑΝΘΡΩΠΙΝΗΝ ἕξιν φαμέν, &c.

Demosth. de Cor. § 55. ὅσα προσῆκε ΤΟΝ ᾿ΑΓΑΘΟΝ πολίτην, &c.

The reason of this position is plain. If, for example, we had read ἐούσης τῆς χώρης, the sense would have been complete; the mind of the reader would be satisfied; the Article would have a sufficient Predicate in χώρης, and we should look no further [1]. When ᾿Αττικῆς precedes χώρης, this does not happen: χώρης or γῆς, or something similar, is expected [2].

---

[1] If, however, explanation or limitation be necessary, something more will be requisite than the addition merely of the Adjective; as we shall see hereafter.

[2] I ought to have acknowledged, that though such is the invariable usage in Prose writers, Homer here, as in some other instances, affords exceptions: thus, Il. Φ. 317. τὰ τεύχεα καλά. And Od. P. 10. τὸν ξεῖνον δύστηνον. See Valckenaër, Adnot. Critic. p. 338 *.

---

* Nearly resembling the latter of these examples is Soph. Trach. 938. κἄνταῦθ' ὁ παῖς δύστηνος· in which, however, it is clear that the Predicate of the Article is παῖς, and not δύστηνος at all. It is not the Poet's object to define *the* unhappy Boy in contradistinction from other Boys; but the Boy being already defined, as in v. 934. the Adjective refers only to the circumstances of his present condition—*unhappy as he was.* I spoke foolishly in my note on *Phœniss.* 536.

POSITION IN CONCORD.

The condition, however, of the canon just laid down was, that the attribute should be *assumed*: where this does not happen, the position will be different.

Of non-assumption we may instance such passages as

Isocr. Pan. § 30. κοινῆς ΤΗΣ ΠΑΤΡΙΔΟΣ οὔσης.
Xen. Symp. p. 509. ΤΗΝ ΦΩΝΗΝ πρᾳοτέραν ποιοῦνται.
Id. Cyrop. lib. i. p. 8. ΤΟΙΣ μὲν ΛΟΓΟΙΣ βραχυτέροις ἐχρῆτο καὶ ΤΗι ΦΩΝΗι ἡσυχαιτέρᾳ.
Id. Hellen. lib. ii. p. 277. ἐκέλευσε φανερὰν φέρειν ΤΗΝ ΨΗΦΟΝ· together with all those which are similar to Homer's ἀλλὰ τὸν υἱὸν Γείνατο εἶο χέρεια μάχῃ· (see Note, p. 87). Such, for instance, is Soph. Aj. 1121. οὐ γὰρ βάναυσον τὴν τέχνην ἐκτησάμην· where the meaning is, "the art, *which*·I have acquired, *is* no mean one." See also Elect. 1500. and Eurip. Suppl. 434. *Ed. Beck.* In all such instances we may, before the Adjective, supply ὥστε εἶναι.

§ 2. We are next to consider what will happen, where both the Substantive and the Adjective have the Article; and there the rule invariably [1] is, that the Substantive, with its Article, shall be placed first.

---

[1] I do not recollect any deviation from this rule, except one in *Sophocles*. In the Trachinians, v. 445. we read, ὥστ' εἴ τι τῷ 'μῷ τ' ἀνδρί, κ. τ. λ. which *Brunck* after his predecessors has published without remark. On looking, however, into the new Sophocles by *Erfurdt*, I observe that the false arrangement has at length been noticed: Erfurdt conjectures ὥστ' εἴ τι τῆσδέ γ' ἀνδρί, κ. τ. λ. and supposes τῷ 'μῷ to have been a marginal annotation explanatory of τῆσδε. This

---

when I threw out even a distant hint of altering the text. The other passages there quoted by Matthiæ are easily explained, as not coming within the Bishop's rule of "concord, where the attribute is assumed of the substance." The same remark applies to many other examples which apparently, and only apparently, violate the rule. Ex. gr. Æsch. Agam. 520. διπλᾶ δ' ἔτισαν Πριαμίδαι θαμάρτια (i. e. τὰ ἁμάρτια), the *price* which *they paid was double.* Soph. Philoct. 1248-9. τὴν ἁμαρτίαν αἰσχρὰν ἁμαρτών—Not, *having committed* the *foul offence,* but, *since* the *offence* which *I have committed is foul.* In such cases it is to be observed, that in the *closer* translation the English idiom would require us to express τὴν by *a: having committed* a *foul offence.*—But see the rule accurately guarded by the Bishop himself in the limitation which follows.—J. S.

EXAMPLES.

Lys. vol. v. p. 139. ἐλθὼν ἐπὶ τὴν οἰκίαν τὴν ἐμήν.
Isocr. Pan. § 1. τῆς ταραχῆς τῆς παρούσης.
Ibid. § 6. πρὸς τοὺς προγόνους τοὺς ἡμετέρους.
Xen. Cyrop. lib. v. p. 86. ἐπὶ τῷ ἀγαθῷ τῷ σῷ πεποιημένα.
Id. Hell. lib. ii. p. 280. τοῖς νόμοις τοῖς ἀρχαίοις χρῆσθαι.
Plato, vol. iv. 61. οἶον τὰ σώματα τὰ καλά.

Apollonius has adverted to this usage. He says that we must write ὁ ἄνθρωπος ὁ ἀγαθός, and not ὁ ἀγαθὸς ὁ ἄνθρωπος· ὁ δοῦλος ὁ ἐμός, and not ὁ ἐμὸς ὁ δοῦλος· ὁ παῖς ὁ γράψας, and not ὁ γράψας ὁ παῖς· and the reason assigned by him accords in substance with the principles which I have attempted to establish[1]. In the legitimate arrangement, the addition of ὁ ἀγαθὸς in apposition to ὁ ἄνθρωπος is admissible, because it says something more than was said in ὁ ἄνθρωπος: to assume of any one that he is a *man*, is less than to assume that he is a *good man*: but in the transposed order the reverse happens; for when we have said ὁ ἀγαθός, (i. e. ὁ ὢν ἀγαθὸς ἄνθρωπος), the addition of ὁ ἄνθρωπος will be wholly without meaning. And so of all similar instances.

Hence we perceive that in cases of explanation or limitation something more is requisite, as was before hinted, than the

emendation is not improbable; it is certain that Sophocles has elsewhere attended to both the rules here laid down: thus in a single sentence,

ὦ θρέμμ' ἀναιδές, ἦ σ' ἐγὼ καὶ Τ' ΑΜ' ἘΠΗ
καὶ Τ' ἌΡΓΑ Τ' ἌΜΑ πόλλ' ἄγαν λέγειν ποιεῖ.

Elect. 622. Ed. Brunck *.

[1] P. 87. ἐπεὶ τὰ ἐπιθετικώτερον ἀκουόμενα φέρεται ἐπὶ τὰ ὑποκείμενα· οὐ μὴν τὰ ὑποκείμενα πάντως ἐπὶ τὰ ἐπιθετικά· εἴγε τὸ ἄνθρωπος οὐκ ἐπιζητεῖ τὸ λόγιος, τό γε μὴν λόγιος τὸ ἄνθρωπος.

* But without having recourse to emendation, ("the worst argument a man can use; so let it be the last,") Seidler has explained the construction with great felicity: τ' ἀνδρί is not τῷ ἀνδρί, as had been hastily supposed, but τε, to which ἢ answers in the next line but one. There are in fact two constructions combined: *if I blame* both *my husband* and *this woman;* and, *if I blame* either *my husband* or *this woman.*—J. S.

addition merely of the Adjective: in explanation of τῆς χώρης we must add ΤΗΣ Ἀττικῆς: for in τῆς χώρης, as was shown, the Article has already a sufficient Predicate, and no other can be admitted: if, therefore, we have more to assume of the subject τῆς, that subject must be repeated; otherwise Ἀττικῆς will be predicated of nothing.

Lastly, it is to be observed, that though this order is never violated, yet instances will occur in which the former Article is omitted: thus,

Herod. lib. ix. p. 327. κατιππάσατο ΧΩΡΗΝ τὴν Μεγαρίδα.

Herod. lib. ix. p. 329. ΤΡΟΠΩι τῷ σφετέρῳ ἐτίμων Μασίστιον[1].

Xen. Cyrop. lib. v. p. 86. εἴ τις ΓΥΝΑΙΚΑ τὴν σήν, κ. τ. λ.

It is plain that this ellipsis does not affect the meaning, since the Article prefixed to the Adjective is alone sufficient to correct the indefiniteness of the Substantive. The use of both Articles is, however, the more common: and in general it may be observed, that ὁ ἀγαθὸς πολίτης and ὁ πολίτης ὁ ἀγαθὸς are, in respect of the order of the several words, the forms which prevail where the Substantive and Adjective are to be taken in immediate concord. The apparent violation of the former order is no other than the ellipsis, which is sometimes observable in the latter.

Still, however, it may be asked, whether between the two complete forms there be any difference in respect of the sense. A most acute critic makes ὁ ἀγαθὸς πολίτης to be the suitable expression, where *goodness* is the idea with which chiefly the mind is occupied; while ὁ πολίτης ὁ ἀγαθὸς implies, that the principal stress is to be laid on *citizen*[2]. That instances may be found which seem to favour this distinction, I will not deny: but to affirm that such a distinction is usually observable, would, I think, be an erroneous conclusion. Ὁ μέγας βασιλεὺς and ὁ βασιλεὺς ὁ μέγας, are, I believe, strictly equiva-

---

[1] This form is of very frequent occurrence in *Herodotus*.

[2] Quum οἱ οἰκτροὶ παῖδες dicimus, primarium est οἰκτροί: quum οἱ παῖδες οἱ οἰκτροί, potius est παῖδες.—*Hermann, Hym. Homer.* p. 4.

The same critic (on Soph. Trach. 736.) says, that ὁ ἐμὸς πατὴρ denotes, "*my* father, and the father of no other person;" while ἐμὸς πατὴρ is simply "the person who is my father, and may be father of others;" and πατὴρ ὁ ἐμὸς is nearly the same, though somewhat more accurate,—H. J. R.

lent: so also are τὸ ἅγιον Πνεῦμα and τὸ Πνεῦμα τὸ ἅγιον in the New Testament: nor would it be easy from the passage of the Electra of Sophocles, cited above in the note on p. 112, to establish the proposed rule. I do not, however, mean that it is a matter of indifference, in all cases, which of the two forms be used: the former, as it is the more simple and natural, is in all the Greek writers by far the more common; in the latter, in which the Adjective is placed last, we may generally, I think, observe one of these two things; viz. either that the Substantive might of itself reasonably be presumed to signify the particular person or thing intended, though by the addition of the Adjective the Substantive is absolutely restricted to the object meant; in which case, the addition is a kind of after-thought: or else, that the Adjective has been purposely reserved by the speaker to mark an *emphasis* or *opposition*. Thus, in the former case, τὸ Πνεῦμα cannot easily be misapplied; yet the addition of τὸ ἅγιον absolutely limits the sense. *Justin Martyr*, ed. 1636. p. 479. has the expression τοῦ Πνεύματος, ΦΗΜΙ, τοῦ ἁγίου, which seems to indicate very clearly what is the force of the addition in that and in all similar instances.—The other case may be illustrated by the following examples: Aristot. de Cura Rei Fam. lib. i. (Opera, vol. ii. p. 387.) says, ἀνδρός τε καὶ γυναικὸς ὁμόνοιαν ἐπαινεῖ ὁ ποιήτης, οὐ τήν γε μὴν ἀμφὶ τὰς θεραπείας ΤΑΝ ΜΟΧΘΗΡΑΣ, ἀλλὰ τὴν νῷ τε καὶ φρονήσει δικαίως συνηλλαγμένην· where μοχθηρὰς is *opposed* to what is implied in νῷ τε καὶ φρονήσει. Demosth. (de Cor. § 27.) exulting in having saved the Chersonesus and Byzantium, exclaims emphatically, these successes ἡ προαίρεσις Ἡ ἘΜΗ διεπράξατο· and our Saviour has said, John x. 11. ἐγώ εἰμι ὁ ποιμὴν Ὁ ΚΑΛΟΣ, as opposed to him who is μισθωτός. I am, therefore, of opinion that ὁ πολίτης ὁ ἀγαθὸς would not, in all cases, be admissible: I should expect to find it only where a *good citizen* had recently been mentioned, and where, consequently, ὁ πολίτης alone might in some measure be understood of the same citizen; or else, where the *good* citizen was to be opposed to another of a different character; though, in the latter case, the other form is not unfrequently employed.

CHAPTER IX.

HOW FAR CLASSICAL RULES RESPECTING THE ARTICLE APPLY TO THE NEW TESTAMENT.

THE foregoing Inquiry having been instituted in order that the result might be applied to the language of the New Testament, it may be expected, before I conclude this part of my work, that I should vindicate the application of rules founded on classical usage to the diction of the Sacred Writers. The sequel, indeed, will show, that from the Evangelists and Apostles, no less than from Xenophon and Demosthenes, those rules may be exemplified and confirmed: and it was principally with a view to the proof of this agreement, that in passages presenting no difficulty I shall be found frequently, though briefly, to refer the reader to the canons previously established; that thus in other passages, where the sense or the reading is disputable, recourse may be had to the same canons, as being of acknowledged authority even in the New Testament. Still, however, it may be right in this place to offer a few remarks on the style of the Sacred Volume, so far only as it may be supposed to affect my plan.

It may be asked, Is it likely that writers, who were confessedly untaught, and whose Greek style is far removed from classical purity, should pay regard to circumstances so minute as are the uses of the Greek Article? In the recent controversy the negative of this question has been assumed, I will venture to affirm, without any right founded on fair reasoning, or on the nature of the case. It will not, indeed, be immediately conceded, that *all* the writers of the New Testament were illiterate persons. To *St. Paul* some have ascribed a considerable degree of learning; much more, probably, than he really possessed: and if the acquirements of *St. Luke* were not pre-eminent, his style gives us no reason to believe, that his education, any more than his condition in life, was mean.

If, therefore, it be recollected, how large a portion of the Sacred Volume was written by these two, and that *St. Paul* is the writer from whom, principally, the controverted texts are drawn, it may well be doubted whether the known simplicity of some of the Apostles could afford any argument to Mr. Sharp's antagonists. My own concern, however, is with the New Testament generally : I shall, therefore, consider the writers under one general character, as being, if the reader so please to call them, illiterate men : to admit that they were illiterate is not to concede that they were not competently skilled in the use of the Greek tongue.

The objectors argue as if they imagined that the Sacred Writers encountered the same difficulties in acquiring Greek, which our own peasants and mechanics would meet with in their attempt to learn French or Italian: but the cases are plainly dissimilar. The greater part of Englishmen pass through life without having ever heard a conversation in any other language than their own : and even of those, who have acquired some knowledge of the continental tongues, there are but few who made the acquisition in their childhood by residing in the countries where those languages are respectively used. But this is not applicable to the writers of the New Testament. Neither were they natives of a country where Greek was rarely spoken ; nor is it probable that any of them made the acquisition late in life. The victories of Alexander, and the consequent establishment of the Seleucidæ, produced a revolution in the language of Syria and Palestine. The Aramæan dialects still, indeed, continued to be in use; but the language of literature and of commerce, and in a great degree, even of the ordinary intercourse of life, was the Greek : without a knowledge of this it was impossible to have any extensive communication. " Greek," says Michaelis [1], " was the current language in all the cities to the west of the Euphrates :" and *Josephus* expressly declares, that he had written in his vernacular idiom a work on the Jewish war, of which the Greek work, still preserved, is a translation, " in order that Parthians, Babylonians, Arabians, and *the Jews who dwelt beyond the*

---

[1] *Introduction* by *Marsh*, vol. ii. p. 39.

Euphrates, might be informed of what had happened [1]." It is, then, manifest, that westward of the Euphrates, a knowledge of Greek was not an accomplishment confined exclusively to the learned and polite, but that it was generally understood, and commonly used by people of all ranks, and must have been acquired in their childhood.

In this state of things, therefore, what were we to expect *à priori* from the writers of the New Testament? I speak not of *St. Luke* and *St. Paul*, of whom Greek was the *native language*, but of the other Evangelists and Apostles. It was not, indeed, to be expected, if we reflect on their circumstances and habits of life, and on the remoteness of Palestine, that they should write with the elegance of learned Athenians; but I know not of any reasonable presumption against their writing with perspicuity and with grammatical correctness; and it is against these, and not against elegance, that the improper use of the Article would offend [2]: to insert it gratuitously will in most instances alter, and in many destroy, the sense: to omit it, indeed, is, as we have seen, not unfrequently the licence of poetry; but no one will suspect that the style of St. John was corrupted by a too familiar acquaintance with Pindar and the Tragic Chorusses, especially when such writers as Xenophon and Plato escaped the contamination. In most cases also the improper insertion or omission of the Article would be a breach of grammatical correctness; since, as has been demonstrated, the uses are not arbitrary, but are subject to rules, the reasons of which are apparent. It is not true, therefore, however prevalent may be the opinion, that the uses of the Greek Article do, for the most part, deserve to be considered as *minutiæ*; unless it be deemed minute in writing to adhere to the ordinary construction of the language, and to employ, in Nouns the Case, and in Verbs the Mood and Tense, which the writer's meaning may require. That there are, indeed, *minutiæ* in all idioms, at least in all polished ones, will be readily conceded. Of this class in Greek is the Attic use of many of the Parti-

---

[1] See Michaelis's *Introd.* vol. i. p. 102. and *Josephus*, ed. Hudson, vol. ii. p. 954.

[2] To put a question from analogy: Would the most unlettered person in our own country say, Shut *a* door, when his meaning was, Shut *the* door?—J. S.

cles; which, without being indispensable to the sense, contribute to mark the feelings of the speaker and the latent operations of his mind; as doubt, conviction, limitation, concession, earnestness. They conduce, therefore, to elegance: they belong to the colouring of discourse: they give it richness and effect: and it is to the very frequent use of them in Plato, that we may impute, in great measure, the spirit and vivacity, which enable his writings, as conversation-pieces, to defy all competition. Now in this particular the Sacred Penmen differ from the Philosophers and Orators of Athens: the former introduce the Particles more sparingly; not so frequently in combination; and sometimes in a manner which the classical practice will hardly justify. But this cannot excite surprise; had the style of St. John's Gospel differed not even in *minutiæ* from that of Plato, the authenticity of such a writing could not easily have been credited.

The objection, however, has been urged in a somewhat different form, so as not to suppose the writers of the New Testament to be altogether *ignorant* of the Greek idiom, but to question the probability that they should *studiously attend* to it: their minds, we have been told, were occupied with matters of greater moment. I am not certain, that in this form the objection deserves notice: however, it shall not be entirely overlooked, μὴ δόξωμεν ἔρημον ἀφεικέναι τὸν ἀγῶνα[1]. It is true, then, that they were occupied with matters of greater importance; so is every man, who either in writing or in speaking has any thing interesting to communicate: so were the several writers, from whose works I have selected the examples, by which the rules are illustrated; but does such occupation of the mind commonly lead men to express themselves in an unauthorized and unnatural manner? to renounce modes of speech, to which they have long been habituated? to unlearn at once all which they have been taught? and to adopt a phraseology, which is not to be understood according to the obvious import? The fact is directly the reverse: men never speak with less ambiguity, nor with less deviation from the usual mode, than when they are least studious of their diction.

[1] Dion. Hal. De Comp. Verborum. Ed. Reiske, vol. v. p. 207. on an occasion not very dissimilar.

It is not true, therefore, that any particular *attention* is supposed by the advocates of grammatical interpretation: the assumption is only, that the Evangelists and Apostles wrote as plain men commonly do write, that is, as habit and the ear direct: they are not supposed, as has been alleged, to have been Grammarians and Philologists. But this is a disingenuous attempt to substitute ridicule for reasoning: nor is it a very defensible kind of criticism, which would put upon an author any construction in preference to that which the genius of the language and his usual practice sanction.

In short, the only tolerable presumption against the correctness with which the Sacred Writers may have used the Greek Article, is founded on their familiar acquaintance with certain Oriental idioms: whence it may be supposed that they have sometimes adopted the Hebrew or Aramæan usage rather than the Greek. Now where languages have a very close affinity, it is conceivable that some such confusion may arise: but it so happens, that between the language of Greece and the dialects of Palestine, the difference was so great in regard to the Article, that the supposed corruption was scarcely possible. The Syriac and Chaldee have, indeed, no Article, but express *emphasis* by a change in the termination of Nouns: and the Hebrew ה, though it corresponds in some of its uses with the Ὁ of the Greeks, is yet, on the whole, so dissimilar, that he who should translate a portion of the Hebrew Scriptures into Greek, inserting the Greek Article where he found the Hebrew one, and no where else, would write a language almost as unlike Greek as is the Hebrew itself: not to insist that Hebrew, properly so called, had, in the time of the Apostles, become nearly obsolete. If any danger were to be apprehended as to the particular of which we are treating, it is rather that the Syriac or Chaldee should have been corrupted from the Greek, than the converse: since it is far more natural that men, who had the use of two languages, should enrich the poorer, than that they should impoverish the richer: and this we find to have been actually the case. There is not any example in the whole New Testament, in which the writer has endeavoured to give to a Noun the *forma emphatica* of the Syriac and Chaldee: yet in the *Peshito* there is at least one instance (John v. 7.) in which the Syriac Pronoun Demonstrative represents the Article of the Greeks; and afterwards, as is well known, this practice became common. It is less to our purpose, yet it is worthy of remark, that for one Syriac word adopted into the Greek, there are at least fifty Greek words transferred into the Syriac: nor is the irregularity noticed in *Philo* (see above, p. 38) to be explained as a Hebraism, it being directly contrary to the Hebrew usage.

I have, however, been considering the New Testament as consisting of original compositions: and I am persuaded, that where the Writers speak immediately from themselves, their use of the Article will be found to be purely Greek. But what has been here adduced will not apply with equal force to translations; since he who translates, rarely writes with the same ease and correctness, as when he is left entirely to himself. Hence it has happened, that in *Quotations from the LXX.*, in some parts of the *Apocalypse*, (see Apoc. x. 7.) and in passages rendered from the *Hebrew*, some licence may be observed. The LXX., notwithstanding the occasional disagreement of the Septuagint and the Hebrew copies still extant, appear to have been servile translators: in respect of the Article, they have every where kept as close to the original as the Greek idiom would admit; and if they have not in any instance violated the rules, they have at least, in conformity with the Hebrew, availed themselves of all the latitude which the rules allow: it is for this reason that I have made so little use of the Septuagint in the preceding investigation. The same may be said of a few passages of the New Testament not derived from the LXX., but translated by the Evangelist or Apostle, in whose writings they occur: such instances will be noticed in the sequel: they will be found to be extremely rare: and with these exceptions, the style of the New Testament has not, in the view in which we are considering it, any peculiarity. If the Notes, which consist merely of references to Part I., and which serve as illustrations of the rules, be observed to occur more sparingly as the reader advances in the volume, he must impute their absence to my unwillingness to fatigue him with proofs of that which he could not any longer doubt.

PART THE SECOND.

ADVERTISEMENT.

The Editions of the Greek Testament which have been consulted in the course of the following *Annotations* are,

 Mill's, 1 vol. fol. ....Oxon. 1707.
 Bengel's, 1 vol. 4to. ....Tubingæ, 1734.
 Wetstein's, 2 vols. fol. ....Amstel. 1751.
 Griesbach's, 2 vols. 8vo.......Halæ, Sax. 1796 & 1806.
 Matthäi's, 12 vols. 8vo...............Rigæ, 1782, &c.
 Alter's, 2 vols. 8vo. ....Viennæ, 1787.
 Birch's Quatuor Evangelia, 1 vol. fol. .....Havniæ, 1788.

The Text which I have adopted is that of Wetstein. The mark + denotes the *insertion* of a word or passage, and — the *omission*.

PART II.

NOTES

ON THE

NEW TESTAMENT.

ST. MATTHEW.

CHAP. I.

VER. 1. γενέσεως Ἰησοῦ Χριστοῦ, υἱοῦ, &c. Both *Campbell* and *Wakefield* translate " a son of David, a son of Abraham ;" and the former remarks "the modesty and simplicity" with which the historian introduces his subject. However ready the reader may be to acquiesce in this commendation, it will be prudent to pause, till he shall have taken into the account some subsequent applications of the same principle of criticism. In this very Chapter the Angel says, Ἰωσὴφ υἱὸς Δαβίδ, not Ὁ υἱός, where "modesty and simplicity" are out of the question : and indeed it has been shown (Part I. Chap. iii. Sect. iii. § 6.) that the Greek usage will readily admit υἱοῦ to be anarthrous. Or if we are to consider the passage as a translation from a Hebrew original, υἱοῦ without the Article will be an accurate version : for it is well known, that the Hebrew in the *status constructus* does not usually admit the emphatic ה: and thus we find υἱὸς used by the LXX. Num. i. 5, 6, 7. *et passim*.
—In the German translation by *Michaelis* (Göttingen, 1790) we find what is equivalent to *the son*, as in the English Version.
—The want of the Article before γενέσεως may also be explained by Part I. Chap. iii. Sect. iii. § 6. Βίβλος γενέσεως is, however, exactly rendered from the Hebrew ספר תולדת, used Gen. v. 1. for what we should call a pedigree.

V. 2. *et seqq*. Throughout the whole of this genealogy there is an use of the Article, which is wholly foreign from the Greek practice, and which in some degree favours the historical account of the Hebrew original of St. Matthew's Gospel. The Greek usage would require 'Αβραὰμ ἐγέννησεν 'Ισαάκ· Ὁ δὲ 'Ισαὰκ ἐγέννησεν 'Ιακώβ· Ὁ δὲ 'Ιακώβ, &c. (See Part I. Chap. iv.) thus introducing the Article on the *repetition* of each Proper Name: the very reverse of which here takes place. The Article, therefore, in this genealogy represents the Hebrew את or the Chaldee ית, and it is thus that the LXX. render the Particle marking the objective case. Compare LXX. with the Hebrew of Ruth iv. 18. 1 Chron. vi. 4. *et passim.*—In the genealogy by St. Luke the use of the Article is strictly Greek, τοῦ being every where an ellipsis of τοῦ υἱοῦ.

V. 16. ὁ λεγόμενος Χριστός. Not Ὁ Χρ. (Part I. Chap. iii. Sect. iii. § 2.) and yet the Coptic Translator reads Ὁ Χριστός: (See *Alter's* N. T. vol. i. p. 752.) unless, indeed, which I suspect to be the truth, he attended to the *sense* of the passage, where, no doubt, Χριστὸς is equivalent to Ὁ Χρ., rather than to the exigency of the Greek idiom. It is certain, that in many other places, in which in the Greek MSS. the Article is wanting before the name *Christ*, the Coptic has prefixed its Article: as John iv. 25. Romans viii. 10. 1 Cor. xv. 3. and elsewhere. That inattention to the difference of idiom has been a fruitful source of alleged various readings in the MSS. used by the Oriental Translators, has been proved by *D. C. B. Michaelis*, the father of the late Professor at Göttingen, in the valuable Tract de Variis Lectionibus N. T. Halæ, Magd. 1749, and more fully by *Bode* in his Pseudocritica Millo-Bengeliana, Halæ, Magd. 1767.

V. 17. A few MSS. want αἱ. It should be inserted. See Part I. Chap. vii. § 2. The mistake probably arose from the uncertain use of πᾶς in the Plural, where there is not reference.

V. 18. ἐκ πνεύματος ἁγίου. *Wakefield*, both in his St. *Matthew*, and in his *New Testament*, 1795, translates "a holy Spirit." There is reason to believe that he laid some stress on the absence of the Article; for I have observed that he generally in such cases adheres to the letter of the original: whence

CHAPTER I.

it is plain, that he did not advert to the anomaly noticed in the Preliminary Inquiry, Chap. vi. § 1. In whatever manner we are to render this passage, it is certain that the absence of the Article after a Preposition does not affect the definiteness of the sense. Since, however, the phrases πνεῦμα and πνεῦμα ἅγιον, both with and without the Article, are of frequent occurrence in the New Testament, it may not be amiss in this place to inquire generally into the meanings which they bear, and especially on what occasions the Article is taken or rejected.

I. The primitive signification of πνεῦμα is *breath* or *wind*: in which senses, however, it is not often found in the New Testament. In the sense of *breath* πνεῦμα takes or rejects the Article, as the circumstances may require. Thus, Matt. xxvii. 50. ἀφῆκε ΤΟ πνεῦμα, *his* breath or life: (Part I. Chap. iii. Sect. 1. § 4.) but Apoc. xiii. 15. we have δοῦναι πνεῦμα, to give life, where τὸ would be inconsistent with the sense: for that, which was possessed already, could not now first be given. In the meaning of *wind* we find, John iii. 8. τὸ πνεῦμα πνεῖ, ὅπου θέλει· where the Article is requisite by Part I. Chap. iii. Sect. 1. § 5.

II. Hence we pass by an easy transition to πνεῦμα, the intellectual or spiritual part of man, as opposed to his carnal part. Thus, πνεῦμα is frequently contradistinguished from σάρξ. In this sense also it may be used either definitely or indefinitely: examples of each will be noticed in the sequel.

III. A third meaning arises by abstracting the spiritual principle from body or matter, with which in man it is associated: hence is deduced the idea of the immaterial agents, whom we denominate *spirits*. Thus, Luke xxiv. 39. πνεῦμα σάρκα καὶ ὀστέα οὐκ ἔχει. John iv. 24. πνεῦμα ὁ Θεός. Acts xxiii. 9. πνεῦμα ἢ ἄγγελος. The πνεύματα also of the Demoniacs are to be classed under this head. It is evident that the word, in this acceptation, must admit both a definite and an indefinite sense.

IV. But the word πνεῦμα is used in a sense not differing from the former, except that it is here employed κατ' ἐξοχὴν to denote the Great and Pre-eminent Spirit, the Third Person in the Trinity: and in this acceptation, it is worthy of remark, that πνεῦμα or πνεῦμα ἅγιον is never anarthrous; except, indeed, in cases where other terms, confessedly the most definite, lose the Article, from some cause alleged in the Preliminary Inquiry. It will be shown in the following pages, as the passages occur, that such is the practice of the Sacred Writers.— The addition of τὸ ἅγιον serves only to ascertain to what class of spirits, whether good or evil, this pre-eminent Spirit is affirmed to belong.—It may here be briefly noticed, that in the passages which, from their ascribing *personal acts* to the πνεῦμα ἅγιον, are usually adduced to prove the Personality of the Blessed Spirit, the words πνεῦμα and ἅγιον invariably have the Article. See particularly Mark i. 10. Luke iii. 22. John i. 32. Acts i. 16. and xx. 28. Ephes. iv. 30. Mark xiii. 11. Acts x. 19. and xxviii. 25. 1 Tim. iv. 1. Heb. iii. 7. &c.—The reason of this is obvious; for there being but one Holy Spirit, he could not be spoken of indefinitely. In Matt. also xxviii. 19. where the Holy Spirit is associated with the Father and the Son, the reading is τοῦ ἁγίου πνεύματος.

V. The fifth sense of πνεῦμα is easily deducible from the fourth; being here not the Person of the Holy Spirit, but his *influence* or *operation*: the addition of ἅγιον is explicable as before. And in this meaning a remarkable difference may be observed with respect to the Article. Though the Holy Spirit himself be but one, his influences and operations may be many: hence πνεῦμα and πνεῦμα ἅγιον are, in this sense, always *anarthrous*, the case of *renewed mention* or other reference being of course excepted. The expressions of being "filled with the Holy Ghost," "receiving the Holy Ghost," "the Holy Ghost being upon one," &c. justify this observation.

VI. The last meaning, or rather class of meanings, for they are several, comprises whatever is deducible from the last acceptation, being not the influences of the Spirit, but the effects of them: under which head we may range πνεῦμα in the senses of *disposition*, *character*, *faith*, *virtue*, *religion*, &c. and also whenever it is used to signify *evil* propensities or desires, with this difference only, that these latter must be supposed to arise from the influence of the Evil Spirit. In all these senses the Article is inserted or omitted according to the circumstances.

Now if we put together the consequences of what has been

shown under the *fourth* and *fifth* heads, we shall perceive the futility of pretending that the Holy Spirit is, as some aver, merely an influence: the Sacred Writers have clearly, and in strict conformity with the analogy of language, distinguished the *influence* from the *Person* of the Spirit. In like manner, the Personality of the Holy Spirit is deducible by comparing the *third* and *fourth* heads: for if πνεῦμα, in the passages adduced under the *third*, mean a spiritual agent, τὸ πνεῦμα, in the places referred to under the *fourth*, where there is no *renewed mention*, nor any other possible interpretation of the Article, but the use of it, κατ' ἐξοχήν, can mean only the one spiritual agent of acknowledged and pre-eminent dignity. But the personality of πνεῦμα, under the *third* head, cannot be disputed, unless by those who would controvert the personality of ὁ Θεός: the personality, therefore, of τὸ πνεῦμα used κατ' ἐξοχὴν must be conceded.

I have thus, at some length, examined the senses of the word πνεῦμα in the first passage in which it occurs, in order to exhibit the result of my observation at a single view; so that in the sequel I need only to refer to what has been here advanced.—With respect to the place in St. Matthew which has given rise to this note, it is impossible to prove incontestably that the Holy Spirit, in the *personal* acceptation, is here meant, inasmuch as the Preposition, (see Part I. Chap. vi. § 1.) may have occasioned the omission of the Articles; and this happens, in some other places also, from the same cause. However, *Mr. Wakefield's* translation, which implies a *plurality* of Holy Spirits, the ordinary Ministers of Almighty Providence, is irreconcileable with the phraseology of the New Testament, in which πνεύματα ἅγια are not once mentioned. *Rosenmüller's* (see Scholia in N. T. 1789.) "*per omnipotentiam divinam*" is less liable to objection.

V. 20. Κύριος, in the sense of *The Almighty*, takes or rejects the Article indifferently; and nearly the same is true of Θεός: but see on Luke i. 15.

V. 21. Ἰησοῦν: not τὸν Ἰησοῦν. Part I. Chap. iii. Sect. iii. § 2.

V. 23. ἡ παρθένος. The Article in this place, as in many others, appeared to our English Translators to be without meaning: accordingly they render "a virgin." That the

Article is never without meaning in the Greek, though it may not always be possible in a Version adequately to express its force, has already been demonstrated. The passage, however, is quoted accurately from the LXX. who have as accurately translated the Hebrew. The force of the Article, therefore, in this place (See Part I. Chap. ix.) can be sought only from the Hebrew of Isaiah vii. 14. That the LXX. did well in expressing the Article, may be inferred from its having been retained in the subsequent Versions of Aquila, Symmachus, and Theodotion, notwithstanding the readiness, of the two former at least, on most occasions to differ from the LXX. Here, indeed, they all three render ἡ ΝΕΑΝΙΣ, Aquila having set the example: on which *Montfaucon* remarks, (Prælim. in Hexapla, vol. i. p. 111. ed. Bahrdt) "*An autem ut locum detorqueret Aquila, sic versionem suam concinnaverit, nescio. Verisimile tamen est, eum a voce* παρθένος *consulto declinasse, quia hac maxime prophetia utebantur Christiani pro sua tuenda fide. Imo, nec vocem* ἀπόκρυφος, *quam ALIBI pro Hebraica* עלמה *exprimenda adhibet, hic usurpare voluit: quia forte hæc interpretatio puellam, quæ virorum adspectui occulta manserat, atque ideo virginem, exprimebat.*" The same Translator, instead of Χριστός, commonly has ἠλειμμένος.

An excellent Dissertation on the Prophecy in Isaiah and on its application by St. Matthew may be found in the Βίβλος Καταλλαγῆς of *Surenhusius*, Amstæl. 1713.

V. 24. ἀπὸ ΤΟΥ ὕπνου· in reference to ὄναρ above, ver. 20. So also in Acts xx. 9.

CHAP. II.

V. 3. πᾶσα Ἱεροσόλυμα. The want of the Article in this place may appear to contradict what has been advanced, Part I. Chap. vii. § 1. Two MSS. indeed, viz. *r* of Matthäi and Vat. 360. of Birch, insert ἡ. These were probably the corrections of persons who had attended to the more usual construction of πᾶς. I am of opinion, however, with *Rosenmüller*, that ἡ πόλις is understood, Ἱεροσόλυμα being always Neuter in the New Testament, unless we are to except this place; on the sole authority of which, so far as I can discover, *Schleusner* (in Lex.) makes it to be Feminine in the Singular. *Kypke* (Obss.

Sacr. ad loc.) says, that in the Feminine it is very uncommon, yet he adduces two passages from Josephus, in which he supposes it to be so used. One of these is a citation from Clearchus, the scholar of Aristotle, in which Clearchus says, that " the city has ὄνομα σκολιόν, ΊΕΡΟΣΟΛΥΜΗΝ γὰρ αὐτὴν καλοῦσιν." But a Greek would hardly have called such a name σκολιόν: and on turning to Josephus I find the true reading to be ΊΕΡΟΥΣΑΛΗΜ: the same passage is so cited by Eusebius.—The force of Kypke's other passage depends on ἀλοῦσα, which is made to refer to Ἱεροσόλυμα preceding: but there the reference may be πρὸς τὸ σημαινόμενον, as is usual even in the best Greek Writers. If, however, the word be Feminine in this place, the Article may still be omitted because of the Proper Name, to which the reason of the rule will not necessarily apply. We find, indeed, in the next Chapter, ver. 5, πᾶσα Ἡ Ἰουδαία: but Ἰουδαία is an Adjective: compare Mark i. 5.

V. 5. διὰ τοῦ προφήτου, viz. Micah v. 2.

V. 11. δῶρα, *by way of* presents. Part I. Chap. iii. Sect. iii. § 4.

V. 23. Ναζωραῖος. Eng. Version, "*a* Nazarene:" I would rather translate, He shall be called "*the* Nazarene." The Article could not be inserted in the Greek. Part I. Chap. iii. Sect. iii. § 2.

CHAP. III.

V. 3. φωνὴ βοῶντος. Eng. Version, "The voice," &c. quoted from LXX. Isaiah xl. 3. It serves, however, to illustrate Part I. Chap. iii. Sect. iii. § 6. *Mr. Wakefield*, not aware of this usage, translates, " *A* voice of one crying," &c. For the same reason, in the next verse, it could not have been ΤΩΝ τριχῶν.

V. 5. Ἱεροσόλυμα. 1 Bodl. prefixes πᾶσα ἡ. The *r* of Matthäi has only ἡ. See above, Chap. ii. ver. 3.

V. 8. τῆς μετανοίας. D alone wants τῆς, which is not a bad reading after ἄξιος: but the uncertainty respecting abstract Nouns has been remarked in Part I.

V. 9. πατέρα. Part I. Chap. iii. Sect. iii. § 4.

V. 11. ἐν πνεύματι ἁγίῳ καὶ πυρί. *Mr. Wakefield*, in his

New Testament, here translates, "with a holy wind and with a fire." *Heylin* had already given a similar Version, urging in behalf of it, that where the Holy Spirit is meant, the Article is generally prefixed; and also that the verse following, which he considers as an illustration of the present, requires such an interpretation. See *Campbell ad loc.* whose remark on the Article is, indeed, of no great value, but whose opinion, that the present verse represents the manner in which Christ will *admit* his Disciples, the next, that in which he will *judge* them at the end of the world, appears to be extremely just. In confirmation of the manner of *admission*, see Acts ii. 3. The words, indeed, καὶ πυρί, are wanting in so many of the MSS. that if they were not found in a few of the older MSS. and Versions, they might be deemed spurious. They have, however, probably, been rejected because they are wanting in Mark: see *Adler's Verss. Syriacæ*, p. 159.—Mr. W. in support of his Translation refers us to his own *Silva Critica*, Part ii. § 83. where, however, his arguments are nearly the same with those of *Heylin*. This he seems not to have known, as appears from his expression of " *quod primus moneo*:" and even Heylin's Version, according to Campbell, was not entirely new.

The meaning of ἁγίῳ πνεύματι, as the reader will have perceived, (See above, Matt. i. 18.) cannot here be inferred from the doctrine of the Article. There can, however, be little doubt, that the fifth sense there deduced is here the true one: because πνεῦμα joined with ἅγιον has only two senses; and the Holy Spirit in his *personal* acceptation cannot well be associated with *fire*. In the connection of fire with the *influence* of the Spirit there is nothing unnatural or violent.

V. 12. εἰς τὴν ἀποθήκην. "*His* garner." Many MSS. with the Syriac add αὐτοῦ. The Article alone has in such instances the force of the Possessive Pronoun; (See Part I. Chap. iii. Sect i. § 4.) but the Syriac, as the genius of the language requires, generally has the addition of the Pronoun. Its insertion or omission in passages of this kind is a fruitful source of various readings: to have noticed them once may be deemed sufficient.

V. 16. τὸ πνεῦμα τοῦ Θεοῦ. *Rosenmüller* does not understand these words in the *personal* sense of the Holy Spirit, but explains the whole to signify no more than a strong emotion in the mind of our Saviour entering on his Ministry. It is observable, however, that Mark and John use precisely the same expression, whilst Luke, speaking of the same event, chap. iii. 22. says, τὸ πνεῦμα τὸ ἅγιον σωματικῷ εἴδει, which appears to give the personal sense of πνεῦμα in the most unequivocal terms.—I have remarked, that the other two Evangelists have also τὸ πνεῦμα τοῦ Θεοῦ· because, if I mistake not, that phrase is to be distinguished from πνεῦμα Θεοῦ, which is also of frequent occurrence in the New Testament, but which signifies no more than "a divine influence," notice of which will be taken in its place. It is worthy of mention, that though πνεῦμα Θεοῦ and πνεῦμα Κυρίου are very common in the LXX. τὸ πνεῦμα τοῦ Θεοῦ does not once occur: for which I have no better reason to assign, than that the Translators attended to the idiom of their original, in which רוח must be anarthrous. *Rosenmüller's* objection, that change of place cannot be ascribed to an Omnipresent Being, is evidently fallacious, unless it could be proved, that a Being, who is also Omnipotent, could not assume a visible form. Such a Being, though present every where, may yet be visible only in a given place.

CHAP. IV.

V. 1. εἰς τὴν ἔρημον. On these words I will translate the Note of *Michaelis* (See *Anmerkungen zu seiner Uebersetzung,* &c. 4to. 1790.) "Not into *a* desert, but into *the* desert; a phrase, which must suggest to the mind of the reader the Great Desert of Arabia, in which the Israelites wandered so many years, and in which Mount Sinai is situate: and this notion, if not elsewhere contradicted by the historian, will appear the more probable, when in reading of a miraculous fast of forty days, we recollect a similar fast of Moses and Elias on Mount Sinai, or on the way to that mountain. See Exod. xxxiv. 28. 1 Kings xix. 8. The instant we imagine ourselves in this Desert, the whole history, including both the artifices of Satan and the answer of our Lord, receives extraordinary light.

"The people of Palestine show the wilderness, in which

Jesus is supposed to have been tempted, and from the forty days it has acquired the name of *Quarantaria:* it is an extremely rugged and wild ridge of mountains, to the north of the road which leads from Jerusalem by the Mount of Olives to Jericho. Its aspect is most hideous: but it can hardly be the Desert of the Temptation; and the assertion of those, who for 1600 years past have been paid by travellers for showing the Holy Places of Palestine, is utterly destitute of weight. Not to insist, that no writer of common sense would call this merely *the Desert* without a more particular description, its situation is at variance with the whole history; no man could there be in danger of perishing with hunger: for in whatever part of that desert he might happen to be, he need travel only for a few hours to reach a place where provisions might be had, viz. Ephraim, Bethel, Jericho, or elsewhere: if any one were there so unreasonable as to say to a famished worker of miracles, 'Command that these stones be made bread,' the proper answer would be, 'Shall God, then, work a miracle merely in aid of our sloth? Let us go and buy bread.' The Angels, also, on this supposition were superfluously employed in bringing food to Jesus. Again, our Saviour could not here have been altogether in solitude, nor as Mark (i. 13.) says, among wild beasts or serpents, but among men, possibly among robbers, who then infested this Desert, and made it dangerous to travel from Jerusalem to Jericho. According to Luke too, (iv. 1, 2.) Jesus, who was baptized beyond the Jordan, proceeds from the Jordan (not over it back again,) a journey of forty days to the Wilderness: can this be any other than the Wilderness of Sinai? Certainly it cannot be the Desert of Quarantaria; for to get to it he must have *crossed* the Jordan, on this side of which it lies: and the journey could not have occupied at the utmost more than a couple of days."

The reasoning of this note is for the most part satisfactory; but the argument last adduced from Luke iv. 1, 2. may admit a doubt. The words ἡμέρας τεσσαράκοντα are usually understood to denote the length of the Temptation, and not the time employed in reaching the Wilderness; and it ought to be observed, that the reading of Wetstein's D and L, and Birch's 1209 (the Vat.) is ἐν τῇ ἐρήμῳ, which, if admitted, confirms the usual acceptation. However, it is true on the other hand, that the Syr. and Vulg. favour the contrary exposition.

Same v. ὑπὸ τοῦ πνεύματος. By the Holy Spirit. So all commentators now understand it: there is no ground, either from the expression, or from the context, to interpret it of the Devil.

V. 3. εἰ υἱὸς εἶ τοῦ Θεοῦ. In this place both *Campbell* and *Wakefield* translate "a Son of God," and the former enters at some length into the reasons of this innovation: they are founded principally on the absence of the Article before υἱός, together with the implied degradation of our Saviour's character arising " either from the ignorance of Satan, as not knowing the dignity of the person, whom he accosted, or from his malignity, as being averse to suppose in Christ more than an equality with other good men."

Now, that the Tempter should be ignorant of our Saviour's character is highly improbable: ignorance is no where in Scripture ascribed to the Evil Spirit, but the reverse; and the expression, *if thou be*, can be understood only as a sneer at our Saviour's known pretensions. Besides, we shall find, that even the Demoniacs knew, if any stress is here to be laid on the Article, (see Mark iii. 11. and Luke iv. 41.) that Christ was, in the highest sense, the Son of God. Neither can malignity be well assigned as the cause, why Satan should designedly suppress any part of the title, which he knew that Christ claimed : malignity would surely have prompted Satan rather to exaggerate those pretensions at the moment, when he was endeavouring to show their futility.

It is plain, therefore, that the degradation, which is supposed to be implied by the absence of the Article, has no foundation in the tenor of the argument: I think it has as little in the expression of the Evangelist; but as doubts have arisen on the various forms of the phrase in question, I shall briefly notice them.

The phrase υἱοὶ Θεοῦ in the Plural, is sometimes used to signify *Saints* or *Holy Men:* but in the Singular, when it is spoken of Christ, there is no reason to infer that such is ever the meaning in the New Testament.

It is evident, that there can be only four combinations arising from the insertion or omission of the Article before υἱὸς and Θεοῦ. Ὁ υἱὸς Θεοῦ is never found, and it would scarcely have been Greek: ὁ υἱὸς τοῦ Θεοῦ is common, but is allowed to be meant in the highest acceptation: we need, therefore, consider only υἱὸς τοῦ Θεοῦ and υἱὸς Θεοῦ. Now there are instances, besides that which has given birth to this discussion, which prove incontestably, that υἱὸς τοῦ Θεοῦ was never meant to be taken in an inferior sense: i. e. on the supposition that Christ was ever declared to be the Son of God in the usual acceptation; which Campbell does not dispute. Thus, Mark i. 1. υἱὸς τοῦ Θεοῦ is spoken by the Evangelist himself of Jesus. John x. 36. the same phrase is employed by Christ himself of himself: and Matt. xxvii. 40. it is used by those, who well knew Christ's pretensions. Stronger proofs derived from the circumstances cannot be expected: for if Christ be admitted ever to be called the Son of God, we cannot believe that less would be affirmed of him in any of these examples.

Neither is υἱὸς Θεοῦ, without either of the Articles, to be taken in an inferior sense: for not to examine all the places in which it occurs, we have Matt. xxvii. 43. the crime laid to Christ, that he said, "I am the Son of God:" which the High Priests would hardly palliate. In Luke i. 35. the same phrase is affirmed of Christ by an Angel; and Rom. i. 4. of Christ by the Apostle Paul. It is plain from these proofs, that the presence or the absence of the Article does not determine the phrase to be used in a higher or lower sense.

Is it, then, to be concluded, that the Article may generally be used at pleasure? This is the very hypothesis which I would combat: but in this particular phrase there is a licence arising out of the nature of the word Θεός, (see on Luke i. 15.) and hence it will be allowable (see Part i. p. 36.) to write either ὁ υἱὸς τοῦ Θεοῦ or υἱὸς Θεοῦ indifferently: the former, however, is the more common. The reason why we meet with both σὺ εἶ Ὁ υἱὸς τοῦ Θεοῦ and σὺ εἶ υἱὸς τοῦ Θεοῦ, is that here two principles interfere: after Verbs Substantive the first Article should be omitted; yet where σὺ precedes, it is not unfrequently inserted: see Part i. p. 44.—The reason for adopting a particular form, where any reason can be assigned, will be noticed as the places occur. For example, in Luke i. 35. the phrase could not be ὁ υἱὸς τοῦ Θεοῦ, because of the Verb Nuncupative, after which the rule is strictly observed.

CHAPTER IV.

V. 4. ἄνθρωπος. Wetstein's C. D. E. &c. prefix the Article, and in the parallel passage, Luke iv. 4. the Article is found in the majority of MSS. As this is an exclusive Proposition (See Part i. Chap. iii. Sect. iii. § 5.) the Article would regularly be omitted. The passage, however, is quoted from the LXX. Deut. viii. 3. who have ὁ ἄνθρωπος, and on turning to the Heb. I found, as I expected, האדם.

V. 5. ἐπὶ τὸ πτερύγιον. There is no word, on the meaning of which the Commentators are more at variance, than πτερύγιον in this and the parallel place in St. Luke. One thing, however, appears certain, viz. that the Article shows πτερύγιον to be something *Monadic:* had there been several πτερύγια, we should probably have read TI πτερύγιον: it cannot, therefore, be "a pinnacle," as the English Version renders it. To determine what is really meant is, perhaps, impossible; since no instance can be found in any author, in which πτερύγιον is applied to a building. It is probable, however, from the meaning of the cognate term πτερόν, that a ridged or pointed roof is intended: for, from some of the passages collected by *Wetstein,* it is evident that πτερὸν is synonymous with ἀετὸς or ἀέτωμα, a term appropriated to the roofs of temples. See Aristoph. Aves 1110, and his Scholiast; Dion. Hal. Antiq. Rom. Edit. Reiske, vol. ii. p. 789; Josephus, vol. i. p. 109. edit. Huds. in which last place it is spoken of the Tabernacle, and so applied, as it should seem, on account of the figure, which the transverse section of a pointed roof, or the gable, presents. Now if this be πτερόν, analogy would lead us to infer, that πτερύγιον was the same thing, only of smaller dimensions: and therefore, if the pointed roof of the Temple be πτερόν, πτερύγιον may be the same kind of roof of the Great Eastern Porch: and this is the spot fixed upon by *Lightfoot.* The height of this roof was 385 feet, and therefore it is not ill adapted to the circumstances of the narration. However, Wetstein and Michaelis (*Anmerk.* ad loc.) understand it of the *Royal Porch,* which overlooked the precipice to the east and south of the Temple. This situation is, perhaps, even better suited to the history: but the difficulty is to account how the roof of this detached building could be called τὸ πτερύγιον τοῦ ἱεροῦ. Michaelis, indeed, in his Introduction (vol. i. p. 144. edit. Marsh) supposes πτερύγιον to have been a kind of *side-*

wall inclosing the Temple: but then there were several such porches or colonnades, each of which might thus be called πτερύγιον: but the πτερύγιον, as was shown, could be only one. On the whole, I have nothing more plausible to offer, than what has been suggested above. The extreme difficulty of the question is admitted by Mr. *Herbert Marsh* on the first part of Michaelis, vol. i. p. 420.

V. 15. ὁδὸν θαλάσσης. "This expression," says *Campbell*, "is rather indefinite and obscure." He appears, notwithstanding, to have given its true meaning; "near the sea." By this sea is plainly meant the sea of Gennesareth. But how happens it, if a particular sea be meant, that θαλάσσης has not the Article? The words are copied literally from the LXX. who have thus translated דרך הים, Isaiah ix. 1. The LXX. appear to have omitted the Article before θαλάσσης, from considering ὁδὸν in the light of a Preposition. Of דרך in the sense of *versus* examples may be found in *Noldius*.

V. 16. ἐν χώρᾳ καὶ σκιᾷ θανάτου, is also a quotation, though not an exact one; but the want of the Articles may be very well defended. See Part i. Chap. vi. § 1. and Chap. iii. Sect. iii. § 7.

V. 20. τὰ δίκτυα, *their* nets: a few MSS. with Syr. have αὐτῶν. See above, iii. 12.

V. 21. ἐν τῷ πλοίῳ. This may mean, in *their* boat: but as there are instances, in which the Article before πλοῖον cannot be so explained, the word will be examined below, xiii. 2.

CHAP. V.

V. 1. ἀνέβη εἰς τὸ ὄρος. This is the reading of all the MSS. Eng. Version and *Campbell* "a mountain." *Wakefield* says, "a particular mountain, well known in the neighbourhood of Capernaum." *Wetstein* and *Rosenmüller* make it definite: the former says, "τὸ ὄρος *significat certum et notum montem, Taborem intelligo.*" *Wolfius* remarks, "*in certum quendam montem, ut* Act. xvii. 1. ἡ συναγωγὴ τῶν Ἰουδαίων," which, however, is not parallel: but see the place. *Schleusner* has only "*montem ascendit*," which of course determines nothing. As no mountain has recently been mentioned,

CHAPTER V. 137

this passage is one among others, which are adduced to prove that the Greek Article is often without meaning. Archbishop *Newcome*, in his Revision of the English Version, 2 vols. 8vo. Dublin, 1796, observes on this place, " In the N. T. the Greek Article is often used without its proper force :" and he refers us to Matt. i. 23. v. 15. viii. 23. ix. 28. Mark xiv. 69. John i. 21. iii. 10. vii. 40. xviii. 3. and to Dr. *Scott* on Matt. i. 23. v. 15. viii. 4. To Dr. Scott's work I have not access: all these texts, however, shall be examined as they present themselves. In the present instance the Article admits a very certain explanation.

" *Judæi in Talmude*," says Reland, Palæst. vol. i. p. 306. " *terram suam in tria dividunt respectu MONTIUM, vallium et camporum.*" Τὸ ὄρος, then, will signify *the mountain district*, as distinguished from the other two. The LXX. have so employed the term. To mention only the following instance: in the destruction of Sodom and Gomorrah, *cities of the plain*, the Angels say to Lot, Gen. xix. 17. εἰς ΤΟ ὄρος σώζου, where no mountain has been mentioned, and none in particular can be meant. And that the LXX. intended to express "the mountain district," may be inferred from Joshua ii. 22, 23. where it is said of the spies, whom Rahab protected, ἦλθον εἰς τὴν ὀρεινήν, and of the same persons in the next verse, that after staying till the danger was over, κατέβησαν ἐκ ΤΟΥ ὄρους. The Article, therefore, in this place is neither without meaning, nor does it necessarily direct us to Mount Tabor: indeed, I am persuaded that Mount Tabor was not the scene of our Saviour's first preaching. If it be admitted that τὸ ὄρος may signify *the mountain district*, and if we attend to the topography of Galilee, it is highly probable that the sermon on the mount was delivered farther to the north. The whole of Palestine is intersected by a ridge of mountains running nearly in the direction of north and south. Now, if our Saviour's object was, as may reasonably be supposed, to lead his disciples into the nearest place of retirement, he would not conduct them to Mount Tabor, because the part of the ridge nearest to Capernaum was at a much less distance. Besides, had Tabor been meant, its name would surely have been mentioned, " *in primis*," as Reland says on a different occasion, " *quum Scriptores sacri adeò diligenter nomina locorum notent, in quibus aliquid memorabile à Christo patratum est.*" On the whole, I am of opinion, that this mountain has been fixed on merely from its celebrity, that thus the force of the Article might be most easily explained.

V. 3. τῷ πνεύματι. D—τῷ *a pr. manu*. The Article should be retained, if τὸ πνεῦμα here mean, as the best Commentators suppose, the sentient and thinking principle in man. So Acts xviii. 25. ζέων ΤΩι πνεύματι. So also in the present Chapter, v. 8. καθαροὶ ΤΗι καρδίᾳ, in *their* heart.

V. 9. οἱ εἰρηνοποιοί. The Article is wanting in two MSS. It is requisite. Part i. Chap. iii. Sect. ii. § 2.

V. 15. ὑπὸ τὸν μόδιον, τὴν λυχνίαν. Campbell vindicates the Article in this place by considering the bushel and the candlestick to be what I have denominated *Monadic* Nouns; one only of each would probably be found in a house: but his concession, that the Article is in some cases redundant, is more liberal than just.

V. 17. τὸν νόμον here clearly means the law of Moses, and this is the import of the term in the four Evangelists and the Acts: but on this word see below, Romans ii. 13.

V. 20. τῶν γραμματέων καὶ Φαρισαίων. That combinations of this kind do not interfere with the principle of the rule contended for by Mr. *Granville Sharp* will be evident from Part i. Chap. iii. Sect. iv. § 2.

V. 21. ἔνοχος τῇ κρίσει. Eng. Version, "to the judgment:" which to the unlearned may seem to signify the punishment of a future state. Campbell says, "to the judges." There can be no doubt that by ἡ κρίσις is meant some Court of Judicature, but not the Sanhedrim. *Schleusner* makes it to be the Court of Seven established in every principal town to decide petty causes. Wetstein understands it of the Court of Twenty-three. Between these two opinions there is probably no real difference. See *Lewis's Heb. Antiq.* vol. i. p. 67.

V. 22. τὴν γέενναν τοῦ πυρός. The second Article is requisite by Part i. Chap. iii. Sect. i. § 7.

V. 25. ὁ ἀντίδικος, ὁ κριτής, ὁ ὑπηρέτης, persons well-known in the courts of law.

V. 32. παρεκτὸς λόγου πορνείας. Part i. Chap. vi. § 1. and Chap. iii. Sect. iii. § 7.

Same v. ἀπολελυμένην. Not "her that is divorced" or dismissed, but *any one* that is divorced[1]. This distinction may appear frivolous, but the principle of the distinction is important. The force of the precept is, indeed, here the same; but that will not always happen. *Piscator* (see Bowyer's Conjectures) supposed τὴν to be wanting.

V. 34. ὅτι θρόνος ἐστὶ Θεοῦ. Here θρόνος is the Predicate, and οὐρανὸς understood the Subject; and so in the verses following: and yet nothing can be more definite than both θρόνος and Θεοῦ. Part I. Chap. iii. Sect. iv. § 1. and Chap. iii. Sect. iii. § 7.

V. 37. ἐκ τοῦ πονηροῦ. The Article here determines nothing, as has been supposed, respecting the question whether the meaning of these words be "of evil," or "from the Evil One:" the decision, however appears to be easy, if the opinion of the Syr. Translator be admitted as satisfactory evidence. The word which he has used in this place is ܒܝܫܐ, the same which he has employed for ὁ πονηρός, Matt. xiii. 19. and its undoubted cases, wherever they occur; and also for τοῦ διαβόλου, Acts x. 38. with which, therefore, τοῦ πονηροῦ in the verse before us is made to be synonymous. But τὸ πονηρόν, which is found only Rom. xii. 9. he has translated by ܒܝܫܬܐ, evil things; as in the same verse τῷ ἀγαθῷ is rendered "to good things." It is manifest, therefore, that in the judgment of the Syr. Translator the passage in question, as well as ἀπὸ τοῦ πονηροῦ in the Lord's Prayer and elsewhere, is to be interpreted of the Evil Spirit. And so, in the Lord's Prayer at least, the Fathers almost unanimously understood it. See *Suicer's Thes. Eccles.* vol. ii. p. 808. edit. 1728; a work, which I venture to recommend to the student in theology, as containing an immense fund of information on the subject of Christian Antiquities.

CHAP. VI.

V. 1. τὴν ἐλεημοσύνην ὑμῶν. *Rosenm.* says, "*Articulus* τὴν *et pronomen* ὑμῶν *adduntur, quia CERTA QUÆDAM GENERA virtutis significantur, in quibus colendis et exer-*

---

[1] Would not the correct translation rather be, "*when* she is divorced?" J. S.

cendis Christiani fugere ostentationem debent." The Article and Pronoun appear not to me to indicate any thing so recondite; but only to imply in our Saviour a presupposition, that his hearers did alms in some way or other; and his precept is, therefore, limited to the *manner* of doing them. "The liberality, which you and all men occasionally exercise, must be free from ostentation." This presupposition having once been signified, the phrase afterwards, v. 2, 3. falls into the more general form of the *Hendiadys*. Part I. Chap. v. Sect. ii. § 1.

Same v. ὑπὸ τῶν ἀνθρώπων. Men *generally*. Part i. Chap. iii. Sect. ii. § 2.

Same v. ἐν τοῖς οὐρανοῖς. D. 1. and a few of Matthäi want τοῖς. This also is a copious source of various readings arising from the anomaly noticed, Part i. Chap. vi. § 1.

V. 2. τὸν μισθὸν αὐτῶν. Mr. *Wakefield* (on St. Matt.) concludes his Note on this passage with a remark, of which I do not perceive the force. He observes, that "the Article prefixed to μισθὸν by the Evangelist, *the* or *this* reward, proves, in his opinion, that human applause, ὅπως δοξασθῶσιν, was intended." But the Article in this place is not to be rendered by *the* or *this*: it is used because of αὐτῶν following; for where a Pronoun depends on a Noun, the Article of that Noun is generally inserted. Of these insertions the N. T. will furnish, probably, a thousand examples: in the Lord's Prayer alone *six* occur. Such fanciful interpretations do much harm to the cause of criticism: from a professed scholar like Mr. W. they were not to be expected; and yet I shall have occasion to show, in several instances, that his notion of the uses of the Greek Article was not derived from attention to the Greek Writers.

V. 6. τῷ ἐν τῷ κρυπτῷ. Wetstein's D. 1. and Birch's Vind. Lamb. 31. and Esc. 11. want the first τῷ. The difference is, that the common reading makes the *Father* to be in secret; whilst the omission of the Article ascribes secrecy to the *worshipper*. Either reading affords good sense; but the received one appears to be preferable.

V. 10. ἐπὶ τῆς γῆς. *Origen* de Oratione, Birch's 1209. or Vat. and one or two others want τῆς: probably, says Wetstein, because " οὐρανῷ *Articulo caret*." After Prepositions, as has

CHAPTER VII. 141

been shown, the usage is anomalous: I think, however, that where Nouns are connected, as in this passage, the general practice is in favour of uniformity.

V. 19. σὴς καὶ βρῶσις. This will illustrate Part i. Chap. vi. § 2. In the next verse the Proposition is exclusive: *no* moth, &c.

V. 22. This verse affords an instance of a convertible Proposition. See Part i. Chap. iii. Sect. iv. § 1.

V. 24. ἢ ἑνὸς ἀνθέξεται. Mr. *Markland* (see Bowyer's Conjectures, 3d edit.) says, " Perhaps ΤΟΥ ἑνός, as Luke vii. 41. xvii. 34, 35, 36. xviii. 10. and yet the Article is wanting, Luke xvi. 13." A single MS. of Matthäi, but of inferior value, has τοῦ. The omission of the Article, therefore, must be considered as the true reading: but why should it be omitted before ἑνός, when in the preceding clause it was inserted before ἕνα? The answer seems to be, that εἷς opposed to ὁ ἕτερος usually takes the Article, where εἷς has not recently been mentioned: but if this practice were to be retained, where εἷς has recently occurred, the Article might be supposed to indicate *recent mention;* a purpose to which in ὁ εἷς it is frequently subservient. Now this objection does not apply to the passages which Mr. *Markland* has quoted in support of his conjecture, but does apply to Luke xvi. 13. which he admits to be against him. This word, however, I shall have occasion to examine more fully hereafter. See 1 John v. 8.

V. 28. τὰ κρίνα τοῦ ἀγροῦ. Supposed by *Michaelis* (Anmerk.) to be the *Crown Imperial*, a plant common in the meadows of the East.

V. 34. τὰ ἑαυτῆς. Many MSS. among which is Birch's 1209. or Vat. omit τά: but μεριμνᾶν elsewhere in the N. T. governs an Accusative, as 1 Cor. vii. 32, 33, 34. Phil. iv. 6.

CHAP. VII.

V. 6. τὸ ἅγιον τοῖς κυσί. This passage illustrates Part i. Chap. iii. Sect. ii. both §.

V. 17. τὸ δὲ σαπρὸν δένδρον. Eng. Version, " a corrupt tree." This is the sense: yet the Article here is not without meaning in the Greek, but is equivalent to πᾶν in the preceding clause. The Version might have been "*every* corrupt tree," as is evident from what was said of the hypothetical use of the Article, Part i. In the next verse neither πᾶν nor τὸ is used, because the Proposition is there exclusive.

V. 24. ἐπὶ τὴν πέτραν. Eng. Version and *Newcome*, "on a rock." *Campbell* and *Wakefield*, "on the rock," but without any remark. *Schleusner* says, "*fundamento ex lapidibus jacto.*" According to the first and last of these interpretations, it will be difficult to account for the presence of the Article. Schleusner, however, seems not in this instance to have given the meaning with his usual success: for in the parallel passage, Luke vi. 48. it is said, ἔθηκε θεμέλιον ἐπὶ τὴν πέτραν· where ἐπὶ τὴν πέτραν must certainly have a different meaning from that which Schleusner assigns it in the present verse; since no writer could speak of laying a foundation on a foundation of stones. But it is well known, and Schleusner admits, that in the parable of the Sower, Luke viii. 6. ἐπὶ τὴν πέτραν signifies *on the rocky* or *stony ground*, and he himself explains it by ἐπὶ τὸ πετρῶδες, Mark iv. 5. It can, therefore, hardly be doubted, that in this place also the words have a similar meaning, especially when we consider that the foolish man is said to build ἐπὶ τὴν ἄμμον. In St. Luke, though the moral is the same, the illustration is somewhat different. There the wise man builds his house, first laying a foundation on the rock: the foolish man builds ἐπὶ τὴν γῆν, and that too χωρὶς θεμελίου.—In these passages at least it is plain that θεμέλιον has not the meaning assigned to it, Apoc. xxi. 19, by Mr. *King*, in his most valuable *Munimenta Antiqua*, vol. ii. p. 9.

V. 25. ἡ βροχή, οἱ ποταμοί, &c. Part i. Chap. iii. Sect. i. § 5. *Bengel* (in his Gnomon) observes, "*Articulus significat pluviam non defuturam.*" When such a man could indulge in this fantastic criticism, it is surely time that the uses of the Article should be examined. Of this, indeed, he himself seems to have been sensible: he says, on Matt. xviii. 17. speaking of this very subject, "*Digna materies, quæ à Philologis curatiùs digeratur.*"

V. 29. ἐξουσίαν ἔχων. Hendiadys. Part i. Chap. v. Sect. ii. § 1. (Page 95.)

CHAPTER VIII.

CHAP. VIII.

V. 1. ἀπὸ τοῦ ὄρους. See above, v. 1.

V. 4. τῷ ἱερεῖ. To the officiating priest, not to the high priest, as supposed by *Wolfius*. The Syr. has, "to the priest." I cannot conceive why Dr. Scott (see above on v. 1.) should think the Article in this place superfluous.

V. 6. ἐν τῇ οἰκίᾳ. In *my* house, or at home.

V. 12. εἰς τὸ σκότος τὸ ἐξώτερον. See below, xxv. 30.

Same v. ἐκεῖ ἔσται ὁ κλαυθμὸς καὶ ὁ βρυγμὸς τῶν ὀδόντων. This is another of the passages which might induce an English reader, but superficially acquainted with the Greek language, to suppose that its Article may be inserted *ad libitum*. The expression occurs in the N. T. seven times, and always in the same form: the usage, therefore, cannot be supposed to be arbitrary: and the reason why the Articles are inserted is plain. The weeping and gnashing of teeth spoken of is that of the persons last mentioned; and the sense is, "there shall *they* weep and gnash *their* teeth." Without the Articles the Proposition would have asserted only that *some persons* should there weep; which falls short of the real meaning. Our English Translations, however, in general say nothing more. The *Complut*. omits the first Article, probably, because it had been observed that in Propositions, which merely affirm or deny existence, the Noun is commonly anarthrous. Part. i. Chap. iii. Sect. iii. § 1. Here, however, the case is different: the affirmation terminates not in ἔσται, but in ἐκεῖ. Bengel observes, "*Articulus insignis: in hâc vitâ dolor nondum est dolor.*" This is not much better than a remark of the same Critic quoted above, vii. 25.

V. 16. ὀψίας δὲ γενομένης. It being evening. The Article could not here be used. Part i. Chap. iii. Sect. iii. § 1.

V. 20. αἱ ἀλώπεκες. Part i. Chap. iii. Sect. ii. § 2.

Same v. ὁ υἱὸς τοῦ ἀνθρώπου. See John v. 27.

V. 23. ἐμβάντι εἰς τὸ πλοῖον. Wetstein's C. 1. Birch's Vat. 1209. and Vind. Lamb. 31. and three of Matthäi's MSS. —τό: but see below on xiii. 2. In this place, indeed, it may be the vessel *implied* above, ver. 18. in the order given to cross the Lake, which I find to have been the opinion of *Bengel:* and it is remarkable that one good MS. of Matthäi places this very verse immediately after ver. 18. Were this arrangement admissible, the reference of the Article would here be sufficiently plain.

V. 26. τοῖς ἀνέμοις καὶ τῇ θαλάσσῃ. Natural objects. Part i. Chap. iii. Sect. i. § 5.

V. 28. ἐκ τῶν μνημείων. These μνημεῖα were in the wildest and most unfrequented situations, amid rocks and mountains. Some idea of their form and arrangement may be gained from the νεκροπόλεις, as described and represented by *Denon* in his Travels in Egypt.

V. 29. πρὸ καιροῦ. Part i. Chap. vi. § 1.

V. 33. εἰς τὴν πόλιν. The obvious use of the Article in this place is to direct the mind to the city of the Gergesenes, Gerasenes, or Gadarenes, (whichever be the true reading) in whose territory Christ then was. *Michaelis*, indeed, (*Anmerk.* ad loc.) maintains, "that the city here meant is not that of Gadara or Gerasa, (Gergesa being only a conjecture of Origen's) because they both lie some miles distant from the sea; but that the town spoken of was the first which presented itself to our Saviour at his landing; the name of which, however, is not given by his Historians, probably, because they knew it not, having all of them been indebted for their information to others." This objection appears to me to have little or no support. In the 28th verse Γαδαρηνῶν is the reading which Michaelis and most critics prefer. Now the distance of Gadara from the border of the Lake was not so great as to authorize us to depart from the common interpretation. According to Josephus, as quoted by *Lightfoot* and *Reland*, from Gadara to Tiberias, which lay on the opposite side of the Lake, was a distance of sixty stadia; the width of the Lake was, on the same authority, forty stadia; the difference, therefore, or the distance of Gadara from the water side, will be less than two and a half English miles; or, supposing the Lake to be here below its average width, we may state the distance at three, or at most at four, English miles: and where is the improbability, that the persons who tended the swine, should carry the tidings of so extraordinary an event to a city, which was at no greater distance? especially when it is considered, that Gadara was the capital of Peræa, and,

CHAPTER IX.

therefore, a place of some importance. Thus far with respect to the circumstances of the case: but, further, I am persuaded that had any other city been meant, than the metropolis of the Gadarenes, the expression would not have been εἰς τὴν πόλιν. Of this indefinite use of so definite a phrase the N. T. furnishes no example. To pass over instances, in which Jerusalem is evidently meant, we find in John iv. 8. ἡ πόλις in reference to Sychar recently mentioned: Acts ix. 6. to Damascus: x. 9. to Joppa: xiv. 19. to Lystra: xvi. 13. to Philippi: and xvii. 5. to Thessalonica. On the contrary, where some city unknown or undeclared is spoken of, we read εἰς πόλιν and ἔν τινι πόλει, as in Luke i. 39. and xviii. 2. On the supposition, therefore, of Michaelis, it is probable that one of these latter forms would have been adopted in the passage under review.

It may be added in behalf of the reading Γαδαρηνῶν, which Michaelis states to be found only in the Syr. that it appears also in Birch's Vat. 1209. and in two MSS. of Matthäi: these readings, however, might be unknown to Michaelis, having been published only in the same year, in which his own work appeared.

V. 34. πᾶσα ἡ πόλις. Part i. Chap. vii. § 1.

CHAP. IX.

V. 1. εἰς τὸ πλοῖον. Wetstein's L. 1. and six others, with Origen, omit τό. So also five MSS. of Birch, including Vat. 1209, and also some of Matthäi's. The vessel, however, may be the same with that already mentioned, waiting to carry Christ back again. But see on πλοῖον below, xiii. 2.

V. 5. σοὶ αἱ ἁμαρτίαι. For σοὶ many MSS. have σοῦ, which Wetstein would admit into the Text. To me σοῦ appears to have been originally the correction of some one, who knew not that αἱ ἁμαρτίαι might signify " your sins:" and this conjecture is strengthened by the addition of σοῦ after ἁμαρτίαι in a few MSS., in both Syr. Versions, in the Æthiopic, Coptic, Origen, &c.

V. 15. ἐλεύσονται ἡμέραι. D. and two others αἱ ἡμέραι. This is an instance, in which, as in Propositions asserting existence, the Predicate is contained in the Verb. It is probable, therefore, that the common reading is the true one: at the same time it must be admitted, that there may be a reference anticipative of ὅταν following. In the parallel places the MSS. are without the Article.

V. 28. εἰς τὴν οἰκίαν. Abp. *Newcome* (see above on v. 1.) did not perceive that the Article in this place had any meaning. It is rightly explained by *Rosenmüller*, who says, " *eam nimirum domum, in quá Capernaumi consueverat habitare.*" Part i. Chap. iii. Sect. i. § 4.

V. 33. τοῦ δαιμονίου. In reference to δαιμόνιον implied in δαιμονιζομένου in the verse preceding. Part i. Chap. iii. Sect. i. § 1.

CHAP. X.

V. 1. πνευμάτων ἀκαθάρτων. Over them *generally*: but the Article is wanting by Part i. Chap. iii. Sect. iii. § 7.

V. 2. πρῶτος Σίμων ὁ λεγόμενος Πέτρος. The word πρῶτος, though found in all the MSS. and also in the Syriac, &c. has been supposed to be interpolated by some zealot, who wished to establish the Pope's primacy. The Papists, however, must be allowed the advantages, if there be any, arising from the undoubted authenticity of the reading: but, probably, more stress would have been laid on it, had it been preceded by the Article, to which their writers have ascribed considerable importance, though they have not always understood its use. (See on Matt. xxvi. 26. and on 2 Thessal. ii. 3.) Πρῶτος, however, being an ordinal is not the less definite by being anarthrous; Part. i. Chap. vi. § 3. and hence Campbell needed not to have apologized for rendering it "the first." Still there is nothing in this text to support the pretensions of the Prelates of Rome. It is a sufficient explanation of πρῶτος, that Peter was the Apostle first called to the ministry. Προτίθησι δέ, says Theophylact, as quoted by *Suicer*, Πέτρον καὶ Ἀνδρέαν, διότι καὶ πρωτόκλητοι. The same interpretation will apply also to the assurance, that Peter should be the rock on which Christ would found his Church; especially if we recollect that the same Apostle was destined to preach to that people, to whom the Covenant of Salvation was first to be proposed.

V. 4. ὁ Ἰσκαριώτης. Many MSS., especially of *Matthäi*, omit ὁ, and it is observable, that almost wherever the word occurs in the N. T. there is either a variation in the MSS. or the Article is wholly omitted. The meaning and origin of Ἰσκαριώτης no Commentator, whom I have seen, pretends satisfactorily to determine. The majority, among whom is Schleusner, suppose that it has reference to the town of *Kerioth*, mentioned in the O. T. I think, however, that the frequent absence of the Article authorizes a suspicion that the word is a surname, and not an epithet significant of a place of birth or residence; because in that case the Article should be prefixed, as in Μαρία ἡ Μαγδαληνή. Mark, indeed, (xv. 21.) has τινὰ Σίμωνα Κυρηναῖον· but this is only on the first mention, besides that τινὰ would make ΤΟΝ Κυρηναῖον absurd. I am not certain whether the same inference is not strengthened by the compound ἐπικαλούμενον, which we find used of the name Iscariot, Luke xxii. 3. and which, so far as I have observed, is confined, as in strictness it ought to be, to *surnames:* thus in the present verse ἐπικληθεὶς Θαδδαῖος.—Acts i. 23. ὃς ἐπεκλήθη Ἰοῦστος.—x. 5. ὃς ἐπικαλεῖται Πέτρος.—xii. 12. τοῦ ἐπικαλουμένου Μάρκου. If this notion be well founded, the Article in this verse and in every other, in which Ἰούδας precedes Ἰσκαριώτης, ought to be omitted. Some curious conjectures on the word may be seen in the works of the most learned *Lightfoot*, vol. ii. p. 176.

V. 5. εἰς ὁδὸν ἐθνῶν. Part i. Chap. vi. § 1. and Chap. iii. Sect. iii. § 7.

V. 8. ἀσθενοῦντας, λεπρούς, &c. without the Article, for not *all* the sick were healed, nor *all* lepers cleansed.

V. 15. ἐν ἡμέρᾳ κρίσεως. Mr. *Wakefield* (on St. Matt.) translates these words "in a day of judgment;" and he assures us in his N. T. that "this phrase has not the least reference to the day of general judgment." But it may be asked, what other judgment could at that time await Sodom and Gomorrha? These cities with their inhabitants had long since been exterminated, and were, therefore, no longer subject to temporal visitations. He quotes, indeed, in support of his opinion ἐν τῇ κρίσει, Luke x. 14. where, however, the expression is too plainly definite to admit any doubt, and where also the argument already adduced will apply with nearly equal propriety, Tyre and Sidon being then in ruins.—Since Mr. W., as appears from other parts of his Version, acknowledges a day of general retribution, all proofs of that doctrine would, so far as he is concerned, be superfluous. A late writer, however, who is said to have devoted forty years to the study of the Bible, could not discover, that the usually received doctrine of a day appointed for the judgment of *all* mankind by Christ in the presence of Angels, had any foundation in Scripture. See *Cappe's Remarks*, vol. ii. p. 278. How, then, are we to explain John v. 28, 29. Rom. ii. 16. and, not to instance other passages to the same purport, the circumstantial description beginning at Matt. xxv. 31?

V. 16. Here we have ὡς πρόβατα, but ὡς ΟΙ ὄφεις. It is not without reason, that even this apparently minute distinction is observed. *All* sheep are not supposed to be in the midst of wolves, but all serpents are assumed to be prudent.

V. 17. ἀπὸ τῶν ἀνθρώπων. Mr. *Markland* (See *Bowyer's* Conjectures) is of opinion, "that some *particular men* are intended; and accordingly τῶν ἀνθρώπων can possibly signify no other than *the men*, i. e. the Jews, as the reasoning requires: ΟΙ ἄνθρωποι, the Jews, as plainly appears from what follows: ἄνθρωποι, the Heathen, frequently in the three first Evangelists; not so in some parts of John, the Acts, and the Epistles, because the distinction had ceased before the writing of those pieces. So xvii. 22. παραδίδοσθαι εἰς χεῖρας ἀνθρώπων, of the Heathen, not ΤΩΝ ἀνθρώπων, which would have been of the Jews, and false: see Mark ix. 31. Luke ix. 44." I have given this Note at length, because the work from which it is taken is now somewhat scarce. It is not true, however, that in εἰς χεῖρας ἀνθρώπων any thing can be inferred from the absence of τῶν. (See Part i. Chap. vi. § 1. and Chap. iii. Sect. iii. § 7.) Nor can the learned Critic have been aware of the difficulties which would arise, if we should adopt his proposed distinction between ἄνθρωποι and οἱ ἄνθρωποι, even in the three first Evangelists. To go no further than to St. Matt. vi. 14. " if ye forgive *men* their trespasses:" vii. 12. " whatever ye wish that *men* should do unto you:" xiii. 25. " whilst *men* slept." In these places *men* must thus be understood to signify the Jews, to the exclusion of the Heathen: on the other hand, xv. 9. " teaching for doctrines the commandments of men;" xix. 26. " with men this is impossible;" *men* must here be taken exclusively to signify the Heathen: than which nothing can be more absurd.—With respect, however, to the passage in question, it is true, that τῶν ἀνθρώπων is more especially applicable to the Jews : but then this appears merely from the context, and not from any *emphasis* in the original, as Mr. *Wakefield* (St. Matt.) as well as Markland maintains¹. In this very Chapter, v. 32, we read of the consequences of denying Christ ἔμπροσθεν τῶν ἀνθρώπων, where there is the same supposed *energy of expression*, but where the meaning of οἱ ἄνθρωποι is adequately conveyed in our English phrase *the world*, as opposed to God, who is mentioned in the same verse. And generally, I think, the word ἄνθρωποι takes the Article, even where " no particular men " are meant, but only men indiscriminately, unless some of the alleged causes interfere ². The *inclusive* use of the Article has been noticed, Part I. Chap. iii. Sect. ii. § 2.

V. 23. εἰς τὴν ἄλλην. The Article here serves to mark the opposition between οὗτος and ἄλλος, two cities only being supposed, and is, therefore, not without meaning in the Greek.

V. 24. οὐκ ἔστι μαθητής. *No* disciple. Part I. Chap. iii. Sect. iii. § 5.

V. 28. καὶ ψυχὴν καὶ σῶμα. Many MSS. of Wetstein and some of Matthäi and Birch have ΤΗΝ ψυχὴν καὶ ΤΟ σῶμα, a reading, which doubtless originated from ignorance of the usage noticed, Part I. Chap. vi. § 2. The transcribers, not adverting to this, altered the reading from the preceding part of the verse.

V. 29. ἀσσαρίου. D. *à pr. manu* and Origen (*Griesb.* Symb. Crit. vol. i.) have τοῦ. This reading, though so feebly supported, is not altogether improbable, as there is a *correlation* between the δύο στρουθία and the ἀσσάριον, for which they are sold. The use of the Article in this sense is perfectly

---

[1] It may be worth mentioning that οἱ ἄνθρωποι is often used for "the enemies," in classical Greek. See Xen. An. IV. 2. 7. VII. 3. 43. and 47. H. J. R.

[2] In Xen. An. I. 7. 6. Krüger edit. οἱ ἄνθρωποι, Poppo and Bornemann omit the art. after several MSS. the sense being *men generally* (" where men cannot live for the heat.") On this omission see Bomem. and Xen. Symp. 11. 24. Buttman. Gr. Gramm. Maj. § 110. not. 3. Thiersch. § 306. 9. Stallbaum (on Plat. Protag. p. 355. A.) cites from p. 322. C. ἐρωτᾷ οὖν Ἑρμῆς Δία, τίνα οὖν τρόπον δοίη δίκην, καὶ αἰδῶ ἀνθρώποις, and within three or four lines, δίκην δὴ καὶ αἰδῶ οὕτω Ὁ φ ἐν τοῖς ἀνθρώποις. H. J. R.

classical. Thus *Demosth.* de Cor. § 30. τοὺς τριηράρχους αἱρεῖσθαι ἐπὶ ΤΗΝ τριήρη συνεκκαίδεκα.

V. 32. τῶν ἀνθρώπων. See above, ver. 17.

V. 36. ἐχθροὶ τοῦ ἀνθρώπου. Eng. Version has "a man's foes." If this be the whole meaning of τοῦ ἀνθρώπου, the force of the Article is not apparent. *Schleusner* explains τοῦ ἀνθρώπου by οἰκοδεσπότης. This, indeed, would be sufficiently definite; for the master of a family, when we are speaking of his domestics, is a pre-eminent person: with this, however, I am not satisfied, and that for the following reason. The passage before us is taken from Micah vii. 6. where the Hebrew is איבי איש אנשי ביתו. Here by איש Schleusner would, I suppose, understand οἰκοδεσπότης: but how did the LXX. interpret Micah? Their words are ἐχθροὶ πάντες ἀνδρὸς οἱ ἄνδρες οἱ ἐν τῷ οἴκῳ αὐτοῦ, "though some MSS." says *Breitinger* in Proleg. vol. iii. "have ἐχθροὶ ἀνδρὸς πάντες οἱ ἄνδρες, &c. *quæ genuina videtur lectio et Hebræo planè consona, nisi quòd vox πάντες sit adjecta, quæ tamen in Veteri Vers. τῶν O,* INIMICI HOMINIS VIRI DOMESTICI EJUS, *non comparet.*" Now though "*vox πάντες sit adjecta,*" it is not difficult to infer what was the reading which it has supplanted. The reader of this work will not, I hope, discover in it any rage for conjectural emendation: yet I cannot doubt, when I observe πάντες and compare the Hebrew, that the LXX. wrote, by the alteration of a single letter, παντὸς ἀνδρός: the *Omicron* and *Epsilon* of the Uncial MSS. are not dissimilar; and I thought it probable, when this Note was first written, that the late Dean of Winchester, Dr. *Holmes*, had Providence permitted him to advance so far in his most important undertaking, would have found this emendation confirmed. The passage of Micah is not contained in the remains of the Hexapla.

If this, then, be the true reading, it is "*Hebræo planè consona,*" without any "*nisi quòd*" whatever: איש, it is well known, commonly means *unusquisque;* the rendering, therefore, could not be closer than by παντὸς ἀνδρός. It is true, indeed, that the Vet. Vers. τῶν O discovers no very evident vestige even of παντός: yet it should be remembered that *hominis* is much nearer to παντὸς ἀνδρός, than is *viri* to πάντες οἱ ἄνδρες: in the one case the sense loses little or nothing;

in the other a great deal. Supposing, then, this conjecture to be admitted, what is the use to be made of it in the passage under review? It was reasonable to expect that the quotation in St. Matt. would bear a close resemblance to the Hebrew of Micah and to the Greek of the LXX.; and that the latter of these, if it did not exhibit the Article as we find it in St. Matt. would at least have something equivalent. This equivalent, I think, is παντός: and τοῦ ἀνθρώπου will then mean every man, or men generally, according to the hypothetic use of the Article so often noticed. In confirmation of this conclusion, the reader may turn to John ii. 24, 25. where he will find that our Saviour is said γινώσκειν πάντας, a truth which immediately afterwards is expressed by ἐγίνωσκε τί ἦν 'ΕΝ ΤΩι 'ΑΝΘΡΩΠΩι [1].

V. 37. πατέρα ἢ μητέρα. Without Articles. Part I. Chap. vi. § 2.

V. 41. μισθὸν προφήτου, not ΤΟΝ μισθόν. Part I. Chap. iii. Sect. iii. § 6.

CHAP. XI.

V. 3. ὁ ἐρχόμενος. The person confessedly expected.

V. 5. τυφλοί, χωλοί, λεπροί. See last Chap. ver. 8.

V. 8. οἱ τὰ μαλακὰ φοροῦντες. It is remarkable that so accurate a Greek scholar as Mr. *Toup* (See Bowyer's Conjectures) should here wish to expunge τά, not perceiving that the passages, which he adduces in support of his conjecture, have no bearing on the present question. That λευκὰ φορεῖν, ἀνθινὰ φορεῖν, &c. are the legitimate phrases in ordinary cases, nobody will dispute: but supposing that λευκὰ ἱμάτια had recently been spoken of, the phrase in such case would certainly be οἱ ΤΑ λευκὰ φοροῦντες· for the *assumption* respects not merely the act of wearing, but also the colour of the garments.

V. 11. ἐν γεννητοῖς γυναικῶν. D. alone *à pr. manu* has ἐν τοῖς γεννητοῖς τῶν γυναικῶν. This is evidently wrong, the Proposition being exclusive; *any* offspring of *any* women.

---

[1] Stallbaum (ad Plat. Protag. p. 355. A.) says that ἄνθρωπος is one of those words which, when used of the genus universally, *may be* without the Article. It is so in that place, while in p. 322. A. we have ἐπειδὴ δὲ ὁ ἄνθρωπος θείας μετέσχε μοίρας.

For the same reason we have in this v. μείζων, *any one* greater. Part I. Chap. iii. Sect. iii. § 5. An *Unknown Writer*, who, in a pamphlet entitled "*Six more Letters*," has attacked Messrs. *Sharp* and *Wordsworth* on their respective publications, and whose petulance is scarcely surpassed by his profound ignorance of the subject, gravely challenges his readers (at p. 24) to assign a reason why the Article was here omitted before γεννητοῖς. That the reason will be satisfactory, to him at least, is more than I dare hope: it is, that the Writer, or rather Translator, of St. Matthew's Gospel, understood Greek somewhat better than does the Author of the *Six more Letters*. See Part I. p. 36, 37. I shall take occasion to adduce other proofs of the Unknown Writer's extraordinary erudition: the tone of confidence and even of triumph, with which his remarks are delivered, gives them a claim to some consideration.

V. 12. βιασταί. D. alone (if we except a reading of Clem. Alex. in *Griesb*. Symb. Crit. vol. ii.) has ΟΙ βιασταί. Respecting the sense of this passage the Commentators are pretty equally divided. The two interpretations are these: βιασταί, says one party, are those who strive with all diligence to enter into the kingdom of Heaven, "who," says *Whitby*, "by their continual attendance on the doctrine of the Gospel preached to them, their care to understand it, and readiness to receive it, show their ardent desires to be made partakers of it." The other party contends, that by βιασταὶ are meant "*publicani et milites, qui concussionibus et rapinâ priùs vixerant*." Wetstein *ad loc*. The difference between these two opinions is sufficiently striking: but it has not been remarked, that the difference is precisely that which arises from the insertion or the omission of the Article: ΟΙ βιασταὶ will include a whole species or class, as was shown in Part I. whilst βιασταὶ will denote only *some individuals* of a class: so μάγοι, Matt. ii. 1. ἄγγελοι, iv. 11. and so Isocr. Panegyr. § 33. ἐν ᾗ ΚΑΤΑΠΟΝ-ΤΙΣΤΑΙ τὴν θάλατταν κατέχουσιν. The question therefore, is only, which of the two interpretations is more favoured by the omission of the Article. On the first supposition, then, i. e. if βιαστὴς be one, who is earnest in the pursuit of everlasting happiness, surely the whole class of such must be affirmed ἁρπάζειν τὴν βασιλείαν, and that too whether ἁρπάζειν

CHAPTER XI. 153

refer to the attempt or to the result : the attempt, indeed, is implied in βιαστής, and the result cannot be doubted, when we know, that to them, who ˙knock, it shall be opened. According, therefore, to the first interpretation, we should expect ΟΙ βιασταί, or the whole class, and even then the assertion would not amount to much.

But supposing the other interpretation to be right, what should we then expect? Not that *all* plunderers and extortioners should find their way into the kingdom of Heaven: that *any* such should be admitted therein might at first be matter of surprise : at any rate we should expect the proposition to be limited, i. e. that the reading would be simply βιασταί. Since, therefore, this is the reading of the MSS. with the exceptions above stated, and since the Article, if it were found in more MSS. would not admit a very easy explanation, we must conclude that βιασταί, meaning persons hitherto of irregular lives, came from the Evangelist.—It is remarkable that Schleusner, who adopts the other explanation, has twice quoted the passage (viz. under βιαστής and ἁρπάζω) ΟΙ βιασταί, whether from accident, or whether he adopted the various reading, I know not. *Michaelis* (in his *Anmerkungen*) understands the place as I do ; provided, he adds, that no mistake has been committed by the Greek Translator of Matthew's Hebrew original.˙ His suspicion arises from a trifling discrepancy between this and the parallel passage in St. Luke xvi. 16. where, however, the word βιαστὴς does not occur, being in the N. T. ἅπαξ λεγόμενον. It is once found in *Philo*.

V. 19. ἡ σοφία. For the personification of Abstract Nouns, see Part I. Chap. v. Sect. i. § 2.

V. 22. ἐν ἡμέρᾳ κρίσεως. See above, x. 15.

V. 23. ἕως τοῦ οὐρανοῦ .... ἕως ᾅδου. A very few MSS. omit τοῦ before οὐρανοῦ, probably with a view to uniformity with what follows. There is, however, this difference, that οὐρανὸς in the N. T. is used equally in all its cases, whilst ᾅδης occurs chiefly in the Oblique cases after Prepositions, which may have caused the Article to be omitted.

V. 25. νηπίοις. Without the Article. In the *inclusive* form the affirmation would not have been true.

V. 29. τῇ καρδίᾳ, in *my* heart. Part I. Chap. iii. Sect. i. § 4.

CHAP. XII.

V. 1. τοῖς σάββασι. D. alone of all the MSS.—τοῖς. This word usually takes the Article, unless where there is an especial reason for dispensing with it.

V. 7. τοὺς ἀναιτίους. Without the Article the Proposition would have been exclusive, and would thus have denied more than the circumstances required. The guiltless persons meant are only Christ and his Apostles.

V. 10. ἦν τὴν χεῖρα. C. Vers. Copt. and Birch's Vat. 1209. —ἦν τήν: a very probable reading, though the received one has nothing objectionable; *his* hand, as elsewhere.

V. 12. ἄνθρωπος προβάτου. D, which is so often singular with respect to the Article, has τοῦ προβάτου. This must be wrong: for though πρόβατον has been mentioned before, there is no reference to it: the assertion is of *any* man and *any* sheep.

V. 20. τὴν κρίσιν. It is now generally agreed, that κρίσις, which in the Hebrew is משפט (See Isaiah xlii. 3.) is here used, like that word, to signify a divine law or rule of life: and it has been well shown by *Raphel*, vol. i. *ad loc.* from Polybius and Plato's Epistles, that ἐκβάλλειν εἰς νῖκος may mean *to render victorious*: whence the whole will signify, Till he make his Gospel triumphant. I affix this meaning to the Article, observing, that one MS. of Wetstein, seven of Matthäi, one of Griesbach (Symb. Crit.) and Philox-Syr. according to Birch, add αὐτοῦ, which, though unnecessary, shows in what sense the Article was here understood. Part I. Chap. iii. Sect. i. § 4.

V. 24. τὰ δαιμόνια. Not all Demons; but those whom he does cast out, he casts out through the aid of Beelzebub.

V. 28. ἐν πνεύματι Θεοῦ. This may signify no more than *by divine co-operation:* and if so, πνεῦμα is here used in the fifth of the senses assigned it on Matt. i. 18.

V. 29. εἰς τὴν οἰκίαν τοῦ ἰσχυροῦ. Mr. *Wakefield* in his St. Matt. observes " the strong person, not ἰσχυροῦ simply without the Article, because it has a more particular reference to Satan mentioned above." And in his N. T. published subsequently, he says " τοῦ ἰσχυροῦ, i. e. Satan." According to

CHAPTER XII. 155

Wolfius, Vitringa (on Isaiah) entertained the same opinion. A comparison, however, of the parallel place, Luke xi. 21, 22. will show that Satan is not here meant : for there we find mention of ὁ ἰσχυρότερος, which destroys the notion that ὁ ἰσχυρὸς was meant κατ' ἐξοχήν : neither am I aware that גבר is ever so employed in the O. T. The Article need not create any difficulty : *Rosenm.* indeed says, that it here has "*significationem indefinitam ;*" and *Schleusner* has something similar : but its true use in this place is no other than that which I have denominated the *hypothetic*, and which I have shown to be, like most other uses of the Article, as old as the age of Homer. Part I. p. 41 [1].

V. 32. κατὰ τοῦ πνεύματος τοῦ ἁγίου. D. alone *à pr. manu* —second τοῦ. This is evidently wrong : for not only does it contradict what was shown, Part I. Chap. viii. § 1. but is also foreign from the practice of the whole N. T. The meaning of πνεῦμα ἅγιον in this place is not absolutely determined by the Article, though it is evidently used either in the personal or fourth meaning, deduced Matt. i. 18. or else according to the fifth sense, to signify the Holy Influence. The context, however, determines at once in favour of the former of these, as is plain from τὸ πνεῦμα τὸ ἅγιον being used in opposition to ὁ υἱὸς τοῦ Θεοῦ in the preceding part of the verse : for an antithesis between a person and an influence would be unnatural. Τὸ πνεῦμα, therefore, in the last verse was also used in the personal sense.

V. 35. ὁ ἀγαθὸς ἄνθρωπος. D. alone *à pr. manu*—ὁ. The Article is here employed hypothetically.

Same v. τὰ ἀγαθὰ, followed by πονηρὰ without the Article. This difference has occasioned some critical discussion. *Markland* (see Bowyer) says, " perhaps τὰ πονηρά :" but adds, referring to *Casaubon's* Notes on the N. T. " such is the difference of the use of the Article in the Greek tongue, *good things* with the Article, *evil things* without it." The name of *Casaubon* must ever command respect ; and the reader, who otherwise might smile at this whimsical distinction, will probably forbear, supposing that Casaubon has authorized the remark. He has, indeed, said, "*notetur diversitas Articuli adjecti et*

---

[1] Winer adopts this as usual without acknowledgment. H. J. R.

omissi," but he has not shown wherein lies the diversity of meaning. *Raphel,* however, (*ad loc.*) explains it to be, that the mind of the one person must be understood to be wholly bad, whilst that of the other has only some admixture of evil; wherefore care is to be taken, that those things alone, which are good, be brought forth, and that the evil things be kept back. That this was Casaubon's meaning is more than I can readily believe: but supposing it to be so, still I cannot perceive that the distinction is well founded: and *Raphel's* illustrations, though often of great value, here illustrate nothing. I am persuaded, however, that no such difference, as that which our received Text now exhibits, originally existed; that either both ἀγαθὰ and πονηρὰ had the Article, or that both were without it: and of these the latter is by far the more probable; for the *assumption,* that the things brought forth, were good, is scarcely allowable, this being the very thing to be *asserted.* The MSS. though some few have τὰ πονηρά, are much more strongly in favour of my supposition: no less than twenty-seven of Wetstein, ten of Birch, including Vat. 1209, and fifteen of Matthäi, among which are several of his best, omitting τὰ before ἀγαθά. In the parallel passage, Luke vi. 45. we have τὸ ἀγαθὸν and τὸ πονηρόν: but Adjectives in the Neuter Singular, used in the abstract sense, require the Article. See Part I. Chap. iii. Sect. i. § 6. *Raphel,* however, would account for τὸ πονηρὸν by supposing the persons spoken of in one Evangelist to be less worthless and abandoned than those mentioned in the other. Both solutions are plainly *ejusdem farinæ.*

V. 41. ἄνδρες Νινευῖται. Men of Nineveh: οἱ ἄνδρες οἱ would not have been true [1].

Same v. ἐν τῇ κρίσει. Not the day of general judgment, says *Wakefield:* but see above, on x. 15.

V. 42. βασίλισσα νότου. English Version, "The Queen of the South." This translation would lead the reader to look for something more definite in the original: yet the original is more natural than our Version. "A Queen of Arabia," says our Saviour, "a mere barbarian, shall rise up in judgment against this generation, whose calls to repentance, though in-

---

[1] This is a mistake. See on Luke xi. 30.

CHAPTER XII.

effectual, have been so much more urgent." The allusion, it is true, is to the Princess recorded in 1 Kings x. 1. but the reference was not necessary, especially when the event alluded to had happened so many centuries before. Indeed the insertion of the Article would rather have directed the mind of the hearer to some Queen then living; whilst the omission would leave him at liberty to make the intended application. Thus I might speak of it as an historical fact, that a Roman Emperor had died at York. I should evidently allude to *Severus*[1]; but I should not think of giving my expression a more definite form.
—Νότος in N. T. is always anarthrous, being considered as a Proper Name.

Same v. Σολομῶντος. D. has τοῦ, which is neither necessary nor very usual in the regimen of Proper Names. Part I. p. 51.

V. 43. ὅταν δὲ τὸ ἀκάθαρτον πνεῦμα ἐξέλθῃ ἀπὸ τοῦ ἀνθρώπου. Mr. *Wakefield*, deviating from our Eng. Version, has, "when the unclean spirit is gone out from *the* man," which certainly is close to the original, but is perhaps scarcely compatible with the idiom of our language. Be this as it may, the case before us is analogous to that of regimen, in which τὸ ἀκάθαρτον πνεῦμα ἀνθρώπου would scarcely, for the reasons already assigned, be allowable in Greek. But, it may be asked, might not both the Articles have been omitted in the place in question? No doubt, they might: and the only difference would have been, that what is now affirmed universally, would then have been asserted only in a single instance; which instance, however, not being particularly selected, would leave the mind to infer, that in other instances also the same will be true. This process is well known to Logicians by the name of *Induction*. I have observed, however, that the genius of the Greek language is, in this respect, unlike our own: it usually precludes the necessity of induction, by asserting all, which could be thus inferred; whilst our own tongue loves to assert the proposed truth only of a single example, and leaves it to the hearer to form the general conclusion. Accordingly *Camp-*

---

[1] No. Constantius also died at York. *Author's MS.* But the grammatical principle contended for in the text is easily intelligible, notwithstanding this slight historical error in the hypothesis. J. S.

bell has, I think, in strict conformity with the idiom of our language, rendered this place, "*an* unclean spirit, when he is gone out of *a* man." Of the Greek form the N. T. has other examples: thus, Matt. xv. 11. οὐ τὸ εἰσερχόμενον εἰς τὸ στόμα κοινοῖ ΤΟΝ ἄνθρωπον, and so also Mark vii. 15. ἔξωθεν ΤΟΥ ἀνθρώπου.

V. 50. ἀδελφὸς καὶ ἀδελφὴ καὶ μήτηρ. This does not contradict what was said above on vi. 3: the Article before ἀδελφὸς is rightly omitted, because of ἐστί: Part I. Chap. iii. Sect. iii. § 2. Instances similar to the present will be adduced on John viii. 44. second Note.

CHAP. XIII.

V. 1. ἀπὸ τῆς οἰκίας. From *his* house. The meaning can be no other than the house, in which our Saviour dwelt at Capernaum. See on ix. 28.

V. 2. εἰς τὸ πλοῖον. In this and in some other places of the Evangelists we have πλοῖον with the Article; the force, however, of which is not immediately obvious. In the present instance, English Version, Newcome and Campbell understand τὸ πλοῖον indefinitely; but that *any ship*, without reference, can be meant by this phrase is grammatically impossible. Many Philologists, indeed, have adduced this passage among others, to show that the Article is sometimes without meaning: but this proves only that its meaning was sometimes unknown to them. Accordingly, *Rosenm.* says, " *Navem aliquam; nam Articulus τὸ hic indefinitè sumitur;*" and *Schleusner* is of the same opinion. There is not, however, as has been shown in this work, any such thing as an indefinite sense of the Article; that, which has sometimes been so denominated, being no other than its *hypothetic* use, explained Part I. Chap. iii. Sect. ii. which is wholly inapplicable to the present case. Mr. *Wakefield* observes in his N. T. "A particular vessel is uniformly specified. It seems to have been kept on the Lake for the use of Jesus and the Apostles. It probably belonged to some of the fishermen (see iv. 22.) who, I should think, occasionally, at least, continued to follow their former occupation: see John xxi. 3." Thus far Mr. W. whose solution carried with it an air of strong probability: and when we look at Mark iii. 9. which appears to have escaped him, his conjecture becomes absolute certainty; for there our Saviour is said to have directed, that a small vessel *should constantly be in waiting for Him*, προσκαρτερῇ αὐτῷ. Moreover, I think we may discover to whom the vessel belonged. In one Evangelist, Luke v. 3. we find a ship used by our Saviour for the very purpose here mentioned, declared expressly to be Simon's: and afterwards in the same Evangelist, viii. 22. we have τὸ πλοῖον definitely, as if it were intended, that the reader should understand it of the ship already spoken of. It is, therefore, not improbable that in the other Evangelists also, the vessel so frequently used by our Saviour was that belonging to Peter and Andrew.—It is observable, that in most of the passages, in which the received Text has τὸ πλοῖον, some MSS. want the Article. In the present instance Wetstein's important MS. C. 1. with six of Matthäi, and two of *Griesbach*, (Symb. Crit.)—τό. This omission can be accounted for only by supposing it to have been originally the emendation of some one, to whom the force of the Article was not apparent.—I observe that *Bengel* (in Gnom.) has remarked, "*Articulus navem innuit ibi haberi solitam.*"

V. 3. ὁ σπείρων. English Version, "A Sower." *Campbell*, "The Sower." And the latter observes, "The Article here is, in my opinion, not without design, as it suggests that the application is eminently to one individual." *Schleusner* and *Rosenmüller* make it synonymous with τίς, " answering," says Rosenm. " to the Hebrew ה prefixed to Verbs and Participles; for the poverty of their language compelled the Hebrews to use participles in the place of Verbal Nouns." Amid this diversity of opinion, one thing at least is certain, that the Article is placed here, not without design, since three of the Evangelists, i. e. all who have the Parable, make use of the same expression. That the Hebrews employ the Participle *Benoni* in place of a Substantive, as mentioned by Rosenmüller, is well known; but it is not true, that the Participles, so used as Substantives, necessarily have the ה prefixed: in proof of which, if the reader have any doubt, he may consult Psalm cxxix. 7. and Prov. xxii. 8, where the Participles קוצר and זורע are both without ה. It cannot, therefore, be inferred, that in ὁ σπείρων the Article is inserted in compliance with the Hebrew usage: and when we observe, that in both the cited passages the LXX. thought the Article necessary in their Version, (for they have Ὁ θερίζων and Ὁ σπείρων) though they found it not in their original, surely we should say that the idiom is Greek, rather than that it is Hebrew: and I take this to be the truth; for σπείρων without the Article in the sense of σπορεύς, a word unknown to the LXX. as well as to the Writers of the N. T. would certainly not be warranted. The Article, therefore, in this place is not, as has been contended, without its use, since it serves to give σπείρων the force and nature of a Substantive, as Campbell supposes, if I rightly understand him: for without doubt σπορεύς τις, had the word been used, would have accurately conveyed the meaning.

V. 6. ἡλίου δὲ ἀνατείλαντος. D. alone has τοῦ δὲ ἡλίου. There are several instances, even in the classical Writers, in which ἥλιος wants the Article; and the reason seems to be, that it is one of those Nouns, which, as *Taylor* on *Æschines* somewhere observes, *inter nomina Propria et Appellativa æqualiter librantur*. In the N. T. it sometimes wants the Article; not only after Prepositions and in anarthrous regimen, but also in some Genitives absolute; in which, as in the present instance, the case differs little from Propositions asserting only existence. The same remark will hold of most of the Propositions, which express merely *the time*, when an event is said to happen: so Acts xvi. 35. ἡμέρας δὲ γενομένης. Matt. xiv. 6. γενεσίων ἀγομένων. Luke xxiii. 54. σάββατον ἐπέφωσκε. See on John v. 1 [1].

V. 14. ἡ προφητεία Ἡσαΐου ἡ λέγουσα. D alone has τοῦ Ἡσ. λέγουσα. Nothing, however, is more common than the

---

[1] Krüger (on Xen. Anab. II. 10. 15.) observes that the article is usually omitted when the word, as in that place, is joined with δύομαι. But he might have spoken more generally. Indeed of the six other instances which he adduces from the Anabasis, one is ἡλίου δύνοντος (II. 2, 3.), one is ἥλιος ἦν ἐπὶ δυσμαῖς (VII. 3. 34.), and the others are ἅμα ἡλίῳ δύνοντι (II. 11. 13.), ἀνίσχοντι (II. 1. 3.), ἀνατέλλοντι (II. 3. 1.), περὶ ἡλίου δυσμὰς (VI. 3. 32.). I observe ἡμέρα ἐγένετο, Xen. An. II. 2. 13. When the reader sees assertions in modern critics that the art. is omitted with *many* nouns (as in Ast. ad Plat. Prot. p. 19.), he will find on examination that most or all of them admit of explanations, as in these cases. See prefatory remarks. H. J. R.

omission of the Article before Proper Names, even when they are governed by Nouns, which have the Article prefixed. Λέγουσα is anarthrous also in two MSS. of Matthäi; which, however, is probably wrong, because the writer would naturally assume that the Prophecy was known to contain the words in question.

V. 16. οἱ ὀφθαλμοί, τὰ ὦτα. Here D wants οἱ and τά, and that without the support of any other MS. It is but rarely that Nouns governing Pronouns in the Genitive are anarthrous. See above on vi. 3.

V. 23. ὁ ἀκούων καὶ συνιών. Spoken of the same person. Part I. Chap. iii. Sect. iv. § 2.

V. 25. ἐν τῷ καθεύδειν τοὺς ἀνθρώπους. *Wakefield* (St. Matt.) observes, "the servants, whose business it was to take care of the field; or the phraseology may be after the Hebrew manner, and mean in general, *during the time of sleep.*" The expression is certainly in the inclusive form, marked by the Article prefixed; but the phraseology is not more that of the Hebrew language, than it is of every other. The Author of the *Night Thoughts* in a celebrated passage has employed the same mode of speech, without regard to the correctness, which philosophy exacts:

> " Night, sable Goddess! from her ebon throne,
> In rayless majesty, now stretches forth
> Her leaden sceptre o'er *a slumb'ring world.*
> Nor eye, nor list'ning ear, an object finds;
> *Creation* sleeps." NIGHT I.

V. 27. ἔχει τὰ ζιζάνια. A great many MSS. of *Wetstein* and *Matthäi*, and some of the best of *Birch*, omit τά. This is probably right: the servants would express their surprise rather at there being *any* tares (darnel) at all, than at the particular tares in question: Wetstein, therefore, and Griesbach, would properly omit the Article [1].

V. 30. ἐν τῷ καιρῷ τοῦ θερισμοῦ. Here also very many MSS. including several of the best, omit τῷ, and Wetstein approves the omission: but in this place I think the omission wrong, because of ΤΟΥ θερισμοῦ following: for the reader will observe, that governing Nouns having become anarthrous on

---

[1] It may be observed, however, that the Article may either be inserted or omitted with perfect correctness; not because there is any laxity in the use of it, but because a different form of expression is used accordingly as it is used or omitted. H. J. R.

M

account of preceding Prepositions, usually [1] impart the same form to those which they govern: had we read ἐν καιρῷ θερισμοῦ, there could have been no doubt. See below, ver. 35.

V. 32. πάντων τῶν σπερμάτων. D and Vind. Lamb. 31. —τῶν. See Part i. Chap. vii. § 2.

V. 35. ἀπὸ καταβολῆς κόσμου. Part I. Chap. vi. § 1. and Chap. iii. Sect. iii. § 7.

V. 38. ὁ δὲ ἀγρός ἐστιν ὁ κόσμος. This is a convertible Proposition; and yet in the next verse συντέλεια and ἄγγελοι want the Article: we find, indeed, in eight of Matthäi's MSS. Ἡ συντέλεια, which is not an improbable reading, though in *Abstract Nouns*, as has been shown, the Article is less necessary than in others: but in ἄγγελοι the same licence is not allowed; and we certainly ought to render, "the reapers are angels," notwithstanding that in other places, as in ver. 49. of this Chap. and in xxv. 31. the task here spoken of is assigned to the angels generally.

Same v. τοῦ πονηροῦ. Satan. See above on v. 37.

V. 42. ὁ βρυγμὸς τῶν ὀδόντων. See on viii. 12.

V. 44. ἐν τῷ ἀγρῷ. Some MSS. principally seventeen of Matthäi's,—τῷ. It is wanting also in Chrysostom, *probante Bengelio*. The Article seems to have been originally inserted from the frequent use of Ὁ ἀγρὸς in the sense of "the country," and not from its being necessary in this place: here it must signify *an estate* or *farm*, as is evident from τὸν ἀγρὸν ἐκεῖνον following. It may not be amiss to remark, that *Matthäi's* MSS. are very important in restoring the true readings of the Article, as might be expected, from their being principally of Greek origin, or of the *Byzantine edition* [2]. And conversely, if we had known nothing of the Writers of these MSS. it might have been inferred, that for the most part they were natives of countries where Greek was well understood, from their frequent correctness in the use of the Article where the MSS. of other editions are faulty. It is true that the *Codex Bezæ* is among the MSS. which have ἐν ἀγρῷ: but of that MS. more will be said in an APPENDIX.

[1] See note on p. 49. H. J. R.

[2] I have here asserted that Matthäi's MSS. are of the Byzantine edition. I did this on the authority of *Michaelis*, Introd. Vol. II. p. 117. This, however, Matthäi himself, on Matt. xxi. 4. positively denies: the dispute is not *hujusce loci nec temporis*.

CHAP. XIV.

V. 2. διὰ τοῦτο αἱ δυνάμεις ἐνεργοῦσιν ἐν αὐτῷ. English Version has, "therefore mighty works do show forth themselves in him." *Newcome* adopts the marginal reading, "are wrought by him." *Wakefield*, (N. T.) "these powers are active in him." The German of *Michaelis* signifies, "and therefore he works miracles." So also *Beausobre:* and *Schleusner* is nearly to the same effect. If, however, it be the object of the Proposition to declare that miracles are wrought by John, it is rather unnatural that their existence should be *assumed*. I think, therefore, that the Article in this place, combined with other circumstances, directs us to further inquiry.

First, there is something remarkable in the sense, which the Commentators, with the exception of *Wakefield* (whose Version, however, I had not seen when this note was first written), ascribe to ἐνεργοῦσιν. Our own Version of the passage seems to be founded on a *lectio singularis* à pr. manu of D, viz. ἐναργοῦσιν, a word, indeed, which wants authority, but which, if it existed, would be deducible from ἐναργής : and when we consider that the Codex Bezæ was presented to the University of Cambridge only about twenty-six years before our present Version was made, it is not altogether improbable that this reading might have been thought of great importance [1]. The other Translators (Wakefield excepted) appear to take ἐνεργεῖν *passively;* whereas it is every where in the N. T. used in a *transitive* or an *absolute* sense ; where the passive is required, we have ἐνεργεῖσθαι. But further, not only is the sense either transitive or at least absolute, but the action is usually referred to some being of extraordinary power ; either to *God*, as 1 Cor. xii. 6. ; Gal. ii. 8. iii. 5. ; Ephes. i. 11. 20. ; Philipp. ii. 13. ; or to the *Holy Spirit*, as 1 Cor. x. 11. ; or to the *Devil*, as Ephes. ii. 2. ; and these are the only instances in which the active Verb occurs, except indeed that in Philipp. ii. 13. we have τὸ θέλειν καὶ τὸ ἐνεργεῖν applied to *men*. The parallel

---

[1] On a better acquaintance with the Codex Bezæ, I think it probable that ἐναργοῦσιν is not a various reading, but is to be ascribed solely to the copyist's mode of spelling : still, however, our translators might consider it as a distinct reading.

passage in Mark is, of course, out of the question. Hence we are led to infer, that in the place also under review, ἐνεργοῦσιν is used in an absolute sense, and that,

Secondly, αἱ δυνάμεις must be some kind of Agents: and that spiritual Agents were so denominated, there can be no doubt. In a curious, but somewhat neglected passage of *Eusebius Præp. Evang.* vii. 15. where he speaks of a *Jewish Trinity*, he tells us that " all the Hebrew Theologians next to God, who is over all, and Wisdom his First-born, ascribe Divinity to (ἀποθειάζουσιν) τὴν τρίτην καὶ ἁγίαν ΔΥΝΑΜΙΝ, whom they call The Holy Spirit, and by whom the inspired men of old were illumined." And again, *Demonst. Evang.* iv. 9. he says, " ΔΥΝΑΜΕΣΙ χθονίαις καὶ πονηροῖς πνεύμασιν ὁ πᾶς τῶν ἀνθρώπων βίος κατεδεδούλωτο." And several others of the Fathers employ the word in the same sense. It is plain, therefore, that δύναμις may be a Spirit either good or bad: and in this manner it is used in the N. T. Compare Ephes. vi. 12. where, indeed, δύναμις does not occur, with Ephes. i. 21. where δύναμις is associated with some of the words in the first-mentioned passage, and with others of similar import, and where Schleusner admits, though his own opinion seems not to be decided, that δυνάμεις is there generally understood of Angels. Such also is probably the meaning of the word, Rom. viii. 38.

It can hardly be doubted, then, that the passage under review, and consequently the parallel one, Mark vi. 14. should be rendered, " the Powers or Spirits are active in him." Mr. Wakefield, by rendering "*these* Powers," has shown that he understood the passage somewhat differently from the manner here proposed.—We are to consider that Herod was a Sadducee, and that he had hitherto believed neither in a resurrection nor in the agency of Spirits. His remorse, however, and his fears, for the moment at least, shake his infidelity; and he involuntarily renounces the two great principles of his sect.

In this way of understanding the passage, the Article may be accounted for as in οἱ ἄγγελοι.

V. 6. γενεσίων ἀγομένων τοῦ Ἡρώδου. This is another instance coming under the head of Propositions of Existence. Part i. Chap. iii. Sect. iii. § 1.

V. 11. ἐπὶ πίνακι. D and 1. have ἐπὶ τῷ πίνακι, which in

CHAPTER XIV. 165

D at least is remarkable, because that MS. at ver. 8, to which τῷ would have reference, wants the words ἐπὶ πίνακι: but the *Cod. Bezæ* sets Criticism at defiance.

V. 15. ὀψίας γενομένης. Part I. Chap. iii. Sect. iii. § 1. So also below, ver. 23.

V. 22. εἰς τὸ πλοῖον. A few MSS. including Vat. 1209—τό. See above, xiii. 2.

V. 23. εἰς τὸ ὄρος. See above v. 1.

V. 25. τετάρτῃ δὲ φυλακῇ. See on Ordinals, Part i. Chap. vi. § 3.

V. 30. τὸν ἄνεμον ἰσχυρόν. This is not an objection to what was advanced, Part I. Chap. viii. § 1. Similar instances were adduced, p. 144.

V. 33. ἀληθῶς Θεοῦ υἱὸς εἶ. Several Translators and Critics understand this to signify only, "Thou art a son of God." That the want of the Articles affords no ground for such an interpretation, has been generally proved above, on iv. 3.; but it may not be amiss briefly to notice the particular circumstances of this passage. It is conjectured by some Commentators, that the mariners who made this declaration were Pagans ; for which supposition, however, I find not the least support: and *Wetstein*, who favours this conjecture, adds, that there is no reason to believe that even the Apostles did as yet recognize the Divinity of Christ. By way of parallelism he adduces the common Heathen phrase προσκυνεῖν ὡς ΘΕΟΝ: he should have quoted some instances of ὡς υἱὸν Θεοῦ, or rather of υἱὸς εἶ Θεοῦ, as an expression of vulgar admiration: for ὡς Θεὸν is no parallelism at all ; and his not having produced any such instance affords a tolerable presumption, considering his immense range of reading, and his eagerness to correct extravagant conceptions of the dignity of Christ, that no such instance exists. The inscription adduced by him (on John i. 1.) αὐτοκράτωρ Καῖσαρ, ΘΕΟΥ Ἀδριανοῦ ΥΙΟΣ, ΘΕΟΥ Τραϊανοῦ ΥΙΩΝΟΣ, κ. τ. λ. proves only what every one knows, that the Roman Emperors were after death called *Divi;* and that frequently they had sons, grandsons, &c. like other men. Admitting, then, that the mariners were Pagans, it is not easy to understand how, if they spake merely in conformity with their own notions, and according to their own phraseology, they came to use the expression. But they were the companions of the Disciples: might they not, therefore, use a phrase which they had borrowed from others? Against this it is urged, that the Disciples themselves were not yet acquainted with our Saviour's Divinity; a position which, though true on the whole, is yet received with too little restriction. That the expected Messiah was to be the *Son of God*, was a Jewish doctrine. See *Allix's Jewish Testimonies*, Chap. xvii. If, therefore, they had believed our Saviour to be the Christ, they must also have regarded him as the Son of God. But allowing their faith to have been unsettled, or that, generally speaking, they rejected the notion that Jesus was the Christ; still it was extremely natural, whenever his extraordinary works induced a momentary acquiescence in his mission, to apply to him the title by which, had their conviction been uniform, they would uniformly have distinguished him; and it is not too much to add, that knowing the pretensions of Christ, they would hardly, whatever were their own opinion, if we recollect how extraordinary and singular these pretensions were, conceal them from their companions and friends. To have heard Christ declare, as they often must have done in their intercourse with Him, that He was *the Son of God*, and yet not once to mention such a declaration to their familiar associates, would not be explicable on the common principles of human conduct. Even on the supposition, therefore, that the Mariners were Pagans, their exclamation, that Jesus was the Son of God, I mean in the highest sense, admits an easy solution; much easier, indeed, than that which would make υἱὸς εἶ Θεοῦ, without any proof, to be a term commonly significant of Pagan admiration. It was not thus that the Heathens of Lystra, Acts xiv. 11. expressed their astonishment at the works of Barnabas and Paul: their language is ΟΙ ΘΕΟΙ ὁμοιωθέντες ἀνθρώποις κατέβησαν πρὸς ἡμᾶς. So also the people of Cæsarea, Acts xii. 22. struck with the eloquence of Herod, exclaim, ΘΕΟΥ φωνή, οὐκ ἀνθρώπου. *Josephus*, recording the same transaction, says, *Antiq*. lib. xix. cap. viii. § 2. ἀνεβόων, ΘΕΟΝ προσαγορεύοντες.

Campbell, indeed, does not insist that the Mariners were Heathens; and he contends that they might mean only to say, that Christ was a Prophet, for that such are denominated *sons of God*. He has not, however, adduced any instance in which υἱὸς Θεοῦ is so used; nor does my memory supply the defect. On the whole, whether the Mariners were Pagans or not, I understand the declaration to signify, that Christ was really what he had professed to be: ἀληθῶς expresses both their former doubt and their present conviction. At the same time, I ought not to suppress that the great *Casaubon*,

O DOCTIORUM QUICQUID EST, ASSURGITE
HUIC TAM COLENDO NOMINI!

distinguished between ὁ υἱὸς τοῦ Θεοῦ and υἱὸς Θεοῦ, in his extremely rare and learned work *Exercitt. ad Baronium*, p. 326. He rests wholly on the authority of Theophylact: of my own opinion I have no other vindication to offer than that which is contained in the Note above, on iv. 3.

CHAP. XV.

V. 1. οἱ ἀπὸ Ἱεροσολύμων Γραμματεῖς. A few MSS. including Vat. 1209.—οἱ. The difference will be, that with the Article we must understand the principal part of the Scribes and Pharisees of Jerusalem; without it, that some Scribes and Pharisees came from Jerusalem. The latter is the more probable; and this is the sense of the Syr. Version, and apparently of the Vulg. See also Mark vii. 1.

V. 5. πατέρα ἢ μητέρα. Part i. Chap. vi. § 2.

V. 9. διδασκαλίας. *By way of*, &c. Part i. Chap. iii. Sect. iii. § 4.

V. 11. τὸν ἄνθρωπον. The Article is here necessary, because, as in the case of *Regimen*, the definiteness of a part supposes the definiteness of the whole: τὸ στόμα ἀνθρώπου would not be Greek, nor in this place ἄνθρωπον. In the same manner must we explain 1 Cor. vi. 16. ὁ κολλώμενος ΤΗι πόρνῃ.

V. 12. τὸν λόγον. This word always in the N. T. except where particular rules interfere, takes the Article, when used in the sense of ὁ λόγος τοῦ Θεοῦ, or τοῦ Κυρίου.

V. 24. οἴκου Ἰσραήλ. And so also above, x. 6. The Greek form would have been τοῦ οἴκου: the Hebrew would reject the Article. The writers of the N. T. waver between the two; for in Heb. viii. 8. 10. we have τὸν οἶκον Ἰσραήλ. The same diversity is observable in the LXX. and probably for the same cause: οἶκος Ἰσραὴλ may be regarded as a single Noun, and that a Proper Name¹. The Syr. Translator, at Acts iv. 8. has rendered Ἰσραὴλ by *House of Israel*.

V. 26. τοῖς κυναρίοις. To those of the family.

V. 22. εἰς τὸ ὄρος. See on v. 1. It may be remarked, that what was there said of the contiguity of the mountain district to Capernaum, derives confirmation from the mention in this place of παρὰ τὴν θάλασσαν τῆς Γαλιλαίας.

V. 30. χωλούς, τυφλούς, κωφούς, κ. τ. λ. Some individuals of each class; as elsewhere.

V. 39. εἰς τὸ πλοῖον. Here only two MSS.—τό. See on xiii. 2.

CHAP. XVI.

V. 1. οἱ Φαρισαῖοι. A few MSS. with Origen—οἱ. This omission is not necessary, since the Article may imply only the greater part of those who resided in the neighbourhood.

V. 13. τὸν υἱὸν τοῦ ἀνθρώπου. There is a difference of opinion (see *Bowyer's* Conjectures) respecting the construction of this passage. The one rendering is that of our Eng. Version, "Whom do men say that I, the Son of Man, am?" the other, "Whom do men say that I am? The Son of Man?" This is one of the very many new senses which the Writers in Bowyer's Collection would derive from a new punctuation; a kind of conjectural criticism, which has experienced unusual indulgence, merely because, as is alleged, it alters nothing of the original Text; but which, if generally allowed, would corrupt the sense of ancient Writers no less effectually than do the rashest and most unauthorized substitutions. It is not true, however, that the most ancient MSS. are without points: that points are found in the A. B. C. D. of Wetstein, i. e. the Cod. Alexand. the Vatican, though rarely, the Cod. Ephrem, and the Cod. Bezæ, has been shown by Mr. Herb. Marsh, (Notes on Michaelis, Vol. II. p. 892.): and the supposition made in the Preface to Bowyer's Conjectures, third edit. p. 6. "that the Apostles inserted no points themselves," is very questionable. We are informed by *Montfaucon*, as quoted by the same learned Critic, p. 889, that the first person who dis-

---

¹ Winer tacitly adopts this explanation on Acts ii. 36. H. J. R.

tinguished the several parts of a period in Greek writing by the introduction of a point, was Aristophanes of Byzantium, who flourished about two hundred years before the Christian æra, and that points have been found in inscriptions written two hundred years earlier. Admitting, however, that the Evangelists and Apostles did not adopt a contrivance which must in their time have been growing into common use, they may be supposed at least to have availed themselves of the same means of becoming intelligible, to which Writers, before the use of points, ordinarily had recourse: and that was *arrangement*. The ancients generally complain of the obscurity of Heraclitus: the Epigram says,

Μὴ ταχὺς Ἡρακλείτου ἐπ᾽ ὀμφαλὸν εἷλυε Βίβλον
τ᾽ουφεσίου· μάλα τοι δύσβατος ἀτραπιτός·
ὄρφνη καὶ σκότος ἐστὶν ἀλάμπετον.

This obscurity, however, was caused not entirely by the closeness of his reasoning or the depth of his researches: he was confused in his arrangement: his words were so *ingeniously* disposed (for according to Cicero de Nat. Deor. lib. iii. cap. 14. he wished not to be understood) that to have pointed his writings would have been a laborious task. *Aristotle* observes, (Rhet. lib. iii. cap. v. § 2. ed. 1728.) τὰ γὰρ Ἡρακλείτου διαστίξαι, ἔργον, διὰ τὸ ἄδηλον εἶναι ποτέρῳ πρόσκειται, τῷ ὕστερον ἢ τῷ πρότερον. Hence it is evident that the position of the words, before the actual use of points, in great measure supplied the defect: and, indeed, otherwise the same sentence would often admit two or three distinct meanings, or might be destitute of all meaning whatever. I cannot, therefore, agree with those who would rashly disturb the established punctuation: new senses may, indeed, be thus deduced *ad infinitum:* but unless great caution be employed, and the difference occasioned in the relative position can be well defended, unnatural and even absurd constructions will be the inevitable consequence. If the reader wish to feel the effect of this kind of criticism when applied to our own language, he may turn to the *Midsummer Night's Dream*, Act v. Sc. 1.

But to return: though the Sacred writers are by no means remarkable for *elegance* of style, their perspicuity, so far at least as their language is concerned, is not to be called in question. Neither do I believe, that had the passage been intended to convey the sense supposed, it would have stood in its present form; for I do not recollect any instance of an interrogation so abrupt as τὸν υἱὸν τοῦ ἀνθρώπου, some interrogative particle, such as μὴ or μήτι, being always prefixed.

I am concerned with this dispute only as D omits τόν; an omission which, had it been sufficiently supported, would have favoured the conjecture, but which, resting on a single authority, like so many of the readings, which respect the Article, in the *Cod. Bezæ*, must be deemed of little or no importance. On the other hand, *Birch's* Vat. 1209, and the Hieros.-Syr. with some other Versions, omit με, and thus strengthen the common interpretation. *Adler* in his *Versiones Syriacæ*, p. 164. very well conjectures that the received reading was made up of two, viz. τίνα με λέγουσιν οἱ ἄνθρωποι εἶναι (which is the reading of Mark and Luke) and of τίνα λέγουσιν οἱ ἄνθρωποι εἶναι τὸν υἱὸν τοῦ ἀνθρώπου, which is the supposed true reading of St. Matthew.—At any rate, the new punctuation gives a most improbable meaning. Had Christ inquired whether he were commonly regarded as the *Son of God*, the case would have been different: this would have been to ask, whether men regarded him as the *Christ*, the promised Redeemer (John xi. 27.) but the *Son of Man* was a name which, though frequently assumed of Himself by himself, as in the present instance, was not applied to Him by others till after His Ascension.

Same v. οἱ ἄνθρωποι. Men generally. See on x. 17.

V. 18. πύλαι ᾅδου. On these words, and on the promise of which they form a part, much has been written, which I shall not attempt even to abridge. It may, however, be observed, that in explaining ἐπὶ τῇ πέτρᾳ preceding, the Protestants have betrayed unnecessary fears, and have referred πέτρᾳ not to Peter, to whose name it evidently alludes, but to his recent confession that Jesus was the Christ: nor is it easy to see what advantage would be gained, unless they could evade the meaning of δώσω σοι τὰς κλεῖς, which follows. But there is no occasion to have recourse to violence. "The Christian Church in matters of doctrine," says *Michaelis*, "rests on the testimony of the Apostles, of whom Simon Peter was one of the most distinguished, in order the first, and who only, in company with James and John, was eye-witness of many important facts." *Anmerk. ad loc.* It may be added, that Peter was the first Apostle who preached to the Jews and also to the Gentiles. See Acts ii. and x. By πύλαι ᾅδου one class of Critics understand simply *death* or *destruction*; so that the meaning will be, The Christian Church shall never be destroyed: whilst others contend that πύλαι refers to the Oriental custom of meeting and deliberating at the gates of palaces and cities; of which usage there are several vestiges both in the Old Testament and in the writings of modern Travellers; and the name *Ottoman Porte* is deduced from this practice. According to this acceptation, the meaning will be, that the power and the machinations of Hell itself shall not be able to subvert the Church of Christ. This latter opinion is plausible, and it is espoused by *Casaub. Exercitt.* p. 356. and also by *Michaelis ad loc.*: but the objection is, that πύλαι ᾅδου is no other than שערי שאל of the Old Test. which is used only to signify death, or the entrance into a new state of being: and the πύλαι ᾅδου of the Classical writers has no other meaning. Πύλαι in this place wants the Article, by Part i. Chap. iii. Sect. iii. § 6.

V. 28. τινὲς τῶν ὧδε ἑστηκότων. Several MSS.—τῶν, which can hardly be right, Part i. Chap. iii. Sect. i. § 8.: but the true reading is probably ἑστῶτες, which Wetstein adopts.

CHAP. XVII.

V. 2. ὡς τὸ φῶς. Τὸ φῶς σελήνης is the conjecture of *J. S. Bernardus* ap. Wetstein. It has no foundation, and would, without the second Article, be false Greek. *Bowyer* treats it with deserved contempt: he calls it a *moonshine emendation*: and yet his Collection has many others, which are not at all more *luminous*.

V. 15. εἰς τὸ πῦρ. *Bengel* (in Gnom.) has here a Note which I do not understand: he says, " *Articulus UNIVERSE innuit naturam horum elementorum, quod lunaticus apud ignem et aquam proclivior sit in paroxysmum:*" and he bids us observe, that the Article is omitted in the parallel passage, Mark ix. 22. It may very well be omitted by Part i. Chap. vi. § 1.

V. 24. τὰ δίδραχμα. Here *Piscator* (see Bowyer) for τὰ

would read τό, alleging that δίδραχμα is a single piece of money. The singular, however, is δίδραχμον, and though only one was to be paid by one individual in one year, the reference is to the practice of paying annually.

CHAP. XVIII.

V. 3. ὡς τὰ παιδία. Children *generally*. Part i. Chap. iii. Sect. ii. § 2. Not, however, the general character of children. "We must not," says *Michaelis (Anmerk.)*, "bring together, in illustration of these words, all the properties of children, which may be either good or bad, as is sometimes done in the pulpit-effusions of well-disposed men : the meaning of the precept, if we attend to the occasion which gave rise to it, can be only, that he who would enter into the kingdom of Heaven, must no more pretend to merit than a child, with any show of justice : I purposely say, *can with any appearance of justice;* for not seldom are children presumptuous, and entertain high opinions of their own deserts." This solution relieves us from a considerable difficulty. Our own language contains a multitude of Sermons, the writers of which seem to have thought themselves bounden to shut their eyes to all the early manifestations of the corruption of human nature; and we have delineations of childhood in which the hearer or reader perceives as little of reality and truth, as in the wildest fictions of Romance. The Copt. Version reads τὸ παιδίον τοῦτο, and six of the Moscow MSS. but those the least valuable, have the same reading.

V. 7. τῶν σκανδάλων. In these words I think there is reference, not, indeed, to any thing which has been mentioned, but to what had previously occupied the mind of Christ. The σκάνδαλα alluded to are the calamities and persecutions which threatened the Christian Church. Such is the opinion of *Noesselt*, approved by *Schleusner*. These, though future, might be present to the mind of Christ, and might, therefore, being uppermost in his thoughts, be made the subjects of reference. *Lord Bacon*, as quoted by Archbishop *Newcome* on our Lord's conduct, 8vo. p. 117. has a most masterly remark, viz. that our Saviour, knowing the minds of men, often replies to the *thoughts* of his hearers, rather than to their actual questions. I am of opinion, that in like manner He sometimes refers to what has recently been the subject of his own meditation, though it may not have been the subject of discourse; and it is not impossible that the present instance may be of this kind: the calamities which threatened the rising Church we know, from other places, strongly moved the compassion of our Saviour; and though the Article in this passage may be otherwise explained, as is done by *Wakefield*, yet his solution will not hold in Luke xvii. 1. which, however, he has not noticed. My opinion that the reference is *anticipative* is in some degree strengthened by the Version of *Michaelis*. After "offences" he inserts, "which the world will take at the Gospel;" without which addition he thinks the passage obscure.

V. 14. οὐκ ἔστι θέλημα. There is no wish. Part i. Chap. iii. Sect. iii. § 5.

V. 17. τῇ ἐκκλησίᾳ. *Collegio presbyterorum*, says Schleusner.

Same v. ὁ ἐθνικὸς καὶ ὁ τελώνης. *Hypothetically*. Here two distinct persons are meant; the second Article, therefore, is inserted: and so it is in all similar instances throughout the N. T. See Part i. p. 60.

CHAP. XIX.

V. 3. οἱ Φαρισαῖοι. Those of the neighbouring district. Many good MSS. omit οἱ.

V. 10. τοῦ ἀνθρώπου μετὰ τῆς γυναικός. Both have the Article, being *Correlatives*.

V. 12. ἐκ κοιλίας μητρός. Part i. Chap. vi. § 1. and Chap. iii. Sect. iii. § 7.

Same v. τῶν ἀνθρώπων. This is another instance in which it is evident that οἱ ἄνθρωποι does not mean exclusively the Jews. See on x. 17.

V. 21. δὸς πτωχοῖς. Here D. and Vat. 1209. have τοῖς πτωχοῖς, and in many other places in which the same phrase occurs, there is the same variety; but the discrepancy is of no importance, being no other than that of giving to the poor, or to poor persons.

V. 28. ἐν τῇ παλιγγενεσίᾳ. *Lightfoot* understands this of a regeneration, or a renewing of manners and doctrine: but *Schleusner* has well observed that the Syr. has what is equivalent to *in seculo novo*, which in the Oriental idioms expresses a future state of being. It is plain, therefore, that with *Campbell* we should join ἐν τῇ παλιγγενεσίᾳ with καθίσεσθε: about which there have been doubts. *Kypke* has a good Note on this passage, which he understands as it is here explained.

V. 30. πρῶτοι ἔσχατοι καὶ κ. τ. λ. *Markland* (ap. Bowyer) infers from what is said in the next Chap. ver. 16. that we should read οἱ πρῶτοι ἔσχατοι καὶ οἱ ἔσχατοι πρῶτοι· but the cases are not similar: for though we may say with strict propriety οἱ πρῶτοι ἔσχατοι, yet after πολλοὶ the Article is not wanted: πολλοὶ πρῶτοι is similar to πολλοὶ σοφοί, &c. 1 Cor. i. 26. nor does any MS. here read πολλοὶ ΟΙ πρῶτοι, or there πολλοὶ ΟΙ σοφοί, πολλοὶ ΟΙ δυνατοί. A few MSS. indeed, with the *Complut.* read the latter clause οἱ ἔσχατοι πρῶτοι· but then this must have been on the supposition that the πολλοὶ of the preceding clause was not here to be understood.

CHAP. XX.

V. 2. τὴν ἡμέραν. Each day, in reference to each Denarius. See above, x. 29 [1].

V. 3. περὶ τὴν τρίτην ὥραν. Very many MSS. want τήν, an omission which *Wetstein* approves: in other places the same variety is observable, on which see Part i. Chap. vi. § 3.

V. 12. οὗτοι οἱ ἔσχατοι. C—οἱ. This is wrong. See Part i. Chap. vii. § 5.

V. 16. οἱ ἔσχατοι πρῶτοι. L. Origen—οἱ. Article requisite by Part i. Chap. iii. Sect. iv. § 1.

V. 22. τὸ ποτήριον. Definite on account of ὃ following.

CHAP. XXI.

V. 12. τὰς περιστεράς. Particular doves are alluded to, viz. the accustomed offering of the poor.

V. 13. οἶκος προσευχῆς. Our own Version is justifiable in translating definitely "the house of prayer," since after the Verb Nuncupative the Articles could not have been employed.

[1] See Note, p. 41.

Campbell and *Wakefield* are, therefore, more literal than the case required.

V. 18. πρωΐας is definite in sense, but the Article is omitted on account of γενομένης understood.

V. 42. εἰς κεφαλὴν γωνίας. Our Translation has "the head-stone of the corner," but it is not very plain what this head-stone was. It may be inferred, however, first, to have been such, that it might be added when the building was otherwise complete; as appears from the present verse. Secondly, that it was so placed, that the passenger might fall against it, and also that it might fall upon him, as is evident from ver. 44. Now nothing which otherwise corresponds with the term can be conceived to answer these conditions, except an upright stone or column added to a building to strengthen and protect it at the corner, which was most exposed to external violence. The Greek expression is equivalent to the Hebrew אבן פנה or ראש פנה: but every rectangular building would have necessarily four פנות, and we find these four spoken of, Job i. 19; but such a protection placed at *each* of the four corners could hardly be the subject of allusion in this place; for Christ, who is the *sole* bulwark of the Christian Fabric, could not aptly be compared with any thing which admits plurality, and in which, indeed, plurality is necessarily implied. Besides, the κεφαλὴ γωνίας is allowed to be the same with the λίθος ἀκρογωνιαῖος, Ephes. ii. 20. where the Apostles and Prophets are said to be the foundation, but Christ the λίθος ἀκρογωνιαῖος, which must therefore be something pre-eminent; for else it would not be a fit illustration: and indeed we find אבן פנה, Job xxxviii. 6. spoken of as being *single* in a building, though nothing can thence be inferred with respect to its form or height. The common interpretations appear to be objectionable in not answering the conditions mentioned at the beginning of this Note. No inference that the κεφαλὴ γωνίας is more than one in one fabric, can be drawn from the absence of the Articles. See Part I. Chap. vi. § 1. and Chap. iii. Sect. iii. § 7.

CHAP. XXII.

V. 10. ἀνακειμένων. D and three others would prefix τῶν. This is not usual after words significant of *fulness*.

V. 14. κλητοί. A few MSS. have ΟΙ κλητοί. Either reading may be right. The called are many, or, there be many called.

V. 23. οἱ λέγοντες. Several MSS. including Vat. 1209. would omit the Article. This can hardly be right: for the meaning seems not to be, that as they came they made this assertion, but only that the dogma subjoined was notoriously maintained by them.

V. 28. τίνος ἔσται γυνή. A very few MSS. have Ἡ γυνή, and in the parallel place, Mark xii. 23. this is the reading of A D *à pr. manu*. In this instance, as in many others, either reading may be tolerated, the difference being only, Whose wife shall she be? or, Whose shall the Woman be?

V. 30. ὡς ἄγγελοι τοῦ Θεοῦ. Some MSS. both of Matthäi and Birch,—τοῦ. This is extremely probable, ἄγγελοι not having the Article.

V. 38. αὕτη ἐστὶ πρώτη καὶ μεγάλη ἐντολή. For Ordinals and Superlatives (for μεγάλη is here equivalent to μεγίστη) see Part i. Chap. vi. § 3 and 4. Wetstein's L, however, would read ἡ μεγάλη καὶ ἡ πρώτη: and Vat. 1209, with Vind. Lamb. 31. Hieros.-Syr. and a few others, ἡ μεγάλη καὶ πρώτη. Where μεγάλη precedes, either of these readings may be tolerated. Μεγάλη, used as a Superlative, is merely a Hebraism; and yet D alone has μεγάλη καὶ πρώτη. In the next verse we have δευτέρα without the Article, being an Ordinal.

CHAP. XXIII.

V. 9. καὶ πατέρα μὴ καλέσητε ὑμῶν ἐπὶ τῆς γῆς. It is curious that *Markland* (ap. Bowyer) has observed on this passage, "it would have been much more agreeable to the Greek Tongue, had the Article τὸν been expressed, ΤΟΝ πατέρα μὴ καλέσητε ὑμῶν ΤΟΝ ἐπὶ τῆς γῆς." Each of these insertions would, if admitted, be not only a corruption of the Sacred Text, but a violation of the Greek idiom. The first Article is contrary to the uniform usage noticed Part i. Chap. iii. Sect. iii. § 2. and the second, ΤΟΝ ἐπὶ τῆς γῆς, would signify some definite person, whereas the Proposition is exclusive, and the meaning is, as our version has it, "Call *no* man," &c. a meaning which the absence of the Article authorizes, but which its presence would destroy. See Part i. Chap. iii. Sect. iii. § 5.

V. 15. υἱὸν γεέννης. Part i. Chap. iii. Sect. iii. § 3.

V. 23. τὸ ἡδύοσμον καὶ τὸ ἄνηθον, &c. The species so called.

V. 24. οἱ διυλίζοντες. D *à pr. manu* and Vat. 1209.—οἱ : but the meaning is, Ye are foolish *on the assumption*, that διυλίζετε. The same remark will apply to ver. 16. where D would omit οἱ.

Same v. τὸν κώνωπα, τὴν κάμηλον. In proverbial allusions like this, it is usual in most languages to make the subject of the remark definite: and this is perfectly natural; for allusions suppose the thing alluded to to be known; and no allusions are more readily apprehended, than those which are made to Proverbs and Fables. Perhaps, therefore, the spirit of the original would have been best preserved by translating " the gnat, the camel." Of this form, in our own language, *Ray's Proverbs* will supply a multitude of examples.

CHAP. XXIV.

V. 9. ὑπὸ πάντων ἐθνῶν. Several MSS. read τῶν ἐθνῶν, which Wetstein approves: in this instance it is safe to go with the multitude, since either reading is alike admissible. See Part i. Chap. vii. § 2.

V. 15. ἐν τόπῳ ἁγίῳ. Eng. Version, "in the holy place." *Campbell*, " on holy ground." The latter of these interpretations is that of *Grotius*, and also of *Spanheim* in his most learned work *de Præstant. et Usu Numismatum*, vol. i. p. 669 : and it is but fair to apprise the Reader, that a great majority of the Translators and Commentators are of the same opinion : but it will be right to state the nature of that opinion, as well as the foundation on which it rests. The point contended for is, that τόπος ἅγιος here means, " the district lying within a certain distance of the Temple, and which even the enemies of the Jews had, at different periods, agreed to regard as sacred;" and *Spanheim* has shown that the Temples of the Pagans frequently possessed similar immunities. This, however, is rather an illustration than an argument: but Grotius contends, that if by τόπος ἅγιος we should understand the Temple itself, the event described would not be an indication of *approaching* calamity, but the very calamity itself. To this, I think we may answer from the following verse, that the admonition is here given not to the inhabitants of the city, to whom no opportunity of escape would then be left, but to the people of Judea, οἱ ἐν τῇ Ἰουδαίᾳ: and immediately afterwards we find ὁ ἐν τῷ ἀγρῷ. Grotius, however, aware of this objection, observes further, that Ἰουδαία frequently signifies no more than *tractus Hierosolymitanus*: yet of this use I find no example, nor has *Schleusner* given any. But, in the next place, what is the usual meaning of the phrase ἐν τόπῳ ἁγίῳ? In the N. T. it occurs (except in the present passage) only Acts vi. 13, and xxi. 28: in neither of which can it be otherwise understood than of some part of the Temple. In the LXX. it is very common, and there it is always meant of the Temple, and generally of the Holy Place properly so called. We have, therefore, no authority from the Sacred Writers to understand τόπος ἅγιος otherwise than of the Temple.—But, lastly, we are to consider that the passage before us is τὸ ῥηθὲν ὑπὸ Δανιὴλ τοῦ προφήτου· now the passage itself in so many words is not found in Daniel; neither does τὸ ῥηθὲν or its equivalent שנאמר in the Talmud, if we may rely on *Surenhusius* in his Βίβλος καταλλαγῆς, authorize such an expectation. In such cases we are to look only for the *sense* conveyed in the passage quoted, and that too, perhaps, dispersed through various places. The places, then, in Daniel, to which our Saviour is here supposed to allude, are ix. 27. xi. 31. xii. 11: and the first of these, in the Version of the LXX. is not very remote from the words of St. Matt. The LXX. there have καὶ ἐπὶ τὸ ἱερὸν βδέλυγμα τῶν ἐρημώσεων ἔσται, and both the Vulg. and Arab. are similar. If, therefore, the matter rested here, the question would at once be decided: but it so happens, that the LXX. differ from the Hebrew: in the Hebrew, however, we find על כנף, and it is observable that כנף is the word by which the Syr. Translator has rendered πτερύγιον, Matthew iv. 5. where some part of the Temple (see above) is unquestionably meant. There is, therefore, a strong presumption that the MSS. which the Greek Translator used, (whether the translation be of the LXX. or, as *Jerome* asserts in his Preface to Daniel, of *Theodotion*,) gave the whole sentence in such a

CHAPTER XXIV.

manner as to justify the Greek and other Versions : the great objection at present is, that the reading of the Hebrew MSS. is שקוצם, whereas the proposed construction would require the omission of the final *Mem*. It is, however, to be observed, that one of *Kennicott's* MSS. gives a reading which, even if it be not authentic, still tends to show in what sense כנף is to be understood. His Cod. 313. preserves the remarkable variation בהיכל (See *Bibl. Hebraica Dissert. Gen.* p. 95.) which is exactly ἐπὶ τὸ ἱερόν, and which, by the way, is one among several testimonies, which one or other of the Hebrew MSS. affords in favour of the LXX. or at least of the old Translations. The value of the LXX. as preserving readings which are no longer visible in our Hebrew Text, is not even at the present day sufficiently understood. Without, however, wishing to assume the authenticity of the reading in question, I may be permitted to suppose, that the accidental substitution of a synonym is more easily to be accounted for, than is the introduction of a reading which gives a totally different sense. It is, then, on the whole, probable, that the Greek Translator has given the true meaning of Daniel, though the vestiges of that meaning be in our present Hebrew Copies so much obscured : and if ἐπὶ τὸ ἱερὸν be admitted in Daniel to be a true rendering of the Hebrew, we can hardly doubt that the Temple is the spot intended by our Saviour in St. Matthew. Nor is the admirable history of the completion of the Prophecy adverse to this exposition. The desolation of abomination was seen to stand *in the Temple*. Ῥωμαῖοι δὲ .... κομίσαντες τὰς σημαίας ΕΙΣ ΤΟ ἹΕΡΟΝ, καὶ θέμενοι τῆς ἀνατολικῆς πύλης ἀντικρύς, ἔθυσάν τε αὐτοῖς αὐτόθι, καὶ τὸν Τίτον μετὰ μεγίστων εὐφημιῶν ἀπέφηναν αὐτοκράτορα. *Joseph. de Bell. Jud.* lib. vi. c. vi.—In the parallel place, St. Mark xiii. 14. we have, instead of ἐν τόπῳ ἁγίῳ, the words ὅπου οὐ δεῖ. This expression is, indeed, so indefinite, that it may admit different interpretations : it appears, however, to be an *Euphemism*, to which the violation of no place less sacred than the Temple could have given rise.

If the Reader wish to know the other expositions of Daniel ix. 27. he may consult the *Thes. Theol. Philol.* vol. i. p. 929, to which, though I have differed from the Writer, I am indebted for some information on the subject. It there appears, that the reading found in *Kennicott's* MS. 313. had been long since conjectured by *Capellus* and other Critics: this is a curious fact.

I observe that *Campbell* and, perhaps, other Translators have preferred the more indefinite sense of this passage, because the words were *anarthrous*. This objection, however, is of no weight. See Part i. Chap. vi. § 1.

V. 17. ἆραι τὶ ἐκ τῆς οἰκίας. Here *Wetstein*, on the authority of a great many MSS. would read ἆραι τά. However, several of Birch's best MSS. including Vat. 1209, have τι: and this is a preferable, because a more exclusive, reading.

V. 27. τοῦ υἱοῦ τοῦ ἀνθρώπου. For this phrase see on John v. 27.

V. 31. ἕως ἄκρων. Birch's Vat. 1209, and Wetstein's i. 69. have τῶν ἄκρων. This reading would suppose τὸ ἄκρον to be here used substantively: which, however, after ἄκρων preceding, is very improbable.

V. 32. τὰ φύλλα ἐκφύῃ. The Article shows plainly that τὰ φύλλα is the Nominative to ἐκφύῃ, and not the Accusative after it, as the English Version, *Campbell*, and the French of *Beausobre* make it: but *Wakefield*, *Schleusner*, and the German of *Michaelis*, understand it in the former manner. The Reader will hardly need to be reminded, that ἐκφύω may be used in a neuter sense [1].

V. 36. τῆς ὥρας. A great many MSS. omit τῆς. *Griesbach* would reject it, but, I think, improperly: for ἐκείνης, which is understood, would require the Article.

V. 40. ὁ εἷς παραλαμβάνεται καὶ ὁ εἷς, &c. A few MSS. including Vat. 1209. omit both Articles. Probably they should be retained, ὁ εἷς being generally used to signify one of two. See on 1 John v. 7.

CHAP. XXV.

V. 2. πέντε μωραί. Several Editors, says *Birch*, as Wetstein, Griesbach, &c. omit αἱ though found *in plerisque Codicibus*. Griesbach, however, in his last edition, admits it into the

---

[1] There seems, however, no objection to retaining the common Version, and rendering the words "*it's* leaves." See the parallel passage in Luke xxi. 30. —J. S.

CHAPTER XXV. 181

Text, though with great hesitation. I have little doubt of its being authentic: the omission may have arisen from the want of the Article before the *former* πέντε: the *first* five, however, are not definite, whilst the latter are so, being those which remain of the ten.

V. 30. εἰς τὸ σκότος τὸ ἐξώτερον. This phrase occurs in two other places, viz. in this Evangelist, viii. 12. and xxii. 13. It is not of very easy interpretation. The opinion generally entertained by the Commentators may be expressed in the words of *Wetstein:* "*Manet in imagine convivii: cœnaculum crebris luminibus per noctem collucebat: expulsus cœnaculo atque domo in tenebris versatur, quoque longiùs removetur, eò crassiores tenebræ ipsi offunduntur.*" It seems not, however, to have been observed, that the "*imago convivii*" does not pervade all the three passages in which the phrase occurs. In the first, we have the word ἀνακλιθήσονται, which in some measure favours the common interpretation: in the second, the subject is a marriage-feast, which is directly to the purpose: but in the present instance, the Parable of the Talents, there is not any the most remote allusion to banqueting; and, consequently, the received interpretation can scarcely in this instance be right. Besides, the person who is here said to be cast εἰς τὸ σκότος, is a slave, who would hardly have been admitted to a feast. It is, however, to be presumed, that the phrase has in all the three places the same meaning, whatever that meaning be, to discover which we should endeavour to detect the idea which pervades the three passages; and this, it is evident, is the future punishment of perverseness and disobedience. It might, therefore, be expected, even before inquiry, that τὸ σκότος τὸ ἐξώτερον was the Greek rendering of a Jewish phrase *generally* understood of the place of punishment after death, not an allusion or metaphor requiring to be explained by the context: and with this the strong expression ὁ βρυγμὸς τῶν ὀδόντων, which every where is added, agrees. *Windet*, in his curious and learned *De vitâ functorum statu*, has some passages which favour the supposition. He says, p. 114. that "both the Paradise and the Gehenna of the Hebrews were subdivided into seven mansions: that the six higher regions of Hell formed the גיהנם עליון, whence Spirits after purgation are supposed to return; whilst the seventh is the dungeon, where the wicked shall abide for ever." And in another place, p. 246. he makes this very phrase τὸ σκότος τὸ ἐξώτερον to be equivalent to the Tartarus of the Heathen Mythology. I have to wish only that this writer had adhered, in the present instance, to his usual practice of noting authorities. *Schleusner* has not adverted to the work of *Windet*, but he appears to understand the words in nearly the same sense; and he refers to ζόφος τοῦ σκότους, 2 Peter ii. 17. as a parallel expression.

V. 32. ὁ ποιμήν. Hypothetically. Part i. Chap. iii. Sect. ii. § 1.

CHAP. XXVI.

V. 26. τὸν ἄρτον. Several of the most important MSS.—τόν. The parallel passages are, Mark xiv. 22. and Luke xxii. 19. in the former of which a very few MSS. only have ΤΟΝ ἄρτον; and in the latter, so far as I have observed, not one. The majority, therefore, of the MSS. of St. Matt. is at variance with those of the other two Evangelists: and the fair inference will be, if we assume the intended agreement of the three Historians, that the received Text of St. Matt. must yield to the combined force of its own various readings, and of the almost uniform reading of the other two Evangelists. *Campbell*, however, *ad loc.* observes as follows: "Had it been ἄρτον without the Article, it might have been rendered either *bread* or *a loaf:* but as it has the Article, we must, if we would fully express the sense, say, *the loaf.* Probably, on such occasions, *one loaf* larger or smaller, according to the company, was part of the accustomed preparation. This practice, at least in the Apostolic age, seems to have been adopted in the Church in commemorating Christ's death. To this it is very probable the Apostle alludes, 1 Cor. x. 17. ὅτι εἷς ἄρτος, ἓν σῶμα, κ. τ. λ." On this Note we may remark three things: first, that it is not certain, as Campbell supposes, that the Article in this place is really not wanting. Secondly, that it does not appear to be the fact, that only *one* loaf was part of the accustomed preparation. And, thirdly, that the practice of the Apostolic age might possibly differ from the Paschal ceremony of the Jews.

1. The first point admits no other decision than that which

is founded on strong presumption. This, however, is a case in which we may suppose that uniformity was intended by the three Evangelists: had any one of them meant to have expressed his belief, that our Lord celebrated the Paschal supper in a manner different from that usually observed, that Evangelist would assuredly have noticed the deviation in unequivocal terms. This not having been done, the majority of voices will be decisive of the question: and two sets of witnesses, I mean the MSS. of St. Mark and St. Luke, must be admitted to be more credible than is one, even if that one consist of individuals who agree among themselves: which, however, is here by no means the case. There is, therefore, a strong presumption against the common reading.

2. The accounts which have reached us of the mode of celebrating the Passover, uniformly speak of *two* loaves of unleavened bread. *Maimonides* and the Talmudists, as quoted by Lightfoot, tell us, " Then (the person officiating) washing his hands and taking *two* loaves, breaks one, and lays the broken upon the whole one, and blesseth it, saying, Blessed be He, who causeth bread to grow out of the earth." These loaves, indeed, were in truth *cakes* cut nearly through, probably by the instrument on which they were baked, into squares or other figures, so that they might afterwards be broken into pieces with perfect ease. See *Rohr's Pictor Errans* in the valuable collection, the *Thesaurus Theol. Philol.* vol. ii. : whence it may be observed, *obiter*, that our own mode of dividing the sacramental bread approaches to the decency of the original ordinance, more nearly, perhaps, than is generally imagined. The round loaf, which appears in paintings of the Consecration of the Elements, is, like many other things of the same sort, a violation of historical truth.

3. But though two cakes were used in the celebration of Christ's last Passover, it is not improbable, that *one* only was from the first introduced in the Eucharist. The passage adduced by *Campbell* from 1 Cor. might alone prove the Christian practice. Indeed, though there are many passages in the Fathers, which rather tend to confirm this statement, I do not recollect any one, which is so pointedly to the purpose. Nor are we to wonder at this deviation from the actual usage of the superseded institution. Of the two cakes usually introduced

at the Passover, only one is recorded to have been broken by Christ, and to have been declared to be the symbol of his body: it was, therefore, natural that his followers, in commemorating the Lord's Supper, should discontinue so much of the Jewish ordinance, as was foreign from the newly established rite. Thus, at no distant period, the bread employed was not necessarily *unleavened*: for though unleavened bread was actually used by Christ, it was not studiously chosen, but was such as the Passover unavoidably presented: yet the Greek and Latin Churches in a subsequent age disputed this very point.

On the whole, I think, we may fairly infer, that a loaf or cake *indefinitely* was here meant by the Evangelist: but how the Article found its way into the great majority of the MSS. of St. Matthew, it may not be easy to determine. To say that it was understood by the Translator to represent the *status emphaticus* of the Syro-Chaldaic original, and that the other two Evangelists want it, not being translations, would be a bold and perhaps a gratuitous conjecture, since some of the oldest MSS. of St. Matthew, such as B. C. D. L. are without τόν. I am, therefore, somewhat surprised that *Griesbach* has not prefixed to it the mark of possible spuriousness.

Same v, τοῦτό ἐστι τὸ σῶμά μου. It may amuse the Reader to be informed, that the Article in this place was once supposed to prove the doctrine of Transubstantiation: " *quasi Articulus vim habeat propositionem contrahendi ad proprium sensum, et tropicum non permittat.*" This is, indeed, most ridiculous, but is yet not incredible: I learn the fact, however, from the testimony of a Reformer. See *Petri Martyris Opera*, p. 869, edit. 1583.

V. 27. τὸ ποτήριον. Here a very few MSS. among which is the Vat.—τό. In the parallel place, Mark xiv. 23. so many of the MSS. want the Article, that *Griesbach* is inclined to reject it: of *Matthäi's* MSS. however, only *three* are without it, and those three are of the lowest order. In St. Luke xxii. 20. the MSS. agree in giving the Article. In this instance, as well as in a preceding one (see first Note on this Chapter) it may be presumed that uniformity was intended by the several Evangelists: the evidence of the MSS. is, however, here more nearly balanced, and to determine the true reading it becomes indispensable to attend to the circumstances of the case.—It does not appear, so far as I can discover, that more than *one* vessel was employed on these occasions; for though *four* cups full of diluted wine were to be emptied by the party celebrating the feast, yet as these were not to be placed on the table at once, but were to be used at different periods of the ceremony according to stated forms, a single cup four times filled was all, which the occasion required. Which of these four cups was that, which our Saviour declared to be the symbol of his blood, is not quite decided. It is usually understood to have been the *third* or the *Cup of Blessing*, so called because over this the company implored the blessing of God on the food which they had eaten; and this cup was regarded as the most important of the four. *Michaelis*, indeed, (in his *Anmerkungen*) infers that the Cup consecrated by our Saviour was the *fourth* and last, because of the expression in St. Luke, μετὰ τὸ δειπνῆσαι: this, however, is by no means decisive, since it was the *third* or the Cup of Blessing, which immediately followed the eating of the Lamb; and this was the last thing eaten.—The Cup used at the Passover is stated by the Rabbinical Writers to have contained one-fourth of an Italian Quart. Of its form nothing can now be known, though *Ven. Bede* relates, that in his time the Cup used by our Saviour was still preserved at Jerusalem; a tale, which the Reader will probably with *Casaubon* (Exercitt. Baron. p. 518.) be disposed to question. Much curious information, respecting the manner of celebrating the Eucharist in the primitive ages may be found in *Suicer* vocc. Ἀγάπη, Εὐχαριστία, and especially Σύναξις. On the Passover the Student may consult *Saubert's* Dissertation *de Ultimo Christi Paschate* in Thesaur. Theol. Philol. vol. ii. and the *Pascha Judæorum abrogatum* in Meuschen's *N. T. e Talmude illustratum*, 4to. Lips. 1736. p. 897.

V. 34. πρὶν ἀλέκτορα φωνῆσαι. This Noun is every where anarthrous in the N. T. unless indeed in Luke xxii. 60. where, however, on the authority of a multitude of MSS. Griesbach has rejected the Article. *Wakefield*, I observe, in his first Translation renders "*a* cock." To English ears this might sound oddly; and we should naturally inquire, whence arises the difference of the usage in the two languages. It appears from a passage in the Talmud, referred to by *Lightfoot* and

Schoettgen, that cocks were not allowed to be kept within the walls of Jerusalem, for the reason that "*animalia immunda eruerent ;*" and on the same plea the Priests were forbidden to keep them throughout the whole Jewish territory. To reconcile the Talmud with the Scripture, *Reland* published a Treatise, the substance of which is detailed in *Schoettgen's Horæ Hebr.* and which proves by sufficient arguments, that the two accounts are not necessarily at variance : for example, the crowing of a cock without the walls might easily, in the stillness of the night, be heard at the house of Caiaphas, from which the walls were at no great distance. The authority of the Talmud may, however, be disputable : but one thing, I think, is manifest from the uniform indefiniteness of the expression, viz. that cocks, if at all tolerated in Jerusalem, were much less common than domestic fowls are with us : for the screaming of an eagle could not have been spoken of in a more indefinite manner. Wakefield's Version, therefore, though apparently unnatural, is perhaps not ill adapted to the actual circumstances ; and it is not clear that he ought to have altered it in his subsequent work.

V. 41. τὸ μὲν πνεῦμα. See on i. 18. under the second head. The Article is requisite by Part i. Chap. iii. Sect. i. § 9.

V. 75. τοῦ Ἰησοῦ. Griesbach on the authority of very many MSS. absolutely rejects τοῦ. Proper Names in the Genitive, as has been shown, deviate from the common rule.

CHAP. XXVII.

V. 8. ἀγρὸς αἵματος. Part i. Chap. iii. Sect. iii. § 2.

V. 15. κατὰ δὲ ἑορτήν. Here D alone, as in other instances, has τήν. Though the Passover ἡ ἑορτὴ be meant, the Article is omitted by Part i. Chap. vi. § 1.

V. 50. τὸ πνεῦμα. *His* spirit. See on i. 18. under the first head.

V. 54. Θεοῦ υἱός. Here *Campbell* renders " a son of God," and defends his version at considerable length. *Bishop Lowth* in his English Grammar had proposed the same translation. Having very fully considered the phrase above, iv. 3. and xiv. 33. I have nothing new to add. The Centurion could scarcely fail to know the alleged blasphemy, for which Christ suffered ;

and had he intended in Heathen phraseology to express his admiration of our Saviour's conduct, he would not have called our Saviour Θεοῦ υἱός. But these points have been already discussed. See as above.

V. 60. *Rosenmüller* remarks, "*Articulus ἐν τῇ πέτρᾳ ostendit, ex unâ rupe sive petrâ excisum et excavatum fuisse monumentum.*" I understand the phrase in the same manner as above, vii. 24.

CHAP. XXVIII.

V. 1. Μαρία ἡ Μαγδαληνή. On v. 56. of the preceding Chapter, *Campbell* well observes, that the meaning is Mary of Magdala or the Magdalene, and that custom only has made the word a Proper Name: and yet, in the present verse, D.— ἡ *à pr. manu.*

V. 18. πᾶσα ἐξουσία. This must be understood in the most unlimited sense. See Part i. Chap. vii. § 3. It is not, therefore, without reason, that *Vitringa* Obss. Sac. (as quoted by Wolfius) "*per ἐξουσίαν hic regnum Providentiæ universalis innui contendit.*"

ST. MARK.

CHAP. I.

V. 1. υἱοῦ τοῦ Θεοῦ. Here *Markland* conjectures that we should read ΤΟΥ υἱοῦ, and he thinks that the Article has been lost by the *homœoteleuton* of Χριστοῦ preceding. Titles, however, in apposition frequently want the Article. It is to the full as probable, that τοῦ before Θεοῦ ought to be omitted, as in the Vat. 1209 [1].

V. 12. τὸ πνεῦμα the Holy Spirit. See Matt. i. 18. D alone adds τὸ ἅγιον.

V. 13. οἱ ἄγγελοι. The Alex. MS. with a few others—οἱ. Matthäi calls it *arguta correctio*. Supposing it, indeed, to be a correction, it may possibly deserve the epithet: but in similar instances, as well as in the parallel place of St. Matthew, Nouns are generally anarthrous.

V. 15. πεπλήρωται ὁ καιρός. The definiteness of this expression proves incontestably the then prevailing expectation of the Messiah.

CHAP. II.

V. 26. ἐπὶ ᾿Αβιάθαρ τοῦ ἀρχιερέως. A great deal of learning and ingenuity has been employed on these words, in order to remove a difficulty, which in reality does not exist. It has been observed, that the fact here referred to happened, *not* in the High Priesthood of Abiathar, but in that of Ahimelech his father. See 1 Sam. xxi. and hence it was thought necessary to vindicate the expression in the best manner possible. *Dr. Owen* (see Bowyer's Conject.) thought ἐπὶ might mean *about*,

---

[1] V. 7. ὁ ἰσχυρότερός μου. Winer observes, that this distinctly points to the Messiah. *That one who is stronger than I is coming.*—H. J. R.

CHAPTER II. 189

or a *little before the time that*: *Wetstein* imagines it to signify, *in the presence of*: *Michaelis* believes that it is a Jewish mode of citing Scripture, as if any one should say, *In the Chapter of*, &c.; an interpretation which *Rosenmüller* and *Mr. Herb. Marsh* (Introd. vol. i. p. 403.) would have thought not improbable, if Mark had added γέγραπται, or λέγει ἡ γραφή, as Rom. xi. 2. Some have supposed that Ahimelech and Abiathar, the father and the son, were called by either name indiscriminately: and *Lightfoot* understands Abiathar to mean the *Urim* and *Thummim*. All this has arisen from imagining that the words of St. Mark, explained in the obvious way, would mean *in the Priesthood of Abiathar*; and, indeed, even the accurate *Schleusner* (*voce* ἐπί) renders the words *sub pontificatu Abiatharis*; a sense which they will not bear. The error consists in having confounded ἐπὶ Ἀβιάθαρ ΤΟΥ ἀρχιερέως with the same words, omitting the Article: for though several recently collated MSS. including the far greater part of *Alter's* and *Matthäi's*, do, indeed, omit the Article; yet none of the solutions which I have noticed, appear to have originated in the belief that such was the true reading. That reading, however, would indeed mean, that Abiathar was actually High Priest at the period in question: thus in Demosth. vol. i. p. 250. edit. Reiske, ἐπὶ Νικοκλέους ΆΡΧΟΝΤΟΣ: and Thucyd. lib. ii. sub init. ἐπὶ Χρυσίδος ἐν Ἄργει ἹΕΡΩΜΕΝΗΣ, καὶ Αἰνησίου ἘΦΟΡΟΥ ἐν Σπάρτῃ, καὶ Πυθοδώρου ἔτι δύο μῆνας ΆΡΧΟΝΤΟΣ Ἀθηναίοις· where the insertion of the Article would imply only, that these persons were subsequently distinguished by their respective offices from others of the same name.

But we find the very form of expression in the LXX. 1 Macc. xiii. 42. ἐπὶ Σίμωνος ἀρχιερέως, and in the N. T. Luke iii. 2. we have ἐπ' ἀρχιερέων Ἄννα καὶ Καιάφα, examples which sufficiently prove that the received reading will not admit the received construction. Of the other form, viz. that which has the Article, I find only Luke iv. 27. ἐπὶ Ἐλισσαίου τοῦ προφήτου, by which phrase, however, is plainly meant, " In the days of Elisha the Prophet," without any reference to his actual exercise of the prophetic office at the period mentioned. Indeed the different import of the two readings of this passage might be theoretically proved, as it has been practically illustrated.—The only question is, therefore, whether Abiathar was a High Priest of distinguished name, so as to justify the use of the Article: and the answer must be obvious to every person acquainted with the Jewish History. Besides, it is not improbable that there might have been other persons of the same name and of some celebrity among the Jews, though no account of them has descended to the present time. The name itself was certainly not uncommon: and this circumstance alone might render the addition of τοῦ ἀρχιερέως natural, if not absolutely necessary. One writer (see Bowyer) has observed, that the expression, Matt. i. 6. Δαβὶδ τὸν βασιλέα is similar to the present; and this is perfectly true: it may be added, that any event which had happened during the early part of David's life, might have been said to have taken place ἐπὶ Δαβὶδ ΤΟΥ βασιλέως· and had this phrase occurred, solutions similar to those before us would probably have been hazarded. See also John xi. 2. ἡ ἀλείψασα, though the act of anointing was subsequent. I observe that Griesbach, in his N. T. has prefixed the mark of possible spuriousness to the Article, though the omission of the Article can alone make the passage really difficult. For this, however, he is not to be blamed, if he thought that the evidence in favour of that reading preponderated. The Oriental Versions appear to have understood the passages, as if the Article were omitted. D and some of the Old Latin Versions omit the clause altogether. See on xii. 26.

CHAP. III.

V. 8. οἱ περὶ Τύρον. A very few MSS. of great note—οἱ. This reading, however, would make Tyre and Sidon to be the scene of action; which is contradicted by the very next verse.

V. 13. εἰς τὸ ὄρος. See on Matthew v. 1.

V. 19. εἰς οἶκον. Two MSS. of little account have εἰς ΤΟΝ οἶκον. Mr. Wakefield, in his N. T., lays some stress on the absence of the Article, and understands οἶκον of the first house which presented itself; adding, " None but those who are ignorant of the Greek language, and are acquainted with *no* language, will treat as pedantic a proper attention to the Article." To this general principle I most readily assent; but that nothing can be here inferred from the want of τὸν is certain, on account of the Preposition preceding. Part i. Chap. vi. § 1.

V. 20. ὄχλος. A. D. Ὁ ὄχλος, which, with πάλιν, is probably right.

V. 28. βλασφημίαι, ὅσας, κ. τ. λ. *Griesb.* admits into the text αἱ before βλασφημίαι. This is not indisputable, ὅσος sometimes allowing its antecedent to be anarthrous. Compare Acts ix. 39. I do not, however, perceive with *Bengel*, that "*Articulus in Edd. omissus magnam sermoni vim addit.*"

CHAP. IV.

V. 1. εἰς τὸ πλοῖον. See on Matt. xiii. 2.
V. 3. ὁ σπείρων. See on Matt. xiii. 3.
V. 22. οὐ γάρ ἐστί τι κρυπτόν. *Griesb.* on the authority of some good MSS. prefixes the mark of possible spuriousness to τι. The word is not necessary. See on Exclusive Propositions, Part i. Chap. iii. Sect. iii. § 5.

CHAP. V.

V. 33. πᾶσαν τὴν ἀλήθειαν. The whole truth respecting the affair in question. See Part i. Chap. vii. § 3.

CHAP. VI.

V. 3. ὁ τέκτων. This term, as *Schoettgen* observes, is of various import, signifying an artificer of any kind whatever. If we may rely on a passage in Justin Martyr's Dial. with Trypho, p. 270. edit. Jebb, the Founder of our Faith τὰ τεκτονικὰ ἔργα εἰργάζετο ἐν ἀνθρώποις ὤν, ΆΡΟΤΡΑ καὶ ΖΥΓΑ. To vindicate the dignity of such an occupation, would be just as absurd, and as foreign from the spirit of the religion of humility, as was the once prevailing fashion of defending the *style* of the Sacred Writers, because, forsooth, it had incurred a sneer from the infidel *Earl of Shaftesbury.* He who can believe that the Almighty Being must select the original promulgers of his will from among those only who possess the advantages of rank and learning, worships not the Universal Father, but the God of his own vain imagination. Still, however, it may be remarked, that our Saviour's employment was not degrading, though, that it was lowly, is evident from the passage now before us. From the Rabbinical writers we learn, that among the Jews, even they who were destined to contemplative life, were yet taught some manual occupation. It was a Jewish maxim, that he who brings not up his son to some kind of work, is as culpable as he who should teach his son to steal. See *Schoettgen* Hor. Heb. vol. ii. p. 898.—In this place there is a variation in a few MSS. and Versions, which makes Christ to be only the *son* of a τέκτων, perhaps, says Wetstein, from the notion that such an art little suited the dignity of our Saviour: and it is remarkable that *Origen* cont. Cels. lib. vi. p. 299. 4to. denies that Christ is ever so denominated by any of the Evangelists: which, however, contradicts the vast majority of MSS. and Versions, as well as general tradition, and the otherwise uniform testimony of the Fathers.

Same v. ἀδελφὸς δέ. C. D. L. have καὶ ὁ ἀδελφός. This must be wrong, because it would make the son of Mary and the brother of James to be distinct persons. See Part i. Chap. iii. Sect. iv. § 2.

V. 14. αἱ δυνάμεις. See on Matthew xiv. 2.

V. 15. ὅτι προφήτης ἐστίν, ἢ κ. τ. λ. According to *Euthymius*, some copies had Ὁ προφήτης, which *Heinsius, Exercc. Sacr.* approves; so that the sense would be, "He is the Prophet predicted of old;" but the almost general consent of the MSS. in omitting ἢ, forbids us to admit the Article and the exposition which is founded on it. The sense is, He is a Prophet resembling one of the Prophets of ancient times.

V. 29. ἐν τῷ μνημείῳ. *Markland* (ap. Bowyer) objects to the Article before μνημείῳ. It is found, indeed, in scarcely any MS. except D, though it was admitted into Stephens's edition, and has since been a part of the received text.

V. 55. ἐπὶ τοῖς κραββάτοις. A. 1. 69.—τοῖς: but the Article may be used for the Possessive Pronoun.

CHAP. VII.

V. 10. τὸν πατέρα σου καὶ τὴν μητέρα σου is here followed by ὁ κακολογῶν πατέρα ἢ μητέρα. These passages are quoted from the LXX. Ex. xx. 12. and xxi. 17; yet there is not in them any irregularity in respect of the Article: see on Matt. vi. 3. and x. 37. To account, however, for the insertion in the one case, and the omission in the other, is among the problems proposed by the *Unknown Writer* alluded to on Matt. xi. 11. He has, besides the present, collected various instances of πατὴρ and μήτηρ (principally from the LXX.) in some of which these words have the Article, and in others are without it. For the insertion, I apprehend no reason will be required: the omissions are all of them, either in consequence of preceding Prepositions, or after an anarthrous governing Noun, or in what I have called Enumeration. In the same page (viz. 25,) he urges, as another unanswerable argument against Mr. Sharp, to whose hypothesis, however, it could not at all apply, that we find in one place περὶ τὴν τρίτην ὥραν, and in another (without the Article) περὶ ἕκτην, which is the common anomaly in Ordinals. He next adduces examples of θεὸς and ὁ θεός, in none of which is the usage violated, (see on Luke i. 15.) and in some the other form could not be adopted. He who is thus ignorant of every thing relating to the point in dispute may, with little invention, find questions to put to his antagonist: it may be doubted, however, whether the interrogative style in controversy be always judiciously chosen.

V. 24. εἰς τὴν οἰκίαν. The Article should be omitted, as in a vast majority of the MSS. Wetstein and Griesbach both reject it.

CHAP. VIII.

V. 8. ἦραν περισσεύματα κλασμάτων. The *Cod. Ephrem* or C has τὰ περισσεύματα. D has τὸ περίσσευμα τῶν κλασμάτων. Neither of these readings appears to conform with the Greek idiom. The former offends against *regimen*, which would require ΤΩΝ κλασμάτων: and the latter contradicts the usage noticed. Part i. Chap. iii. Sect. iii. § 4.

CHAP. IX.

V. 15. πᾶς ὁ ὄχλος. D and edit. Colin.—ὁ, which, however, is indispensable. Part i. Chap. vii. § 1.

V. 41. ὅτι Χριστοῦ ἐστε. It is a question of some interest in Biblical Criticism, whether Χριστός, as used in the N. T. be a Proper Name or an Appellative; and though Dr. *Campbell*, in his Prelim. Vol. D. v. P. iv. has several pages on this very subject, his remarks, however valuable, are not altogether so accurate as to preclude further inquiry.

That Χριστὸς was originally merely an Appellative, descriptive of office or dignity, as Campbell makes it, no one can doubt: he truly observes, that ὁ Χριστὸς was as much an Appellative as ὁ Βαπτιστής, and that the commonness of the name *Jesus* among the Jews, both rendered an addition necessary, and also contributed to the gradual substitution of that addition for the real name. The point to be determined is, How early did this substitution take place, and was Χριστὸς used as a Proper Name, while Christ was still on earth? Campbell says, "This use seems to have begun soon after our Lord's Ascension: in his lifetime it does not appear that the word was ever used in this manner:" and he adds, that in the Titles and some other places of the Gospels, the Writers only adopt the practice of their time. This conclusion would merit our assent, if the learned author had been able satisfactorily to explain away the instances which, as he felt, might appear to be exceptions: but this, I think, he has not done. Thus he adduces John xvii. 3. where our Lord calls himself Ἰησοῦν Χριστόν, but which, from its *singularity*, Campbell suspects should be read ΤΟΝ Χριστόν, to make it an Appellative, though not a single MS. has the Article. Next, respecting the passage which has given rise to this Note, he observes, that in this, as in all other terms, there is an ellipsis of the Article, where the common usage would require it: but what are the limits of this licence he pretends not to show, nor does he adduce any similar example: that the use of the Article is not thus vague, I have every where endeavoured to demonstrate. A similar expression occurs in 1 Cor. iii. 23. ὑμεῖς δὲ Χριστοῦ, Χριστὸς δὲ Θεοῦ, where Campbell, I am persuaded, would readily allow Χριστὸς to be a Proper Name; for in the Epistles he admits it to be common. By way of further exception to his rule, viz. that the absence of the Article generally determines Χριστὸς to be a Proper Name, he adduces Luke ii. 11. Χριστὸς Κύριος; where, however, again, there is no reason for the omission of the Article before Χριστός, if it be an Appellative: and the same is true of Luke xxiii. 2. In one or two other cases instanced by Campbell, the absence of the Article is not decisive either way: but then the ground of this may be assigned. Thus John ix. 22. Χριστὸν might be either Christ or the Messiah, because of the Verb Nuncupative ὁμολογήσῃ;

for as to the Pronoun αὐτόν, it has not, though Campbell supposes the contrary, any thing to do with the business: the sense, however, of the passage compels us, with him, to understand Χριστὸς of the Messiah. For a similar reason it might be doubted in which way Χριστὸς should be taken in Matt. xxvii. 17. and 22. ὁ λεγόμενος Χριστός· for ὁ λεγόμενος Ὁ Χριστὸς would not be Greek: see on Matt. i. 16. Campbell, conformably with his notion, that Pilate, during the lifetime of our Saviour, could not have meant to call him *Christ*, decides for rendering it Messiah: the turn of the expression is, however, so entirely similar to Σίμων ὁ λεγόμενος Πέτρος, that I think its tendency is rather to prove that *Christ* was, even before the ascension, our Saviour's familiar appellation. That He is not so addressed by his disciples is true; but this leads to no conclusion: for in scarcely any instance do they address him by the name Jesus; Κύριε, διδάσκαλε, Ραββί, being the forms usually employed. Besides, as Campbell observes, Vocative Cases would decide nothing, because there the Article could not be used.

On the whole, it can hardly be doubted that the word Χριστός, even during our Saviour's lifetime, had become a Proper Name, though its Appellative use was by much the more frequent: it is, however, very remarkable, that *Michaelis* in his Introduction (edit. Marsh, Chap. vi. Sect. xiii.) says, "*In the time of the Apostles* the word Christ was never used as the Proper Name of a Person, but as an epithet expressive of the ministry of Jesus;" and hence he infers the spuriousness of a passage, Acts viii. 37. which will be noticed in its place. But if Χριστὸς be never used as a Proper Name in the Apostolic Epistles, how are we to explain, among other instances, Rom. v. 6; 1 Cor. i. 12. 23; 2 Cor. iii. 3; Gal. ii. 17; Coloss. iii. 24; 1 Peter i. 11? Are we to translate, "*an anointed person* died," &c.? for to say, "the anointed," or "the Messiah," is more than any of the passages will bear: and no reason can be assigned why, if Ὁ Χριστὸς in such places be really meant, the Article is in all the MSS. omitted. Considering the stress which Michaelis elsewhere lays on the Article, it is surprising that he overlooked this objection.

CHAP. X.

V. 6. ἀπὸ δὲ ἀρχῆς κτίσεως. Part i. Chap. vi. § 1. and Chap. iii. Sect. iii. § 7.

V. 25. διὰ τῆς τρυμαλιᾶς τῆς ῥαφίδος. A. C. F. &c. with a few of Birch and Matthäi—τῆς *bis*; and Griesbach has prefixed to each Article the mark of *possible spuriousness*. There can be no doubt that they are spurious; the latter, because any needle indefinitely is meant, and the former by Part i. p. 51.

V. 29. οἰκίαν ἢ ἀδελφοὺς ἢ κ. τ. λ. *Enumeration*. Part i. Chap. vi. § 2.

V. 31. καὶ οἱ ἔσχατοι πρῶτοι. Many MSS.—οἱ, and Griesbach has removed it to the margin. See above on Matt. xix. 30.

V. 35. οἱ υἱοὶ Ζεβεδαίου. A with some others—οἱ. In this reading there is an appearance of accuracy; for nothing is more prevalent than υἱὸς or υἱοί, without the Article prefixed: but in such cases, if I mistake not, the parentage of the person is, generally speaking, then first announced: here the case is different; for James and John had been declared to be the sons of Zebedee already in this Evangelist, i. 19, 20. The Article, therefore, in this place may serve to recall to the Reader's recollection, that James and John had, in this particular relation, been already introduced to his notice. Vat. 1209. reads οἱ ΔΥΟ υἱοὶ κ. τ. λ.

V. 46. υἱὸς Τιμαίου Βαρτίμαιος. Here several MSS. including B. C. D. L. and five of Matthäi's, but those *among the worst*, have Ὁ υἱός; and Griesbach has, though with the mark of the lowest degree of probability, admitted the Article into the Text. *Wakefield* believes that υἱὸς Τιμαίου is the interpolation of some one who wished to show that he knew the meaning of Bartimæus: the Syr. however, has " Timæus, the son of Timæus," which affords a strong presumption that Bartimæus was not all which was found in the original of St. Mark; and had υἱὸς Τιμαίου been interpolated as an explanation of Bartimæus, it would probably have followed, and not have preceded, the word which it was intended to explain. It appears to me not unlikely that the name of the person was really as the Syr. represents it, Timæus, but that from the circumstance of his father's name likewise being Timæus, he was called also Bartimæus: in this case it was very natural in the Evangelist to add υἱὸς Τιμαίου (the Greek form of expression,) the name by which the person in question was sometimes called: but the Syr. Translator was here compelled to make a slight deviation; for a literal rendering from the Greek would have been " Bartimæus Bartimæus," a repetition which the Syriac Reader would not have understood. The Translator, therefore, very properly consulted the sense of the passage, rather than the literal phrase, by rendering it ܒܪ ܛܝܡܝ ܛܝܡܝ, which expresses, indeed, something more than the supposed Greek original, but not more, possibly, than the Translator knew to be true.—If this conjecture as to the original of St. Mark be right, a step will be gained towards deciding on the Article; for if Βαρτίμαιος came from the Evangelist, and be not a subsequent interpolation, (which is, of the two, more plausible than the opinion of Mr. Wakefield,) the Article should most likely be omitted, since there is an apparent contradiction in announcing the son as already known, and then immediately subjoining his name. I admit, however, that this is only a presumptive argument; for certainty in such cases is not looked for, except where the natural and usual practice cannot be disregarded without positive absurdity.

CHAP. XI.

V. 4. τὸν πῶλον. Very many MSS.—τόν. Probably without the Article, this being all which the sense requires.

V. 13. οὐ γὰρ ἦν καιρὸς σύκων. This passage, as explained by Wetstein and Campbell, though less liable to objection than it had been heretofore, is still not perfectly plain. They have observed that the fig-tree has the property of forming its fruit before the leaves appear: the fruit, therefore, of the tree here spoken of ought to have been now well advanced: it could not, however, have been gathered, because the καιρὸς σύκων, the season of gathering, had not yet arrived: the absence of fruit, therefore, could be accounted for only by the barrenness of the tree. But *Michaelis*, who in his *Anmerk.* on Matt. xxi. 19. has examined the subject at great length, objects that the figs at this time of the year (April) must have been so unripe, as to be wholly unfit to eat. *Shaw*, however, of whom Michaelis has made great use, tells us in his Travels, p. 342. edit. 1757, "that some of the more forward and vigorous trees will now and then yield a few ripe figs six weeks or more before the full season."—But my concern is more immediately with Mr. Wakefield. He observes, that the reason why the Article is wanting (he should have said Articles, for ὁ καιρὸς σύκων would not have been Greek, notwithstanding that Origen and one or two MSS. have this reading) is, because there are in Judæa two seasons of ripe figs in a year. Michaelis affirms, after Shaw, that there are *three;* but this is not the reason why the Articles are wanting, nor could it have been, if we consider, that whatever be the number of gatherings in a year, there can be only one gathering of a given crop. Mr. W. appears to have been misled by observing, Matt. xxi. 34. ὁ καιρὸς τῶν καρπῶν applied to grapes: and no other solution seems to have occurred to him, why the Articles should be used in the one case, but in the other omitted. Whoever compares the two passages will perceive, that in this place the Proposition is confined to *Existence:* see Part i. Chap. iii. Sect. iii. § 1. whilst in St. Matthew *near approach* is predicated of the vintage.

CHAP. XII.

V. 23. ἔσται γυνή. A. D. *à pr. manu* Ἡ γυνή. See above on Matt. xxii. 28. In this verse all the MSS. properly omit the Article before γυναῖκα, by Part i. Chap. iii. Sect. iii. § 4.

V. 26. ἐπὶ τῆς βάτου. This is an undoubted instance of the Rabbinical mode of citing Scripture, and signifies, "in the section which treats of the burning Bush." See above, on ii. 26. If the Reader should be of opinion that the conjecture of *Michaelis* on that place is strengthened by the present passage, (and the word ἀνέγνωτε, which is found in both, though in the former it is placed rather too far from ἐπὶ Ἀβιάθαρ, in some degree removes the objection,) the Article before ἀρχιερέως will be necessary, and its force will be that which I have assigned it: the difference will be confined to the Preposition.

V. 27. ὁ θεὸς νεκρῶν, ἀλλὰ θεὸς ζώντων. In this passage

there is a great variety in the reading, arising probably from an apparent difficulty in the construction of the Article. Ὁ Θεὸς νεκρῶν, if the words were in Regimen, could not be tolerated: νεκρῶν must, therefore, depend on a second Θεὸς understood. This in many MSS. is inserted, whilst a few would obviate the supposed difficulty by omitting the Article, and making the Proposition exclusive, "There is no God," &c. which, though it offends not against the idiom, is but a lame expedient. The insertion of Θεὸς before νεκρῶν accurately explains the Ellipsis, but is wholly unnecessary, and Θεὸς before ζώντων, in the received Text, is yet more superfluous. Griesbach, on the authority of many MSS. has removed it into the Margin.

V. 36. ἐν τῷ πνεύματι τῷ ἁγίῳ, A multitude of MSS. and several editt.—τῷ bis: and Griesbach rejects the Articles. If, as the context seems to require, we are here to understand *the influence* of the Spirit, the omission is right. See on Matt. i. 18.

V. 41. βάλλει χαλκόν. Wetstein's 1. 69. and Origen have τόν. In Luke xxi. 1. it is τὰ δῶρα αὐτῶν: in the same manner τὸν χ. would mean *their* money. I am, however, of opinion, that the Article is spurious; and indeed it is well known that Wetstein's 1. 69. and Origen (to which in general may be added his 13 and 33) amount to little more than one evidence.

CHAP. XIII.

V. 11. τὸ πνεῦμα τὸ ἅγιον. Evidently the Holy Spirit in the personal acceptation. See on Matt. i. 18.

V. 28. τὴν παραβολήν. The Article here is not without its use, as a superficial Reader might conclude: a particular similitude is founded on a particular tree.

CHAP. XIV.

V. 10. ὁ Ἰούδας ὁ Ἰσκαριώτης εἷς τῶν δώδεκα. The first Article in a great many MSS. including A. B. C. D. is wanting; and Griesbach prefixes to it the mark of *probable* spuriousness. Judas had never been mentioned by this Evangelist excepting once in Chap. iii. which is so far back, that the use of the Article would hardly be justifiable on the ground of previous mention; and when it is subjoined, that the Judas here spoken of was one of the twelve, the spuriousness of the Article is fully established.—The second Article also is absent from a few MSS. and probably should have been omitted in all. See on Matt. x. 4. The Vat. 1209. alone prefixes Ὁ to εἷς, which is altogether without meaning.

V. 23. τὸ ποτήριον. Here again several MSS.—τό, and Griesbach has the mark of possible spuriousness. See on Matt. xxvi. 27.

V. 36. Ἀββᾶ ὁ πατήρ. *Heinsius* (ap. Bowyer) conjectures Ὁ πατήρ, i.e. ὅ ἐστι μεθερμηνευόμενον πατήρ, and even *Schleusner* considers ὁ πατήρ to be an interpretation of Ἀββᾶ, though he does not adopt the conjectured Ὁ. The word Ἀββᾶ occurs three times in the N. T. and always with the same addition: the MSS. have no various reading, except that in this place Wetstein's 69. and Birch's Vind. Lamb. 31. subjoin μου. This reading accords with the Syr. whence, no doubt, it was taken; and that excellent Version, if we compare it in the three places with the Greek, shows plainly in what manner ὁ πατήρ must be understood: for it renders ὁ πατήρ, *my* Father, or *our* Father, as the circumstances of the case require. The Article, therefore, has here, as elsewhere, the force of a Possessive Pronoun: and ὁ πατήρ must be taken for a Vocative Case, like ὁ υἱὸς in this Evangelist, x. 47; ὁ βασιλεύς, Matt. xxvii. 29; Κύριε ὁ θεός, Apoc. xv. 3. which answers the objection of *Lightfoot.* Mr. *Wakefield*, indeed, thinks, that "every Reader of sensibility would rejoice at the suppression of ὁ πατήρ, as in the Arabic and Persian Versions." Other Critics, however, (and I must request to be admitted of their number) have regarded the addition as expressive of the most impassioned feeling. Ἀββᾶ was the Oriental term, by which children *familiarly* addressed their parents: the addition of "my Father" was requisite to give it solemnity and force.

V. 41. τὸ λοιπόν. A great many MSS. including several of Wetstein's best,—τό, and Griesbach prefixes his mark of *probable* spuriousness. In the sense, however, in which the word is here used, I do not find that the Article is ever omitted in the N. T. nor, so far as I recollect, even in the classical Writers. Some of Matthäi's MSS. also want the Article, but not any of those which he deems most valuable.

V. 69. ἡ παιδίσκη. The Article in this place, as Biblical Scholars well know, has been a source of great embarrassment. St. Matthew, relating the same transaction, has instead of ἡ παιδίσκη, (the maid recently mentioned) ἄλλη, another maid. To get rid of this difficulty *Michaelis* had proposed (Introd. by Marsh, Chap. x. Sect. iv.) to read simply παιδίσκη. *Rosenmüller*, with less apparent temerity, has recourse to the common expedient of making ἡ παιδίσκη equivalent to παιδίσκη τις, "*quomodo interdum sumi Articulum, certum est:*" than which nothing is more absurd in theory, or more false in practice. The whole difficulty, however, has arisen from the vain expectation that the Evangelists must always agree with each other in the most minute and trivial particulars; as if the credibility of our Religion rested on such agreement, or any reasonable scheme of inspiration required this exact correspondency. The solution which Michaelis afterwards offered in his *Anmerkungen*, affords all the satisfaction, which a candid mind can desire. After stating that Matthew had said " another maid," Mark " the maid," and Luke " another *man*" (ἕτερος), he observes, " the whole contradiction vanishes at once, if we only attend to John, the quiet spectator of all which passed: for he writes, xviii. 25, *They* said to him, Wast not thou also one of his disciples? Whence it appears, that there were several, who spake on this occasion, and that all, which is said by Matthew, Mark, and Luke, may very easily be true: there might probably be more than the three, who are named: but the maid, who had in a former instance recognized Peter, appears to have made the deepest impression on his mind, and hence in dictating this Gospel to Mark, he might have said, *The* maid."

I have since perceived that the remark from *Rosenmüller*, given in this Note, belongs to *Grotius:* but its value is not by this discovery either increased or diminished. It may not be amiss to mention once for all, that Rosenmüller, whose *Scholia* are for the most part a compilation, very rarely points out the particular source, from which his information is derived. Hence in the explanations which he offers, he has in general no other merit or demerit, than that of the selection.

CHAP. XV.

V. 43. Ἰωσὴφ ὁ ἀπὸ Ἀριμαθαίας. *Bengel* (in Gnom.) observes, "*Articulus ostendit hoc Josephi cognomen esse factum: Matthæus Articulum non ponit, quia ante Marcum scripsit.*" I think that there is something in this remark, and that it is capable of being extended: not, indeed, that the Article could, in the present form of expression, have been omitted; but the whole expression might have been different.

It is well known, that considerable doubts prevail respecting the order, in which the four Gospels were written. All, which is certain, is that John's Gospel was written last: it is thought probable, that St. Matthew's is the oldest; though some are of opinion that the first place is to be given to St. Luke. St. Mark, according to the majority of Critics, for here again they are divided, followed both St. Matthew and St. Luke. The probability that this is the true place of St. Mark, is, I think, somewhat strengthened by the manner in which the four Evangelists first make mention of Joseph of Arimathea. St. Matt. xxvii. 57. says ἦλθεν ἄνθρωπος πλούσιος ἀπὸ Ἀριμαθαίας, τοὔνομα Ἰωσήφ. This is the language of an Historian, who wrote before Joseph had acquired celebrity. St. Luke xxiii. 50. has, ἀνὴρ ὀνόματι Ἰωσήφ, ἀπὸ Ἀριμαθαίας πόλεως τῶν Ἰουδαίων. This is even more explicit than the former: but is, perhaps, not so much an argument for the priority of St. Luke's Gospel over that of St. Matthew, as for the generally received opinion, that St. Luke wrote in Greece. St. Mark (in this place) has, ἦλθεν Ἰωσήφ, ὁ ἀπὸ Ἀριμαθαίας, εὐσχήμων βουλευτής· here it is supposed that the addition of ὁ ἀπὸ Ἀριμαθαίας will enable the Reader to recognize the person meant. Lastly, John xix. 38. has ἠρώτησεν ὁ Ἰωσὴφ ὁ ἀπὸ Ἀριμαθαίας· if this be the true reading, we have here language adapted to still increased notoriety: many MSS. however, omit the first ὁ.—Something similar may be observed in the manner, in which the four Evangelists introduce the name of Pilate. Matthew xxvii. 2. has παρέδωκαν αὐτὸν Ποντίῳ Πιλάτῳ τῷ ἡγεμόνι. Luke's first mention of him is iii. 1. ἡγεμονεύοντος Ποντίου Πιλάτου τῆς Ἰουδαίας, and again xiii. 1. ὧν τὸ αἷμα Πιλάτος ἔμιξε. Mark in this Chapter, ver. 1.

introduces Pilate with merely παρέδωκαν τῷ Πιλάτῳ, one MS. only (viz. the Vat.) omitting the Article. John xviii. 29. ἐξῆλθεν οὖν ὁ Πιλάτος, no MS. omitting the Article.—If similar instances abounded, they would form, perhaps, somewhat of a criterion, by which we might be assisted in determining, if not the order of the four Evangelists, at least the place of St. Mark.

CHAP. XVI.

V. 1. διαγενομένου τοῦ σαββάτου. The Sabbath being *over*: hence this does not contradict Part i. Chap. iii. Sect. iii. § 1.

V. 15. πάσῃ τῇ κτίσει. Eng. Version, " to every creature:" Campbell, "to the whole creation:" the latter is the more correct. See on πᾶς, Part i. Chap. vii. § 1.

V. 16. ὁ πιστεύσας καὶ βαπτισθείς. In the *Complutens.* edit. the second Participle also has the Article, which would materially alter the sense. Part i. Chap. iii. Sect. iv. § 2. It would imply, that he, who believeth, as well as he who has been baptized, shall be saved; whereas the reading of the MSS. insists on the fulfilment of both conditions in every individual.

ST. LUKE.

CHAP. I.

V. 1. Ἐπειδήπερ πολλοὶ ἐπεχείρησαν ἀνατάξασθαι διήγησιν, κ. τ. λ. The Reader cannot be unacquainted with *Mr. Herb. Marsh's* most ingenious and profound Dissertation on the Origin of the Three first Canonical Gospels; in which he assumes as the basis of all the three, a Hebrew Document marked in his notation by א. This Document, he thinks, (p. 197.) may have been entitled in Greek, Διήγησις περὶ τῶν πεπληροφορημένων ἐν ἡμῖν πραγμάτων, καθὼς παρέδοσαν ἡμῖν οἱ ἀπ' ἀρχῆς αὐτόπται καὶ ὑπηρέται γενόμενοι τοῦ λόγου· in which case it is actually referred to in the Preface to St. Luke. This had been the conjecture of *Lessing*. Mr. Marsh, after stating several objections to another way of understanding this Preface, and after observing that the proposed conjecture will obviate them all, leaves it to others to determine, whether the attempt is not rendered abortive by the want of the Article before διήγησιν. His general hypothesis, it is truly remarked by him, will at any rate remain unaffected: the conjecture, however, if it could be confirmed, would afford so direct and decisive evidence of the existence of the supposed Document, that I cannot without reluctance proceed to offer the following observations.

With respect to the Article the rule is, I believe, that the Title of a Book, as prefixed to the Book, should be anarthrous; but that when the Book is referred to, the Article should be inserted. *Dion. Hal.* ed. Reiske, vol. i. p. 182. has Καλλίας δὲ ὁ ΤΑΣ Ἀγαθοκλέους Πράξεις ἀναγράψας· the Title of this Book was probably Πράξεις Ἀγαθοκλέους similar to Πρ. τῶν Ἀποστόλων. So also p. 172. Σάτυρος ὁ ΤΟΥΣ ἀρχαίους μύθους συναγαγών· the Title must have been Ἀρχαίοι μῦθοι: as Plutarch has denominated a work Ἐρωτικαὶ διηγήσεις.

CHAPTER I. 205

Longinus also (§ 9.) has εἴγε Ἡσιόδου καὶ ΤΗΝ Ἀσπίδα θετέον· the Title, as prefixed to the Poem, is Ἀσπὶς Ἡρακλέους. The reasons for the assumption, and also for the non-assumption, are sufficiently obvious. The Reader may further consult what was said Part i. p. 106. on the names of Dramas: we must, indeed, except instances, where the name of the work is governed by a Preposition, or where any other of the causes already alleged will account for the omission: to say that a passage is found ἐν Μηδείᾳ is perfectly admissible: for this is the common anomaly. Part i. Chap. vi. § 1.

I must further express my doubts, whether the supposed difficulties require us to understand Διήγησιν, &c. as the title of a document. Mr. Marsh has stated four objections, which I will not transcribe, because his work is in every body's hands. To the First, it may be answered, that if διήγησιν in the Singular be exceptionable, the Plural would not be less so; since it might imply that each individual of the πολλοὶ had written *several* narratives: the Syr. however, has the Plural. Secondly, With respect to the word ἀνατάξασθαι, which Mr. M. would understand as signifying to "re-arrange a narrative already written," it is certain, that the Preposition ἀνὰ does not always in composition retain its proper force: ἀναγράφω very frequently is no more than γράφω, as has been shown by *Raphel*: it is so used also in the first of the citations above from Dion. Hal. and so also very commonly in Josephus. The word itself ἀνατάσσομαι is so rarely found, that it is difficult to determine any thing respecting it with certainty: in the N. T. it is ἅπαξ λεγόμενον: in the LXX. we are referred by Trommius to Eccl. ii. 10. where, however, it does not appear: in ii. 20. we have ἀποτάξασθαι. Plutarch, in his Treatise Πότερα τῶν ζώων, &c. Ed. 1674. p. 479. uses the word, I think, equivocally: he says, that some elephants having been previously taught certain attitudes and movements, one of them, who had often been punished for his dulness, was seen by moonlight ἀνατατόμενος τὰ μαθήματα καὶ μελετῶν· this instance, however, the Reader will, perhaps, deem favourable to Mr. Marsh: it is the only one, which my small library enables me to adduce. Hesychius has explained the word by εὐτρεπίσασθαι, unless this be one of the sacred Glosses subsequently inserted: see *Bentley's* Letter to *Biel*, in Alberti's Hesych., or in Bentley's Correspondence, which has been so splendidly published by *Dr. Ch. Burney.* That ἀνατάξασθαι διήγησιν is simply to write a narrative, seems probable from what follows, ἔδοξε κἀμοὶ γράψαι. Thirdly, It will not be necessary to substitute αὐτοῖς for ἡμῖν in ver. 2. unless we reject the Syr. and (if I may trust the Latin) some other ancient renderings of πεπληροφορημένων : they explain it to signify " things of which we are firmly persuaded:" the Syriac word is the same which is employed, Luke xx. 6. to express πεπεισμένος : Schleusner has shown that this rendering may be vindicated from the N. T.; and if so, we may understand the second verse as assigning the *ground* of the firm conviction which had been mentioned in the first : καθὼς not unfrequently signifies *siquidem, propterea quòd :* (see Schleusner) ἡμῖν will be, "to us Christians." The Fourth objection will be answered, if we admit the answer to the third : they were not eye-witnesses who had composed narratives; these, probably, were credulous persons, who had blended falsehood with truth, for which reason St. Luke, in ver. 4. uses the word τὴν ἀσφάλειαν: the eye-witnesses were those on whose authority rested the conviction mentioned in ver. 1.

On the whole, then, so far as I can judge, (and I offer my opinion with great deference,) no difficulties really exist: if they do, I fear that the omission of the Article destroys the conjecture by which it is proposed to remove them.

V. 15. Τοῦ Κυρίου. *Griesb.* on the authority of many MSS. rejects τοῦ : and *Matthäi* thinks that the Article was originally interpolated by some one who wished it to be understood that Κύριος, in this place, signifies God. It has already been observed, on Matt. i. 20. that Θεὸς and also Κύριος, in the sense of *God*, either take or reject the Article indiscriminately ; a licence which these words derive from their partaking of the nature both of Appellatives and of Proper Names. It may be right, however, to fix the usage with somewhat more precision than was done in the Note referred to.

With respect to Θεός, there is, I believe, no instance in the N. T., though the word occurs more than thirteen hundred times, in which it does not conform to that law of Regimen which forbids an anarthrous Appellative to be governed by one having the Article prefixed : and hence such a phrase as ὁ υἱὸς

Θεοῦ is not to be found. In some other respects also it follows the common rule of Appellatives, e. g. in rejecting the Article where it (Θεὸς) is the Predicate of a Proposition which does not reciprocate, as in John i. 1. for as to Θεὸς being sometimes used in an inferior or qualified sense, an opinion which Mr. *Wakefield* and others have found it convenient to adopt, there is not a single example of such an use in the whole N. T. Θεὸς is God, or *a* God, either true or false, real or imaginary; but never *superior* or *inferior*. But more of this on Romans ix. 5. For the present it is sufficient to show that the absence of the Article affords not, as some have affirmed, any indication of this pretended subordinate sense; for in many of the passages in which, without dispute, Θεὸς is meant of the Supreme Being, the Article is not used: see Matt. xix. 26.; Luke xvi. 13.; John i. 18. ix. 33. xvi. 30.; Romans viii. 8.; 1 Cor. i. 3.; Gal. i. 1.; Eph. ii. 8.; Heb. ix. 14.— But Κύριος, in Regimen at least, is not so strictly limited; since we find Matt. i. 24. ὁ ἄγγελος Κυρίου. Luke i. 38. ἡ δούλη Κυρίου. Acts ii. 20. τὴν ἡμέραν Κυρίου. James v. 11. τὸ τέλος Κυρίου. The word Κύριος, therefore, differs in the manner in which it is used, from Θεός, by approaching more nearly to a Proper Name; for Proper Names, it will be remembered, are very commonly anarthrous, though depending on Appellatives which have the Article: thus in the verse just cited from St. James, τὸ τέλος Κυρίου is immediately preceded by τὴν ὑπομονὴν Ἰώβ. The LXX. indeed, have frequently translated the incommunicable names of the One True God, יהוה and יה, by Κύριος, and that too most commonly without the Article: so that the interpolation of the Article, according to the probable conjecture of Matthäi mentioned above, tended rather to defeat the purpose of the interpolator; for though both Κύριος and Ὁ Κύριος are used in the N. T. to signify God, yet Κύριος without the Article, without the addition of the name of Christ, and so circumstanced that none of the rules for Appellatives will show why the Article is wanting, signifies *God* almost invariably: I say *almost* invariably; for undoubted instances of the contrary occur. The learned and excellent Bishop *Pearson*, in his great work on the Creed, (p. 150. edit. 1723,) has, indeed, collected about a hundred examples to prove that Κύριος, without the Article, is used to signify the *Son:* but on examining them I found by far the greater part of them to be wholly inconclusive: thus, at least half of them consist of such phrases as ἐν Κυρίῳ, ὑπὸ Κυρίου, κατὰ Κύριον, where the Article may have been omitted because of the Preposition; and in some of them this was plainly the reason, for ἐν Κυρίῳ is immediately preceded or followed by Ὁ Κύριος used in the same sense: see 1 Cor. ix. 1. xv. 28.; 2 Cor. x. 17. In others of his examples we have Κυρίου after some anarthrous Noun: in some, Κύριον follows a Verb *Nuncupative,* or one of *appointing*: in a few, the *reading* is doubtful: in some, we may fairly question whether the Son be meant. He has quoted even Ephes. iv. 5. εἷς Κύριος, "there is one Lord," not considering that εἷς Ὁ Κύριος would have conveyed a totally different meaning. His least exceptionable instances are, Matt. iii. 3. and the parallel places, τὴν ὁδὸν Κυρίου, and 1 Thess. v. 2. with 2 Pet. iii. 10. ἡ ἡμέρα Κυρίου, though the first of them is not entirely free from objection, being a quotation from the LXX. where Κύριος represents the Heb. Jehovah: the latter may be admitted to be satisfactory. To these examples we may add 2 Cor. iii. 17, 18. τὸ πνεῦμα Κυρίου and τὴν δόξαν Κυρίου, with a few others, which the Bishop has not noticed: also Rom. xiv. 6. which is decisive. The instances adduced by him of the form Κύριος Ἰησοῦς Χριστὸς are certainly to his purpose, but do not affect my remark.

The same illustrious writer complains, that "the Socinians will have ὁ to be an *accession* to Θεός, but a *diminution* from Κύριος." That Θεὸς in the N. T. is equivalent to ὁ Θεὸς has already been shown: but what if we admit that ὁ Θεός, where there is no reason for omitting the Article, be, though not universal, at least the more common? The writers of the N. T. adhered, in great measure, to the usage established before their time. Now if we turn to the LXX. we shall find that they call the false gods of Egypt and of Canaan θεούς, but never Κυρίους; which is the more remarkable, when we consider the etymology and meaning of בְּעָלִים: this, however, they have never rendered by Κύριοι, but have commonly left untranslated, by giving the word Βααλείμ. The Jews, indeed, from their proneness to idolatry, seem to have regarded the false gods, as not wholly without power, though fatal experience so frequently convinced them, for the moment at least, how wretched was their delusion: hence the true God was generally called ὁ Θεός, as distinguished from other Θεοί: but in Κύριος, a name exclusively appropriated to the true God, no such mark of distinction was necessary: Κύριος assumed the rank of a Proper Name; and yet sometimes it took the Article; for though used as a Proper Name, it was not a name arbitrarily imposed, but was evidently derived from the dominion of Him, to whom it was given.—There is, then, no just ground of alarm, if the Socinian remark be in part admitted: the doctrine of the Article, if well understood, can tend only to the confirmation of the true Faith.—It is evident, however, that the reading in respect of the verse before us cannot with any certainty be determined, ἐνώπιον having the nature of a Preposition, and that Editors of the N. T. can have no other guidance on similar occasions, than the majority of the best MSS.

Same v. πνεύματος ἁγίου. The *influence* of the Holy Spirit. See Matt. i. 18.

V. 17. Κυρίῳ. A and a few others insert τῷ. See above on ver. 15.

V. 32. υἱὸς ὑψίστου. Here Mr. *Wakefield*, with his usual attention to the *letter* of the original, translates "*a* son of the most High God:" why he did not from regard to consistency write also "*a* most High God," I do not pretend to know; yet assuredly that rendering would have been equally defensible. If the phrase be not here meant in a pre-eminent sense, the declaration of the angel amounts to very little, at the same time that it ill accords with what immediately follows: the prophecy must be either, that Christ should be called the Son of God, in the sense in which he afterwards so styled himself, or else that he should merely be one of the υἱοὶ Θεοῦ, of which number is every righteous person in every age. See Rom. viii. 14. Υἱός, it is true, wants the Article in the original, and so it must have done, allowing the sense to be the most definite: for Ὁ υἱὸς after κληθήσεται would not be Greek. With respect to ὑψίστου, this word in the LXX. also is frequently without the Article. See Part i. Chap. vi. § 4. *Regimen* may also affect the present instance.

V. 35. πνεῦμα ἅγιον. This is commonly understood in the

Personal sense, but I think improperly. "A divine influence" equally well suits the occasion, and conforms better with the general usage: and indeed δύναμις ὑψίστου in the next clause appears to be explanatory of πνεῦμα ἅγιον in the present.

Same v. υἱὸς Θεοῦ. Here also, of course, Mr. *Wakefield* translates "*a* son of God." See on ver. 32. Besides, if υἱὸς Θεοῦ be here to be taken in the inferior sense, what becomes of the inference implied in διό? To announce to the Virgin that she shall have offspring by the extraordinary agency of God, and to add "*therefore* that offspring shall be called (or shall be) *a holy man*," really appears to me to be a downright anti-climax. It is also observable, that when Zacharias below (ver. 75.) prophesies of John, he does not say that John shall be called υἱὸς ὑψίστου or υἱὸς Θεοῦ, which in Mr. Wakefield's way of understanding that phrase, he might very well have done, but he says προφήτης ὑψίστου κληθήσῃ, which is not more appropriate when applied to him, of whom it was afterwards said, that there was not a greater Prophet (Luke vii. 28.), than is υἱὸς ὑψίστου or υἱὸς Θεοῦ in the highest acceptation, when applied to Christ.

V. 66. χεὶρ Κυρίου. So also in the other work of St. Luke, Acts xi. 21. and xiii. 11. (for so we should read in the last instance with the best MSS.) χεὶρ wants the Article by Part i. Chap. iii. Sect. iii. § 6.

V. 78. διὰ σπλάγχνα ἐλέους Θεοῦ ἡμῶν. Every attentive reader of the two songs of Thanksgiving of Mary and Zacharias, contained in this chapter, must have remarked in them certain peculiarities of style: but the only one, with which I am concerned, is, that they are extremely *anarthrous*. I do not, indeed, mean to affirm, that they ever violate the rules, but only that they display the utmost *latitude of omission*, which the rules allow: and this is nothing more than we might antecedently have expected: they might be supposed to retain some traces of the character of their originals, which certainly were not Greek. Michaelis says (in his *Anmerk.*) of the latter of them, "that it appears to have been spoken in Hebrew, not in Chaldee the vernacular idiom, for that the Jews still used Hebrew in their prayers. Its not having been composed in the mother-tongue may explain," he adds, "why the periods are so unrounded, consisting of many short clauses forcibly brought together." Both compositions have unquestionably a Hebrew air; and if we add to their Hebrew origin, that they are also *poetical* compositions, their frequent omission of the Article in cases, in which it would probably have been found in an original Greek narration, can excite no surprise. Whoever will compare the LXX. translation of the Song of Deborah with the Hebrew, will perceive that it has in most instances, so far as the Article is concerned, conformed with the strict letter of the original, and that it is so far anarthrous as scarcely to be tolerable Greek.

I have been led into these observations, not at all more by the words which introduce the present note, than by some other passages to be found in the two Thanksgivings: in those passages, indeed, the Article might have been employed, where it is now omitted; in the present instance, διὰ ΤΑ σπλάγχνα would have made it necessary to write ΤΟΥ ἐ. ΤΟΥ Θ. ἡμῶν· as it stands, the whole precisely agrees with the Hebrew form, and is also perfectly defensible on principles, with which the Reader is by this time well acquainted.

V. 80. ἐκραταιοῦτο πνεύματι. The same phrase and the same sense of πνεῦμα occurs below, ii. 40. The sense is plainly *in mind*, mentally, as opposed to corporeally. But the question is, Can any general rule be laid down respecting the Article, where πνεῦμα is so used? I think not. In this sense we find it without the Article in Rom. viii. 13. Gal. v. 16, 18, 25. 1 Pet. iii. 18. (for such should be the reading): but then, in other places, as John xi. 33; xiii. 21. Acts xviii. 25; xx. 22. 1 Cor. xiv. 15. we have ΤΩι πνεύματι, and in one instance, Mark viii. 12. τῷ πνεύματι ΑΥΤΟΥ, an addition which, however, adds nothing to the sense, but shows only in what manner the Article in that and the preceding instances should be understood. Would it, therefore, have been allowable in the Evangelist to have written ἐκραταιοῦτο ΤΩι πνεύματι? I doubt not that it would. He has, however, used the more indefinite and adverbial form, the sense not requiring the limitation of πνεύματι, though such a limitation might very well be admitted. Yet I do not affirm, that in all the anarthrous instances above adduced the Article might be inserted: thus in Gal. v. 16. πνεύματι περιπατεῖτε, the insertion of τῷ would injure the sense; for the precept is to walk spiritually, i. e. in such a manner as the spiritual or better part, not merely of the persons addressed, but of men without limitation, would suggest and approve. Although, therefore, it may not be possible so to circumscribe the rule, that it shall not be liable to partial objection, still the reason of the case will commonly point out a preference in the form: and where either form is equally well adapted to the particular case, no exception can justly be taken against the uncertainty of the practice. See Part I. Chap. v. Sect. ii. § 2.

CHAP. II.

V. 1. Καίσαρος Αὐγούστου. Here L and *Euseb.* have ΤΟΥ Αὐγούστου, a reading which supposes Augustus not to have been as yet recognized as a Proper Name. In the Acts we have Σεβαστός, the translation of Augustus, *with* the Article, as might be expected; for by translating we lose the Name and revert to the Epithet, in which the Article is required. This may serve to illustrate more fully what was said on Χριστός, Mark ix. 40.

V. 2. αὕτη ἡ ἀπογραφὴ πρώτη ἐγένετο. On this passage so much has been written, that a mere abstract of the whole would far exceed my limits. It will be recollected, that the difficulty consists in reconciling the Evangelist with *Josephus*, who makes the taxing here spoken of to have taken place ten or eleven years later than the period of our Saviour's birth. Hence a multitude of solutions have been attempted, and various conjectures risked. Many Interpreters have thought, that πρῶτος is here put for πρότερος, of which use there are examples, as John i. 15. πρῶτός μου ἦν. Of this opinion are *Beausobre* and *Schleusner*. But the cases are not similar: to say that one person was before another, is unexceptionable: but to say that a taxation was before Quirinius, is harsh in the extreme; or if the meaning be, before the *presidency* of Quirinius, the original, as *Campbell* well observes, would have been τῆς ἡγεμονίας Κυρηνίου or τοῦ ἡγεμονεύειν Κυρήνιον. Others have thought that πρὸ τῆς before ἡγεμονεύοντος has been lost by the Copyists; a conjecture, which is adopted by *Michaelis* both in his *Anmerk.* and in his *Introduction*, but of which, besides that it is mere conjecture, our learned Translator of the latter work has well observed, that "according to the proposed emendation, the Greek of this passage is really too bad to have been written by St. Luke, and the whole construction savours neither of Greek nor of Hebrew." *Lardner* supposed, that we ought to supply *afterward* Governor of Syria; but then we must have read ΤΟΥ ἡγεμονεύοντος or ΤΟΥ ἡγεμόνος; for which see on Mark ii. 26. And it is remarkable, that in the only instance, which he produces, the Article is prefixed. *Newcome's* translation after Lardner is faulty in another respect also, as will be shown hereafter. *Casaubon* in his *Exercitt. ad Baron.* p. 115—130. has examined the subject at great length: he supposes Quirinius to have been, at this time, sent into Judea for the purpose of the enrolment, and that this was a distinct mission from that of his Presidency mentioned by Josephus. This interpretation differs from the last, inasmuch as it makes ἡγεμονεύοντος to be significant of this particular duty, and not of the subsequent Presidency. This explanation, as well as a former one, must be pronounced to be mere unsupported hypothesis, and it is also incompatible with the words of St. Luke, as will be seen. Amidst all this perplexity the most probable solution (for probability is all which can be pretended) is that preferred by *Wetstein* and *Campbell*. They understand St. Luke to mean, that though the *census* was actually set on foot about the period of our Saviour's birth, it was presently laid aside, or at least no consequences followed the imperial decree, till ten or eleven years afterwards in the Presidency of Quirinius. Campbell rests this interpretation principally on the meaning of ἐγένετο, which he explains to signify not merely to be, but *to be completed* or *to take effect:* and numerous instances of this and kindred meanings of γίνομαι are produced by Schleusner; though, as was remarked, he has preferred a different interpretation. It is true, that Josephus has not related that any order for enrolment was issued at this time: yet he adverts to circumstances, which make it not improbable, that some measure of this kind might be thus early adopted. In the latter part of Herod's reign, which terminated only two years after the birth of Christ, we learn from Josephus, (lib. xvi. p. 735. edit. Huds.) that Augustus became offended with Herod, and in an angry letter threatened henceforth to treat him as a slave: by this threat it might fairly be understood, that he meant to reduce Judea to the state of a Roman Province; and it is not unreasonable to suppose, though the threat was not executed in the lifetime of Herod, that steps might have been taken to make him believe, that the Emperor was in earnest. In the reign of Archelaus, Herod's successor, the enrolment actually took effect: Archelaus was deposed, and Judea was made subject to Augustus.

But not only is the opinion of Campbell, as stated by himself, the most plausible, which I have met with; but further, I think it may be strengthened by an argument, of which he seems not to have been aware. His translation is, "This first register took effect," &c. whence it is evident that he understood πρώτη to agree *immediately* with ἡ ἀπογραφή, not to follow ἐγένετο. The same construction is adopted also by Wakefield. Newcome, following Lardner, has, "this was the first enrolment." Different from these and more correct is our English Version; which separating πρώτη from ἡ ἀπογραφὴ gives it the adverbial sense: "this taxation was first made." Had our Translators understood ἐγένετο as explained by Campbell, their Version of this passage would then have been perfect, and it would have expressed the sense, which that Critic has adopted, more strongly than he has done it, merely by being in stricter conformity with the original Greek. He did not perceive that πρώτη is without the Article: and that consequently his mode of rendering, as well as Newcome's, is inadmissible; ἡ ἀπογραφὴ πρώτη being a form of speech, which, if the words be meant to be taken in *immediate concord*, is without example either in the N. T. or the LXX. The ground of the impropriety was explained Part i. Chap. viii. I am aware that πρῶτος is an Ordinal; but even Ordinals have not this licence. The more usual form would be ἡ πρώτη ἀπογραφή; but if ἡ ἀπογραφὴ precede, Ἡ πρώτη must follow. So Apoc. xx. 5. αὕτη ἡ ἀνάστασις Ἡ πρώτη· see also iv. 1. 7; xxi. 19. And in the LXX. Dan. viii. 21. αὐτός ἐστιν ὁ βασιλεὺς ὁ πρῶτος· also Joel ii. 20. Exod. xii. 15, 16. 1 Reg. xiv. 14. Zach. xiv. 10. and in many other instances, which *Trommius's Concordance* will supply; for though he has a few apparent exceptions, they turn out, on examining the places, to be either false readings or inaccurate quotations. It is plain, therefore, notwithstanding the great authority of *Casaubon*, who affirms the contrary, and who appears to have been implicitly believed, that the absence of the Article before πρώτη is not unimportant: it points to a solution different from that which has usually been given, by making it probable that πρώτη must be understood in the adverbial sense, as was done by the English Translators. Of this sense of the word in the N. T. instances may be found in *Schleusner*, and for the classical use see *Thieme's Lex. Xenoph.* and *D'Orville* in *Charit.* p. 313. The meaning will then be, that "the enrolment here alluded to first took effect (or did not take effect till) under the Presidency of Quirinius."

Three MSS. including Vat. 1209. omit the Article: on that supposition, ἀπογραφὴ must not be taken with αὕτη, since οὗτος in its Adjective use requires its Noun to have the Article. Part i. Chap. vii. § 5.

I learn from Michaelis (Introd. vol. i. p. 267. edit. Marsh) that *Kluit* has grounded his explanation of this passage chiefly on the use of the Greek Article. In what way he has done this, and what is his explanation, I know not. It is possible, that in this and in some other instances our conclusions may be the same: in which case, it may be presumed that they are not wholly unfounded, having been independently deduced.

V. 7. ἐν τῇ φάτνῃ. A few of Wetstein's best MSS. but not any of Matthäi's—τῇ, and Griesbach has prefixed to it the mark of possible spuriousness. The presence of the Article in the received Text has been drawn into the dispute respecting the place of our Saviour's birth. *Baronius*, principally on the authority of a passage in *Justin Martyr's Dial.* with *Trypho*, makes the birth-place of Christ to have been in the *vicinity* of Bethlehem, and not in Bethlehem itself: and the place of his nativity is frequently by the Fathers denominated σπήλαιον or ἄντρον. *Casaubon* (Exercitt. p. 145.) has considered this subject also at great length; and he argues that the Article shows the φάτνη in question to be that which belonged to the stable of the κατάλυμα mentioned in the same verse: " *illud præsepe, quod erat in stabulo pertinente ad diversorium.*" His argument is not altogether invalidated, supposing the various reading to be the true one (which, however, is not probable), for the Preposition might cause the absence of the Article, even though φάτνη were intended definitely. But the great difficulty is, to ascertain the *meaning* of φάτνη: for though the Article would prove that not *any* φάτνη was meant, still it would leave the import of the word undetermined. Casaubon would render it "the manger:" Campbell, Beausobre, Michaelis, and the English Version, have "*a* manger;" which, of course, supposes ἐν φάτνῃ to be the true reading. Wakefield and Rosenmüller say, "in the *stable*;" a sense which the word is known to bear: and Schleusner understands it of the *area* before the house, a space inclosed, but without any covering, in which stood the cattle and implements of agriculture; it was, therefore, according to this notion, not unlike a farm yard.

With respect to Casaubon's opinion, that the Article refers us to something certain and definite, so as to make φάτνη Monadic, it can hardly be doubted: but I think he is mistaken in supposing that a *manger* would be spoken of thus definitely in relation to the κατάλυμα. The stable and the inn might very well be thus contradistinguished, but not so well the inn and the manger: of mangers there would probably be several; but if not, the very circumstance that there *might* be several, would render this definite mode of speaking somewhat unnatural. But there is another consideration which seems to be of importance, though I am not aware that any attention has been paid to it. The context of the whole passage convinces me that the φάτνη was not merely the place in which the Babe was laid, but the place also in which he was born and swaddled: I understand the words ἐν τῇ φάτνῃ to belong as much to ἔτεκεν as to ἀνέκλινεν, for else where did Mary's delivery happen? Certainly not in the κατάλυμα, for there we are immediately told that there was not room: not room for whom? not merely for the new-born infant, but αὐτοῖς, for Mary and Joseph. By φάτνη, therefore, we must understand some place in which they might find accommodation, though less convenient than that which the κατάλυμα would have afforded them, had it not been occupied; and such a place could not have been a manger. It might be either a stable or an inclosed area; but more probably the former; for an inclosed area without any covering, seems not to afford the shelter and privacy which the situation of Mary rendered indispensable, and, moreover, is not to be reconciled with the

Fathers, who called the birth-place of Christ an ἄντρον or σπήλαιον, nor indeed with the tradition which, according to all the Travellers, still prevails in the East, that the scene of the Nativity was a Grotto. That the *stable* might be really such, is made highly probable by the remark of Casaubon, who has observed, after *Strabo*, that the country for many miles round Jerusalem is rocky; and he adds, that an Arabian Geographer has described such excavations to be not unfrequently used in those parts for dwellings. The stable of the κατάλυμα, if it were so hewn out, might very well be called a σπήλαιον, or if it were formed chiefly by nature, it would still better merit the appellation. But Casaubon's other reason, that the meanness of the place might also justify the term, in the same manner as in Theocritus we have ἰλεόν, οὐκ οἴκησιν, is much less satisfactory: from the mouth of *Praxinoe* such a figure of speech is perfectly natural, as is, indeed, every syllable in the *Adoniazusæ*; but such a ludicrous hyperbole would ill accord with the character of *any* of the Fathers, and was still less to be expected from *several* of them: indeed their agreement plainly indicates that they meant to be understood literally.

The remaining difficulty is to explain why Justin Martyr has made the birth-place of Christ to be *near* and not *in* Bethlehem: and on this I have nothing better to offer than the obvious remark, that even though the inn were without the village, still, inasmuch as it belonged to Bethlehem, whatever had happened at an inn so situated, might fairly be said to have happened at Bethlehem: this laxity of expression, if it must be so considered, cannot require to be exemplified or defended. It may be added, that, according to *Volney*, the Traveller, as quoted in a very useful compilation, *Burder's Oriental Customs*, the houses of public reception in the East " are always built without the precincts of towns." Supposing this to have been the case in the time of the Evangelist, his manner of expressing himself must have been understood by others, as it appears to have been by Justin.

Casaubon, for having, among other things, laid some stress in this place on the Greek Article, is warmly attacked by one *Peter Lansselius*, a champion of Baronius, in a Tract annexed to Justin's Works, edit. Paris, 1615. This Writer is one of the multitude who teach that Articles are very unmeaning things; and he instances in this Chap. ver. 11 and 12, σωτὴρ without the Article, and σημεῖον with it. He should have told us on what principle the contrary might have been expected: σωτὴρ is there very properly without the Article, because it is then first mentioned; and σημεῖον as properly has the Article, because not *any* sign indefinitely is spoken of, but the sign of the thing in question. This Peter Lansselius appears to have been a good Catholic, but a sorry Critic.

V. 12. ἐν τῇ φάτνῃ. Here the best MSS.—τῇ, and Griesbach very properly rejects it.

V. 25. πνεῦμα ἅγιον. A divine influence. Τοῦ πνεύματος τοῦ ἁγίου following may be intended of the same divine influence, and the Article may signify only the renewed mention: however, I am disposed to believe that the latter is meant in the personal acceptation, because of the act there imputed. See on Matt. i. 18.

V. 32. φῶς εἰς ἀποκάλυψιν ἐθνῶν, κ. τ. λ. This song of Simeon has, as might be expected, something of the anarthrous character mentioned above on i. 78.

CHAP. III.

V. 21. καὶ 'Ιησοῦ βαπτισθέντος. *Markland* (ap. Bowyer) conjectures τοῦ 'Ιησοῦ, and he thinks that wherever the Article is wanting before the name Jesus, the want has always proceeded from the negligence of the Transcribers, except, indeed, where the name begins a sentence, or where some descriptive epithet is subjoined, as 'Ιησοῦς Χριστός, 'Ιησοῦς ὁ Ναζωραῖος, &c. I have not been able to discover that this conjecture, or the general emendation of which it is a part, has any support. It is not true, as Markland supposes, that the omission of the Article gives to the name the contemptuous sense *one Jesus*, or that the respect and reverence which the disciples entertained for him, rendered the insertion of the Article necessary. The uses of the Article before Proper Names, and the limitations, so far as they can be assigned, have been noticed in the former Part: it may be observed, however, that it is not in the manner of the Sacred Historians to impute celebrity to Christ, or to assume that he is known to the Reader: on the contrary, they all, at the beginning of their narratives, tell us who is the subject of their story. That they usually write Jesus with the Article, affords no presumption that they did so always: they observe the same practice with respect to other Proper Names, which have recently been mentioned.

But Markland has the two exceptions mentioned above. He says of the first, that it prevails, though he sees not the reason of it; and he instances the first verse of the next Chapter. I do not perceive, however, that the exception is at all constant: see Matt. ii. 1; xiii. 57; xvii. 11; xxvi. 6. and other places in which we find ὁ δὲ Ἰησοῦς, or some one of its cases beginning sentences; and there can be no doubt that the next Chap. might in like manner have begun with ὁ δὲ Ἰησοῦς: it is, therefore, needless to look for the *ground* of this exception, since the fact alleged does not exist. If there can be any reason assignable why the next Chap. should rather begin as it does, I should suppose it to be, that since the last mention of the name of Jesus, a whole catalogue of names has intervened, so that Jesus could hardly have been uppermost in the mind either of the Historian or his Reader. If it be thought that ὁ Ἰησοῦς, at the beginning of the Acts, contradicts this reasoning, let it be remembered that a reference to St. Luke's former work precedes the mention of Jesus, and might therefore recall him to the mind of Theophilus antecedently to the actual mention. On a nicety of this kind, however, I mean not to lay undue stress, but only to show that Markland's opinion appears to be unsupported. Of his second exception he says, that the reason is obvious, meaning, I suppose, that the addition makes the Article superfluous. It should be observed, however, that ὁ Ἰησοῦς Χριστὸς is admissible, when Χριστὸς is not an Appellative, but a Proper Name: which, as was shown on Mark ix. 40. is sometimes the case. See Matt. i. 18. and Acts viii. 37.

V. 3. υἱὸς Ἰωσὴφ τοῦ Ἡλὶ τοῦ, κ. τ. λ. *Lightfoot*, in order in some measure to lessen the difficulty attending this genealogy, tells us that υἱός, and not υἱοῦ, should be supplied throughout, so that the sense may be, "the son of Joseph, consequently the son of Heli, and therefore ultimately the son of Adam and of God." Now this is to suppose that the Article τοῦ is every where not an ellipsis of τοῦ υἱοῦ, but the Article of the Proper Name subjoined: in that case, however, we should certainly have found, τοῦ prefixed to Ἰωσήφ, for no reason can be imagined why it was not as necessary there as elsewhere; and further on in the Genealogy we actually meet with τοῦ Ἰωσὴφ twice. But on the usually received construction, the first-named Joseph is rightly without the Article, since such an omission guards the Reader, so far as it is possible, against the very mistake into which Lightfoot, and others after him, have fallen. *Raphel* has given from Herodotus a Genealogy which in form exactly accords with this of St. Luke; Λεωνίδης ὁ Ἀναξανδρίδεω τοῦ Λέοντος τοῦ; κ. τ. λ. . . . . . τοῦ Ἡρακλέος. The ancient interpreters, the best judges in a question of this kind, explained St. Luke in the same manner.

With the various hypotheses invented to reconcile the Genealogies by Matt. and Luke I have no concern: they may be seen fully detailed in the Βίβλος καταλλαγῆς of *Surenhusius*.

CHAP. IV.

V. 1. ἐν τῷ πνεύματι. It is not universally agreed, in what sense πνεῦμα is here to be taken. *Wakefield* renders "by that spirit," meaning πνεῦμα ἅγιον just mentioned, which, according to the rule of interpretation laid down Matt. i. 18. must mean the *influence* of the Spirit: I think, however, that in this case the Evangelist would have written ἐν τῷ πνεύματι ἐκείνῳ or ἐν τῷ αὐτῷ πνεύματι. As the reading now stands, I am inclined to interpret πνεῦμα of the *Person* called the Holy Spirit, and to make ἐν equivalent to ὑπό, signifying *through the agency of*, a common Hebraism; once, indeed, I was of opinion, that the hypothesis, which some Critics have adopted, of our Saviour's Temptation being a *visionary*, not a *real* transaction, was favoured by this expression of St. Luke; for τῷ πνεύματι frequently signifies *in his mind or spirit*. This inquiry, however, has led me to observe, that then the Preposition is always omitted; as in Mark viii. 12. John xi. 33; xiii. 21. Acts x. 20 [1]. Besides, of ἐν τῷ πνεύματι meaning "by the agency of the Holy Spirit," we have

[1] There is a mistake in this reference. It has been suggested to me that it should be Acts xx. 22. but I think rather xviii. 5. or 25.—J. S.

an instance in this Evangelist, ii. 27. If to these considerations we add that Matt. and Mark in the parallel passages have expressed themselves less equivocally, we need not hesitate to understand ἐν τῷ πνεύματι in the personal sense. Many cogent arguments against the doctrine of a visionary temptation are detailed with great perspicuity in the fourth of the "Lectures on St. Matthew" by the *Bishop of London*, a work, which would have done honour to the better ages of Christianity.

V. 4. ὁ ἄνθρωπος. *Griesb.* on the authority of several MSS. prefixes to ὁ the mark of probable spuriousness. But see on Matt. iv. 4.

V. 38. ἡ πενθερὰ δὲ τοῦ Σίμωνος. A great majority of the MSS.—ἡ, and it is rejected both by *Wet.* and *Griesb.* I do not perceive on what principle the Article can here be omitted: it is true, that the received reading can hardly be right, since it throws δὲ too far from the beginning of the sentence : but Wetstein's C. and 106. Birch's 360. and Matthäi's *x*, which are mostly MSS. of repute, have ἡ δὲ πενθερά, which, I doubt not, came from the Evangelist.

CHAP. V.

V. 29. καὶ ἦν ὄχλος τελωνῶν. *Complut.* has Ὁ ὄχλος, which before τελωνῶν *without the Article*, is so gross a deviation from the usage, that supposing it to have been found in any MS. it excites some curiosity respecting the history and quality of such a MS. The Cod. Esc. 8. of Birch, according to *Moldenhawer*, by whom the Escurial MSS. were collated (See Birch's Proleg. p. 79.) "*abundat otiosis Articulorum additamentis*," but I do not know of any affinity between this MS. and the Complut. Between this celebrated Edit. and the Cod. 1 Havn. the agreement is said to be very remarkable. See same Proleg. p. 90.

CHAP. VI.

V. 12. εἰς τὸ ὄρος. See Matt. v. 1.

Same v. ἐν τῇ προσευχῇ τοῦ Θεοῦ. There exists a difference of opinion, whether this mean "in prayer to God," as our Eng. Version renders it, or "in the *proseuche* or oratory of God," which is the interpretation of *Camp.* and others. The following are the reasons, which induce me to prefer the common explanation. 1. It is well known, that the προσευχαὶ of the Jews were not usually situated among mountains, to which, however, Christ is here said to have retired. It appears from Acts xvi. 13. and from the well-known decree of the Halicarnassensians, recorded in Josephus Antiq. xiv. 10. 23. that προσευχαὶ were always situated near water, either that of some river or of the sea : the mountain district was not likely to afford the requisite convenience. 2. If an oratory had been meant, it is not likely that τοῦ Θεοῦ would have been added, for all oratories were τοῦ Θεοῦ. 3. It is objected, that if prayer to God were here intended, the idiom would require πρὸς τὸν Θεόν : but this may be doubted. At least it is certain that the *genitive* of the object after εὐχὴ is unexceptionable Greek : see Eurip. Ion, 638. Troad. 889. Soph. Œd. Tyr. 239. Of προσευχή, indeed, the compound, I do not find any similar use : but the word is of rare occurrence in profane writers. 4. To pass the night in prayer, without (so far as I know) going to an oratory, appears to have been a common act of Jewish devotion. This is noticed by *Schoettgen*, Horæ Hebr. 5. Some stress has been laid on the presence of the Article in this place : but this is not unusual before προσευχὴ in the sense of prayer : see Matt. xxi. 22. Acts i. 14. 1 Cor. vii. 5.

V. 35. υἱοὶ τοῦ ὑψίστου. *Griesb.* on the authority of many MSS.—τοῦ. See on i. 32.

V. 48. ἐπὶ τὴν πέτραν. See on Matt. vii. 24.

CHAP. VII.

V. 5.[1] τὴν συναγωγήν. Eng. Version "a synagogue." But this implies, that there were several synagogues in Capernaum ; which is contrary to the spirit of the original. The Article, as is observed by *Campb.* and *Markl.* (apud Bowyer) shows that there was at that time only one synagogue in the place.

V. 28. ὁ μικρότερος. That the Comparative is here by an *Enallage* put for the Superlative, is generally admitted : the only question is, whether ὁ μικρότερος here refer to any person

---

[1] V. 3. πρεσβυτέρους τῶν Ἰουδαίων. There is an ellipse of τινὰς here. Τοὺς πρεσβυτέρους would be nonsense.—H. J. R.

in particular. Some have thought, and of this number are a few of the Fathers, that we are by ὁ μικρότερος to understand Christ, from his being junior in ministry and indeed in age to John. I cannot but suspect that in this decision, as in so many others, the force of the Article has been mistaken. See especially on Matt. xii. 29. The tenor of the argument seems not to require any such restriction, but rather, I think, rejects it: for that Christ should say of Himself that He was greater than the person, whom He had just described as having been sent to prepare His way, amounts to nothing: besides, the expression is ὁ μικρότερος ἐν τῇ βασιλείᾳ τοῦ Θεοῦ, i. e. under the Gospel Dispensation; so that the comparison must be, not, as the interpretation supposes, between the Baptist and Christ, but between Christ and the body of Christians, in respect of whom Christ, assuredly, cannot be called ὁ μικρότερος. *Michaelis* (Introd. by Marsh, vol. i. p. 79.) understands μικρότερος, from the context, to signify the least *prophet*; and on this he grounds a curious argument for the inspiration of the N. T. That interpretation certainly may be tolerated; but if προφήτης be not supplied from the former clause, then the assertion will be still more comprehensive; viz. that every person enjoying the light of the Christian Revelation shall possess advantages, which were denied to the most favoured of mankind under the former Dispensation. In this sense the promise of Christ has been abundantly fulfilled: the most unlettered Christian, who has ever attended to religious instruction, being endued with a knowledge of divine truths which the Almighty did not vouchsafe to the Prophets of the O. T. nor even to the Baptist. In this manner the passage is understood by *Schoettgen*, Hor. Hebr. and, I believe, by the majority of Critics. According to either of these latter interpretations, the Article is used in the *Hypothetic* sense.

CHAP. VIII.

V. 5. ὁ σπείρων. See on Matt. xiii. 3.

CHAP. IX.

V. 20. τὸν Χριστὸν τοῦ Θεοῦ. According to *Mill*, the Copt. here read σὺ εἶ Χριστὸς Ὁ Θεός· which *Wet.* has represented as being Χριστὸς Θεός. For the omission of the Article he is sharply reprehended by *Matthäi*: "Puerile autem est, quod Wetsteinius ex ista lectione furtim sustulit Articulum : cur non potius supra I. 16. sustulit τὸν Θεόν? ibi enim Christus diserte appellatur Κύριος ὁ Θεὸς 'Ισραήλ." It would not always be an easy task to vindicate the manner in which Wet. has treated passages relating to our Saviour's Divinity: mere accident, however, may, in the present instance, have led to the omission of a single letter; which, after all, is of no importance, even if the Copt. reading had been confirmed by the best MSS., except that Χριστὸς ὁ Θεὸς is more consonant with the Greek usage. I have, however, already on Matt. i. 2. hinted at the extreme difficulty of ascertaining with precision what readings were found in the MSS. used by the Oriental Translators. The Coptic has here what is equivalent to 'Ο ΧΡΙΣΤΟΣ ΦΘΑ [1] : *Phtha* was an Egyptian name of the Deity, for which see the authors referred to by the Commentators on Cicero de Nat. Deor. Lib. iii. Cap. 22. "*in Nilo natus OPAS*, &c. ;" and also Jablonski's Pantheon Ægyptiacum: but whether *Phtha* be more fitly represented by Θεὸς or ὁ Θεός, it is not, I should think, possible to determine ; since the One undoubted God is signified by both these terms in various places of the N. T.

V. 48. τοῦτο τὸ παιδίον. *Beza* and *Grotius* (ap. Bowyer) would here read ΤΟΙΟΥΤΟ τὸ παιδίον. This reading, however, would not be Greek ; for though οὗτος requires its Substantive to take the Article, this is not the case with τοιοῦτος either in the N. T. or in profane writers. It is needless to adduce examples of the contrary use, since they are so common.

V. 60. θάψαι τοὺς ἑαυτῶν νεκρούς. Mr. *Herb. Marsh*, in his Origin of the Three first Gospels, p. 129. mentions a conjecture by *Bolten*, that the Syriac of this and the parallel passage, Matt. viii. 22. is to be rendered by "*relinque mortuos* SEPELIENTIBUS *mortuos suos*." Mr. Marsh observes, that "if

---

[1] In this remark I followed Wilkins, the Editor of the Coptic Version, who makes *Phtha* to be a single word ; and he adds, that they who understand it to be an abbreviation representing the noun *Noudi* (God) with its Article, " *rem acu haud tetigerunt*." Proleg. p. 10.—I find, however, that *La Croze*, Lex. Ægypt. p. 62. is of a different opinion. *Non nostrum tantas componere lites:* I know nothing more of Coptic, than any man may acquire in a month.

the passage occurred either in St. Matt. alone, or in St. Luke alone, one might conjecture that the Greek text was originally ἄφες τοὺς νεκροὺς ΘΑΨΑΣΙ τοὺς ἑαυτῶν νεκρούς, and that through an oversight of the Transcribers the Σ in θάψασι was omitted, and the Participle thus converted into the infinitive θάψαι. But that the same oversight should have happened in both places, is not probable."

I much doubt, however, whether a single Evangelist would have translated Syriac or Chaldee words signifying " Leave the dead to those whose office it is to bury the dead," by the Greek given above: for neither does the Participle of the first Aorist θάψασι, notwithstanding some remarkable uses of that Tense, seem well adapted to express "those whose office it is," nor will it be easy to account for the omission of the Article. In Acts v. 9. οἱ πόδες τῶν θαψάντων τὸν ἄνδρα σου, the Participle marks a past act: the *office* appears rather to require the Present Tense, as in the LXX. 2 Kings ix. 10. οὐκ ἔστιν ὁ θάπτων, and John ii. 16. τοῖς τὰς περιστερὰς πωλοῦσιν εἶπεν. With respect to the Article, had the Proposition been negative and exclusive, the case would have been different: as it now stands, τοῖς is, I believe, indispensable: so John i. 22. ἵνα ἀπόκρισιν δῶμεν ΤΟΙΣ πέμψασιν ἡμᾶς.

The conjecture of Bolten has the approbation both of Mr. Marsh and of Eichhorn: is it not, however, an objection of some weight, that ܡܝ̈ܬܝܗܘܢ has the affix, *mortuos suos*? In the usual way of understanding the passage, the affix strengthens the sense.

CHAP. X.

V. 6. ὁ υἱὸς εἰρήνης. A great majority of the best MSS.— ὁ and *Griesb.* properly rejects it. *Beza, without the authority of MSS.* says Wet., inserted the Article, supposing it to be necessary: on the contrary, the *Regimen* will scarcely endure it. *Raphel*, however, so far from thinking the Article necessary in this place, has recourse to the solution common in all difficulties, viz. that ὁ is here used *indefinitely*.

V. 14. ἐν τῇ κρίσει. See on Matt. x. 15.

V. 21. τῷ πνεύματι. Several MSS. and most of the old Verss. including the *three* Syr. and all the Lat. add τῷ ἁγίῳ, possibly, says *Wolfius*, because it was imagined that πνεῦμα with the Article could be intended only of the Holy Spirit. I believe this to have been the cause of the interpolation; which, however, must have been made at a very early period. Τῷ πνεύματι, as has been elsewhere observed, frequently means no more than *in his mind* or *within himself*. See above iv. 1. It ought to be mentioned, that of Matthäi's MSS. only *one*, and that among the least considerable, has the addition.

V. 29. πλησίον. *Markl.* would read Ὁ πλησίον, and two or three inconsiderable MSS. have this reading. It must be confessed that the conjecture is at the first view plausible, but yet I suspect that it is not sound. In ver. 27. we have indeed τὸν πλησίον, but there the Article was necessary; for *without* it the meaning would be, " thou shalt love near thee," which obviously is not sense: τόν, therefore, was requisite to give the signification of *the person* near thee, or thy neighbour. But how stands the case in the present verse? The question is, Who is near me? i. e. *near* in the same sense in which the word had just been employed. I do not, then, perceive any defect in this construction, and I am persuaded that the received reading is the true one, on comparing it with ver. 36. where not a single MS. has ventured to interpolate the Article. It is there asked, Who of the three appears to have been *near* him, who fell, &c. [1]

CHAP. XI.

V. 4. ἀπὸ τοῦ πονηροῦ. See on Matt. v. 37.

V. 7. εἰς τὴν κοίτην. Eng. Version says, " My children are with me in bed." A difficulty has arisen in determining whether they were all in the *same* bed : some Critics, whom Bishop *Pearce* and *Campbell* have followed, make μετ' ἐμοῦ to mean only " as well as myself." Possibly, however, κοίτη may signify the bed-chamber; in which case, the same κοίτη held the whole family. According to *Chardin*, as quoted by *Harmer*, it is usual in the East for the whole family to sleep in the same chamber, on different beds or mattresses laid on the floor. *Newcome*, I observe, has adopted this interpretation.

---

[1] Winer says that Döderlein compares Æsch. Prom. 940. Ἐμοὶ δ' ἔλασσον Ζηνὸς ἢ μηδὲν μέλλει, where he says that μηδὲν seems to be for τοῦ μηδέν.— H. J. R.

CHAPTER XI.

V. 13. δώσει πνεῦμα ἅγιον. The *aid* of the Holy Spirit: see what was remarked above on Matt. i. 18. under the fifth head; of which the present instance is a good illustration: accordingly the Greek Scholiasts have χάριν πνευματικήν. See *Matthäi ad loc.*

V. 15. ἄρχοντι τῶν, κ. τ. λ. Several good MSS. have τῷ ἄρχοντι, and *Griesbach* has admitted the Article into the Text. In this admission there was something of temerity. Ἄρχων is one of those words which, being liable to be considered either as a Participle or a Substantive, may in this case either take or reject the Article: as a Substantive it would reject the Article, as a Participle it would require it. The substantive use appears to be that here meant, and it is, indeed, the more common in the N. T. In the parallel place, Matt. xii. 24. not a single MS. has the Article. In the present instance only three of Matthäi's MSS. and those not the best, have τῷ.

V. 30. τοῖς Νινευίταις. The Article is here properly inserted, though it was omitted Matt. xii. 41. I ought not, however, there to have said, that with the Articles the assertion would not have been true; since in Jonah ii. 5. the repentance of the Ninevites is affirmed to have been general. Still, however, the Articles were not necessary: it was sufficient to declare simply, that "men of Nineveh should," &c.— I observe that Dr. *Gillies* in his valuable "History of the World from Alexander to Augustus," (Prelim. Survey) has assigned several strong reasons to prove that the Nineveh here spoken of was situate in the neighbourhood of Babylon, and was not the city which stood opposite to the modern Mosul, between 36 and 37 deg. of Northern Latitude, near the Tigris. Yet *D'Anville* (Euphrate et Tigre, p. 88.) treating of Mosul, says, "On sait que la rive opposée, ou la gauche du fleuve, conserve des vestiges de Ninive, et que la tradition sur la prédication de Jonas n'y est point oubliée." Is this merely one of the unfounded Mohammedan traditions which are so prevalent in the East? Ἀλλὰ ταῦτα ὡς ἐν παρόδῳ.

V. 34. ὁ ὀφθαλμός. The proposition is convertible. See Part i. p. 74.

V. 36. ἔσται φωτεινὸν ὅλον. *Michaelis* (Introd. vol. ii. p. 404.) observes, that "this verse would be more intelligible, if we inserted the Article, ἔσται φωτεινὸν ΤΟ ὅλον. The meaning of the passage would then be, If in consequence of one perfect eye the whole body is light, take care that the whole, i. e. the whole man, body and soul, become light. The eyes give light to the body; but that which Christ calls light, shall enlighten, or give true knowledge to the whole man." The sense which would thus arise is, indeed, unexceptionable: but, perhaps, nearly the same meaning is conveyed in the reading of the MSS. In the sense of *wholly*, ὅλον does not require the Article: see Part i. Chap. vii. § 4.: the meaning, however, will be the same, whether we render, " it will be wholly enlightened," or "the whole will be enlightened." In the former case, it is true, the reference will be to σῶμα: but I much doubt whether, if we had read TO ὅλον, we could have understood it of the "body and soul," nothing more than the body having been mentioned, though the soul be the object which our Saviour has in view: and to this, probably, by a tacit inference the application is to be made. In ver. 35. the analogy between external and internal light had been established: in the present, the complete illumination described in the concluding clause, though intended of the mind, is affirmed only of the body, the application, after what had been said, being supposed to be obvious. *Rosenmüller* appears to have understood the passage somewhat in this manner, when he says, "*permixta est nempe rei comparatæ ipsa comparatio.*" If these remarks have any weight, the conjecture of Michaelis becomes gratuitous.

V. 42. τὸ ἡδύοσμον. Part i. Chap. iii. Sect. ii. § 2.

CHAP. XII.

V. 6. καὶ ἓν ἐξ αὐτῶν. Three editt. of *Erasmus* here read TO ἕν. This, in speaking of *five* things, would not conform with the Greek usage. See 1 John v. 7.

V. 10. εἰς τὸ ἅγιον πνεῦμα. The Holy Spirit, the *Person* so denominated. See on Matt. xii. 32. Compare also Mark iii. 28. In these places it may be observed, in confirmation of what was said on Matt. i. 18. that the Article is employed. The only difference is, that in two of them the phrase is τὸ πνεῦμα τὸ ἅγιον, which, however, is equivalent. A few MSS. indeed, have in this place also the same form. D, as in

CHAPTER XII.

St. Matthew, omits the second Article. The *Compiler* of that MS. was not always sufficiently on his guard.

V. 14. δικαστήν. Part i. Chap. iii. Sect. iii. § 3.

V. 54. τὴν νεφέλην. A few MSS. (among which are A. B.) —τήν. Dr. *Owen* (ap. Bowyer) approves the omission; but in this, as in other instances, the Article has its meaning. We read in 1 Kings xviii. 44. that the appearance of a certain cloud rising out of the sea was regarded as a prognostic of rain. Now the sea lay westward of Palestine; and, therefore, the cloud which rose out of the sea, might also be said to rise from the West. If, then, we put these circumstances together, there is good reason to suppose that the cloud here spoken of was a well known phenomenon, which would naturally and properly be adverted to as Ἡ νεφέλη. Mr. *Bruce* in his Travels has noticed a similar appearance attending the inundation of the Nile. *Newcome*, in his Revision of the Common Version, has adopted this explanation, and yet he translates " *a* cloud." I cannot help thinking that a Revision would be extremely imperfect, or indeed would be nearly useless, if it were to overlook minute circumstances, such as that before us. It is in niceties of this sort principally, that our English Translation admits improvement: its general fidelity has never been questioned; and its style, notwithstanding the captious objections of Dr. *Symonds*, is incomparably superior to any thing which might be expected from the finical and perverted taste of our own age. It is simple; it is harmonious; it is energetic; and, which is of no small importance, use has made it familiar, and time has rendered it sacred. Without the least predisposition to decry the labours of the Writer to whom I have alluded, I may express the hope, that whenever our Version shall be revised by authority, the points last attended to will be those which respect a pretended inelegance of language. A single instance of the suppression of a local custom or popular opinion, which can be shown to have existed among the Jews in the age of the Apostles, appears to me to be of infinitely higher importance; because, by concealing from the notice of the Reader circumstances which are beyond the reach of fabrication, we withhold from him perhaps the strongest evidence of the authenticity of the Scriptures, and consequently of the credibility of our Religion.

CHAP. XIII.

V. 27. πάντες οἱ ἐργάται. *Griesbach* following several MSS. prefixes the mark of possible spuriousness to οἱ : but, as I think, without reason; especially when ΤΗΣ ἀδικίας follows.

CHAP. XIV.

V. 28. τίς ὑμῶν θέλων, κ. τ. λ. Many MSS. have Ὁ θέλων. This reading implies that there is an *assumption* of his wishing to build, as if we should say, Who of you, *supposing that* he wished. It is, therefore, not an improbable, though by no means a necessary, reading.

V. 34. τὸ ἅλας. (Part I. Chap. iii. Sect. ii. § 2.)

CHAP. XV.

V. 22. τὴν στολὴν τὴν πρώτην. A few good MSS. have στολὴν without the Article, and *Griesbach* thinks that it may possibly be spurious. It was shown, Part i. Chap. viii. § 2. that the Article of the Substantive is in such cases frequently omitted : it is, however, much more frequently inserted, as in the very next verse, ΤΟΝ μόσχον τὸν σιτευτόν.

CHAP. XVI.

V. 22. εἰς τὸν κόλπον τοῦ Ἀβραάμ. *Griesbach* rejects τοῦ : it is totally unnecessary, and the best MSS. are without it.

CHAP. XVII.

V. 1. τὰ σκάνδαλα. See Matt. xviii. 7.

V. 4. τῆς ἡμέρας. The Article here, though lost in the English, is not without its use, as has been already shown: see on Matt. xx. 2. : so also Hebrews ix. 7. and LXX. Exod. xxiii. 14.

V. 17. οἱ δέκα. A Reader of our Common Version, "Were there not ten cleansed?" might suppose the Article in the Greek to be a mere expletive. The original, however, means to say, "Were not the whole ten (recently mentioned) cleansed?" which, though it make no alteration in the tenor of the argument, is very different in the turn of the expression. *Wakefield's* Translation accords with the Greek.

V. 34, 35. ὁ εἷς, ἡ μία. The first Article *Griesb.* has rejected, and to the second he has prefixed his mark of probable spuriousness. I do not perceive any difference in the two cases, except that the MSS. which omit ὁ are rather more numerous than those which want ἡ. This, however, is a very insufficient criterion; nor can it be well doubted, that both ὁ and ἡ are genuine or spurious alike: I am disposed to think them genuine. See on Matt. vi. 24.

CHAP. XVIII.

V. 2. ἄνθρωπον μὴ ἐντρεπόμενος. Not regarding *any* man. It is not said, in like manner, *any God*, because only one God was in the Historian's contemplation [1].

V. 13. ἐμοὶ τῷ ἁμαρτωλῷ. *Wet.* here remarks, "*τῷ habet emphasin,* τῷ καθ' ὑπερβολὴν ἁμαρτωλῷ." The influence thus ascribed to the presence of the Article is, I believe, unfounded; and the mistake seems to have arisen from inattention to an usage which, though sufficiently common, I do not remember to have seen noticed. It prevails in the Profane Writers, no less than in the N. T. and in Verse as well as in Prose: it is, that When any of the words which in the First Part of this Work I have denominated Attributives, is placed in apposition with a Personal Pronoun, that Attributive has the Article prefixed. An instance occurs in this Evangelist, vi. 24. ὑμῖν ΤΟΙΣ πλουσίοις, where *pre-eminent* wealth cannot be intended. So also xi. 46. ὑμῖν ΤΟΙΣ νομικοῖς. We find the same form of speech in Xenoph. Cyrop. lib. iv. p. 66. κἀγὼ μὲν Ὁ τάλας; and ibid. lib. vii. p. 109. ἐγὼ ἡ μωρά. In both these instances, it is true that *Sturz*, in his Continuation of *Thieme's* Lex. Xenoph. vol. iii. p. 232. supposes *emphasis*; and so also in another example adduced by him, viz. ἐγὼ ἡ παρακελευομένη, where the very notion of emphasis is ridiculous: indeed his

---

[1] V. 9. πρός τινας τοὺς πεποιθότας ἐφ' ἑαυτοῖς. Here, says Winer, to τινας, by which persons not accurately defined are designated, is added a more exact description by means of a definite quality: *He said to some persons, and they were such as trust in themselves.* Bp. Middleton would probably have said, *Some persons,* viz. *those who (were known) to trust in themselves.* See note on v. 13. Winer refers to Herm. ad Soph. Œd. C. 167. Döderlein ad Œd. C. p. 296.—H. J. R.

whole account of the Article is liable to much objection. See also Herod. lib. ix. p. 342. μὲ τὴν ἱκέτιν. Plut. Conviv. Sept. Sap. p. 95. ἐμὲ τὸν δύστηνον. The same usage occurs in Theocritus Idyll. iii. 19 and 24. μὲ τὸν αἰπόλον, and ἐγὼ ὁ δύσσοος, and Idyll. ii. 132. See also Soph. Electra, 282. Edit. Brunck. ἐγὼ ἡ δύσμορος. Eurip. Ion, Edit. Beck, 348. σφὲ τὸν δύστηνον. Aristoph. Aves 5. Achar. 1154. Eccles. 619. Many other examples will present themselves to the reader, nor need so many to have been produced, had the opinion of Wetstein been of less weight: it seems, indeed to have been implicitly followed: thus on μὲ τὸν ταλαίπωρον, Eurip. Hec. 25. *Ammon* informs us that "the Article in this place strengthens the expression of misery and misfortune," &c. &c.: but if Ammon's Edition of the Hecuba had nothing worse in it, it might be tolerated. Of the usage in question the ground is sufficiently obvious: the Article here, as elsewhere, marks the assumption of its Predicate, and the strict meaning of the Publican's Prayer is, "Have mercy on me, who am *confessedly* a sinner," or, "*seeing that* I am a sinner, have mercy on me."

V. 27. τὰ ἀδύνατα . . . . . δυνατά. There cannot be a better example than this, of the use of the Article in marking *assumption* as distinguished from *assertion*. Part i. Chap. iii. Sect. iv. § 1.

V. 29. γονεῖς ἢ ἀδελφούς, κ. τ. λ. Part i. Chap. vi. § 2.

CHAP. XIX.

V. 2. ἀρχιτελώνης. What was the rank and office of this person? Our Version calls him "the chief among the Publicans:" to this *Campbell* objects, that it seems to imply the chief of the whole order in Palestine, in which case the word would most probably have been attended with the Article. Thus, he adds, it is always said Ὁ ἀρχιερεύς, when the High Priest is spoken of: and he concludes with making this ἀρχιτελώνης the chief Publican of that particular city or district; which interpretation, however, will, on Campbell's principle, require the Article just as much as would that which he rejects. But the truth is, that be the meaning of the word what it may, the Article must here be omitted; ἦν Ὁ ἀρχιτελώνης would offend against the usage noticed, Part i. Chap. iii. Sect. iii. § 2.

(unless, indeed, there had been a dispute whether Zaccheus or some other person were the ἀρχιτελώνης;) and with respect to what Campbell says of ὁ ἀρχιερεύς, his error has arisen from his not adverting to that usage: for though ὁ ἀρχιερεὺς be the common appellation, yet the Article here, as elsewhere, is omitted whenever the word follows a Verb Substantive. Thus, by this Evangelist, in Acts xxiii. 5. St. Paul is made to say of him, who in the preceding verse is called τὸν ἀρχιερέα τοῦ Θεοῦ, " I knew not ὅτι ἐστὶν ἀρχιερεύς:" which is strictly similar to the passage under review. So also St. John xi. 49. 51; xviii. 13. and in the LXX. 2 Macc. xv. 12. τὸν γενόμενον ἀρχιερέα. There is, therefore, no reason to infer that ἀρχιτελώνης is at all less definite in its import, than would Ὁ ἀρχιτελώνης be, if the circumstances had permitted the Article to be employed.

The precise nature of the office it is not easy to determine. *Michaelis*, in his German work so often quoted, understands Zaccheus to have been a *Publicanus*, or Farmer of the Tolls, as distinguished from a *Portitor*, or mere Collector; and a passage of Josephus, adduced by Wetstein, makes it probable that Jews were sometimes admitted to this rank, though, as every one knows, it properly belonged to Roman knights. Such a person might without impropriety be called ἀρχιτελώνης, a Head-Collector, as being a Publican in the strict sense, under whom the τελῶναι acted. The *Publicani*, indeed, formed a Society, or College, under the direction of a President residing at Rome; and this President managed the concerns of the Society by means of Representatives appointed in the Provinces. The President himself was called *Magister*, and each Representative *Pro-Magister*, as the Reader will learn on consulting *Grævius's* Note on *Cicero ad Fam. lib.* xiii. *Epist.* 9. Zaccheus might, perhaps, be this Representative; for though he was a Jew, it might be the policy of the Romans sometimes to employ Jews in offices of trust and emolument. Of these two conjectures,—for I confess they are nothing more,—I am inclined to prefer the latter. The word ἀρχιτελώνης is ἅπαξ λεγόμενον in the N. T.

V. 23. ἐπὶ τὴν τράπεζαν. A great many MSS. omit τήν, to which *Griesbach* prefixes the mark of probable spuriousness. The omission will not, in this instance, affect the sense: I am disposed, however, to retain the Article, observing that in Demosthenes ἐπὶ τὴν τράπεζαν is common, whilst ἐπὶ τράπεζαν is not found. See *Reiske's* Index Demosth. *voce* τράπεζα.

V. 29. ἐλαιῶν. We have not in this instance any infringement of the rule of Regimen. The Mount of Olives is commonly called τὸ ὄρος τῶν ἐλαιῶν, and the second Article is then never omitted. But the insertion of καλούμενον makes a difference; for then we have an *ellipsis* of ὄρος understood after καλούμενον, where ΤΟ ὄρος would be contrary to the rule. See Part i. Chap. iii. Sect. iii. § 2. Notwithstanding this, one or two inferior MSS. have τῶν.

V. 30. οὐδεὶς πώποτε ἀνθρώπων. It might be expected that ἀνθρώπων, after the Partitive οὐδείς, would have the Article; but see Part i. p. 54.

CHAP. XX.

V. 36. καὶ υἱοί εἰσι τοῦ Θεοῦ. Here the Alex. MS. has the remarkable reading, οἱ υἱοί εἰσι Θεοῦ, which, however, can scarcely be right: it would mean, "the children are of God [1]."

---

[1] In v. 38. of this chapter, we have our Saviour's argument in proof of a resurrection, expressed with some difference, in respect of the Article, from the corresponding terms in Matthew and Mark : Θεὸς δὲ οὐκ ἔστι νεκρῶν, ἀλλὰ ζώντων· πάντες γὰρ αὐτῷ ζῶσιν. This passage furnishes us with a specimen of the Scriptural criticism of some of the opponents of Bishop Middleton's hypothesis. " The Article ought to be inserted before Θεός," says the Monthly Reviewer, (June, 1810.) Not necessarily; as the present reading may very well be rendered, "*But he is not the God of the dead, but of the living.*" But the Reviewer proceeds: "The additional words in Luke, πάντες γὰρ αὐτῷ ζῶσι, which are rendered in our common Version, 'all live unto him,' mean, we think, ' all who are his are rewarded with life and happiness,'"—"no good man loses his reward." This is sufficiently startling to one accustomed to the sober criticism of Bishop Middleton; but the surprise excited by it is increased by the examples brought to confirm the novel interpretation : " See the dative so used in Luke v. 33. John xvii. 6 and 9." And he further appeals to some *Hebrew* usages in the Old Testament. Passing by these latter as proving nothing, the Greek references deserve to be examined. The first is Luke v. 33. οἱ δὲ σοὶ ἐσθίουσι καὶ πίνουσι· where σοί is evidently the nominative plural of the adjective σός, and if the writer had intended it for the dative of σύ, he would have used the dative also in the beginning of the verse, 'Ιωάννῃ instead of 'Ιωάννου.• The examples from John are of the same kind, σοὶ ἦσαν and σοί εἰσι· though if there *could* be a doubt of the construction, the tenth verse would remove it : τὰ ἐμὰ πάντα σά ἐστι. In the same way, the construction of Luke xx. 38. should be compared with Romans

CHAPTERS XXI. XXII.

V. 42. ἐν βίβλῳ ψαλμῶν. Some MSS. have ἐν τῇ βίβλῳ τῶν ψαλμῶν. Both Articles may be omitted by rules, which have often been referred to.

CHAP. XXI.

V. 25. ἐν ἡλίῳ καὶ σελήνῃ καὶ ἄστροις. Part I. Chap. vi. § 2 [1].

V. 37. ἐλαιῶν. Here again two or three MSS. read τῶν. See on xix. 29.

CHAP. XXII.

V. 3. ὁ σατανᾶς. Very many MSS. omit ὁ, and *Griesbach* rejects it. This word is used both with and without the Article, as partaking of the nature both of a Proper Name and of an Appellative, q. d. the Adversary.

V. 11. ὁ διδάσκαλος. I remember to have seen it somewhere remarked, that the Article in this place indicates the pre-eminent dignity of the Teacher: but this notion may easily be shown to be groundless, if we consider that διδάσκαλος, without the Article, would here scarcely have been sense. The disciples of a particular Teacher could not well have spoken of their Master in any other manner. See *Aristoph. Nub.* 868. 1150. 1329. 1335. 1337. 1447. Edit. *Hermann:* and these instances, it will be remarked, are taken from a Poet.

V. 17. ποτήριον. A few MSS. including the *Alex.* prefix τό. Michaelis *(Anmerk.)* says that "this is not the Cup used at the institution of the Holy Supper, but an earlier one, perhaps the *first*, which was drunk before the meal." That only one vessel was used during the celebration is probable, as I have remarked on Matt. xxvi. 27. in which case the reading would be τὸ ποτήριον: the MSS. however, are, for the most part, against the supposition. But this is not the only difficulty attending the passage. Our Saviour is here said to have given thanks, εὐχαριστήσας: this Cup seems, therefore, to have

---

xiv. 8. τῷ Κυρίῳ ζῶμεν.—The reader will probably be disposed, from this specimen, to consider Bishop Middleton and our own Translators safer guides to follow.—J. S.

[1] Winer says that the Article is omitted before ἥλιος, when it is mentioned *with the moon and stars!*—H. J. R.

been the *Cup of Blessing*, or the *Third* of the Four, and in that case it probably *was* the Cup used at the institution of the Lord's Supper, contrary to Michaelis's supposition. But then, on the other hand, how are we to understand what is said below, ver. 20? The perplexities attending the present passage are such as almost to induce me to believe it spurious. "It is wanting," says *Adler* (in his *Verss. Syr.* p. 183.) "in all the MSS. of the *Peshito*, and in the first or *Vienna Edit.* and also in the *Codex Veronensis* of *Blanchini*." The Latin Translation contained in that Codex cannot, in the opinion of a consummate judge, (see Marsh's Note on Mich. Introd. vol. ii. p. 559.) be shown, with any colour of argument, to have been made *in the first Century*: its very remote antiquity, however, neither Mr. *Marsh* nor any other Critic, so far as I know, appears disposed to question.

V. 19. τοῦτό ἐστι τὸ σῶμά μου. Mr. *Wakefield*, having translated these words in the usual manner, observes, "The original is more emphatical and striking, *This is this body of mine*, laying his hand probably at the same time upon his breast." I do not perceive that the original expresses any thing of this sort; and if it did, I should not well understand it.

V. 60. ὁ ἀλέκτωρ. *Griesbach*, on the authority of very many MSS. rejects Ὁ. See on Matt. xxvi. 34.

CHAP. XXIII.

V. 18. τὸν Βαραββᾶν. In this place, and in the corresponding one in St. John, Βαραββᾶς, when first mentioned, has the Article. Here, indeed, several MSS. including A. G. H. and a large proportion of *Matthäi's* omit τόν: but in St. John the MSS. are uniform in exhibiting the Article. The celebrity of this robber, at the time, at least when St. John wrote his Gospel (see above on Mark xv. 43.) may have caused the name to be thus introduced.

According to Origen, the name was Jesus Barabbas, but the name Jesus was omitted, lest it might appear to be profaned: and a few MSS. do actually insert it in Matt. xxvii. 17. The Armenian Version also of that passage has, according to *La Croze*, Jesus Barabbas: it is found too in the Vers. Syr-

CHAPTER XXIII.

Hieros. : and *Adler* says (Verss. Syr. p. 173.) that there is a tradition among the Syrians, that Barabbas was called also Jesus. *Schleusner* doubts not that the Copyists expunged that name wherever Barabbas occurs. The presence, however, of the Article in all the MSS. of St. John (for here it ought probably to be omitted) is rather unfavourable to this hypothesis. If Barabbas's name had been Jesus Barabbas, it must in Greek have been written 'Ιησοῦς Βαραββᾶς, as is the case with Σίμων Πέτρος, not 'Ιησοῦς 'Ο Βαραββᾶς: consequently, the reading in St. John, at least, affords a presumption that 'Ιησοῦν never in that instance preceded ΤΟΝ Βαραββᾶν. It may be said, indeed, that τὸν was inserted in the place of the name expunged : but this is highly improbable, since the name Barabbas, *without* the Article, would have accorded rather better with the ordinary usage. On the whole, I am disposed to think that the authority of Origen influenced some of the Copyists to *insert* the name of Jesus, and that even the tradition mentioned by Adler may have arisen from the same source.

V. 26. τοῦ ἐρχομένου. The Article should probably be omitted, as in many MSS. and in Griesbach.

V. 38. ἐπιγραφή. Many MSS. have 'Η ἐπιγραφή. This is not absurd, since the practice of putting up inscriptions on similar occasions was not unusual; and to this practice reference might be made.

V. 43. ἐν τῷ παραδείσῳ. The reference in this place is to the Jewish notion of the state of the dead. See *Lightfoot*.

V. 47. δίκαιος ἦν. In Bowyer's Collection we have a conjecture by *Wasse*, 'Ο δίκαιος: in support of which he quotes Acts vii. 52; xxii. 14. James v. 6. That δίκαιος in this place, if used κατ' ἐξοχήν, may dispense with the Article, is more than I dare affirm ; though, considering the tendency of the Verb Substantive to render the Noun following anarthrous, and especially that Names and Titles (see above, xix. 2.) so situated reject the Article, I think the case somewhat disputable. There is, however, another view in which the question may be regarded. St. Luke was not present : he had heard the exclamation of the Centurion from others : and in what manner did the relater represent it? The Roman said, probably, *Reverà hic vir Justus erat*. If St. Luke understood not Latin, the reporter was to translate the phrase into Greek : but would he have been justified in representing the Centurion to have said what was equivalent to Ὁ δίκαιος? This would have been rather to act the part of a Commentator than of a narrator. Besides, a Roman who had heard merely that the Messiah was to be distinguished by the attribute of justice, or that he was to be called the Just One, would very naturally, according to the practice of his nation, suppose Justus to be a *cognomen* of Christ; to which he might thus allude : that it was a *cognomen* in some instances we know from Acts i. 23; xviii. 7. Col. iv. 11 : and if the Reporter or Translator viewed the case in this light, I do not see that he would think of inserting the Article in the Greek. Had Pompey died gloriously, I can conceive a Greek by-stander to have exclaimed, Ἀληθῶς ὁ ἀνὴρ οὗτος ἦν Μέγας, in allusion to *Magnus*; and I believe he would have said no more. Such allusions, it is well known, are very much in the manner both of the Greeks and Romans. But see more on Acts vii. 52.

V. 54. ἡμέρα and σάββατον are illustrations of Part I. Chap. iii. Sect. iii. § 1.

CHAP. XXIV.

V. 10. Μαρία Ἰακώβου. Markland conjectures Ἡ Ἰακώβου. This is the reading of the best MSS. including a large proportion of Matthäi's.

V. 18. ὁ εἷς. Some MSS.—ὁ: but this is wrong, there being only two persons mentioned.

V. 21. τρίτην ταύτην ἡμέραν. This is contrary to what was said on οὗτος in Part i. Chap. vii. § 5. A few MSS. indeed, and Syr. Philox. want ταύτην, by which omission the difficulty would be removed : it is evident, however, from Wetstein's Note, that the phrase accords with the practice of the Greek writers. In the whole N. T. I find no other instance of οὗτος in immediate concord with an anarthrous Noun, except Acts i. 5. μετὰ πολλὰς ταύτας ἡμέρας, and xxiv. 21. περὶ μιᾶς ταύτης φωνῆς : unless, indeed, we add τοῦτο τρίτον, John xxi. 14. and 2 Cor. xiii. 1. where, however, the Substantive is understood. Now in all these instances it will be observed, that either a Numeral Adjective occurs, or something which is analogous to it : whence I infer that the anomaly noticed Part i. Chap. vi. § 3. sometimes extends its influence so far as to cause the omission of the Article in cases like the present. I am aware that some Critics would at once have recourse to the *homœoteleuton*: but I am disposed to believe that almost every word which existed in the Autographs is found in some one at least of the MSS. still extant. If there be many instances in which the original reading is wholly lost, they will probably, for the most part, respect the Article: yet rarely, if ever, has a case occurred, in which the reading of some MS. or other did not agree with the principles previously established in this Work.

Same v. *Markland* here conjectures Ἡ σήμερον, making it, I suppose, the Nominative to ἄγει: no emendation, however, is requisite: the Nominative to ἄγει is Christ. Σήμερον is wanting in the Vat. MS. and in the Syr. Arab. Copt. Æth. and Arm. Verss. It is not necessary to the sense.

ST. JOHN.

CHAP. I.

V. 1. Θεὸς ἦν ὁ λόγος. Certain Critics, as is well known, have inferred from the absence of the Article in this place, that Θεὸς is here used in a subordinate sense: it has, however, been satisfactorily answered, that in whatever acceptation Θεὸς is to be taken, it properly rejects the Article, being here the Predicate of the Proposition: and *Bengel* instances the LXX. 1 Kings xviii. 24. οὗτος Θεός, as similar to the present passage. It may be added, that if we had read Ὁ Θεός, the Proposition would have assumed the convertible form, and the meaning would have been, that whatever may be affirmed or denied of God the Father, may also be affirmed or denied of the Logos; a position which would accord as little with the Trinitarian as with the Socinian hypothesis. It is, therefore, unreasonable to infer that the word Θεὸς is here used in a *lower sense:* for the Writer could not have written Ὁ Θεὸς without manifest absurdity. The meaning of that clause in the Athanasian Creed which affirms that " the Father is God, the Son God, and the Holy Ghost is God," is adequately expressed by Θεὸς ὁ Πατήρ, Θεὸς ὁ Υἱός, Θεὸς τὸ Πνεῦμα τὸ ἅγιον: nor will the most zealous Trinitarian, if he understand Greek, be dissatisfied with this interpretation of his belief. It is, therefore, not very easy to perceive what *Origen* could mean in his Commentary on this verse, when he commends the *caution* of the Evangelist in omitting the Article before Θεός, as applied to the Logos: whatever degree of divinity that Father might impute to the Logos, the Article could not have been used in this place, for the reasons already alleged. Besides, it is not true that the Sacred Writers have distinguished between Θεὸς and ὁ Θεός, as was shown above, Luke i. 15.

CHAPTER II. 241

V. 21. ὁ προφήτης. This is another of the instances referred to by *Abp. Newcome*, to prove that the Article is sometimes redundant: see above on Matt. v. 1. Accordingly he translates " Art thou *a* Prophet ?" and he appeals to this Evangelist, vii. 40, 41; where, however, the Article is no more redundant than in the place before us. Here, indeed, the very answer of the Baptist is of itself sufficient to show that ὁ προφήτης must be rendered as the idiom requires: for else how could John have answered in the negative? Does not Christ declare of John (Matt. xi. 9.) that he was a Prophet, and even more than a Prophet? See also Luke i. 76. The reference is, I believe, properly explained in the *Anmerk*. of Michaelis, who says, " Namely, the Prophet promised in Deut. xviii. 15—19. The Jews understood these words of an individual resembling Moses in greatness and in miracles: I am of a different opinion, and understand them of all and singular the true Prophets, whom God from time to time was to send to the people of Israel: the question, however, is put to John according to the then prevailing interpretation." *Lightfoot* supposes ὁ προφήτης to mean " one of the ancient Prophets" spoken of, Luke ix. 8, 9.: but this is as inconsistent with the presence of the Article, as is the rendering of Newcome.

V. 42. ὁ Χριστός. The best MSS. omit ὁ. It is remarkable that any should insert it. See Part i. Chap. iii. Sect. iii. § 2.

V. 46. τὸν Ναθαναήλ. The Article here is of use to show that Ναθαναὴλ is in the Accusative, and not a *Cognomen* of Φίλιππος preceding.

V. 47. τι ἀγαθόν. *Dr. Owen* (apud Bowyer) conjectures ΤΟ ἀγαθόν, than which nothing is more improbable: the meaning is, that *nothing* good could come from Nazareth; much less, therefore, could τὸ ἀγαθόν.

CHAP. II.

V. 11. τὴν ἀρχήν. A. B. 1. and Origen—τήν. These are considerable authorities: but see on οὗτος, Part i. Chap. vii. § 5. Matthäi's MSS. as usual, comply with the idiom [1].

[1] V. 25. τοῦ ἀνθρώπου. I observe, that the Article is here used for the purpose of Hypothesis only, because Winer, I. § 14. and II. § 3. seems to consider it as indicating that ἄνθρωπος is one of two correlatives,—*the man with whom he had to do*.—H. J. R.

CHAP. III.

V. 10. ὁ διδάσκαλος τοῦ Ἰσραήλ. Eng. Version, "a Master of Israel." *Campbell* observes that the Article here is remarkable, and that it is omitted in no MS. Many MSS. have been for the first time collated since his work appeared, but in none of them is the Article omitted. It must, therefore, be concluded to have a sense which is indispensable to the passage; and Campbell is certainly right, when he contends that it ought to be expressed in Translations. It is, indeed, the more remarkable that we should find the Article in *all* the MSS. since, even if we should admit the definiteness of διδάσκαλος, it might still have wanted the Article on account of the Verb Substantive preceding; though the subject σὺ would favour the insertion.

To determine the precise meaning of the appellation is a task which, I believe, no Commentator pretends to have accomplished. We know that Nicodemus was a person of high consideration, and a member of the Sanhedrim: and some suppose him, and not without reason, to have been the same Nicodemus who is frequently mentioned in the *Talmud*: in which case, he was not in wealth and consequence inferior to any Jew of that time. Still it will be asked, why did our Saviour say to Nicodemus, Art thou the Teacher of Israel? I have only conjecture to offer; but even this may be tolerated, where nothing certain is known, and when even conjecture has scarcely been attempted. It has been observed, that the Jews gave their Doctors high and sounding titles: "*Splendidis valde nominibus Doctores suos Judæi ornárunt vel potius onerárunt,*" says *Danz* apud Meuschen, N. T. *ex Talm. illustr.* p. 579, in the same manner, probably, as among the Schoolmen in the middle ages, one was called the *Angelic* Doctor, another the *Admirable*, and a third the *Irrefragable*. Might not, then, Nicodemus have been styled by his followers, ὁ διδάσκαλος τοῦ Ἰσραήλ [1]? On this supposition, nothing is more probable than

---

[1] There is a remarkable passage in the *Theætetus* of Plato, § 60. Bekk. which strikingly illustrates the supposed use of the Article in the case before us. Protagoras is represented as repressing the triumph which Socrates would indulge

CHAPTER IV.

that our Saviour should have taken occasion to reprove the folly of those who had conferred the appellation, and the vanity of him who had accepted it: and no occasion could have been more opportune than the present, when Nicodemus betrayed his ignorance on a very important subject. Our Saviour's readiness to condemn the practice here referred to, may be proved from Matt. xxiii. 7. and it is observed by *Schoettgen Hor. Hebr.* on James iii. 1. μὴ πολλοὶ διδάσκαλοι γίνεσθε, that "*cum nomine Magistri res ipsa simul a Christo et Apostolis ejus est prohibita.*" If it be said that Christ would rather have asked, "Art thou *called* the Master of Israel?" I think it may be answered, that this objection is the same with that made by the High Priests to the *Inscription on the Cross:* see this Evangelist, xix. 21. in which case it cannot be deemed of weight. Besides, the reproof is more severe in the present form of expression, since it seems to signify not only that the followers of Nicodemus distinguished him by this appellation, but also that he thought himself not altogether unworthy of it[1].

V. 29. νυμφίος. *Markland* (ap. Bowyer) conjectures Ὁ νυμφίος. No MS. has this reading, nor is it wanted. See Part i. Chap. iii. Sect. iv. § 1.

V. 34. τὸ πνεῦμα. This is generally understood of the *gifts* of the Spirit: I rather prefer the *personal* sense. That τὸ πνεῦμα here follows δίδωσιν is no ground of objection; since we find the same word applied to *the Son* in the 16th verse of this very Chapter.

CHAP. IV.

V. 27. μετὰ γυναικός. Eng. Version, "With the woman." But *Campbell* lays some stress on the absence of the Article, and thinks the meaning is, with any woman at all. From the absence of the Article nothing can be inferred, because of the Preposition: on the whole, I am inclined to believe that the surprise felt by the Apostles was rather at our Saviour's con-

---

over him, the famous Master, when in fact he had gained it only over one of his Disciples. Οὗτος δὴ ὁ Σωκράτης ὁ χρηστός, ἐπειδὴ αὐτῷ παιδίον, κ. τ. ε. . . . . γέλωτα δὴ ΤΟΝ 'ΕΜΕ ἐν τοῖς λόγοις ἀπέδειξε.—J. S.

[1] Winer quietly adopts the Bishop's conjectural interpretation, without any acknowledgment.—H. J. R.

versing with this particular woman, than with any woman indiscriminately. It is true, that we learn from the Rabbinical Writers that it was not thought decorous in a man to hold conversation with any woman in public : it may be observed, however, that not only was this woman a Samaritan, a circumstance which made her peculiarly obnoxious, but also, as *Schoettgen Hor. Hebr.* vol. i. p. 343. has remarked, the very place rendered her character somewhat suspicious. The business of fetching water belonged exclusively to females; and wells had, from that cause, become places of resort for the loose and licentious of both sexes. It is possible, therefore, that the surprise of the disciples might be excited more especially by our Saviour's conversing with this particular woman, whom he had found in such a place; and her appearance, probably, bespoke somewhat of her real character, as exhibited in the sequel of the story. It may be added, that in other places our Saviour is represented to have conversed with women, without having given rise to particular observation.

V. 37. ὁ ἀληθινός. *Beza* remarks on this place, that every person moderately acquainted with Greek must perceive that the Article is here inadmissible. A few MSS. indeed, are without it: but, as Matthäi well observes, "*et abesse et adesse potest.*" If we render, " in this instance the saying is true," the Article must be omitted: but if " in this is exemplified the true saying," the Article is absolutely necessary, as in this Evangelist, i. 9; vi. 32; xv. 1. *Markland* refers us in behalf of the Article to 2 Peter ii. 22. which has nothing to do with the question, for there the Adjective *precedes* the Substantive instead of following it. I cannot but observe of *Matthäi*, that he is the most accurate Greek scholar who ever edited the N. T.—Griesbach prefixes to the Article the mark of possible spuriousness. In this instance, however, the great majority of the MSS. ought, I think, to prevail: they are at least as fifty to one.

CHAP. V.

V. 1. ἑορτὴ τῶν Ἰουδαίων. If we could accurately ascertain what was the Festival here meant, it would go far towards determining the much controverted question respecting the duration of Christ's ministry; the various opinions concerning which the reader will find very ably detailed in

CHAPTER V. 245

Marsh's Michaelis, vol. iii. Part i. p. 56. of the Notes. It seems to be admitted, that if the reading had been Ἡ ἑορτή, (which, indeed, is found in several MSS.) the Festival here spoken of could be no other than the Passover, and that then there were *four* Passovers, according to St. John, during our Saviour's Ministry: otherwise, it is contended that some other Feast, probably of Pentecost, is here meant, and that the Passovers of our Saviour's Ministry were only *three*. In proof, indeed, that ἑορτή without the Article may mean the Passover, *Grotius* refers us to the phrase κατὰ ἑορτήν, Mark xv. 6. and Luke xxiii. 17. where, however, the omission of the Article, as in other instances, is to be accounted for by means of the Preposition. The present case, therefore, is wholly dissimilar; and on the supposition that the Passover is here intended, we must explain the absence of the Article on a different principle. That principle, if I mistake not, was developed in Part i. Chap. iii. Sect. iii. § 1. which treats of Propositions affirming or denying existence. In this Evangelist, xix. 14. we have an example similar to the present in the word παρασκευή, ἦν δὲ ΠΑΡΑΣΚΕΥΗ τοῦ Πάσχα, than which nothing can be imagined more definite; where there is no reason against admitting the Article, we find it called ἡ παρασκευή. So also we usually read τὸ σάββατον: yet in this Chapter, ver. 9. we have ἦν δὲ σάββατον, and elsewhere. So likewise Æschines, in the *Orat. Gr.* vol. iii. p. 456. ὅτ᾽ ἦν ΠΡΟΑΓΩΝ, which was the prelude to the games. It may, indeed, be supposed that the Proposition under review is not strictly confined to the assertion of Existence, on account of μετὰ ταῦτα: but this objection is of little or no force, because μετὰ ταῦτα is not here emphatic, i. e. it is not the principal purpose of the Writer to affirm, that the Festival was *after*, rather than *before*, the events last recorded: he means simply to say, Then came the Festival of the Jews. The case is different in this Evangelist, vii. 2. ἦν δὲ ἐγγὺς ἡ ἑορτὴ τῶν Ἰουδαίων, ἡ σκηνοπηγία· for there the *nearness* of the Feast of Tabernacles is an important part of the Proposition; indeed the assertion of this fact was the chief or sole object of the Writer. It is also to be observed, that lest the phrase ἡ ἑορτὴ τῶν Ἰουδαίων should be ambiguous, he adds ἡ σκηνοπηγία. It is, therefore, probable, that in the passage before us, if the principal Festival had not been meant, something explanatory would have been subjoined.

On the whole, I think it certain that the Passover *may* here be intended, and that the arguments against this supposition are not strengthened, as is commonly supposed, by the absence of the Article. On the other hand, the opinion that the Passover *is* here meant, is somewhat favoured by the various reading, since the insertion of the Article in several MSS. may have arisen from a desire in the Copyists to make the definiteness of ἑορτὴ more evident: that most of the MSS. want ἡ, affords no support to the contrary opinion, because it was to be expected that the majority would conform with the established usage.

V. 27. ὅτι υἱὸς ἀνθρώπου ἐστί. The term ὁ υἱὸς ἀνθρώπου has already occurred above seventy times, but now, for the first time, without either of the Articles: and on this circumstance some stress has been laid by *Beza, Michaelis, Campbell,* and others. They contend that the Articles are here purposely omitted, for that our Saviour meant only to assert, that the person to whom power was thus given, was himself a man: and that here, by a common Syriasm, *son of man* and *man* are synonymous. "The Syrians," says Michaelis *(Anmerk. ad loc.),* "cannot express the word *man* otherwise than by *son of man*: accordingly, 1 Cor. xv. 47. Adam, in the Syriac Version, is called *the first Son of Man*, though no mortal was his father." I am fully aware that ܒܪܢܫܐ and ܒܪ ܐܢܫܐ are used for ἄνθρωπος, and mean no more than the Latin *homo*, or the German *mensch*: but, if I mistake not, the Syriac expressions above mentioned are no where employed by the Authors of the *Peshito* as equivalent to ὁ υἱὸς τοῦ ἀνθρώπου, nor even to the υἱὸς ἀνθρώπου of the present verse. This term (for I consider the absence of the Articles as making no difference) they every where translate by ܒܪܗ ܕܐܢܫܐ: whence it may be inferred, that in the verse under review, no less than in other places, they held υἱὸς ἀνθρώπου, applied to Christ, to be significant of something different from ἄνθρωπος.—It appears, then, that the argument founded on the Syriasm is rather against the conclusion which it was meant to establish: the omission, however, of the Greek Articles ought to be explained from the Greek usage, if any such exist. The question is, How came the

Articles in the phrase Ὁ υἱὸς ΤΟΥ ἀνθρώπου ever to be employed? Obviously, because our Saviour assumed to Himself this appellation; and the very *assumption* forbad Him to use the phrase otherwise than as ὁ υἱὸς τοῦ ἀνθρώπου. He was to be designated as Ὁ υἱὸς, for otherwise He would not have been distinguished from any other individual of the human race; and if ὁ υἱὸς, then ΤΟΥ ἀνθρώπου, for ὁ υἱὸς ἀνθρώπου would offend against *Regimen*. Hence it is plain, that the Article before ἀνθρώπου is not, if I may say so, *naturally* and *essentially* necessary, but is so only *accidentally;* and consequently it will not be admitted, unless where Regimen requires it, i. e. where ὁ υἱὸς precedes. Now in the present instance υἱὸς, and not ὁ υἱὸς, properly follows ἐστί. See Part i. Chap. iii. Sect. iv. § 1. and, therefore, the phrase could not be any other than υἱὸς ἀνθρώπου. We find, indeed, such phrases as σὺ εἶ υἱὸς τοῦ Θεοῦ, or even ὁ υἱὸς τοῦ Θεοῦ, as was explained above, Matt. iv. 3: but the Reader will recollect that the word Θεοῦ commonly takes the Article even where Regimen does not make it necessary, besides that the Pronoun ΣΥ contributes to give the Predicate a definite form. See Part i. p. 44. —If it be thought remarkable, and therefore unfavourable to the foregoing interpretation, that υἱὸς ἀνθρώπου, as applied to Christ, now first occurs without the Articles, it is sufficient to answer that now, for the first time, has Christ *asserted* his claim to the title: in all other places he has assumed it. It is moreover to be observed, that the Fathers, in similar cases, appear always to use the phrase υἱὸς ἀνθρώπου, I mean where the Canons require υἱὸς to be without the Article. See *Suicer's Thesaurus, voce* υἱός.

On the whole, I am convinced that the rendering of our common English Version "the Son of Man" is correct, contrary to the opinion of those who would conform with the letter rather than with the spirit of the original. The import of the passage is, indeed, as they contend, "that God hath made Christ the Judge of Man, for that He, having taken our nature, is acquainted with our infirmities." But the same meaning will be deducible from the Common Version, if we consider that the very Title, "Son of Man," has every where a reference to the *Incarnation of Christ*, and is, therefore, significant of his acquaintance with human weakness. I have, indeed, observed, that in a majority of the places in which our Saviour calls himself the Son of Man, (and he is never in the N. T. so called by others before his Ascension,) the allusion is either to his present humiliation, or to his future glory : and if this remark be true, we have, though an indirect, yet a strong and perpetual declaration, that the human nature did not originally belong to Him, and was not properly his own. He who shall examine the passages throughout with a view to this observation, will be able duly to estimate its value: for myself, I scruple not to aver, that I consider this single phrase so employed, as an irrefragable proof of the Pre-existence and Divinity of Christ [1].

V. 35. ὁ λύχνος ὁ καιόμενος. *Campbell* objects to our Version, "a burning and a shining light," on the ground that the Article indicates something more. So far I agree with him: but I do not believe, that in this place there is any reference to the LXX. Psalm cxxxi. 17. I suppose, rather, that the allusion is to some phrase then in vogue among the Jews, to signify a wise and-enlightened Teacher: and on turning to *Lightfoot*, one of the best illustrators of the N. T. I find that "a person famous for life or knowledge was called *a candle:* hence the title given to the Rabbins, the *Candle of the Law*, the *Lamp of Light*." I conclude, therefore, that our Saviour meant to say, " John was," to use your own phrase, " the burning and shining light." Allusions of this kind are much in our Saviour's manner. Compare what was said on iii. 10.

V. 36. τὴν μαρτυρίαν. An inattentive Reader might object to the Article: but see similar instances, Part i. Chap. viii. § 1.

CHAP. VI.

V. 40. ὁ θεωρῶν καὶ πιστεύων. See on Mark xvi. 16.

V. 63. τὸ πνεῦμα, ἡ σάρξ. I do not here understand τὸ πνεῦμα of the Holy Spirit; for πνεῦμα and σάρξ are evidently opposed to each other, as co-existent in the same whole. So we find them Matt. xxvi. 41. Rom. viii. 5. James iv. 5. In

---

[1] V. 32. ἄλλος ἐστὶν ὁ μαρτυρῶν περὶ ἐμοῦ. In this place, Winer explains the Article, by saying that a definite witness, viz. God, was in the writer's mind. *He that witnesseth rightly about me is another.* This falls in nearly with Bishop Middleton's observation in iii. 3. 2. (p. 44.) on reciprocating propositions.—H. J. R.

CHAPTER VI. 249

like manner, 2 Cor. iii. 6. we have πνεῦμα opposed to γράμμα; for as in an animated substance there are the flesh and the animating principle, so in the Levitical Law there was the *letter*, which was intelligible to the most carnal understandings, and the *spirit* or ulterior design of the Institution, which for the most part eluded notice: and, by an easy metaphor, in speaking of any system or body of instruction, the term *spirit* and *flesh* may be substituted for *spirit* and *letter*. Indeed we learn from *Philo*, vol. ii. p. 483. (as quoted by Michaelis, *Anmerk. ad loc.*) that the Essenes actually used this illustration with regard to the Mosaic Law. I suppose our Saviour, therefore, to say, "Does this, then, stagger you? How much more would ye be surprised, if ye were to witness my ascension! But it is the *spiritual* part of Religion which is of avail in opening the understanding: the mere *letter* is nothing: my words, however, are the spirit and the life of all, which ye have hitherto known only in the literal and carnal sense." Michaelis explains this passage nearly in the same manner.

Mr. *Wakefield* apologizes for "having in so many instances conformed with *unconquerable prejudice*," and translates πνεῦμα by *breath*. This might be endured; but he adds, that "there is *not one place* in the Scriptures where the original word would not *more properly and intelligibly* be so translated." He says, "the *scrupulous* and *unlearned* may consult for their satisfaction Gen. ii. 7; vi. 17. 1 Kings xvii. 17. 21. and the margin of our Common Version at James ii. 26." These places, and many others which he might have adduced, prove, what is universally admitted, that πνεῦμα frequently retains its primitive meaning of *breath*. Mr. W. as he rightly insinuates, wrote for a class of persons who, though perhaps endowed with good intentions, are not generally the most capable of judging for themselves on subjects of erudition. He became, therefore, their instructor: and in what manner has he discharged his trust? His Readers may possibly be "scrupulous and unlearned:" that he himself was either not very learned or not very scrupulous, is the inevitable conclusion. But the doctrine of the personality of the Spirit is not to be subverted by random and unsupported assertion. If the Reader wish to try the effect of *breath* as a *general* translation of πνεῦμα, he may begin the experiment with the passages referred to, Matt. i. 18. under the fourth head.

CHAP. VII.

V. 23. περιτομήν. In the preceding verse it is THN περιτομήν: but there the *institution* is spoken of generally; here, only a *single act*[1].

V. 39. οὔπω γὰρ ἦν πνεῦμα ἅγιον. Πνεῦμα ἅγιον is here plainly to be understood of the *extraordinary influence* of the Spirit. There is a trifling difference, indeed, in the reading. Some MSS. omit ἅγιον, and some insert διδόμενον[2]: by both sets of Copyists it was, I suppose, imagined, that the words of the received Text could mean only the *Person* of the Holy Spirit, which they justly regarded as an impiety. But no MS. or Version, so far as I know, omits the passage: it cannot, therefore, be an interpolation: it is then, not indeed *direct* evidence, but what is much more valuable, an *indirect appeal* to the world for the truth of what St. Luke has recorded in Acts ii. The unavoidable inference is, either that this Evangelist contrived obliquely to countenance a notorious falsehood, and that his Readers conspired to give it currency, or else that our Religion is true.

V. 40. ὁ προφήτης. See above on i. 21[3].

V. 52. προφήτης. Dr. *Owen* (apud Bowyer) would read Ὁ προφήτης, for that *some* Prophets had come from Galilee. Campbell very justly replies, that men who are angry are apt to exaggerate.

---

[1] V. 24. τὴν δικαίαν κρίσιν κρίνετε. This is easily explained on the principles noticed in Bp. Middleton's concluding note to Chap. iv. *Let the judgment which you pass be just.* Winer says awkwardly, *The just*, in opposition to *The unjust*, as only one judgment can be passed on one case.—H. J. R.

[2] In our English Version διδόμενον is properly *expressed*, though not found in the original: "The Holy Ghost was not yet *given*." And with this should be compared Acts xix. 2. which exactly answers to it in the *Greek*, though it is strangely translated in our Version: "We have not so much as heard whether there be *any* Holy Ghost." Ἀλλ' οὐδὲ εἰ πνεῦμα ἅγιόν ἐστιν, ἠκούσαμεν.— J. S.

[3] V. 51. τὸν ἄνθρωπον, *the man who falls under the cognizance of the law.* Winer. H. J. R.

CHAP. VIII.

V. 7. τὸν λίθον. The eleven first verses of this chapter, containing the story of the Adulteress, are wanting, as is well known, in a great many of the best MSS. and Versions, and the majority of Critics appear to regard them as spurious. *Michaelis*, however, is the advocate of their authenticity, and thinks that the Copyists omitted them from scruples about their tendency, as being liable to be misinterpreted or perverted. I regard it as a circumstance rather in favour of their authenticity, that λίθον has the Article prefixed. The allusion is to the particular manner of stoning, which required that one of the witnesses (for two at the least were necessary, see Deut. xvii. 6.) should throw the stone, which was to serve as a signal to the by-standers to complete the punishment. There is, therefore, strict propriety in calling this stone TON λίθον, in order to distinguish it from *other* stones. But would an interpolator have been thus exact in his phraseology? or would he have adverted to this apparently trifling circumstance? Probably he would not, especially since the expression of βάλλειν τὸν λίθον is not elsewhere found in the N. T. Some MSS. indeed, though but few, omit the Article; but this, I think, proves only that the Copyists knew not what to make of it, and that had *they* undertaken to interpolate the passage, they would have done it less skilfully than did the present interpolator, supposing that we must consider the passage to be spurious.

Erasmus Schmidt, in his N. T. 1658, infers from TON λίθον, that each of the by-standers was prepared with a stone, which is thus referred to: but I prefer the former solution.

V. 44. ἐκ τοῦ πατρὸς τοῦ διαβόλου. The MSS. differ as to the insertion or omission of the first Article: the best of Matthäi have it, and he thinks that the Copyists omitted it, lest it should seem to ascribe a Father to the Devil: I do not perceive that after the Preposition any difference will arise, whether the Article be inserted or omitted. Some MSS. have the addition of ὑμῶν, which, if authorized, would leave no doubt of the construction.

Same v. ὅτι ψεύστης ἐστί, καὶ ὁ πατὴρ αὐτοῦ. Our English Version says, "He is a liar, and the father of it." One of my earliest recollections is that of my surprise at this uncouth and scarcely intelligible phraseology; and that surprise did not abate on my becoming acquainted with the original of the N. T.

One thing must be evident to all who accurately observe the construction; viz. that καὶ ὁ πατὴρ αὐτοῦ is equivalent to καὶ ὁ πατὴρ αὐτοῦ ἘΣΤΙ ΨΕΥΣΤΗΣ, "he is a liar, and *so is his father.*" It has been said, indeed, that αὐτοῦ here refers, not to the Nominative to ἐστί, but to ψεῦδος above, and in behalf of this strange and unnatural construction we are reminded of Acts viii. 26. Heb. ix. 4. and Iliad XXIV. 499. passages which have not the slightest similitude to the present. But further, not to insist that phrases in the form of ὁ πατὴρ αὐτοῦ, meaning *his father*, are extremely common, there is another difficulty, which for some centuries seems not to have been thought of: indeed I have no evidence that it ever was directly drawn into the dispute, though there is reason to believe that it was tacitly regarded; I mean, that if we are to affirm that any one is the father of us, him, it, &c. i. e. if ὁ πατὴρ αὐτοῦ is to *follow* ἐστί, the Article is wholly intolerable, and in such cases is always omitted. Thus in this single chapter we have, ver. 31, ἀληθῶς ΜΑΘΗΤΑΙ μου ἐστέ; ver. 42, εἰ ὁ Θεὸς ΠΑΤΗΡ ὑμῶν ἦν; ver. 54. ὅτι ΘΕΟΣ ὑμῶν ἐστι, not ΟΙ μ., Ὁ π., Ὁ θ. We may, therefore, safely determine that our Common Version, which, however, is the interpretation of *Campbell, Newcome, Mill, Beausobre, Erasmus Schmidt, Casaubon, Heinsius, Suicer, Whitby, Wolfius, Rosenmüller, Schleusner*, and indeed of most modern Critics, is erroneous; and I am persuaded, that had these eminent men attended to the Article, they would have had recourse to some different explanation. Indeed it is evident from the manner in which some of the Fathers quoted the passage, what idea they entertained of the *construction*: for some of them (see Griesbach) for καὶ read ὡς, or καθὼς καί. I do not suppose that they found either in their MSS. or that they pretended to have found it; but only that they thus endeavoured to prevent misconception.

This passage, however, it must be confessed, was attended with difficulty, even in the earlier ages of Criticism. See *Suicer*, ii. 635. Some of the Fathers,—for instance, *Jerome*,— interpreted the place as is usually done at the present day.

Others inferred (and indeed the construction leads directly to this inference) that the *Father of the Devil* was here spoken of: "this being the sentiment," says Whitby, "not only of the *Cajani* and *Archontici*, who held that the God of the Jews was the Father of the Devil, as *St. Austin* saith, but also of the orthodox, as *St. Jerome* testifies; and *Origen* leaves it as a thing doubtful." To detail other opinions of the ancients might be tedious to the Reader; but I think that, generally speaking, they admitted the true *construction*. Among the moderns, *Grotius* in part adheres to the ancient interpretation. He supposes that the Devil here spoken of as the Father of the Jews and a manslayer, was not the Prince of Devils, ὁ ἄρχων τοῦ κόσμου τούτου, but an inferior evil Spirit, ἄγγελος Σατανᾶ, 2 Cor. xii. 7. This explanation, it must be admitted, accords very well both with the construction and with the general tenor of the passage: but it may be doubted how far the doctrine on which it rests is warranted by Scripture. This is an objection which Grotius has not endeavoured to remove.

It may, then, be imagined, that nothing is to be made of the text in its present state, and that recourse must be had to conjecture. Of this opinion was Mr. *Wakefield*: for in the place of τὸ in τὸ ψεῦδος, he would substitute ΤΙΣ. This conjecture, like most others, makes every thing plain; for who, with the unlimited licence of invention, would recommend a reading which does not entirely suit the place? I have professed myself to be altogether unfriendly to conjectural emendations of the N. T.; but is it not possible that the sense of the passage may, by an allowable ellipsis, be the same as if we had actually found ΤΙΣ inserted? and may not Mr. W. in this instance, as has happened to other Critics, have corrupted his author by attempting to supply an imaginary defect? The learned Reader will judge. In *Hesiod*, Op. et Dies, 291. Ed. *Le Clerc*, we have ἐπὴν δ' εἰς ἄκρον ῾ΙΚΗΑΙ, though, as we are told in the Note, Philo, Clemens, Xenophon, and others confirm the common reading ῾ΙΚΗΤΑΙ: *Heinsius*, the author of the alteration, tells us, that *Scaliger* and *Meursius* approved it: they did not then perceive that τις before ἵκηται might be *understood*. So also *Soph.* Œd. Tyr. 315. ἔχοι τε καὶ δύναιτο. sc. ΤΙΣ. In *Xenoph.* the same Ellipsis is not very uncommon: in the Memorab. I. 2. 55. ἐὰν βούληται τιμᾶσθαι, without any Nominative; *subaud.* ΤΙΣ. Œcon. I. 12. ἦν ἐπίστηται, sc. ΤΙΣ. In the Apol. 7. ὑγιὲς δὲ (τις) τὸ σῶμα, κ. τ. λ. where, however, says *Sturz*, in *Lex. Xen.* ΤΙΣ was first interpolated by Leunclavius. So also de Re Eq. VIII. 13. ὡς ἂν βούληται, ἀντιχαρίσηται, (sc. ΤΙΣ,) which *Leunclavius* and *Wells* altered into βούλῃ, ἀντιχαρίσῃ. For these passages, excepting one, I am indebted to *Sturz;* and I have little doubt that a multitude of such might be found, if every vestige of them had not in many instances been obliterated by unauthorized departure from the MSS. I suppose, then, the same Ellipsis in St. John; and, if I mistake not, a similar form of expression is found Heb. x. 38: so at least ἐὰν ὑποστείληται is understood by our Translators. In this way of interpreting the passage, every thing is plain and consistent: in the beginning of the verse it had been said, " Ye are of your Father the Devil:" it is here added, " When (any of you) speaks that which is false, he speaks after the manner of his kindred: for he is a liar, and so also is his Father [1]."

CHAP. IX.

V. 17. προφήτης. *Wolfius* is of opinion that the man cured of blindness does not here speak of Christ merely as a *Prophet*, but as *the one Prophet* foretold by Moses; and he adds, that though the Article be here wanting, yet it is frequently omitted where "*res singularis indicatur:*" in proof that Ὁ προφήτης is here meant, he refers us to ver. 22. I do not think this reasoning conclusive; for it does not follow, because the parents were cautious in their answer, that the son should have been incautious; his caution, indeed, is apparent in ver. 25. and the conduct of the Pharisees leads us to infer, that though they were little pleased with his answer, they did not consider him

---

[1] That the learned Author is right in his general view of this passage, I can have no doubt: my only wonder is, that he did not carry his improvement a little farther, and translate, taking away the comma after ἐστί, "for his father also is a liar."—I cannot but wonder also that there are found any competent judges of the question, who do not immediately approve of the Bishop's proposed improvement; but either adhere to the old method, or understand τὸ ψεῦδος to be the nominative to λαλῇ.

The ellipsis of τις needs no further support to justify it: but perhaps it is unnecessarily supplied in the passage from the Hebrews.—J. S.

CHAPTER IX. 255

as having pronounced Jesus to be the Messiah. Their further interrogation of him rather confirms this opinion: in ver. 31. the man says only, that " if any one be a worshipper of God, and doeth his will, him God heareth:" this seems to prove that the man considered Christ to be only $\theta\epsilon o\sigma\epsilon\beta\eta\varsigma$, a term applicable to the *meanest* Prophet; and in ver. 36. he shows plainly that he did not acknowledge our Saviour to be the Son of God, a phrase which, among the Jews, was equivalent to Christ. I am, moreover, of opinion, that if the man had meant to declare that Christ was the promised Prophet, the Evangelist would either have inserted the Article, or he would otherwise have prevented what, at any rate, must be regarded as an ambiguity. An expression perfectly similar occurs Mark xi. 32. applied to John the Baptist; from which, however, it never was inferred that John was believed to be the Christ.

After all, however, the argument of Wolfius proceeds on the supposition that the Prophet promised in Deut. xviii. 15. is the Messiah. I have already had occasion, on i. 21. to advert to this subject: it may be useful in this place to consider it somewhat further. The principal reason for confining the promise to the coming of Christ is founded on the apparent application of the passage to our Saviour by St. Peter, Acts iii. 23. and by St. Stephen, vii. 37. On the former of these places, *Michaelis* (Anmerk.) has the following observations: " The Prophet like unto Moses, whom God would raise up unto the Israelites from among their brethren, and whom they were to hear, many Christians have understood to be Christ himself: in which case they will have it, that the passage is adduced by Peter as a Prophecy respecting the Messiah. But this opinion appears to me to be improbable. The phrase, ' A Prophet like myself,' used of Christ, would, in the mouth of Moses, seem very indecorous and offensive; and to judge from the context, the discourse is not of one, but of several true Prophets, whom God from time to time would oppose to soothsayers and diviners: to these impostors, set up by Superstition, the Israelites were not to give ear, but only to the true Prophets resembling Moses, whom God would occasionally send them. Many of the Jews, it is true, in the time of Peter, interpreted the promise of an extraordinary Prophet, in greatness rivalling Moses, but not of Christ: for they distinguish this Prophet from Christ, calling the former simply *the Prophet*: John i. 21. 25; vii. 40, 41. I understand Peter, then, to mean, Moses says, God will raise up to the people of Israel prophets to whom they must give ear; and whosoever will not hear them, him will God call to an account : all the Prophets bear witness of Jesus; what answer, then, shall he be able to give, who is disobedient to all the Prophets?"—*Dathe* also, in his Latin Version of the Pentateuch, Deut. xviii. 15. agrees for the most part with Michaelis, except, indeed, that he admits the application of the passage by St. Peter and St. Stephen to the Messiah. He inculcates the doctrine, that "*multa Vet. Test. loca præter sensum proximè intentum (literalem vocant) habere quoque sensum sublimiorem.*" My own reason for adopting this opinion will be given on Hebrews ii. 6.

CHAP. X.

V. 33. ποιεῖς σεαυτὸν θεόν. It is not to be inferred that θεὸς is here used in an inferior sense, because the Article is omitted. See Part i. Chap. iii. Sect. iii. § 3.

CHAP. XI.

V. 33. τῷ πνεύματι. The injudicious zeal of some of the ancients was exercised in attempting to prove that the Holy Spirit was here intended; and the same opinion has found abettors in later times: but it must be obvious to the dispassionate Inquirer, that τὸ πνεῦμα here, as in a multitude of places, means only the *mind* or *spirit of man*: this is evident on comparing ver. 38. where it is said, ἐν ἑαυτῷ. The eagerness which has been sometimes shown to explain πνεῦμα indiscriminately of the Holy Spirit, has greatly contributed to countenance the temerity which I have already noticed and condemned. It is thus that extremes generate their opposites. I have endeavoured to assist the younger Student in distinguishing the different senses of πνεῦμα, though it must be confessed, that in a few cases, generally however of inferior importance, some doubt may still remain [1].

---

[1] The meaning, therefore, in the present passage will be, "in *his* spirit."—J. S.

CHAP. XII.

V. 1. ὅπου ἦν Λάζαρος ὁ τεθνηκώς. *Markland* (ap. Bowyer) rightly censures the *Latin Versions* for rendering *ubi Lazarus fuit mortuus*, and thus overlooking the Article. The sense, as he observes, is, " where Lazarus was, he who had been dead." Had this celebrated Critic elsewhere exercised the same discrimination, by far the greater part of his Conjectures would never have seen the light. His objection does not, and is not, meant to apply to the English Version.

V. 24. ὁ κόκκος. Mr. *Wakefield* renders "*this* grain:" he says, it is "an elegant designation of Himself (Christ); on which circumstance the propriety and beauty of the Article depends." This is not the only instance in which Mr. W. has confounded 'Ο with ΟΥΤΟΣ 'Ο : he might as well have said that ἡ γυνή, xvi. 21. is "an elegant designation" of some particular woman ; whereas nothing can be more remote from the sense : he did not perceive that the Article may be used *hypothetically*.

CHAP. XIII.

V. 5. εἰς τὸν νιπτῆρα. The Article seems to indicate, that only one basin or ewer was used on this occasion.

V. 13. ὁ διδάσκαλος καὶ ὁ Κύριος. The editt. of Erasm. Colin. and Bogard omit the latter Article, I suppose, from a belief that it interfered with the usage which has lately been defended by Mr. Granville Sharp. No MS. however, warrants the omission ; nor is it at all necessary : for though both titles are meant to be applied to our Saviour, yet they are not spoken of as being applied *at the same time*, but distinctly and independently, as if our Saviour had said, One of you calls me ὁ διδάσκαλος, another ὁ Κύριος. The Article, then, is necessary to each of the Nouns, as must be evident on considering the reason of the rule. Part i. Chap. iii. Sect. iv. § 2.

V. 21. τῷ πνεύματι. See above, xi. 33.

CHAP. XIV.

V. 16. εἰς τὸν αἰῶνα. This word, both in the Singular and in the Plural, always has the Article in the N. T. unless after

s

Prepositions, or from other assignable causes. The reason is, that in the Singular it is *Monadic*, life, eternity, the Jewish or the Christian Dispensation, &c. being but one : in its Plural sense, of *the worlds*, it requires the Article by Part i. Chap. iii. Sect. i. § 5. In the Classical Writers we meet with αἰῶνα διάγειν, which is a Hendiadys. See Part i. p. 94. The multifarious meanings of the word αἰὼν are well deduced by Schleusner.

CHAP. XV.

V. 18. πρῶτον ὑμῶν. It is rightly contended by *Campbell*, that Lardner's interpretation of these words, *your prince* or *chief*, is unwarranted by the construction: it would then rather have been τὸν πρῶτον ὑμῶν. The use of the Superlative for the Comparative is a known Hebraism.

CHAP. XVI.

V. 13. πᾶσαν τὴν ἀλήθειαν. Our English Version has "into all truth." This, however, is somewhat too comprehensive: for though I have admitted in the former part of this Work, that it is frequently difficult and even impossible to ascertain when the Article should be used before abstract Nouns; yet, as was there observed, there is not the same difficulty, when such Nouns are preceded by πᾶς. See Part i. Chap. vii. § 3. and I think that the Examples there adduced clearly prove that ἀλήθεια, in this place, is not truth universally, but only in reference to the particular subject: "He shall lead you into all the truth," as Campbell has translated it, though without any remark. Compare also Mark v. 33.

V. 21. ἡ γυνή. See above xii. 24.

CHAP. XVII.

V. 3. σὲ τὸν μόνον ἀληθινὸν θεόν, κ. τ. λ. there are, says *Rosenmüller*, "*tres potissimum* FERENDI *constructionis modi*," not all of which, however, appear to me to merit this indulgent appellation. The first is, "*ut te et quem misisti Jesum Christum solum verum Deum agnoscant.*" This is said to be the manner in which the passage was explained by Chrysostom; but for want of reference, I cannot find the place. With this

CHAPTER XVII. 259

first interpretation the use of the Article does not directly interfere. I would remark, however, that such a construction appears very violent and unnatural; whilst, on the other hand, σὲ τὸν ἀληθινόν, supposing the words to be taken in immediate connexion, is so common a form of expression, that the Writer could hardly intend that they should be taken in any other way. See on Luke xviii. 13. A second interpretation is, " *ut te agnoscant* (sc. esse) *unum verum Deum et quem misisti Jesum* (esse) *Christum vel Messiam.*" Here the doctrine of the Article *does* interfere, for thus we must omit τὸν before μόνον, as well as before Χριστόν: not to insist that 'Ιησοῦς Χριστὸς cannot be separated without violence. It may be imagined, indeed, that the subject σὲ may justify εἶναι TON μόνον: but this is to suppose a dispute, whether Jehovah or some other were the one true God. See on St. Luke xix. 2. The third construction, which Rosenmüller ascribes to *John Melch. Faber*, a learned German Professor, is, ἵνα γιγνώσκωσί σε (εἶναι) τὸν μόνον ἀληθινὸν θεόν, καὶ 'Ιησοῦν Χριστὸν (εἶναι ἐκεῖνον,) ὃν ἀπέστειλας· but this seems to be objectionable, partly on the same ground with the former, and is besides so involved, that I question whether any thing parallel to it can be found in any author, sacred or profane.

I cannot but remark, that the first interpretation appears to have originated in a wish to evade the consequences which this Text has been supposed to establish. It has usually, I believe, been regarded as one of the strong holds of Socinianism; and much use is made of it by *Crellius* in his Tract *de Uno Deo Patre*, in the Collection of the *Polish Brethren*. But, as *Schleusner* and others have observed, τὸν μόνον ἀληθινὸν θεὸν is here opposed to the false gods of the Pagan worship: compare 1 Thess. i. 9. 1 John ii. 8; v. 20. Apoc. iii. 7. It ought, then, to be considered, that the Socinian, in quoting this text in support of what he calls *Unitarianism*, commits the common mistake of interpreting phrases rather from opinions subsequently adopted, than from those which prevailed at the time when the words in question were employed, and to which alone the words were intended to refer. The Socinian argues as if, in our Saviour's days, there had been the same controversy about the *nature* and *essence* of the One True God, which arose afterwards; whereas the dispute then was, whether there were a *plurality* of Gods, or only *One*: the Jews held the latter opinion, and the whole Pagan world the former. Our Saviour, therefore, keeping, if I may so call it, this controversy in view, tells his hearers that eternal life is to be obtained only by a knowledge of the One True God and of Jesus Christ; thus at once directing the mind to the truths both of natural and of revealed religion: and the hearers of our Lord could not possibly have understood him in any other sense. It is, therefore, perfectly frivolous to introduce this passage into the Trinitarian dispute: and the stress which has been laid on it, can be accounted for only from the extreme difficulty of giving to the opposite hypothesis any thing like the sanction of Scripture.—The English Version appears to me to give the sense of the original.

CHAP. XVIII.

V. 1. τῶν κέδρων. English Version, "the brook Cedron." It is very remarkable that only three MSS. viz. A, Vat. 354. and Vind. Lamb. 30. have τοῦ Κεδρών, which, however, is the reading of Jerome, as well as of both Syr. Verss. the Vulg. and some others, and is probably the true one, notwithstanding that τῶν κέδρων occurs twice in the LXX. The received reading might originate in a mistake of the Copyists, or possibly even in design: for we know that the Greeks were accustomed to give a Greek appearance to barbarous names, wherever this could be done by a trifling alteration: in many instances, indeed, they seem not to have been so scrupulous. See *Richardson* on the Languages, &c. of the Eastern Nations, p. 40. The Persian names in the *Persæ* of Æschylus, and many of the names of places in Strabo, may also serve as examples. It is, therefore, highly probable that the name of this brook, or rather torrent, was Κεδρών, and it is spoken of under this appellation by Josephus. The name is supposed to be derived from קדר, and hence Κεδρὼν will mean the *black* or *gloomy torrent*. It is curious, supposing this account of the corruption of the reading to be just, that a perfectly similar corruption has happened in the name of the river *Kison*, which *Suidas* (voce Ἰαβὶν) has called χειμαρρόυς τῶν Κισσῶν, the Torrent of Ivy, just as the common reading makes Κεδρὼν the Torrent of Cedars. See *Rel. Palæst.* vol. i. p. 289 and 294.

CHAPTER XVIII.

for an excellent account of Cedron.—Griesbach has admitted ΤΟΥ Κεδρὼν into the text.

V. 3. τὴν σπεῖραν. This is spoken of definitely, as being the particular Cohort which, by order of the Procurator, attended on the Sanhedrim at the great festivals, and preserved tranquillity. See *Rosenm.*

V. 15. ὁ ἄλλος μαθητής. *Grotius* says, " it is certain that in these, as well as in other writings, the Article is frequently redundant." *Schleusner* too adduces some other instances, besides the present, in proof of the same assertion (see Lex. *voce* ὁ, ἡ, τό :) in the principal, however, of which it has already been shown, that the assertion is wholly groundless; and it is to be considered as the refuge of ignorance, though of the ignorance of learned men. I am, indeed, ready to confess, that the Article in this place is a subject of some difficulty; of greater, perhaps, than in any other in the whole N. T.: yet, though it should be altogether impossible to assign its use with absolute certainty, it is surely more reasonable to impute the obscurity to our own want of knowledge, than to attempt to subvert the whole analogy of language; for to say that ὁ ἄλλος and ἄλλος may be used indifferently, is an assertion which is contradicted alike by experience and by common sense. It is better to understand phrases according to their obvious import, even though we should be compelled to leave the proof of their fitness to more diligent or more fortunate inquiry. Thus τὸ πλοῖον, Matt. xiii. 2. and elsewhere, has always been regarded as signifying merely *a certain ship:* I should not, however, have acquiesced in this vague interpretation, even if I had found it impossible to account for the Article in a satisfactory way. I entertain the same feeling with respect to the present passage.

It is not at once to be taken for granted, that the received is the true reading. The Article is omitted in A. D. and two other MSS. and in the Syr. Pers. and Goth. Versions, according to Griesbach. He might have added the Vulg. for *alius* does not express Ὁ ἄλλος: this would be *alter.* *Nonnus* also in his Paraphrase has νέος ἄλλος ἑταῖρος : but on a poetical Paraphrase little stress can be laid. The Edition also of *Erasmus, Colin.* and *Bengel,* omit ὁ. Griesbach has thought this evidence sufficient to justify the mark of possible spuriousness, which he has prefixed to the Article. It is easier, however, to account for the omission of the Article in a few MSS. supposing it to be authentic, than for its insertion in almost all of them, supposing it to be spurious: for the apparent difficulty, which might operate as an inducement in the one case, would be a powerful discouragement in the other. Besides, I observe that all the MSS. collated by Birch, as well as those of Matthäi, which last are probably, on the whole, the best existing, exhibit the Article. I am, therefore, disposed to retain it, whatever be the difficulties with which the reading is accompanied.

Commentators have generally admitted, that by "the other disciple" here mentioned, St. John means himself; and *Michaelis* (in his Anmerk.) well observes, that "John has never named himself in the whole Gospel, nor has ever said *I:* and yet the occurrences which took place in the hall of Annas, as well as St. Peter's Denial of Christ, he has described so circumstantially, and has thrown so much light on the dark and seemingly contradictory narratives of the other Evangelists, that we cannot but conclude that he was present." Supposing, then, that St. John himself is meant by ὁ ἄλλος μαθητής, it may not be impossible to assign something like a plausible reason why he should call himself *the other disciple*. This phrase obviously implies *the remaining one of two persons*, who not only were, in common with many others, disciples of Christ, but between whom some still closer relation might be recognized to exist: and if it could be shown that Peter and John stood towards each other in any such relation, the term *the other disciple* might not unfitly be used, immediately after the mention of Peter, to designate John; especially, if from any cause whatever John was not to be spoken of by name. Now it does appear, that a particular and even exclusive friendship existed between Peter and John: the circumstance has been noticed in that admirable manual of Christian piety, the *Companion for the Fasts and Festivals*. "Upon the news of our Saviour's resurrection, they two hasted together to the Sepulchre. It was to Peter that John gave the notice of Christ's appearing at the sea of Tiberias in the habit of a stranger: and it was for St. John that St. Peter was solicitous what should become of him. See John xxi. 21. After the ascension of our Lord, we find them both together going up to the Temple at the hour of prayer ; both preaching to the people, and both apprehended and thrown into prison, and the next day brought forth to plead their cause before the Sanhedrim. And both were sent down by the Apostles to Samaria, to settle the plantations Philip had made in those parts, where they baffled Simon Magus."—See p. 77. It might have been added, that the same two were sent by Christ to prepare the last Passover, Luke xxii. 8. It is moreover to be observed, that the same expression of ὁ ἄλλος μαθητής, with some addition indeed, occurs in this Evangelist, xx. 2. where, however, I do not perceive that the addition affects the question : it is repeated also in verses 3, 4, and 8, of the same Chapter, in a manner which, to the modern Reader, will appear extraordinary, but which, combined with the circumstances already related, leads me to infer that this phrase, when accompanied with the mention of Peter, was readily, in the earliest period of Christianity, understood to signify John : and it is not impossible that the Evangelist may have employed this expression in order to remind his Readers, that of the Twelve Apostles, two were distinguished from the rest by their closer friendship and connexion. If this be a reasonable solution of the difficulty, (and I cannot help thinking it preferable to the bungling expedient uniformly adopted,) the Article ought to be expressed in all future Translations : by the omission of it, we withhold from the Reader's notice a circumstance of considerable interest and beauty. See also below, Acts i. 13.

CHAP. XIX.

V. 7. υἱὸν τοῦ Θεοῦ. The Editt. of Erasmus and Colin. have τὸν υἱόν : but this must be wrong. See Part i. Chap. iii. Sect. iii. § 3. The Article before Θεοῦ is wanting in a multitude of MSS. including the greater part of the best of Matthäi's : Griesbach has dismissed it from the text. The true reading, therefore, is υἱὸν Θεοῦ, as is usual in such cases, however definite be the sense. Yet Mr. Wakefield, *qualis ab incepto*, goes on translating " *a* Son of God," thus at once disregarding the idiom and the obvious sense of the passage : for that the Jews should talk of putting Christ to death for pretending merely to *sanctity of character* (which is all that " he made himself *a* son of God" can mean, see Rom. viii. 14.) is unnatural and absurd, and is contrary to what we learn from the other Evangelists: the charge was evidently not that of *hypocrisy*, but of *blasphemy;* and Christ, in affirming that He was the Son of God, did in fact affirm his Messiahship. See on Matt. xiv. 33. and compare Luke xxii. 66. with 70. But the bigotry of heterodoxy seems to be to the full as blind as the orthodoxy which it professes to enlighten.

V. 29. οἱ δὲ, πλήσαντες. This is one of the instances in which the Article is supposed to have an indefinite sense: and *Elsner*, Obss. Sacr. *ad loc.* has collected several similar passages from the Profane Writers. In such places, however, the Article retains its original pronominal use, no Predicate being annexed, probably because it is supposed to be superfluous. In the present instance, the Pronoun can refer only to the bystanders: the same is true in Luke v. 33. Sometimes there is a preceding Ellipsis of οἱ μέν, or what is equivalent: in which case οἱ δὲ will mean *others:* so in Matt. xxviii. 17. where we have ἰδόντες, which is equivalent to οἱ μὲν τῶν ἰδόντων. *Valckenaër*, in his Adnot. Crit. would there read ἰδόντες αὐτὸν ΟΙ ΜΕΝ: which, however, appears to me to be unnecessary.

V. 31. ἦν γὰρ μεγάλη ἡ ἡμέρα ἐκείνη τοῦ σαββάτου. We have here a considerable variation. A majority of the MSS. for ἐκείνη have ἐκείνου: this reading is adopted by both Wetstein and Griesbach, and, I think, on the best grounds. Several also of the same MSS. omit ἡ, so as to make the whole run ἦν γὰρ μεγάλη ἡμέρα ἐκείνου τοῦ σαββάτου. No Editor, that I know of, has adopted this reading, and yet I am persuaded that it is the true one. I understand the sense to be, "there was a high-day, or, it was high-day, on that sabbath," in which case the Article Ἡ ought to be omitted, just as in ἦν παρασκευὴ and similar expressions. Nor is its insertion in the MSS. difficult to explain; for when once ἐκείνη had gained admission, the addition of ἡ became necessary. See Part i. Chap. vii. § 7.

V. 38. ὁ Ἰωσήφ. Many MSS. omit the Article; but see on Mark xv. 43.

CHAPTER XX.

CHAP. XX.

V. 22. λάβετε πνεῦμα᾽ ἅγιον. Here the MSS. as I expected, uniformly omit the Article, the meaning being, the *influence* of the Spirit. See on Matt. i. 18.

V. 28. ὁ Κύριός μου καὶ ὁ Θεός μου. It might be supposed that the former Pronoun and the latter Article should here have been omitted, in conformity with Part i. Chap. iii. Sect. iv. § 2. It must be confessed that this would have been the usual Greek form: but in this instance the Greek idiom seems to have given way to the Hebrew or Syro-Chaldaic: in those languages the Affix must be subjoined to *both* Nouns; for if it be added only to the latter, it will not comprehend the Noun preceding. Thus we read, Psalm v. 3. מלכי ואלהי, and Ps. xxxv. 23. אלהי ואדני; and it is not unreasonable to suppose, that as the expression of St. Thomas was so remarkable, the Evangelist might wish to record it with the utmost exactness. This he has done; for supposing the exclamation to have been (allowing for the difference of dialect) אדני ואלהי, or as the Syriac Version has it, ܡܪܝ ܘܐܠܗܝ, the Greek translation is the closest possible. The two passages above cited from the Psalms, the LXX. have rendered respectively by ὁ βασιλεύς μου καὶ ὁ Θεός μου and ὁ Θεός μου καὶ ὁ Κύριός μου· in both which instances, as well as in the present and many others, the Nominative with the Article prefixed is used for the Vocative. —It will hence be perceived, that I do not understand the words of Thomas in the way of assertion, as some have done, by supposing an Ellipsis of σὺ εἶ: of such an Ellipsis I have not noticed any example. But though the words seem to have been spoken by way of exclamation, this exclamation is not to be construed into a mere expression of astonishment. *Michaelis* has justly observed, that if Thomas had spoken *German*, (he might have added, English, French, or Italian,) it might have been contended with some degree of plausibility, that "my Lord and my God" was only an irreverent ejaculation. But that Jewish astonishment was thus expressed, is wholly without proof or support. Add to this, that the words are introduced with εἶπεν αὐτῷ, i. e. to Christ; but a mere ejaculation, such as that here supposed, is rather an appeal to Heaven. But our Saviour's reply makes it absolutely certain, that the words of Thomas, though in the form of an exclamation, amount to a confession of faith, and were equivalent to a direct assertion of our Saviour's Divinity. Christ commends Thomas's acknowledgment, while he condemns the tardiness with which it is made: but to what did this acknowledgment amount? That Christ was Κύριος καὶ Θεός.—It is true that attempts have been made to lessen the value of this recognition. Thus *Servetus*, in a passage cited by Wetstein, remarks that Thomas did not call Christ *Jehovah*, to which the Affix is never applied. This objection is so frivolous, that I should not have thought it worth notice, but for the sanction which may seem to have been thus given it: for just as well might it be urged that the God invoked by Christ was not the true God, since Christ, Matt. xxvii. 46. and Mark xv. 30. exclaims, "My God, my God:" yet was it ever doubted whether Jesus in these words addressed Jehovah? The same address is common also in the LXX. and is incapable of being otherwise understood, than in the obvious and common way. It is much to be lamented, that the bias of Wetstein's mind inclined him to countenance such absurdity.

CHAP. XXI.

V. 4. εἰς τὸ πλοῖον. Grotius, wishing, I suppose, to account for the Article, says, "*relictum aut commodatum antehac.*" The Pronoun seems here, as frequently elsewhere, to be used in the possessive sense: they went on board *their* vessel.

ACTS OF THE APOSTLES.

CHAP. I.

V. 5. μετὰ πολλὰς ταύτας ἡμέρας. See on Luke xxiv. 21.

V. 8. τοῦ ἁγίου πνεύματος, in the personal sense. Matt. i. 18.

V. 13. Dr. *Owen* (ap. Bowyer) observes, that from the latter part of this verse it seems that the Apostles were here originally distinguished *by pairs;* for which reason he would omit the καὶ between Ἰάκωβος and Ἰωάννης. If, however, the Apostles are here to be taken in pairs, we might expect that Peter should be associated either with Andrew, his brother, or with John, his friend. See above, John xviii. 15. The received arrangement, it will be seen, disappoints both these expectations, by placing the brothers James and John between the brothers Peter and Andrew. It is remarkable, however, that in the MSS. A. C. D. the Versions Vulg. Syr. Copt. Armen. Æthiop. and in Augustine, John is placed next to his friend Peter. The very high authority for this arrangement, and its coincidence with what was noticed above, render it exceedingly probable. I do not, indeed, find that any MS. omits καὶ so as to distinguish the first two pairs: the Syr. places the Conjunction before the names of John and all who follow.

V. 14. σὺν γυναιξί. It has been doubted whether the translation in this place should be *with the women* or *with their wives*. *Campbell*, vol. i. p. 501, 4to. chastises Beza for adopting the latter sense, and contends that it would then have been σὺν ταῖς γυναιξὶν αὐτῶν. The Article, however, alone might signify *their*, as has been seen in a multitude of instances; and this Article, as has been shown, may be omitted on account of the Preposition preceding. Campbell's argument, therefore, founded on the meaning of the French, *avec les femmes*, is wholly inconclusive; and so, indeed, are most of the reasonings which attempt to prove what will happen in one language, from what actually happens in another: the Greek Preposition has the power of dispensing with the Article; the French Preposition has it not. But not only is it true, that σὺν γυναιξὶ *may* signify *with their wives:* we see below in this Writer, xxi. 5. that it is actually so used; for σὺν γυναιξὶ καὶ τέκνοις has no ambiguity. On the whole, I am inclined to think this the true interpretation. *Grotius,* indeed, with the majority of Commentators, prefers the other; and he supposes the women alluded to, to be those mentioned Matt. xxvi. 55. with some others of Jerusalem: but, surely, if this be the sense, it is most obscurely expressed. It might be better to say, that the women meant are those spoken of by the Writer of the Acts in his own Gospel, xxiii. 49. than to send us to St. Matthew: yet even if these had been meant, St. Luke would hardly have left us to make it out by mere conjecture.

CHAP. II.

V. 36. πᾶς οἶκος Ἰσραήλ. If the whole house of Israel be here meant, of which there can be no reasonable doubt, the Greek usage would require οἶκος to have the Article prefixed. See Part i. Chap. vii. § 1. I can account for the omission only by referring the Reader to what was said on Matt. xv. 24.

V. 47. τοὺς σωζομένους [1]. I do not at all understand the remark of *Beza,* (ap. Bowyer,) that if τοὺς σωζομένους meant those who *should* be saved, τοὺς is inserted contrary to the use of the Greek tongue; and that, therefore, perhaps it should be τινάς. If τοὺς σωζομένους be used in this sense, it is made to be equivalent to τοὺς σωθησομένους, where the Article would be proper and even necessary. But this expression signifies only, as *Markland* has well observed, those who are in a state

---

[1] I have already noticed Winer's explanation of the Article here. He says that it is used in consequence of the persons spoken of being thought of *definitely,* and that the place is to be translated, "The Lord added daily to the Church new members, those, namely, who embraced the Christian faith, and were thereby saved." He compares Plat. Menex. p. 236. B. ὅτι μέλλοιεν Ἀθηναῖοι αἱρεῖσθαι τὸν ἐροῦντα.—H. J. R.

CHAPTER II. 269

of salvation, as οἱ ἀπολλύμενοι, 1 Cor. i. 18. and 2 Cor. ii. 15. are the opposite. See also Luke xiii. 23. The tense employed shows this to be the meaning; and it is remarkable that this is the only tense which excludes the Calvinistic interpretation; both the Future and the Past tenses would have favoured it: yet Calvinism has made great use of this text, and important consequences have been deduced from it. It has been rightly observed, that τοὺς σωζομένους may be illustrated by σώθητε above, ver. 40. If the salvation of men were either already effected, or could be spoken of as a thing which must inevitably happen, an exhortation to be saved, or to save ourselves, would in the case of the Elect be superfluous, and in that of the Reprobate an unfeeling mockery.—This passage, however, may seem to countenance the same doctrine from its similitude to xiii. 48. which text is a principal fortress of the Calvinists. With that text I have no immediate concern: I will, however, briefly observe, that the words τεταγμένοι εἰς ζωὴν αἰώνιον are not necessarily to be understood of an absolute decree. The fullest illustration which I have seen of them is in *Krebs's Obss. in N. T. ex Josepho;* which, as well as *Loesner's Obss. in N. T. e Philone,* ought to be in the hands of every Reader of the Greek Testament. *Krebs's* Note is too long to be here transcribed: the substance of it is, that it is plain who are the τεταγμένοι εἰς ζωὴν αἰώνιον *ex lege oppositionis;* for they are expressly opposed to those, οἳ οὐκ ἀξίους κρίνουσιν ἑαυτοὺς τῆς αἰωνίου ζωῆς, *nempe* τῷ ἀπωθεῖσθαι τὸν λόγον τοῦ Θεοῦ: see ver. 46. and that hence οἱ τεταγμένοι is no more than οἱ ἑαυτοὺς τάξαντες. This remark, is, indeed, found in Wetstein, and even in Grotius. It may be difficult to discover to whom it properly belongs; for Theologians, as I have had occasion to know, are not very nice in acknowledging their obligations. Krebs goes on to show from Josephus, that the Præt. Pass. is commonly used in a middle sense: but none of his quotations appear to me to be so apposite as that from *Max. Tyr.* Diss. x. p. 102. edit. Heins. cited by *Loesner,* ἐπὶ σαρκῶν ἡδονὰς συντεταγμένος [1]. The text, therefore, seems to mean no more than that "they believed, as many as felt *a longing after immortality.*"

---

[1] Exod. xxxv. 21. *Author's MS.*

CHAP. III.

V. 11. τὸν Πέτρον καὶ Ἰωάννην. A. and two or three other MSS. prefix τὸν to the second name also: but this is not necessary. See Part i. Chap. iii. Sect. iv. § 2.

V. 21. πάντων ἁγίων αὐτοῦ προφητῶν. *Wetstein*, on the authority of several MSS. admits τῶν before ἁγίων into the text. It is, however, not necessary in this place. Part i. Chap. vi. § 1. and Chap. iii. Sect. iii. § 7.

V. 25. ὑμεῖς ἐστε υἱοί, κ. τ. λ. Several MSS. read οἱ υἱοὶ *probante Bengelio.* Either reading may be right; for here, as has been elsewhere observed, two rules interfere, one of which must give way: the received reading appears to me to be the more probable.

CHAP. IV.

V. 1. ὁ στρατηγὸς τοῦ ἱεροῦ. It may be asked, why this person is here and below, v. 24. spoken of in the Singular Number, and as if there were only one; when we find that in Luke xxii. 4. and 52. there were several such στρατηγοί. The most probable opinion is that of *Lightfoot* on Luke xxii. 4. who has shown from Jewish Writers, that in various parts of the Temple bodies of Levites constantly mounted guard. The persons commanding these several parties were called στρατηγοί: but that, besides these, there was an officer, who had the supreme authority over all of them: and this is he whom Lightfoot supposes to be called, by way of eminence, ὁ στρατηγὸς τοῦ ἱεροῦ, and to be the same with *the Man of the Mountain of the House*, mentioned in the *Talmud.* Michaelis calls him the *Commandant of the Temple;* and Wolfius supposes that Pashur, the son of Immer, mentioned Jer. xx. 1. held the same office [1].

V. 17. μηδενὶ ἀνθρώπων. A very few MSS. some Editt. and Theophyl. have ἀνθρώπῳ. This seems to me to be preferable, on account of the Partitive μηδεὶς preceding: see Part i.

---

[1] V. 12. ἡ σωτηρία, *the expected salvation.* This is Winer's remark. This case nearly answers to Bp. Middleton's reciprocating proposition in pronouns. It is assumed, in short, that there is salvation from a Messiah. The question is, Is Jesus Christ that Messiah?—H. J. R.

Chap. iii. Sect. i. § 8. though I am willing to admit that the rule is not always observed even in the Classic Writers.

V. 31. πνεύματος ἁγίου. A. D. and one of Matthäi's have τοῦ ἁγίου πνεύματος. This is contrary to the usage so frequently noticed, when the sense is the *Influence* of the Spirit.

CHAP. V.

V. 4. τῷ Θεῷ. From a comparison of this verse with the preceding one, as well as from other passages, Theologians have in all ages inferred that the Holy Ghost is God. The opinions of the Fathers may be seen in *Suicer*, vol. ii. p. 769. Wetstein, indeed, has remarked, that ὁ Θεὸς with the Article is always confined to *God the Father:* I have, however, already shown that no such distinction is observed: ὁ Θεὸς and Θεὸς are used indiscriminately, except where grammatical rules interfere. In this place Θεῷ and τῷ Θεῷ would have been equivalent: thus we have in this Chapter, ver. 29. πειθαρχεῖν Θεῷ μᾶλλον ἢ ἀνθρώποις [1]. If, however, the Article had been wanting in the present passage, we should probably have been told that the Holy Spirit is God, only in an inferior sense.

It is worthy of notice, that though the Writer has in the preceding verse made ψεύδομαι to govern an Accusative, it here has a Dative. Of the usage in the N. T. nothing can be said: for elsewhere this Verb is used absolutely. The classical use of the word, if I mistake not, requires an Accusative: at least there is no instance of a Dative in any of the passages cited by Wetstein; and in many others which I could adduce, the Case is the Accusative. *Erasmus Schmidt*, a good Greek Scholar, tells us, that this Verb governs different Cases, according to the difference of the signification. I do not perceive, however, that he has been able to make any distinction between the senses of the word as used in the third and fourth verses; nor does he adduce any instance of a Dative, except the one in question. Schleusner says, that in the LXX. the Verb sometimes governs a Dative and sometimes an Accusative:

---

[1] Which again is expressed by Plato *Apolog. Socr.* § 17. Bekk. with the Article: πείσομαι δὲ μᾶλλον τῷ Θεῷ ἢ ὑμῖν.—J. S.

but even there, I believe, the Dative is employed only where the Translators wished to represent the Dative of their original expressed by ב or ל; elsewhere they prefer the Accusative.

V. 32. τὸ πνεῦμα τὸ ἅγιον. It will, perhaps, be supposed, that these words are not here to be understood in the personal sense, because of ἔδωκεν in the next clause: we read, however, John iii. 16. that God τὸν ΥΙΟΝ αὐτοῦ ἔδωκεν.

CHAP. VI.

V. 10. τῷ πνεύματι. Here, though the Article be prefixed, πνεῦμα must be taken for the influence of the Spirit, or inspiration. The Article is inserted in reference to ᾧ ἐλάλει immediately subjoined; and it is for this reason that in the next Chapter, ver. 3. some good MSS. would read εἰς ΤΗΝ γῆν, ἥν, κ. τ. λ. though there the Article is made unnecessary by the Preposition. The same solution would, indeed, be applicable in the preceding note; but there the association of τὸ πνεῦμα with ἡμεῖς favours the personal sense, as σοφία, with which it is here connected, leads us to an Attribute.

CHAP. VII.

V. 36. ἐν ἐρυθρᾷ θαλάσσῃ. Part i. Chap. vi. § 1. Otherwise it has the Article.

V. 52. τοῦ δικαίου. This term is evidently used κατ' ἐξοχὴν to signify Christ: it may be asked, however, How early did this name come into use? In a note on Luke xxiii. 47. in which I remarked on the conjecture of *Wasse*, I assumed the possibility that it was the intention of the Centurion to call Christ emphatically the Just One; as if the name were used by the Jews to signify the expected Messiah; in which case it might easily be known to a Roman residing in Jerusalem: I ought, however, to have inquired whether there be any reason to conclude, that the expected Messiah had ever been thus denominated, or referred to under this appellation. The strongest evidence which I have met with, that Christ was foretold as the Just One, may be found in § 65. of the *Diss. Gen.* at the end of *Kennicott's Heb. Bible.* As some of my Readers may not have immediate access to that work, I will translate the passage. ".We read in St. John xix. 36, 37, These things were done, that the Scripture might be fulfilled, A bone of Him shall not be broken : again, another Scripture saith, They shall look on Him whom they pierced. In these words the Evangelist cites two passages, in which, as he says, are foretold certain events relating to the Messiah; and he affirms that these predictions were fulfilled in Christ. The first of them is not found in any part of the O. T. at this day in express terms, so as to be incapable from the context of being otherwise applied than to Christ. The Commentators, therefore, have, for the most part, had recourse to the type of the Paschal Lamb, Exod. xii. 46. and Num. ix. 12. though in neither of those places do the words exactly correspond with those of the Evangelist. I am of opinion that this circumstance of not breaking a bone of the Messiah, not only was from early times prefigured by this type, but was also predicted of the Messiah somewhere among the Prophetic Oracles, and that too in express terms; for by the correction of a single word in Psal. xxxiv. the former of the testimonies adduced by John may be as easily vindicated as the other." He then proceeds to give an accurate analysis of the whole Psalm. He concludes, that " after the just and humble have been spoken of in the Plural Number seven times, mention is made in ver. 20. of a certain Just individual, the Just One, a name by which, as all know, the Messiah is distinguished. Of Him, then, it is said, Many are the afflictions of the Just One; but Jehovah delivers Him from all of them. He preserves all his bones: not one of them shall be broken. In the next verse the Just One is again introduced, and in such a way, that the words can be understood only of the Messiah. They that hate the Just One shall be made *desolate:* where, it is plain, that the punishment is characteristic of the crime; for the punishment of *desolation* was inflicted on the Jews for their hatred of Christ. This interpretation of the three verses, 20, 21, 22, is attended with no difficulty or violence, and would no doubt have been adopted by others, but for the Singular רשע, ver. 21: for it was supposed, that as no Impious Person definitely is here meant, so no Just One in particular was intended in the verse preceding. It is, therefore, to be remarked, that the word רשע was corrupted from רשעים: and this is proved from all the Antient Versions, which agree in having the Plural; viz. Gr. Syr. Arab. and Vulg." He might have added the Æthiop. "And the evidence of these Versions is confirmed by a Hebrew MS. of repute, comprehending besides the Hebrew Text a Chaldee Paraphrase much purer than the printed one, in which MS. the Paraphrase also has דרשיעיא in the Plural. This Codex is preserved in the Barberini Library at Rome. The same word is likewise in the Plural in the Chaldee part of the Dresden MS. marked in my work 598. Add to this, that in the citation of the Evangelist we find συντριβήσεται, which is the very word used in the Greek Version of the Psalm, and corresponding with the Hebrew: whereas, in the passage relating to the Paschal Lamb, we have συντρίψετε and συντρίψουσιν." Kennicott afterwards notices the other citation from Zech. xii. 10.

This reasoning appears to me to be satisfactory; yet, while I entirely assent to the conclusion, I will not conceal the fact, that the LXX. have αἱ θλίψεις ΤΩΝ ΔΙΚΑΙΩΝ, and so have the Vulg. the Arab. and the Æthiop. thus differing from all the Heb. MSS. With respect, however, to the LXX. whose Version had considerable influence on the Oriental Translators, it is not to be considered as absolutely certain that their MSS. had צדיקים; for supposing that they found the Singular, unless they understood it of the Messiah, they equally well expressed the meaning of their original by writing τῶν δικαίων plurally; for though τοῦ δικαίου, in the *hypothetic* use of the Article, would mean of just men universally, yet it would have been less free from ambiguity. At any rate, we cannot suspect the Jews of substituting the Singular צדיק for the Plural: of substituting a Plural for a Singular in Psalm xvi. 10. the Jews have been suspected: see *Kennicott, on the Heb. Text*, vol. i. pp. 218. 496. but there the alteration was favourable to their views; here it would have been directly the reverse. The *Targum*, as printed in Walton's Polyglott, has צדיק and רשע: the Syr. favours the proposed interpretation in both instances.

There are one or two other passages in the O. T. which have been referred to in proof, that in Prophetic language Christ was called the Just One. *Whiston*, in his "Essay on the Text of the O. T." supposed that in Isaiah xli. 2. צדק was originally

צדיק. Wolfius lays great stress on liii. 11. where, however, on the authority of three MSS. צדיק is rejected by Bishop *Lowth*, and also by Bishop *Stock* in his Version lately published. The opinion that the Just One was a Prophetic name of our Saviour, is not ill defended in a Note on Isaiah iii. 9. in the " New Translation by a Layman," (Michael Dodson, Esq.) 1790 : and evidence of the same fact, deducible from the *Talmud*, may be seen in *Schoett. Hor. Hebr.* vol. ii. p. 18.

Supposing, then, *the Just One* to have been a Jewish appellation of the expected Messiah, it will not be difficult to strengthen the presumption, that the Centurion (Luke xxiii. 47.) intended to allude to it. It is said of him, that ἐδόξασε τὸν Θεόν, which would hardly accord with the simple assertion that Christ was a just man. Δοξάζειν is the word employed, as often as believers in the true God acknowledge the greatness of his power, and do homage to his name. Our Saviour himself is said δοξάζειν τὸν Πατέρα, and in 1 Pet. ii. 12. δοξάζειν τὸν Θεὸν is applied to the conversion of the Pagans : it is not impossible that the scene of the Crucifixion might have produced this effect on the Centurion, and that St. Luke might thus mean to record the event. It has, indeed, been affirmed, that this officer became a convert to Christianity in consequence of what he had seen; and *Michaelis* inclines to the opinion. At any rate, the term employed is much too strong, if τὸ δοξάζειν τὸν Θεὸν consisted merely in saying, " Truly this man was just." Besides, in what manner had the justice of Christ displayed itself, so as to impress the mind of the Centurion ? Or was this the language in which a Roman, not having reference to a title of the Messiah, would signify his admiration at what had passed ? I think not. He is made also to say ὄντως, which seems to imply that he now recognized Christ in some character previously ascribed to Him ; a sense which I have already affixed to the ἀληθῶς of the other Evangelists. To this, indeed, it may be said, that the Centurion had heard that Christ was a just man, and that now he believed it : but surely this confession amounts to very little, when we consider how it was extorted, viz. by the prodigies which attended the Crucifixion. The Centurion had probably known numerous examples of fortitude under suffering; but had he ever witnessed the manifest interposition of the Almighty at a public execution? If not, I cannot help thinking that his remark, if he meant merely to say, Truly this man was just, is so tame and cold, as to be absolutely unnatural, and, considering the circumstances, scarcely intelligible.

It seems to me, therefore, nearly certain, that in Luke xxiii. 47. the Centurion alludes to an appellation which he had heard applied to the expected Messiah; and the probability is not lessened by the agreement, which will thus be established between the narrative of St. Luke and the account given by St. Matthew and St. Mark, who represent the Centurion as having said that Christ was υἱὸς Θεοῦ. In what sense that expression is to be taken, I have endeavoured to show in a proper place. It is highly improbable, as was there stated, that such a phrase as υἱὸς Θεοῦ should have been used by a Roman, without any reference to the pretensions of the Messiah: but that another of the Messiah's titles should have been stumbled upon by mere accident, and without any allusion whatever, is improbable to a degree, which staggers all reasonable belief. There will still, indeed, remain a discrepancy in the expressions of the Evangelists, but not any in the sense. Nor is it impossible that the Centurion might have said what is imputed both by Matthew and Luke: in which case Luke would be very likely to lay hold of the Centurion's recognition of the Messiah as the *Just One*, because, as we know from the Acts, he much delighted to speak of our Saviour under that appellation. See Acts iii. 14. the Verse on which this Note is written, and xxii. 14: in the first of these he has combined the two titles of the Holy One and Just One.

It is scarcely worth mentioning, nor do I lay any stress on it, that in the exclamation of the Centurion, the Syr. Translator has rendered the word *Just* in the *stat. emphat.* exactly as in the passages in the Acts and in James v. 6. where Christ is confessedly meant. This is not done in giving the characters of Simon and Cornelius: however, I am ready to admit, that in many instances the *stat. emphat.* of ܙܕܝܩܐ, as well as of other words, is used without any apparent cause. In James v. 16. the Translator seems to have found a reading in his Greek MSS. which would justify the *stat. emphat.* in his Version.

CHAP. VIII.

V. 5. εἰς πόλιν τῆς Σαμαρείας. A. 31. 40. have the Article before πόλιν. I have frequently observed, that in cases like the present, in which the Article may be inserted or omitted indifferently, the *Alex. MS.* usually prefers the insertion, and is sometimes unsupported by any other. These various readings appear to me to have been the corrections of a Copyist, who was not acquainted with the licence allowed after Prepositions; and such a Copyist could hardly have been a native Greek. This remark, unimportant as it may seem, may not be wholly useless to those who would trace this celebrated MS. to its origin. The prevailing opinion had always been, that it was written in Egypt, till *Wetstein* in his *Proleg.* contended that it came from Mount Athos. See *Woide's Pref.* Sect. ii. § 11. In that case, however, the writer would, I think, have been better acquainted with the language. The Moscow MSS. (Matthäi's) are supposed to have come from Athos: yet they, as I have had repeated occasion to observe, show, on the whole, that the Writers were by no means ignorant either of the rules or the anomalies of the Greek Tongue.

V. 37. *Michaelis* (as translated by Marsh, vol. i. 337.) infers the spuriousness of this verse, not only from its being unknown to so many of the MSS. but from the circumstance that Christ is here used as a Proper Name; whereas that word, in the age of the Apostles, was merely an epithet expressive of the ministry of Jesus. My reasons for dissenting from this opinion have been fully detailed on Mark ix. 40. The verse, indeed, may nevertheless be spurious: it is wanting in a great number of MSS. but is found in *Irenæus*.

CHAP. IX.

V. 2. τῆς ὁδοῦ. Two MSS. + ταύτης : but this is unnecessary. Comp. xix. 9. 23; xxiv. 22. *Schoettgen* has remarked, that "in *the way* of the Nazarenes" is still the phrase used by the Jews to express "according to the manner of the Christians."

V. 12. ἐπιθέντα αὐτῷ χεῖρα. The phrase is elsewhere τὴν

χεῖρα or τὰς χεῖρας. E. Vulg. and Copt. have τὰς χεῖρας, and this is the reading below, ver. 16.

V. 17. εἰς τὴν οἰκίαν: that of Judas, mentioned ver. 11.

CHAP. X.

V. 38. ἔχρισεν πνεύματι ἁγίῳ. This is a good example of what was noticed on Matt. i. 18. under the fifth head. In ver. 47. where it is τὸ πνεῦμα τὸ ἅγιον, the words, though spoken of the influence, may be understood in *reference*, viz. to the recent dispensation of divine gifts: this may be inferred from καθὼς καὶ ἡμεῖς.

CHAP. XI.

V. 5. τέσσαρσιν ἀρχαῖς. English Version. By four corners. Mr. *Wakefield* translates " by four strings," and refers us to *Diod. Sic.* Ed. Rhod. p. 32. The passage respects the manner of harpooning the Hippopotamus: εἶθ' ἐνὶ τῶν ἐμπαγέντων ἐνάπτοντες ΑΡΧΑΣ ΣΤΥΠΙΝΑΣ ἀφίασι μέχρις ἂν παραλύθῃ. Here the meaning of ἀρχαὶ is evident, and the same sense is well adapted to the place under review. This illustration of Mr. W.'s is singularly happy, and is, probably, worth all that remains of his New Testament. I think it is confirmed by the absence of the Article. A sheet ὀθόνη (see above, x. 11.) could scarcely be other than quadrangular, in which case we should expect ΤΑΙΣ τέσσαρσιν ἀρχαῖς, as in Matt. xxiv. 31. τῶν τεσσάρων ἀνέμων.

CHAP. XII.

V. 3. ἦσαν ἡμέραι τῶν Ἀζύμων. This is strictly a Proposition of Existence; for nothing is affirmed of the days of unleavened bread, but that they were. Yet several MSS. have αἱ ἡμέραι *probante Bengelio,* and *Griesbach* has admitted the Article into the text. I am convinced that the received reading is the true one; and it is an additional confirmation of what was said on John v. 1.

V. 15. ὁ ἄγγελος αὐτοῦ ἐστιν. English Version. " It is his angel." This supposes an Ellipsis, so that the meaning will be, That which thou hast seen and supposed to be Peter,

CHAPTER XII. 279

is his angel. In this case, however, if I mistake not, it should have been ἄγγελος without the Article, (see on John viii. 44. second Note;) indeed one of the Medicean MSS. viz. Wetstein's, 56 and 59, and Chrys. omit ὁ: this, however, will hardly be deemed sufficient to justify its rejection; and, therefore, we are to seek some other explanation. I am much struck with the arrangement of the words in the *Alex. MS.* ὁ ἄγγελός ἐστιν αὐτοῦ : it seems to indicate that αὐτοῦ was not meant to depend on ἄγγελος, but that it is the Adverb; and this is the sense which, as I conceive, St. Luke here intended : "His angel is there." According to Schleusner, the Adverb αὐτοῦ is found four times in the N. T. and it is remarkable, that *three* of these instances occur in the Acts of the Apostles: it is, therefore, a word which the writer would not be unlikely to employ; and the present verse, probably, supplies a fourth example. This interpretation will accord as well with the context, as does the received one. The maid had just announced that Peter was standing *before the Porch*: the Persons assembled think her mad; but finding that she persists in her story, they exclaim, "His angel is there:" viz. before the Porch. I suppose ὁ ἄγγελος to signify *his* angel by virtue of αὐτοῦ understood : Part i. Chap. iii. Sect. i. § 4. At the same time, I think that on comparing the Alex. with the other MSS. we may discover vestiges of a reading which no MS. has preserved entire : St. Luke may have written ὁ ἄγγελος αὐτοῦ ἐστιν αὐτοῦ· the Copyists agreed in considering one of the two *Pronouns* to be superfluous : the greater part expunged the second, the writer of the Alex. MS. the first. I have, indeed, endeavoured to discountenance critical conjectures : but a reading compounded of the readings of different MSS. is hardly so to be regarded. At the same time, the proposed explanation does not require the Reader to assent to this hypothesis; it is rather an attempt to account for the arrangement in the Alex. MS. than the ground-work of a new interpretation.

V. 23. τὴν δόξαν. Several MSS. including six out of seven of Matthäi's — τήν, and Griesbach has removed the Article into the margin. In this expression the Article is usually omitted, except where the glory of some particular act is meant.

CHAP. XIII.

V. 11. χεὶρ τοῦ Κυρίου. I do not perceive why, according to this reading, χεὶρ should want the Article. Griesbach, on the authority of many MSS. rejects τοῦ from the text.

V. 23. σωτῆρα Ἰησοῦν. Instead of these words, some MSS. including the greater part of Matthäi's, have σωτηρίαν: and *Mill* endeavours to explain the manner in which the various reading originated. It is adopted by Matthäi. If the received be the true reading, which probably is the case, σωτῆρα properly wants the Article by Part i. Chap. iii. Sect. iii. § 4.

V. 29. καθελόντες. *Rosenm.* observes, "*Deest Articulus, ut sæpe; vult enim dicere* ΟΙ καθελόντες." Had this been intended, the Article would have been inserted: for it is not true, that in such instances it is ever omitted. Strictly speaking, indeed, the persons who interred the body of Jesus were not the same who had put him to death; but the case will not be mended, at least the sense will not agree with the accounts expressly given by Matthew and Mark, or with the inference deducible from the other two Evangelists, if we should read ΟΙ καθελόντες; for thus Joseph of Arimathea and his companions will be represented to have *taken down the body*, as well as to have interred it: but the persons who actually took it down, appear to have been the executioners. There is, however, no need to deviate from the plain sense of the passage. St. Paul is addressing his discourse to the Jews, and is recounting the several particulars of their treatment of Jesus: and whether his murderers be said to have interred him, or, as St. Matthew represents it, " to have commanded the body to be delivered" to others for the purpose of interment, the Apostle's argument will be the same. He is hastening to the grand subject of the Resurrection, on which he is about to expatiate; and he evidently cared not to avoid a trifling inaccuracy, by which none of his hearers could be misled, because they were able to correct it.

CHAP. XIV.

V. 13. ὁ ἱερεὺς τοῦ Διὸς ὄντος, κ. τ. λ. *Valckenaër*, in his *Adnot. Crit.* in N. T. would here read ὁ ἱερεὺς ΤΟΥ τοῦ Διός.

CHAPTER XIV.

He says that the Interpreters suppose a statue of Jupiter to have been placed before the gate of the city; but that statues of the gods standing thus in the open air, and encompassed with a ἕρκος or περίβολος, certainly had not Priests allotted them. He contends, therefore, that the *Temple* of Jupiter is here to be understood, and that consequently we must read as above, so that the first τοῦ may mark an Ellipsis of ἱεροῦ : and he commends Casaubon for having similarly corrected a passage of Plato.—Notwithstanding the high authority of Valckenaër and Casaubon, I cannot suppress my suspicion, that both their emendations are false. With respect to that with which I am more immediately concerned, I do not perceive the necessity, admitting, which seems to be true, that mere statues had not Priests assigned them, and that a Temple is here supposed, of inserting τοῦ to mark the Ellipsis of ἱεροῦ. It is not unusual, indeed nothing is more common in Greek, than to say, " the Priest of such a God:" thus *Soph. Œd. Tyr.* ver. 17.

οἱ δὲ σὺν γήρᾳ βαρεῖς
Ἱερῆς, ἐγὼ μὲν ΖΗΝΟΣ·

and even elliptically, *Demosth.* cont. Mid. Edit. Reiske, vol. i. p. 531. ὁ ΤΟΥ ΔΙΟΣ. And as to what follows of " being before the city," though it be said, indeed, of the God, it may very well be understood of the Temple, in which the God was worshipped, and in which his statue was placed. Thus *Pausan.* lib. iv. p. 337. edit. Kühn, Μάντικλος δὲ καὶ τὸ ἱερὸν Μεσσηνίοις τοῦ Ἡρακλέους ἐποίησε, καὶ ἔστιν ἐκτὸς τείχους Ὁ ΘΕΟΣ ἱδρυμένος. He evidently means to say, that the *Temple* in which stood a statue of Hercules, was without the wall.—But further, supposing that St. Luke could not have said the Priest of Jupiter, but only the Priest of his Temple, the emendation is still gratuitous; for τοῦ, as the reading now stands, may as well mark the Ellipsis of ἱεροῦ as be the Article of Διός, which, as a Proper Name, may dispense with the rule which elsewhere prevails in Regimen: τὸ Διός, meaning τὸ Διὸς ἱερόν, (for ἱερόν, as Valckenaër admits, is often understood,) is just as good Greek as τὸ τοῦ Διός. However, I greatly prefer the former explanation.

The emendation by *Casaubon* may be found in the *Animadv.* on *Athenæus*, IX. 12. It respects a passage in the *Gorgias*,

p. 183. *edit. Routh*, where it was proposed to read ΤΟΥ τοῦ Πυριλάμπους, because not Pyrilampes himself, but the son of Pyrilampes, is meant: but this again is needless; for why may not the single τοῦ mean τοῦ υἱοῦ, or, to preserve the pun, τοῦ Δήμου? The Proper Name requires not the Article; and accordingly we find immediately afterwards, πρὸς τὸν Πυριλάμπους νεανίαν. Dr. *Routh* very properly mistrusts the proposed correction, and adheres to the common reading.

CHAP. XV.

V. 11. Κυρίου Ἰησοῦ Χριστοῦ. A very great number of MSS. and Editt. have τοῦ Κυρίου, and *Wetstein* and *Griesbach* admit it into the text. Nearly as many MSS. reject Χριστοῦ, which may possibly be an interpolation. There is not, however, any other reason than the preponderance of MSS. for either of these deviations from the received text.

CHAP. XVI.

V. 6. ἐν τῇ Ἀσίᾳ. Mr. *Wakefield* translates "in that part of Asia," and thinks that in the N. T. Asia Minor is meant, whenever the Article accompanies the Name. How the Article can affect the meaning, I am not able to conjecture. The fact, however, is, as *Schleusner* remarks, that in the N. T. Asia always signifies either Asia Minor, or else only the part of it adjacent to Ephesus, and of which Ephesus was the capital.

V. 7. τὸ πνεῦμα. If this be the true reading, I understand it in the personal sense of the Holy Spirit. But the MSS. A. C. D. E. &c. add Ἰησοῦ, and some, with several Old Versions and two or three Fathers, have τοῦ Ἰησοῦ. *Mill*, *Wetstein*, and *Griesbach*, approve the addition of the name of Jesus; and it appears from Jerome, as quoted by Wetstein, that the *Nestorians* were suspected of having expunged Ἰησοῦ from the modern copies. It is true that the evidence for inserting the name of Jesus is very strong. *Wolfius* urges against this reading, that the addition of Ἰησοῦ to πνεῦμα is not to be found in the N. T. In this, however, he is mistaken: we have in Philipp. i. 19. τὸ πνεῦμα Ἰησοῦ Χριστοῦ, though in a sense different from that which most Readers would annex to the

CHAPTER XVI.

passage in question. *Abp. Newcome*, indeed, who adopts the reading, explains it by "the Spirit imparted by Jesus:" but this is, I fear, unsupported by analogy, to which alone we can here have recourse. But the context affords the strongest argument against the addition: for in the preceding verse we are told that the Apostles were forbidden of the Holy Ghost to preach the word in Asia; in the present, that on their attempting to go into Bithynia, the Spirit suffered them not. It is, therefore, highly unnatural that τὸ πνεῦμα of the latter verse should be meant of any other than τὸ ἅγιον πνεῦμα in the former. It is also to be observed, that of Matthäi's MSS. only one, and that not one of the best, has the proposed addition: were the remainder written by Nestorians, or taken from Nestorian copies?

V. 12. ἥτις ἐστὶ πρώτη τῆς μερίδος τῆς Μακεδονίας πόλις, κολωνία. English Version, "which is the chief city of that part of Macedonia." Mr. *Wakefield* translates, "by which city there is an entrance into that part of Macedonia." This differs from the former in making πρώτη to signify *first* or *nearest* in situation; a sense which, indeed, it sometimes bears, though usually with something in the context to show that such is the sense intended: in the instances adduced by *Raphel*, it is πρώτη κεῖται or πρώτη ἰόντι ἀπό, κ. τ. λ.: besides, the Apostles, before they reached Philippi, had passed through Neapolis. But my principal objection is to the manner in which both the Versions render the Article in τῆς μερίδος, as if it were ἘΚΕΙΝΗΣ τῆς μερίδος: of such an Ellipsis I have not seen any example.

A Writer (apud Bowyer) for πρώτη τῆς had conjectured πρώτης, so as to make the meaning to be, Which is a city of the First Part of Macedonia, or Macedonia Prima. See *Livy*, lib. xlv. 29. And ΜΑΚΕΔΟΝΩΝ ΠΡΩΤΗΣ is found also on Coins. See *Spanheim de Usu*, &c. vol. i. p. 651. This conjecture, which Wetstein gives to *J. Pearce*, and Griesbach says is "*Artemonii et aliorum,*" appears to me to be the most ingenious and most probable of all which Bowyer has collected: still, however, it is but conjecture. *Wetstein* thinks, that after the battle fought at Philippi, this city became the metropolis of its district, though before that time Amphipolis had been the capital. *Michaelis* also appears to have been of the same opinion, though he adds, that πρώτη is not necessarily confined to the capital, but may mean merely "a principal town." He translates, however, " of this quarter of Macedonia," which is objectionable on the same ground as our own Version. On the whole, I see nothing better than to translate, " which is the chief of its district, a city of Macedonia, a colony." It is rather in favour of this construction, that some good MSS. and Chrysost. omit τῆς before Μακεδονίας: Griesbach prefixes to the Article the mark of probable spuriousness. If the Reader prefer the less definite sense of πρώτη, the construction will still be the same.

V. 13. παρὰ ποταμόν. D has τόν, which Dr. *Owen* thinks necessary to the sense: but he was not aware of the usage so common after Prepositions.

CHAP. XVII.

V. 1. ἡ συναγωγὴ τῶν Ἰουδαίων. English Version, *Newcome* and *Wakefield*, " a synagogue." *Wetstein* remarks, and after him *Rosenmüller*, that the Article in this place is emphatic; for that in the other cities of Macedonia there was no synagogue, but only a *proseucha* or oratory. This assertion, however, is contradicted by what follows: see below, ver. 10. Neither do I perceive with *Michaelis*, that the Article necessarily marks the *greatness* or *celebrity* of this synagogue, or that it justifies his inference, that the Jews were then very numerous at Thessalonica, as they are at the present day. The passage seems to signify merely that the Jews, I suppose of the surrounding district, had their synagogue there. Οἱ Φαρισαῖοι is frequently used in the same limited sense. Or if with the MSS. A. 40. we omit ἡ, then the Jews must be taken in a larger acceptation, and the meaning is that the people of that persuasion had there a synagogue.

V. 23. Ἀγνώστῳ Θεῷ. It would far exceed the limits of a Note to give merely a meagre sketch of the different opinions which learned men have entertained of the origin and purport of this Inscription: and, indeed, the only question with which I am concerned, respects the proper translation of it. It is usually rendered, " To the unknown God." Mr. *Wakefield* has ventured, " To *an* unknown God." This Version, if I mistake not, more correctly expresses the original.

An Inscription is still preserved, which some suppose to be the very same noticed by St. Paul: it is the first in the *Syntagma* of *Reinesius*, fol. 1682.

ΘΕΟΙΣ ΑΣΙΑΣ ΚΑΙ ΕΥΡΩΠΗΣ
ΚΑΙ ΛΙΒΥΗΣ
ΘΕΩι ΑΓΝΩΣΤΩι
ΚΑΙ
ΞΕΝΩι.

Michaelis speaks of this Inscription, as if it were the one referred to: yet there are strong objections to this opinion. *St. Jerome*, in his *Comm. Epist. Tit.* tells us that the altar was inscribed, " DIIS ASIÆ ET EUROPÆ ET AFRICÆ DIIS IGNOTIS ET PEREGRINIS ;" but that the Apostle, not wishing to argue against a plurality of unknown Gods, chose to quote only a part of the Inscription, and that too altered from the Plural to the Singular, the better to suit his purpose. This, however, is on many accounts a most improbable supposition: indeed, the very manner in which the Inscription is introduced, " I found an altar with this Inscription," &c. makes it incredible that St. Paul could intend merely a remote and vague allusion. That the altar was inscribed simply with the words 'ΑΓΝΩΣ- ΤΩι ΘΕΩι, must either be conceded, or all inquiry on the subject will be vain. As to the Greek inscription above cited, *Reinesius*, though he has given it a place in his Collection, believes it to be a forgery.—But that St. Paul might have met with an altar inscribed, as he himself asserts, is probable in the highest degree. We know from *Pausanias* and *Philostratus* that there were at Athens altars to *Unknown Gods:* and even if this be meant to signify that 'ΑΓΝΩΣΤΟΙΣ ΘΕΟΙΣ was the Inscription of every altar, (for their expressions are ambiguous,) still it will be probable, that if there were several such Deities, an altar might sometimes be erected to one of them: but the words of the Author of *Philopatris*, usually printed with the works of Lucian, νὴ τὸν ῎Αγνωστον τὸν ἐν 'Αθήναις, are decisive that 'ΑΓΝΩΣΤΩι ΘΕΩι in the Singular was a well-known Inscription. The only question, then, is, Was it intended to be applied to one of a possible multitude, as if we should impute any kindness or any injury to an unknown benefactor or enemy, or was it meant to be significant of the One True God, whom the worshipper chose to call ἄγνωστος, as possessing unknown attributes? The latter way of understanding it has been preferred by the Translators, though I know not on what grounds. If Inscriptions of this kind, and so intended, had been common in Athens, Paganism and Polytheism could scarcely have been tolerated: if they were rare, we might expect to read that the authors of them were given up to the bigotry of the populace: the Philosophy of Socrates, which excited so much resentment, could not have been more offensive. It may be urged, however, that the Apostle reasons as if the Inscription had been so intended: and yet if we recollect his zeal and eagerness to convert his hearers, the mention of any unknown Deity must be admitted to have afforded him ἱκανὴν ἀφορμήν. Indeed, admitting that the Inscription was *To an Unknown God*, the discourse of the Apostle is still extremely pertinent.

Little notice, however, appears to have been taken of the order of the words, and the omission of the Article. In ordinary language, as distinguished from that of Inscriptions, we should most probably, meaning a particular God, say either τῷ θεῷ τῷ ἀγνώστῳ, or τῷ ἀγνώστῳ θεῷ: though in the former of these we might omit the first or even both the Articles ; but where the Adjective precedes the Substantive, we must retain the Article; for else we shall fall into the indefinite form, and thus be misunderstood. Thus Acts xxiv. 14. τῷ πατρώῳ θεῷ. Rom. i. 23. τοῦ ἀφθάρτου θεοῦ. Titus i. 2. ὁ ἀψευδὴς θεός. Nor does the language of Inscriptions appear to admit any other usage. Of the omission of both Articles, where the Substantive precedes, may be instanced from *Reinesius*, p. 199. ΘΕΟΥ ΜΕΓΑΛΟΥ 'ΟΔΗΣΙΩΤΩΝ: p. 202. ΘΕΟΙΣ ΣΩ-ΤΗΡΣΙΝ. *Spon* and *Wheeler*, vol. ii. p. 390. Ed. 1724. ΘΕ-ΟΙΣ ΣΕΒΑΣΤΟΙΣ. But where the Adjective is placed first, the Article is retained. *Spon*, vol. ii. p. 270. ΤΟΝ ΛΑΜΠΡΟ-ΤΑΤΟΝ 'ΑΝΘΥΠΑΤΟΝ. Vol. i. 320. ΟΙ ΘΕΙΟΤΑΤΟΙ ΑΥ-ΤΟΚΡΑΤΟΡΕΣ: p. 306. ΤΩι ΣΩΤΗΡΙ ΘΕΩι: for here σωτὴρ may be considered as an Adjective: I conclude, therefore, that had the altar noticed by St. Paul been dedicated to the One True, though Unknown God, the Inscription would have been either ΤΩι 'ΑΓΝΩΣΤΩι ΘΕΩι, or ΘΕΩι 'ΑΓΝΩΣΤΩι: since it is neither of these, I accede to Mr. Wakefield's translation.—

CHAPTER XVIII.

If the Reader would know what has been written on this text, he will find it amply detailed in a dissertation by *Wonna*, Thesaur. Theol. Philol. vol. ii. 464.

V. 24. Κύριος. Ed. Bogardi ὁ Κ. This is very faulty: γῆς ὁ Κύριος offends against Regimen. Οὐρανοῦ and γῆς are anarthrous by Part i. Chap. vi. § 2.

V. 28. τοῦ γὰρ καὶ γένος ἐσμέν. D. and another for τοῦ have τούτου. The Latin *hujus* would easily suggest this reading to a writer, who did not consider the original and poetical use of the Article. See the *Appendix*.

V. 30. τοὺς μὲν οὖν χρόνους τῆς ἀγνοίας ὑπεριδὼν ὁ θεός. It would seem almost impossible for a Translator to go amiss in rendering this passage, at least so far as respects the construction; for ὑπεριδὼν has been differently understood, though hardly any reasonable doubt can be entertained that it signifies, *having overlooked*, or *having regarded with lenity*. See *Krebsii Obss. Flav.*: yet even the construction was not sufficiently plain for Mr. Wakefield. He renders "condemning *such* ignorance in *these* times;" and this he thinks correspondent with the scope and phraseology of the context. He adds, indeed, that "some of the ancient Translators seem to have had the same notion of the passage." Who these were, I cannot discover: but if it could be proved that their Greek MSS. had the present reading, their Versions would not, from so curious a specimen, rise in credit.—Ὑπερείδω most commonly in profane writers, and always in the LXX. governs an Accusative: in the N. T. it is ἅπαξ λεγόμενον.

CHAP. XVIII.

V. 13. τοὺς ἀνθρώπους. Dr. *Owen* (ap. Bowyer) supposes that here the Jews are meant, on account of the Article: but see Matt. x. 17. where, however, Mr. Markland admits that his remark is not applicable to the Acts.

V. 24. Ἀπολλὼς ὀνόματι Ἀλεξανδρεὺς τῷ γένει. D. has γένει Ἀλεξανδρεύς: but τῷ γένει, at least in the N. T. is the usual form. It is not, however, a case in which uniformity should be expected: for whether we say *by birth* or *by his birth*, there will be no difference, except that the latter will be marked by unnecessary though allowable precision. Ὀνόματι so used, I think, never takes the Article, possibly because of the frequent occurrence of the word, which may have given it the more careless and colloquial form. This is one of the instances in which we may admit the force of custom without endangering the Philosophy of Language: where no principle is violated, custom and reason are not brought into competition; nor can the authorized latitude of the one be made an argument against the rigorous restrictions of the other.

CHAP. XIX.

V. 6. τὰς χεῖρας. A. and few others — τάς. The Article is elsewhere inserted in this phrase, nor do I perceive why it should be here omitted.

V. 28. Ἐφεσίων. A single MS. has τῶν: but this is wholly unnecessary: national appellations have in Regimen the same licence which is allowed to Proper Names.

V. 29. συγχύσεως. A. and very many MSS. and Edd. have τῆς, and Griesbach admits it into the text. There may, indeed, be a reference to what is related in the verse preceding: at the same time, if the Article be here to be inserted, it will be almost the only instance after a Verb *of filling* in the whole N. T.

CHAP. XX.

V. 9. ἐπὶ τῆς θυρίδος. English Version, "in a window." I think it may be inferred from the Article, that the ὑπερῷον had only one window.

V. 11. ἄρτον. A. C. D. *à pr. manu*, have τόν. I do not know any reason for the insertion of the Article. The breaking of bread seems not here to be meant of the Eucharist, but only of taking ordinary refreshment: and even where the Eucharist is intended, as above, ver. 7. and elsewhere, ἄρτον is without the Article; for though the loaf used was only *one*, yet from the double meaning of ἄρτος, *a loaf* and *bread*, it was not necessary to mark that circumstance.

V. 13. ἐπὶ τὸ πλοῖον. No ship has been recently mentioned: above, however, ver. 6. mention was made of sailing from Philippi: this, therefore, is the ship which was there implied, and in which St. Luke, and his party performed their

CHAPTER XX. 289

coasting voyage, touching at Troas, Assos, Mitylene, Chios, Samos, Trogyllium, Miletus, Coos, Rhodes, and finishing at Patara : there they embark on board another vessel, a trader bound to Phœnicia. See next Chap. ver. 1. Michaelis in his *Anmerk.* adduces some plausible reasons to show that the ship here spoken of was one which Paul had hired, in order to have it entirely at the disposal of himself and his friends.

V. 22. δεδεμένος τῷ πνεύματι. This, as *Wolfius* remarks, resembles συνείχετο τῷ πνεύματι above, xviii. 5. In both places I understand τὸ πνεῦμα, not of the Holy Spirit, but of the spirit or mind of Paul ; a sense in which τῷ πνεύματι frequently occurs, as John xiii. 21. Acts xviii. 25. *et passim.* Archbishop *Newcome* renders, " I go to be bound according to the Spirit," i. e. he says, " the Spirit foretelling that I shall be bound." I cannot help thinking this interpretation somewhat unnatural, nor am I aware that any parallel construction can be found in the N. T.

V. 28. τοῦ Θεοῦ. The Reader is probably aware of the variations with which this passage is perplexed. We find, besides τοῦ Θεοῦ, the reading of the received text, τοῦ Κυρίου, τοῦ Χριστοῦ, τοῦ Κυρίου Θεοῦ, τοῦ Θεοῦ καὶ Κυρίου, and τοῦ Κυρίου καὶ Θεοῦ, in all, six readings. It is foreign from my purpose to examine minutely the relative degrees of probability which each of them may claim : this task, indeed, has already been performed by *Wetstein* and *Griesbach*, who decide in favour of τοῦ Κυρίου. Since, however, two of these readings bring the text within the limits of the Canon revived by Mr. *Granville Sharp*, it may be right briefly to state the evidence by which they are all severally supported : and this I shall do in the words of Michaelis, (in his *Anmerk.*) with such additional remarks as may be requisite.

1. " The reading τοῦ Θεοῦ has hitherto been found in but few MSS. and among those none is of high, or even of considerable antiquity. It stands in the present Vulg. ; but some of the older Latin MSS. have τοῦ Κυρίου, and it is not found in any other ancient Version whatever. If I were called upon to speak in its defence, I should say that the Copyists wished to avoid the strong expression of *God's blood ;* and this they have done, some in one way, some in another : at the same

U

time I confess, that on impartial attention to the evidence, I dare not adopt it as the true and genuine reading. The MSS. in which it is found, amount to fourteen; and it is quoted or referred to by a great many of the Fathers.

2. "Τοῦ Κυρίου is found in several of the most ancient MSS. or other early documents; and, on weighing the evidence, this will be preferred to the other readings. Here ὁ Κύριος, as is usual in the N. T. is Christ: and thus not a syllable is said of his Eternal Godhead; for as to the notion that thus the Divinity of Christ will be more strongly maintained, ὁ Κύριος being equivalent to Jehovah, it is a barefaced, and I may add, a dishonest attempt to employ an argument which has been long exploded. It is true, that the LXX. and others who followed them, render Jehovah in the O. T. by Κύριος: but ὁ Κύριος spoken of Jesus in the N. T. has not this signification." If it be meant, that in the N. T. God is never called Ὁ Κύριος, this is a mistake: see James iv. 15. Luke i. 6; ii. 15. Acts iii. 20. I would not, however, willingly rest a doctrine of so much importance on equivocal evidence. In the O. T. this usage is not uncommon.—The authorities alluded to in support of this reading, are the MSS. A. C. D. E. and five others more modern, and the Copt. and Syr.-Philox. Verss. with several of the Fathers.

3. "Τοῦ Χριστοῦ has less support than the preceding: and this, like the former, affords no proof of the Divinity of Christ." It is found in no MS. whatever, but only in the Syr. and Erp.-Arab. Verss. and in a few of the Fathers: it appears, however, from *Adler* (Verss. Syr. p. 17.) that one MS. of the *Peshito* has τοῦ Θεοῦ. What are the "*plurimi Codd. Græci,*" which, as Adler says, (p. 18.) support the reading τοῦ Χριστοῦ, I cannot conjecture: they were unknown to Wetstein, Matthäi, and Griesbach.

4. and 5. The two next readings have so little authority, that, as Michaelis observes, they are scarcely worthy of notice.

6. "Τοῦ Κυρίου καὶ Θεοῦ is found in a very great multitude of MSS. If numbers," says Michaelis, "were to decide the question, this reading would be preferred; but of the MSS. which contain it, none is of high antiquity." Of these MSS. one is in Uncial letters, viz. G. or Harl. 5684, preserved in the British Museum. It is also the reading of the Edd. Com-

CHAPTER XX. 291

plut. and Plant. and of the Slavon. Vers. and Theophylact. It is remarkable, and it could not be known to Wetstein, that *all* of Matthäi's MSS. have this reading, even his Codex 1, which in the Acts usually differs from all the rest: this was the MS. alluded to above, on xvi. 7. The greater part of Alter's have the same reading.

These three last readings are supposed by Michaelis to have been compounded of the two first: but is it not just as probable, that the two first may have arisen by dividing the reading τοῦ Κυρίου καὶ Θεοῦ? The reading τοῦ Κυρίου Θεοῦ, which is in one MS. and in the Arab. of Walton's Polyglott, might very well, by the accidental omission of the Copulative, be the intermediate step; for in that case subsequent Copyists, rightly observing that τοῦ Κυρίου Θεοῦ is a phrase unknown to the writers of the N. T. and indeed to the LXX. who always write Κύριος ὁ Θεός, judged one of the words to be superfluous: some, therefore, might retain Κυρίου, and some Θεοῦ.

The remark, however, of Michaelis, with which I am most concerned, is, that the two last readings would not carry with them any proof of the Divinity of Christ; for that the subjoined expression "of his own blood," would then be referrible not to Θεοῦ, but to Κυρίου. Now in the case of the fifth reading, τοῦ Θεοῦ καὶ Κυρίου, the most which can be admitted is, that there is an ambiguity arising from the uncertainty of the usage with respect to Κύριος; for if Christ be ever called Κύριος without the Article, as he sometimes is, (see on Luke i. 15.) then it may be contended that the newly revived Canon will not here necessarily apply: though it may be answered that Κύριος without the Article so seldom means Christ, that the application of the Canon will not be at all violent. However, Michaelis appears not to have thought of this Canon: according, then, to his distinction between Κύριος and ὁ Κύριος, if the former mean Jehovah, the reading in question will be tautological, for it will mean, "of God and Jehovah." It has, however, so little authority, that it is needless to inquire into its import.

With regard, however, to τοῦ Κυρίου καὶ Θεοῦ, I can by no means admit, that if it be authentic, it affords no proof of the Divinity of Christ: on the contrary, it will establish this

u 2

important point in a manner the most satisfactory. Allowing Michaelis to have been unacquainted with a Canon which once was well known and very generally adopted, it is still surprising that he did not feel the extreme violence of making τοῦ ἰδίου αἵματος refer to Κυρίου, the *former* of the two Nouns, by passing over Θεοῦ, the *latter:* and, I think, it may be maintained, that had not the writers of the numerous MSS. which exhibit this reading, understood Κυρίου and Θεοῦ of one and the same person, most of them would infallibly have transposed the words, so as to make αἷμα refer to the Noun immediately preceding. Their constant acquiescence in the other arrangement is a very strong presumption, supposing them to have understood what they wrote, (which I believe to have been the case with most of the Copyists of the Moscow MSS. as well as with many others,) that they perceived no awkwardness in the structure, because they had no idea that τοῦ Κυρίου καὶ Θεοῦ could be taken otherwise than of one person. As to the proof, that they ought so to be understood, I must refer the Reader to the First Part of this Work, where I have endeavoured not only to exemplify the usage, but to develope the principle. I will, however, add, that I consider the phrase τοῦ Κυρίου καὶ Θεοῦ, if it be authentic, which is more than I maintain, to be among the best possible illustrations of the rule: why it is less exceptionable than τοῦ Θεοῦ καὶ Κυρίου, has already been hinted. Ὁ Θεός, though when it is unconnected it possesses, for a reason formerly assigned, the privilege of rejecting the Article, (which privilege, however, it exercises but rarely,) is in all cases of combination with other Nouns, subject to the rules which affect the commonest Appellative: thus in Regimen we never find ὁ υἱὸς Θεοῦ, ἡ εἰρήνη Θεοῦ, &c. but ΤΟΥ Θεοῦ: so also it is always Ὁ Θεὸς καὶ πατήρ, not Θεός. The rule respecting ὁ Θεὸς plainly is, that its privilege of rejecting the Article shall in no wise interfere with the usage common in other cases. It is, therefore, indisputable, that if there be authority for admitting the reading, Mr. Sharp is right in understanding the phrase of one person. His proposed rendering of καὶ by *even* is, indeed, erroneous; because it is in direct opposition to the principle on which the truth of the rule depends. Καὶ is in all such instances no other than the common Copulative, so that the sense will here be, "of Him being (or who is) both Lord and God." It may be replied, however, that Mr. Sharp had nothing to do with the principle, and was concerned only with the fact.

It is obvious, that if the reading τοῦ Θεοῦ of the received text be authentic, the passage will still afford a proof of the Divinity of Christ; for the name *God* will then be applied to Him, who in the next verse is said to have purchased the Church *with his own blood*. Yet where is the inference which may not be evaded by human ingenuity;

Πολλὰ τὰ δεινά, κοὐδὲν ἀνθρώπου δεινότερον πέλει.

Mr. *Wakefield* has a Note which may amuse the Reader; and the little amusement which I can procure for him, I feel that I ought not to withhold. After having preferred τοῦ Θεοῦ, which, considering his bias, must excite surprise till the mystery is explained, and having stated that Griesbach's testimony respecting the Æthiopic Version is "*infamously false*," Mr. W. thus proceeds to comment on his own rendering of τοῦ ἰδίου αἵματος:

"*His own son*: literally, *his own blood*: but, as this expression could answer no good purpose, and would unavoidably lead those unacquainted with the *phraseology* of these languages into erroneous doctrines and impious conceptions of the Deity, I could not justify myself in employing it in this place. So *blood* is used for *man* in xvii. 26. and Matt. xxvii. 4. So *Homer* Il. Z. 211.

" Ταυτης τοι γενεης τε και ΑΙΜΑΤΟΣ ευχομαι ειναι.
ΑΙΜΑ σοφου Φοιβοιο, και ευπαλαμοιο Κυρηνης,

"says *Nonnus* D. lib. v. p. 152. and the *scholiast* on Eur. Orest. 1239, says ΑΙΜΑ δε οἱ ΠΑΙΔΕΣ, γενος οἱ αδελφοι, συγγενεια οἱ γαμβροι. And Virgil Æn. vi. 836.

"*Projice tela manu*, SANGUIS MEUS!

"See farther *Davies* on *Cicero* de finn. i. 10. note 2. This is well known, and supplies the most easy and obvious interpretation of this most·disputed passage. See also Mr. *Henley's* Note in the *Appendix* to Bowyer's *Criticisms*, who first excited in my mind the notion of this acceptation, and to whom, therefore, the entire applause justly due to this excellent solution of so great a difficulty, ought in all reason to be given. If no passage of the N. T. quite parallel can be found, we should recollect that *Luke* is an elegant writer, and does not confine himself to the narrow limits of *Hebrew phraseology*, as might be shown by many instances."

The Note of Dr. Henley's referred to by Mr. W. is as follows :

" διὰ τοῦ ἰδίου ΑΙΜΑΤΟΣ. An expression explanatory of αἵματος occurs in Tibullus, lib. i. 6. v. 66.

"Te semper, natamque tuam te propter, amabo,
Quicquid agit, SANGUIS est tamen illa tuus.

" But there is one still more analogous in the Alexander of Lucian, ed. Reitz. tom. ii. p. 225 :

" Εἰμὶ Γλύκων, τρίτον ΑΙΜΑ Διός, φάος ἀνθρώποισι."

To whom the merit of this notable contrivance properly belongs, I shall not inquire: it may, possibly, be Dr. Henley's ; or if any other Critic should assert his claim to it, Dr. Henley's high reputation may very well spare "the entire applause :" perhaps, indeed, he feels the justice of Mr. W.'s acknowledgment quite as much as the generosity. Mr. W. has undertaken to defend the " excellent solution ;" and he cannot be suspected, here at least, of *prevarication*, I mean in the *Latin* sense of that word : yet what has he been able to establish? only that ἀθῶον αἷμα has been used of blood unjustly shed, (which, by the way, is the blood spoken of in the present passage,) and that God has of *one blood* made all the nations of the earth. But then Luke was " an elegant writer:" at this rate he, or rather St. Paul, must have been to his hearers a perfect barbarian ; for it is almost impossible that they should have understood him ; because the very mention of doing any thing "by his own blood" must have directed their minds to the sacrifice made by Christ, the efficacy of whose blood was an idea extremely familiar to the first Christians, whatever it may be to those of the present day ; so familiar, that the phrase διὰ τοῦ ἰδίου αἵματος otherwise applied could not but have misled them. A few of the passages in which mention is made of Christ's blood are, Rom. iii. 25; v. 9. Ephes. i. 7; ii. 13. Col. i. 14. and in Heb. ix. 12. and xiii. 12. we find the very phrase, διὰ τοῦ ἰδίου αἵματος, plainly intended, though not more plainly than in the present verse, of the sacrifice made by Christ. Besides, in what part of Scripture do we find the Son of God, so often mentioned, called the *blood of God?* and is it not to the full as revolting to all *human* notions (for they, as it should seem, are alone to be regarded) to impute *blood* to the *Father*, as *Divinity* to the *Son?* I agree with Mr. Wakefield in thinking that such a translation might lead men into "erroneous doctrines and impious conceptions of the Deity," unless the context made it evident that *God* in this place could mean only *God the Son:* yet if this be really the language of Scripture, if *God* and *Blood* be so associated, why is it to be concealed by a false rendering, and then acknowledged in a Note, which the majority of Mr. Wakefield's Readers will never examine, deterred by its learned aspect? Has Christianity its *exoteric* teaching for the vulgar, and its *esoteric* for the advantage of the few, who possess the erudition of the late Mr. Wakefield? ῎Αρα πρὸς Χαρίτων πάνσοφός τις ἦν ὁ Πρωταγόρας, καὶ τοῦτο ἡμῖν μὲν ἠνίξατο τῷ πολλῷ συρφετῷ, τοῖς δὲ μαθηταῖς ἐν ἀπορρήτῳ τὴν ἀλήθειαν ἔλεγε.

I know not whether it be in consequence of being acquainted with the discovery said to have been made by Dr. Henley, that Michaelis mentions this very rendering, as one of the ways by which the inference from the common reading may be evaded by the opponents of the Divinity of Christ. The same Writer suggests another mode of avoiding this stumbling-block; one which is in all respects as "excellent" as the former, and is just as defensible by an appeal to the language of Scripture: it is that of translating διὰ τοῦ ἰδίου αἵματος " by the blood of his own (Son):" and it is added that several of the oldest MSS. place the Adjective after the Substantive, reading τοῦ αἵματος τοῦ ἰδίου, (as in τὸ πνεῦμα τὸ ἅγιον, &c.) a circumstance by which this construction is supposed to be somewhat favoured. Whether, indeed, Tibullus or Virgil will in this case supply any thing parallel, is a question which I forbear to examine.

CHAP. XXI.

V. 4. τοὺς μαθητάς. English Version has simply, "finding disciples." Many MSS. and Editt. omit the Article: among the MSS. are six of Matthäi's, including the best.

V. 6. εἰς τὸ πλοῖον. *Michaelis* is of opinion, that when the ship in which St. Paul sailed from Patara to Tyre had unladen her cargo, he hired it, in order to make a day's voyage to Ptolemais. The Article seems to strengthen this conjecture.

V. 8. τοῦ ὄντος. A very great number of MSS. and Editt. —τοῦ. Since it had not been already said that Philip was one of the Seven, there can be little doubt that the Article should be rejected, as it is by both Wetstein and Griesbach [1].

CHAP. XXII.

V. 14. τὸν δίκαιον. See above, vii. 52.

V. 25. τοῖς ἱμᾶσιν. The Article is not here without meaning: there is reference to the thongs or cords usually employed for this purpose.

CHAP. XXIII.

V. 5. ὅτι ἐστὶν ἀρχιερεύς. Ananias had just before been called ὁ ἀρχιερεύς: still the Article in this place, whichever of the proposed interpretations be the true one, is necessarily omitted. Our English Version understands St. Paul to say, that he knew not that Ananias was the High Priest: *Lightfoot* adduces reasons why the Apostle might affirm that he knew not that there was then *any* High Priest. *Michaelis* supports the former opinion, and shows that from particular circumstances St. Paul might very easily be ignorant of the dignity which Ananias had assumed [2].

---

[1] But see Chap. vi. 5. Whereas, if the Article be omitted, it will be more naturally rendered, " *Since* he was one of the seven."—J. S. Winer concurs in this remark.—H. J. R.

[2] V. 6. Τὸ ἓν μέρος ἐστὶ Σαδδουκαίων. Compare this with Mark xii. 27. In both, as the Predicate would be the same word as the Subject, it is omitted. See too Gal. iii. 20. and the note on Col. ii. 17. Compare also Rom. iii. 29 ; ix. 9. 1 Cor. xiv. 33. and perhaps Eph. ii. 8.—H. J. R.

CHAPTER XXIII.

V. 8. τὰ ἀμφότερα. Mr. *Harris*, in his Hermes, p. 226, observes, after Apollonius, that we cannot say in Greek ΟΙ ἀμφότεροι, nor in English, he adds, *the both*. This is one of the instances in which these profound Grammarians appear to be mistaken on the subject of the Greek Article: we find it prefixed to ἀμφότεροι no less than three times in Ephes. ii. 14. 16. 18. So also Plato, vol. ii. p. 180. ΤΑ ἀμφότερα γινώσκει. It is true, that we cannot in English say *the both*; but we can say *they* or *them both*, or *both of them*, which is precisely the meaning of ΟΙ ἀμφότεροι, or ΤΑ ἀμφότερα, in the text. The reason assigned why ἀμφότεροι and *both* reject the Article is, that they are in themselves " sufficiently defined :" but to *define* is not, strictly speaking, the use of the Greek Article. Harris, however, sets out on this principle; and it is the source of most of the mistakes which follow. But of this enough has been said in Part I.—The two things referred to are the Resurrection and the Existence of Immaterial Beings, for πνεῦμα and ἄγγελος are considered as falling under the same head. It has, indeed, been supposed that ἀμφότερα may, by Writers who are not very attentive to correctness, be used of things which are more than two: but of this I have seen no example. Mr. *Wakefield* understands the passage in the same way with myself.

V. 9. οἱ γραμματεῖς. A great number of Wetstein's MSS. though not any in Uncial letters, omit the Article: so also do the best of Matthäi's. Griesbach prefixes the mark of possible spuriousness, and not without reason. Several MSS. instead of οἱ γραμματεῖς, have τινὲς τῶν γραμματέων, which was evidently the marginal illustration of some one who wished to show that γραμματεῖς, which he found in his copy without the Article, signified *some* scribes. This is one of many instances in which the MSS. written in small characters appear to have preserved the true reading, where the Uncial MSS. have lost it: nor is this surprising, since it is not at all improbable that some of the former may be lineally descended, that is, be copies of copies, from MSS. much older than any which now exist. The *lectiones singulares*, observable in some of the less ancient MSS., where they are neither mistakes of the Transcriber, nor apparent corrections, can scarcely be accounted for on any other hypothesis. The deference, therefore, which is usually paid to the Uncial MSS. may in some instances be unmerited: at least it may be affirmed, that the evidence of A. B. C. D. E. &c. is not so decisive as to supersede further inquiry.

CHAP. XXIV.

V. 14. τῷ πατρῴῳ Θεῷ. It is worthy of remark, that the Editt. of *Erasmus*, and after him of *Colin*. and *Bogard*, have τῷ πατρῴῳ ΤΩι Θεῷ. This reading is so faulty, that I cannot believe it to have been found in any MS.: in that case it was, probably, one of the corrections of Erasmus, a curious specimen of the philological skill of so learned a man. See Part i. Chap. viii. § 2.

V. 15. δικαίων τε καὶ ἀδίκων. An English Reader might here expect ΤΩΝ δικαίων: but see Part i. Chap. vi. § 2.

V. 23. τῷ ἑκατοντάρχῃ. English Version and *Newcome*, " to a centurion." I need hardly observe, that this must be wrong. Mr. *Wakefield* translates the Article, but without any remark. It may be shown, I think, that the Article here, as elsewhere, has its meaning. It will be recollected, that in the preceding Chapter, ver. 23. the Chief Captain, or χιλίαρχος, called unto him *two* Centurions, and ordered them with a body of horse and foot to escort Paul to Cesarea. Having arrived at Antipatris, (ver. 32.) the infantry return to Jerusalem, and leave the prisoner in custody of the cavalry, who conduct him to Felix. It is plain, therefore, that the Centurion here spoken of as a person known to the Reader, was no other than the Commander of the Horse, who had the sole charge of Paul, after the Captain of Infantry, who made part of the escort as far as to Antipatris, had returned to Jerusalem. That Felix should remand Paul to the same Officer who had brought him to Cesarea, is the conduct we should expect. The fidelity of this Centurion had been tried, and might therefore be trusted.

CHAP. XXV.

V. 26. τῷ Κυρίῳ. This is the only passage in the N. T. in which we find ὁ Κύριος applied to the Roman Emperor: instances of this early usage of the title are at least uncommon. See *Spanheim de Præst. Numism.* vol. ii. p. 483.

CHAP. XXVI.

V. 30. ἀνέστη ὁ βασιλεὺς καὶ ὁ ἡγεμών. All the MSS. rightly insert the second Article, two different persons being here intended. The same care has been observed in the 11th verse of the next Chapter.

CHAP. XXVII.

V. 9. τὴν νηστείαν. Two or three different, but wholly needless and unsupported, conjectures have been proposed in place of the reading of all the MSS. The νηστεία here mentioned, as is now generally admitted, is the Day of Expiation, the great Fast on the 10th of the month Tisri. See *Lewis's Heb. Antiq.* vol. ii. p. 569. The 10th of Tisri is, according to *Michaelis*, about the 10th of our October; and consequently, if the great Fast was now past, the season of the year could not well be favourable to navigation. The objection of *Markland* (ap. Bowyer,) that a Heathen would take no notice of a Jewish Fast, is wholly inexplicable: it is not said or insinuated that the Alexandrian Mariners *did* take any notice of the νηστεία: the remark is made by St. Luke, to whom, as a Jew, or at least a person much acquainted with Jewish habits, the mention of the Fast was a natural and obvious mode of marking the time of the year: and to say that "τὴν νηστείαν must be something which *increased* the danger of sailing, to which the Fast of the Jews has no more relation than Circumcision has," would certainly, had it proceeded from any man less eminent than Markland, be thought ridiculous. The Poets represent the stormy season as beginning soon after the rising of *Hædi*, or the setting of *Arcturus*: yet it never was seriously supposed, that the rising or setting of a star produced a storm. —In short, few texts of the N. T. appear to be less difficult than the present: and yet he who should read Markland's Note without attending to the passage, would suppose it to be corrupted beyond the possibility of restitution. The same Fast, as *Loesner* has shown, is adverted to by *Philo de Vitâ Mosis*, whence we may collect, that it was commonly called *The Fast* κατ' ἐξοχήν: his words are τὴν λεγομένην νηστείαν.

Besides, as *Michaelis* observes, it was the only Fast in the whole year of Divine appointment.

V. 16. τῆς σκάφης. On this passage a Criticism of mine appeared, many years ago, in one of the periodical publications of the day: it is to the following effect.

The learned Michaelis has established it as a rule, that critical conjectures are not to be admitted into the sacred text; and yet he confesses that some emendations have forced themselves upon him, which, in a profane author, he should not hesitate to adopt. One of these proposed readings (vid. Marsh's Michaelis, vol. ii. p. 406) respects Acts, Chap. xxvii. ver. 16. Νησίον δέ τι ὑποδραμόντες καλούμενον Κλαύδην, μόλις ἰσχύσαμεν περικρατεῖς γενέσθαι τῆς σκάφης, where the Critic would reject the Article from τῆς σκάφης, because it implies that they had before let down the boat into the sea, and had afterwards great difficulty in recovering it. "This," says he, "is improbable; because, 1st. No reason can be assigned why they should have let it down into the sea in a storm. 2dly. If they *had* let it down, they would have been able to draw it up again; unless we suppose, what is contrary to reason, they had let it entirely loose. 3dly. Supposing the boat to have been loose, it does not appear that the circumstance of the ship's being near an island, has any connexion with the recovery of this boat. I would therefore omit the definite Article, and explain the passage thus: Being near an island, we sought for help, but could not procure a boat to our assistance." Thus far Michaelis.

Now, in the first place, to say nothing farther of this construction, it is impossible to adopt it, because μόλις ἰσχύσαμεν, κ. τ. λ. must signify, we found a *difficulty* in gaining the boat, and not that we could not procure a boat at all: so μόλις is twice used in this very Chapter, ver. 7, 8. But, secondly, a very easy and obvious supposition will remove all the objections urged by the Professor against the acknowledged reading of the MSS. St. Luke is describing the storm, in which St. Paul at last suffered shipwreck; and it is well known that the boat, with every thing on deck, is frequently washed overboard by the violence of the waves. This seems to have happened in the voyage of St. Paul; and as the sea was running high, μόλις properly expresses the difficulty of regaining the boat. To the objections, therefore, of Michaelis, I would answer, with respect to the first and the second, that the boat was not *purposely* let down into the sea, and that nothing of that kind is implied; but that it had broken loose: and to the third, that the circumstance of the ship's being near an island, was not intended to have any other connexion with the recovery of the boat, than, in the following sentence, the vicinity of a promontory has with the loss of a mast: "Being a league S. W. of the Lizard, our foremast went by the board:" the mention of place, no less than of time, is essential to the accuracy of a journal.

V. 20. μήτε ἡλίου μήτε, κ. τ. λ. Part i. Chap. vi. § 2.

V. 38. τροφῆς. A few MSS. τῆς τροφῆς. There may be reference to former mention: but see on xix. 29.

CHAP. XXVIII.

V. 4. ἡ Δίκη. No MS. wants the Article. See Part i. Chap. v. Sect. i. § 2.

ROMANS.

CHAP. I.

V. 4. υἱοῦ Θεοῦ. Mr. *Wakefield*, as usual, avails himself of the absence of the Article, not considering that by the usage the Article could not be here inserted. Part i. Chap. iii. Sect. iii. § 2. Neither does the context very well accord with his Translation; for if the meaning be merely that Christ was shown to be *a Son of God*, (a term explained by St. Paul in this Epistle, Chap. viii. 14.) surely Christ's "miraculous resurrection from the dead" was a much stronger instance of Divine interposition than the occasion required.

We are told (ap. Bowyer) that ὁρισθέντος is supposed by some to be a gloss from the margin : I see no pretence for this suspicion; which must be unfounded, since τοῦ υἱοῦ Θεοῦ would offend against Regimen.

V. 17. δικαιοσύνη γὰρ Θεοῦ. It may be right in this place to apprise the Reader, that the style of St. Paul, in respect to the Article, as well as otherwise, somewhat differs from that of the Evangelists. It was to be expected, from the general vehemence and quickness of his manner, that he would, in the use of the Article, adopt a mode of expression the most remote from precision and formality, which the Greek idiom admits. *Dion. Hal.* in his description of what he calls the *austere style*, among many other remarks distinguished by nice discrimination, observes, that it is ὀλιγοσύνδεσμος, 'ΑΝΑΡΘΡΟΣ : see de Comp. Verb. § 22. and these, perhaps, are not the only characters of that style, as represented by Dionysius, which are applicable to the language of St. Paul. In the Evangelists, as has been noticed, there are a few instances in which Θεὸς is without the Article, but in the Epistles of St. Paul such

CHAPTER II.

instances occur very frequently; and hence, in conformity with the rule of Regimen, we meet with so many expressions similar to that in question: so ὀργὴ Θεοῦ in the next verse: so also Ἡ βασιλεία ΤΟΥ Θεοῦ, the phrase which is every where used in the Gospels and Acts, sometimes in the Epistles rejects both the Articles. Other examples, in which the Apostle has preferred the *anarthrous* form, will be noticed in the sequel.

V. 21. τὸν Θεὸν οὐχ ὡς Θεόν. Here the second Θεὸν necessarily refuses the Article, the sense in such cases requiring us to supply οὐχ ὡς (ὄντα) Θεόν.

CHAP. II.

V. 13. τοῦ νόμου, *bis*. It is remarkable, that A. D. G. and two others, in each place omit τοῦ : but it is more remarkable that *Griesbach* has prefixed to each his mark of *probable spuriousness*: for the form οἱ ἀκροαταὶ νόμου, as I have repeatedly observed, is not admissible. It was, however, I imagine, inferred that the context here did not allow the mention of the Mosaic Law, which the presence of the Article might seem to imply; and hence the omission of the Article was originally the correction of some one who knew not the Greek usage, and moreover, as I think, misconceived the sense of the passage. It must, indeed, be admitted, that there is scarcely in the whole N. T. any greater difficulty than the ascertaining of the various meanings of νόμος in the Epistles of St. Paul. In order to show that, "by the Gospel alone men can be justified, and that the Mosaic Revelation is in this respect of no more avail than is the Light of Nature," a proposition, the proof of which is the main object of the whole Epistle, he has occasion to refer to the different Rules of Life with which the Gentiles and Jews had respectively been furnished: to the latter, more than one Revelation had been granted; for from the earliest ages to the time of Malachi, the Almighty favoured them, through the Patriarchs and Prophets, with repeated indications of his will. Hence νόμος is used by St. Paul of every Rule of Life, of every Revelation, especially of the Mosaic Law, and even of the moral and ceremonial observances, one or both of which it is the object of every νόμος to inculcate. The various senses, then, of this word are calculated to produce perplexity, especially since, as will be seen, there are passages in which more than one meaning of the word will accord with the tenor of the argument. It had, indeed, very early been remarked, that where the Law, as promulgated in the Pentateuch, is spoken of, and even where the whole body of the Jewish Scriptures is meant, there νόμος for the most part, though not without exception, has the Article prefixed. See *Macknight* on Rom. ii. 12. and on vii. 1. Now it is obvious, that were this rule *without exception*, an important step would be gained; for at least we should know, when the *Jewish Law* is meant by the Apostle, which is now so often, even among the best Commentators, a subject of dispute: but if there be exceptions, and these have no certain character, then plainly they destroy the rule, and it is on account of these exceptions that the rule seems now to be pretty generally abandoned. My observation, however, has led me to conclude, that the rule is liable to no other exceptions than those by which, as has been shown in this work, words the most definite are frequently affected. For example, we have in this Epistle, vii. 7. διὰ νόμου, where, as is rightly contended, the whole tenor of the passage requires us to interpret νόμου of the Law of Moses. Here, then, we have an exception, which, no doubt, has with some others been thought to invalidate the rule; as unquestionably it would, if it were not an example of an anomaly which every where prevails: Part i. Chap. vi. § 1. As it is, the Law of Moses may there be meant, and the context shows that νόμου cannot be otherwise interpreted: but this is not to be regarded as an instance in which the Mosaic Law is called simply νόμος, because the omission of the Article may be accounted for. And similar reasoning may be employed in behalf of the other places, where the Law κατ' ἐξοχὴν may appear to be called simply νόμος: in all such, if I mistake not, the Article is omitted by some licence allowed in like circumstances to all words, however definitely meant, and of which the limits have already been ascertained. How far this may be true, will be seen as we proceed.

It is scarcely necessary to observe, that our English Version, by having almost constantly said "the Law," whatever be the meaning of νόμος in the original, has made this most difficult Epistle still more obscure: for the English reader is used to

CHAPTER II.

understand the term of the Law of Moses, as in the Evangelists.

With respect to the passage under review, I am of opinion, that by τοῦ νόμου the Law κατ' ἐξοχὴν is meant, though it must be confessed that the purpose of the Apostle would not be altogether defeated, if the word were here used in a less restricted sense. I understand, however, with *Macknight* and *Whitby*, that the Apostle means to reprove the presumption of the Jews, who thought themselves sure of eternal life, because God had favoured them with a Revelation of his Will: in which case the reasoning will be, As many as have sinned without a Revelation, shall be punished without incurring the additional penalties which such a Revelation would have enacted: and as many as have sinned under a Revelation, shall suffer the severer punishment which that Revelation, whatever it be, has denounced against their crimes. If it be thought strange, says St. Paul, that such indulgence should be shown the former class of persons, I will add, that not the hearers *even of the Law itself*, but, &c. Besides that the other interpretation would have required ἀκροαταὶ νόμου, this turn is more forcible, and more in the manner of St. Paul. The verse following seems also to prove that τοῦ νόμου in the present is so to be understood: for the Apostle subjoins, For when Gentiles, who have not any Revelation, practise, by a natural impulse, morality as pure as that which even the Mosaic Law enjoins, though they have not actually a Revelation, they become a Revelation to themselves, and may, therefore, hope for all the rewards of virtue, which an actual Revelation would have taught them to expect. And the same argument, with the same attention to the use of the Article, is prosecuted to the end of the chapter.

V. 17. τῷ νόμῳ. Here *Griesbach*, on the authority of A. S, B. D. and a few others, prefixes to τῷ the mark of probable spuriousness. Thus, it is true, we shall not, as in the former instance, have questionable Greek; and the reasoning will be consistent, if the Apostle be made to say to the Jew, " Thou restest on a Revelation," instead of *on the Law:* the received reading is, however, more pointed and direct, and the authority for altering it is so trifling, as to be of no avail, even supposing the sense either way to be equally good. Griesbach might

x

possibly be influenced by observing that the Article is wanting in ἐν νόμῳ, ver. 23. but from this nothing can be inferred, because of the Preposition.

V. 25. νόμον πράσσῃς. Here it is plain, that by νόμον without the Article we are to understand, not the Law itself, (nor indeed would πράσσειν ΤΟΝ νόμον be very intelligible,) but *moral obedience* or *virtue*, such as it was the object of the Law to inculcate, and of which Circumcision was the outward and visible sign. Thus in the next verse, instead of νόμον, we have, in the same sense, τὰ δικαιώματα τοῦ νόμου. We have also, 1 Macc. ii. 21. νόμον καὶ δικαιώματα, where νόμον is used as it is here by St. Paul. So also Sirac. xxxiii. 2, 3 ; xxxv. 1. The same explanation will serve for νόμου below, ver. 27.

V. 27. σὲ τὸν διά, κ. τ. λ. See below, 1 Cor. xiv. 9 [1].

CHAP. III.

V. 11. ὁ συνιῶν, ὁ ἐκζητῶν. The former Article is omitted in A. B. G. and the latter in B. G. Though we have for the omission of the Articles the authority of only a few MSS. I am disposed to prefer the reading which those MSS. exhibit. See Part i. Chap. iii. Sect. iii. § 1. Thus we have immediately afterwards οὐκ ἔστι ποιῶν, one MS. only reading ὁ, probably a correction for the sake of uniformity. The quotation is from Ps. xiv. 1—3. and from Ps. liii. 1—3. on turning to which I find that the Articles are every where omitted. I have, indeed, above, on Luke ix. 60. quoted from the LXX. οὐκ ἔστιν ὁ θάπτων· which, however, differs from the present instances in expressing an occupation.

V. 20. ἐξ ἔργων νόμου. The absence of the Article proves nothing in this place as to the meaning of νόμου. Part i.

---

[1] V. 27. It will appear from the note on 1 Cor. xiv. 9. that the Bishop allows Mr. Wakefield's explanation, i. e. that he would take σὺ ὁ διὰ γράμματος for *tu literatus*, i. e. *qui literam vel legem Mosaicam profiteris*. When we look to the original, we can have little doubt of this, for ἡ ἐκ φύσεως ἀκροβυστία, in the first clause, is opposed to σὲ τὸν διὰ γράμματος καὶ περιτομῆς, in the second. But the Apostle, as is usual with him, is led into a form contrasting in *sense*, not in *words*, with the former. Gersdorf (rightly) explains the sentence to be, σὲ τὸν διὰ γ. κ. π. ὄντα, παραβάτην νόμου εἶναι.

Winer rightly says, that as τελοῦσα has not the Article, it is here truly participial, and does not serve for definition. *If it fulfils the law.*—H. J. R.

Chap. iii. Sect. iii. § 7. *Rosenmüller* says, that it signifies the whole law as revealed to the Jews, and contained in the O. T.; and *Michaelis* is of the same opinion. But this explanation appears to me to fall short of the Apostle's argument. It is his purpose to show that *no man whatever* can be justified by the works either of the Jewish Law or *of any other*: πᾶσα σάρξ, like ὁ κόσμος in the preceding verse, cannot but be understood universally; and what follows, διὰ γὰρ νόμου ἐπίγνωσις ἁμαρτίας, is also plainly an universal Proposition. *Macknight* here takes νόμος in the same sense that I do; though his reasoning is somewhat different. In the next verse, χωρὶς νόμου is well explained by Macknight to signify "without perfect *moral obedience.*" See above on ii. 25. But in this very verse, where the Law, meaning the Pentateuch, is mentioned, we have ὑπὸ τοῦ νόμου.

V. 25. ἱλαστήριον. The Article which is found in G. is inadmissible by Part i. Chap. iii. Sect. iii. § 4.

V. 31. νόμον. Here νόμος without the Article must be taken in the sense of *moral obedience*, as is plain from the context; for it is opposed to *faith*. Few texts of Scripture, rightly understood, are more important. Our own Version, from a cause which has been already noticed, does not place in the clearest light the truth herein taught.

CHAP. IV.

V. 4. τὸ ὀφείλημα. *Wetstein* and *Griesbach* reject the Article. It is wanting in a great majority of the MSS. and how it found its way into any, it is not easy to discover.

V. 11. πατέρα. Article wanting by Part i. Chap. iii. Sect. iii. § 2.

V. 13. τοῦ κόσμου. Several MSS. omit τοῦ: *Griesbach* rejects it. The omission may certainly be vindicated by Part i. Chap. iii. Sect. iii. § 7: but it is by no means necessary to deviate from the received text. *Matthäi's* MSS. all retain the Article.

CHAP. V.

V. 13. ἄχρι νόμου. Here, as in an instance already noticed on ii. 13. νόμου is equivalent to τοῦ νόμου, but the Article is omitted on account of the Preposition. So also ἐν κόσμῳ is ἐν τῷ κόσμῳ.

V. 15. τοῦ ἑνός: the one mentioned in the preceding verse, viz. Adam. By τοῦ ἑνὸς ἀνθρώπου, in the same verse, there is reference to Him, who had just before been called τοῦ μέλλοντος.

V. 20. νόμος δὲ παρεισῆλθεν. *Locke, Rosenmüller, Schleusner,* and *Michaelis,* and indeed most of the Commentators, understand this of the Law of Moses: in which case it must be admitted, that the rejection of the Article is not here authorized by any of the Canons. *Macknight,* however, has a different explanation of the passage. He well contends, that παρεισῆλθεν cannot be said of the Law of Moses, since it signifies " entered privily," as in Galat. ii. 4. the only instance, besides the present, in which the word occurs in the whole N. T. so also the similarly compounded words παρεισάγω, 2 Pet. ii. 1; παρεισακτούς, Galat. ii. 4; παρεισδύω, Jude ver. 4. But the Mosaic Law was ushered into the world with all possible pomp and notoriety: Macknight, therefore, understands νόμος of the Law of Nature: he asks, " Can any one with Locke imagine, that no offence abounded in the world which could be punished with death, till the Law of Moses was promulgated? And that grace did not superabound, till the offence against the Law abounded? The Apostle himself affirms, Rom. i. 30. that the Heathens, by the light of nature, knew not only the Law of God, but that persons who sinned against that Law, were worthy of death. The offence, therefore, abounded long before the Law of Moses entered. For these reasons, I conclude that *the Law which silently entered,* the moment Adam and Eve were reprieved, was *the Law of Nature:* and its taking place, the Apostle very properly expressed by its *entering;* because if Adam and Eve had been put to death immediately after they sinned, the law of man's nature would have ceased with the species. But they being respited from immediate death, and having a new trial appointed them, by the sentences recorded Gen. iii. 15, 16, 17. the law of their nature took place anew, or *entered silently* into the world." Perhaps, however, in such cases νόμος had best be rendered, *a Rule of Life:* this exactly accords with Macknight's notion, for in his Commentary he says, " Law secretly entered into the world as the rule of man's conduct;" and such a rendering would be more generally intelligible than the term *Law*, to which the English Reader annexes no very precise idea.

Same v. τὸ παράπτωμα, and in the next verse, ἡ ἁμαρτία, are supposed by *Wetstein* to express κατ' ἐξοχὴν the wickedness of the Jews, as being more heinous than that of the Gentiles. I am afraid that this explanation is without authority from the use of the Article in similar instances, and is also foreign from the purport of the argument. By τὸ παράπτωμα I understand the offence of Adam already spoken of, the consequences of which were more and more visible in the corruption of his posterity. Ἡ ἁμαρτία is sin *universally: Macknight* thinks that it is here personified: in either case, the Article is properly inserted, though in the anarthrous style of St. Paul, the latter usage is not always observed.

CHAP. VI.

V. 13. ὅπλα ἀδικίας, and so also ὅπλα δικαιοσύνης. Part i. Chap. iii. Sect. iii. § 4.

V. 14 and 15. ὑπὸ νόμον. Here again, I believe, we must desert the multitude of Commentators, and interpret the passage with *Macknight*, whose "Translation of the Epistles" has contributed more largely to our Theological knowledge, than perhaps any other exegetical work which appeared in this country during the last century. It is true, that if by ὑπὸ νόμον we understand the law of Moses, the argument will be coherent with respect to the Jews: but it ought to be remarked, that the design of the Apostle is far more comprehensive, and that he means to contrast the nature of all *Law*, i. e. of every Rule of life, which offers neither mediation nor atonement, and consequently makes no provision for the inevitable weakness of man, with *Grace*, i. e. with a gracious dispensation, which requires not an unsinning obedience, but only the best exertions of frail creatures, giving assurance of pardon through Faith, where our obedience has been imperfect.

CHAP. VII.

V. 1. γιγνώσκουσι γὰρ νόμον. *Macknight* appears to doubt whether by νόμον we are here to understand the Mosaic Law, or Law generally: the absence of the Article inclines him to the latter interpretation, though he thinks that the Apostle's reasoning in this Chapter admits either of them. My own notion of the passage is, that St. Paul here addresses his Readers with some degree of rhetorical complaisance. He might, indeed, have said merely, that they knew τὸν νόμον, the Mosaic Law; for the greater part of them, probably, had not extended their view to the imperfection which must belong to every Dispensation not providing an Atonement. He takes it, however, for granted, that they had made a general application from their own particular experience; and the design of the Epistle (see on ii. 13.) led him to speak, directly or indirectly, of the imperfection of all the possible schemes of salvation which afforded not a Redeemer.

V. 7. διὰ νόμου. This has already been considered on ii. 13. *Macknight*, though he admits that this can be understood only of the Mosaic Law, translates indefinitely "through Law:" he was, probably, unacquainted with the licence allowed after Prepositions.

V. 13. ἀλλ' ἡ ἁμαρτία, ἵνα φανῇ ἁμαρτία. English Version, "but sin, that it might appear sin." *Macknight*, "but sin (hath become death) that sin might appear." Here this excellent Translator deviates from the Common Version, not only without reason, but in neglect of a plain distinction arising from the omission of the Article before the second ἁμαρτία. Had the Apostle meant to make this the Nominative *before* φανῇ, he would probably, I do not say certainly, have written ἡ ἁμαρτία, as in the clause preceding: but supposing the sense to be as represented in our English Version, the omission of the Article is absolutely necessary: there can, therefore, be little doubt that our Version is right. Three, indeed, of the least considerable of Matthäi's MSS. have ἡ ἁμαρτία, but this was possibly the correction of some one who understood the passage in the same manner with Macknight. The Syr. and the Vulg. render the words as in the English.

V. 18. ἀγαθόν. F. G. and Cyril, with *l* of Matthäi, read

τὸ ἀγαθόν. This appears to be a mistake, arising from the use of τὸ ἀγαθὸν just before: the Article is here rightly omitted. Part I. Chap. iii. Sect. iii. § 5.

V. 21. τὸν νόμον. The Article here is anticipative of what is subjoined; the law or principle, which the Apostle is about to describe as impelling him to evil,. even when he is endeavouring to practise virtue. *Hemsterhusius* (ap. Wetstein) would expunge τὸ καλόν, so as to make τὸν νόμον dependent on ποιεῖν. This reading would understand τὸν νόμον of the Mosaic Law; a sense which accords not with the argument.

CHAP. VIII.

V. 9. πνεῦμα Θεοῦ ...... πνεῦμα Χριστοῦ. *Michaelis* in his Anmerk. says, " Here, at least in my opinion, and so far as can be collected from the context, St. Paul is not speaking of the Holy Ghost, the Third Person in the Godhead, who had not hitherto been mentioned, but rather of what in the Platonic Philosophy is called the Spirit, or the rational Soul, which is named likewise *the Spirit of God*, because it is formed after God's image, and is, like God, a Spirit, a thinking essence, eternal, &c. &c." He proceeds to observe, πνεῦμα Θεοῦ, πνεῦμα Χριστοῦ, and Χριστὸς ἐν ἡμῖν, are mere variations of phrase, without any difference of sense. Πνεῦμα Χριστοῦ he makes to signify, "those higher faculties of the soul which, in Christ, had entire dominion over the body, and by which the body was subdued."

It is extremely difficult, perhaps impossible, to fix the precise import of these terms; but if any thing be certain, it is, I think, that this passage, notwithstanding the opinion of so great a Critic, is not to be explained from the phraseology of Platonism. I much question, indeed, whether πνεῦμα Θεοῦ be a phrase in use with Plato; at least I do not recollect to have seen it in his Works, though, considering their extent, it may have escaped my notice: or if it be meant only that it was common with the Platonists of the School of *Ammonius*, it is obvious that St. Paul could not have borrowed their language. The misfortune is, that the plan of Michaelis's Work perpetually restrains him from adducing quotations and authorities which only men of some erudition could require or understand: it is true that he meditated a similar work for the Learned; but this, unhappily, he lived not to execute. Notwithstanding this inconvenience, "*The Annotations for the Unlearned*" is a work by which the most learned may profit: it contains much which is original and profound; it was the last labour of its author, and may, therefore, be regarded as the depository of his settled convictions; and the arguments which it affords in behalf of some important doctrines, are the more valuable, because they are the arguments of an Advocate whose occasional concessions attest his regard to truth. A Translation of this Work, or rather a Selection from it, (for to German prolixity it sometimes adds German indelicacy,) would doubtless be acceptable to English Readers; and a knowledge of the German language, which so many have acquired for no very commendable purpose, might thus be employed in promoting the best interests of man.

But though it may be questioned whether πνεῦμα Θεοῦ can be explained from the language of Platonism, I incline to the opinion that it is not here to be understood of the Holy Ghost, and also that the three phrases are nearly of the same import; for this is evident from the context. The sense of πνεῦμα, in this and in several other places, will probably be best deduced from Luke ix. 55. οὐκ οἴδατε οἴου πνεύματός ἐστε, where it means indisputably *spirit, mind, temper,* or *disposition*: in like manner we meet with πνεῦμα δουλείας, πνεῦμα σοφίας, πνεῦμα πρᾳότητος, &c. all common Hebraisms, in which the Genitive is to be construed, as if it were the corresponding Adjective agreeing with πνεῦμα. Two of the phrases in question appear to me to be of the same character, so that πνεῦμα Θεοῦ and πνεῦμα Χριστοῦ will signify a godly and a Christian frame of mind: so also 1 Cor. vii. 40. πνεῦμα Θεοῦ cannot be taken of the Holy Spirit in the personal sense, but must mean Divine aid or inspiration. The proposed interpretation exactly suits the context: "they who are carnal," says St. Paul, "cannot please God: ye, however, are not carnal, but spiritual, if, indeed, a godly spirit dwell in you; but if any one have not a Christian spirit, then he is not Christ's. If, however, Christ be in you, your body, it is true, shall die in consequence of (the original) transgression (of Adam), but your soul shall live through the righteousness (of the Redeemer)." I admit, however, that in ver. 11. τὸ πνεῦμα τοῦ ἐγείραντος Ἰησοῦν can be taken only of the Holy Spirit, for there the Hebraism has no place: and even τὸ πνεῦμα τοῦ Θεοῦ, 1 Cor. iii. 16. I would interpret in the same sense.

V. 13. πνεύματι is here evidently used in the adverbial sense, to mean *spiritually*, for it is opposed to κατὰ σάρκα, *carnally*, in the preceding clause: πνεύματι Θεοῦ also, in the next verse, seems to mean little more, and is in some degree a confirmation of what was said in the last Note. *Macknight*, however, understands both these of the Holy Spirit, as if we had read ὑπὸ or διὰ τοῦ ἁγίου πνεύματος· for some Preposition is, I think, always used, when an act is said to have been accomplished through the agency of the Holy Spirit. See on Luke iv. 1.

V. 16. αὐτὸ τὸ πνεῦμα .... τῷ πνεύματι ἡμῶν. Here we have two important senses of πνεῦμα plainly contradistinguished: "the Holy Spirit," and "the spirit or mind of man."

V. 22. πᾶσα ἡ κτίσις. English Version has "the whole creation:" *Macknight*, "every creature." The former is the right translation: see Part i. Chap. vii. § 1. though I am not aware that the settling of this point will be of any avail in ascertaining the meaning of the whole passage, beginning at verse 19. They who would know the several senses in which it has been interpreted, may consult *Wolfius*; whose Work, besides its other merits, is an excellent Index to the various interpretations of difficult passages of Scripture. There is likewise a Dissertation on the same subject in the *Thesaur. Theol. Philol.* vol. ii. On the word κτίσις I shall have occasion to remark, Col. i. 15.

V. 23. υἱοθεσίαν. We have here an illustration of Part i. Chap. iii. Sect. iii. § 4; so that the construction will be, "even we also, though we have received the first-fruits of the Spirit, wait for a deliverance from death, *as our adoption.*" *Macknight* thinks that there is an allusion to our Lord's words, Luke xx. 36; in that case, the proposed construction is still more evidently the true one. The Translators have inverted the order, though without much injury to the sense. In D. F. G. the word υἱοθεσίαν is omitted.

V. 24. βλεπομένη. Better with the Article, as in F. G.: the circumstance, that *it is seen*, should be assumed.

CHAP. IX.

V. 5. ὁ ὢν ἐπὶ πάντων Θεός, κ. τ. λ. It is well known that this text has been the subject of much controversy; yet not of more than was to be expected, considering how strongly and directly it attests the Divinity of Jesus Christ: if, however, I mistake not, the doctrine of the Article has much more to do with the question, than is commonly imagined.

1. One method which has been employed to evade the received interpretation, is *conjecture*. *Schlictingius* would transpose ὁ ὢν, and likewise alter the accent and breathing of the latter word, so as to make it ὧν ὁ. The meaning would thus be, "whose (viz. of the Jews) is the Supreme God." It may be asked, however, whether St. Paul was likely to affirm that the Jews had an exclusive interest in the One True God, when he had already in this very Epistle (see iii. 29.) asserted the contrary: "Is He the God of the Jews only, and not also of the Gentiles? Yes, also of the Gentiles." Nor is this all: an Article is wanting to authorize the proposed interpretation; for by thus making ὁ the Article of Θεός, we ought also to have an Article before εὐλογητός, taken in immediate concord with Θεός: Part i. Chap. viii. § 2. the form ὢν (ἐστι) ὁ Θεὸς εὐλογητός, (for the words discarded affect not the construction,) is without example in the N. T. But see on 1 Tim. i. 17. and Heb. ix. 1. places which may seem to contradict this remark. This conjecture, therefore, though it ranks among the happiest efforts of Socinian Criticism, obtrudes on the passage an argument which is improbable, and Greek which is impossible: yet *Griesbach* has, in his new edition, honoured this conjecture with a place among his various readings. An instance of the form which the proposed emendation would require, is Acts iv. 24, 25. σὺ (εἶ) ὁ Θεὸς Ὁ ποιήσας τὸν οὐρανόν, κ. τ. λ. Ὁ διὰ στόματος, κ. τ. λ.

I scarcely know whether I ought to consider under the same head a remark of *Wetstein*, who observes at the end of his long Note, "*Denique si id voluisset Paulus, quod quidam putant,*

CHAPTER IX.   315

videtur potius scripturus fuisse ὁ ὢν Ὁ ἐπὶ πάντων Θεὸς εὐλογητός, ut Eph. vi. 6." In the opinion of *Michaelis,* Wetstein was the most learned of the opponents of the Divinity of Christ: it may, therefore, be thought incredible that he should have expressed the received interpretation in false Greek: yet such, I fear, is the case. Ὁ ὢν Ὁ, so intended that the latter Article shall be predicated of the former, is, I am persuaded, a form of expression not to be met with in the uncorrupted remains of Greek literature, whether sacred or profane: for ὁ ὢν Ὁ would in fact amount to ὁ ὢν Ὁ ʼΩN: accordingly, throughout the N. T. even in cases where the sense of the Noun following ὢν is the most definite, we always find the Article omitted. Thus John x. 12. οὐκ ὢν ποιμήν, though a particular Shepherd is meant, viz. of the sheep in question: xi. 49. ἀρχιερεὺς ὤν, declared immediately to be the High Priest of that year. Heb. v. 8. ὢν υἱός, the Son, who is always, where no rule interferes, called ὁ υἱός. Acts v. 17. ἡ οὖσα αἵρεσις τῶν Σαδδουκαίων, not Ἡ αἵρεσις, though in xv. 5. we have τῆς αἱρέσεως τῶν Φαρισαίων. 2 Cor. xi. 31. ὁ ὢν εὐλογητός, though in Mark xiv. 61. we find the Father called κατ᾿ ἐξοχήν, Ὁ εὐλογητός. And not to accumulate examples, we have in *Philo,* p. 860. and p. 1040. Ed. 1640. τοῦ πρὸς ἀλήθειαν ὄντος ΘΕΟΥ, and τὸν ὄντως ὄντα ΑΛΗΘΗ ΘΕΟΝ. It is inconceivable how the terms *God* and *true God*, in these two passages, could be meant more definitely; yet after ὄντος and ὄντα the Articles are necessarily omitted. Wetstein, indeed, refers us to Eph. iv. 6. where, however, the Participle ὢν has no place: to have supported this hypothesis, it should have been ʼΩN ὁ ἐπὶ πάντων, for as the reading stands, and must stand, it is no more to his purpose than is every other clause in that whole chapter.—I see, then, no reason to admit, that if St. Paul had meant what is commonly understood by his words, he would have written ὁ ὢν Ὁ: a specimen of Greek which is worse even than the conjecture of Schlictingius; for, besides the fault just noticed, it involves the same error of using εὐλογητὸς without the Article, when Θεὸς is with it.— I find, however, in *Clarke's Reply to Nelson,* p. 68, the remark, that " if the words ὁ ὢν ἐπὶ πάντων Θεὸς be *allowed* to be certainly spoken of Christ, yet it is not the same as if the Apostle had said, ὁ ὢν Ὁ ἐπὶ πάντων Θεός."

2. But conjecture, in defiance of MSS., Versions, and Fathers, has by many been thought a desperate resource. This uniformity, indeed, seems not always to have been known. *Schoettgen, Hor. Hebr.* holds himself obliged to concede that "*quamplurimi Codd. et quidam ex Patribus*" want Θεός, and in the more popular work on the Trinity, by *Clarke*, we find a similar assertion. Some, therefore, may have inferred that this text cannot fairly be adduced in support of the Trinitarian scheme; and yet the received reading is confirmed by all the MSS. which have been hitherto collated, by all the ancient Versions, and by all the Fathers, except Cyprian in the *printed* copies, and also Hilary and Leo, who, according to Griesbach, have each of them *once* referred to this text without noticing Θεός. Whence the notion arose that Θεὸς is wanting in many MSS. I am not able to discover: there is scarcely a verse in the N. T. in which ancient authorities more nearly agree. It has, therefore, been deemed a safer expedient to attempt a *construction* different from the received one, by making the whole, or part of the clause, to be merely a doxology in praise of the Father; so that the rendering will be either "God, who is over all, be blessed for ever," or, beginning at Θεός, "God be blessed for ever." These interpretations also have their difficulties, though of a kind unlike the former; for thus εὐλογητὸς will properly want the Article. On the first, however, of these constructions it is to be observed, that in all the Doxologies, both of the LXX. and of the N. T. in which εὐλογητὸς is used, it is placed at the beginning of the sentence: in the N. T. there are five instances, all conspiring to prove this usage, and in the LXX. about forty. The same arrangement is observed in the *formula* of *cursing*, in which ἐπικατάρατος always precedes the mention of the person cursed. The reading, then, would on this construction rather have been, εὐλογητὸς ὁ ὢν ἐπὶ πάντων Θεὸς εἰς τοὺς αἰῶνας.—Against the other supposed Doxology, which was approved by *Locke*, the objection is still stronger, since that would require us not only to transpose εὐλογητός, but to read Ὁ Θεός. This word, as has already been remarked, though it have some latitude in taking or rejecting the Article, never uses its licence so as to create the least possible ambiguity: thus it can make no difference whether we write (viii. 8.) Θεῷ or ΤΩι Θεῷ ἀρέσαι, but εὐλο-

CHAPTER IX.

γητὸς Θεὸς will appear to signify, not "blessed be God," but that the words are to be taken in immediate concord with each other: accordingly, in all instances where a Doxology is meant, we find εὐλογητὸς Ὁ Θεός. See also below on 1 Cor. i. 9. For these reasons I conclude that both the proposed constructions are inadmissible. But,

3. Mr. *Wakefield* would *qualify* the meaning of Θεός. He says, "I adopt, with the Æthiopic Translator, *a lower sense* of Θεὸς common in the *O. T.:* so 2 Thess. ii. 4. and elsewhere:" and he renders "who is, *as* God, over all, blessed for evermore." On looking at the *Latin* of the Æthiopic Version, I find "*qui est Deus benedictus in sæcula.*" Whether this be the true rendering of the Æthiopic, I am wholly incapable of judging; certainly it discovers nothing of a lower sense of Θεός. Mr. W. indeed, every where professes his high opinion of this Version; but I do not recollect that he has any where informed us on what ground his esteem of it is founded; whether on the merits of the Version itself, of which, according to Michaelis, we know less than of any other Oriental Version, but which, so far as respects the Epistles, he says, was made by a person who was very unequal to the task: or merely on the Latin, which, according to the same Critic, is of little value. Be this as it may, I have, on the alleged lower sense of Θεός, already in part stated my opinion. See on Luke i. 15. In order to show that the lower sense is common even in the Old Testament, it is to be regretted that Mr. W. did not produce a few examples. One, to which possibly he might allude, is Judges xiii. 22. where the Hebrew has אלהים translated by the LXX. ΘΕΟΝ ἑωράκαμεν, though what Manoah had seen was in reality no more than מלאך, an angel. Now here, it is true, that we have Θεὸν in a lower sense; but then the circumstances of the case are not at all applicable to the New Testament. The LXX. were Translators, and not Commentators; and, therefore, it is not surprising if they sometimes adhered to the letter, rather than to the spirit, of their original. In the Hebrew they found אלהים, which usually signifies Θεὸς in the strict sense: they still, however, rendered the Hebrew by Θεός, even where the strict sense was not intended, the discovery of which they left to the discernment of the Reader, and possibly to his knowledge, that the original was ambiguous.

Nothing of this will apply to the Writers of the New Testament, who came to their task unfettered and unbiassed, and were at liberty every where to choose the word which best suited their purpose: they have not, therefore, in any instance, though the opportunities were so frequent, called an angel Θεός. But Mr. W. refers us to 2 Thess. ii. 4: there the word Θεὸς occurs repeatedly; but in which of the places he supposed it to be meant in a lower sense, I am unable to determine. It is the Prophecy respecting the Man of Sin: of whom it is not said, that he shall assume *inferior Divinity*; that he shall arrogate to himself the *plenitude of Divinity*, is asserted in the strongest terms. We there find, indeed, mention of " every one that is called God," which, however, is not to be understood as indicating that there are several Θεοί, whose divinity differs not in kind, but in degree, but only as including the objects of human adoration, whether men worship the true God, or any of the creatures of their own superstition: for the Apostle has cautiously said, not πάντα Θεόν, which was liable to perversion, but πάντα ΛΕΓΟΜΕΝΟΝ Θεὸν ἢ ΣΕΒΑΣΜΑ: and the same caution with respect to λεγόμενος is observable in 1 Cor. viii. 5. But I suppose Mr. W. more particularly to allude to the words ὡς Θεόν, since he translates Θεὸς in the passage under review by "*as a God*." He should, however, rather have produced an instance of a similar Ellipsis of ὡς, for he has inserted *as* into his Verse without any other apparent reason than that he might weaken the force of Θεός. Ellipses of ὡς, I well know, may be found; but can an instance be adduced, in which ὡς may be supplied between ὁ ὢν and its Predicate? Besides, that ῺΣ Θεὸν in 2 Thess. ii. 4. marks any Diminution of Divinity, it would be absurd to imagine, if we look at the context; for to say that the Man of Sin " shall sit in the Temple of the True God, (εἰς τὸν ναὸν τοῦ Θεοῦ,) as if he were an *inferior God*," is a violation of common sense[1]. It may be observed too, that the words ὡς Θεόν, to which I suppose Mr. W. to allude, are wanting in many MSS. and in many of the old Versions, among others, in his favourite the Æthiopic: Griesbach has removed ὡς Θεὸν into the margin. Lastly, if Mr. W. inferred

---

[1] See Rom. i. 21.—H. K. B.

any thing from the absence of the Article before Θεὸς in the verse from 2 Thess. I will remind the Reader, that it is not once omitted where, consistently with the rules, it could have been inserted.—I have been obliged to examine Mr. Wakefield's solution at some length, because it is impossible to know precisely on what it rests. The inquiry, however, might have been evaded by the previous question, Whether it be agreeable with the usage of Scripture to apply to an inferior Divinity the solemn *formula*, εὐλογητὸς εἰς τοὺς αἰῶνας?

Having thus endeavoured to refute the principal hypotheses which have been adopted to weaken or destroy the force of a most important text, I shall conclude this Note in the words of Michaelis: " I, for my part, sincerely believe that Paul here delivers the same doctrine of the Divinity of Christ, which is elsewhere unquestionably maintained in the N. T."

V. 9. ἐπαγγελίας γάρ, κ. τ. λ. The Rule of Regimen is not here violated, as might be inferred from the English Version, by the omission of the Article before ἐπαγγελίας : the construction is, For this word is of promise. The sense, it is true, will be the same [1].

V. 27. τὸ κατάλειμμα. This is another of the instances wherein the Article may be supposed to be redundant. The passage is quoted from Isaiah x. 22. where the LXX. inserted the Article, though they found it not in the Hebrew. This appears to have been right: for τὸ κατάλειμμα is the remnant or portion of the Israelites reserved by the Almighty for the purposes of his promises: see *Taylor's Heb. Concord. voce* שאר. It would be better that this circumstance should be noticed in any future Translation.

CHAP. X.

V. 4. τέλος γὰρ νόμου. Νόμος is here plainly ὁ νόμος, the Law of Moses: the Article is omitted by Part i. Chap. iii. Sect. iii. § 7.

V. 10. καρδίᾳ . . . . . στόματι. Both used *adverbially*.

---

[1] See above, note on Acts xxiii. 6.—H. J. R.

CHAP. XI.

V. 12. πλοῦτος κόσμου, similar to τέλος νόμου, ver. 4. of last chapter, and to καταλλαγὴ κόσμου below, ver. 14. 15

V. 19. οἱ κλάδοι. Many good MSS. including some of *Matthäi's*, omit οἱ, to which *Griesbach* prefixes his mark of probable spuriousness. Matthäi, however, observes, " I doubt not that the Article ought to be retained ; it marks the arrogance of the Gentile. It was, perhaps, rejected because in ver. 17. we read τινὲς τῶν κλάδων, for κλάδοι is τινὲς κλάδοι, whereas οἱ κλάδοι is πάντες οἱ κλάδοι." This remark discovers a very just notion of the hypothetic use of the Article (see Part I. p. 55 :) at the same time, I am rather inclined to understand οἱ κλάδοι in reference to the τινὲς τῶν κλάδων mentioned just before : the argument of the Gentile is continued.

V. 33. ὦ βάθος πλούτου καὶ σοφίας καὶ γνώσεως Θεοῦ. This is a good instance in illustration of what was said in the Note, Part I. p. 68. The *meaning* is ΤΟΥ π. καὶ ΤΗΣ σ. καὶ ΤΗΣ γν. ΤΟΥ Θ. But βάθος being in the Vocative cannot have the Article prefixed : the whole clause, therefore, is anarthrous.

CHAP. XIII.

V. 8. νόμον here appears to be used in the same sense as above, ii. 5. *Markland* and *Dr. Owen* (ap. Bowyer) make νόμος here to signify the *second* Table of the Law. It is true, that the moral observances which respect our neighbour are the subjects of that Table ; and so far this interpretation accords with my own notion of the meaning of νόμος in similar passages : it is, however, better in all cases to deduce the meanings of words generally, than to trust to their accidental application [1].

---

[1] In v. 9. of this Chapter, there is an use of the Article somewhat uncommon, but strictly classical, which is not happily preserved in our Version : indeed the whole verse is far from being a favourable specimen of that admirable work. Τὸ γάρ· Οὐ μοιχεύσεις, κ. τ. ἑ. It should be rendered : " For the *commandment*, Thou shalt not commit adultery, Thou shalt not kill, Thou shalt not steal, Thou shalt not bear false witness, Thou shalt not covet, and WHATEVER (εἴτις) other commandment there is, is briefly comprehended in THE *precept*, Thou shalt love thy neighbour as thyself."—J. S.

V. 14. τῆς σαρκὸς πρόνοιαν μὴ ποιεῖσθε. See Chap. iii. Sect. iii. § 9. and Heb. i. 3.—H. J. R.

CHAP. XIV.

V. 8. Τῷ Κυρίῳ. Mr. *Wakefield* translates " to *this* Master," as if it were τῷ Κυρίῳ ΤΟΥΤΩι. Similar instances of mistranslation have already been noticed. See above on John xii. 24.

V. 9. καὶ νεκρῶν καὶ ζώντων. The dead and the living *generally*. Articles wanting by Part i. Chap. vi. § 2.

V. 13. τῷ ἀδελφῷ. Mr. *Wakefield* rightly renders the Article by *your:* in ver. 15. and 21. σου is added.

CHAP. XV.

V. 6. τὸν Θεὸν καὶ πατέρα. No MS. violates the usage by inserting the Article before the second Noun. See Part i. Chap. iii. Sect. iv. § 2.

I. CORINTHIANS.

CHAP. I.

V. 1. Σωσθένης ὁ ἀδελφός. It has been inferred, says *Rosenmüller*, from the Article prefixed to ἀδελφός, that Sosthenes was a person of eminence in the Church. That he was not inconsiderable, is evident from his being joined with St. Paul in this prefatory address; but the Article seems not to authorize any conclusion of this sort. *Such an one*, ὁ ἀδελφός, is nothing more than the accustomed manner of mentioning a fellow Christian: so Rom. xvi. 23. Κουαρτὸς ὁ ἀδελφός, who is no where else spoken of, and of whom nothing is known. The practice of calling each other Brethren, as we learn from *Suicer*, (*voce* ἀδελφός,) continued long in the Christian Church.

V. 9. πιστὸς ὁ Θεός. C—ὁ. In this form Θεὸς never wants the Article. See 2 Cor. i. 18. ix. 8. Heb. vi. 10. *et passim*. And these are further confirmations of what was said respecting εὐλογητὸς ὁ Θεός, Rom. ix. 5.

V. 17. ἐν σοφίᾳ λόγου. Bp. *Pearce* conjectures either οὐκ ἐν λόγῳ σοφίας, or οὐκ ἐν τῷ σοφίας λόγῳ. The latter of these is very questionable Greek; nor do I perceive any thing difficult or exceptionable in the reading of the MSS.

V. 20. ποῦ σοφός; ποῦ γραμματεύς; ποῦ, κ. τ. λ. Commentators have usually supposed this exclamation to be quoted from Isaiah xxxiii. 18. *Michaelis*, however, *Introd.* vol. i. p. 209. and also in his *Anmerk*. thinks that there is no ground for this supposition, and that the whole similarity consists in the threefold repetition of *Where is?* In this opinion I entirely agree with him, and so probably will the Reader, if he turn either to the Hebrew, to the LXX., or to the late Translation by the *Bp. of Killala*[1], whose rendering of that passage, though

---

[1] Dr. Stock.

expressed in modern and familiar terms, conveys the true sense of the original: " Where now is the Commissary? Where the Collector? Where is the Barrack-master?" As to the phraseology, I recollect nothing more closely resembling it than the language which *Demosth. de falsâ Leg.* vol. i. Ed. Reiske, p. 400. imputes to Æschines : ποῦ δ' ἅλες ; ποῦ τράπεζαι ; ποῦ σπονδαί ; To account for the omission of the Articles, it might in each case seem sufficient to say, that it marks a vehemence and rapidity of style : but the principles laid down in the former part of this Work will afford a more satisfactory explanation. It is the object of the Speaker, in each instance, to deny that the things or persons spoken of have any longer either effect or existence : this case, therefore, falls under Part i. Chap. iii. Sect. iii. § 1.

CHAP. II.

V. 9. ὀφθαλμός, κ. τ. λ. Part i. Chap. iii. Sect. iii. § 5.

CHAP. III.

V. 13. ἡ γὰρ ἡμέρα. Commentators are much divided about the meaning of ἡμέρα in this place. *Schleusner* supposes it to mean merely *futurum tempus*, so that the sense may be, as we say in English, " time will show :" but he has not produced any parallel instance. I rather suppose with *Macknight*, that ἡ ἡμέρα is *the day*, the dreadful day of persecution. His reasoning, which appears to be just, accords best with this interpretation.

V. 22. κόσμος. This word usually has the Article, except where some rule interferes : here it is wanting, by Part i. Chap. vi. § 2. See on Gal. vi. 14.

CHAP. IV.

V. 5. ὁ ἔπαινος. The praise due, in reference to the act by which it will be acquired. So Winer.

V. 9. καὶ ἀγγέλοις καὶ ἀνθρώποις. *Enumerated* as the constituent parts of ὁ κόσμος preceding. Part i. Chap. vi. § 2.

CHAP. V.

V. 9. ἐν τῇ ἐπιστολῇ. An important question, which has been much agitated, and on which, at this day, the learned are not agreed, turns partly upon the reference of the Article in this place. It has been inferred from this text, that St. Paul had already written to the Corinthians an Epistle, which is no longer extant, and to which he here alludes: while others contend, that by τῇ ἐπιστολῇ, he means only the Epistle which he is writing. Of the former opinion we may reckon *Calvin, Beza, Grotius, Le Clerc, Capellus, Witsius, Heinsius, Mill, Wetstein, Bishop Pearce, Beausobre, Rosenmüller, Schleusner, Michaelis*: against these may be opposed the names of *Fabricius, Wolfius, Glass, Whitby, Jer. Jones, Lardner, Macknight, Abp. Newcome*, and the *Bishop of Lincoln*[1]. It is not probable that this question can ever be decided, so as to preclude all future doubt; for it is rightly contended that the reference of the Article may be either to the Epistle which St. Paul was then writing, or to a former one; and the meaning of ἔγραψα, on which also, in part, the dispute depends, is unfortunately not less ambiguous. One thing alone is certain, that our own Version, "in an Epistle," is not correct: the Article is no more redundant in this place than in others, in which its meaning has been shown, though none was supposed to exist. Schleusner, indeed, explains ἐν τῇ to mean ἔν τινι, a sense of the Article which cannot be established by any instance from the N. T.: the examples which he adduces have most of them been already otherwise accounted for. If, indeed, Schleusner imagines this to be an instance of the *Attic* usage, he is further mistaken, since του for τινος is Feminine as well as Masculine: see the *Scholiast* on the *Ajax* of *Soph.* 290. Ἐν τῇ ἐπιστολῇ, then, must be rendered "in the letter," or, "in my letter:" but the question is, What letter? the present, or a former one? It may be right to state the evidence on both sides.

That τὴν ἐπιστολὴν may be said of the letter which St. Paul is writing, is beyond dispute: thus Tertius, who was Paul's Amanuensis, speaks of the Epistle to the Romans xvi. 22; so also Coloss. iv. 16. 1 Thess. v. 27. 2 Thess. iii. 14. Lardner

---

[1] Dr. Prettyman, afterwards Tomline.

too, vol. vi. near the end, has produced two passages from the Epistles of Libanius, which prove the same usage. It is, therefore, very obvious, so far as the Article is concerned, to understand τῇ ἐπιστολῇ of the present Epistle. On the other hand, there is a single passage, 2 Cor. vii. 8. in which ἡ ἐπιστολή can mean only the former Epistle: there, indeed, the Philox-Syr. adds the word *former*; but a single authority is not to be insisted on. There is, however, this difference, which has not, I believe, been noticed, that there the reference to a former letter is at once evident, because the Apostle had in the preceding verse been speaking of the effects which that letter had produced. In the case under review nothing of this kind takes place: hence the argument for a lost Epistle ought not to be founded on the ambiguity of the phrase ἐν τῇ ἐπιστολῇ, which every where considered *per se* refers to a *present* Epistle. As to the passage 2 Cor. x. 10. it scarcely merits notice; for as Lardner has observed, ἐπιστολαὶ is often used plurally in a singular sense; and even if it were not, the Corinthians might very well speak of the character of St. Paul's Epistles from a single specimen.

There seems, therefore, to be no internal evidence for a lost Epistle, unless ἔγραψα and the general import of the passage compel us to suppose one. That ἔγραψα is not necessarily to be understood in a past sense, Lardner infers from John iv. 38. where ἀπέστειλα is used by Christ of the Mission of the Apostles, which, however, had not yet taken place. Of this use of the first Aorist I entertain no doubt. That it has frequently a *present* signification, is admitted by *Hermann* in his Treatise *de Emend. Ratione Græcæ Gramm.* p. 194; a work which every Scholar must wish to see completed: and I have as little doubt, that it has the sense also of the Latin Future Perfect *Scripsero* or ἔσομαι γράψας, which Hermann will not allow, though ἀπέτισαν, which he adduces from Iliad IV. 161. appears to admit no other explanation. Lardner, therefore, instead of supposing ἔγραψα to refer to verses 5 and 6, as is usually done by the Commentators on his side of the question, considers it to be anticipative of what the Apostle will be found to have written in the 10th Chapter. I do not, however, perceive that any considerable part of that Chapter treats of the crime of fornication: I am, therefore, disposed to consider the reference as made generally to the excommunication of the incestuous person, which was an important object with St. Paul in writing this Epistle; so important, that the subsequent penitence of that person is adverted to in the Epistle following. "I have written to you," says St. Paul, "in my letter, not to associate with fornicators:" and the Readers of the Epistle could not but perceive that the Apostle had done so; for the incestuous person was instantly excommunicated.—Some stress, indeed, is laid on the subjoined νυνὶ δὲ ἔγραψα in verse 11. as if this were meant by way of distinction from what the Apostle had said on some former occasion: the very contrary, however, is the inference which I draw from these words. It is to be remarked, that the same Tense ἔγραψα is here used again, which could scarcely happen if νυνὶ were not meant to be synonymous with ἐν τῇ ἐπιστολῇ. In Philipp. iii. 18. we read πολλάκις ἔλεγον, νῦν δὲ κλαίων ΛΕΓΩ: in like manner, I think, if a different occasion had been intended, we should have read νυνὶ δὲ ΓΡΑΦΩ. I question also whether, if the supposed opposition had been designed, we should not have found in verse 9. ἔγραψα MEN to correspond with νυνὶ ΔE, for though μὲν sometimes suffers Ellipsis, this rarely happens, so far as I have observed, where the opposition is so strong as that here alleged.

Putting, then, all the circumstances together, even the internal evidence seems to be unfavourable to the hypothesis, that a letter to the Corinthians had preceded that which St. Paul was now writing. As to the *external* evidence, it is entirely against the same supposition; for besides the extreme improbability that a Canonical Book should have been lost, a point which is well established by Jones (on the *Canon*, vol. i. p. 158, 1st edit.) and also by Lardner, as above, no instance has been produced in which an ancient Writer has cited the pretended first Epistle, or even alluded to its existence, though both the *received* Epistles are quoted by the Fathers perpetually, and that too from the earliest period. On the whole, therefore, I entertain no doubt myself that the two Epistles still preserved are the only ones which St. Paul ever addressed to the Corinthians: at the same time, I cannot hope that the little light which I have been enabled to throw on this controversy, will avail towards its decision.

V. 13. τὸν πονηρόν. The incestuous person who is the subject of this Chapter. A few MSS. have τό.

CHAP. VI.

V. 1. πρὸς τὸν ἕτερον. This word, used in the sense of one's *neighbour*, usually has the Article. So Rom. xiii. 8. and this Epistle, x. 24. 29. The reason is, that in such cases two persons are supposed, who stand in a certain relation the one to the other. I do not, therefore, see any reason to agree with Mr. *Wakefield* in preferring ἑταῖρον, which is found in no MS. but was, as he says, the reading of most of the old translators. I suspect, however, that they intended only to give the *sense*, not to show that they read ἑταῖρον: the Syriac renders "his brother;" yet I do not thence conclude that the Translator found in his copy τὸν ἀδελφόν. Dr. *Mangey* also conjectured ἑταῖρον.

V. 16. ὁ κολλώμενος τῇ πόρνῃ. Here πόρνῃ has the Article, being spoken of in relation to ὁ κολλώμενος: see last Note. It is as if he had said ὁ κολλώμενος καὶ ἡ πόρνη εἰσὶν ἓν σῶμα. See also on Matt. xv. 11.

CHAP. VII.

[1] V. 28. ἡ παρθένος, in the hypothetic use of the Article, she who is a virgin, i. e. virgins generally. So below, verse 34. See on John xii. 24. B &

V. 34. σώματι καὶ πνεύματι. A few MSS. prefix Articles, but probably they should be omitted by Part i. Chap. vi. § 2.

V. 39. νόμῳ, by moral obligation, by the *spirit* of every law, divine or human. See on Rom. ii. 25. But MS.s Eds. omit

V. 40. πνεῦμα Θεοῦ, Divine guidance. See on Rom. viii. 9.

---

[1] Vv. 10 and 11. Ἀνὴρ and γυνὴ are without the Article, but the Propositions are exclusive.

V. 20. τήρησις may want the Article because Θεοῦ does, on grounds familiar to the reader; or the Proposition may not be universal, τήρησις not being one act like περιτομή, but a continued line of conduct. The Apostle's meaning and the correct Translation may be, 'Circumcision and uncircumcision are nothing, but *an attention to* God's commands, (is what is required,') and not 'the full, entire, and unsinning observation of God's commands.'—H. J. R.

I. CORINTHIANS,

CHAP. IX.

V. 20. ὑπὸ νόμον, the Mosaic Law: the Article is wanting by Part i. Chap. vi. § 1.

V. 22. τὰ πάντα. Many good MSS. and some Fathers omit τά: probably right after γέγονα: so *Achilles Tatius* πάντα ἐγενόμην, quoted in *Rosenmüller*.

V. 26. ἀέρα δέρων. It might be expected that ἀέρα should have the Article, but I take this to be an instance of what I have called a *Hendiadys*, Part i. Chap. v. Sect. ii. § 1.

CHAP. X.

[1] V. 13. τὴν ἔκβασιν, in reference to the temptation from which escape is to be made.

CHAP. XI.

V. 3. παντὸς ἀνδρὸς ἡ κεφαλή. We have not here a real, though an apparent, breach of the rule of Regimen: for παντὸς ἀνδρὸς is equivalent to τοῦ ἀνδρός, using the Article in the hypothetic or inclusive sense. Besides, παντὸς τοῦ ἀνδρὸς would have a different meaning. The next κεφαλὴ wants the Article, which could not be admitted.

V. 7. εἰκών. A. and three others have ἡ εἰκών, which cannot be right, when Θεοῦ wants the Article. Two of them, indeed, but not A. have τοῦ Θεοῦ; but even this, I fear, will not do after ὑπάρχων. Thus Acts xvii. 24. οὐρανοῦ καὶ γῆς Κύριος ὑπάρχων. This is, I think, another presumption against the Greek origin of A. See above, Acts viii. 5.

Vv. 8, 9, 10, 11, 12. In these verses the words ἀνὴρ and γυνὴ repeatedly occur both with and without the Article; and I know not any passage in the whole N. T. from which an inconsiderate opponent would be so likely to infer that the Article may be inserted or omitted *scribentis arbitrio*. *Macknight* indeed, in his Version, has in this passage closely adhered to the original, without producing any awkwardness or

---

[1] V. 10. τοῦ ὀλοθρευτοῦ. The destroyer mentioned by Moses. Comp. Heb. xi. 28.—H. J. R.

confusion. I might, therefore, perhaps be excused, if I were to pass over these verses without notice : I would not, however, incur the imputation of having expatiated on instances favourable to my purpose, whilst I suppressed others which may be thought of less easy explanation.

In verse 8. then, ἀνὴρ and γυνὴ must be understood of individuals, a single man and a single woman, the progenitors of the human race ; for in any greater latitude the assertion would be untrue. In verse 9. the Apostle says, that in no instance was a man (ἀνήρ, any man) created on account of the woman, (i. e. one assumed already to exist, διὰ τὴν γυναῖκα,) but a woman *was* formed on account of the man (already existing.) In verse 10. whatever be the meaning of the remark, it is plain that *women generally* are spoken of, and ἡ γυνὴ accords with the usage in such cases. Verse 11. I understand to mean, " Notwithstanding, (such is the ordinance of God,) neither is any man brought into being without the intervention of a woman, nor any woman without that of a man : for as (ver. 12.) the woman (i. e. women generally) is originally from the man, so the man (i. e. men generally) is brought into being by the intervention of the woman (i. e. women :) these and all other things are ordained by the wisdom of God." If this be the true sense of the passage, the Article is throughout inserted and omitted according to the principles laid down in this work. I have given the meaning of verses 11 and 12. as they are understood by *Whitby* and others; and I think, leaving the Article entirely out of the question, it is that which is most consonant with the tenor of the argument. Χωρὶς I interpret in its most common acceptation, *without the aid* or *operation of*, as in John i. 3. χωρὶς αὐτοῦ ἐγένετο οὐδέν· *et passim* : χωρὶς γυναικὸς in verse 11. I take to be the contrary of διὰ τῆς γυναικὸς in verse 12. Some Commentators, indeed, among whom is Mr. *Wakefield*, understand verse 11. to signify, that the Christian Dispensation extends alike to both sexes, as is affirmed Gal. iii. 28 : but I do not perceive how such a remark could be introduced in this place, where the Apostle appears to be treating of the relative dignity of the sexes, as deducible from their origin, and from the laws by which the species is continued.

With the difficulties of verse 10. I have not properly any

concern. *Michaelis* confesses that he does not understand it. It seems on all hands to be admitted, that ἐξουσία signifies *a veil*, or something of that kind worn by females. It was generally supposed that this was called ἐξουσία, as being an emblem of the *authority* of the husband: but this opinion is exploded both by *Michaelis* and *Schleusner*. The former supposes ἐξουσία to be a provincial term, understood only at Corinth; but pretends not to account for this application of the word. Schleusner is of opinion that this term was thus applied from the authority and consequence by which, among the Jews, married were distinguished from unmarried women. For myself, I have sometimes thought that a veil might have acquired the name ἐξουσία from the *power* or *licence* which it gave the wearer to appear in public; for without it she was not permitted to leave her chamber. This conjecture, however, is possibly of no more value than are the multitude which have been already offered in illustration of this most obscure passage [1].

V. 20. Κυριακὸν δεῖπνον. The Article may here be omitted by the same licence by which it is so frequently wanting before Κύριος; in the same manner as *National Appellations* partake of the licence which is allowed to Proper Names. On this passage *Michaelis*, Introd. vol. iv. p. 61. has a valuable remark:

"In the first Epistle to the Corinthians we find the plainest indications that they celebrated *Sunday*. They assembled on the first day of the week (κατα μιαν σαββατων:) and the expression κυριακον δειπνον, 1 Cor. xi. 20. may be translated, as in the Syriac Version, 'a meal which is proper for the Lord's day,' or a Sunday meal. In the controversy relative to the celebration of Sunday, it is extraordinary that this translation of κυριακον δειπνον, in so ancient a Version as the Syriac, should never have been quoted."

V. 27. αἵματος. A multitude of MSS. and several Fathers have τοῦ αἵματος, which is probably the true reading.

---

[1] It may be mentioned here, that Valkenaer lays much stress on the difference between κεφαλή and ἡ κεφαλή in this place. This is only one of a thousand proofs that Bishop Middleton's observation as to the omission of the Article after a Preposition, without any consequent change of meaning, had escaped the most eminent scholars.—H. J. R.

CHAP. XII.

V. 4. τὸ δὲ αὐτὸ πνεῦμα. It is plain that πνεῦμα must here be taken in the Personal sense: nor do I see how it is possible to elude the observation of *Markland*, that in this and the two following verses we have distinct mention of the Three Persons of the Trinity. Dr. *Owen* (ap. Bowyer) asks, Whether τὸ πνεῦμα of this verse be not the same, who in the next two verses is called Κύριος and Θεός? This opinion likewise is, to say the least of it, highly probable: for the structure of the whole passage leads us to understand ὁ ἐνεργῶν τὰ πάντα ἐν πᾶσι, as intended to be applied alike to the Three Persons; else the two preceding verses will be defective, and only the last will be complete. There we are told that it is the same God who works all in all: this is very intelligible: but in the two former, that it is the same Spirit—who does what? and the same Lord—who does what? unless we are to understand the concluding clause as applicable alike to the Three Persons: and if so, then the Three Persons must in some sense be the same. The Reader, indeed, of our English Version might suppose that the two verses, 4 and 5, assert only the Unity of the Spirit, and the Unity of our Lord. Had the words been ἓν δὲ πνεῦμα and εἷς δὲ Κύριος, this might have been alleged; and the propositions, though ill according with what follows, would have been complete in themselves: but this is not the case: yet εἷς is, I believe, the term employed wherever the assertion of Unity in the thing spoken of is all which is intended. So Ephes. iv. 5. εἷς Κύριος, μία πίστις, ἓν βάπτισμα. It is, therefore, to be concluded, that in verses 4 and 5 a clause is understood; and if it be not that which is subjoined to the whole passage, what are we to supply? But see the next Note.

V. 11. τὸ ἓν καὶ τὸ αὐτὸ πνεῦμα.—Some MSS.—τὸ *prius*. This would be right, if there were not reference to the Spirit recently spoken of: but that such reference was intended is most certain, both from the whole tenor of the argument, and also the addition of τὸ αὐτό. Of the personal sense of πνεῦμα in this place, it might be thought that the blindest prejudice could not entertain a doubt, since He is here said to "distribute gifts according to his pleasure," which surely is the attribute not merely of a Person, but of a Being who is Omnipotent. Then again, the term ἐνεργεῖν is applied to Him; though, as was shown on Matt. xiv. 2. it is never used in the New Testament but of an agent, and that commonly a very powerful one. Now it is observable that πάντα ταῦτα ἐνεργεῖ, spoken in this verse of the Holy Spirit, is very similar to what is said in verse 6. of Θεός, or, as I am inclined to think, (see last Note,) of each of the Three Persons of the Trinity: the question is, Whether these words identify τὸ πνεῦμα, to which they are applied, with the other two Persons, or at least with Θεὸς mentioned in verse 6? The Spirit is said to work πάντα ταῦτα; but what are these? They plainly comprehend all the miraculous powers enumerated from verse 7. to verse 11. inclusive, among which are χαρίσματα spoken of in verse 4. and ἐνεργήματα in verse 6. The διακονίαι of verse 5, it is true, are not expressly noticed; but if this term according to *Theodoret*, and as it is usually explained, relate principally to the office of preaching, διακονίαι will be included in the enumerated operations of the Spirit; for λόγος σοφίας and λόγος γνώσεως, verse 8. are the qualities by which διακονίαι are rendered efficacious. It appears, therefore, that *all* the miraculous powers mentioned in verses 4, 5, and 6, are here imputed to the influence of the Spirit. The result is, that if we understand the clause ὁ ἐνεργῶν, κ. τ. λ. verse 6. to belong, in the manner which I have supposed, to each of the three verses 4, 5, and 6, then the Spirit must in some sense be the same with the other two Persons, since he is here, verse 11. made *solely* to be the cause of effects above severally ascribed to the *Spirit*, to the *Lord*, and to *God*. Or if it be *not* admitted that the clause in question was intended to be so applied, then the present verse identifies the Spirit only with God, (ver. 6.) to whom the clause is *confessedly* applied: though still it will be very difficult to account for the introduction of the *Spirit*, verse 4. and the *Lord*, verse 5. if it be not meant that they are respectively the authors of χαρίσματα and διακονίαι, in which case the consequence will be the same as if the concluding clause be admitted to be common to verses 4, 5, and 6.

The observations of *Markland* and Dr. *Owen*, which gave rise to the Note on verse 4. are, it should be known, very ancient (see *Wolfius*;) though this could not be inferred from any thing that is said in Bowyer. Theologians would do well to notice the antiquity of the opinions which they defend, because that antiquity is sometimes no inconsiderable evidence of truth.

V. 21. ὀφθαλμός. With a multitude of MSS. we should read Ὁ ὀφθαλμός. Griesbach has admitted the Article into the text.

CHAP. XIII.

V. 2. πᾶσαν τὴν γνῶσιν . . . . . τὴν πίστιν. The knowledge and the faith here spoken of must be understood in reference, viz. to the Gospel. See Part i. Chap. vii. § 3. Mr. *Wakefield* has rendered the Article in his translation.

Vv. 3, 4. ἀγάπην ἔχειν . . . . . ἡ ἀγάπη. Abstract Nouns after ἔχω are commonly anarthrous; Part i. p. 124. But ἡ ἀγάπη, verse 4. is used in its most general sense, or may even be considered as personified. See Part i. Chap. v. Sect. i. § 1, 2. In verse 13, πίστις, ἐλπίς, ἀγάπη, want the Article, probably by Part i. Chap. vi. § 2.

CHAP. XIV.

V. 2. πνεύματι. Used *adverbially*.

V. 4. ἐκκλησίαν. I do not perceive why, according to the received reading, this word wants the Article. Mr. *Wakefield*, indeed, translates " a whole Church :" F. G. and the Vulg. add Θεοῦ, which appears to be the true reading.

V. 9. ὑμεῖς διὰ τῆς γλώσσης, κ. τ. λ. Mr. Wakefield translates, " Ye, who speak with a different language, unless ye speak plainly, &c." He says that this phrase, ὑμεῖς διὰ τῆς γλώσσης, is of the same kind as σὲ τὸν διὰ γράμματος, κ. τ. λ. Rom. ii. 27. which he explains, *Silv. Crit.* P. I. p. 123. by *te literatum*, i. e. *qui literam vel legem Mosaicam profiteris.* In *this* explanation Mr. W. may be right; for if τὸν were immediately the Article of παραβάτην, νόμου depending on it could not be anarthrous. It is, however, impossible to accede to his interpretation of the present verse, in which ὑμεῖς διὰ τῆς γλώσσης differs from σὲ τὸν διὰ γράμματος by wanting the Article οἱ before ὑμεῖς. To this difference Mr. W. did not attend: yet without the Article, διὰ τῆς γλώσσης must depend on δῶτε. Moreover, it is probable that he has mistaken the sense of τῆς γλώσσης, which does not here signify a foreign language, (for then it wants the Article, as may be seen throughout the chapter,) but *the tongue*, the organ of speech, which is here opposed to the musical instruments recently spoken of. Besides, Mr. W.'s rendering does not accord with the Apostle's argument, which is, that he who speaks " in a foreign tongue " *cannot* speak " plainly." St. Paul, wishing to repress the vanity of those who valued the gift of tongues more than other gifts, which, though less splendid, were more generally useful, contends, that he who speaks in a foreign tongue, can rarely, if ever, edify the hearer. " If the trumpet give an unintelligible sound, who will prepare for battle? *so also*, if ye by the tongue speak not so as to be understood, how shall men be benefited?"

V. 17. ὁ ἕτερος. See above, on vi. 1.

V. 32. καὶ πνεύματα προφητῶν προφήταις ὑποτάσσεται. On the meaning of these words there are two opinions: according to some Expositors, they signify, that "the inspiration with which true Prophets are gifted, does not, like the phrensy which agitated the Priests of the Heathens, hurry them away irresistibly, but that they have power to controul its operation, as occasion may require." Others affirm that the passage means, that " they who are divinely inspired, are bound at proper seasons to give place to others who have been gifted with the same inspiration." Neither of these interpretations is at variance with the context: one of them tends to show the *practicability*, the other the *duty*, of observing good order in publicly declaring the suggestions of the Spirit; and both senses accord very well with the verse following: " for God is not the author of disturbance, but of peace." The partisans of the former opinion appear to be the more numerous: I incline, however, to the latter, because I believe that in the other way of understanding the passage, the expression would have been different; perhaps something of this sort, κυριεύουσι γὰρ τῶν πνευμάτων οἱ προφῆται· at any rate προφήταις would not have been anarthrous; if the same Prophets be meant with those just mentioned, it will be difficult to assign a reason why we should not read τοῖς προφήταις. On the other hand, if other Prophets be intended, the phrase is precisely that which

CHAPTER XV. 335

might be expected: thus Mark xiii. 2. λίθος ἐπὶ λίθῳ, one stone upon another: in this Epist. vi. 6. ἀδελφὸς μετὰ ἀδελφοῦ, one brother with another: xv. 41. ἀστὴρ γὰρ ἀστέρος διαφέρει, one star, another star: in such cases I have observed that in classical writers also both Nouns are anarthrous. On the whole, though either explanation may be reconciled with the context, that which I have adopted seems to be preferable: since the *practicability* of doing what is enjoined is proved in the verse preceding, δύνασθε γάρ, &c.: in the present, the Apostle intends to show that it is also a *duty*, being an ordinance of that Being who is not the author of confusion. To avoid this consequence, *Macknight* renders καὶ in this verse by *for*, a Hebraism which is not very common in the N. T.— *Schleusner* is among the few moderns who understand the passage as here explained: he renders ὑποτάσσεται by *sibi invicem cedere debent.* Many MSS. for πνεύματα have πνεῦμα, which, however, affects not the question. *Bentley's* conjecture, ὑποτάσσηται, would, if admitted, produce no other difference than that of *commanding* subjection, instead of affirming that such subjection is the will and ordinance of God; as far as I see, it amounts to the same thing, whichever explanation be approved. It is to be observed, however, that the commands of St. Paul are usually given in the *Imperative*, of which this chapter affords several examples [1].

CHAP. XV.

V. 8. ὡσπερεὶ τῷ ἐκτρώματι ὤφθη κἀμοί. There is no passage in the N. T. which has given rise to more dispute on the subject of the Article, than has the present. Two MSS. indeed, viz. F. G.—τῷ, but these, as it is known, (see *Marsh's Michaelis,* ii. 226.) amount to little more than one evidence: it is wanting also in one of Matthäi's Euchologies. There can, therefore, be little or no doubt that the received reading is right: though Griesbach, on this evidence, thinks the various reading of equal value with that of the text.

Some Critics will have the Article here to be a Hebraism:

---

[1] V. 33. See note on Acts xxiii. 6.

others affirm that it is the Enclitic τῳ, for τινί: and a third class thinks that τῷ ἐκτρώματι is used κατ' ἐξοχήν. The first of these opinions is preferred by *Loesner, Obss. e Philone*. Of Hebraisms, however, in the use of the Article in the N. T. I have met with no example, unless in translations, or quotations from the LXX.: see Part I. p. 156 : neither am I aware that the Article could thus be accounted for, even if the Hebraism were to be admitted ; since the LXX. who, as translators from the Hebrew, abound in Hebraisms, have said, Job iii. 16. ὥσπερ ἔκτρωμα, and Num. xii. 12. ὡσεὶ ἔκτρωμα. The second mode of explaining the Article in this place is as little satisfactory : it was, I believe, first proposed by *Ritterhusius* in his Notes on Porphyry's Life of Pythagoras, and it has been adopted by many succeeding Critics, among whom is *Schleusner*. I have, however, already observed that this Attic usage is unknown to the Writers of the N. T. : (see above, on v. 9.) besides, would it not be extraordinary that these writers should Atticize in only two or three examples, though the occasions are so frequent ? In the writers who are generally allowed to have used this mode of speaking, we find an instance of it in almost every page.—To the third solution, which is approved by *Wolfius*, I object, because I do not perceive that ἔκτρωμα, in whatever sense we understand the word, admits the idea of pre-eminence : in one ἔκτρωμα there cannot be any superiority over others. My own opinion is, that the Article might here be accounted for nearly in the same manner as in Luke xviii. 13. It appears to be the purport of the writer to apply the term ἔκτρωμα to *himself*, and to say that *he* is, as it were, ἔκτρωμα : to express which, it was necessary to use the Article, for otherwise the meaning would have been, " as by *an* ἔκτρωμα," as if ἐκτρώματα sometimes in other cases saw what he had seen. There is no doubt, that if he had left out ὡσπερεί, and had inverted the clauses, he must have written ὤφθη κἀμοὶ τῷ ἐκτρώματι, as in Luke, ἐμοὶ τῷ ἁμαρτωλῷ : see on Luke, as above. I do not perceive any difference in the sentence as it actually stands, except that ὡσπερεὶ is an apology for an application which might seem to be too strong. That this is an allowable use of ὡσπερεὶ is evident from *Longinus*, (noticed by Wetstein,) Sect xxxii. Ed. Toup. 8vo. p. 111, who calls this word one of the μειλίγματα τῶν θρασειῶν μεταφορῶν.

CHAPTER XV.   337

This method, however, of explaining the Article supposes, for the most part, that the common interpretation of ἔκτρωμα, viz. *fœtus immaturus*, or what the French call *avortement*, is the true one: but of this I have sometimes doubted; and herein, as I suspect, and not in the Article, lies the principal difficulty of the passage. It is true, that whenever the word occurs in the LXX. it is used in this sense: but how, it may be asked, could any thing be *seen* by an ἔκτρωμα in this acceptation? In Job iii. 16. and Eccles. vi. 3. compared with verse 5. the ἔκτρωμα is expressly said to be that which *never sees the light*: and the same thing is asserted in the Hebrew of Psalm lviii. 9. though this does not appear in the LXX. who, instead of נפל אשת, must, from their translation, (ἔπεσε πῦρ,) have read נפל אש; and in the only remaining place in which ἔκτρωμα occurs in the LXX. they have made it to represent what in the original signifies, "as one who is dead in the womb." It is, therefore, hardly to be believed, that St. Paul meant to use ἔκτρωμα in the same sense with the LXX.; for according to this, to say "he was seen by me, ὡσπερεὶ τῷ ἐκτρώματι," would involve a contradiction. Judging merely from the context, and from the tenor of the argument, ἔκτρωμα might be supposed to signify a last-born child, especially if there were a prevalent notion that such children in one respect resembled ἐκτρώματα by being smaller and less perfect than others, as is the opinion at this day among our country people, with respect to the last-born offspring of multiparous animals at a given birth: this meaning would suit both the ἔσχατον πάντων, which precedes, and the ἐλάχιστος, which follows, and the whole of the reasoning would be clear and connected. That the word, indeed, ever has this sense, is more than I can prove; and yet that some such idea was entertained by Commentators of considerable antiquity, may, I think, be collected from an expression of *Theophylact*, who, after stating the common reasons why St. Paul should call himself ἔκτρωμα, subjoins τινὲς δὲ τὸ ὕστερον γέννημα ἔκτρωμα ἐνόησαν. In that way of understanding the passage, ἐκτρώματι would have the Article, being opposed to the other Apostles just mentioned, and being therefore in its nature definite and monadic.

V. 15. νεκροὶ οὐκ ἐγείρονται. An exclusive Proposition;

z

and so throughout the Chapter. Part i. Chap. iii. Sect. iii. § 5. F. G. improperly have OI νεκροί[1].

V. 29. ὑπὲρ τῶν νεκρῶν, *secundo loco*. A great many MSS. have ὑπὲρ αὐτῶν. *Wolfius* vindicates the received reading, "*propter emphasin, quam in voce* νεκρῶν *collocasse Apostolum vel ex præposito Articulo* τῶν *apparet.*" I am not sure that I perceive the drift of this remark: there is, however, no *emphasis* in the Article here, and this may be affirmed of nine places out of ten where Commentators suspect an emphasis. The dead taken generally are οἱ νεκροί; though there may be reasons for *omitting* the Article, as in the last Note. It is foreign from my purpose to detail the different attempts to explain this very obscure text, since the Article is not in question: I may be permitted, however, to notice the opinion of *Matthäi*. He understands ὑπὲρ τῶν νεκρῶν to be equivalent to ὑπὲρ ἑαυτῶν, taking the word νεκρῶν in the figurative sense, as in Matthew viii. 22: this notion is at least ingenious; how far it may be satisfactory, the Reader must judge for himself.

V. 41. ἡλίου .... σελήνης. These words want the Article by Part i. Chap. iii. Sect. iii. § 7. and δόξα by § 1.

CHAP. XVI.

V. 24. ἡ ἀγάπη μου. It is observed by *Estius*, (ap. Bowyer,) that "St. Paul does not use to conclude his Epistles with the benediction of his own love: and that for μου we should probably read Θεοῦ." Regimen would require ΤΟΥ Θεοῦ, which, of course, renders the conjecture less probable.

---

[1] See prefatory remarks as to this word.—H. J. R.

II. CORINTHIANS.

CHAP. I.

[1] V. 20. ὅσαι γὰρ ἐπαγγελίαι Θεοῦ, ἐν αὐτῷ τὸ ναί, καὶ ἐν αὐτῷ τὸ ἀμήν. The Authors of our English Version, from not attending to the Articles, have here, I think, obscured the perspicuity of the original: they have rendered "for all the promises of God in him are Yea, and in him Amen:" and the other English Translators, *Macknight*, *Wakefield*, and *Newcome*, have taken the words in the same order. I would render "for how many soever be the promises of God, in Him (Christ) is the Yea, and in Him the Amen;" meaning, Whatever God hath promised, He will through Christ assuredly fulfil, ναὶ and ἀμὴν being strong and well-known asseverations of the truth.

V. 22. τὸν ἀρραβῶνα τοῦ πνεύματος. I understand this of the Holy Spirit, and so did many of the Ancients, as appears from *Suicer*; the pledge spoken of consists of those various gifts of the Spirit which were an earnest of immortality to the persons on whom they were conferred.

V. 24. κυριεύομεν ὑμῶν τῆς πίστεως. *Macknight* distinguishes between ὑμῶν τῆς πίστεως and τῆς ὑμῶν πίστεως, though if he mean by the latter the more usual arrangement, he should have put the Pronoun last: and he translates "lord it over you through the faith," making τῆς πίστεως to depend on a Preposition understood. He remarks, "that this is a proper translation of the passage, is evident from the position of the Greek Article." In this, however, he is mistaken; for this position of the Article is extremely common: thus in this Epistle, x. 6. ὅταν πληρωθῇ ὑμῶν ἡ ὑπακοή, which Macknight

---

[1] V. 17. τῇ ἐλαφρίᾳ. Ἐλαφρία, says Winer, is here spoken of objectively, as a quality inherent in human nature: *the well-known sin of light-mindedness.*—H. J. R.

renders, "when your obedience is completed." The very same position is found also in the next Chapter, ver. 11. Philipp. i. 7; ii. 2. 1 Tim. iv. 15. 2 Tim. i. 4. Coloss. ii. 5. 1 Thess. i. 3, *et passim*, where this excellent Theologian has adhered to the common interpretation. He further, indeed, contends, that St. Paul could not consistently disclaim all authority over the faith of the Corinthians, since by the inspiration of the Spirit given to the Apostles, they were authorized to judge or rule the Twelve Tribes of Israel: Matt. xix. 28. This remark is just; yet I do not perceive that it is at all at variance with the common construction of the present text. By κυριεύειν I understand the exercise of a domineering and arbitrary power, (as in Luke xxii. 25.) as if the Apostle had said, Though I speak of punishment, I would not have you think that we tyrannize over your faith by wanton acts of severity, but rather that we are fellow-workers of your joy; i. e. that we have your welfare at heart; for by your faith alone, that faith which we seek to strengthen in you, can you attain to salvation.—This appears to be a natural and reasonable vindication, not only of the threat already employed, but of any severities to which the Apostle might afterwards be driven in the discharge of his duty.

CHAP. III.

V. 3. πνεύματι Θεοῦ ζῶντος. Mr. *Wakefield* translates, "with *a* power of *a* living God." The original, however, is very different. The English Reader might hence infer, that the term the "living God," instead of being a name of the one True God, as distinguished from idols, may be applied with equal propriety to *several* Divinities. The Article is omitted before πνεύματι, as is usual, where not the Spirit in the personal sense, but the *inspiration* of the Spirit is intended; and Θεοῦ ζῶντος wants the Articles by Part i. Chap. iii. Sect. iii. § 7. Abp. *Newcome* says, "not written with ink, but by the Spirit of the living God;" but besides that a person or agent is not well opposed to an instrument, it may be objected, that if the Apostle had intended what is here expressed, he would have prefixed some Preposition to πνεῦμα. See above on Rom. viii. 13.

V. 6. οὐ γράμματος ἀλλὰ πνεύματος, I would render "not

a literal, but a spiritual one." Καινῆς διαθήκης may want the Article, by depending on the anarthrous word διακόνους, and this last wants the Article by Part i. Chap. iii. Sect. iii. § 3 [1]. We ought, however, probably to understand καινῆς διαθήκης in this place definitely. In the same verse, τὸ πνεῦμα is that which is spiritual, viz. the Gospel, as opposed to that which is literal, or the Mosaic Law.

V. 17. ὁ δὲ Κύριος τὸ πνεῦμα, i. e. the spiritual Religion mentioned in ver. 6.

V. 18. ἀπὸ Κυρίου πνεύματος. English Version has "by the Spirit of the Lord;" but in the margin, "by the Lord of the Spirit [2]:" this is adopted by *Macknight:* Abp. *Newcome* says, "by the Lord, who is that Spirit;" but this, I believe, would have been in the Greek τοῦ πνεύματος, in like manner as the Article is always inserted in Κύριος ὁ Θεός. The phrase, "Lord of the Spirit," Macknight explains to mean the Author of the Gospel, called τὸ πνεῦμα in the last verse; but I do not remember that this construction has any parallel in the N. T. or that Christ is ever called the Lord of the Gospel, of the Faith, or of the Spirit. I prefer the common interpretation, the sense of which appears to me to be free from all objection: the Spirit of the Lord is that mentioned in the verse preceding. It ought, however, to be observed, that much doubt has always existed about the true construction of the words in question.

CHAP. V.

V. 1. ἡ ἐπίγειος ἡμῶν οἰκία τοῦ σκήνους. English Version has " our earthly house of *this* Tabernacle," which is more than is warranted by the Greek. The Syr. understands the whole to signify, " our earthly abode of the *body;*" so also do *Michaelis* and *Schleusner*. The former, in his *Anmerk.* observes, "This word σκῆνος in Greek frequently signifies no more than *body:* it is so used by the Philosophers, especially the Pythagoreans, and even by the writers on Physic. The expression is not uncommon in Hebrew, but the Greeks borrowed it from the Egyptians, to whom it is so familiar, that regard is no

---

[1] i. e. After Verbs of *creating, appointing, choosing,* &c.—H. J. R.
[2] The common marginal reading is, " Of the Lord the Spirit."—J. S.

342   II. CORINTHIANS,

longer paid to its derivation or primitive sense : thus the Physician speaks of the *Tent,* and to paint the Virgin Mary is expressed by the phrase, To paint the *Tent* of the Mother of God. The reason is, that in countries like Egypt, inhabited by Nomadic tribes, human life was represented as the peregrination of roving shepherds dwelling in tents. Paul, indeed, may have adverted to the literal meaning of the word, and may have contrasted the temporary tent, the body, with the eternal and immoveable habitation which we shall occupy hereafter : this allusion, however, could not well be conveyed in German, the phrase *House of the Tent* not being very intelligible." The same objection must lie in English against *House of our Tabernacle.* The proposed interpretation is much strengthened by comparing ver. 4. with ver. 6 [1].

CHAP. VI.

V. 6. ἐν πνεύματι ἁγίῳ. Not merely the omission of the Articles, but the Nouns, which are here associated with πνεύματι ἁγίῳ, forbid us to understand it in the personal sense : I suppose it, therefore, to signify the *influence* of the Spirit. *Macknight* appears to have understood πνεῦμα in this place of the *human mind,* for he explains it by " a well regulated

---

[1] In v. 15. εἰ εἷς ὑπὲρ πάντων ἀπέθανεν, ἄρα οἱ πάντες ἀπέθανον, the Article inserted on the renewed mention of πάντες refers us back to πάντων, preceding, and marks the meaning of the two words as co-extensive. Whatever conclusion this may lead to, it is quite certain that ἀπέθανον is wrongly translated *were dead,* a sense which it never did, and never could, bear. Where the Apostle wishes to express *were dead,* as in Ephes. ii. 1. he does it by the periphrasis, νεκροὺς ὄντας. On the contrary, he uses ἀπέθανον frequently in its proper sense, they *died* or ARE dead. See Rom. v. 15 ; vi. 2. 8 ; vii. 2. Galat. ii. 19. Coloss. ii. 20 ; iii. 3. Once only, in Luke viii. 53. it is *properly* translated, " *was* dead :" but this is owing to the difference between the Greek and English idioms, the latter properly taking a past tense after a past, while the former, by a very common anomaly, admits the present. The construction, therefore, in κατεγέλων αὐτοῦ, εἰδότες ὅτι ἀπέθανεν, is precisely the same as in Plato, Apolog. § 6. Bekk. and a thousand other places, ἠπόρουν τί ποτε λέγει· *I was at a loss to know what in the world he means* (Angl. *meant.*) Compare John xi. 13—4.—The passage of St. Paul, therefore, ought to be translated, *Then all died,* or *are dead,* as Coloss. iii. 3. The meaning I am not concerned with : my business is with the point of criticism not of doctrine.—J. S.

spirit :" I have no where, however, observed it to be so used, where it has the epithet ἅγιον [1].

CHAP. VII.

V. 8. ἐν τῇ ἐπιστολῇ. See on 1 Cor. v. 9.

V. 11. ἐν τῷ πράγματι. In the affair, viz. of the incestuous person: the readiness with which the Corinthians, at the instance of the Apostle, had excommunicated the offender, justified the acknowledgment of St. Paul, that they were not any longer to be blamed for what had happened. Some Commentators understand τῷ πράγματι as in 1 Thess. iv. 6. See on that place.

CHAP. VIII.

V. 12. ἐὰν ἔχῃ τις. A great many MSS. &c. omit τις. *Griesbach* prefixes to it the mark of probable spuriousness; and Mr. *Wakefield* says, that it has been foisted in by some ignorant Scribe, to mend what he supposed a defective construction. In this conjecture Mr. W. may be right; but when he makes προθυμία, repeated from the last clause, to be the Nominative to ἔχῃ, I think he is mistaken. If τὶς be an interpolation, it was still meant to be understood; and we shall then have another instance of the usage noticed John viii. 44. It is remarkable that the Ellipsis in this place did not put Mr. W. on the true construction of that passage, especially as he saw that τὶς was there wanting to the sense.

CHAP. IX.

V. 8. πᾶσαν χάριν, rendered rightly by *Macknight*, " every blessing." English Version has " all grace." See Part i. Chap. vii. § 3.

---

[1] V. 17. ἀκαθάρτου. Our version has *the unclean thing*, where the Article wears the appearance of renewed mention. Probably our Translators did not intend it, but meant to express only *that which is unclean, any unclean thing*. The Article is wanting here by Chap. iii. Sect. iii. § 5. the proposition being *exclusive*.
—H. J. R.

CHAP. X.

V. 10[1]. αἱ μὲν ἐπιστολαί. See on 1 Cor. v. 9. *Abp. Newcome* has, however, observed, that St. Paul's Epistles were sent from one church to another to be publicly read; he refers to Col. iv. 16. This is a valuable remark.

CHAP. XI.

[2] V. 25. ἐν τῷ βυθῷ. Some Commentators have understood this of a *prison*, and others of a *well*: in either case, even if we admit the word ever to bear these senses, the Article would have been omitted.

CHAP. XII.

V. 18. τὸν ἀδελφόν. English Version has "a brother;" but it is evident that this is merely to evade the difficulty of the original. Commentators have usually supposed, that by τὸν ἀδελφὸν is meant St. Luke, and the Subscription of this Epistle expressly informs us, that the bearers of it were Titus and Luke, though in the Syr. (not also in the Copt. as affirmed by Wetstein) the name of the latter is omitted. The Subscriptions, however, are not regarded as of high authority, and that of this Epistle is believed by *Michaelis* to be founded on Chap. viii. 18. Now to show that St. Luke is not the person there intended, the same Writer has (*Introd.* by *Marsh*, vol. iii. p. 254.) assigned the following reasons; and if they be valid, neither can St. Luke be the ἀδελφὸς spoken of in the present verse. He says, "I have already observed in the preceding section, that the word εὐαγγέλιον, as used by the Apostles and Evangelists, does not denote a written narrative of the life of Christ, and therefore that St. Paul can hardly be supposed, in the passage in question, to allude to the Gospel of St. Luke.

---

[1] V. 13. ὁ Θεὸς μέτρου. Macknight translates "The God of measure," which is impossible. The Article would have been inserted, as in Rom. xv. 5. I apprehend that μέτρου, by a common Greek figure, is in concord with οὗ.—τὸ μέτρον τοῦ κανόνος οὗ (sc. μέτρου) ἐμέρισεν κ. τ. λ.——H. J. R.

[2] V. 4. ὁ ἐρχόμενος. This, says Winer, is *that person who will, I think or fear, come among you.* It is assumed, as Bishop Middleton would say, that a person will come.—H. J. R.

CHAPTER XII.   345

It is, moreover, probable that by the expression, *the brother, whose praise is in the Gospel*, he meant a totally different person from St. Luke. For this brother, as appears from the quoted passage, was sent by St. Paul to Corinth: yet though St. Paul himself went to Corinth soon after he had written this Epistle, St. Luke was not with him when he again departed from that city; for, according to Acts xx. 3—6. St. Luke went from Philippi (where he had stayed several years) to join company with St. Paul at Troas. Besides, as this brother was sent with Titus, in order to remove all suspicions of St. Paul's making an improper use of the contributions of the Corinthians, St. Luke, who was his intimate friend and companion, was by no means qualified to answer that purpose. And if we may judge from what St. Paul says, 2 Cor. viii. 23, 24. both of the brethren, who are there opposed to Titus, whom St. Paul calls his partner and fellow-helper, were deputies from the churches in Macedonia. Who they were, it is impossible to determine: but as Sopater, Aristarchus, and Secundus were Macedonians, (see Acts xx. 4.) it is not impossible that two out of these three persons were the brethren of whom St. Paul speaks, 2 Cor. viii. 18—23." This appears to me to be conclusive against St. Luke's being the brother spoken of in the two places, viii. 18. and the present verse: but independently of this, there is something remarkable in the manner in which this brother is here mentioned; for even if St. Luke had been meant, I do not perceive why he should be called τὸν ἀδελφόν, unless indeed in the general sense of τὸν ἀδελφὸν ἡμῶν, as in viii. 22. and even then he will be oddly distinguished from Titus, who must have been entitled to the same appellation, and so likewise must the third person; for that *three* were commissioned to be bearers of the Epistle, is plain from viii. 16. 18. 22. I rather wonder, therefore, that neither Mill, Bengel, Wetstein, nor Griesbach, have noticed in this place the reading of the Syr. which has *the brethren*, though *Schaaf*, it is true, in the V. R. subjoined to his Syr. N. T. mentions two Edd. which read *brother* in the Singular, but the original Ed. of *Widmanstad*, which Critics hold in the highest esteem, has the Plural; and so have the other Edd. which are most valued. If this reading, then, be genuine, and if the Translator found in his copy τοὺς ἀδελφούς, the difficulty, so far as it respects the

Article in the present passage, entirely vanishes; for τοὺς ἀδελφοὺς will mean the brethren, whoever they may be, who in viii. 18. and 22. are mentioned as the colleagues of Titus.

It may be added, that the opinion of *Schleusner*, which is adverse to what *Michaelis* has said on the Scriptural sense of εὐαγγέλιον, is not sufficiently established. To show that this word signifies *a Gospel*, as we say *the Gospel of St. Matthew*, *the four Gospels*, &c. he refers us in his Lex. to Matt. xxvi. 13. and Mark xiv. 9. in both which places the judicious reader will, I think, discern that the word εὐαγγέλιον is used in a different sense. *Schleusner* mentions, indeed, the Inscriptions of the Gospels; but these, though ancient, do not appear to have been of the apostolic age. It is of importance to mention this circumstance, because the notion that εὐαγγέλιον, viii. 18. signified a Gospel in the alleged sense, has operated very powerfully in producing the decision, that the brother there mentioned is St. Luke.

GALATIANS.

CHAP. II.

[1] V. 16. ἐξ ἔργων νόμου. *Macknight* rightly, I think, understands this of Law indefinitely, and so also ver. 19. See on Rom. iii. 20. But with this interpretation of ver. 19. I am not wholly satisfied: " Besides, I through law have died by law, so that I must live by God:" he makes νόμῳ and Θεῷ to be " Datives, not of the *object*, but of the *cause* or *instrument*," and he refers us to former passages of his work. I do not know, however, that any thing can be produced analogous to ζῆν Θεῷ, signifying to live by the agency of God. He quotes, indeed, at Rom. xiv. 7. *Soph. Ajax* 970. Ed. *Brunck.* θεοῖς τέθνηκεν οὗτος, which the Scholiast explains by θεῶν βουλομένων. That explanation may, perhaps, be disputed: at any rate, it is contrary to sound criticism to appeal to *Sophocles*, when phrases similar to that in question occur in the N. T. See Luke xx. 38. Rom. xiv. 7, 8. 2 Cor. v. 15. Coloss. iii. 3. and this very Epist. vi. 14. The meaning, therefore, of ver. 19. of this Chapter, I understand to be, " For I through law (i. e. the imperfection belonging to law of every kind, in not providing an atonement) died unto law, (i. e. renounced the harsh conditions on which alone it offered me salvation,) that I might live unto God (i. e. that I might embrace the more merciful scheme by which eternal life is offered

---

[1] V. 7. οἱ ταράσσοντες, says Winer, are here *thought of definitely as such*, and the passage is similar to the well-known Grecism, εἰσὶν οἱ λέγοντες, *They who trouble you are some*. What Bishop Middleton says on such points is clearer, though it perhaps is not very different, i. e. that it is assumed that there are persons who trouble the Galatians, and they are identified with τινές. See III. 3. 2.—H. J. R.

me through Christ.") And with this interpretation the remainder of the Chapter very well agrees. *Abp. Newcome*, indeed, supposes " dying through the law" to mean, " by the tenor of the law itself, which foretels a better covenant." But this arises from making νόμῳ to signify the Law of Moses; in which case it would have the Article. See on Rom. *passim*. Besides, this explanation appears not to harmonize with the reasoning which St. Paul pursues through the whole Epistle to the Romans, and which he repeats in the present, that the great defect of *all law* is its inevitable condemnation of imperfect obedience.

Mr. *Wakefield, Silv. Crit.* Part i. p. 125. observes, that the phrase ἐγὼ διὰ νόμου resembles Rom. ii. 27. σὲ τὸν διὰ γράμματος, " *ut ovum ovo non potest esse similius.*" A want of similitude, however, arises from the want of the Article in the present instance. See on 1 Cor. xiv. 9.

CHAP. III.

V. 2. τὸ πνεῦμα. Though the word here has the Article, I suppose it to mean the gifts of the Spirit, the *well-known* gifts: after the Galatians had received them, ἐλάβετε, they became subjects of reference.

V. 3. πνεύματι and σαρκὶ are here used adverbially for πνευματικῶς and σαρκικῶς.

V. 11. ὁ δὲ δίκαιος ἐκ πίστεως ζήσεται. These words, which are an allusion to Habakkuk ii. 4. occur also Rom. i. 17. and Heb. x. 38. *Macknight* and others render " the just by faith shall live;" but I much doubt whether this deviation from our Common Version can be vindicated. If I mistake not, we should thus have read, ὁ δίκαιος Ὁ ἐκ πίστεως, or else ὁ ἐκ πίστεως δίκαιος. Nor is this all: to say that he who is just or justified by faith, shall live, amounts to very little; but to affirm that the good man, he whose obedience, though imperfect, is sincere, shall reap life everlasting from faith, (as opposed to a law of works,) and from faith alone, is a most important declaration; and it agrees exactly with the context. " That no man," says the Apostle, " is justified under the law, ἐν νόμῳ δικαιοῦται, is evident, for one of the Prophets hath said, The just man shall live by faith." The second Proposition, as it is represented in the new Translation, affords no proof of the truth of the former.

CHAP. IV.

V. 4. ὑπὸ νόμον. The Mosaic Law. Part i. Chap. vi. § 1.

V. 24. αἱ δυὸ διαθῆκαι. *Wetstein* and *Griesbach*, with all the best MSS. reject αἱ. The Article is by no means requisite to the sense: it was, probably, a subsequent interpolation of some one who did not attend to the purport of the Apostle's declaration; which was only, that the bond-woman and the free-woman were emblems of two Covenants: that these, indeed, were the Mosaic and the Christian dispensations, is true; but the application, being so obvious, was left to the Reader.

V. 31. παιδίσκης τέκνα. A distinguished Prelate, the present Bishop of *Durham*[1], observes, (ap. Bowyer,) " The Article being prefixed to παιδίσκης in the preceding verse, suggests the probability of its being wanting to it here." This is certainly very plausible: but perhaps the omission may be accounted for by the Negative form of the Proposition.

CHAP. V.

V. 5. πνεύματι. *Spiritually*, as in iii. 3. *et passim*. *Rosenm.* says that πνεῦμα is either *the mind*, or else *the Holy Spirit*, " *nisi malis intelligere perfectiorem illam mentis indolem, qua Christiani gaudent*," &c. This is saying only, that πνεῦμα is here used in some one of the principal senses in which it is found in Scripture. About the real meaning in this place, there cannot, I think, be any reasonable doubt: the same *adverbial* use, and always without the Article, occurs in a multitude of instances: in this Chapter, besides the present, see verses 16. 18. 25.

V. 13. τὴν ἐλευθερίαν. *Your* liberty, as elsewhere; so the Syr. and Syr.-Philox. *Macknight* has " this liberty," a sense which the Article will, indeed, sometimes bear, but which it is not any where necessary to introduce.

[1] Dr. Barrington.

V. 25. εἰ ζῶμεν πνεύματι, πνεύματι καὶ στοιχῶμεν, if we be spiritually affected, let us also walk spiritually. This I take to be the sense of the passage, and I understand it as a caution against the mischievous consequences of trusting to the all-sufficiency of Faith. *Schleusner*, who pays no regard to the Article in distinguishing the different senses of πνεῦμα, has nearly the same interpretation.

CHAP. VI.

V. 8. εἰς τὸ πνεῦμα. That which is spiritual, generally.

V. 13. οὐδὲ γὰρ οἱ περιτεμνόμενοι αὐτοὶ νόμον φυλάσσουσιν. Νόμον is here understood by *Schleusner* and *Macknight* and the other Critics, of the Law of Moses: but the absence of the Article led me to suspect that this is not the true meaning; and this suspicion is not without confirmation. It is the object of the Apostle to show that the Jews, who were so zealous for the circumcision of the Gentile Christians, were ostentatious hypocrites. He says, that though they adhered to the Ritual of their Religion, of which Circumcision was so important a part, they paid no attention to its spirit and design, and being thus insincere, were unworthy of regard. They had the ἐν σαρκὶ περιτομή, (see Rom. ii. 28, 29.) but not the περιτομὴ καρδίας, which ought to follow: περιτομὴ γὰρ ὠφελεῖ, ἐὰν νόμον πράσσῃς. (Rom. ii. 25.) There, indeed, both *Schleusner* and *Macknight* make νόμον to signify *moral obedience*: the strict parallelism of the two passages affords the strongest presumption that they are both to be interpreted in the same manner; and of the former there is not, nor can there be, any doubt.—*Michaelis*, understanding νόμον as others have done, proceeds to show the impossibility of closely adhering to all the ordinances of the Levitical Law in foreign countries: but this, I believe, is not the subject of complaint. In Acts xxi. 24. where the Brethren are urging the necessity of adhering to the ceremonies of the Jewish Religion, we find ΤΟΝ νόμον φυλάσσων.

V. 14. κόσμος. This word throughout the N. T. meaning *the world* in its common acceptation, has the Article wherever the rules will not account for its omission, except in two instances, viz. the present and 2 Cor. v. 19. for in 2 Pet. ii. 5.

CHAPTER VI.

the word is to be understood somewhat differently. It appears to me that κόσμος, like Θεός, is one of those words which partake of the nature of Proper Names. The same uncertainty prevails in the classical use, as will be evident on a cursory view of the Greek philosophical writers, though the Article is there, as in the N. T., almost always inserted. The word is used as a Proper Name by *Plutarch*, περὶ Στωικ. ἐναντ. p. 470. fol. Basil 1574. ὁ δὲ Ζεὺς καὶ Κόσμος.—F. G. in this place prefix ὁ, and some good MSS.— τῷ before κόσμῳ: the former reading is probably the correction of some one who knew not the latitude allowed to κόσμος: the latter is probably genuine, and is so considered by Griesbach.

EPHESIANS.

CHAP. I.

V. 1. τοῖς ἁγίοις τοῖς οὖσιν ἐν Ἐφέσῳ. It is a well-known subject of dispute among learned men, whether this Epistle was addressed to the Ephesians, or whether it be the *Epistle to the Laodiceans* mentioned Coloss. iv. 16: the external evidence is in favour of the former opinion; the internal, as is alleged, of the latter. They who would know the arguments on both sides, detailed at great length, may consult *Michaelis's* Introd. by *Marsh*, vol. iv. chap. 20: my immediate concern is with a passage of *St. Basil*, quoted by *Michaelis*, and before him by *Wolfius* and others; it is as follows: Ἀλλὰ καὶ τοῖς Ἐφεσίοις ἐπιστέλλων, ὡς γνησίως ἡνωμένοις τῷ Ὄντι δι' ἐπιγνώσεως, ΟΝΤΑΣ αὐτοὺς ἰδιαζόντως ὠνόμασεν, εἰπών, τοῖς ἁγίοις τοῖς Οὖσι, καὶ πιστοῖς ἐν Χριστῷ Ἰησοῦ. Οὕτω γὰρ οἱ πρὸ ἡμῶν παραδεδώκασι, καὶ ἡμεῖς ἐν τοῖς παλαιοῖς τῶν ἀντιγράφων εὑρήκαμεν. Basilii Opera, tom. i. p. 254. Ed. Garnier. From this it has usually been inferred, that in St. Basil's judgment the addition of ἐν Ἐφέσῳ was spurious: and yet nothing is more certain than that he acknowledged this Epistle to have been addressed to the Ephesians, from the mention of τοῖς Ἐφεσίοις above: and in another place, de *Spir. Sancto*, cap. v. cited by *Matthäi*, he says, γράφων ὁ Ἀπόστολος πρὸς Ἐφεσίους φησίν, Ἀληθεύοντες ἐν ἀγάπῃ, κ. τ. λ. which words are still found in this Epist. iv. 15. Besides, we learn from Ignatius, who lived in the first century, that St. Paul wrote an Epistle to the Ephesians, the description of which, as given by that Father, corresponds with the Epistle which is still extant. See the Bishop of *Lincoln's Elem. of Christ. Theol.* vol. i. p. 401. The same very learned Prelate observes, that it is recognised likewise by Irenæus, Clemens Alex. Tertullian,

Origen, Cyprian, Eusebius, and others. The question, therefore, is, What is the meaning of the latter part of the quotation from St. Basil? " For thus our ancestors have delivered it to us, and thus have we found it in ancient copies." *Mill*, in his *Proleg.* 1st Edit. p. 9. and *ad loc.* contends, that certain ancient MSS. which St. Basil had seen, omitted the words ἐν 'Εφέσῳ, and the late Dr. *Paley*, in his invaluable *Horæ Paulinæ*, chap. vi. No. 4. thinks that Mill, notwithstanding the objections which have been made, is right. Dr. Paley, however, would perhaps have thought differently, if Mr. Marsh's Translation of Michaelis had at that time existed. The German Critic has shown, vol. iv. p. 144. that the context of the passage in St. Basil is very important to its true interpretation, for that the Father, after having accumulated instances where the word ἐστὶ is applied to the True God, endeavours to prove, that as the True God is called ὁ 'ΩN, to distinguish Him from false Gods, so true Christians are called οἱ ὄντες, in opposition to the Heathens, τὰ μὴ ὄντα, 1 Cor. i. 28 : now a man who was prosecuting this puerile conceit, might very naturally omit the words ἐν 'Εφέσῳ, as not making for his purpose, without meaning that they were wanting in the old MSS.; especially when he had said in the preceding sentence, that the Epistle was addressed to the Ephesians. Dr. Paley was possibly the more disposed to accede to Mill's opinion from a belief that "the name ἐν 'Εφέσῳ is not read in all the MSS. now extant;" and if I understand him rightly, he supposes that a few have ἐν Λαοδικείᾳ. In this, however, he must have been mistaken; for not a single MS. hitherto collated omits the words in question, or has any various reading: unless, indeed, we except an *emendation* in one of the Vienna MSS. noticed in the new edition of Griesbach's N. T., but which Dr. Paley could not have in view : ἐν 'Εφέσῳ, according to that emendation, is to be expunged. But this is no authority.

If not, then, in behalf of the omission of ἐν 'Εφέσῳ, why did Basil appeal to the ancient MSS.? Some have thought that a few copies might before οὖσιν have omitted τοῖς, the genuineness of which the Father vindicated as being necessary to his argument; and Wolfius affirms that a MS. was in his time still extant, in which τοῖς was wanting. It is true, that one inconsiderable MS. in Griesbach (not known to him, however, when he published his former Edit.) does omit τοῖς: whether this be, or be not, the MS. alluded to by Wolfius, I cannot believe the supposed omission to be that to which St. Basil refers, partly because it would offend against the general usage to omit the Article in this place, on which account such an omission is the less probable; and partly because St. Basil's argument, such as it is, could suffer nothing from the absence of τοῖς, its whole weight resting on οὖσιν. The omission of οὖσιν, therefore, I suppose with Michaelis to be the subject of St. Basil's implied censure, as being contrary to τὰ παλαιὰ τῶν ἀντιγράφων: and this omission would not only be hostile to his whimsical inference, but moreover is one with which it is highly probable that some MSS. were chargeable; for though οὖσιν would not imply the subintellection of τοῖς, yet the Article might, and consequently does, imply the subintellection of the Participle of Existence. So in the very first clause of the Lord's Prayer; an instance, by the way, not very favourable to St. Basil's reasoning. I conclude, therefore, that this Father's appeal to the old MSS. was in behalf of τοῖς ΟΥΣΙΝ ἐν Ἐφέσῳ, against some few copies which had what is in truth exactly equivalent, viz. τοῖς ἐν Ἐφέσῳ, though not likely to be approved by St. Basil, as not being at all to his purpose.

In answer to the objection that the Epistle contains no intimation of its being addressed to persons with whom the writer was acquainted, though St. Paul had resided two years at Ephesus, Macknight contends that there are passages in which this acquaintance is implied. Michaelis, however, gets rid of the difficulty by supposing the Epistle to have been *circular*, being addressed to the Ephesians, Laodiceans, and some other Churches of Asia Minor. It could hardly be circular in the sense in which Michaelis understands that term; for he supposes that the different copies transmitted by St. Paul had ἐν Ἐφέσῳ, ἐν Λαοδικείᾳ, &c. as occasion required, and that the reason why all our MSS. read ἐν Ἐφέσῳ is, that when the Books of the N. T. were first collected, the copy used was obtained from Ephesus: but this seems to imply that the Canon was established by authority, and that all copies of this Epistle not agreeing with the approved edition were suppressed. Neither does the ingenious conjecture of Dr. *Paley*, who thinks that this is actually the Epistle to the Laodiceans referred to

CHAPTER I. 355

Coloss. iv. 16. altogether accord with the fact, that all the extant MSS. have ἐν 'Εφέσῳ : he says, " Whoever inspects the map of Asia Minor will see, that a person proceeding from Rome to Laodicea would probably land at Ephesus, as the nearest frequented sea-port in that direction. Might not Tychicus, then, in passing through Ephesus, communicate to the Christians of that place the letter with which he was charged? and might not copies of that letter be multiplied and preserved at Ephesus? Might not some of the copies drop the words of designation ἐν τῇ Λαοδικείᾳ, which it was of no consequence to an Ephesian to retain? Might not copies of the letter come out into the Christian Church at large from Ephesus; and might not this give occasion to a belief that the letter was written to that Church? And, lastly, might not this belief produce the error which we suppose to have crept into the inscription?" According to this account we should surely expect, that if not all the MSS. at least the greater part of them, would read ἐν Λαοδικείᾳ, which, however, is not found in one. Besides, though the Ephesians, who might thus be disposed to multiply copies of the Epistle which Tychicus had shown them, were numerous, yet it ought to be considered that the Christians of Laodicea, Colossæ, and Hierapolis, (mentioned Coloss. iv. 13.) three considerable cities which lay very near each other, were probably not less numerous; and therefore the copies disseminated from that quarter cannot well be supposed to be fewer than those which issued from Ephesus; not to insist that Tychicus, thus charged with a letter to the Laodiceans, would hardly of his own accord communicate to the Christians of Ephesus what was intended for those of another city. On the whole, I see nothing so probable as the opinion of *Macknight* on Col. iv. 16. " that the Apostle sent the Ephesians word by Tychicus, who carried their letter, to send a copy of it to the Laodiceans, with an order to them to communicate it to the Colossians." This hypothesis will account, as well as that of Michaelis, for the want of those marks of personal acquaintance which the Apostle's former residence at Ephesus might lead us to expect: for every thing local would be purposely omitted in an Epistle which had a further destination.

If ever there were a Letter from St. Paul to the Laodiceans

distinct from the present, it is lost, that preserved in *Fabricius* and in *Jones's* Work on the *Canon* being universally admitted to be a forgery; and yet the loss of a canonical writing is of all suppositions the most improbable. See on 1 Cor. v. 9. and Macknight, Essay II. p. 59. Mr. *Wakefield*, however, explains Col. iv. 16. τὴν ἐκ Λαοδικείας by " the Laodicean Epistle, viz. that sent to them by St. Paul;" and this he would vindicate by the phrase ἀνὴρ ἐκ τῆς πόλεως, Luke viii. 27. a citizen of Gadara; as if, because in one place the Preposition ἐκ marks *origin* or *derivation*, it must in another denote the *destination* or *end*. The instances which *Raphel* has adduced from Polybius in support of the same construction, are not much better: the embassy from Rome, sent thither by the Lacedæmonians, τὴν ἐκ τῆς Ῥώμης πρεσβείαν, ἣν ἀπέστειλαν οἱ Λακεδαιμόνιοι, returned without having accomplished the object of its mission; and the other instance is similar, having only *ambassadors* for *embassy*. But between the case of an embassy and that of a letter, there is a manifest difference: ambassadors, such as were those of the ancients, were expected to return from the place to which they had been sent, so soon as their business was completed; and when the ambassadors *from* a given place are expressly said to be on their *return*, as happens in both of *Raphel's* examples, they are necessarily understood to be the same who had already gone thither: but a letter is not sent to a place for the purpose of being sent back again to the writer, which, however, must be supposed before the cases can be admitted to be parallel. In short, nothing appears to me more certain, than that τὴν ἐκ Λαοδικείας must be rendered, " the Letter *from* Laodicea," whether, as some imagine, it was one which the Laodiceans had written to St. Paul, or one which had been transmitted to Colossæ from Laodicea, though addressed to a different Church.

Once, indeed, I thought that the Epistle referred to might be the First to Timothy, (which others have supposed,) and that on the following grounds: 1st. The subscription of that Epistle declares it to have been written from Laodicea; and *Schleusner*, I know not for what reason, but doubtless on some better authority, affirms this to have been the case: see Lex. in Λαοδίκεια.—2. It was not improbable that the Colossians should have been referred to that Epistle, because, as Michaelis

CHAPTER II. 357

has shown, though not with a view to any such hypothesis, the 1st Epistle to Timothy, no less than that to the Ephesians, relates partly to the same subject which gave rise to the Epistle to the Colossians. See *Introduct.* Vol. IV. Chap. xv. Sect. iii. —3. It is not difficult to conjecture why that Epistle should be called by St. Paul *the one from Laodicea*, because not being addressed to a whole Church, but merely to an individual, it might seem more respectful to the Church of Phrygia, the country in which both Colossæ and Laodicea were situated, to describe the Epistle by the place where it was written.—4. The Syr. Version seems to favour the notion that the Epistle in question was *written from Laodicea*: the Latin of *Schaaf's* Edition is, "*illam quæ scripta est* EX *Laodicensibus* :" the Syr. Preposition may, indeed, be rendered "*by* the Laodiceans ;" *Schaaf* had probably some ground of preference.—5. According to the Chronology adopted by Michaelis, the 1st to Timothy had been written a few years before that to the Colossians, and might therefore be the Epistle in question.—I am aware, however, of strong objections to this hypothesis, which, therefore, I am not disposed to urge, especially that founded on Col. ii. 1. to which *Lardner* has, indeed, attempted to give an interpretation different from the received one, but without, so far as I know, having made any one convert to his opinion.

CHAP. II.

[1] V. 21. πᾶσα ἡ οἰκοδομή. Very many MSS., including a large proportion of those of *Matthäi*, omit ἡ, and many Editors adopt this reading; among others, *Bengel* and *Griesbach* are disposed to think the Article spurious. But thus the sense will be "*every* building," (see Part i. Chap. vii. § 1.) which the context, as will be evident on looking at the passage, will not admit. This is, therefore, one of the instances in which the smaller number of MSS. has preserved the true reading. *Macknight* rightly renders "the whole building," but observes, " πᾶσα for ὅλη," which I do not understand: is not πᾶς with a Substantive, which has the Article prefixed, always equivalent to ὅλος ?

[1] V. 8. Θεοῦ τὸ δῶρον. See perhaps Acts xxiii. 6.—H. J. R.

CHAP. III.

V. 1. ἐγὼ Παῦλος ὁ δέσμιος, κ. τ. λ. I cannot better state the difficulty attending this passage than by abridging *Wolfius*. " There are two distinct opinions by which the Interpreters are here divided : since a Verb is wanting to make the sense complete, some supply γράφω, some πρεσβεύω or κεκαύχημαι, which two last are found in some MSS. or, which is more generally adopted, the Verb εἰμί. Others, however, suppose a parenthesis, the limits of which are variously represented ; some making the sense to be continued at ver. 8. some at ver. 14. and others at the beginning of the next Chapter." Wolfius concludes by giving his own opinion, that " *in ambages illi incidunt, qui commati primo plenum et absolutum sensum, subintellecto verbo* εἰμί, *non vindicant.*"

On this I have to remark, that πρεσβεύω is found in only three MSS. and that κεκαύχημαι exists in only one still preserved : *Mill*, indeed, speaks of it, as having been found by *Stephens*, but it is not now known where. On these various readings, therefore, no stress is laid : the subintellection of εἰμὶ is the favourite solution : let us, therefore, consider wherein lies the objection to adopting it.

This Ellipsis, we are told by Wolfius, is in other instances very common : I think, however, that it is not at all common in cases strictly similar to the present. After the Verb Substantive, the Predicate, for the most part, rejects the Article, Part i. Chap. iii. Sect. iii. § 2. but this, for a reason there assigned, does not always happen when the subject is a Pronoun Demonstrative, as *Glass* has observed, *Philol. Sac.* p. 325. Ed. 1711. Thus John x. 7. ἐγώ εἰμι Ἡ θύρα τῶν προβάτων. My objection, therefore, is not to the insertion of the Article before δέσμιος, but to the subintellection of εἰμί. Among the examples which Glass has enumerated in proof of his remark, he quotes the verse in question. One thing, however, seems to have escaped his notice : it is, that in every passage adduced by him, excepting this one, the Verb Substantive is *expressed ;* a strong presumption at least, that however frequently in other cases it is understood, in this particular case its subintellection is not allowable. But it is not merely from the examples collected by Glass, that I infer the impossibility of supplying εἰμὶ before ὁ δέσμιος: the N. T. abounds with instances in which, where ἐγὼ is the subject, the Verb Substantive is *expressed*, both where the Predicate has the Article, and where it is anarthrous. Thus Matt. xxiv. 5. ἐγώ ΕΙΜΙ ὁ Χριστός. Luke i. 19. ἐγώ ΕΙΜΙ Γαβριήλ. John viii. 12. ἐγώ ΕΙΜΙ τὸ φῶς τοῦ κόσμου; xv. 1. ἐγώ ΕΙΜΙ ἡ ἄμπελος ἡ ἀληθινή. Acts xxiii. 6. ἐγὼ Φαρισαῖός ΕΙΜΙ. 1 Tim. i. 15. ὧν πρῶτός ΕΙΜΙ ἐγώ. Rev. i. 17. ἐγώ ΕΙΜΙ ὁ πρῶτος; xxii. 16. ἐγώ ΕΙΜΙ ἡ ῥίζα Δαβίδ.

Rosenmüller, however, one of the multitude who would insert εἰμί, as if conscious of the difficulty of defending it, refers us to the idiom of the Hebrew: he says, "*sicut Hebr.* האסר אני *explices* ἐγώ εἰμι ὁ δέσμιος· comp. Mark xii. 26. Rom. viii. 33." The latter of these examples is dissimilar, because no Pronoun Demonstrative is there employed: the former is more deserving of consideration; it is ἐγὼ ὁ Θεὸς Ἀβραάμ, κ. τ. λ. where unquestionably εἰμὶ is understood: but the Reader, who has accompanied me thus far in these remarks, will have perceived the necessity of distinguishing original passages from *citations*. Now Mark xii. 26. is cited from Exod. iii. 6. and in the Hebrew, as every one knows who has but the most superficial knowledge of that language, the Verb Substantive in such Propositions is almost always understood. The Hebrew says, "I (am) the God of your father, the God of Abraham, &c." Our Saviour omitted the clause, "the God of your father," as having no relation to his argument, and appears to have quoted in a cognate dialect, "I (am) the God of Abraham," which his Evangelist has faithfully, and even scrupulously, recorded, though even here a few MSS. and so also Origen, have inserted εἰμί. But how, it will be asked, have the LXX. rendered the Hebrew? Translators are not restricted so closely as are the reporters of the sayings of illustrious persons: the LXX. therefore, though generally not averse from Hebraisms, have rendered the Hebrew by ἐγώ ΕΙΜΙ ὁ Θεὸς τοῦ πατρός σου, ὁ Θεός, &c. a plain intimation that in their judgment ἐγὼ ὁ Θεὸς would be hardly tolerable. And I could show that elsewhere they have adopted the very same usage, or else, not inserting εἰμί, they have omitted the Article of the Predicate, as in Isaiah xli. 4. ἐγὼ Θεὸς πρῶτος, not Ὁ Θεὸς Ὁ πρῶτος· and so in many other examples.

There is, therefore, no force whatever in the imaginary Hebrew instance (for I cannot find it in the O. T.) adduced by Rosenmüller: there is no doubt that he who should meet with it, would render it as Rosenmüller says, ἐγώ ΕΙΜΙ ὁ δέσμιος: but would he have sufficient authority for writing, for that is the question, ἐγὼ ὁ δέσμιος, meaning εἰμὶ to be understood? If not, which I think has been abundantly proved, the case stands on the same footing as if the Hebrew, instead of omitting the Verb Substantive, constantly inserted it.

Thus far I have endeavoured to show that εἰμὶ cannot be understood before ὁ δέσμιος: to make the argument complete, I ought to remind the Reader that ἐγὼ ὁ δέσμιος, on the hypothesis that εἰμὶ is *not* to be supplied, is the very form usual in similar instances: see on Luke xviii. 13. So also ἐγὼ ὁ δέσμιος, ver. 1. of next Chapter. The result of the whole seems to be, that εἰμὶ is not understood before ὁ δέσμιος, and that consequently we must have recourse to a Parenthesis.

As to the *limits* of this Parenthesis, I think that the whole reasoning will be perfectly connected and conclusive, if we suppose the thread to be resumed at the 14th verse. The principal truth announced in the preceding Chapter was, that the Ephesians, who had been Gentiles, were in common with the Jews admitted to all the privileges and blessings of the new Dispensation. "For this cause," (τούτου χάριν, ver. 1.) says St. Paul, "I the prisoner of Jesus Christ, (for ye cannot but" (εἴγε, see *Hoogeveen de Part. Gr.* who quotes this passage,) "have heard both of my divine commission and of the nature of the doctrine which I am commanded to teach," (ver. 2—13.) "for this cause" (τούτου χάριν repeated ver. 14—19.) "I pray to God, who has been thus merciful in calling you, that ye may be strengthened with might by his Spirit, (ver. 16.) that so Christ may dwell in your hearts." After this prayer is subjoined (vers. 20, 21.) a Doxology, with the concluding Amen.—The opinion that the sense is not resumed till the next Chapter, is certainly somewhat plausible: the reasons, however, which tend to show that it is continued at ver. 14. of the present Chapter, are also reasons against its being first resumed elsewhere: in addition to them I would observe, that the solemn Doxology with which the present Chapter concludes, forbids us to imagine that the sense is still incomplete.

CHAPTER IV.

Nor is it difficult to explain the παρακαλῶ οὖν of the next Chapter, without supposing it to be the resumption of the argument. At ver. 1. Chapter iv. begins an exhortation, which is continued to the end of the Epistle: the οὖν, which some suppose to indicate a resumption, is no other than the "*quæ cum ita sint*" of Cicero, which usually introduces his perorations. "These things being so," says St. Paul, i. e. God having thus called you to partake in the Covenant of mercy, "I exhort you to walk worthy of your vocation:" and accordingly the remainder of the Epistle is devoted to moral precepts.

I have entered into this subject the more fully, from the perplexity which appears to have attended it. Our English Version supposes a Parenthesis, of which, however, the boundaries are not very clearly marked. *Macknight* and *Wakefield*, as well as the French Translator, *Beausobre*, supply the Verb Substantive, and *Michaelis* goes on to the next Chapter. It is, moreover, a question of some curiosity, as tending to illustrate the style of St. Paul.—If I have not attempted to refute the notion, that the resumption is at ver. 8. it is because I know not of any thing which can be alleged in its behalf. It was, indeed, the opinion of *Grotius*, but he has not assigned the grounds of it.

V. 15. πᾶσα πατριά. All the modern Versions which I have met with, here render πᾶσα by *all*, in the sense of *the whole*, or something equivalent thereto. It is, however, to be observed, that the reading is not πᾶσα Ἡ πατριά, and that therefore the sense is *every* family. And so the Ancients appear to have understood it, i. e. they understood several πατριὰς or *Families* on earth, and several in Heaven. See *Theophyl. Œcumen.* and others in *Suicer*, vol. ii. p. 633.

CHAP. IV.

V. 30. μὴ λυπεῖτε τὸ πνεῦμα τὸ ἅγιον. I believe that I have already shown ἐκ περιουσίας, that wherever in the N. T. either *action* or *passion* is ascribed to the Spirit, πνεῦμα has the Article. See on Matt. i. 18.

CHAP. V.

V. 5. ἐν τῇ βασιλείᾳ τοῦ Χριστοῦ καὶ Θεοῦ. This is, strictly speaking, the first of the Examples adduced by Mr. *Granville Sharp* in proof that the same Person is in Scripture called Christ and God: for in Acts xx. 28. as was there shown, the reading is doubtful. The principle of the rule was sufficiently demonstrated in Part i. p. 78; and it cannot be pretended that the present instance in any respect deviates from the conditions there prescribed, since both Χριστὸς and Θεός, the former retaining its more usual sense, and not being taken as a Proper Name, are as plainly what I have denominated Attributives, as are any of the words which appear in illustration of the rule: Θεός, indeed, is itself adduced in one or two of the examples. I must, however, repeat, that this word never uses its licence with respect to the Article in such a way as to interfere with the construction usual in the case of the most common Appellatives. If Θεοῦ, therefore, be here meant otherwise than as a joint Predicate of τοῦ, the construction is wholly destroyed; an inconvenience which might easily, and unquestionably would have been avoided by writing ΤΟΥ Θεοῦ, in the same manner as ὁ βασιλεὺς καὶ Ὁ ἡγεμών. See on Acts xxvi. 30. Matt. xviii. 17. second Note: *et passim*.

The *Unknown Writer*, already noticed on Matt. xi. 11. contends that " Χριστὸς being an epithet, the expression is harsh and intolerable: and that he must be a rude Writer who should say, The anointed and God," p. 74. Rude he would be indeed: but this is not similar to the Greek, and therefore ought not to have been so represented; and yet this very misrepresentation is made to be the ground-work of the Writer's whole fabric. Without deigning to inquire whether the Greek and English Articles have any and what degree of analogy, he sets out with the bold assertion, that the rule laid down by his Opponent, and by all Antiquity, " may be tried *just as well* in English as in Greek. Now in English," he says, " we have such phrases as the King and Queen, the Husband and Wife, &c. &c. which cannot be understood of the same person." See p. 19. And hence he concludes that Mr. Sharp and all the Greek Fathers, who, according to Mr. Wordsworth, support Mr. Sharp's interpretation, must be wrong. If it be so, for

CHAPTER V. 363

Mr. Sharp's error I cannot pretend to account; but that of the Fathers should thus appear to have arisen from their ignorance of English.

A mind accustomed to any thing like proof would have shrunk from such temerity. It *might* have been thought of some importance in a question of Greek criticism, to have ascertained the practice of the Greek Writers in cases precisely parallel: it *might* have been a consequence of this examination to have investigated the *ground* of an usage which, in the Greek Writers, both profane and sacred, was found to prevail universally: the result of this inquiry *might* have induced at least a suspicion, that the Greek idiom in some respects differed from our own; and on a subject of a very serious nature, which after all could be decided only by learning and calm discussion, it *might* have been deemed neither necessary nor decent to catch at the applause of illiterate Unbelievers, by attempting to raise a laugh. On all these points, however, the *Unknown Writer* thought differently from persons accustomed to sober and grave deliberation: at the outset he is satisfied with a mis-statement of the question, and he is not ashamed to triumph in the consequences.—The truth is, that the Article of our language not being a Pronoun, has little resemblance to that of the Greeks; and the proper rendering of τοῦ Χριστοῦ καὶ Θεοῦ is not "of the anointed and God," but "of Him (being, or) who is the Christ and God;" in which, I believe, there is nothing approaching to the "rudeness" of the burlesque translation, nor to the vulgarity of such phrases as "the King and Queen." Of the objection, that Χριστὸς is an *epithet*, I do not see the drift: for epithets, being descriptive of *quality*, are more especially and strictly subject to the rule; though epithets in many instances, as in ξενός, &c. and in this also, become Substantives; and to them this Writer, being ignorant of the *principle* on which the rule is founded, seems to have supposed it chiefly, if not exclusively, to apply. But it is the strange infelicity of the *Unknown Controversialist*, that when he would reason, which rarely happens, he can only cavil.

But not only the principle of the rule, Part i. Chap. iii. Sect. iv. § 2. and the invariable practice in the N. T. with respect to Θεὸς and all other Attributives, compel us to acquiesce in the identity of Χριστοῦ καὶ Θεοῦ, but the same truth is evinced by the examination of the Greek Fathers so ably executed by Mr. Wordsworth; who affirms, " we shall have the consolation to find, that no other interpretation than yours (Mr. Sharp's) was ever heard in all the Greek churches:" p. 26. He then adduces, among other examples, some very decisive passages from Chrysostom, Cyril Alex. and Theodoret, in which this very text is cited with the common Trinitarian texts, John i. 1. Rom. ix. 5. These passages, indeed, the *Unknown Writer* would evade by saying, that the arguments of the Fathers are a deduction from the *unity of dominion;* meaning, I suppose, that Christ and God are no otherwise one, than as they jointly reign over one kingdom. But here again is the mischief of not inquiring into the *principle* of the rule which does and must apply perpetually in cases where a reference to community of dominion cannot be supposed. Besides, how will this accord with Theodoret's explanation of Titus ii. 13. (see *Wordsworth*, p. 32.) " He" (the Apostle) " hath called the same person the Saviour and the Great God and Jesus Christ?" It may here, indeed, with as much reason as in the former instance, be urged, that this is a deduction from the *unity of appearance*, ἐπιφάνειαν τῆς δόξης: but then why is it not ΤΟΥ σωτῆρος ἡμῶν, as in the former case why was it not ΤΟΥ Θεοῦ? Almost every chapter of the N. T. contains some exemplification of the rule in question, with which, therefore, the Sacred Writers were well acquainted, and must have supposed their Readers to have been acquainted also; and if in Titus ii. 13. they did not mean to identify the Great God and the Saviour, they expressed themselves in a manner which they well knew would mislead their Readers, and to mislead must have been their object: so absurd are the conclusions to which the subterfuges and conjectures of this Writer inevitably conduct us. It ought to be observed, that Theodoret's explanation of Titus ii. 13. introduces the present text as a similar passage.—Mr. Wordsworth avers, (p. 132.) " I have observed more, I am persuaded, than a thousand instances of the form ὁ Χριστὸς καὶ Θεός, (Eph. v. 5.) some hundreds of instances of ὁ μέγας Θεὸς καὶ σωτήρ, (Tit. ii. 13.) and not fewer than several

CHAPTER V. 365

thousands of the form ὁ Θεὸς καὶ σωτήρ, (2 Pet. i. 1 :) while in no single case have I seen, where the sense could be determined, any one of them used, but only of *one* person."

The same Writer, however, laments his inability to ascertain the sense of the Oriental Versions: though, as he rightly states, they are, in comparison with the interpretation of the Fathers, but of secondary importance; for it is obvious that the Oriental Translators could not be *better* skilled in Greek than were such men as Chrysostom and Cyril Alex.: and the probability is, that some of them not being native Greeks, understood it not so well : still, however, this is a question of some curiosity, and I wish with Mr. Wordsworth, that I were capable of answering it satisfactorily.

The Syriac does not appear to me to have any method, generally applicable, of expressing the idiom noticed in Part i. Chap. iii. Sect. iv. § 2. I had, indeed, once thought that in Genitives resembling the present instance, *diversity* of persons might be signified by inserting the Preposition ? before the second Syriac Noun, as well as before the first, and that *identity* was marked by the omission: this would show the Translator to have understood Χριστοῦ καὶ Θεοῦ of two persons: but in 2 Pet. iii. 18. where the Syr. Translator, after Ἰησοῦ Χριστοῦ, read καὶ Θεοῦ πατρός, which could not be taken of Jesus Christ, he has, instead of ܐܠܗܐܕ as in the present example, simply ܐܠܗܐ. This, therefore, cannot be the rule. In one of Mr. Sharp's texts (viz. Jude 4.) identity is clearly expressed by *apposition*, the Copulative being omitted: but in Heb. iii. 1. τὸν ἀπόστολον καὶ ἀρχιερέα, this does not happen. In the present text, at least, I suspect that the Syriac is ambiguous: others, perhaps, may detect some distinction which has escaped my notice.

In examining the Coptic, I believe we shall be more successful. This language has Articles, both determinate and indeterminate: they seem not to be employed to mark the difference distinguishable in the usage, which we are now considering; yet, if I mistake not, the Coptic has a Canon, which is equivalent to the Greek one. In that language there are two Copulatives, ouoh and nem: the latter, indeed, is a Preposition corresponding with the Hebrew עם or Greek μετά: but it is also commonly employed where the Greek has καί.

I have observed, however, that these Copulatives are not used indiscriminately: where the Translator understood two Attributives of the *same* person, καὶ is always, I think, rendered by ouoh; where of different persons, as in ὁ βασιλεὺς καὶ ὁ ἡγεμών, by nem. A single example will illustrate my meaning: the Translator read ver. 20. of the present chapter, ἐν ὀνόματι τοῦ Κυρίου ἡμῶν Ἰησοῦ Χριστοῦ καὶ τοῦ Θεοῦ καὶ πατρός· his Version is nem τοῦ Θεοῦ ouoh τοῦ πατρός. Supposing, then, that we have here a Coptic Canon equivalent to the Greek one, what is the result? It is, that of Mr. Sharp's seven texts, (for at Acts xx. 28. the Coptic read Κυρίου,) the present was understood of two persons, contrary to the interpretation of the Greek Fathers: the three next, viz. 2 Thess. i. 12. 1 Tim. v. 21. and 2 Tim. iv. 1. also of two persons: but there the Fathers are silent: Titus ii. 13. and 2 Pet. i. 1. were interpreted of one person: and Jude 4. where, however, the Coptic did not read Θεόν, is expressed, as in the Syriac, by apposition.

For the Arabic and Æthiopic I must avail myself of the assistance of Mr. *Wakefield*. His rendering of this passage is very curious, "of the anointed Teacher of God." He observes in his Note, that the Arabic and Æthiopic Versions omit καί, and he refers us in behalf of the phrase "anointed of God," to Luke ii. 26. and ix. 20. On examining the places, I find ὁ Χριστὸς Κυρίου and ὁ Χριστὸς ΤΟΥ Θεοῦ· both of which accord with the Greek usage: see on Luke i. 15: but where are we to look for ὁ Χριστὸς Θεοῦ? It is somewhat singular that a man who had devoted the greater part of his life to Philology, who had translated the N. T. and who had written the *Silva Critica* in illustration of it, should not have known that ὁ Χριστὸς Θεοῦ is not Greek. But the Arabic and Æthiopic Versions, says Mr. W., omit καί: was he, then, to learn Greek from Arabs and Æthiopians, when they presented him with a construction founded on a solecism? But after all, how does it appear that they omitted καί? I suspect, from the known analogy of the Oriental Languages, that neither the Arabic nor the Æthiopic Translator meant to indicate what Mr. Wakefield's rendering implies, that καὶ was wanting in the copies which they respectively used: for I know that in the *Peshito* ὁ Θεὸς καὶ πατὴρ is frequently, though not always, rendered by "God the Father:" I think it probable, therefore, that the

Arabic and Æthiopic Translators have here employed the same method of expressing identity.—On turning to *Bode's Pseudocritica*, which I had not seen till some part of this work had been printed off, I found the very same solution. It appears, therefore, that the Arabic and Æthiopic Translators did actually understand this passage of Him, who is Christ and God.

On the whole, I regard the present text, as it stands in the Greek, to be among the least questionable of the authorities collected by Mr. Sharp, and as being, when weighed impartially, a decisive proof, that in the judgment of St. Paul, Christ is entitled to the appellation of God.

V. 20. τῷ Θεῷ καὶ πατρί. *Macknight* would improve the English Version, " to God and the Father," which implies that *God* and *the Father* are distinct persons, by rendering " to God, *even* the Father ;" and *Abp. Newcome* does the same. I have already shown, (p. 292, and in Part i.) that καὶ in such cases is no other than the common Copulative, and if it signifies *even*, there could be no reason for omitting the second Article: the Father κατ᾽ ἐξοχὴν is always Ὁ πατήρ. It is rather remarkable, that almost all the modern Translators should, in some instances at least, have been compelled to adopt the Canon, (Part i. Chap. iii. Sect. iv. § 2.) and yet that none of them should have stumbled on the principle which must have led them to a more general application of it.

V. 23. ὁ ἀνήρ. Many MSS.—ὁ, which is not absolutely necessary. A. alone has Ὁ σωτήρ, where, however, the Article is dispensed with, as in the same verse is ἡ before κεφαλή.

CHAP. VI.

V. 2. ἐντολὴ πρώτη. *Markland* conjectures Ἡ πρώτη, though he admits that this word is elsewhere without the Article. So, frequently, are all Ordinals: see Part i. Chap. vi. § 3 [1].

[1] V. 12. ἡ πάλη, the contest referred to in the preceding verse, as Winer notes.—H. J. R.

PHILIPPIANS.

CHAP. I.

V. 25. εἰς τὴν ὑμῶν προκοπὴν καὶ χαρὰν τῆς πίστεως. Of these words there are various translations, which I forbear to enumerate. My objection to the greater part of them is, that they disjoin προκοπὴν and χαράν, as if πίστεως did not depend on the former of these as well as on the latter. That this, however, is the construction, I infer from the omission of the Article before χαράν. So in verse 7. of this chapter, ἐν τῇ ἀπολογίᾳ καὶ βεβαιώσει τοῦ εὐαγγελίου, though even there *Macknight* disjoins the two governing Nouns without any apparent reason: for the words ἀπολογία εὐαγγελίου are found in the present chapter, verse 17. Neither in the passage under review would there be any thing harsh in joining προκοπὴν with πίστεως, for in verse 12. it is joined with εὐαγγελίου, which in sense is not very dissimilar. I understand the translation, therefore, to be, "to promote your advancement and joy in the faith," i. e. for your religious improvement and your religious comfort. Macknight renders "for the advancement of the joy of your faith," which does not seem to be deducible from the Greek.

CHAP. II.

V. 2. τὸ ἓν φρονοῦντες. This reading is remarkable on two accounts, both as it is so nearly a repetition of a phrase which had already occurred in the same verse, viz. τὸ αὐτὸ φρονῆτε, and as having the Article (supposing the common interpretation to be right) prefixed to ἕν, which always is anarthrous in the N. T. except where there is some kind of reference. A. C. 17. 73. of Griesbach and the Vulg. have, indeed, the reading

CHAPTER II. 369

τὸ αὐτό : this relieves us from the difficulty attending the Article in τὸ ἕν, but it rather increases that which arises from the repetition. Those MSS. however, are of considerable authority, and it may well be contended, that even without admitting τὸ αὐτὸ the tautology is sufficiently evident : indeed *Schleusner* makes τὸ αὐτὸ φρονεῖν and τὸ ἓν φρονεῖν to be equivalent. *Markland* and the Bishop of *Durham* (apud Bowyer) suspect that one of those clauses is a marginal explanation : in the collection of Conjectures, many are much more improbable ; the suspicion, however, is not confirmed by any MS. or Version. *Rosenmüller* tells us that τὸ αὐτὸ φρονεῖν and τὸ ἓν φρονεῖν are different things : the former marking consent in doctrine, as below, iii. 16. the latter, conformity in moral conduct, as in Rom. xv. 5. But in this there must be some mistake ; for in Rom. xv. 5. it is not τὸ ἓν φρονεῖν, but τὸ αὐτό ; neither does the phrase τὸ ἓν φρονεῖν occur in the whole N. T. except in the present instance. *Blackwall* (Sacr. Class.) according to the fashion of his day, when it was presumed to be impossible that inspired thoughts could be expressed in any other than classical Greek, admits the tautology, but defends it on the authority of *Xenophon ;* the two clauses, συνεστηκότα εἰς τὸ αὐτὸ and συνεστήκοιεν εἰς ἕν, being found in the same sentence, Cyrop. p. 13. Edit. 1581. This, however, proves at most that the best writers are sometimes inattentive ; but even the reading is not indisputable ; for according to *Sturz, Lex. Xen. voce* συνίστασθαι, the Cod. Guelf. wants the latter clause : at any rate, it is observable that in Xenophon it is not εἰς ΤΟ ἕν : and in τὸ ἓν φρονοῦντες, even though the tautology could be shown to be of the essence of elegance, the Article is still to be accounted for, which can be done only by supposing some kind of reference ; since there is not in the LXX. or the N. T. any instance of τὸ ἓν in which the Article is not to be so explained : and in the profane Greek writers the usage is the same. But see on 1 John v. 7. This reference, then, I suppose here to be to what immediately follows, μηδὲν κατ' ἐριθείαν ἢ κενοδοξίαν, as if the Apostle had said, "minding *the one thing,* viz. &c." This interpretation is favoured by the Vulg. " ID IPSUM *sentientes, Nihil per contentionem neque per inanem gloriam.*" But what principally confirms my opinion is the construction of the sentence following,

B b

μηδὲν κατ' ἐριθείαν, which in having no Verb assumes the form of a proverbial admonition, such as might naturally be made a subject of reference. Thus in μηδὲν ἄγαν we must supply ποιεῖτε, exactly as in the instance before us. I observe that *Grotius* understood the passage in the manner here proposed: his words are, " HOC UNUM *studentes, maximè* SCILICET, *nequid contentiosè*," &c.

V. 4. ἀλλὰ τὰ ἑτέρων. Some good MSS. have τὰ τῶν, which is probably right.

V. 6. ἐν μορφῇ Θεοῦ. I do not recollect that any one has, in consequence of the absence of the Article, asserted that Θεοῦ is here to be taken in a lower sense; yet Mr. *Wakefield's* translation, " in a divine form," savours somewhat of this kind of criticism. The Article, however, may be omitted by Part i. Chap. iii. Sect. iii. § 7. Many modern Divines, and among the Fathers Theodoret, understand the clause οὐχ ἁρπαγμὸν ἡγήσατο somewhat differently from our English Version. The remark of Theodoret, as quoted by *Wolfius*, is, that " Christ being by nature God, and having equality with the Father, did not pique himself on this His dignity, as is the manner of those who have obtained unmerited honour ; but having renounced His high station, he condescended to the extreme of humility, and assumed the form of man." To this interpretation of ἁρπαγμὸν ἡγήσατο, the few parallel expressions which Commentators have collected, appear to me to be favourable: since the terms most nearly approaching to ἁρπαγμὸν are λαφυρόν, ἑρμαῖον, φωρίον ; and no difficulty arises from the context, the passage being introduced by the admonition, " Let this mind be in you, which was also in Christ Jesus." Not dissimilar is the praise bestowed on *Athanasius* by Greg. Naz. vol. i. p. 377. οὐ γὰρ ὁμοῦ τε καταλαμβάνει τὸν θρόνον, ὥσπερ οἱ τυραννίδα τινὰ ἢ κληρονομίαν παρὰ δόξαν ΑΡΠΑΣΑΝΤΕΣ, καὶ ὑβρίζει διὰ τὸν κόρον· a passage which I have no where seen quoted in illustration of the present verse. If, however, we admit even this explanation, the text affords the most decisive evidence of the Divinity of Christ. He is said to have been in the form and nature of God: I know not, indeed, whether ὑπάρχων may not be rendered *pre-existing;* for *Suidas*, edit. Kust. vol. iii. p. 532. observes, τὸ ὑπάρχειν οὐχ ἁπλῶς τὸ εἶναι σημαίνει ἀλλὰ τὸ πάλαι εἶναι, καὶ ΠΡΟΕΙΝΑΙ, φθάνειν· even, however, if the word be taken in its looser sense, the inference will be the same: since Theodoret's interpretation makes the humility of Christ to have consisted in His relinquishing the dignity of being equal to the Father, which, of course, it admits Him to have enjoyed; and if it was enjoyed, it could be only in a state of pre-existence. Unbelief has, indeed, endeavoured to explain away the force of the expression ἐν μορφῇ Θεοῦ: but, as is well observed by the Bishop of *Lincoln*, (Elem. of Theol. vol. ii. p. 112.) "Being in the form of God, signifies being really God, just as the phrase, 'took upon him the form of a servant, and was made in the likeness of man,' signifies, that He was really a man in a low and mean condition." Besides, the Fathers explain μορφὴ by οὐσία: see *Suicer*, vol. ii. p. 377.

V. 11. εἰς δόξαν Θεοῦ πατρός. A good instance of Part i. Chap. vi. § 1. and Chap. iii. Sect. iii. § 7.

V. 13. ὁ Θεὸς γάρ, κ. τ. λ. Many MSS.—ὁ, possibly right: so Θεὸς ὁ δικαιῶν, Rom. viii. 33.

CHAP. III.

V. 1. Many MSS. and Editt. have TO ἀσφαλές, of which I do not perceive the meaning.

V. 3. οἱ πνεύματι Θεῷ λατρεύοντες. The majority of MSS. with some of the Fathers, have here Θεοῦ: and to this reading modern Editors, as *Wetstein*, *Matthäi*, and *Griesbach*, give the preference, though *Mill* and *Bengel* prefer Θεῷ. I know of no ground for adopting Θεοῦ, except the preponderance of MSS. and I am persuaded that Θεῷ is genuine, both because πνεῦμα Θεοῦ is no where, that I recollect, used to signify the Holy Spirit, unless there be a reason for omitting the Articles, which here is not the case, and because the context plainly requires us to understand πνεύματι in the *adverbial* sense, and consequently to read Θεῷ: unless, indeed, πνεύματι Θεοῦ mean no more than πνεύματι. See above on Rom. viii. 13. The design of the Apostle is here to depreciate the rite of circumcision, as no longer of any efficacy, which therefore he contemptuously calls the κατατομή, or mutilation: he says, "beware of the *concision:* we (viz. the Christians) are the *circumcision* (ἡ περιτομὴ) who worship God spiritually, πνεύματι, and glory in Jesus, and have no trust in the flesh." Here, plainly, to worship God spiritually is made to be the essence of true Religion, as distinguished from the barren ceremonial observances on which principally the Jewish opponents of Christianity appeared to set a value. The very same argument is elsewhere urged by the Apostle, especially Rom. ii. 25. to the end of the Chapter.—He who keeps in view these remarks, can hardly fail to acquiesce in the reading Θεῷ; which is further confirmed by the Syr. and Vulg. and, if we may trust the Latin, by the Arab. and Æthiop.—Mr. *Granville Sharp*, in his Tract, second edit. p. 32. endeavours to vindicate Θεοῦ, and contends, that if Θεῷ be the reading, it ought to be rendered "the Spirit God," because the Preposition ἐν is not prefixed to πνεύματι. But of πνεύματι without ἐν, when used in the adverbial sense, many instances have been pointed out, and the N. T. supplies probably more than fifty. Besides, the Spirit God, or πνεῦμα Θεός, is a phrase which no where exists, not to insist that the duty of worshipping the Holy Spirit is entirely foreign from the reasoning.

V. 5. περιτομῇ ὀκταήμερος. Some Editions, among others that of *Matthäi*, with whom agrees *Schleusner* in his Lexicon, have περιτομὴ in the Nominative: in that case we must construe "*my* circumcision was," &c.; but then I should have expected the Article, whereas in the more common construction the Article is properly omitted. Moreover, Adjectives of time ending in ημερος and αιος are applied to *persons*, rarely to *things*. So in a passage quoted by Wetstein, we read Χριστὸς ἀνίσταται τριήμερος, and in John xi. 39. τεταρταῖος γάρ ἐστι. Thus the construction will be, "in respect of circumcision (circumcised) on the eighth day." The structure also of the whole passage will be disturbed, if we make περιτομὴ the Nominative; for the Apostle, both before and after the words in question, is himself the subject of the discourse; "I more, circumcised on the eighth day, of the race of Israel," &c.: if, therefore, περιτομὴ be the Nominative, it is strangely inserted, nor do I perceive how we can, without great violence, restore ἐγὼ in the next clause, ἐκ γένους Ἰσραήλ.

COLOSSIANS.

CHAP. I.

V. 15. πρωτότοκος πάσης κτίσεως. Our Version has "of every creature:" *Macknight* and *Wakefield*, "of the whole creation:" *Newcome* says it may be either. But this, I apprehend, is a mistake: the absence of the Article shows that κτίσις is here used for an individual, as in our Version, and not of the creation inclusively, which would have required πάσης ΤΗΣ κτίσεως : so Mark xvi. 15. and Rom. viii. 22. I do not, however, perceive that this distinction throws any light on the controversy respecting the meaning of the passage. *Michaelis,* after *Isidore the Pelusiot,* would accent the Penult πρωτοτόκος, so as to make the sense active: but then it will signify, not simply having borne or begotten, but that *for the first time :* so Homer, Il. XVII. 5. The Socinians understand πρωτότοκος to represent the Hebrew בכור, and to be thus expressive only of the dignity of primogeniture. I am surprised that this interpretation should have been adopted by *Schleusner ;* for surely nothing can be more incompatible with the whole context : in illustration of the truth that Christ is πρωτότοκος πάσης κτίσεως, the Apostle adds, that through Him (Christ) were created all things in heaven and on earth, visible and invisible, with the several orders of Angels: thus, then, it will be said that Christ was the Eldest born of his own Creation; which is so absurd, that it requires no common hardihood to defend it. Schleusner, indeed, it must be admitted, adopts the derived, not the primitive sense of πρωτότοκος, making it to signify *princeps et dominus ;* but this does not relieve the difficulty, unless an instance can be produced in which πρωτότοκος signifies *dominus* otherwise than in reference to the brethren over whom the first-born among the Jews had authority. Of the *literal* sense, the instances cited by Schleusner are, Gen. xxvii. 29. 37. and 1 Sam. xx. 29. about which there can be no doubt: for the *metaphorical* he quotes Jeremiah xxxi. 9. in which, however, there is no confusion of metaphor, the words being, " I am Father to Israel, and Ephraim is my first-born;" i. e. Ephraim shall have authority over the other tribes, who are his brethren; exactly as in Rom. viii. 29. we have πρωτότοκον ἐν πολλοῖς ἀδελφοῖς. What is wanted is an instance in which πρωτότοκος is so used in the metaphorical sense, that it not only has lost sight of its origin as a metaphor, but is used in direct contradiction to it, as is alleged in the present instance.—On the whole, I know of no better expedient than to understand the words as meaning "begotten before every creature," i. e. before any created being had existence: thus it was explained by the majority of the ancients [1]. See *Suicer*, vol. ii. p. 879. That πρῶτος may be thus used is evident from John i. 15. and 30. *Michaelis* has observed, that in the language of the Rabbins, God is called the First-born of the World. At any rate, be the meaning of this text what it may, the utmost which can be expected by the malice of heresy, and achieved by the perversion of criticism, is to detach it from the verses which immediately follow; with which, however, it seems to be most closely connected. But even this will be of no avail: with the 16th, and especially with the 17th verse, the reasonable Advocate for the Pre-existence and Divinity of Christ might, if he had no other evidence in his favour, be abundantly content. The positive assurance that Christ was before all things, and that by Him all things συνέστηκε (the word used both by *Josephus* and *Philo* of the acknowledged Creator : see *Krebs's Obss. in N. T. e Josepho;* and also by many other writers) leaves no question as to the dignity of the Redeemer of Mankind.

Mr. *Wakefield* translates, " *an* image of the invisible God, *a* first-born," &c. as if there were several such : it is difficult to suppose that he was ignorant of the usage after the Verb Substantive.

---

[1] That this is the true interpretation, can hardly be doubted ; and the doctrine is that which is more fully expressed in the Nicene Creed : " Begotten of his Father before all worlds."—The substitution of the superlative for the comparative in such cases, is too common to need illustration.—J. S.

V. 23. ἐν πάσῃ τῇ κτίσει. Several considerable MSS.—τῇ, and *Griesbach* thinks the Article probably spurious: but see the last Note. Not a single MS. of *Matthäi* omits the Article. The phrase here is equivalent to ver. 6. of this Chapter, ἐν παντὶ τῷ κόσμῳ.

CHAP. II.

V. 10. ἡ κεφαλὴ πάσης ἀρχῆς. See on 1 Cor. xi. 3.

V. 14. τὸ χειρόγραφον τοῖς δόγμασιν. There are few passages of the N. T. in the interpretation of which the Translators and Critics have more widely differed from each other. Our English Version has "hand-writing of ordinances," and this is adopted by *Macknight* and *Newcome*; though how this meaning can be deduced from the words of the original, I am at a loss to discover. *Rosenmüller* explains the Greek by "*legem illam scriptam præceptis variis constantem;*" and some have made τοῖς δόγμασιν to have no dependence on τὸ χειρόγραφον, but to be governed by ἐξαλείψας. I believe that the true construction must be sought in an Ellipsis of σύν, examples of which are common in the profane Writers: the same Ellipsis occurs also in Revel. viii. 4. ταῖς προσευχαῖς τῶν ἁγίων, which is well rendered by Abp. Newcome, "*together with* the prayers of Saints." It is some confirmation of this solution, that the Armenian adds αὐτοῦ: that two or three authorities have ΣΥΝ τοῖς δόγμασιν: and that in the Second Homily of *Clemens Romanus* (Coteler. vol. i. p. 631.) Moses is said to have delivered τὸν νόμον σὺν ταῖς ἐπιλύσεσι. The sense will thus be, "Having cancelled the bond, *together with* all its covenants [1]:" these covenants or conditions were the numerous expiations prescribed by the Levitical Law; the Bond was the Law itself. The same Ellipsis is known to the Hebrew: see *Noldius*, p. 576.

V. 17. τὸ σῶμα τοῦ Χριστοῦ. Here many MSS. including a large proportion of Matthäi's—τοῦ. This is probably right, especially since Χριστοῦ is not immediately dependent on τὸ σῶμα.

---

[1] See below, ver. 20. and Eph. ii. 15. *Author's MS.*

CHAP. IV.

V. 5. τὸν καιρὸν ἐξαγοραζόμενοι. *Macknight* renders this by "gaining time." But καιρὸς is not equivalent to χρόνος, being always used in reference to something which is to be done. It seems to be the intention of St. Paul in this place, as well as Ephes. v. 16. to admonish his Christian Readers to "purchase the opportunity, (viz. of gaining over the Heathens,) by judicious concessions, and by a virtuous example." The reason subjoined is, "that the days are evil:" i. e. the times in which ye live are so unpropitious to the conversion of the Jews and the Pagans, that the zeal and circumspection which I have recommended are indispensable.

V. 16. ἡ ἐπιστολή. See on 1 Cor. v. 9.

I. THESSALONIANS.

CHAP. II.

V. 5. Θεὸς μάρτυς. Two MSS. have ὁ Θεός. The Article is not necessary, since if μάρτυς were the subject, its Article could not be omitted [1].

CHAP. IV.

V. 6. ἐν τῷ πράγματι. Our Version has "in any matter." *Wolfius* thinks that τῷ πράγματι is equivalent to τοῖς πράγμασι, by which he understands *in business*, i. e. in commercial transactions. Our own Version has the sanction of *Schleusner*, who explains τῷ by τινι, though this, as has been shown, is an usage unknown to the N. T. He wavers, however, and supposes, that the words may mean, as they are explained by Wolfius. This Writer is supported by *Schoettgen*, (Hor. Hebr.) who reasons from what he considers as a parallelism, 2 Tim. ii. 4. ταῖς τοῦ βίου πραγματείαις : this, however, is not a parallelism, as might easily be shown. The only passage in the N. T. which is at all similar, is 2 Cor. vii. 11. ἐν τῷ πράγματι, signifying *in the matter*, viz. that of which the Apostle was speaking, the misconduct of the incestuous person; an interpreta-

---

[1] The Reader will perhaps pardon me if I stop him for a moment, to offer a gratuitous piece of service, unconnected with the doctrine of the Article, in the correction and illustration of a passage somewhat remarkable in its construction. It occurs in this Epistle, iii. 5. ἔπεμψα εἰς τὸ γνῶναι τὴν πίστιν ὑμῶν, μή πως ἐπείρασεν ὑμᾶς ὁ πειράζων, καὶ εἰς κενὸν γένηται ὁ κόπος ἡμῶν. "I sent to know your faith *whether* the tempter have tempted you by any means, and *lest* (in that case) our labour be in vain." Exactly similar is Eurip. *Phœniss.* 91-2. μή τις πολιτῶν ἐν τρίβῳ φαντάζεται, Κἀμοὶ μὲν ἔλθῃ φαῦλος, ὡς δούλῳ, ψόγος, Σοὶ δ', ὡς ἀνάσσῃ.—In both cases μή has different senses, according to the different moods with which it is connected.—J. S.

tion which Wolfius admits. And why should not the same words in this place be similarly explained? Business or commercial dealing has no relation whatever to the context. Verses 3, 4, 5, and 7, enforce the obligation to chastity: would it not, then, be extremely unnatural that the 6th should enjoin honest dealing in affairs of trade? especially when τὸ πρᾶγμα is a known euphemism for impurity. I have, therefore, no doubt that Macknight's way of understanding the passage, "in this matter," is the true one; except, indeed, that "*the* matter" suits the place as well, without needlessly multiplying the meanings of the Article. Mr. Wakefield, in his *Silva Crit.* Part i. p. 107. commends the Syr. Translation for rendering the passage, "*quasi esset ἐν τούτῳ πράγματι:*" this is not very accurate Greek.—Among the advocates for the explanation which I have adopted, are *Michaelis* and the Bishop of *Durham* (ap. Bowyer). It is remarkable, that *Grotius* should have conjectured ἔν τινι.

CHAP. V.

V. 19. τὸ πνεῦμα. If this be understood of the influence of the Spirit, the Article will be in reference to that portion of influence which each had received. I prefer, however, understanding it of the Person: compare Acts vii. 51.

V. 22. ἀπὸ παντὸς εἴδους πονηροῦ. In this place πονηροῦ cannot be used substantively for ΤΟΥ πονηροῦ, in which sense, however, modern Translators usually understand it. It is an Adjective agreeing with εἴδους: so Vulg. "*ab omni specie malâ.*"

V. 27. τὴν ἐπιστολήν. See on 1 Cor. v. 9.

II. THESSALONIANS.

CHAP. I.

V. 12. κατὰ τὴν χάριν τοῦ Θεοῦ ἡμῶν καὶ Κυρίου Ἰησοῦ Χριστοῦ. This is another of the texts on which Mr. *Granville Sharp* would rest the doctrine of the Divinity of Jesus Christ, by rendering " of our God and Lord." To the validity, however, of this and of one or two others of his proofs, there are objections, which I ought not to suppress.

Κύριος is a word which has a peculiar construction: it so far partakes of the nature of Proper Names, that it sometimes dispenses with the Article, where other words would require it. Thus, for example, had we in the present instance, instead of Κυρίου, read ΣΩΤΗΡΟΣ, no reasonable doubt could have been entertained that identity was here intended, there being no reason derived either from theory or from practice for omitting the Article before σωτῆρος, if different persons be meant. So 2 Pet. iii. 2. no one will deny that τοῦ Κυρίου καὶ σωτῆρος are spoken of one person. But Κύριος Ἰησοῦς Χριστὸς collectively is a title of our Lord familiar to the Writers of the Epistles. We have repeatedly ἀπὸ Θεοῦ πατρὸς ἡμῶν καὶ Κυρίου Ἰησοῦ Χριστοῦ· Rom. i. 7. 1 Cor. i. 3. 2 Cor. i. 2. Gal. i. 3. *et passim*. We have also, Philipp. iii. 20. Κύριον Ἰησοῦν Χριστόν. Hence it is manifest, that in the present passage there is no absolute *necessity* for detaching Κυρίου from Ἰησοῦ Χριστοῦ, in order to couple it with Θεοῦ. It is true that we find also Ὁ Κύριος Ἰησοῦς Χριστός, as Rom. xiii. 14. and 1 Cor. xvi. 21. though in both those places some MSS. after Κύριος add ἡμῶν, which would make the Article necessary. Admitting, however, the title to have been sometimes Ὁ Κύριος Ἰ. Χρ. still such is the ambiguity, that we shall not be *compelled* to apply the Canon Part i. Chap. iii. Sect. iii. § 2.

Another, however, and a much stronger doubt may arise from the little notice which the Fathers have taken of this text. Mr. *Wordsworth*, indeed, finds a passage in the 121st of the Discourses (in Latin) of *Theodorus Studites*: of this passage, in which occurs " *secundum gratiam Dei Dominique nostri Jesu Christi*," he offers what he conjectures to have been the original Greek: and that particular clause he renders by κατὰ τὴν χάριν τοῦ Θεοῦ ἡμῶν καὶ Κυρίου Ἰησοῦ Χριστοῦ. He then observes, that on this arise two questions; both of which, he presumes, must be answered in the affirmative: viz. Does not the writer (Theodorus) quote the Epistle to the Thessalonians, and does he not understand τοῦ Θεοῦ ἡμῶν καὶ Κυρίου of the same person, even Jesus Christ? for does he not, says Mr. W., use them just as *St. Cyril of Jerusalem* writes τοῦ Κυρίου καὶ σωτῆρος ἡμῶν Ἰ. Χρ.: or *St. Basil*, τοῦ Θεοῦ καὶ σωτῆρος ἡμῶν Ἰησ. Χρ.: or *St. Gregory*, τοῦ μεγάλου Θεοῦ καὶ ἀρχιποιμένος ἡμῶν Ἰ. Χρ.? The affirmative of the former of these questions, viz. that Theodorus quotes this verse, can hardly be disputed; but the second may, perhaps, be otherwise determined. It is scarcely fair to conjecture from the Latin of his Translator, *Johannes Livineius*, how Theodorus understood the passage: moreover, if the Latin of Livineius be an exact rendering of Theodorus, then must the Greek be, I think, not as Mr. W. represents it, but τοῦ Θεοῦ καὶ Κυρίου ἡμῶν: or, on the other hand, supposing Mr. W.'s Greek to be that of Theodorus, then should the Latin translation have been, " *Dei nostri et Domini;*" for to say that the present Latin is better suited to the place, would be to assume the very point in dispute. In short, the whole question appears to turn on the arrangement of the words in the original Greek, which might easily be ascertained by a reference to the Greek MS. preserved in the Bodleian: if Theodorus has τοῦ Θεοῦ καὶ Κυρίου ἡμῶν instead of τοῦ Θεοῦ ἡμῶν καί, κ. τ. λ. he presents us, indeed, with a various reading, which, had it been found in a few of the more considerable MSS. of the N. T. would have had its value: but if the Greek of Theodorus be as conjectured by Mr. W., which probably it is, it is obvious that we have

CHAPTER I. 381

here, not an illustration of the Apostle's meaning, but only the same ambiguity transcribed.

Again, as to the similarity between the supposed Greek of Theodorus and the expressions of Cyril, Basil, and Gregory, it must be observed, that in the passages recited, Κυρίου is either not found at all, or else is so placed as not to be involved in the difficulty arising from its peculiar usage. Had St. Paul written τοῦ Κυρίου ἡμῶν καὶ Θεοῦ Ἰ. Χρ. no person who had attended to the manner in which Θεὸς is used, could doubt the identity; for, otherwise, it would have been ΤΟΥ Θεοῦ : see on Ephes. v. 5. It is true, that the passage from Theodorus concludes with a Doxology, " to whom with the Father and the Holy Ghost be glory," &c. and nearly the same is immediately subjoined to the expressions cited from Cyril, Basil, and Gregory: but even this will hardly authorize the inference, that Theodorus understood the disputed words of the same Person, since even if he applied them to *two* Persons, the Doxology will still be free from absurdity, *to whom* referring to the latter.

In a subsequent Letter, (p. 57.) Mr. W. has collected various examples of the form ὁ Θεὸς καὶ Κύριος ; " and it is something," he observes, " to see that the phrase is always used of *one person*." These examples amount to twenty-six : but few of them appear to me to be much to the purpose. That Κύριος is commonly subject to the rule, there can be no doubt : the question is, whether Κύριος, being the second Attribute, may not be excepted from the rule in the particular form, Κύριος Ἰ. Χρ. : and of this form the instances adduced are not numerous: for even those which have ὁ Θεὸς καὶ Κύριος ἩΜΩΝ Ἰ. Χρ. are not admissible, because this position of ἡμῶν leaves no ambiguity : if identity were not intended, Κύριος ἡμῶν would be preceded by ὁ, as in the beginning of this very verse: the difficulty arises from the single circumstance, that Κύριος Ἰ. Χρ. is a common title of Christ, and is often used independently of all which precedes it. Now of unexceptionable instances, Mr. W. brings only two, the one from Gregory of Nyssa, ὁ δὲ Θεὸς ἡμῶν καὶ Κύριος Ἰ. Χρ. ὁ παρακαλῶν, &c. and another from the Scholiast on Jude, quoted by *Matthäi*, N. T. vol. vi. p. 235. These examples prove, I think, that Κύριος *may* be disjoined from Ἰησ. Χριστός, and be identified with a preceding Attributive; but that Κύριος may be detached from Ἰησ. Χρ. was already probable from 1 Cor. viii. 6. καὶ εἷς Κύριος Ἰησοῦς Χριστός, and also from Philipp. ii. 11: and yet those passages have been otherwise interpreted: the proof required is, that in the form Κύριος Ἰ. Χρ. so frequently occurring in the N. T. Κύριος *commonly* is to be separated from the Proper Name, in order to be joined with some preceding Attributive: and this proof, I fear, cannot be obtained. On the whole, then, I am disposed to think, that the present text affords no certain evidence in favour of Mr. Sharp. We have seen that the words Κύριος Ἰησ. Χριστὸς are usually taken together; and the acquiescence of antiquity induces a strong suspicion, that in this instance such was the received construction. On the other hand, the Syriac renders the passage by "of our God and our Lord Jesus Christ:" to modern ears, at least, this sounds like an expression of identity.

The *Unknown Writer* already alluded to, " prefers, even to the Common Version, a construction which should apply both Nouns to one Person, viz. not to Jesus, but to the God of Jesus:" and he is persuaded that the true rendering is, " by the blessing of the God of us and Lord of Jesus Christ:" p. 85. The same writer, consistent in his folly, would translate 2 Pet. i. 1. " the Saviour of Jesus Christ."

CHAP. II.

V. 3. ἡ ἀποστασία. English Version, "a falling away:" Abp. *Newcome* observes, " from the true Christian faith and practice. Some render *the* Apostacy by way of eminence: but in many places of the Greek Testament the Article is used without its exact force." Of the truth of this latter assertion, it has now, I hope, become needless that I should urge my doubt: see on Matt. v. 1. Ἀποστασία, from its use in the LXX. (for in the N. T. it is found only here and in Acts xxi. 21.) appears to denote an *act* rather than a *quality;* and if so, the Article cannot here be inserted without signifying that a *particular* act is meant. Neither do I see the necessity for denying that the Article has here its proper force: since Apostacy, however long continued, might fitly be spoken of as *the* Apostacy, the several acts marking its progress being considered as one whole.

Same v. ὁ ἄνθρωπος τῆς ἁμαρτίας. The Papist, *Bellarmine*, vol. i. p. 839. ed. 1590. contends from these words, that Antichrist must be a definite individual, being called Ὁ ἄνθρωπος τῆς ἁμαρτίας ; and he wonders that this had not been observed. This criticism, however, is well answered by *Newton* on the *Prophecies*, Diss. xxii. who says that " it is agreeable to the phraseology of Scripture, and especially that of the Prophets, to speak of a body or number of men under the character of *one*. Thus *a king* (Dan. vii. viii. Rev. xvii.) is often used for the succession of kings, and *the high priest* (Heb. ix. 7. 25.) for the series and order of high priests. A single beast (Dan. vii. viii. Rev. xiii.) often represents a whole empire or kingdom in all its changes and revolutions, from the beginning to the end. The *woman clothed with the sun* (Rev. xii. 1.) is designed as an emblem of the true Church ; as the *woman arrayed in purple and scarlet* (Rev. xvii. 4.) is the portrait of a corrupt communion. No commentator ever conceived *the whore of Babylon* to be meant of a single woman : and why then should *the man of sin* be taken for a single man?" The remark, therefore, of Bellarmine is true, that ὁ ἄνθρωπος τῆς ἁμαρτίας must primitively mean an individual ; but the inference from his remark is of no force ; since this is a case in which an individual may represent a multitude.

V. 11. τῷ ψεύδει. *Markland* (ap. Bowyer) conjectures τῷ ψευδεῖ, "the false one, or the false thing, which he uttereth." The received reading appears not to need correction ; τὸ ψεῦδος is falsehood generally: so John viii. 44. ὅταν λαλῇ τὸ ψεῦδος.

CHAP. III.

V. 3. ἀπὸ τοῦ πονηροῦ. See on Matt. v. 37.

V. 14. τῷ λογῷ ἡμῶν διὰ τῆς ἐπιστολῆς, τοῦτον σημειοῦτε. *Grotius* and others would alter the punctuation, placing a comma at ἡμῶν, and making διὰ τῆς ἐπιστολῆς depend on σημειοῦτε. According to this explanation, τῆς ἐπιστολῆς will signify a letter to be written by the Thessalonians to St. Paul. But then, I think, the Apostle would have omitted the Article, and have written either δι' ἐπιστολῆς or δι' ἐπιστολῶν, for this direct reference to a letter, which was not yet in existence, and of which, so far as I know, the future existence was not with any certainty to be presumed, appears to be unnatural, and to be unsupported by any parallel example. If, indeed, it could be shown that the Thessalonians had *promised* to write to St. Paul, then διὰ τῆς ἐπιστολῆς might mean "in *your* letter:" but this is not alleged. That δι' ἐπιστολῆς, or ἐπιστολῶν, is the proper mode of expressing " by letter," where the case admits not reference, is evident from 1 Cor. xvi. 3. and this Epist. ii. 2.

I. TIMOTHY.

CHAP. I.

V. 9. δικαίῳ νόμος οὐ κεῖται. Here we have another passage in which the Article, usually placed before νόμος, is omitted, and, as I conceive, not without design. *Macknight's* remark, that νόμος, meaning the law of Moses, commonly, but not always, has the Article, was noticed on Rom. ii. 13: and, judging from his translation, I suppose him to have considered this as one of the exceptions; for he renders " the Law," and so he explains it in his Note. Rosenmüller also informs us, that " *in explicando hoc loco mirificè a se invicem dissident et discrepant interpretes. Sed omnia sunt facilia, si animadvertas, νόμον h. l. non esse in universam legem moralem de officiis agentem (hæc enim viris etiam probis lata est,) sed severam illam legis Mosaicæ disciplinam cum suis pœnis.*" Notwithstanding these authorities, I am still of opinion that νόμος is here to be understood in the indefinite sense in which it is so frequently used in the writings of St. Paul; and that Mr. *Wakefield's* translation, " that no law lieth against a righteous man," expresses the true meaning. The Apostle had said in the preceding verse that καλὸς ὁ νόμος, ἐάν τις αὐτῷ νομίμως χρῆται, i. e. the Mosaic law is an excellent institution, if men would make it subservient to the purposes for which it was given, viz. the restraining and subduing of their vicious desires and evil habits, (for we read, Gal. iii. 19. " the law was given because of transgressions;") recollecting, continues the Apostle, that neither the Mosaic, nor *any other law*, is directed against the just and good, but only against the lawless and disorderly. So also Gal. v. 23. St. Paul, having enumerated the fruits of the Spirit, love, joy, peace, &c. subjoins, " against such there is no law," οὐκ ἔστι νόμος, which appears to be exactly equivalent to νόμος οὐ κεῖται in the present verse. In the former of these passages, Macknight explains νόμος in the same manner in which I would interpret it in both.

Neither am I aware that the objections which may be urged against this interpretation are unanswerable. It may be said that the Apostle had confessedly been speaking of the Law of Moses in the verse preceding, and that, therefore, he must be presumed to do so here also. I do not, however, deny that the Mosaic Law is *comprehended* in νόμος : I contend only, that νόμος in this place is not *limited* to that Law, but that it comprises every law written and unwritten, human and divine; nor could the argument of the Apostle be stated with greater force, than by his extending what was primarily meant of the Law of Moses to Law universally : the Mosaic Law, says St. Paul, was intended to restrain the wicked ; against the just, neither it nor any other law was ever promulged.—Again, it may be alleged that νόμος seems to be limited to the Law of Moses, inasmuch as the lawless and disorderly are explained to be those who violate the precepts of the Decalogue. This position may, perhaps, be doubted : it ought, however, to be remembered, that the precepts of the Decalogue are for the most part the precepts of the Law which is written on the heart; and that the several vices which St. Paul has enumerated, are such as every system of ethics condemns. Even, therefore, supposing him to have alluded more immediately to the Decalogue, this allusion will not be inconsistent with the supposition, that νόμος was meant of law indefinitely : and in speaking of the vices which all laws are designed to restrain, a Jew would naturally specify those which his own Law had particularly prohibited.—Lastly, it should be observed that this interpretation does not authorize any dangerous inferences, a commendable dread of which has, I suspect, led some Commentators to give the passage a different meaning from that which I defend. *Wolfius* informs us, that " *comma hoc à profanorum hominum abusu vindicat* SPENERUS in Vindiciis, &c. p. 376 :" without, however, stating either the abuse or the vindication. The work of *Spener* I have never seen : but it is easy to conjecture the nature of the abuse of this and some other passages in the writings of St. Paul, when they fall into the hands of ignorance or enthusiasm. The verse under review affords no countenance to the frenzy of those who, like the Anabaptists of Munster, first persuade themselves that they are just, and then conclude that therefore they are not amenable to the laws of the Government under which they live. There is a wide difference between affirming that the just, in the number of whom, however, no man will rank himself without extreme temerity and presumption, are not subject to any law, and saying that such are not its proper objects: the most virtuous man is and ought to be subject to the laws of his country, but he is not the object which those laws have principally in view, being the least likely to incur their penalties.

I know not of any other objections which can be opposed to the grammatical interpretation of the passage : and the weight of those adduced is not such as to preponderate against an usage, the ground of which has been explained. See Part i. Chap. iii. Sect. iii. § 5.

V. 17. τῷ δὲ βασιλεῖ τῶν αἰώνων, ἀφθάρτῳ, ἀοράτῳ, μόνῳ σοφῷ Θεῷ. English Version has, " Now unto the King eternal, immortal, invisible, the only wise God :" (and *Newcome* and *Macknight* are similar :) thus making ἀφθάρτῳ and ἀοράτῳ to agree with τῷ βασιλεῖ τῶν αἰώνων. If, however, they be meant to be taken in *immediate concord* with τῷ βασιλεῖ, it is, as has been shown, against the usage (Part i. Chap. viii.) that they should be anarthrous; and I do not perceive that they can be taken otherwise, if they agree with τῷ βασιλεῖ at all. The true construction is, " To the eternal King, the immortal, invisible, only wise God;" the Article before ἀφθάρτῳ being, as frequently elsewhere, omitted before a Title in apposition.

I have pleasure in being able, however rare the opportunities, to commend Mr. *Wakefield*; who, in this instance, has deviated from his predecessors, not without reason, though without remark. I observe that *Griesbach* in his *new* edition has put a comma after αἰώνων, as I have done above. I have no cause to infer from the Latin of any of the Oriental Versions, and certainly not from the Syriac of the *Peshito*, that the old Translators saw the true construction: yet *Gregory of Nyssa* (as cited by *Suicer*, vol. i. p. 596.) has these words:

ὅταν λέγει ὁ Θεῖος ἀπόστολος, ἀφθάρτῳ, ἀοράτῳ, μόνῳ σοφῷ Θεῷ, κ. τ. λ. If the Fathers have generally been thus correct, a question which I leave to others to examine, they were, at least in this instance, better acquainted with the Greek idiom than were the Authors of the Oriental Versions. See above on Eph. v. 5.—The word σοφῷ is wanting in many authorities, and is rejected by Griesbach.

CHAP. II.

V. 5. ἄνθρωπος Ἰησοῦς Χριστός. Such is the reading of all the MSS. *Pricæus*, however, conjectures Ὁ ἄνθρωπος, as in 1 Cor. xi. 2. Matt. xix. 17; xxiii. 9. 20. Mark xiv. 20. James iv. 12. John vi. 8; viii. 41. But none of these instances are similar to the present. For my own part, I do not perceive that the Article is wanted in this place. I understand ἄνθρωπος Ἰησ. Χρ. to be used as a Title, in the same manner with Κύριος Ἰησ. Χρ. nor could Christ be called κατ' ἐξοχήν, *the* man, not possessing the human nature in a preeminent degree. *Michaelis* observes, that *Luther* and other Translators have inserted the Article, but that he himself has been careful to omit it.

If any one be still disposed to contend for the Article, I can afford him no assistance, except by reminding him of what *Reiske* has remarked, *Orat. Gr.* vol. iii. p. 490. that before ἄνθρωπος, ἀνήρ, &c. the *Attic* Writers usually omitted the Article; though I believe that Reiske should have said rather, that they expressed the Article by the aspiration, viz. ἄνθρωπος. See *Dawes's Misc. Crit.* ed. *Burgess*, p. 123. Even this, however, will avail but little, since the vestiges of Attic usage are not in the N. T. very common.

V. 6. τὸ μαρτύριον. Of this abrupt and difficult passage, there are various readings and interpretations. D. F. G. and Codd. Latini have οὗ τὸ μαρτύριον καιροῖς ἰδίοις ἐδόθη, the sense of which is plain. A. omits τὸ μαρτύριον, and *Matthäi*, though he does not adopt this reading, thinks it better than most others of that MS. *Abp. Newcome* is of opinion that we may render "*for a testimony* to the world at the proper season:" but this, I fear, is impossible: see Part i. Chap. iii. Sect. iii. § 4. Mr. *Wakefield*, in his usual way of rendering the Article, says, "*that* testimony." I know of nothing better, if the received reading be genuine, than to put the clause into a parenthesis: "the proof of it in due season[1]."

CHAP. V.

V. 21. ἐνώπιον τοῦ Θεοῦ καὶ Κυρίου Ἰησ. Χριστοῦ. This also is one of the texts which, by applying the rule Part i. Chap. iii. Sect. iv. § 2. Mr. *Granville Sharp* would interpret as an evidence of the Divinity of Christ. Several MSS., Versions, and Fathers here omit the word Κυρίου, according to which reading the passage falls not under the rule: *Griesbach* prefixes the mark of probable spuriousness. The received reading may, however, be the true one; and in that case, the present verse will deserve consideration.

Mr. *Wordsworth*, in his examination of the Fathers, candidly avows, that "not in one instance out of fourteen quotations from the Greek Fathers, and as many at least from the Latin," is the passage explained, so as to favour Mr. Sharp. "Some of them determine nothing either way; while the greater part correspond strictly in meaning with our English Translation." I really think, supposing the copies used by these Fathers to have had the received reading, (and that *some* of them read Κυρίου, may be inferred from evidence adduced by Mr. Wordsworth,) on this supposition I cannot doubt that the particular form, Κύριος Ἰησ. Χριστὸς ought to be excepted from the rule. The grounds of this opinion have been fully detailed above, 2 Thess. i. 12: and the whole of that Note was intended to be applicable to the present verse.

Mr. W. concludes his Inquiry with stating, that "once, indeed, he thought that the Appellation Κύριος might have become so appropriate to our Saviour, as to be considered as a Proper Name." I believe that Κύριος, in the form Κύριος Ἰησ. Χρ. became, as a Title, so incorporated with the Proper Name, as to be subject to the same law: and that the Fathers, in withholding the wished for testimony from the texts in which

---

[1] V. 12. γυναικὶ διδάσκειν οὐκ ἐπιτρέπω, οὐδὲ αὐθεντεῖν ἀνδρός. Here the Article is omitted, because the Proposition is *exclusive,—any woman whatever*, Chap. iii. Scct. iii. § 5.—H. J. R.

this form occurs, corroborates the proposed interpretation of the other passages.—The Syriac has, "before God and our Lord Jesus Christ."

CHAP. VI.

V. 5. πορισμὸν εἶναι τὴν εὐσέβειαν. English Version has, "supposing that gain is godliness." But the Article, as *Abp. Newcome* has remarked, shows that εὐσέβεια is the Subject, not the Predicate.

V. 6. ἡ εὐσέβεια. F. G. add Θεοῦ, a reading which is impossible, on account of the Article before εὐσέβεια. *Matthäi* here observes, "*Est hoc recensionis Occidentalis, quod miror ab oculatissimo Griesbachio non esse animadversum.*"

II. TIMOTHY.

CHAP. I.

V. 8. συγκακοπάθησον τῷ εὐαγγελίῳ κατὰ δύναμιν Θεοῦ. Mr. *Wakefield* here acknowledges that " he is quite at a loss whether the clause κατὰ δύναμιν Θεοῦ should be joined with the Verb, or be connected with εὐαγγελίῳ, the Gospel, which is after the power of God." I cannot perceive that there is any ambiguity, for had the clause in question meant that the *Gospel* was after the power of God, the Article would have been repeated, τῷ εὐαγγελίῳ˙ ΤΩι κατὰ δύναμιν, &c. i. e. τῷ ὄντι. So in the next Chapter, ver. 1. ἐν τῇ χάριτι τῇ, κ. τ. λ. *et passim*. Nor do I know that this rule is ever violated: cases resembling 1 Pet. i. 11 ; iii. 16, &c. are rather confirmations of it. Abp. *Newcome's* Note is, " according to the support which God affords: the early Preachers of the Gospel had great support, from the certainty that God was with them."

CHAP. III.

V. 6. τὰ γυναικαρία. The best MSS. omit the Article, which has the appearance of an interpolation.

V. 16. πᾶσα γραφὴ θεόπνευστος καὶ ὠφέλιμος. This is one of the texts usually adduced in support of the inspiration of the Jewish Scriptures: but it has been doubted whether the rendering of the English Version be the true one. Some of the ancient Versions, with a few of the Fathers, would omit καί, and thus join θεόπνευστος in immediate concord with πᾶσα γραφή. In this, however, they are not supported by a single MS. still extant. Besides, it is much more easy to perceive why καὶ does not appear in these ancient Versions, than how, supposing it not to have been in the earliest MSS. it found its way into those which remain: for a Translator, who had understood θεόπνευστος as agreeing immediately with πᾶσα γραφή, as was the case with the Syr., might find it difficult to express καί, which, indeed, even in the original would thus have little meaning: on the other hand, and for the same reason, if καὶ had been wanting in the Autograph, as its introduction could tend only to embarrass the sense, it could hardly be interpolated, and still less retained, by the consent of all the Transcribers.

Mr. *Wakefield* remarks, that the "Æthiopic alone of the old Versions does not omit καί, and that the Æthiopic is with him equivalent to all the rest in a difficult or disputed passage." Notwithstanding this declaration, Mr. W. without assigning any reason, renders in defiance of the Æthiopic, "every writing inspired by God *is* useful," &c. I agree, however, with him in his translation of πᾶσα γραφή. See Part i. Chap. vii. § 1. and I take the assertion to be, "every writing (viz. of the ἱερὰ γράμματα just mentioned) is divinely inspired, and is useful," &c. I do not recollect any passage in the N. T. in which two Adjectives, apparently connected by the Copulative, were intended by the Writer to be so unnaturally disjoined. He who can produce such an instance, will do much towards establishing the plausibility of a translation, which otherwise must appear, to say the least of it, to be forced and improbable.

CHAP. IV.

V. 1. ἐνώπιον τοῦ Θεοῦ καὶ τοῦ Κυρίου Ἰησ. Χρ. There is so little authority for omitting the Article before Κυρίου, which, however, must be done before this text can be subject to the rule Part i. Chap. iii. Sect. iv. § 2. that I am rather surprised at Mr. *Granville Sharp*'s having adduced the present passage as an example. Many MSS. &c. omit τοῦ Κυρίου, and have Χριστοῦ Ἰησοῦ: the reading which is preferred by Griesbach. Some have τοῦ Κυρίου ἡμῶν. If, however, any one should prefer the few which have the requisite reading, I must, to save repetition, refer him to 1 Tim. v. 21.

TITUS.

CHAP. II.

V. 13. τοῦ μεγάλου Θεοῦ καὶ σωτῆρος ἡμῶν Ἰησ. Χρ. This text also Mr. *Granville Sharp*[1] has brought forward to notice: he translates it, "of our great God and Saviour, Jesus Christ."

---

[1] Mr. Winstanley first chooses to introduce a Comma after Θεοῦ, as he does also in the place of Jude. He then argues that μεγάλου applies both to Θεοῦ and σωτῆρος, and that this explains why the Article is not repeated. But he obviously feels that this is very forced, for he adds, ' If it be said that our Lord is no where else called the *Great Saviour,* neither is he called ὁ μέγας Θεός, *nor any thing* like it.' Now really in speaking of a human being, it may be worth while to observe, (if the case be so,) that he is often called a Saviour, but that the expression, *a Great Saviour,* does not occur. But if a being is called GOD at all, he is called something *very like* the great GOD indeed [*]. And Mr. Winstanley, of course, does not doubt this. He then states very candidly, that it is *very rare* to meet with Nouns Personal in the Singular Number thus constructed relating to *different* persons. But he thinks, that as there are instances of Nouns not personal, or where one is, and one is not, so constructed, and as he has found *one* instance in Clem. Alex. 266. viz. τῷ μόνῳ πατρὶ καὶ υἱῷ, where both are personal, (which instance is obviously one of those noted by Bp. Middleton, where the Article is omitted, because no ambiguity *could* arise,) he thinks himself justified in differing from Mr. Sharp. This needs no further remark. His only argument besides these is a mere *petitio principii,* viz. that the words τοῦ μεγάλου Θεοῦ have a *just* claim to be considered as one of the *incommunicable* titles of GOD the Father. He seeks to answer the argument that ἐπιφάνεια is never used but of Christ, by saying that it is of no consequence, for (as he found in Erasmus) St. Paul is not speaking of the appearance of GOD but of the glory of GOD; and our Lord has told us that He will come in the glory of His Father. Mr. Winstanley might as well have added Erasmus's observation, that the omission of the Article *makes something* for the opposite (i. e. Mr. Sharp's) opinion.—H. J. R.

---

[*] St. Athanasius *(De Communi Ess.* 27.) undertakes to show ὅτι μέγας Θεὸς ἐκλήθη ὁ υἱός, and he quotes Rom. ix. 5. as well as this place : so that he differed from Mr. Winstanley. See Dr. Wordsworth, p. 69.—H. J. R.

According to the principles already laid down, it is impossible to understand Θεοῦ and σωτῆρος otherwise than of one person, (see on Ephesians v. 5. and 2 Thess. i. 12.) the word σωτὴρ not being exempted from the operation of the rule : nor is there a single instance in the whole N. T. in which σωτῆρος ἡμῶν occurs without the Article, except in cases like the present, and in 1 Tim. i. 1. κατ᾽ ἐπιταγὴν Θεοῦ σωτῆρος ἡμῶν, where σωτῆρος wants the Article, on account of the preceding omission before Θεοῦ, exactly as in the common forms, ἀπὸ Θεοῦ πατρὸς ἡμῶν, ἐν Θεῷ πατρὶ ἡμῶν, &c. *Clarke*, indeed, (*Reply to Nelson*, p. 88.) endeavours to get rid of the true rendering, by observing that σωτὴρ is sometimes put for Ὁ σωτήρ : and he instances Luke ii. 11. Phil. iii. 20. and 1 Tim. i. 1. These examples, however, are wholly inapplicable to the present case : the last has been adverted to in this Note ; the first, in its proper place ; and for Phil. iii. 20. I refer the Reader to the Note on Acts xiii. 23. Clarke thinks that σωτήρ, like Θεὸς and Κύριος, partakes in some degree of the nature of Proper Names : that Κύριος and even Θεὸς have some peculiarities, has been shown above, on Luke i. 15. I know not, however, of any proof that σωτὴρ has the same peculiarities ; and even Θεὸς and Κύριος are not used with the latitude supposed by Clarke : where, for instance, are we to look for Θεὸς ἡμῶν, no rule or usage accounting for the omission of the Article? But this is only a weak attempt to embarrass an antagonist. Accordingly, we learn from Mr. *Wordsworth*[1], that all antiquity agreed in the proposed interpretation ; and many of the passages which he has produced from the Fathers, could not have been more direct and explicit, if they had been forged with a view to the dispute.

Some Critics, indeed, of great name, besides Clarke, seem to have been aware of the ancient interpretation : of this number was *Wetstein*, who, without adverting to any of the *Greek* Fathers, informs us that μέγας Θεὸς is to be understood

---

[1] Dr. Routh (Reliq. Sacr. ii. p. 26.) adds two more to Dr. Wordsworth's very large collections, viz. Didymus Alexandr. De Trinitate, tom. iii. 2. § 16. Εἰ τοῦ μόνου Θεοῦ ἐξαίρετον τὸ ὑμνεῖσθαι μέγας Θεός· ἀναφθέγγεται δ᾽ ὁ Παῦλος τοῦ μεγάλου Θεοῦ καὶ Σωτῆρος ἡμῶν Ἰ. Χ. ; and the title of the first Homily ascribed to Amphilochius, Εἰς τὰ γενέθλα τοῦ μεγάλου Θεοῦ καὶ σωτῆρος ἡμῶν Ἰ. Χ.— H. J. R.

of *Deus Pater;* and he concludes with observing, that it was so understood by *Hilary, Erasmus,* and *H. Grotius:* i. e. by a *Latin* Writer, a native of *Sardinia,* who probably had at most but a smattering of Greek, and by two modern Scholars, confessedly great men, but, compared with ancient Greeks, extremely incompetent judges of the question. Of Erasmus, especially, this may be affirmed; for an acquaintance with Greek criticism was certainly not among his best acquirements; as his Greek Testament plainly proves: indeed he seems not to have had a very happy talent for languages. But what says Erasmus on this text? he tells us that the expression is *equivocal:* he is inclined to think that two persons are meant; yet he allows that the omission of the Article before σωτῆρος *(facit nonnihil)* is somewhat in favour of the contrary opinion. Grotius, it must be admitted, went very far beyond Erasmus in the knowledge of Greek: yet what does he urge which could thus influence the mind of Wetstein against the concurring judgment of antiquity? Grotius tells us only, that Ambrose (i. e. the aforesaid Latin writer, Hilary, the author of the Commentary printed with the works of Ambrose) understood the words as of two distinct persons: and that though the reading is not ΤΟΥ σωτῆρος, yet " it should be recollected that in these writings the Article is often inserted where it is not necessary, and omitted where the usage would require its insertion." *Tædet jam audire eadem millies.* Grotius's statement amounts only to this, that he preferred one interpretation, yet knew not well what could be said against the other.— That the Reader may not be misled by high authority, I will refer him to Matt. xviii. 17. Mark xvi. 16. John vi. 40. Acts xxvi. 30; xxvii. 11. 2 Cor. i. 3. Coloss. ii. 2. 1 Thess. iii. 11. 2 Thess. ii. 16. *et passim.* These instances prove, that by the Sacred Writers the rule, both as it respects diversity and identity, has been observed: and where is the instance in which it has been violated? It is idle to tell us, that a certain Canon is applicable to other Greek writings, but not to these, without attempting to prove so remarkable a difference by a single example.

The *Unknown Writer* here again attacks Mr. Sharp and Mr. Wordsworth; but, as usual, has proved only his utter ignorance of the idiom on which he pretends to write. He says, p. 88.

"the Article which precedes the first Noun, must be supplied by Ellipsis before the second:" and on this *axiom* he founds a sort of *reductio ad absurdum*. But where did he learn that a second Article was thus to be supplied by Ellipsis? In such a phrase as ὁ Κύριος καὶ σωτήρ, a second Article is *not* to be supplied; for then it might as well be expressed; and if it were expressed, ὁ Κύριος καὶ Ὁ σωτήρ, then we should have two Pronouns, and consequently two different subjects, with their distinct attributes, instead of one Subject, to whom two attributes are assumed to belong. See Part i. Chap. iii. Sect. iv. § 2. This writer seems still to have had floating in his mind his English illustration of "the King and Queen." See on Ephes. v. 5. To that his reasoning may, for any thing that I know, apply: that it has nothing to do with the Greek idiom, he might possibly have discovered, had he taken the pains to inquire. But what absurdities were not to be expected in a philological discussion which sets out with the principle, that what is true of one language, must be equally true of another?

The Syriac has in this place, "of the Great God and our Redeemer Jesus Christ."—In the *Annotations* of the *Assembly of Divines*, 1651, it is observed on this passage, "To the confutation and confusion of all that deny the Deity of Christ, the Apostle here calleth him not only God, but the great God." It would be a curious inquiry, but probably an unsuccessful one, to attempt to discover the reason why King James's Translators, about forty years before, rejected the true rendering of the passage: if, indeed, their own rendering (which may, perhaps, be questionable) were not intended to convey the real sense.

CHAP. III.

V. 4. ἡ φιλανθρωπία τοῦ σωτῆρος ἡμῶν Θεοῦ. This and some other similar passages ought in strictness to be rendered, "of our Saviour God," as if σωτὴρ had been an Adjective: the common rendering would require τοῦ Θεοῦ τοῦ σωτῆρος ἡμῶν. Τῷ σωτῆρι Θεῷ has been already quoted from an Inscription, Acts xvii. 23. It may be questioned whether, in this place, as well as Chap. i. 3; ii. 10. and 1 Tim. ii. 2. the "Saviour God" be not *Christ*, though usually understood of

CHAPTER III.

the Father. The Nouns which severally govern these Genitives, more especially διδασκαλία, ii. 10. strongly support this conjecture.

V. 5. διὰ λουτροῦ παλιγγενεσίας. A. alone has ΤΟΥ λουτροῦ. This is another instance of a reading which could scarcely have proceeded from a Greek copyist. See on Acts viii. 5.

Same v. πνεύματος ἁγίου. I understand this of the *influence*.

V. 8. τὰ καλά. I do not perceive the force of the Article: many of the best MSS. omit it.

PHILEMON.

V. 9. ὡς Παῦλος πρεσβύτης. The common reading, "as Paul the aged," conveys the idea that the Apostle was thus distinguished from others of the same name. The want of the Article in the original shows that nothing of this kind was meant: " Paul, an old man," is all which there appears. In Arist. Eth. Eudem. lib. i. cap. 5. we read Σωκράτης μὲν οὖν Ὁ πρεσβύτης ᾤετο, κ. τ. λ.

HEBREWS.

CHAP. I.

V. 3. ὃς ὢν ἀπαύγασμα τῆς δόξης καὶ χαρακτήρ, &c. *Macknight* is induced, by the absence of the Article, to translate "an effulgence," which impresses on the English Reader a somewhat different notion. This caution was wholly unnecessary after ὢν. See on Rom. ix. 5 [1].

V. 7. τοὺς ἀγγέλους αὐτοῦ πνεύματα καὶ τοὺς λειτουργοὺς αὐτοῦ πυρὸς φλόγα. Abp. *Newcome*, adopting the opinion of many eminent critics, translates, "who maketh the winds his angels, and flames of lightning his ministers." His translation, however, would require τὰ πνεύματα ἀγγέλους αὐτοῦ καὶ τὴν φλόγα τοῦ πυρὸς λειτουργούς. No usage in the language is more strictly observed: so in this chapter, ver. 13. See Part i. Chap. iii. Sect. iii. § 2. The passage is quoted *verbatim* from the LXX. Ps. civ. 4. *Michaelis*, (Introd. Chap. xxiv. Sect. xi. vol. iv.) on this and some other similar quotations, founds an argument for the Hebrew original of this Epistle.

V. 8. ὁ θρόνος σου, ὁ Θεός, εἰς τὸν αἰῶνα, κ. τ. λ. The English Version here makes ὁ Θεός, as is common elsewhere, to be the Vocative case: but Mr. *Wakefield* ventures to translate, "God is thy throne;" and in defence of this translation, which indeed may boast the support of *Grotius* and *Rosenmüller*, and also of *Semler* and *Döderlein*, (see *Abresch* Paraphr. in Epist. ad Hebr.) he refers us to his work on *Early Opinions concerning Christ*, p. 274. The substance of his defence is contained in the remark, that it is "contrary to the scope of the Psalm," (viz. the xlv. from which the passage is

---

[1] Again, καθαρισμὸν ποιησάμενος τῶν ἁμαρτιῶν. This is explained on the same principle, and by a reference to Chap. iii. Sect. iii. § 3.—H. J. R.

cited,) " and to the rules of grammatical interpretation," to understand ὁ Θεὸς of an address to the Deity. As to the *scope* of the Psalm, Mr. W. supposes the subject of it to be the marriage of Solomon with Pharaoh's daughter. But the Rabbins (see *Schoettgen's* Hor. Hebr. and *Macknight*, and some good remarks in *Surenhus*. Βιβλ. καταλλ.) explained that Psalm of the Messiah : and, what is still more important, the verse in question is positively applied to the Messiah by the Writer of the Epistle, in the chapter under review ; the whole of which is clearly intended to prove the superiority of Christ over all created beings : and he cites the verse as having reference πρὸς τὸν υἱόν. It is, therefore, most certain that the Psalm relates, if not in a primary, at least in a *secondary* sense (see below on ii. 6.) to the Messiah ; and the *scope* of the composition by no means excludes an address, if I must not, in deference to Socinian prejudices, say " to the *Deity*," at least to One who, in the Hebrew, is called *Elohim*, and even *Jehovah*, (Isaiah xl. 3. Jer. xxiii. 6.) and in the N. T. Θεός.—With respect to the "rules of grammatical interpretation," Mr. W. is, if posssible, even more unfortunate. As a Philologist, he should have produced a few unquestionable instances in proof that the construction which he would vindicate, is not without its parallel : for to suppose him ignorant that it is attended with some difficulty, is scarcely possible. The difficulty alluded to lies in the Article prefixed to θρόνος σου. I have, indeed, generally objected to the LXX. as evidence in questions respecting the Greek idiom : but as the present passage is a citation from the Septuagint Version of the Psalms, I am bounden in this instance to place those Translators, so far at least as the Psalms are concerned, on the same footing with the Writers of the N. T., reserving to myself, however, the right of objecting to the reading, where circumstances render it suspicious, in a work which abounds with corruptions. Now the point for which I contend is, that the Socinian interpretation would require simply θρόνος σου ὁ Θεός. Thus Rom. i. 9. μάρτυς γάρ μου ἐστὶν ὁ Θεός· which is repeated Philipp. i. 8. So also in the LXX. Psalm xxiv. 1. Κύριος φωτισμός μου καὶ σωτήρ μου. Ps. xxvii. 7. Κύριος βοηθός μου καὶ ὑπερασπιστής μου. Ps. liii. 6. ὁ Κύριος ἀντιλήπτωρ τῆς ψυχῆς μου. Ps. lxi. 7. αὐτὸς Θεός μου καὶ σωτήρ

CHAPTER I. 401

μου. Ps. lxxiii. 12. ὁ δὲ Θεὸς βασιλεὺς ἡμῶν πρὸ αἰῶνος. I will add another instance, because it is adduced by Mr. W. himself, to show that God may be styled the rock, the fortress, &c. of David: it is Ps. xvii. 3. where, though he speaks of grammatical interpretation, the Critic has never noticed the grammatical objection which that very passage opposes again and again to the translation which he defends: the Psalmist is by the LXX. made thus to express himself; Κύριος στερέωμά μου καὶ καταφυγή μου καὶ ῥυστής μου, ὁ Θεός μου, βοηθός μου, καὶ ἐλπιῶ ἐπ' αὐτόν, ὑπερασπιστής μου καὶ κέρας σωτηρίας μου, ἀντιλήπτωρ μου. Now in this accumulation of examples in a single verse, there is but one which even apparently favours Mr. W., while the rest are decidedly against him; and that one on examination vanishes; I mean Ὁ Θεός μου, where the reader of the English Version might suppose that the Article, according to my argument, should not appear. This Psalm, however, is found likewise in 2 Sam. xxii. where, instead of ὁ Θεός μου, βοηθός μου, we read ὁ Θεός μου φύλαξ ΕΣΤΑΙ μου, whence it is to be inferred, that in Ps. xvii. also we should translate, not "my God my helper," as Predicates of Κύριος, but "my God *is* (or, shall be) my helper:" for in Hebrew the Verb Substantive frequently suffers Ellipsis.—Many more proofs might easily be adduced of an usage which is constant; and fewer would have been sufficient, if there were not persons who regard Mr. W. as an oracle of erudition.

I ought not, however, to suppress, that Mr. Wakefield, apprehending, as I suppose, that his translation of this verse might not be satisfactory to *all* his Readers, subjoins in his *Early Opinions,* " Or perhaps, *Thy throne is the everlasting God.*" Mr. W. found, no doubt, in common with other men, that it is sometimes easier to devise false solutions, than it is to discover the true one, or, where the truth is unwelcome, ingenuously to avow it: and here also, as usually happens to those who once equivocate, the progress is from bad to worse. The former interpretation has been shown to be incompatible with the idiom of the Greek language: the latter offends, if I mistake not, against both the Greek and Hebrew idioms, and also against common sense. I cannot easily believe that even the LXX. would admit such a solecism as "thy throne is ὁ Θεὸς εἰς τὸν αἰῶνα," meaning Θεὸς ὁ εἰς τὸν αἰῶνα: and if an

D d

example can be found in the Hebrew, where God is called אלהים עולם ועד, meaning *the Everlasting God*, it has escaped my notice; while the instances in which עולם ועד are used to mark the duration of the action, passion, or existence signified in the Verb, are numerous; thus, as a single example, Psalm lii. 10. בטחתי בחסד אלהים עולם ועד, the meaning is not, " I confide *in the Eternal God*," but " I confide to all eternity in God."—As to the Proposition, " thy throne is the everlasting God," if it be a mere inversion of the Subject and Predicate, it is resolvible into the former rendering, and has only the semblance of novelty: but if ὁ θρόνος σου be really to be taken as the Subject, then is this second attempt of the very essence of absurdity; for what can be understood by saying, " thy throne (i. e. according to Mr. W., *Solomon's* throne) is the everlasting God?"

I will conclude with noticing what, indeed, is already known, that *Eusebius*, in his *Dem. Evang.* has, for ὁ Θεός, quoted ὦ Θεέ; and that *Wetstein*, whose bias is elsewhere sufficiently manifest, candidly admits, at ver. 9. that ὁ Θεὸς is here the Vocative, and that the Writer has called Christ by the name of God.

CHAP. II.

V. 4. ἁγίου πνεύματος. This is evidently meant of the *influence*.

V. 6. ἄνθρωπος ἢ υἱὸς ἀνθρώπου. From the present, and from one other application of the 8th Psalm, some persons have supposed that it was exclusively intended of the Messiah; and the mention of υἱὸς ἀνθρώπου may possibly have contributed, though without reason, towards confirming them in their opinion : for υἱὸς ἀνθρώπου is here no more than a common Hebraism, and cannot, as is plain from the context, be meant of the Messiah. What is the Messiah, that thou hast such regard unto Him? is a question which the Psalmist would hardly ask. It signifies, therefore, no more than "any son of man." I mean not to insist on the absence of the Articles, because in the Hebrew, before בר, the Article could not be admitted; the LXX. therefore, adhering closely to the original, have rendered υἱὸς ἀνθρώπου: and they have done so in Dan. vii. 13. But other reasons for supposing this Psalm

CHAPTER II.

to be meant exclusively of Christ, demand fuller consideration.

I scruple not to confess myself of the number of those who believe that various passages of the O. T. are capable of a twofold application, being *directly* applicable to circumstances then past, or present, or soon to be accomplished; and *indirectly* to others which Divine Providence was about to develope under a future Dispensation: nor do I perceive that on any other hypothesis we can avoid one of two great difficulties; for else we must assert, that the multitude of applications made by Christ and his Apostles are fanciful and unauthorized, and wholly inadequate to prove the points for which they are cited; or, on the other hand, we must believe that the obvious and natural sense of such passages was never intended, or that it is a mere illusion. The Christian will object to the former of these positions; the Philosopher and the Critic will not readily assent to the latter. The 8th Psalm, as well as some other parts of the O. T. quoted in this Epistle, and indeed throughout the N. T., furnishes an illustration of my statement.

Of the 8th Psalm, the primary and direct purport appears to be so certain, that it could not be mistaken. The excellent *Macknight*, however, has here a Note, in which he endeavours to prove, that the apparent and obvious sense of this Psalm has no existence. His words are, " The place here referred to is Psalm viii. which hath been generally understood of that manifestation of the being and perfections of God, which is made by the ordination of the heavenly bodies; and by the creation of man in the next degree to angels; and by giving him dominion over the creatures.—But this interpretation cannot be admitted, 1. Because at the time the Psalmist wrote, God's name was not rendered excellent in all the earth by the works of creation, as is affirmed in the first verse of the Psalm. The true God was then known only among the Israelites in the narrow country of Canaan. Neither had God displayed his glory above the manifestation thereof made by the heavens. Wherefore the first verse of the Psalm must be understood as a prediction of that greater manifestation of the name and glory of God, which was to be made in after times, by the coming of the Son of God in the flesh, and by the preaching of his Gospel.—2. Next, our Lord, Matt. xxi. 15, 16. hath expressly declared, that the second verse of this Psalm foretels the impression which the miracles wrought by God's Son in the flesh, would make on the minds of the multitude, called *babes and sucklings* on account of their openness to conviction, as well as on account of their want of literature. Struck with the number and greatness of Messiah's miracles, the multitude would salute him with hosannas, as the son of David. And thus his praise as Messiah would be perfected out of their mouth.—3. Farther, it is declared in the Psalm, that this strong proof of his Son's mission was to be ordained by God, for the confutation of infidels, his enemies, and that he *might still* or restrain the devil, the great enemy of mankind, called in the Psalm *the avenger*, because he endeavours to destroy mankind, as the avenger of blood endeavoured to destroy the manslayer, before he fled into the city of refuge.— 4. With respect to the 6th and following verses of this Psalm, they are not to be interpreted of the manifestation which God hath made of his glory by the creation of man, in regard St. Paul hath assured us, that these verses are a prediction of the incarnation, and death, and resurrection of the Son of God, and of his exaltation to the government of the world. For, having quoted these verses, he thus explains and applies them; Heb. ii. 8. *By subjecting all things to him, he hath left nothing unsubjected. But now, we do not yet see all things subjected to him.* 9. *But we see Jesus, who for a little while was made less than angels—for the suffering of death crowned with glory and honour.* Wherefore, according to the Apostle, the person who, in the Psalm, is said to be made for a little while less than angels, and whom God crowned with glory and honour, and set over the works of his hands, and put all things under his feet, is not Adam, but Jesus.—5. And whereas in the Psalm, *the beasts of the field, the fowls of the air, and the fish of the sea*, are mentioned as subjected, they were with great propriety subjected to Jesus, that he might support and govern them for the benefit of man, his chief subject on earth : seeing the happiness of man, in his present state, depends in part on the sustentation and government of the brute creation. —Here it is proper to remark, that if τὰ πάντα, the expression in the Psalm, includes *all things* without exception, as the

CHAPTER II. 405

Apostle affirms, Heb. ii. 8 : 1 Cor. xv. 27. angels as well as men being subjected to the person spoken of in the Psalm, Adam cannot be that person, since no one supposes that the angels were subjected in any manner to him."—To the 1st objection the answer is obvious, that the Hebrew כל־הארץ was quite as limited in its acceptation as Macknight could wish : see *Reland's Palæst*. B. i. C. v. : and as to the remark that " God had not yet displayed his glory above the manifestation thereof made by the heavens," it may be replied, that nothing of this kind is affirmed ; the glory of God is elsewhere said to be above the heavens, Ps. cxiii. 4 ; cxlviii. 13. meaning only, that He is the Most High.—2. The quotation made by our Saviour proves the secondary sense, against which I do not argue, whilst it by no means disproves the primary : for unquestionably the benevolence of God is conspicuous in the protection of helpless infancy against violence and oppression.—3. Macknight understands the Avenger to mean the Devil: but this, though an allowable application, is not necessarily the only sense : see Ps. xliv. 16.—4. The fourth objection seems to require no other answer than that which was offered to the second : it proves the secondary sense, without disproving the primary.—5. As to what is said of τὰ πάντα, I think the extent of that term in the Psalm is ascertained by the subjoined enumeration of the several classes of brute creatures : to say that under the same term angels must be included, because angels are subject to Christ, is to assume that the Psalm has no other than the secondary sense ; which is the very point in dispute.

The real difficulty of the Psalm as applied in the Epistle, seems to me to lie in the word מעט, which signifies both *in a small degree*, and also *for a short time :* the former sense is adapted to man, the latter to our Saviour. Macknight, indeed, alleges that man is *not* in a small degree inferior to the angels: this, probably, is true, yet it is not a truth to which the writer of the Psalm was required to attend : in proclaiming the dignity of human nature, the remark was sufficiently just, since between men and angels the writer knew not, in the chain of being, of any intermediate link. Macknight, however, adopts an expedient which, if it were authorized, would make every thing plain : he supposes the Pronoun Him, in " Thou hast made *Him*," &c. to refer, not to the immediate antecedent *Man*, or *the Son of Man*, "but to a Person not mentioned in the Psalm, of whom the Psalmist was thinking, viz. the Son of God." His proofs, however, of this usage are extremely unsatisfactory; they are, 2 Pet. ii. 11. 1 John iii. 2. 16. and 1 Pet. iii. 14. besides the present instance. Now in 1 Pet. iii. 14. τὸν δὲ φόβον ΑΥΤΩΝ pretty plainly refers to the persons from whom the suffering was to be expected, as implied in πάσχοιτε. In 2 Pet. ii. 11. the difficulty is even less; for nothing can be plainer than that κατ' αὐτῶν is against the τολμηταί, αὐθάδεις, &c. mentioned in the verse preceding. And in 1 John iii. 2. 16. I really wonder that the reference should have escaped Macknight's notice: in ver. 2. we have αὐτῷ referring to Θεοῦ in the former part of the verse; and as to ἐκεῖνος in ver. 16. it is the same with ἐκεῖνος in verses 7. 5. 3; and in ver. 3. it is the same with αὐτῷ in the verse preceding: i. e. it refers to Θεοῦ; it is first introduced with the strictest propriety, the reference being to an antecedent at some distance. A question, indeed, may be raised about the sense of Θεοῦ: is the Father meant, or is it the Son? Ver. 5. seems strongly to favour the latter supposition, for no manifestation had been made but of the Son; and in this case we have here a close parallelism to the received, though disputed, reading of 1 Tim. iii. 16. deserving some notice in the controversy.—Macknight's proofs, then, of the usage alleged, are not the most convincing: but supposing the reference in the cited passages to have been somewhat more doubtful, how will indistinctness of reference, which is all that can be pleaded, and that only in a single instance, apply to Ps. viii. ver. 6? In ver. 5. we have αὐτοῦ and αὐτόν, and in ver. 6. we have αὐτὸν again: and is it to be inferred from any proof adduced, that the last αὐτὸν relates to a person who has never been mentioned or even alluded to in any the remotest manner? This would not be indistinctness of reference, but the confusion and destruction of all reference whatever. Besides, we want a few examples of this strange anomaly deduced from the Hebrew Affixes, rather than from the Greek Pronouns Relative.—On the whole, therefore, I am persuaded that the meaning of מעט derives no illustration from Macknight's conjecture, but that it must be determined on some other ground. Three suppositions appear possible; either that the Psalmist has used this word to signify *in a small degree*, which is the more common meaning, and that the Apostle, availing himself of its ambiguity, has employed βραχύ τι in the other sense; or else that the Psalmist had by inspiration a knowledge of man's future resurrection and exaltation to the condition of angels, in which case he might properly say, *for a little time*; or, lastly, that the Apostle was content to use the phrase, as the Psalmist had used it, to signify *in a small degree*, since this was sufficiently expressive of the condition of human nature, though the other sense would have been more immediately applicable to the condescension of Christ; and of these the last appears to me to be the least embarrassed with difficulties. If the Psalmist has declared man to be little inferior to the angels, the application of this phrase to Christ will signify, that He took the human nature: the only difference will be, that what in the one case is made a matter of pride and exultation, is a subject of humiliation in the other.

I cannot, then, discover any ground for rejecting the obvious sense of the Psalm under review; and the secondary sense can as little be questioned, for a reason already assigned. And the same will be true in many other cases. Against the doctrine, therefore, of a twofold explanation, what is to be urged? I know of no objection worthy of regard, unless, indeed, it be said that the door will thus be opened to the caprice of mystics and enthusiasts. But it is not for unauthorized applications that I contend; it is only for those which have been made by Christ or his Apostles; and unless we admit that such future applications were originally intended by the Holy Spirit, who influenced the minds of the Inspired Writers with a view to this very end, it will be impossible to place any of the citations in the N. T., except, indeed, direct and avowed prophecies, on any better footing than that of being accidentally apposite to the occasion. A quotation from the Psalms by St. Paul will not, in its application, possess any advantage over a quotation from Horace by Addison.

That the difficulties on which this reasoning is founded have been felt by wise and good men, is evident from the attempt which we have witnessed in Macknight, to explain away the obvious meaning of Psalm viii.: he saw that its reference to

Christ was not to be denied nor disputed; and not admitting a double sense, he had no alternative but that which he adopted: but this is to save the application at the expense of the passage which is applied, and ultimately even of the Christian Revelation: for when once we begin to withhold from words their ordinary and natural signification, we must not complain, if Infidels charge our Religion with mysticism, or its Expositors with fraud. But to assign, on the authority of Christ and his Apostles, to certain passages of the O. T. a further and remote meaning, cannot give offence to any one who admits the possibility of Inspiration. The Being who directs the mind and its operations is Omnipotent; and he who shall concede to such a Being any purpose at all, must also concede any variety of purposes not inconsistent with his Benevolence and Wisdom. These his Attributes are known to man, chiefly by the scheme of human redemption. It is, therefore, neither unreasonable nor improbable, that having the Gospel Dispensation in view, He may not only have suggested to the Writer of the O. T. expressions and descriptions adapted to affect the minds of those who should witness their future and secondary signification, but may also have ordained various events to be the forerunners and types of others of greater moment. In examples of both these kinds of coincidence, the Sacred Volume abounds: and when we perceive how numerous are the phrases and circumstances occurring in the O. T., which admitted a hitherto unthought of application in the New, we can hardly fail to acknowledge in the transactions recorded, and in the language employed in both, one directing hand, and One Omniscient Spirit.

V. 9. τὸν δὲ βραχύ τι παρ' ἀγγέλους, κ. τ. λ. *Abresch* remarks, that "it is inconceivable how the Interpreters are embarrassed in settling the construction and sense of this passage." Yet the *construction* is very clearly defined, nor does it meet with any opposition from the context. "Him, who was made somewhat lower than the Angels," i. e. who took the human nature, "even Jesus, we behold, on account of his having suffered death, crowned with glory and honour:" the Subject is, τὸν δὲ βραχύ, κ. τ. λ. . . . . Ἰησοῦν, and the Predicate is all which follows. The subjoined clause, ὅπως . . . . . . θανάτου, I understand to be the reason assigned why

CHAPTER III.

Christ suffered death as mentioned in διὰ τὸ πάθημα. It is remarkable that the Syr. instead of χάριτι Θεοῦ, reads χάριτι Θεός, "that God might graciously taste of death." *Adler*, however, says, that some Nestorian MSS. of the Syr. have what is equivalent to *ipse enim præter Deum pro omnibus gustavit mortem:* the words *præter Deum* are explained to signify, "in his human nature." See *Verss. Syr.* p. 37.

V. 16. σπέρματος Ἀβραάμ. The Article is omitted before σπέρματος by Part i. Chap. iii. Sect. iii. § 6 : thus also οἶκος Ἰσραήλ, &c. *passim.* Mr. *Wakefield* had, therefore, no occasion to translate "*a* race of Abraham :" the Greek idiom does not require it, and the English will not endure it. These, it is true, are little things : but occurring in almost every page of his Translation, they give it the appearance of having been made by a person of whom English was not the mother-tongue. So also in the preceding chapter, ver. 2. he renders ἐν υἱῷ " by *a* Son," which of course implies a plurality of Sons : yet nothing is plainer than that the Son here spoken of is the same who, in John i. 18. is called ὁ μονογενὴς τοῦ Θεοῦ.

CHAP. III.

V. 3. τοῦ οἴκου. *Abresch* explains τοῦ by τινός, an usage unknown to the N. T. The same Critic would in the next verse make τὰ to mean ταῦτα : but see below, on vi. 3.

V. 6. οὗ οἶκος ἐσμὲν ἡμεῖς. Two MSS. read οὗ Ὁ οἶκος, and several ὃς οἶκος. It is observed by *Abresch*, that if οὗ be the true reading, the idiom requires the Article before οἶκος, and he cites Heb. xii. 26. Acts xviii. 7. John iv. 46. Rom. ii. 29. But in all these instances, the Noun governing οὗ is the Subject : here οἶκος is the Predicate, in which case the Article is usually omitted : I say *usually*, for where the Subject is a Pronoun Demonstrative, it is not improbable that an exception may exist. There is not, therefore, any reason to infer, that the received reading is faulty, and on that account to adopt the reading ὅς, which, after all, does not alter the sense : " whose household we are," is equivalent to " which household," if the former be taken in connexion with what immediately precedes.

CHAP. IV.

V. 12. ψυχῆς τε καὶ αἵματος. Part i. Chap. vi. § 2. So ἐνθυμήσεων καὶ ἐννοιῶν, after which καρδίας wants the Article by Part i. Chap. iii. Sect. iii. § 7.

CHAP. V.

V. 4. ὁ καλούμενος ...... ὁ 'Ααρών. With many MSS. we should probably omit both these Articles. The latter, indeed, may be tolerated: but the former disturbs the sense: καλούμενος is opposed to ἑαυτῷ, as if the Writer had said, "not of his own accord, but being called thereto by God."

CHAP. VI.

V. 4. τῆς δωρεᾶς τῆς ἐπουρανίου. *Abresch* here, as in some other instances, supposes the Article to supply the place of οὗτος, and renders " this heavenly gift :" and on this hypothesis principally, he founds remarks which occupy a note of considerable length. I have already had occasion to observe, that there is no authority for such a supposition. There may, indeed, be cases in which the sense will not be affected, whether we insert the Pronoun Demonstrative or not : this will depend on the context. But that τῆς is frequently put for ταύτης, is not true ; for if it be, what are the cases in which this usage is allowable ? Besides, they who make this assertion do not appear to consider, that if ταύτης, to use the present instance, were inserted, τῆς would still be requisite. See Part i. Chap. vii. § 5. They should, therefore, rather affirm, that οὗτος often suffers Ellipsis : of which, however, I have not seen any example.

V. 5. δυνάμεις τε μέλλοντος αἰῶνος. *Markland* conjectures τε ΤΟΥ μέλλοντος. This may at the first view appear requisite: yet, I believe, that the received reading is genuine, the clause being part of an *enumeration* of particulars ; hence δυνάμεις is anarthrous, and μέλλοντος αἰῶνος may be so likewise by Part i. Chap. iii. Sect. iii. § 7. In the clause preceding, had there been no enumeration, we might have expected ΤΟ καλὸν ῥῆμα ΤΟΥ Θεοῦ. So also the whole second verse of this Chapter is made up of Nouns which would not have been anarthrous in other circumstances. Very similar to the present instance is προαγούσης ἐντολῆς in the 18th verse of the next Chapter: the προάγουσα ἐντολὴ is the Law of Moses, than which nothing can be more definite: yet the Article is wanting, because ἀθέτησις is anarthrous by Part i. Chap. iii. Sect. iii. § 1. It is thus that conjectures the most plausible are often found on inquiry to be gratuitous.

The words δυνάμεις τε μέλλοντος αἰῶνος, are rendered by Tertullian *occidente jam ævo*, in accounting for which much labour had been bestowed to very little purpose: among others, *Griesbach* attempted to solve the problem, but without success. They who would see an admirable specimen of conjectural criticism, may consult *Matthäi* on this passage: his Note discovers the hand of a consummate master, as indeed does every part of his edition of the New Testament.

V. 12. τὰς ἐπαγγελίας. Mr. *Wakefield* thinks it "not improbable that we should read τῆς for τάς," and observes, that "so several of the ancient Translators appear to have read. The Participle," he adds, " is used as a Substantive as often." —What is to be gained by this emendation, he does not even hint: the word ἐπαγγελία is as frequently used in the Plural as in the Singular; and as to the remark, that Participles are often used as Substantives, if he mean that οἱ κληρονομοῦντες τῆς ἐπαγγελίας would be tolerable Greek, I apprehend that he is mistaken. "The Creator of all things" may in Greek be expressed by ὁ ποιήσας τὰ πάντα: but he who should write τῶν πάντων, would do little honour to his teacher. Yet on some points Mr. Wakefield is extremely fastidious. Thus he complains that the usual rendering of the 7th verse of this Chapter is " unintelligible and absurd ;" and he would therefore join ἀπὸ τοῦ Θεοῦ, placed at the end of the sentence, with ἐρχόμενον, which stands near the beginning. He then refers us to Acts xiv. 17. Zech. x. 1. and to a few passages of the Classics, which represent rain as *coming from God*, though not to a quarter of those which ascertain the same undisputed fact. If this and some others of his Notes were not written with the intention of making criticism ridiculous, it will be difficult to assign to their Author any thing like an adequate motive:

compared with them, the *Virgilius restauratus* of *Martinus Scriblerus* scarcely maintains its pre-eminence.—In proof that μεταλαμβάνει εὐλογίας ἀπὸ τοῦ Θεοῦ, applied to the earth, is unexceptionable, the Reader may consult Gen. xxvii. 27. and xlix. 25.

V. 16. πάσης ἀντιλογίας πέρας εἰς βεβαίωσιν ὁ ὅρκος. Translators generally connect εἰς βεβαίωσιν with ὁ ὅρκος. But then we should have read ὁ εἰς βεβαίωσιν ὅρκος: in which remark, however, I find that I have been anticipated: see *Abresch*. The meaning is, " The oath (implied in ὀμνύουσι preceding) is to them the termination of all controversy unto confirmation :" i. e. it causes uncertainty to end in assurance.

CHAP. VII.

V. 1. οὗτος γὰρ ὁ Μελχισεδέκ. Some doubt has arisen whether these words are to be taken in immediate concord: the Article appears to me to prove that they are.

Same v. τοῦ Θεοῦ ὑψίστου. With many MSS. *Wetstein* and *Griesbach* have ΤΟΥ ὑψίστου, which is absolutely necessary. Part i. Chap. viii. § 1. Scarcely any of *Matthäi's* MSS. want the true reading.

V. 12. καὶ νόμου. Here it is not denied that the Levitical Law is meant. See what is said on ver. 18. of this Chapter; above, vi. 5.

CHAP. VIII.

[1] V. 4. ὄντων τῶν ἱερέων τῶν προσφερόντων. Three MSS. and as many Versions want the words τῶν ἱερέων, and three of *Matthäi's* omit only the former Article. This latter reading is to be preferred; "there being Priests," &c. Part i. Chap. iii. Sect. iii. § 1.

Same v. τὰ δῶρα, *the* gifts, in reference to the Law just mentioned.

---

[1] V. 2. τῶν ἁγίων λειτουργός. Λειτουργὸς is here the Predicate of ὅς in v. 1. —H. J. R.

CHAPTER IX.

CHAP. IX.

V. 1. τό, τε ἅγιον κοσμικόν. English Version, "a worldly sanctuary." This rendering is wholly inadmissible; it would require us to read either τὸ ἅγιον ΤΟ κοσμικόν, or else τὸ κοσμικὸν ἅγιον· of the present form, the whole N. T. furnishes not, I believe, one unexceptionable instance: *apparent* examples may always be corrected by the help of the MSS.: see on vii. 1. and on 1 John v. 20. Or if it be thought that where a Copulative follows the Article, the rules may be dispensed with, I offer to the reader's notice, out of a multitude of instances, the following: Xen. Hell. iv. p. 314. τά τε μακρὰ τείχη· Arist. de Rep. v. cap. 12. τῆς τε γὰρ ἀρίστης πολιτείας· LXX. Ex. xx. 10. τῇ δὲ ἡμέρᾳ τῇ ἑβδόμῃ· Matt. vii. 17. τὸ δὲ σαπρὸν δένδρον. It is, therefore, matter of surprise, that this difficulty has not been generally observed; yet, so far as I know, Translators both ancient and modern, with a single exception, have acquiesced in the common construction. Mr. *Wakefield*, indeed, tells us, "that the reading ΤΟΝ τε ἅγιον ΚΟΣΜΟΝ, so suitable to the context, was a conjecture of his in very early life, and that he afterwards found it to be the reading followed by the Coptic Translator." He then refers us to his *Silva Crit.* Part v. § 216; where, however, he abandons his emendation, on discovering in *Josephus de B. J.* lib. iv. the phrase τὴν ἱερὰν ἐσθῆτα περικείμενοι καὶ τῆς κοσμικῆς λατρείας κατάρχοντες. This Critic, therefore, was led to his conjecture merely by the exigency of the context; but he did not perceive that the short quotation from Josephus contains *two* examples so unfavourable to the common construction of the passage, that they should rather have encouraged him to proceed in attempting a new interpretation. It is neither τὴν ἐσθῆτα ἱερὰν nor τῆς λατρείας κοσμικῆς· he saw, however, that κοσμικῆς might be an Epithet of λατρείας, and with this he was satisfied.

The Coptic was supposed by Mr. W. to have read conformably with his conjecture. This is a very curious circumstance. The Latin of *Wilkins* is, "*primum quidem igitur tabernaculum habuit justitias ministerii et* SANCTUM SPLENDOREM:" the Coptic word, which is here rendered *splendorem*, is by La Croze (Lex. Ægypt.) explained by *ornamentum*. Had, then, the Coptic Translator the reading ΤΟΝ ἅγιον ΚΟΣΜΟΝ, the sacred furniture? I believe not; but that his interpretation was founded on the reading of all the MSS. τὸ ἅγιον κοσμικόν. In Rabbinical Hebrew we meet with the very word קוזמיקון, explained by *Buxtorf* (Lex. Talm. p. 2006, who cites a passage from the Bereschith Rabba, § 19.) to signify *ornamenta*; and *Schoettgen*, Hor. Hebr. adduces a Gloss on the same passage, which interprets the words by מיני תבשימין *species vestium pretiosarum*. It is, therefore, conceivable that the Coptic Translator's *et sanctum splendorem* or *ornamentum*, may be accounted for without having recourse to conjecture; and that too, on either of the hypotheses as to the language in which this Epistle was originally written. If it were written, as several of the Fathers assert, and as *Michaelis*, Introd. vol. iv. p. 215. attempts to prove by very ingenious arguments, in *Talmudic Hebrew*, it is not impossible that the Coptic Version might have been made immediately from an original, in which there was no ambiguity: for supposing the Hebrew to have been קוזמיקון קדיש, something equivalent to *sanctum ornamentum* would be the almost inevitable translation. It is true, that this is to assume either that the Coptic Version was made very early, or else that the original Hebrew of the Epistle was extant for a considerable time. In the opinion of *Wilkins*, the Editor of that Version, it was made in the middle of the third century; but supposing it to have been of somewhat later date, I do not discover any difficulty in the supposition, that a copy of the original might have been preserved through such a period, and yet afterwards have disappeared. Every one knows that Greek MSS., which were in use among Scholars two or three centuries ago, are no longer to be found.— On the other hand, if we assume that the present Greek is the original of the Epistle, or, which is here the same thing, that the Coptic Version was made from the Greek Translation, there are two points to be conceded; one of which is certain, and the other not extremely improbable: first, That the word κοσμικὸν existed as a Greek Substantive: of which there cannot be any doubt, since we have found the very word written in Hebrew characters, any more than there could be of the existence in Greek of a multitude of other Talmudic Substantives, פרהסיא, דיתיקי, παῤῥησία, διαθήκη, &c. supposing them of less frequent occurrence in the Greek Writers; — and, secondly, That the Coptic Translator might know κοσμικὸν in this place to be a Substantive, though three or four other Translators from the Greek were either ignorant of this usage, or did not advert to it: the extent of this improbability every one sees at once.

The next question respects the context, in deference to which Mr. Wakefield was led to risk his conjecture: but of the context we cannot judge, unless we first agree as to the Substantive to be joined with ἡ πρώτη. If we read with some authorities, ἡ πρώτη σκηνή, then, as *Wolfius* observes, ἅγιον, meaning the sanctuary, will not suit the passage, since the Tabernacle cannot well be said to comprise itself: for which reason, by τὸ ἅγιον he would understand *vasa sacra totumque apparatum Leviticum*, which is precisely what I suppose κοσμικὸν to mean. *Schleusner*, indeed, explains ἡ πρώτη σκηνὴ by *œconomia Mosaica*, to which the objection of Wolfius will not apply.—The great majority, however, of MSS. and other authorities, omit σκηνή, and make ἡ πρώτη to agree with διαθήκη mentioned in the preceding verse; a reading which Mr. Wakefield, with most Critics, adopts. According to this, if the substantive sense of κοσμικὸν be not necessary, it is at least perfectly admissible; for nothing can be more apposite than to say, that " the former Covenant had ordinances of worship, and the splendour of the Levitical Priesthood."

Lastly, if it should be thought that, after all, κοσμικὸν must be rendered as an Adjective, I am ready to allow that this sense is possible, though not so the received construction: κοσμικὸν cannot be *assumed* of τὸ ἅγιον, but must be *asserted* of it by an Ellipsis of ἦν or ὥστε εἶναι: " the sanctuary (was) κοσμικόν," or it had its sanctuary (so as to be) κοσμικόν, which in this case I should render *emblematic of the mundane system*. *Macknight*, though he did not attend to the construction, appears to have thought that κοσμικὸν might be so translated; since in his view of this Chapter he observes, " The Apostle begins with acknowledging that the Covenant made at Sinai, of which the Levitical Priests were the Mediators, had ordinances of worship appointed by God himself, and *a sanctuary which was a representation of the world or universe*." He afterwards refers us to the well-known account of the Tabernacle, given by *Josephus, Antiq.* lib. iii. § 7. edit. Hudson. According to this construction, it will follow that the Coptic Translator mistook the Adjective κοσμικὸν for the Substantive; which, however, is extremely improbable: he could not fail to know the adjective sense of the word, though other Translators may easily be imagined to have been unacquainted with its substantive sense. On the whole, I prefer the construction adopted by the Coptic Version.—A friend of mine, whom I shall characterize as another *Nicias*,

- - - - - - - ἰατρὸν ἐόντα,
Καὶ ταῖς ἐννέα δὴ πεφιλαμένον ἔξοχα Μοίσαις,

on having read this Note, suggested that τὸ ἅγιον κοσμικὸν may mean *the Holy Beauty*, or *Beauty of Holiness*, mentioned Ps. xxix. 2. and elsewhere. To say the least of this conjecture, it is too good to be thrown away.

V. 7. ἅπαξ τοῦ ἐνιαυτοῦ. So Luke xviii. 12. δὶς τοῦ σαββάτου. See above, on Matt. xx. 2 [1].

V. 8. τοῦ πνεύματος τοῦ ἁγίου. With the Articles, as usual, where an act is imputed to the Holy Spirit. So above, iii. 7. and below, x. 14. Also in the 14th verse of this Chapter, διὰ πνεύματος αἰωνίου may be taken in the Personal sense, the Articles being omitted on account of the Preposition: though many with *Vitringa, Obss. Sacræ*, vol. i. 1031. understand it of the Divine Nature of Christ. For myself, I prefer the former: compare Rom. viii. 11. Some authorities, indeed, for αἰωνίου have ἁγίου, which would leave no doubt: but the other reading greatly preponderates.

Mr. *Wakefield* would not omit either epithet. He translates, "who offered himself with a spotless mind unto God;" and in his Note he observes, "διὰ πνεύματος ἄμωμον" (ἀμώμου I suppose to have been an error of the press) "more literally, spotless in his mind," adding that the Æthiopic has no epithet to πνεύματος. Thus this single Version, whenever it can be made subservient to the purpose of getting rid of an obnoxious phrase, is to be paramount to all other authorities. Perhaps, however, Mr. Wakefield's affection for the Æthiopic would not have increased, on a more intimate acquaintance with it.

---

[1] See Note, p. 41.—J. S.

CHAPTER X.

On one occasion at least (see above, p. 366.) he was by this very Version " deserted at his utmost need," and that too at the moment when it was practising on his credulity by insidious offers of support. And how far, in the present instance, does it succour him in his distress? Not, as I suspect, in the smallest degree: for the Latin, which from its similarity to the Greek, can here hardly be incorrect, has "*qui obtulit seipsum per Spiritum Deo absque maculâ:*" the whole of which amounts to nothing more than that this Translator has said, "the Spirit," meaning the Holy Spirit, than which nothing is more common. Or would Mr. W. render "*per Spiritum absque maculâ*" by *spotless in his mind*? It will bear this translation just as well as does the Greek: for supposing διὰ πνεύματος to be the true reading, and conceding to Mr. W. the privilege of forcing ἄμωμον out of its place, where are we to look for a phrase similar to διὰ πνεύματος ἄμωμον, *spotless in his mind?* When Christ is said to be *troubled* in his mind or spirit, we read, John xiii. 21. ἐταράχθη τῷ πνεύματι: and " the humble in spirit" are called (Matt. v. 3.) πτωχοὶ τῷ πνεύματι, not διὰ πνεύματος.—The reading ἁγίου, the same Writer thinks, " is not amiss," meaning *with a holy mind:* but here again we have to seek for authorities which may justify such a translation. It is painful to behold a man whose general character and conduct betrayed no want of pride, thus condescending to subterfuge after subterfuge, and ready to submit to any expedient, however humiliating, if it promised but for a moment to aid the cause which he had at heart. Ἀλήθειαν καὶ Παρρησίαν was the Motto which Mr. Wakefield caused to be inscribed on his portrait: in the exercise of the latter of these, he yielded to no controul; it were much to be wished that his adherence to the former had been equally unshaken. Candour, indeed, requires us to impute to ignorance, that which cannot be proved to originate in malice. There is, however, in the ignorance of this writer, if so we must regard it, the consistency which usually marks design: his ignorance uniformly operates to a given end: and if this be the ground on which his advocates shall choose to defend his integrity, they must concede that his learning was prodigiously overrated, and must assign him a place among scholars of far more modest pretensions [1].

---

[1] V. 13. Τὸ αἷμα ταύρων καὶ τράγων. See Chap. vi. § 2. *et infra.*—H. J. R.

¹ V. 21. τῷ αἵματι, *the* blood; mentioned above, ver. 19.

V. 27. κρίσις. This word, though used of the final judgment, very properly wants the Article in this place; the Proposition not asserting the notoriety or magnitude of the event, but only that it will happen.

V. 28. εἰς τὸ πολλῶν. Here *Bentley* conjectured εἰς τὸ ΤΩΝ πολλῶν: but this, like the multitude of conjectures on the N. T., remains unconfirmed by subsequent collations of MSS.; neither do I perceive, *pace dixerim viri tanti*, the absolute necessity for deviating from the common reading. We are told that οἱ πολλοὶ is often equivalent to πάντων: it is not, however, quite certain that the Apostle here meant to express πάντων; the verse concludes with the mention of those "who wait for Him," i. e. who wait for Christ's second coming, in humble hope of receiving their reward: and these manifestly are not the whole human race. So also in this Epist. ii. 10. it is said that Christ bringeth *many* sons, πολλοὺς υἱούς, unto glory: see also Matt. xx. 28; xxvi. 28. Mark x. 45. The reason why, in some places, Christ is said to give Himself a ransom for *all*, and in others, only for *many*, seems to be, that when all are mentioned, it is meant that to *all* He has offered the terms of salvation; and where *many* are spoken of, it is considered that by *all* the terms will not be accepted. There is, therefore, no ground for the Calvinistic interpretation of this and similar texts.

CHAP. X.

V. 10. ἐσμὲν διὰ τῆς προσφορᾶς. Many MSS., all indeed of *Matthäi's*, except one, have ἐσμὲν ΟΙ διά, κ. τ. λ. This reading has so little the appearance of an interpolation, that it is scarcely possible to doubt its authenticity; for without the Article the whole is plain. The passage will thus be similar to Rom. ii. 27. σὲ ΤΟΝ διὰ γράμματος. See on 1 Cor. xiv. 9: and the meaning will be, "by which will we of the sacrifice" (or who partake in the sacrifice) " of Jesus Christ are sancti-

¹ V. 19. τῶν μόσχων καὶ τράγων. This is an excellent instance of what is said in the latter part of Chap. iii. Sect. iv. § 2.—H. J. R.

fied once for all: I know not what else can be made of it. The Arab. Lat. has evident traces of the same reading, "*sanctificati, ut qui sanctificati sumus.*"

V. 25. τὴν ἡμέραν. The day of the dissolution of the Jewish State. See on 1 Cor. iii. 13.

V. 29. τὸ πνεῦμα τῆς χάριτος. Mr. *Wakefield* would translate, " the mercies of the Gospel," but laments that " the present ignorance of Scriptural phraseology will not allow, in this and many other instances, alterations which he gladly would have made." I am afraid, however, that no very intimate acquaintance with Scriptural phraseology is to be inferred from the proposed correction. He tells us that "spirit of grace, favour, or kindness, signifies spiritual kindness, or spiritual mercy; viz. the mercy of the Gospel." There certainly is in the ancient Oriental Tongues an usage, of which Mr. W. could not have been wholly ignorant, but of which his recollection was so indistinct, that he has adduced from it an inference directly contrary to the fact: it is, that Attributes are frequently expressed, not as with us by means of Adjectives, but by the Genitives of the names of Attributes, made to depend on the Noun to which the Attribute belongs. See *De Dieu, Gramm. Ling. Orient.* p. 68. Thus we find that, in Ps. xxiii. 2. "tranquil waters" are called in the Hebrew, *the waters of quietness*, in the LXX. ὕδατος ἀναπαύσεως: in Zech. xii. 10. "a benign influence" is, in the Hebrew, *an influence of benignity*, in the LXX. πνεῦμα χάριτος: "the Holy Spirit" is continually named in the Syriac Version, the *Spirit of Holiness:* and "the Gracious Throne," a title of the Almighty, is in this Epist. iv. 16. ὁ θρόνος τῆς χάριτος: lastly, "the all-gracious God" is, 1 Pet. v. 10. ὁ Θεὸς πάσης χάριτος. A hundred similar examples might easily be collected. It appears, therefore, that in reality it is the Noun *governed* which expresses the Attribute, and not the governing Noun, as Mr. W. supposed: and the sense will be, not "spiritual grace," but the *gracious Spirit*, i. e. the Holy Ghost. And this interpretation exactly suits the context: that the Writer should in the same verse speak of *trampling on the Son of God*, and of *insulting the gracious Spirit*, will seem very intelligible and natural to those who admit the personality of the Holy Ghost: and they who do not, ought at least to show that ἐνυβρίζειν in Greek has for its object *things* and even *qualities*, and that to "insult the mercies of the Gospel" is tolerable sense. This chasm in the evidence I am unable to fill up; and I confess myself to be one of those to whom, as Mr. W. supposed, his rendering "would appear a most strange and unaccountable perversion of the original."

V. 38. ὁ δὲ δίκαιος. See above, Rom. i. 17 [1].

Same v. ἐὰν ὑποστείληται. See on 2 Cor. viii. 12 [2].

CHAP. XI.

[3] V. 35. τὴν ἀπολύτρωσιν. The *proffered* deliverance: the History is that of Eleazar, 2 Macc. vi. The deliverance was definite and specific, one obtained by submitting to an act of base dissimulation. — Mr. *Wakefield* understands the passage exactly in the same manner.

CHAP. XII.

V. 2. ὑπέμεινε σταυρόν. Endured *a* cross. To have written TON σταυρόν, as one MS. reads, would have been improper: the cross on which Christ suffered, was not at the time of his suffering pre-eminent above any other cross; which, however, the presence of the Article would imply. We have, therefore, Philipp. ii. 8. "the death of a cross."

V. 9. τῷ πατρὶ τῶν πνευμάτων. *Macknight* translates, "the Father of *our* spirits," I suppose because of the phrase, "fathers of our flesh," preceding. I consider both to be Hebraisms for *fleshly* and *spiritual*: so also does Mr. *Wakefield*; which was not to be expected after what we have seen above at x. 29; nor is it probable that he would have adopted this interpretation, had it interfered with his known prejudices. "*Mihi res, non me rebus subjungere*" is as much the principle of the criticism of Mr. Wakefield, as of the philosophy of Aristippus. The Syriac is very remarkable, "to our spiritual

---

[1] See also Gal. iii. 11.—H. K. B.
[2] Also on John viii. 44. pages 347-8.—J. S.
[3] V. 7. κληρονόμος. See Chap. iii. Sect. iii. § 1, 2, and 3, and compare 1 Pet. iii. 13.—H. J. R.

Fathers:" *Schaaf*, however, refers us to the Notes of *Tremellius*, which I have not at hand.

V. 24. παρὰ τὸν Ἀβελ. There does not appear to be any difficulty in this reading, though it has been the subject of conjecture. Παρὰ here, as in many other places, marks comparison; and "speaking better things than Abel" must mean, than the blood of Abel. I much prefer τὸν to τό, the various reading.

CHAP. XIII.

V. 14. τὴν μέλλουσαν. The Heavenly Jerusalem. See last Chapter, ver. 22.

JAMES.

CHAP. I.

V. 11. ὁ ἥλιος σὺν τῷ καύσωνι. The word καύσων, which occurs in two other places of the N. T., Matt. xx. 12. and Luke xii. 55. is usually rendered *heat*: I understand it, however, of a *burning wind*, the Hebrew קדים, which in the LXX. is sometimes called καύσων, and sometimes Νότος. In the passage of St. Matthew, if the mere heat of the day had been meant, it is probable that we should have found τῆς ἡμέρας placed after τὸν καύσωνα: and of St. Luke there is an apposite illustration in *Maillet*, as quoted by *Burder, Orient. Cust.* vol. i. No. 58. "If the north wind happens to fail, and that from the south comes in its place, then the whole caravan is so sickly and exhausted, that three or four hundred persons are wont in common to lose their lives by the fire and dust of which this fatal wind is composed." This quotation is applied to Numbers xi. 1. to which, however, it is perhaps less suitable. As to the verse under review, there is something unnatural in representing the sun to rise *with its heat;* which cannot be intense compared with that of noon; though a *hot wind* may as well blow at the rising of the sun, as at any other period. I conclude, therefore, that καύσων in the N. T. has been commonly misunderstood.—I should add, however, that *Schleusner* admits the meaning for which I contend to be possible in the present passage.

V. 27. παρὰ τῷ Θεῷ καὶ πατρί. Many MSS.—τῷ. This may be on account of the Preposition, and the rule will remain inviolate.

CHAP. II.[1]

V. 8. νόμον βασιλικόν. Our Eng. Version, "the royal law," leads the Reader to expect in the Greek τὸν νόμον τὸν βασιλικόν. I suppose, however, that νόμον is here used as in Rom. ii. 25. for that St. James, as well as St. Paul, occasionally employed the word in this sense is evident from ver. 11. and from iv. 11. Βασιλικὸς I interpret *excellent*, in which case the Article is unnecessary. Wetstein quotes from the *Meno* of *Plato* τὸ μὲν ὀρθὸν νόμος ἐστὶ βασιλικός, which is very much to the purpose. Similar to the present passage in its general form, though without βασιλικὸν, is Romans xiii. 9. *Michaelis* (Anmerk.) explained νόμον βασιλικὸν to signify "a law made not for slaves, but for kings," which I do not altogether understand.

V. 11. παραβάτης νόμου. That νόμος is here to be taken in the general sense of *morality*, is, I think, evident from the tenor of the argument : " He, who said, Thou shalt not commit adultery, said also, Thou shalt not kill : if then thou abstainest from one of these crimes, yet committest the other, thou art a violator of that morality, which the whole and every part of the Law was designed to promote." What immediately follows (ver. 12.) is a further confirmation ; since it shows that [2] the παραβάτης νόμου does not act, as one, who shall be judged by the Law of Liberty : and this Law certainly is not the Law of Moses. *Michaelis* understands it of Law in the most general sense, the Law of morality and virtue [3].

---

[1] The 14th verse of this Chapter is entitled to notice on account of the Article. Πίστιν first occurs without the Article ; and then on the Renewed Mention it is ἡ πίστις. The meaning therefore is, Can *his* faith save him—the faith which he possesses ? And this the following argument shows to be merely a speculative profession of faith.—J. S.

[2] V. 20. ἡ πίστις χωρὶς τῶν ἔργων νεκρά ἐστιν. Winer observes, that the Article here shows that the works referred to are *the works naturally produced by a lively faith*. In short, πίστις and ἔργα are here correlatives. Bishop Middleton has taught us, that in exclusive propositions the Article is omitted, and χωρὶς ἔργων would thus be, I think, *without any works whatever*, which is not what the sentence requires. The sense is, that *faith, without the right or full performance of its proper works, is dead*.—H. J. R.

[3] V. 13. See Heb. xi. 7.—H. J. R.

CHAP. III.

V. 18. καρπὸς τῆς δικαιοσύνης ἐν εἰρήνῃ σπείρεται. Mr. *Wakefield* would join ἐν εἰρήνῃ with καρπός, so as to mean *peaceable fruit*, and not with σπείρεται. But see above, 2 Tim. i. 8. Many MSS.—τῆς, which is probably right, καρπὸς being anarthrous.

CHAP. IV.

V. 5. τὸ πνεῦμα. Whatever be the import of this passage, (and a multitude of interpretations may be found in *Wolfius*,) τὸ πνεῦμα appears to be used in the personal sense [1].

V. 11. καταλαλεῖ νόμου. On this passage *Macknight* observes, " In Bengelius's opinion against *the Law of Moses*. But why may not the Law in this passage be *the Gospel*, called twice in this Epistle the Law of Liberty? Bengelius says, that this is the last time the Law of Moses is mentioned in the N. T." These very different opinions may justify a presumption, that neither interpretation is right: I believe that the argument of the Apostle is not confined either to the Law of Moses or to the Gospel, but extends to Religion or Moral Obligation in its most general sense. " To all religion," says the Apostle, "candour and good-will are essential, whether we be Jews, Christians, or even of the number of those who are a Law unto themselves:" Rom. ii. 14. A rabbinical Writer in *Schoettgen, Hor. Heb.* has said, *Nemo alteri detrahit qui non simul Deum abneget.* I understand, therefore, that the word νόμος is used here as in Rom. ii. 25. *Rosenmüller* and *Schleusner* explain it of Christianity.

V. 12. ὁ νομοθέτης. Mr. *Wakefield* remarks, that all the old Versions, except the Arabic, add καὶ Ὁ κριτής. He should have omitted the Article, as do the very numerous MSS., of which he has not made mention: the Lawgiver and

---

[1] " Do ye think that the Scripture *speaketh* in vain? *And* does the Spirit *of God* that dwelleth in us lust to envy?" But if the passage be taken as in our own Version, τὸ πνεῦμα will signify *the disposition* which dwelleth in us; where the force of the Article is obvious. The passage has great difficulties, in whatever way we understand it.—J. S.

Judge must be taken of the same person. The additional καὶ κριτὴς is probably the true reading.

CHAP. V.

V. 6. τὸν δίκαιον. It is doubted, whether by this be meant *the Just One*, viz. Christ, as in several other places, or whether just persons *generally* be intended: Part i. Chap. iii. Sect. ii. § 2. *Macknight* is of the former opinion; *Rosenmüller* of the latter. I incline to the former of these: the address is to the rich and more powerful Jews, who had actually "condemned the Just One:" on any other supposition, therefore, than that the passage was meant of the condemnation of our Saviour, terms so obviously applicable to that event would hardly have been employed. Besides, the *hypothetic* use of the Article will here be much too strong. To say that ye have condemned and put to death *all the just*, is more than the truth would authorize.—There is, indeed, a difficulty in ἀντιτάσσεται immediately following. Some would understand it *impersonally*, "resistance is not made;" but this is not supported by any parallel instance, neither does the Greek language love Impersonals so formed. *Bentley, Phileleuth. Lips.* p. 74. very ingeniously conjectured ὁ Κύριος for οὐκ, i. e. ΟΚΣ for ΟΥΚ: and certainly it is in favour of this conjecture, that in Prov. iii. 34. (which was quoted in the preceding Chapter, ver. 6. with the various reading ὁ Θεὸς) we find ὁ Κύριος ὑπερηφάνοις ἀντιτάσσεται· still, however, no MS. is found to read ὁ Κύριος.—I am of opinion that *he* (meaning Christ), carried on from τὸν δίκαιον, is the Nominative to ἀντιτάσσεται: and that the sense is, "The Saviour opposes not your perverseness, but leaves you a prey to its delusion." The Old Versions in part confirm this interpretation; they all have in the Latin, *et non restitit vobis*, or something equivalent: they have only changed the Tense, unless indeed this Latin Preterite be a too close translation of something in the several originals, which, like the Benoni Participle in the Hebrew, has the meaning of the Present Tense. Some Commentators appear to have perplexed themselves by supposing that ἀδελφοὶ in ver. 7. is addressed to the same persons, who in ver. 1. are called πλούσιοι, and that thus the discourse is continued from the beginning: a little attention will show that this is a mistake.

V. 9. κριτής. So many MSS. have Ὁ κριτής, that it ought to have been admitted into the received text.

V. 10. ὑπόδειγμα . . . . τοὺς προφήτας. Part i. Chap. iii. Sect. iii. § 4.

I. PETER.

CHAP. I.

V. 11. ἐδήλου τὸ ἐν αὐτοῖς πνεῦμα Χριστοῦ. A few MSS. have in one word ἐδηλοῦτο: there is, however, no objection to the Article, Χριστοῦ being frequently a Proper Name. See on Mark ix. 40.

V. 23. Θεοῦ. Dr. *Mangey* conjectured τοῦ instead of Θεοῦ, but without any apparent reason.

CHAP. II.[1]

V. 13. εἴτε βασιλεῖ. Most Commentators understand this of the Roman Emperor: the Article may be omitted by Part i. Chap. vi. § 2. Below, ver. 17. where the same reason does not apply, we have τὸν βασιλέα. In the LXX. indeed, we find βασιλεὺς without the Article, though used in the most definite sense, as in Prov. xxiv. 21. φοβοῦ τὸν Θεόν, υἱέ, καὶ βασιλέα, an instance which some have supposed to invalidate the canon contended for by Mr. *Granville Sharp*. This example, however, is inconclusive, partly as being a close translation from the Hebrew, and partly because the word βασιλεύς, even in the Attic Writers, may when definite reject the Article. See *Apollonius* de Synt. edit. 1590. p. 90.

V. 24. ἵνα ταῖς. Dr. *Owen* (ap. Bowyer) observes, "Probably a marginal Note." Does he mean that the two words

---

[1] I have never been satisfied with the common translation of ver. 7. of this Chapter: ὑμῖν οὖν ἡ τιμὴ τοῖς πιστεύουσιν· "Unto you, therefore, which believe, he is *precious.*" The Article seems to lead to a different construction: it refers to ἔντιμον in the preceding verse; and the force of it, if I mistake not, is, "Unto you which believe, is *the preciousness,*" viz. which I speak of.—J. S.

ἵνα ταῖς are a marginal Note? But they are necessary to the sense. Or is it meant that *the whole clause* has been introduced from the margin? Of this I perceive no other probability, than that the passage is somewhat similar to Rom. vi. 11: but even in this similarity there is a remarkable discrepancy; for ἀπογενόμενοι occurs in no other place than the present throughout the N. T.

CHAP. III.

V. 3. ὁ ἔξωθεν ἐμπλοκῆς τριχῶν . . . . κόσμος. The Reader will perceive, that we have here a deviation from an usage, which has so often been noticed: according to which ὁ ἔξωθεν κόσμος cannot govern ἐμπλοκῆς: yet Ὁ is indispensable: we should, therefore, have expected ΤΗΣ ἐμπλοκῆς ΤΩΝ τριχῶν. On turning, however, to the various readings, it will be found that the difficulty may not have originated with the Apostle, but in the error of some Copyist. We learn from *Wetstein* that six MSS., three Edd. and one Father, instead of ἐμπλοκῆς have ἐκ πλοκῆς: none, indeed, of these MSS. is in Uncial characters. From *Griesbach, Symb. Crit.* it appears that the same reading is found in his Cod. 60. and in some MSS. of Origen. Of Matthäi's MSS. likewise *five* have this reading: among them is his Cod. *f*, of which he says in his Pref. to the Catholic Epistles, that " *in Actis et Epist. Catholicis cuilibet præstantissimo par haberi debet.*" In his Note this excellent Critic remarks " ἐκ πλοκῆς *haud indocta est correctio: retinui vulgatam, etiam ob similitudinem membrorum, quæ est in* ἐμπλοκῆς τριχῶν, περιθέσεως χρυσίων *et* ἐνδύσεως ἱματίων." He then adduces an instance of ἐμπλόκιον and also of πλόκιον, but not of ἐμπλοκή: for this word see *Harpocration* and *Hesychius voce* κρώβυλος; also *Clem. Alex.* Pædag. ii. p. 199: the want of authority, therefore, will not be a sufficient reason for rejecting ἐμπλοκῆς. On the other hand, πλοκὴ is not at all an unusual word, being found in the LXX. Exod. xxviii. 14. where our Version renders it *wreathed work*, and in *Lucian's Amores* we have the very phrase ἡ πλοκὴ τῶν τριχῶν. The cognate πλέγματα occurs 1 Tim. ii. 9. The reading, then, ἐκ πλοκῆς is far from being " *indocta correctio,*" supposing it indeed to be a correction; which is not very pro-

CHAPTER III. 429

bable: for it is much easier to conceive that ἐκ πλοκῆς written 'ΕΚΠΛΟΚΗΣ, should have offended a Copyist, who therefore wrote ἐμπλοκῆς, than that ἐμπλοκῆς should have been altered into ἐκ πλοκῆς : one of these corrections required only a knowledge that the word ἐκπλοκὴ is without authority and without analogy, ἐκπλέκω not being found : the other indicates a better acquaintance with the language, and somewhat, perhaps, of critical skill ; for ἐμπλέκω, as well as ἐμπλόκιον, is a legitimate word ; and even ἐμπλοκή, as we have seen, is not without example: the difficulty arising from the want of the Article would not occur to every Copyist. *Matthäi*, indeed, retains the common reading merely "*ob similitudinem membrorum :*" I do not, however, perceive that this harmony is at all injured by the var. reading : ὁ ἔξωθεν ἐκ πλοκῆς τριχῶν καὶ (ἐκ) περιθέσεως, &c. appears to me to have all the regularity, which could be desired even in an Attic Writer. I am, therefore, disposed to adopt the var. reading, unless it can be shown that no considerable difficulty attends the received one; and I have the greater confidence in proposing this emendation of the received text, from having observed, that scarcely in any instance, which seemed unfavourable to the rules laid down in Part i. of this Work, have the MSS. of the N. T. unanimously withholden the assistance required. Some of them have either supplied or rejected the Article as the case demanded, or have exhibited a reading, which places the passage, as in the present instance, entirely on a different footing.

It is scarcely necessary to observe, that the old Versions, the *Latin* of them at least, and probably the Versions themselves, afford no evidence either way, the *sense* being much the same: neither do I insist that the construction κόσμος ἐμπλοκῆς τριχῶν, *the adorning of the plaiting of the hair*, is somewhat unnatural: *Suidas* explains κρώβυλος by ὁ 'ΕΚ τῶν τριχῶν πεπλεγμένος ΚΟΣΜΟΣ : and Arist. de Repub. lib. vii. cap. ii. has καθάπερ ἐν Καρχηδόνι φασὶ τὸν 'ΕΚ τῶν τριχῶν ΚΟΣΜΟΝ λαμβάνειν. That a few authorities omit τριχῶν in St. Peter does not relieve the objection.—It may be supposed that the common reading is to be vindicated by Part i. Chap. vi. § 2 : I have not, however, observed that this usage ever interferes with the law of Regimen.

V. 4. τοῦ πραέος καὶ ἡσυχίου πνεύματος. Of the disposition which is, &c. Part i. Chap. iii. Sect ii. § 1.

V. 18. τῷ πνεύματι. Eng. Version, "quickened *by the Spirit*." So also *Newcome*, *Macknight*, and *Wakefield*. I have had occasion to signify (see on Rom. viii. 13.) that there is no indisputable instance in the N. T., in which any thing is said to have been done or suffered by the Holy Spirit, where πνεῦμα, whether in the Genitive or Dative Case, is not governed by some Preposition. But not only is the Preposition here wanting; even the Article has so little authority, that it is rejected from the text by *Wetstein*, *Griesbach*, and *Matthäi*; though the last, indeed, I know not from what cause, wished to retain it, had not the MSS., as he confesses, compelled him to abandon it. For what would happen, supposing the Article authentic? Not that the passage would speak of the Holy Spirit: the sense would be, in *his* Spirit, viz. the spirit or mind of Christ, as John xiii. 21. and elsewhere. And this is not remote from what I consider to be the true meaning "dead carnally, but alive *spiritually:*" the only difference is, that by retaining the Article, for which there is very little authority, we destroy the form of the Antithesis between σαρκὶ and πνεύματι, an Antithesis, which may be found in the next Chapter, ver. 6: also Galat. iii. 3. We find likewise 'ΕΝ πνεύματι, 'ΕΝ σαρκί, κατὰ πνεῦμα, κατὰ σάρκα: in none of which instances is the Antithesis ever violated by the insertion of the Article before one of the Nouns, while it is wanting to the other.

Soon after the writing of this Note, (for it cannot be dissembled that my Work has been long in hand,) a Sermon on this and the two following verses was published by the late *Bp. Horsley*; a man in whose death the Church of England has sustained a loss which it may not easily repair: to various and recondite learning, to nervous and manly eloquence, and to powers of reasoning which have rarely been equalled, he added a zeal and intrepidity of spirit which enabled him to prosecute a glorious, though an unpopular, career, in an heretical and apostate age. In the Sermon alluded to, "*The descent into Hell*," this Prelate objects to the English Version of πνεύματι, on the ground that the Prepositions are not in the original, and that such a translation destroys the Antithesis. He thinks that the exact rendering would be, "being put to death in the flesh, but quick in the spirit." This accurately agrees in substance with what I had written.—I observe also, that *Michaelis* (in his Anmerk.) gives a similar interpretation, and refers us to Matt. x. 28. Luke xii. 4, 5. The ancient Versions, with the exception of the Æthiopic, seem likewise to have understood the passage in the same manner.

CHAP. IV.

V. 17. ὁ καιρὸς τοῦ ἄρξασθαι τὸ κρῖμα ἀπὸ τοῦ οἴκου τοῦ Θεοῦ. This is usually translated, "the time *is* come," &c. Thus we shall have a Proposition of Existence, Part i. Chap. iii. Sect. iii. § 1. which would require the omission of ὁ, as in the Alex. and in a good MS. of *Matthäi*. The received reading demands a different construction; which, however, the context appears not to admit.

CHAP. V.

V. 8. ὁ ἀντίδικος ὑμῶν διάβολος. *Markland* (ap. Bowyer) observes, "This seems to be meant of the Jews: it is not said, Ὁ Διάβολος." It is true that the word usually has the Article, but I do not see on what ground its omission could alter the sense in the manner supposed. *Campbell*, indeed, remarks, *Prelim. Diss.* p. 184. 4to. that when *the Devil* is meant, the Article is prefixed; and he instances as the only exceptions, Acts xiii. 10. and Revel. xx. 2. besides the present verse. The two former agree with usages established in Part i.: of the present example, I believe the translation should in strictness be, "your opposing evil Spirit," as if ἀντίδικος had been an Adjective. An instance of the same construction has been noticed above, Titus iii. 4.

II. PETER.

CHAP. I.

V. 1. τοῦ Θεοῦ ἡμῶν καὶ σωτῆρος Ἰησ. Χρ. The Note of *Wetstein* on τοῦ Θεοῦ is, "*scilicet πατρός, ut* Tit. ii. 13. *et comm.* 2." This indicates a knowledge of some different interpretation; and that interpretation, it cannot be doubted, is the same which has lately been supported by Mr. *Granville Sharp*[1]. In his examination of the Fathers, Mr. *Wordsworth* has not been able to collect any important evidence in behalf of the proposed explanation: but the reason has been assigned by him: the Second Epistle of Peter is rarely quoted by the

---

[1] On this text Mr. Winstanley is able to make a very weak case. He allows explicitly that the arrangement of the words suggests no objection to Mr. Sharp's rendering; nay, that it agrees *exactly* with the arrangement in ver. 11. τοῦ Κυρίου ἡμῶν καὶ σωτῆρος Ἰησοῦ Χριστοῦ, and this parallelism, he adds, would undoubtedly support Mr. S. as a mere Grammarian or Philologist; 'but on the broad principles of general criticism, there arise very strong objections to Mr. S.'s interpretation.' The strength of these objections is equal to that usually found in objections raised on the broad grounds of general criticism, in opposition to the narrow grounds of grammatical accuracy. 'The Attributes Lord and Saviour, applied to the same Person, are usually connected by the Copulative; but the Nouns σωτήρ and Θεὸς are *as regularly* connected without it, as in Tit. i. 4; ii. 10; iii. 4; and therefore the Copulative must *appear* to render St. Peter *somewhat ambiguous*.' The words σωτὴρ and Θεὸς occur together *only* five or six times in the whole N. T.! Does general criticism teach us to make Canons thus, and say that because two words, not necessarily connected at all, are used in one way five or six times, they cannot be used in another, when that other is just as agreeable to nature and good sense? 'It will be said,' says Mr. W. 'why, then, do you not understand the writer according to the *prevailing idiom* of the language?' I answer, because he appears to me to have explained himself in the very next verse, ἐν ἐπιγνώσει τοῦ Θεοῦ καὶ Ἰησοῦ τοῦ Κυρίου ἡμῶν. It is not *very probable* that he would thus, in immediate consecution, use the words God and the Saviour Jesus Christ, and God and our Lord Jesus Christ, first to signify one Person and then two, without any assignable reason for so remarkable a difference.' That is to say, Mr. W. does not think it *very probable* that two different meanings should be expressed in two different forms!—H. J. R.

CHAPTER I. 433

Fathers: their evidence, therefore, in a question like the present, is not easily obtained. The only passage adduced by Mr. W. is from the *Scholia*, under the name of *Œcumenius*; and the passage proves little or nothing, because it is rather in the way of reference or allusion than of actual quotation.

As this instance differs not in any point of importance from Titus ii. 13. I can have little new to advance with respect to its interpretation. The passage is plainly and unequivocally to be understood as an assumption, that "Jesus Christ is our God and Saviour." The only difference between the present text and Titus ii. 13. is, that ἡμῶν is here placed after the first Noun, not after the second; but for a plain reason, the position of the Pronoun does not affect the sense: in all such cases, strictly speaking, the Pronoun ought to be repeated after each and every Noun, (supposing more than two,) τοῦ Θεοῦ ἡμῶν καὶ σωτῆρος ἩΜΩΝ καί, κ. τ. λ. and if it be only once inserted, for the repetition is unnecessary, it is wholly unimportant, whether it be after the first or after the last Noun; if after the first, then it is understood after the remaining ones; if after the last, it comprehends those which precede: the only mode, in the present instance, of limiting the effect of ἡμῶν to τοῦ Θεοῦ, would have been to prefix an Article to σωτῆρος; and why that second Article, on the supposition that *two* persons were intended, was not employed, as (among a multitude of examples) in 1 John ii. 22. τὸν πατέρα καὶ τὸν υἱόν, it might be difficult to show; in that instance, indeed, it may be said, that the very sense makes the distinction, and yet no MS. has ventured to read τὸν πατέρα καὶ υἱόν.

Scholars, probably, will feel that this reasoning is altogether superfluous: but Scholars are not they for whom it was intended: the *Unknown Writer* was unable to comprehend this subtilty; and it is not impossible that some of his admirers may have experienced the same embarrassment. It is likewise for the same class of Readers, if into the hands of such this Work should fall, that I notice the 11th verse of the present Chapter, τοῦ Κυρίου ἡμῶν καὶ σωτῆρος Ἰησοῦ Χρ. and also ii. 20. Than the former, it is impossible to conceive an example more similar to that under examination: even the position of ἡμῶν is the same: the reason why it is not drawn into the controversy is, that no one doubts that "our Lord

F f

and Saviour" are there meant of the same Person: I have said *no one;* but perhaps the *Unknown Writer* ought to be excepted; for he thinks that the present verse would be best rendered by "the God of us, and Saviour of Jesus Christ:" and it is to be presumed that he would render verse 11. in the same manner. But thus he will be involved in a dilemma: if he mean that "God and Saviour," or in verse 11. "Lord and Saviour," are to be taken of *different* Persons, who, it may be asked, even according to his own theology, is the Saviour of Jesus Christ, as contra-distinguished from God? Or if he mean them of the *same* Person, what was his Book designed to prove? Only, that a certain theory is "fanciful and unfounded," of which, however, he is glad to avail himself, when it suits his purpose: for it ought to be observed, that in *his* construction he virtually admits and applies the rule, though he chooses to divest Jesus of the title of Saviour: his translation will differ from that proposed, only in making Ἰησ. Χρ. to be in *Regimen* instead of *Apposition*, in which difference neither the rule nor the principle of the rule is at all concerned: the offence is merely against the uniform tenor of Scripture, which represents Christ as the Saviour of men, but has no where called the Father the Saviour of Jesus Christ.—The expression, τοῦ Κυρίου καὶ σωτῆρος, occurs again at iii. 2. and that too, unless we regard three or four obscure MSS., *without* the addition Ἰησ. Χρ. There, perhaps, we shall be told that something is to be supplied. Still it will be necessary to understand them of *one Person*, and the mention of *the Apostles* leaves no doubt that the Person is Christ. But *quorsum hæc tam putida?*

If the position of ἡμῶν be thought of any importance, though the contrary has been shown, it may be right to observe, that in three of *Wetstein's* MSS., and in the greater part of *Matthäi's*, including all his best, ἡμῶν is wanting.—The Syriac has "of our Lord and our Redeemer," the Preposition not being repeated before the second Noun. For the Coptic, see on Ephes. v. 5.

Clarke (*Reply* to *Nelson*, p. 83.) says on this place, " I do acknowledge that these words may, in true grammatical construction, equally be rendered, either *The righteousness of our God, and of our Saviour Jesus Christ,* or, *The righteousness of our God and Saviour Jesus Christ.*" Below he adds, " that neither of these opinions can be demonstrably disproved:" and that " the English Translation in our Bibles determines it according to my explication;" i. e. to mean *two* persons. I do not, however, allow that " neither of these opinions can be demonstrably disproved;" the contrary, I think, has been shown: and as to " the Translation of our Bibles," if he mean the earlier Bibles, as well as that in present use, he appears to be exceedingly mistaken: for if we may rely on Mr. *Cruttwell*, as quoted by Mr. *Sharp*, the words were rendered, "*of our God and Saviour Jesus Christ*," in the Versions of Wickliff, Coverdale, Matthews, Cranmer, in the Bishops' Bible, the Geneva, the Rhemish, as well as by Doddridge, Wesley, and others who have lived since Clarke wrote. To the above-mentioned English Translators may be added the name of *Tindal*, the author of the first printed English Version of the N. T., who has given the very same rendering. Or if Clarke meant to speak only of the authorized Version, I must repeat what was said above on Titus ii. 13. that even this is questionable: it is true that King James's Translators have expressed themselves incautiously, if they understood the words of one person; but so they have elsewhere: and in Col. i. 3. " We give thanks to *God* and the *Father* of our Lord Jesus Christ," it would be absurd to affirm that they distinguished between God and the Father of Jesus Christ, however the improved accuracy of modern writing might justify such an inference. At any rate, King James's Translators are not to be regarded, to the exclusion of all who preceded them: nor is it a question in which the opinion of any Translator is of great weight.

V. 19. ἔχομεν βεβαιότερον τὸν προφητικὸν λόγον. English Version has "a more sure word of Prophecy," as if βεβαιότερον were to be taken in immediate concord with what follows. Subsequent English Translators have rightly rendered, " we have the word of Prophecy more firm, or confirmed [1]." A good Note on this text, by *Markland* and *Bowyer*, may be found in *Bowyer's Conjectures*.

Same v. ἡμέρα. Many Editions have Ἡ ἡμέρα: the Editors did not consider that the day spoken of was not yet in exist-

---

[1] Or, " The prophetic word which we have is more sure."—J. S.

ence, in which case the Article is more properly omitted.—Φωσφόρος is used as a Proper Name.

CHAP. II.

V. 5. ἀρχαίου κόσμου. The English usage, and that probably of most nations, would lead us to expect ΤΟΥ ἀρχαίου κόσμου: yet no MS. has the Article. How are we to explain the omission? I do not think that what was observed on the anarthrous use of κόσμος, Gal. vi. 14. will apply in the present instance. Ἄρχαιος κόσμος appears to be the same with κόσμος ἀσεβῶν in this verse, "a multitude of wicked persons," where the Article is not required. May not, then, ἀρχαίου κόσμου be regarded as equivalent to κόσμου ἀρχαίων? At one time I thought that ἄρχαιος might want the Article in the same manner as πρῶτος and other Ordinals: but the former solution appears preferable.

V. 8. βλέμματι γὰρ καὶ ἀκοῇ ὁ δίκαιος ἐγκατοικῶν, κ. τ. λ. It has been made a question whether βλέμματι καὶ ἀκοῇ depend on ὁ δίκαιος or on ἐβασάνιζεν. Of the ancient Versions, the Vulg. and Æthiop. appear to have adopted the former opinion; the Syr. and Arab. the latter: the Copt. seems to have followed a totally different reading: which, however, is not very intelligible. Among the moderns, I know of no Translator, except Mr. *Wakefield*, who makes βλέμματι to depend on ὁ δίκαιος: but in this case, as *Raphel* has observed after Beza, the order would have been ὁ βλέμματι καὶ ἀκοῇ δίκαιος· it may be added, that οὗτος would probably have been inserted at the beginning of the sentence. See on Gal. iii. 11.

V. 15. τὴν εὐθεῖαν ὁδόν. The MSS. &c. almost with one consent omit τήν, which therefore seems to be spurious. In the LXX. Isaiah xxxiii. 15, I find λαλῶν εὐθεῖαν ὁδόν, where the Translators were under no restraint from the Hebrew. "A straight road" appears to be equivalent to *rectitude*. I cannot, however, but remark, that the style of St. Peter is even more anarthrous than that of St. Paul, a circumstance which is not at all at variance with the vehemence of his character. See on Rom. i. 17.

V. 20. εἰ γὰρ ἀποφυγόντες. Three MSS. for εἰ have οἱ, a reading which is much approved by *Abresch*, (Paraph. in Heb.

CHAPTER III. 437

p. 385.) but which I do not understand. According to the common reading, the sense is very plain; the *Apodosis* beginning at γέγονεν. That proposed, seems to make the *Apodosis* begin and end with ἡττῶνται, while the clause which follows γέγονεν, κ. τ. λ. becomes wholly detached from the context.

CHAP. III.

V. 10. οἱ οὐρανοί. Many MSS. want οἱ, and, I think, rightly: the Article is wanting before στοίχεια and γῆ, which naturally require it, as much as does οὐρανοί. Part i. Chap. vi. § 2. Below (same verse) the Alex. alone — τὰ before ἐν αὐτῇ: but there the Article was indispensable; without it, ἐν αὐτῇ would not be connected with ἔργα. See on 2 Tim. i. 8.

I. JOHN.

CHAP. I.

V. 2. τὴν ζωὴν αἰώνιον. It is so printed in *Wetstein*: other Editions confirm the rule by having τὴν ζωὴν ΤΗΝ αἰώνιον. The omission may be an error.

V. 6. τὴν ἀλήθειαν. This I understand of the Gospel, or rather of its precepts: so the same Writer in his Gospel, iii. 21.

CHAP. II.

V. 1. Ἰησ. Χριστὸν δίκαιον. Mr. *Wakefield* would make δίκαιον to agree immediately with παράκλητον; in which, I perceive, that he is supported by the Arabic and the Æthiopic. I am not satisfied with the disjunction of δίκαιον from the Proper Name: at the same time, I think that our Version, "Jesus Christ the righteous," is rather beyond the original: the Writer might, indeed, so have expressed himself; as it is, he has said only "Jesus Christ, a righteous person."—*Markland's* conjecture, ΤΟΝ δίκαιον, does not appear to be necessary.

V. 13. ἐγνώκατε τὸν ἀπ' ἀρχῆς. This is the reading, so far as I know, of all the MSS.; and it might be thought impossible that so plain a sentence should be liable to misconstruction. "Ye have known the Person who was from the beginning, or, who has existed from eternity." So ὁ ἐν τοῖς οὐρανοῖς means Him who is in heaven: but it is needless to adduce examples of an usage which continually presents itself to the notice of all readers of Greek.—There have, however, been Critics who were dissatisfied with the received reading, and with the sense which that reading conveys. Dr. *Mangey* would for τὸν ἀπ' ἀρχῆς read ΑΥΤΟΝ ἀπ' ἀρχῆς: this resembles most of the emendations of the N. T.; or is, perhaps, somewhat worse than the greater part of the collection: for Dr. Mangey appears to have been the *Davus*, not the *Œdipus*, of conjecturers. Mr. *Wakefield* adopts the translation which such a reading would authorize: " Ye have known Him from the beginning;" where, as is evident, ἀπ' ἀρχῆς is thrown upon ἐγνώκατε: and he does not even hint in his Notes that such a Version is not justified by the original, and that it entirely alters the sense of a very important text. His ardent love of truth might have been gratified by such an acknowledgment: he might have added, that all the ancient Versions, on which he usually lays so much stress, understand τὸν ἀπ' ἀρχῆς according to its obvious sense, and that the Latin of his *instar omnium*, the Æthiopic has *(quasi* κατ' ἐξοχὴν*) Primum:* in short, it would have done him honour to have confessed that he had nothing to bear him out, but his prejudices and the conjecture of Dr. Mangey. I would not, however, be thought uncandid; I would speak of men only according to their pretensions; and I would not try modest merit by a criterion from which it shrank. It cannot be forgotten that Mr. W. was a philologist by profession; the editor of Greek Tragedies; the author of a celebrated *Diatribe;* the projector of a Greek Lexicon; and a Grammarian, whose loss has been publicly lamented, *si qua est ea gloria*, by Mr. *Horne Tooke*. These remarks will not apply to *Macknight*, who, indeed, has rendered the passage in the same manner with Mr. W., but who, besides that he never professed any extraordinary degree of philological skill, has honestly and fairly told us what he knew. His Note is, "So I translate τὸν ἀπ' ἀρχῆς; because the Article is often put for the Pronouns Ὅς and αὐτός, see Ess. IV. 72. also because the Apostle is speaking of Jesus Christ, mentioned ver. 6.—If the Reader does not admit this use of the Article, he may consider the expression as elliptical; and may supply it in this manner; *because we have known*, τὸν Ἰησοῦν ἀπ' ἀρχῆς, *Jesus from the beginning:* have known his disengagement from the world, and his contempt of its riches, honours, and pleasures." On turning, however, to Essay IV. I do not find a single instance to support the translation: we there learn, indeed, that ὁ δὲ εἶπεν signifies "and he said," and that ὁ ἀδικῶν is " he that doeth wrong;" and there are other similar instances: as to Rom. vi. 10. I have no doubt that this excellent Divine is mistaken : ὅ there is the Neuter of ὅς, and signifies *in that*, or something equivalent. There is, therefore, no foundation for the rendering which he would adopt; and the only part of his Note to which I can accede, is, that τὸν ἀπ' ἀρχῆς is Jesus Christ. This is to be inferred, not only from the context, but from the circumstance that there was no occasion to assert the eternity of the Father, and the Father is expressly mentioned (τὸν πατέρα) in this very verse. This text, therefore, is another of those which affirm the eternal pre-existence of Christ ; and it harmonizes exactly with the language of the same Writer in the exordium of his Gospel, "In the beginning was the Word."

V. 22. ὁ ψεύστης. English Version, "Who is a liar." It is certain that something more is meant; and the context leaves no doubt that ὁ ψεύστης is the same with ὁ Ἀντίχριστος following.

Same v. τὸν Πατέρα καὶ τὸν Υἱόν. No MS. omits the second Article. There are, however, instances to be found in the writings of the Fathers, in which the omission is observable, the word Υἱὸς applied to Christ having gradually become, in some sort, a Proper Name ; besides, this deviation could not easily, from the very nature of the case, be productive of ambiguity.

V. 25. τὴν ζωὴν τὴν αἰώνιον. *Erasmus*, Editions 1 and 2. omits the latter Article. See on v. 20.

CHAP. III.

V. 4. ἡ ἁμαρτία ἐστὶν ἡ ἀνομία. A convertible Proposition. Part i. Chap. iii. Sect. iv. § 1 [1].

V. 18. γλώσσῃ. A great many MSS. have τῇ γλώσσῃ. This is preferred by *Griesbach*. The organ of speech is here meant : but the Article may be omitted by Part i. Chap. vi. § 2.

---

[1] It is true that ἁμαρτία and ἀνομία have just been mentioned, but in that mention the Article serves the purpose of hypothesis, or shows that each word is taken in its fullest sense—*all sin*, &c. And it is clear enough that the Article is used in the same sense here, and not for renewed mention.—H. J. R.

CHAP. IV.

V. 9. τὸν μονογενῆ. *Erasmus* and some of his followers omit the Article, though it is necessary: no MS. supports this reading. See on Acts xxiv. 14.

CHAP. V.

Vv. 7, 8. Τρεῖς εἰσιν οἱ μαρτυροῦντες [ἐν τῷ οὐρανῷ, ὁ πατήρ, ὁ λόγος, καὶ τὸ ἅγιον πνεῦμα· καὶ οὗτοι οἱ τρεῖς ἕν εἰσι. Καὶ τρεῖς εἰσιν οἱ μαρτυροῦντες ἐν τῇ γῇ,] τὸ πνεῦμα καὶ τὸ ὕδωρ καὶ τὸ αἷμα· καὶ οἱ τρεῖς εἰς τὸ ἕν εἰσιν. Every one knows of how much controversy this passage has been the subject, and that the words which I have enclosed in brackets are now pretty generally abandoned as spurious. It is foreign from my undertaking to detail the arguments by which this decision has been established; and as little is it my purpose to call in question their justness and solidity. He who would see the controversy briefly, yet clearly, stated, may consult the Preface to Mr. *Marsh's* Letters to Mr. *Travis*, and an Appendix to the second volume of Mr. *Butler's Horæ Biblicæ*: and if he wish to enter more fully into the inquiry, the same Appendix will direct him to almost every thing of importance which has appeared on the subject. The probable result will be, that he will close the examination with a firm belief that the passage is spurious; more especially if he be of opinion that it rather obscures than elucidates the reasoning.

It has, however, been insisted, that the omission of the rejected passage rather embarrasses the context: *Bengel* regards the two verses as being connected "*adamantinâ cohærentiâ*:" and yet, it must be allowed, that among the various interpretations there are some which will at least endure the absence of the seventh verse. But the difficulty to which the present undertaking has directed my attention, is of another kind: it respects the Article in εἰς τὸ ἕν in the final clause of the eighth verse: if the seventh verse had not been spurious, nothing could have been plainer than that TO ἓν of verse 8. referred to ἓν of verse 7: as the case now stands, I do not perceive the force or meaning of the Article; and the same difficulty is briefly noticed by *Wolfius*. In order to prove that this is not merely *nodum in scirpo quærere*, I think it right to examine, at some length, what are the occasions on which, before εἷς, the Article may be inserted.

The Article, when prefixed to εἷς, is not used in any peculiar manner, but is, as in all other cases, subservient to the purpose either of *reference* or of *hypothesis*.

The passages of the N. T. in which εἷς or ἓν occurs with the Article, are somewhat more than twenty; without the Article, it is extremely common. Of its *hypothetic* use, I have observed no instance: in the way of *reference*, we find it opposed to ὁ ἕτερος, Matt. vi. 24. Luke xviii. 10: sometimes to ὁ ἄλλος, Rev. xvii. 10: sometimes to εἷς, 1 Thess. v. 11: also to ὁ εἷς, Matt. xxiv. 40. Rom. v. 15. We find also ὁ εἷς used for one of two, Luke xxiv. 18. In like manner, in an Inscription preserved by *Gruter*, p. cccc. 1st ed. we have προξενιαν ἀναγραψαι εἰς χαλκωματα δυο και ΤΟ ἓν δουναι, κ. τ. λ. In these and similar instances, it is obvious that ὁ εἷς is properly used in reference to some one other person; for where three or more persons or things are in question, there the Article is omitted: so Mark iv. 8. and xiv. 10: unless, indeed, in such instances as Herod. lib. iv. p. 152. ed. 1570, where, in speaking of a quadrangular temple, he observes, τὰ μὲν τρία τῶν κώλων ἐστὶν ἀπότομα, κατὰ δὲ ΤΟ ἓν ἐπιβατόν: here three sides are spoken of *together*, and thus we revert to the case in which only two things are mentioned.—The Article may likewise be prefixed to εἷς where one person or thing has been recently mentioned: so Matt. xxv. 18. ΤΟ ἓν, the one talent mentioned in ver. 15; 1 Cor. xii. 11. ΤΟ ἓν καὶ τὸ αὐτὸ πνεῦμα, though some MSS. omit the former Article: in ver. 12. we have τὸ σῶμα ἕν ἐστι followed by ΤΟΥ σώματος ΤΟΥ ἑνός, though here several authorities omit τοῦ ἑνός: 1 Cor. x. 17. we have εἷς ἄρτος followed by ἐκ ΤΟΥ ἑνὸς ἄρτου. Τὸ ἓν φρονοῦντες, Philipp. ii. 2. I have explained *ad loc*. From some of these instances, it is evident that, had the seventh verse been authentic, the usage would have allowed us to refer ΤΟ ἓν of ver. 8. to ἓν of ver. 7. and the meaning would have been, that the three earthly witnesses concurred in testifying *the one thing* testified by the heavenly witnesses. Since, however, the interpolation of the seventh verse has been proved, the difficulty remains, and it is not diminished by a comparison of the present with the other passages of the N. T., which most nearly resemble it : for in them we shall perceive that the Article is uniformly omitted. These passages are to be found principally in the Gospel of the Writer of this Epistle: for the phrase ἓν εἶναι see John x. 30; xvii. 11. 21, 22. 1 Cor. iii. 8; and probably Gal. iii. 28. for there the authorities differ: for εἰς ἓν see John xi. 52. ἵνα συναγάγῃ εἰς ἕν; xvii. 23. ἵνα ὦσιν τετελειωμένοι εἰς ἕν. If more examples of this kind be required, as being more exactly to the purpose than are the former, I will observe that five instances of συνάγειν, or ἀθροίζειν εἰς ἕν, collected from Plato, Aristoph., Dion. Hal. and Plotinus, have been adduced by *Wetstein*, on John xi. 52; to which may be added, Plato, vol. iii. 8vo, p. 255. συντιθέμενα εἰς ἓν δηλοῖ τὴν φύσιν τοῦ Θεοῦ. Xenophon, Athen. Polit. Opera, 1681, p. 405. ταῦτα πάντα εἰς ἓν ἠθροῖσθαι. Apost. Const. cap. iii. τὰς τρίχας ποιεῖν εἰς ἕν. St. Basil, vol. i. p. 620. εἰς ἓν συγκολλώμενοι. *Suidas (voce ἕνωσις)*, ἕνωσις δὲ εἴρηται διὰ τὸ εἰς ἓν συνωθεῖσθαι τὰ πράγματα· he instances ten kinds, among which are ἐπὶ τῶν ὑποστάσεων and ἐπὶ τῶν γνωμῶν. And this I believe to be uniformly the usage, where the reason of the case does not require that the Article should be inserted.

It is manifest, however, that I suppose ἓν εἶναι in ver. 7. to be expressive only of *consent* or *unanimity*, and not of the consubstantiality of the Divine Persons; for otherwise τὸ ἓν of ver. 8. could not be imagined to have any reference to ἓν in ver. 7; I mean here and throughout the Note, on the assumption of the authenticity of that verse. Now that ἓν εἶναι in the supposed ver. 7. would not bear any other sense, has been admitted by very zealous Trinitarians; of which number was the late Bishop *Horsley*. But not to argue from authority, let it be considered how the phrase ἓν εἶναι is elsewhere used in the N. T. In 1 Cor. iii. 8. ἓν εἶναι is affirmed of him that planteth, and him that watereth: where nothing more than unity of purpose is conceivable. With St. John ἓν εἶναι was, as we have seen, a favourite phrase : in John xvii. 22. Christ prays to the Father, that the disciples ἓν ὦσιν, καθὼς ἡμεῖς ἕν ἐσμεν. These passages, I think, decide the import of the expression in John x. 30., and wherever else it occurs in the

N. T. That some of the Fathers used it in the other sense, does not affect my argument.

I have asserted above, that of the *hypothetic* use of the Article before ἕν, I have seen no instance in the N. T. In the philosophical Writers, especially in the Metaphysics of Aristotle, and in the Parmenides of Plato, this use is extremely common: so Arist. Met. lib. iv. cap. 15. τὸ πολλαπλάσιον πρὸς τὸ ἕν, that which is manifold, to that which is (supposed to be) only one, or *Unity*. That τὸ ἓν in this verse is not found in the LXX. the Reader will readily believe: if I may rely on the Concordance of *Trommius*, there is not a single instance of τὸ ἕν, where the Article is not subservient to *reference* of some kind or other. The only passage at all deserving notice in the present inquiry is Exod. xxxvi. 18. καὶ ἐγένετο ἘΝ, applied to the various parts of the Tabernacle, forming one whole. The Hebrew of Job xxiii. 13. והוא באחד promises a very important illustration: but there the LXX. *in alia omnia abeunt*: and in the remains of the *Hexapla* the passage is not preserved.

Out of τὸ ἕν, supposing the Article to be employed as in Part i. Chap. iii. Sect. i. § 6. seems to have arisen the use of the term as a philosophical name of the Deity. We are told by *Maximus*, the scholiast on the Pseudo-Dionysius the Areopagite, vol. i. p. 701. ed. 1634, that ἘΝ ὠνόμασαν τὸν Θεὸν οἱ πάλαι· and we know that the Platonic Trinity had for its Hypostases τὸ ἓν or τἀγαθόν, Νοῦς, and Ψυχή. This also is a sense of τὸ ἕν, which the Reader will hardly expect to find in the N. T. I was compelled, however, to notice it, as will be evident from what follows.

The Complut. edition reads, ὅτι τρεῖς εἰσιν οἱ μαρτυροῦντες ἐν τῷ οὐρανῷ, ὁ πατὴρ καὶ ὁ λόγος καὶ τὸ ἅγιον πνεῦμα· καὶ οἱ τρεῖς εἰς τὸ ἕν εἰσι· καὶ τρεῖς εἰσιν οἱ μαρτυροῦντες ἐπὶ τῆς γῆς, τὸ πνεῦμα καὶ τὸ ὕδωρ καὶ τὸ αἷμα. The final close of ver. 8. is wanting. Mr. Porson (Letters to Mr. Travis, p. 51.) gives it as his opinion, that the Complutensian Editors "transplanted the clause καὶ οἱ τρεῖς εἰς τὸ ἕν εἰσι to the end of the seventh verse." And (p. 53.) he observes, in answer to an objection of Mr. Travis, "to me, I confess, the Complutensian εἰς τὸ ἓν appears full as orthodox as the more common ἓν alone; and may be thus paraphrased: οἱ ΤΡΕΙΣ τὸ ἘΝ

CHAPTER V. 445

ΘΕΙΟΝ ἅμα συντελοῦσιν, *hi TRES conjuncti UNUM efficient DEUM;* in the same manner as ἔσονται οἱ ΔΥΟ εἰς σάρκα ΜΙΑΝ is exactly synonymous with οὐκέτι εἰσὶ ΔΥΟ, ἀλλὰ σὰρξ ΜΙΑ : Matt. xix. 5, 6." That the Preposition makes no alteration in the sense, is well known; this usage is a common Hebraism; but, perhaps, it may still be doubted in what way we are to explain the Complutensian ΤΟ ἕν : Mr. Porson says, by supplying Θεῖον. But here two questions may be asked : viz. In τὸ ἕν, the name of the Deity, is Θεῖον the Noun *usually* understood ? And further, Is it in the manner of the Sacred Writers to employ such an Ellipsis ? To the affirmative of the former, the origin of the term may not seem to be very favourable; and to that of the latter it may be objected, that τὸ Θεῖον, a Pagan appellation of God, is not found at all in the LXX., and only once in the N. T. Acts xvii. 29. where St. Paul, in addressing the philosophers of Athens, adopted their own phraseology. Neither does the term τὸ ἕν, whatever Noun be understood in it, (and in this respect I should have thought that it differed not from τὸ πρέπον, τὸ ἀγαθόν, τὸ ὄν, &c.) appear to have been very familiar to the Writers of the N. T. nor to the LXX.: for though they speak of God some thousands of times, and of his Unity in particular very frequently, they no where call Him τὸ ἕν : they say of Him, that he is εἷς Θεός: the Fathers do the same; they say also μία θεότης.

But the point with which I am immediately concerned is, whether the Professor meant to give this explanation of εἰς τὸ ἕν, as it now stands in ver. 8. On this head I am justified in expressing a doubt, from his having alleged, that the clause which he thus interprets was transplanted from the eighth verse. At the same time, I am disposed to believe that Mr. Porson intended this explanation to apply to the *seventh* verse only, as we find it in the Complutensian, because, applied to ver. 8. of the common editions, it would require us to understand the *Spirit* and the *Water* and the *Blood* of the three Persons of the Trinity, a mystical interpretation adopted by some of the Fathers, but unwarranted by Scripture, and discountenanced, I think, by Mr. Porson. At any rate, if this explanation of εἰς τὸ ἕν in ver. 8. and of the Spirit, the Water, and the Blood be admitted, the rejected passage was never worth contending for, inasmuch as the eighth verse will thus affirm all which Athanasius himself could have desired.

There are, however, a few passages in the Fathers and elsewhere, which bear some resemblance to the final clause of ver. 8: they have usually been adduced as citations of the seventh verse; they are now brought forward in order to ascertain the probability whether or not St. John would have written εἰς TO ἓν in ver. 8. supposing the seventh verse not to have preceded. The assumptions which I mean to make are, that as many of these passages as have τὸ ἕν, and are admitted, or can be shown, to be citations of the final clause of ver. 8. (for the seventh verse is here out of the question,) afford evidence only of the antiquity of the reading to which I object, not of the propriety or legitimacy of the phrase; because citations from Scripture are intended to be literal: and that as many as, without being citations, affirm *three to be one*, or any thing similar to it, yet omit the Article before ἕν, are evidence that the εἰς TO ἓν of St. John (supposing that there is no reference) is a deviation from the ordinary usage. If a third class exist, i. e. if there be well authenticated instances, differing from those last mentioned only in having TO ἕν, I admit that they invalidate my objection.—In examining the passages I will adhere to the order observed in Letter IX. of Mr. *Porson.*

The first Greek authority examined by Mr. Porson is the *Synopsis* printed with Athanasius; by appealing to which Mr. Travis certainly did not serve his cause, since neither τρεῖς nor ἓν occurs in it, neither does τριὰς nor any thing of the kind. It is, therefore, no more to my purpose than it was to Mr. Travis's; except, indeed, as it affords me an opportunity of expressing my surprise, that in default of the seventh verse no use was made of the mystical interpretation of the eighth.— The next also of the cited passages is found among the spurious works ascribed to Athanasius. The words are πρὸς δὲ τούτοις πᾶσι Ἰωάννης φάσκει, Καὶ οἱ τρεῖς τὸ ἕν εἰσι Mr. Porson says, that it is found in the Dialogue between an Athanasian and an Arian, and that *Cave* believes it to be the composition of some doating monk: "in general," adds the Professor, "it is attributed to *Maximus*, who lived in the seventh century." In the works of Athanasius, 2 vol. fol. Paris, 1627, there is a Dialogue in five parts between an Athanasian and an

Arian, in which, indeed, the passage does not appear; I find it, however, in the " Disputation in the Nicene Council against Arius," a work, of which Cave has actually said, that it is "*figmentum monachi cujusdam delirantis.*" This, therefore, should seem to be the Treatise alluded to; and yet, on the other hand, of the Dialogue between the Athanasian and the Arian, *Maximus* is named by Cave as being possibly the author. In whatever way this apparent contradiction be accounted for, we have here plainly a citation of ver. 7. or of ver. 8, though, as Mr. Porson remarks, it is not in the exact words of either: he says, that it more nearly resembles those of the eighth; that the Preposition has been absorbed by τρεῖς; and that the same omission has happened in the copies of *Cyril*, of *Euthym. Zigab.* and of *Dionys. Alex.* The Reader should know, that πρὸς τούτοις in the Disputation is preceded by an allusion to the baptismal formula at the conclusion of St. Matthew: hence it is evident that the Writer is speaking of the Trinity: still he might be one of those, who adopted the mystical interpretation; and in that case the eighth verse might be the passage, which he had in view. On this supposition, the citation will show to a certain degree, that in the time of Maximus or of "the doating monk" the final clause of the eighth verse existed nearly in its present form. I say, *to a certain degree;* for it is well known that such writers do not always cite Scripture very accurately, not to insist on the incorrectness, which some of them owe to the Copyists.

Mr. Porson next considers a passage from *Euthym. Zigab.* who has said τὸ ἓν ἐπὶ τῶν ὁμοουσίων λέγεται, ἔνθα ταυτότης μὲν φύσεως, ἑτερότης δὲ τῶν ὑποστάσεων, ὡς τὸ Καὶ τὰ τρία ἕν. Mr. Porson grants, that if this passage be a quotation from Scripture, it is from 1 John v. 7. He discovered, however, that Euthymius took it from *Greg. Nazianzen,* who had said, Ἓν γὰρ ἐν τρισὶν ἡ θεότης, ΚΑΙ ΤΑ ΤΡΙΑ ῾ΕΝ. My inference is, that Greg. Nazianzen, who confessedly is speaking of the Trinity, but does not cite St. John, considered ἓν without the Article, to be the natural expression of his meaning. He uses ἕν, it is true, of *consubstantiality:* but I do not perceive that, if it had been used of *consent* as in ver. 8. the Article could have been more wanted.

The passage, which is next to be examined, is also from

Euthym. Zigab. where that Writer has given the seventh and eighth verses entire, as they stand in our common editions. Mr. Porson, however, objects, that Euthymius's reasoning proves him to have been ignorant of the seventh verse, for that his argument derives all its force from the close connection of verses 6, 8, and 9. Euthymius, as translated by Mr. Porson, reasons thus: " See now again how the Preacher of truth calls the Spirit by nature God and of God; for having said that it is the Spirit of God that witnesses, a little onward he adds, the witness of God is greater; how then is he a creature," &c. So far as I understand Euthymius's argument, I do not perceive that he has made more use of the eighth verse, than he has of the seventh. Euthymius, however, derived all these arguments and testimonies from *Cyril's Thesaurus;* where Mr. Porson " saw with his own eyes not a word more than, *For there are three that bear record, the Spirit, the Water, and the Blood, and the three are one.*" I can corroborate the accuracy of Mr. Porson's statement as to the point, which he was considering, viz. the absence of the seventh verse. It is, however, observable, that the words of Cyril are ὅτι ΟΙ τρεῖς εἰσιν οἱ μαρτυροῦντες, so that the rendering should be, " for *the three* are they who bear record:" *the* three are in reference to ver. 6. where Cyril has the reading of some extant MSS. δι' ὕδατος καὶ αἵματος ΚΑΙ ΠΝΕΥΜΑΤΟΣ. This instance, therefore, is totally distinct from that which follows; for Cyril in this place has εἰς τὸ ἕν. In those words he appears to have cited accurately what he found in his copy; while in οἱ τρεῖς he wrote as from himself. It may be inferred, however, from Griesbach, that even in the final clause of ver. 8. Cyril sometimes shook off the yoke, which the MSS. imposed on him, and wrote not merely ΤΟ ἕν, which is just as exceptionable, and in which, as Mr. Porson supposes, the Preposition might be absorbed in the preceding τρεῖς, but sometimes simply ʽΕΝ : that is to say, Cyril has sometimes so far forgotten or disregarded the precise words of Scripture, as, in quoting them, to have expressed himself according to the common usage.

The *Apostolos*, which comes next in order, requires no notice.

The passage from *Basil* is, I imagine, for Mr. Porson has given only the Latin, that which I find *advers. Eunom.* lib. v.

CHAPTER V. 449

πιστεύουσιν εἰς Θεὸν καὶ λόγον καὶ πνεῦμα μίαν οὖσαν Θεότητα. On this I would merely observe, that μία Θεότης and εἷς Θεός, predicated of the Three Persons, are so common in all Treatises on the Trinity, that it is improbable that the Fathers had any knowledge of τὸ ἓν for τὸ ἓν Θεῖον, as being a Scripture phrase.

The *Scholion* ascribed to *Origen*, on Psalm cxxiii. 2. ends with οἱ γὰρ τρεῖς τὸ ἓν εἰσιν· and nothing is more evident, than that this is a citation from the eighth verse: the Writer had just said τὰ δὲ τρία (viz. the Spirit, the Body, and the Soul) κύριος δ' Θεὸς ἡμῶν ἐστι· he immediately subjoins ΟΙ ΓΑΡ ΤΡΕΙΣ, &c. the sudden change of the Gender and the γὰρ together demonstrate, that the words were borrowed by way of proof. These Scholia, though imputed to Origen, are generally allowed to be *sequioris ævi*. Many of them, like the present, are models of mysticism and absurdity.

We next learn, that *Andreas Cretensis* has from Greg. Nazianzen the words τὰ τρία εἷς Θεός: and that the *Nomocanon*, published by Cotelerius, has ἓν ταῦτα τὰ τρία, not ΤΟ ἕν. Lastly, the Author of the *Philopatris*, published with Lucian, has said, in ridicule of the faith of his Christian contemporaries, ἓν τρία, τρία ἕν.

Supposing, then, that these are all the Greek passages, which have any similitude to the controverted verse, (and if there were many more, the controversy could not easily have failed to bring them to light,) I think I may state it as the general result, that they belong either to the first or to the second of the classes above described: they are either citations of the words of St. John, and therefore afford no other evidence affecting my inquiry than that of the antiquity of the reading; or else they are instances tending to prove that the reading of the eighth verse, on the supposition that the seventh is spurious, is not authorized by ordinary usage. Of the third class, consisting of passages similar to the final clause of the eighth verse, not being citations of that clause, yet having τὸ ἓν so used as to form a vindication of the Article in the clause, I have not found any example. There is, however, in *Origen*, as quoted by *Griesbach*, *Symb. Crit.* vol. ii. p. 611. a passage, which is remarkable, as tending to show what would have been the meaning of εἰς ΤΟ ἓν in ver. 8. if the seventh had not been spurious. I transcribe Griesbach. "*Origenes, in transfiguratione, ait, Christi, postquam ipse discipulos attigisset, hi non viderunt, nisi Jesum solum.* ἘΝ μονον γεγονε μωσης (ὁ νομος) και ἠλιας (ἡ προφητεια) ἰησου (τῳ εὐαγγελιῳ.) και οὐχ ὥσπερ ἠσαν προτερον τρεις, οὑτω μεμενηκασιν, ἀλλα γεγονασιν οἱ τρεις εἰς ΤΟ ἑν." According to this account Moses and Elias, respectively emblematic of the Law and of Prophecy, became *one* with Jesus or the Gospel: there were no longer three, but the three were transformed into *the one* (before mentioned). The reference of the Article in τὸ ἓν is here as evident as it is in οἱ τρεῖς of the same passage.

The difficulty, then, attending the final clause of ver. 8. remains thus far not only unobviated, but in some degree confirmed; and I do not perceive how the present reading is to be reconciled with the extermination of ver. 7. The only alternative left us, is the possibility, that the Article in εἰς τὸ ἓν may be spurious, or even that the whole final clause of ver. 8. may be an interpolation. All the evidence, with which I am able to support the former of these conjectures, consists in the reading of the Vienna MS. published by *Alter*, which has εἰς ἕν, in a var. reading of Cyril (ἓν for εἰς τὸ ἓν) already alluded to, as noticed by Griesbach *ad loc.* and in the same var. reading in the MS. of Euthym. Zigab. which once belonged to Chrysanthus, as cited by Matthäi. That MS. omits the rejected passage, and says of the Spirit, the Water, and the Blood, καὶ οἱ τρεῖς ἕν εἰσι: such also is the reading (according to Griesbach) of the Armenian, and in one place of Œcumenius. There is likewise a passage in Origen in his Commentary on St. John's Gospel, which I give on the authority of Griesbach, Symb. Crit. ii. 610: "*Joannes* τὸ πνεῦμα καὶ τὸ ὕδωρ καὶ τὸ αἷμα ἀνέγραψε, τὰ τρία ΕΙΣ ἘΝ γενόμενα." I am not, perhaps, entitled to consider this also as a var. reading, because it seems to be intended to express the sense rather than the exact words of St. John: it is important, however, in another point of view, as it shows in common with some other instances already noticed, that εἰς ἕν, and not εἰς ΤΟ ἕν, is, where there is no reference, the natural phraseology.

De Missy, in his MS. Notes on his copy of Mill's Test. preserved in the British Museum, has a conjecture, which may be noticed in this place. Commenting on the words of Tertul-

CHAPTER V. 451

lian, "*Qui tres UNUM sunt, non UNUS*," he supposes that Father to reject the reading of some MSS. in which was *et tres unus sunt*: which, he says, might have arisen from the Greek καὶ οἱ τρεῖς εἷς εἰσιν: for supposing such a reading in some copies, the rest admits a probable solution. Somebody, dissatisfied, for the same cause as Tertullian, with εἷς, wrote in the margin ἕν, either from authority or from conjecture: thence came the reading of the Lateran Council οἱ τρεῖς ἕν εἰσιν, by adopting ἕν for εἷς: in other copies, for the sake of emphasis, TO might be added: hence the reading of the Author of the "Disputation at the Council of Nice" represents this part of the text to be καὶ οἱ τρεῖς τὸ ἕν εἰσιν. Others, lastly, changing the accent and breathing of εἷς, out of the three readings made a fourth, or, if you will, restored the true one, καὶ οἱ τρεῖς εἰς τὸ ἕν εἰσιν. See Mr. *Beloe's Anecdotes of Literature*, vol. i. p. 116. The best argument which I have to offer in support of this theory, is the variety of readings in the clause: for in addition to those which my immediate purpose required me to notice, three or four authorities have οἱ τρεῖς τὸ ἕν εἰσι, thus omitting the Preposition: it is not, however, at all evident that the passage of Tertullian, which is the basis of the whole, is to be so explained: nor has any extant MS. εἷς.

It is, then, barely possible that the *Article* may be spurious: the authorities are, in general, hostile to this supposition.

The other conjecture, that the *whole clause* may be spurious, is scarcely more defensible; and, indeed, if the last cited passage from Origen be authentic, (and, so far as I know, it has not ever been suspected,) it will, as does the Syr. Version, prove the clause to have existed at an early period. On the other hand, of the Latin MSS., which are the principal support of the seventh verse, many omit the final clause of the eighth. Mr. Porson (p. 139.) has given us his collation of fifty MSS. of the Vulgate: " of this number," he informs us, "thirty-two omit the final clause of the eighth verse: eighteen retain it, but one has it in the text underlined with red lead, two in the margin, one from the first, the other from a second hand." Further on, however, (p. 155.) the Professor has as follows: "Abbot Joachim compared the final clauses of the seventh and eighth verses, whence he inferred, that the same expression ought to be interpreted in the same manner. Since, therefore, said he, nothing more than unity of testimony and consent can be meant by *tres unum sunt* in the eighth verse, nothing more than unity of testimony and consent is meant in the seventh. This opinion the Lateran Council and Thomas Aquinas confuted, by cutting out that clause in the eighth verse. Thomas tells us, that it was not extant in the *true copies*, but that it was *said* to be added by the Arian heretics, to pervert the sound understanding of the foregoing authority." What is here said of the Lateran Council derives some confirmation from what the Professor has asserted, (p. 152.) that twenty-nine Latin MSS., " in general the fairest, the oldest, and the most correct," have the clause of ver. 8.—*Grotius* supposed the clause to be spurious : in his Commentary, he speaks of a very ancient MS. in which it is wanting : this MS., however, was no other than the Alexandrian, in which the words are found: see Mr. Porson, p. 71. It is wanting in Bryennius and in the Correctorium Biblicum.—I do not know whether any inference can be drawn from a citation of the verse by Greg. Nazianz. Orat. xxxvii. p. 603. though the final clause is there omitted. He is arguing against a sophism which turned on the difference between *connumeration* and *subnumeration* : it was contended, that persons or things equal in dignity and homöusian are *connumerated*; e. g. we say *three men three Gods*: whereas things unequal and not homöusian are enumerated, and that, which as being the lowest in dignity is placed last, was said to be *subnumerated* : thus from the formula, *Father, Son, and Holy Ghost*, the objectors inferred the inferiority of the last named Person. With this explanation the passage from Gregory will be intelligible : " What, then, are we to say of John, when in his Catholic Epistles he affirms, that there are three, who bear witness, the Spirit, the Blood, the Water ? Does he appear to you to write nonsense, in having in the first place ventured to connumerate things not homöusian, which you allow to be done only in things homöusian ? For who will pretend, that these are of the same substance ?" It may here be urged, that Gregory omitted the clause purposely, as not contributing to strengthen his argument. The same may be alleged of a similar passage in Nicetas, the Commentator on Gregory, as adduced by Matthäi: Nicetas is there illustrating a different part of his author; but has evidently borrowed his reasoning, and almost his words, from that which I have translated. He too omits the final clause.—At any rate it is remarkable, that the clause in question appears so seldom in the writings of the Fathers: connected with the sentence preceding, it was capable of being converted to some use by persons, who knew the mystical interpretation of Spirit, Blood, and Water, and who for the most part were not averse from that kind of exposition. If it be said, that the clause existed in the time of Origen and of the Syr. Translator, the little use which has been made of it, will still leave a presumption, that some copies were without it: and when we remark in reading the Fathers, that in order to illustrate the Trinity in Unity they have collected all imaginable instances, in which three things in any manner coalesce in one, it becomes matter of surprise, leaving the mystical interpretation out of the question, that a Triad, the unity of which in some sense or other was asserted in Scripture, should not have been more frequently insisted on.

In concluding this Note, I think it right to offer something towards its vindication. I am not ignorant, that in the rejection of the controverted passage learned and good men are now, for the most part, agreed; and I contemplate with admiration and delight the gigantic exertions of intellect, which have established this acquiescence: the objection, however, which has given rise to this discussion, I could not consistently with my plan suppress. On the whole I am led to suspect, that though so much labour and critical acuteness have been bestowed on these celebrated verses, more is yet to be done, before the mystery, in which they are involved, can be wholly developed.

V. 19. ἐν τῷ πονηρῷ. "Lieth under the power of the Wicked One," as translated by *Macknight*. See on Matt. v. 37.

V. 20. ἡ ζωὴ αἰώνιος. Some MSS. omit ἡ, and some insert a second Article before αἰώνιος. One of these emendations is necessary: I prefer the latter, because of οὗτος preceding.

II. JOHN.

V. 1. ὁ πρεσβύτερος ἐκλεκτῇ κυρίᾳ. Commentators and Critics have found it difficult to determine the meaning of the address of this Epistle. Some, with whom agree Eng. Version, *Wakefield, Macknight*, and *Newcome*, make ἐκλεκτῇ to be an Adjective, and render "to the elect, or excellent, or chosen Lady." Others, as *Schleusner*, making Κυρίᾳ a Proper Name, understand "to Cyria the Elect;" and a third class think that Ἐκλεκτῇ is a Proper Name, "to the Lady Electa." A little attention to the position of the words and to the uses of the Article may, perhaps, contribute to remove the uncertainty. The first interpretation would require either τῇ Κυρίᾳ τῇ ἐκλεκτῇ or else τῇ ἐκλεκτῇ Κυρίᾳ, for these, as we have seen, are in such cases the only definite forms of expression. According to the second explanation we should read Κυρίᾳ τῇ ἐκλεκτῇ: so the Epistle following is inscribed Γαΐῳ τῷ ἀγαπητῷ, and so Apollon. de Synt. p. 46. directs us to write Τρυφῶνι τῷ ἀγαθωτάτῳ. On the third hypothesis the phraseology is unexceptionable ; for Κυρίᾳ being a title of honour belonging to others, as well as to *Electa*, would not admit the Article. So Παῦλος ἀπόστολος *passim*. One of the early Fathers, Clement of Alex., so understood the passage. To this explanation it may, indeed, be objected, that in the concluding verse we read τῆς ἀδελφῆς σου τῆς Ἐκλεκτῆς, which seems to intimate that the sister's name also would thus be Electa. *Grotius*, who adopts the same interpretation with myself, tells us that "*alii libri sine Articulo habent* ΕΚΛΕΚΤΗΣ, whilst others have Εὐδέκτης:" the latter reading he approves, and shows that both Electa and Eudecte are names acquired by

II. JOHN.

translation from the Hebrew. But where are these *alii libri?* I cannot learn that any extant MS. has either of the readings alleged. The words τῆς Ἐκλεκτῆς have, however, very much the appearance of being originally the Gloss of some one, who wished to mark the meaning of σου; and indeed, such information might not seem altogether useless, as the address had latterly been in the Plural form, comprehending both Electa and her children: at any rate, a Reader who had observed, that the Singular form had latterly been discontinued, might very naturally on its resumption, if he understood Electa in the Inscription to be a Proper Name, write τῆς Ἐκλεκτῆς in the margin of his copy opposite to σου. The probability that the words in question were a Gloss, is rather strengthened, when we remark that for τῆς ἐκλεκτῆς two MSS. have τῆς ἐκκλησίας: this was evidently the Gloss of some one, who interpreted ἐκλεκτῇ Κυρίᾳ in ver. 1. mystically, as was done by many, to signify the Christian Church; and who wished to give a marginal explanation of σου, in the same manner as I suppose the other Annotator to have been contented with showing its reference to ver. 1. For the most part, indeed, I have endeavoured to defend the incorruptness of the Sacred Text: we are arrived, however, at a part of the N. T. of which the MSS. were always comparatively few, and where, consequently, in suspected passages the genuine reading is less likely to be extant. If we had as many MSS. of the 2d Epistle of St. John, as we have of the Gospel of St. Matthew, I think it highly probable, that in some of them the sentence would terminate with ἀδελφῆς σου.

Michaelis in his Introd. to this Epistle conjectures Κυρία to be an Ellipsis of Κυρία Ἐκκλησία, the Athenian Assembly meeting at stated times; and that since the Sacred Writers adopted the term ἐκκλησία from its civil use among the Greeks, κυρία ἐκκλησία might here mean the stated assembly of the Christians held every Sunday: thus τῇ ἐκλεκτῇ Κυρίᾳ with ἐκκλησίᾳ understood would signify to the Elect Church or Community, which comes together on Sundays. He admits, however, that he knows not of any instance of such an Ellipsis; nor do I think that this explanation can very easily be established. As to his remark, *Introd.* vol. iv. p. 449, that ἐκλεκτῇ cannot here be a Proper Name, "for, if it were, St.

John would not have written τῇ ἐκλεκτῇ Κυρίᾳ, but τῇ Κυρίᾳ Ἐκλεκτῇ, or at least without the Article, Ἐκλεκτῇ Κυρίᾳ," there must be some mistake: what Michaelis alleges, that St. John *would* have written, is actually the reading of the MSS. viz. Ἐκλεκτῇ Κυρίᾳ; and thus far at least, his opinion coincides with my own. It may be added, that on the proposed interpretation the Inscription of this Epistle corresponds with the Greek usage, in which the Name precedes, and the rank, character, or condition in life is subjoined. So St. *Basil's* Letter lxxx. is inscribed Εὐσταθίῳ ἰατρῷ; lxxxiii. Λεοντίῳ σοφιστῇ; lxxxvi. Βοσπορίῳ ἐπισκόπῳ; ccccx. Μαγνημιανῷ κόμητι.

V. 7. οὗτός ἐστιν ὁ πλάνος καὶ ὁ Ἀντίχριστος. Two good MSS. want the latter Article: the omission is not necessary, because the intention of the Writer is not to *assume* the identity of the two characters, but to *assert*, that they are united in those, who denied that Christ had appeared in the flesh.

V. 10. ταύτην τὴν διδαχήν. *Erasmus* and some of his followers omit τήν. This is contrary to Part i. Chap. vii. § 5. and to the uniform practice in all similar cases throughout the N. T. I cannot believe that any MS. justified this or many others of his deviations from the Greek usage. See on 1 John iv. 9.

III. JOHN.

V. 7. ὑπὲρ τοῦ ὀνόματος αὐτοῦ. Very many MSS. omit αὐτοῦ: yet it is found in the Syr. and in the Lat. of the other ancient Versions, except the Coptic. *Rosenmüller* tells us that ὄνομα is sometimes put κατ' ἐξοχὴν for Christ, and he instances James ii. 7. With this, however, no Reader will be satisfied: a less apposite illustration could not easily have been found.—The reading is of considerable importance: if αὐτοῦ be genuine, its antecedent must be θεοῦ immediately preceding, and yet ὀνόματος can be meant only of the name of Christ; and thus Christ will here also, as elsewhere, be called God. If αὐτοῦ be spurious, and the Article be used, as frequently happens, to signify *his*, the inference will be the same. To evade these consequences, it must be shown, that τὸ ὄνομα is used in the same sense with ἡ ὁδός, Acts ix. 2. which, however, may not be an easy task [1].

[1] But see Euseb. Eccl. Hist. v. 18. *Author's MS.*

JUDE.

V. 4. τὸν μόνον δεσπότην θεὸν καὶ Κύριον ἡμῶν Ἰησ. Χρ. This is the last of the passages adduced by *Mr. Granville Sharp* to show that Christ is called God. There is, however, some difficulty in ascertaining the true reading, since very many authorities omit θεόν, and *Griesbach* has rejected it from his text. Yet of *Matthäi's* MSS. all, except one, have θεόν: so also the Syr. Arab. and Æthiopic. Further, *Mr. Wordsworth* has remarked against Wetstein and Griesbach, that Œcumenius, of whose works Mr. W. examined four Editions, has the word θεόν. Supposing the common reading to be the true one, I see no reason to doubt the proposed interpretation, which explains δεσπότης θεὸς (a form resembling σωτὴρ θεός, see on Titus iii. 4.) and Κύριος of one Person, Jesus Christ: for had *two* Persons been meant, we should have read ΤΟΝ Κύριον ἡμῶν. That the Syr. Translator understood the passage of one Person is most certain: he puts Κύριον in *apposition* with δεσπότην θεόν, and renders " the only Lord God (viz.) our Lord Jesus Christ." The Copt. does the same.

V. 11. τῇ πλάνῃ τοῦ Βαλαὰμ μισθοῦ. Many Commentators and Translators (among whom is *Macknight*) make τοῦ to be the Article of μισθοῦ, so that the sense may be, " in the error of Balaam's hire." This is, however, extremely improbable. It is true that Proper Names in Regimen frequently dispense with the Article: but then the arrangement would, I think, have been τοῦ μισθοῦ Βαλαάμ. Besides, before Proper Names which are indeclinable, I do not perceive that in this Epistle the Article is usually omitted: the clauses which are on each side of the present, contain two examples of the contrary ; viz. τοῦ Κάϊν and τοῦ Κορέ. It is scarcely necessary to observe, that μισθοῦ does not require the Article. Thus *Æsch. de fals. Leg.* ed. Reiske, p. 328. λόγους γράφοντα μισθοῦ. I believe, therefore, that the English Version is right.

V. 25. Θεῷ σωτῆρι ἡμῶν. The Reader might, perhaps, expect ΤΩι σωτῆρι ἡμῶν: in apposition, however, the Article is frequently omitted ; so in the phrase ἀπὸ Θεοῦ πατρὸς ἡμῶν *passim*. See above, p. 393.

REVELATION.

CHAP. I.

V. 3. τῆς προφητείας. Some authorities add ταύτης. This addition is unnecessary: the prophecy is that which is laid before the Reader: in the same manner St. Paul sometimes writes ἐν τῇ ἐπιστολῇ. See on 1 Cor. v. 9.

V. 4. ἀπὸ τοῦ ὁ ὢν καὶ ὁ ἦν καὶ ὁ ἐρχόμενος. Many MSS. omit τοῦ, which, however, appears to be requisite, though *Griesbach* has rejected it: a few for τοῦ have Θεοῦ, which *Matthäi* justly regards as a Scholium. Of the Article in ὁ ἦν, I have to observe, that there are many peculiarities in the style of this work, which it may not be easy nor even possible to reconcile to the Greek usage. The difficulty, however, in this place respects not so much the Article as ἦν, which is used as if it had been a Participle of Past Time.

V. 11. ὁ πρῶτος καὶ ὁ ἔσχατος. See on 2 John 7. These words are wanting in some MSS.: they occur, however, repeatedly in other parts of the Book.

V. 13. ὅμοιον υἱῷ ἀνθρώπου. It was remarked on John v. 27. that when our Saviour, in speaking of Himself, assumes the title, *the Son of Man*, the Greek is always ὁ υἱὸς τοῦ ἀνθρώπου: and a reason was assigned why the Articles in that particular instance were omitted. The same reason will not apply to the example before us, in which Christ is not directly and primarily meant. In the Apocalypse, as is well known, many of the expressions, and much of the imagery, is borrowed from the Prophets; and this passage, as the Commentators have remarked, is taken from Dan. vii. 13: see above, p. 402, 3.

CHAP. III.

V. 17. σὺ εἶ ὁ ταλαίπωρος καὶ ἐλεεινός, κ. τ. λ. English Version, "thou art wretched," &c. *Grotius* thinks that the Article is here employed in the κατ' ἐξοχὴν sense: with this solution, supposing it to be founded on the *Greek* usage, I am not entirely satisfied, because I do not know of any thing similar in the Profane Writers, nor even in the N. T. But the Hebrew ה is frequently so used before Adjectives: see *Noldius*, p. 212. and it is not improbable that the Greek Article may, in this place, have the force of the Hebrew one. The Hebraisms of this book are so numerous, that some Critics have assigned it a Hebrew original: see below, on x. 7. Many MSS. have likewise Ὁ ἐλεεινός, which, in the same way of reasoning, may have proceeded from the Author.

CHAP. IV.

V. 2. ἐπὶ τοῦ θρόνου καθήμενος. Dr. *Mangey* conjectures Ὁ καθήμενος, whilst Dr. *Owen* thinks that we have here an uncommon Ellipsis of τὶς. Had the MSS. read ὁ καθήμενος, I should have been somewhat perplexed to explain the force of the Article, for it would not be subservient either to reference or to hypothesis. That there is an Ellipsis of τὶς is true; but not that the Ellipsis is uncommon: the very same takes place in ἡγούμενος, Matt. ii. 6. and in many other instances. It is curious to observe, that these two Critics, while they agree in discovering a difficulty in the text, in order to remove it, adopt expedients which are diametrically opposite to each other.

CHAP. VI.

V. 2. νικῶν. A. has Ὁ νικῶν. But this would not accord with ἵνα νικήσῃ following.

V. 8. ὄνομα αὐτῷ ὁ θάνατος. C. and one MS. of *Matthäi*, with the Complut. omit ὁ: their reading is confirmed by the general usage: so below, ix. 11.

V. 10. ὁ ἅγιος καὶ ὁ ἀληθινός. Several MSS. omit the second Article. It is properly rejected by *Bengel, Griesbach*, and *Matthäi*.

V. 14. οὐρανός. Ὁ οὐρανός, as in several MSS. is the true reading.

CHAP. VIII.

V. 6. ἄγγελοι ἔχοντες. It should be ΟΙ ἔχοντες, as in many MSS. The angels had already been affirmed (ver. 2.) to have the seven trumpets.

V. 10. τὰς πηγὰς ὑδάτων. Many MSS. have ΤΩΝ ὑδάτων: it is surprising that *Wetstein* did not admit the Article into the text. We find it in *Matthäi* and in the *new* edition of *Griesbach*.

V. 11. ἄψινθος. A great many MSS. have ὁ ἄψινθος, and the Article has found its way into the text of *Bengel* and *Griesbach*, and even of *Matthäi*: yet nothing can be more certain than its spuriousness; I mean, on the supposition that the present Greek of this writing is the original. I have not observed any violation of the rule, Part i. Chap. iii. Sect. iii. § 2. In the next Chapter, ver. 16. we should read ΤΩΝ στρατευμάτων. See the last Note.

CHAP. X.

V. 1. ἶρις ἐπὶ τῆς κεφαλῆς. The authorities which direct us to read ἡ ἶρις, are very numerous; and the best modern Editors have admitted the Article into the text. Compare, however, iv. 3. It is true that the names of the great objects of nature, the sun, the moon, the air, &c. usually have the Article: but these are permanent and monadic: the word ἶρις seems to have no other claim to it than have σεισμός, ἔκλειψις, and the names of other transient phenomena.

V. 3, 4. αἱ ἑπτὰ βρονταί. Why the Article is inserted in the former of these verses, I am unable to discover. It is somewhat remarkable, that a few MSS. and Editions omit it in both places. Were *the Seven Thunders* any thing well known and pre-eminent? If not, the omission must be right in the former instance, but wrong in the latter: if they were pre-eminent, then is it wrong in both. *Bengel* omits the Article in ver. 3. but has it in ver. 4. I am inclined to suppose, that αἱ ἑπτὰ βρονταὶ is in both places the true reading, and that there is a reference to some Jewish opinion, of which,

CHAPTER X. 463

however, I find not any vestige either in *Lightfoot, Schoettgen,* or *Meuschen.*—*Storr,* in the *Comment. Theol.* (collected by *Velthusen* and others) vol. iv. p. 457, observes, that we are not here to seek for any Jewish notion; that nothing is to be inferred from the Article; and that in xii. 14. ὁ ἀετὸς ὁ μέγας signifies "*magnam QUANDAM aquilam, &c. æquè ac si Articulus abesset.*" But see on Matt. v. 1.

V. 7. καὶ ἐτελέσθη τὸ μυστήριον. Readers of the N. T. for the most part find a difficulty in rendering this passage: they are led by the context to expect, instead of ἐτελέσθη, a Future Tense to correspond with ἔσται in the preceding verse; and καὶ perplexes the sense, which requires the *Apodosis* to begin at ἐτελέσθη, whereas, if we retain καί, the *Protasis* is continued. The various readings of this passage sufficiently attest, that great also has been the embarrassment of Copyists and Editors. A. 10. 17. *à pr. manu* omit καί: some MSS. and Editions have τελεσθῇ, as more nearly approaching to a Future signification. *Arethas* and three Editions of *Beza* have τελεσθήσεται, which, with the rejection of καί, would make the whole plain: the same reading is said by *Griesbach* to appear in some of the Oriental Versions: perhaps, however, they have given the sense rather than the idiom; see on Matt. i. 16. Abp. *Newcome* observes, "if we omit καί and read τελεσθήσεται," (for which, however, there is scarcely any authority,) "by the mystery of God, we must understand the glorious state of the Church." That some ancient Versions are cited as omitting καί, I mean not to suppress: but the inference, I think, is not justified, that καὶ was wanting in the copies of those Translators, any more than that they found τελεσθήσεται.

I have already remarked, that some Critics have been disposed to assign to the Apocalypse a Hebrew original: I do not know that in behalf of this opinion any stronger argument could be adduced, than that which might be founded on the present passage. The Hebrew language employs what Grammarians call the *Vau Conversivum*: that is, it uses the Copulative in such a manner, that one of its offices is to give to a Past Tense the sense of the Future; the Copulative itself very frequently becoming redundant. For the sake of those who have no knowledge of Hebrew, I will illustrate the usage by a single example. We read, Judges iv. 8. "if thou wilt go with me, *I will go:*" (והלכתי) literally, "*and I went.*" Now nothing can be more evident than the resemblance between the literal rendering of Judges iv. 8. and that of the passage under review: "in the days of the voice of the Seventh Angel, when he shall begin to sound, *and the mystery was finished.*" What is this, if we adopt the Hebrew idiom, but *the mystery shall be finished?* thus superseding the reading of Beza's Editions, countenanced by Abp. Newcome, viz. τελεσθήσεται, instead of καὶ ἐτελέσθη. The ancient Versions which are cited to support the omission of καί, ought rather to be adduced in proof of the true construction: thus the Vulg. has "*cum cœperit tuba canere, CONSUMMABITUR mysterium Dei.*" Whether the translator adverted to the Hebraism or not, he plainly saw what the context required: that he read τελεσθήσεται is highly improbable, as it is not found in any MS. extant.

Of this Hebraism there is not, I believe, a single instance in the Gospels, the Acts, or the Epistles. *Storr*, indeed, (l. l. p. 463) after remarking that the sense is the same as if we had read τελεσθήσεται, refers us to xv. 1. where, however, a Past Tense is indispensable: he cites also John xv. 6. 8; but there the Aorists are used, as frequently they are in purer writers, to mark, not a single act, which is all that can be supposed in the present instance, but the *frequency* of an act: besides that in those places καί does not appear. For καί he cites out of the N. T. only Luke ii. 21. καὶ ἐκλήθη, where indeed, as in some other places, it is equivalent to τότε: but there we have not κληθήσεται.

As to the hypothesis of a Hebrew original of this singular composition, the Reader, probably, will not readily assent to it, unsupported as it is by the evidence of history: at the same time he will recollect, that if it could be established, it would relieve us from all difficulties attending the objection, that the style of the Apocalypse differs from that employed by St. John in his Gospel and Epistles. Without having any such theory in view, I notice a peculiarity, which, so far as I know, had hitherto escaped remark, that the Reader may feel the less surprise, if the Article be sometimes used in this book in a manner, which I am wholly unable to explain: if the style in some instances deviate so widely from the Greek usage, it cannot be expected that rules founded entirely on that usage should in such a composition always apply.

V. 8. ἐν τῇ χειρὶ ἀγγέλου. The Greek practice requires τοῦ ἀγγέλου, with many MSS. and the best modern Editors; so also in ver. 8. of the next Chapter, it should be τῆς πόλεως.

CHAP. XI.

V. 11. τὰς τρεῖς ἡμέρας. Some MSS. improperly omit τάς: it refers to ver. 9.

V. 12. ἐν τῇ νεφέλῃ. Eng. Version, "a cloud." No cloud had been mentioned, yet there is not any instance in the N. T. in which νεφέλη has the Article, where there is not reference.

CHAP. XII.

V. 1. γυνὴ περιβεβλημένη. The four first Edd. of *Erasmus* have Ἡ περιβεβλημένη. This is another of the instances, in which the MSS. of Erasmus, if indeed he always published from MSS., differed both from all those, which are still extant, and also from the exigency of the sense: for Ἡ περιβεβλημένη would mean, that the circumstance of being thus clothed had been already signified. See on 1 John iv. 9.

V. 9. ὁ Σατανᾶς. Very many MSS. omit the Article, as was to be expected after καλούμενος.

V. 11. ἄχρι θανάτου. I do not perceive why our Translators used the uncouth phrase "unto the death," especially as they were not led to it by the original.

V. 14. δύο πτέρυγες τοῦ ἀετοῦ τοῦ μεγάλου. Here it may be asked, Why ΤΟΥ ἀετοῦ ΤΟΥ μεγάλου, or else why not ΑΙ δύο πτέρυγες? The latter difficulty, indeed, is removed, if we admit the reading of a few MSS. which have αἱ: but what is to become of the former? *Michaelis* (Anmerk.) corrects the Version of Luther, and observes, "it must allude to a particular eagle already mentioned in the Apocalypse: yet I do not recollect any other than that, which (see viii. 13.) flew through the heaven and proclaimed the threefold woe, which now is past." It is not improbable that *the Great Eagle*, a species so denominated, may be meant: we find in Ezek. xvii. 3. from whom the expression, as well as other things in

H h

this book, may be borrowed, ὁ ἀετὸς ὁ μέγας ὁ μεγαλοπτέρυγος, κ. τ. λ. *Bochart,* vol. i. Part ii. p. 169. tells us, that the Great Eagle of Ezekiel was the 'Αστερίας said by *Ælian* to be μέγιστος ἀετῶν.

CHAP. XIII.

V. 8. τοῦ ἀρνίου ἐσφαγμένου. With the best MSS. we should read ΤΟΥ ἐσφαγμένου.

V. 18. ἔχων τὸν νοῦν. With many MSS. we should reject the Article: νοῦν ἔχειν is the usual phrase.

CHAP. XIV.

V. 1. ἀρνίον. Probably with several MSS. ΤΟ ἀρνίον, a name of Christ κατ' ἐξοχήν.

Same v. A. reads ΤΟ γεγραμμένον. See above, on xii. 1. unless indeed both be Hebraisms.

V. 6. εὐαγγέλιον αἰώνιον. Our Eng. Version "the everlasting Gospel," says rather more than does the original Greek, and more than the context requires.

V. 14. υἱῷ ἀνθρώπου. See above, on i. 13.

CHAP. XVI.

V. 5. καὶ ὁ ὅσιος. Here many MSS.—καὶ ὁ, and many omit only καί. *Wetstein, Matthäi,* and *Griesbach,* approve the former reading; I should more readily become the advocate of the latter: the former, indeed, I scarcely understand; the latter will mean, Just art Thou, the Being that is and that was, the Holy One: so i. 8. ὁ παντοκράτωρ. The reading of the common Edd. καὶ ὁ seems to have originated with some one, who wished to make the whole passage agree with the form ὁ ὢν καὶ ὁ ἦν καὶ ὁ ἐρχόμενος: some *Edd.* indeed, have this reading.

CHAP. XVII.

V. 4. ἡ περιβεβλημένη. The best MSS. for ἡ have ἦν, which the passage requires.

Same v. γέμον βδελυγμάτων καὶ τὰ ἀκάθαρτα τῆς πορνείας

CHAPTER XVIII.

τῆς γῆς. We have here another passage, which will probably for ever resist the powers of criticism: indeed the task of the Critic throughout this book scarcely yields in difficulty to that of the Expositor: there is, however, this difference, that the fulfilment of Prophecy will gradually dissipate the obscurities which perplex the one, while those, which bewilder the other, may possibly never be elucidated. The common text, it is true, has ἀκαθάρτητος τῆς πορνείας αὐτῆς, for which I find no other advocate than *Schleusner;* the Nominative ἀκαθάρτης being contrary to analogy, and the reading unsupported by MSS. On the other hand, τὰ ἀκάθαρτα after γέμον offends against grammatical construction, which, however, in this book seems not to be regarded; since the best MSS. in the verse preceding have γέμον ὀνόματα, a reading, the very singularity of which proves that it did not originate with the Copyists. But then why was it not also βδελύγματα? My motive for noticing these difficulties has been stated above, on x. 7.

CHAP. XVIII.

V. 17. πᾶς ἐπὶ τῶν πλοίων ὁ ὅμιλος. The Greek usage would require the Article to be placed before ἐπί: the majority of MSS., however, for ἐπὶ τῶν πλοίων ὁ ὅμιλος have ὁ ἐπὶ τόπον πλέων: which is preferred by *Wetstein* and *Griesbach:* a few have πᾶς ὁ ἐπὶ τῶν πλοίων πλέων. The ancient Versions exhibit vestiges of all these readings: the Vulg. has "*omnis qui in lacum* (some MSS. *locum*) *navigant:*" the Syr. "*qui ad locum navigat:*" the Arab. "*qui maria sulcant:*" the Copt. "*omnes navigantes in mari:*" and the Æthiop. "*turba navium.*" *Matthäi* observes, "*Primasius*" (who lived in the sixth century) "has *omnis per mare navigans. Forte ergo* πόντον *legit pro* τόπον. Πᾶς ὁ ἐπὶ τόπον πλέων καὶ ναῦται, *ut ego edidi, binis vocabulis nuncupantur* VECTORES *et* NAUTÆ. *Hæc ergo, ut videtur, aliquis Græcè interpretatus est,* πᾶς ἐπὶ τῶν πλοίων ὁ ὅμιλος. Ὅμιλος *dubito, an idoneâ auctoritate nitatur.*" Notwithstanding the opinion which I entertain of the critical acuteness of Matthäi, I am not satisfied with these conjectures. With respect to ὅμιλος, not only are vestiges of it visible in some of the ancient Versions just cited; but, further, from the manner in which it is here proposed to account for the origin of the reading ὅμιλος, we should not expect to find καὶ ναῦται immediately subjoined; for, if I rightly understand Matthäi, ὁ ὅμιλος was intended to comprehend both *vectores* and *nautæ*. Then, again, the reading *mare* or πόντου seems not to depend wholly on the possible mistake of Primasius ; it is observable in the *lacum* of the Vulg., or if we must allow that reading to be corrupt in the Arabic of the Polyglott, as well as in the Coptic, which could not well be affected either by the Vulgate or by the error of Primasius: and I am not certain that even ἐπὶ πλοίων may not have been considered as an equivalent to ἐπὶ τῆς θαλάσσης. I suspect, therefore, that readings so discordant as those which this passage exhibits, are not thus easily to be accounted for, but are to be explained as being, the one of them (for they are resolvible into two) a supposed or really inaccurate rendering of some Hebrew phrase, and the other the correction. It is well known, that a great part of this prophecy of the fall of Babylon is taken from Ezekiel's prophecy of the destruction of Tyre, Chap. xxvii. where, however, I do not find any thing at all applicable to the solution of our difficulty. The problem seems to be, to discover a Hebrew sentence, which, from its ambiguity, or from a slight, and therefore not improbable, variation in the reading, may explain the rise of the very different readings in the present verse : that is to say, which may account for the difference of *per mare* (or ἐπὶ τῶν πλοίων) and ἐπὶ τόπον, and also show the origin of ὅμιλος. Now in the O. T. I do not recollect any passage which is better, however imperfectly, suited to our purpose, than is Isaiah xlii. 10. the Hebrew of which (יורדי הים ומלאו) the LXX. have rendered οἱ καταβαίνοντες εἰς τὴν θάλασσαν καὶ ΠΛΕΟΝΤΕΣ αὐτήν. Here we observe that ומלאו, which is equivalent to καὶ ὁ ὅμιλος αὐτῆς, is rendered by ΠΛΕΟΝΤΕΣ, and it would not have been a looser translation than is very frequently found in the LXX. to have written either πᾶς ὁ ἐπὶ τῆς θαλάσσης πλέων, or πᾶς ὁ ἐπὶ τῆς θαλάσσης ὅμιλος. As to the difference between πόντον and τόπον, it is much less in Hebrew than in Greek: the Copyist or Translator has only to confound הים *ad mare*, and היד *ad locum*. It is true that we have here nothing to correspond with ἐπὶ τῶν πλοίων : I think, however, that *sailing in ships* and *sailing on the sea* are expressions which might easily be substituted the one for the other: in Psalm cvii. 23. we find the two united.

I have here reasoned on the supposition that the passage was taken from the Hebrew of the O. T.; it is obvious, that on the hypothesis of a *Hebrew original* of the Apocalypse, the argument might be rendered much more conclusive. See above, on x. 7.—In this and the following verses I observe that future events are announced by ἔστησαν, ἔκραζον, &c. This has certainly a Hebrew air: so in Ezek. xxvii. 29, 30. which are parallel to the present and following verse, we find Past Tenses used in a Future signification by the help of the *Vau Conversivum*. The Latin of the Pol. Arab. has in the present instance *stabunt, clamabunt*, as if the Translator had noticed the peculiarity.

CHAP. XIX.

V. 9. οἱ λόγοι ἀληθινοί. If ἀληθινοὶ be meant to be taken in immediate concord with λόγοι, the Article should be repeated, as in A. 4. and Ed. Beng.

V. 10. ἡ γὰρ μαρτυρία τοῦ Ἰησοῦ ἐστι τὸ πνεῦμα τῆς προφητείας. The best interpretation which I have seen of this passage, is that of *J. F. à Stade*, given by *Wolfius*: it supposes the angel to say, " Do not offer me the worship due to God; I am unworthy of the honour, since I am not superior to yourself, but exercise the same function. We both testify of Christ; you to the present generation, I to posterity. Wherefore, love me as a brother and fellow-labourer, but do not worship me as God." If this be the meaning of a text, which has created much dispute, and nothing, I think, can be more clear and satisfactory, we have here a convertible Proposition. See Part i. Chap. iii. Sect. iv. § 1. " Ἡ μαρτυρία τοῦ Ἰησοῦ, the office of an Apostle, which you fill," says the angel, " and τὸ πνεῦμα τῆς προφητείας exercised by me, are not different in value or dignity, but are one and the same thing."

V. 13. ὁ λόγος τοῦ Θεοῦ. *Origen* has omitted the former Article: it is contrary to the usage.

V. 20. εἰς τὴν λίμνην. This lake had not been previously mentioned: it seems to be spoken of as a well-known name for a place of punishment.

CHAP. XX.

V. 2. καὶ Σατανᾶς. Some MSS. have ὁ Σατανᾶς, which, however, the Greek usage will not allow.

CHAP. XXI.

V. 2. Ἱερουσαλὴμ καινήν. So in *Strabo* Καρχήδων νέα.
V. 7. υἱός. Some MSS. improperly prefix the Article.

CHAP. XXII.

V. 2. ξύλον ζωῆς. Our English Version has "the tree of life." Yet it seems more proper to translate "*a* tree of life." Mr. *Wakefield*, indeed, makes ἐντεῦθεν καὶ ἐντεῦθεν to mean that "the river flowed all around;" whereas the words clearly signify that "a tree was *on each side* of the river:" in which case a plurality of trees is implied. This interpretation is corroborated by Ezek. xlvii. 12. It is also assisted by a citation in *Schoettg. Horæ Hebr.* viz. "that in the times of the Messiah God shall create *trees*, which shall produce fruit every month," &c. Mr. W., however, is not the only Critic who has objected to our Common Version in this place. Dr. *Owen* (ap. Bowyer) asks, "Can this translation possibly be right? How could the *single* tree of life, as here represented, possibly stand on *both* sides of the river? The difficulty, in my apprehension, is somewhat considerable: nor can I think at present of any other way to solve it, but by inclosing the words καὶ τοῦ ποταμοῦ ἐντεῦθεν καὶ ἐντεῦθεν, scil. πορευομένου, in a parenthesis; and rendering the passage as follows: in the midst of the street (and consequently of the river that flowed around) stood the tree of life, which bare," &c. The Reader must decide.

V. 17. τὸ ὕδωρ ζωῆς. The best MSS. properly omit τό[1].

---

[1] V. 19. ἀπὸ τῶν λόγων βίβλου. A very large number of MSS. (and some of the best) read τοῦ βιβλίου.—H. J. R.

END OF PART II.

APPENDIX I.

CONTAINING SOME REMARKS ON THE

CODEX BEZÆ,

OR CAMBRIDGE MS. OF THE FOUR GOSPELS AND
THE ACTS OF THE APOSTLES.

BY BISHOP MIDDLETON.

In the earlier pages of the Second Part of the preceding Work, I have sometimes had occasion, in my endeavour to ascertain the true reading or rendering of passages in which the Article was concerned, to condemn the *Codex Bezæ*. I soon found, however, that the deviations of this MS. were so frequent and so extraordinary, that to notice them as they occurred, would greatly swell the bulk of a volume which even then threatened to exceed the limits originally proposed, and that the subject could not be properly considered, but by being reserved for an Appendix.

Before Biblical Criticism had made the progress which it owes principally to the diligence and acuteness of men yet living, the Cambridge MS. though acknowledged to be of very high antiquity, was by many supposed to be a *farrago* compiled from various sources, but principally from the Latin Versions. *Arnauld* pronounced it to be a forgery of the sixth century; *Mill* insisted on its corruptness; *Bengel* held it in no esteem; *Wetstein* not only charged it with latinizing, but of this fact adduced proofs, which were for some time deemed conclusive; *Semler* adopted Wetstein's opinion, though he afterwards revoked it. At the present day, no Critic of eminence, so far as I know, believes the Codex Bezæ to be enormously corrupt, except *Matthäi*, whose judgment on this subject, as it seems to me to come very near the truth, I shall give in his own words: "*De Codice Wetstein. D. ita suspicor. Monachus quidam Latinus, Græcè mediocriter doctus, Græco Novo Testamento suo adscripserat marginibus loca Patrum, cum Græcorum, tum Latinorum, quæ locos singulos N. Testamenti spectare videbantur. Notaverat enim discrimina Codicum aliquot Græcorum et Latinorum N. Testamenti. Adjecerat etiam loca literarum sacrarum parallela. Ex hác farragine deinde vel ipse, vel alius, confecit textum sibi probabilem. Id utrum per stultitiam, an per fraudem fecerit, incertum est. Ex hujusmodi exemplari autem, abhorrenti ab reliquis omnibus, ductus est Codex Cantabrigiensis seu Wetsteinii* D." See Matthäi on Luke xiii. 24. Very different, however, is the opinion of *Michaelis*, *Griesbach*, *Adler*, Professor *Marsh*, and the Editor of the MS., Dr. *Kipling*, the learned Dean of Peterborough.

The defenders of the *Codex Bezæ*, for the most part, content themselves with endeavouring to repel the charge of its *latinizing;* though its very remarkable agreement with the Latin is a fact which, more or less, they feel themselves compelled to admit. It will be remembered that I am concerned only with its frequent and generally unsupported variations from the other MSS. in the insertion or omission of the Article; and that whether these variations arise from its being in many places unskilfully translated from the Latin or from any other language, the conclusion will, in my view of the subject, be the same: viz. that the *Codex Bezæ* is entitled to little or no regard: if, on the contrary, this MS. be a tolerably accurate representation of the Autographs, then is the criticism of the Second Part of this volume extremely fallacious; and the canons which I have endeavoured to establish, however applicable they may be to the Orators and Historians of Athens, are not to be trusted in the Writings of the Evangelists, nor probably in those of the Apostles.

The *Codex Bezæ* is known to harmonize not only with the Latin, but in a great degree with the Old Syriac, with the Sahidic, and with the Coptic, that is to say, probably with the oldest Versions which exist. Hence its advocates would infer not only the *value* of its readings, but also their *authenticity*, which, however, appear to me to be two very different things, not sufficiently distinguished in the controversy: a reading is *valuable* when it preserves the *sense* which was originally expressed by the Writer of the work: to be *authentic*, it must be in his own *words*. I cannot, therefore, accede to the conclusion of *Michaelis*, (Introd. vol. ii. p. 168.) that "the remarkable coincidence with the Syriac and Coptic Versions, is a proof that such MSS. (viz. those which are suspected of latinizing,) instead of being corrupted from the Latin, were *faithfully* taken from very ancient copies, which had readings that are not extant in modern MSS." From this circumstance I infer no *fidelity*, because that which is excellent, may yet be stolen. It is, indeed, possible, and by no means improbable, that the *Codex Bezæ* may have had for its *basis* a MS. older than itself by two or three centuries: in which case, some of its deviations from more modern MSS. may be authentic readings; and unquestionably we ought so to conclude of all of them, if they exactly accorded in sense with the old Versions and with Origen, and if the words in which they are expressed betrayed no marks of their being *re-translated translations*. Every one will assent to the remark of *Münter* (de Vers. Sahid. p. 6.) "*neque probaverit facilè quis, lectionem ex Græcis Codd. deperditam IDEO esse latinizantem.*"

The warmest apologists of the *Codex Bezæ* are *Griesbach* in his Symb. Crit. vol. i. p. 111. and Professor *Marsh* in his Notes to Michaelis, vol. ii. p. 679. The latter observes (p. 683.) that "the purity of a reading is no proof of its authenticity, in a work that is confessedly written in impure

Greek; and that of these fourteen examples," (adduced by Wetstein, Proleg. p. 32.) "there are several which may rather be ascribed to accident than design. In short, there is no reason whatsoever for ascribing any reading of a Greek MS. to the influence of the Latin, unless it can be proved that it could not have taken its rise in the Greek, and that it might easily have originated in the Latin." I cannot otherwise enable the Reader to form an opinion where many of the readings of the *Codex Bezæ* probably originated, and whether their impurity be merely a want of that classical elegance which we ought not to expect, than by laying before him the following Collation: the readings, where nothing is signified to the contrary, are, so far as appears from Griesbach, *lectiones singulares*. Nothing has been omitted, except that in a few instances, to save room, I have passed over readings differing from our common text only in the peculiar spelling of this MS. or in having the paragogic ν, which it constantly inserts before a consonant.

ST. MATTHEW, CHAPTER V.

Received Text.	*Codex Bezæ.*
3. πτωχοι τῳ πνευματι.	— τω.
4. and 5.	transposed. So also in 33. Vulg. Verc. Corb., &c. mostly Latin authorities. See Griesb.
11. ὁταν ὀνειδισωσιν ὑμας και διωξωσι.	οταν διωξουσιν υμας και ὀνειδισουσιν.
Same v. εἰπωσι παν πονηρον ῥημα καθ' ὑμων.	και ειπωσιν καθ' ὑμων παν πονηρον. Hoc ordine Syr. et Syr. Philox. ed.
Same v. ῥημα.	— ρημα. So B. Copt. Æth. Syr. Hieros. the old Italic, the Vulg. The Latins, except the Opus Imperf.
Same v. ψευδομενοι.	— ψευδομενοι. Several Latin Verss. and Fathers, with Origen.
Same v. ἑνεκεν ἐμου.	ἑνεκεν δικαιοσυνης. Many Latin authorities.
12. ἐν τοις οὐρανοις.	εν τω ουρανω.
Same v. οὑτω.	ουτως.
Same v. τους προ ὑμων.	+ ὑπαρχοντας.
13. εἰς οὐδεν ἰσχυει ἐτι.	— ετι. Syr. Erp.-Arab. Latin Versions and Latin Fathers.
18. ἑως ἀν παντα γενηται.	εως αν γενηται παντα.
19. ὁς ἐαν οὐν λυσῃ.	ος οὐν λυσει. Αν was added by a later hand.
Same v. οὑτω.	— ουτω.
20.	deest.
21. ἐῤῥεθη.	ἐρρηθη. E. alii. It is usually so spelt in the Codex Bezæ.

APPENDIX I.

Received Text.	Codex Bezæ.
22. ῥακα.	ραχα.
24. διαλλαγηθι.	καταλλαγηθι.
25. ἐν τῃ ὁδῳ μετ' αὐτου.	μετ' αὐτου ἐν τῃ οδω. L. 1. 13. 33. 124. Lat. Verss. and Lat. Fathers. Three at least of the above MSS. have been suspected of latinizing.
Same v. παραδῳ, bis.	παραδωσει, bis.
Same v. βληθησῃ.	βληθησει.
26. κοδραντην.	χοδραντην.
27. τοις ἀρχαιοις.	deest. A multitude of MSS. of all classes. Some old Verss.
28. ἐπιθυμησαι αὐτης.	ἐπιθυμησαι αὐτην. A multitude of MSS.
29. σου ὁ δεξιος.	ὁ δεξιος σου.
Same v. βληθῃ.	απελθη. Old Latin Versions.
30.	deest. Lost by the homœoteleuton.
31. ἐρρέθη δε ὁτι.	ερρηθη δε. BL. 1. 33. &c.
32. λεγω ὑμιν ὁτι ὁς.	λεγω υμιν ος.
Same v. μοιχασθαι.	μοιχευθηναι. B. 1. 13. 33. &c. and some Greek Fathers.
Same v. και ὁς ἐαν ἀπολελυμενην γαμησῃ, μοιχαται.	deest. 64. Two old Lat. Verss. Codd. Gr. et Lat. ap. Aug. Orig. ut videtur.
36. οὐ δυνασαι μιαν τριχα λευκην ἠ μελαιναν ποιησαι.	ου δυνασαι ποιησαι τριχα μιαν λευκην η μελαιναν.
38. και ὀδοντα.	ὀδοντα. Old Lat. Verss. Latin Fathers.
39. δεξιαν.	deest. Arab. pol. Other authorities mostly Latin.
Same v. σου σιαγονα.	σιαγονα σου. B.
40. τῳ θελοντι.	ὁ θελων. Latin, *Qui voluerit.*
Same v. ἀφες.	αφησεις.
41. μετ' αὐτου δυο.	μετ' αυτου ετι αλλα δυο. Old Lat. Verss. and Writers. Irenæus.
42. διδου.	δος. B. 124. Clem.
Same v. τον θελοντα.	τω θελοντι, 38. and two others.
44. καλως ποιειτε τους μισουντας ὑμας.	καλως ποιειτε·τοις μισουσιν υμας. Many MSS. of different classes.
Same v. ἐπηρεαζοντων ὑμας.	επηρεαζοντων. Vulg. *Persequentibus.*
46. ἐχετε.	εξεται, i. e. εξετε.
47. οὐχι και οἱ τελωναι οὑτω ποιουσιν.	ουχι και οι εθνικοι το αυτο ποιουσιν. Many unexceptionable authorities for both variations.
48. ὁ πατηρ ὑμων ὁ ἐν τοις οὐρανοις.	ὁ πατηρ υμων ὁ ουρανιος. Very many authorities.

Having proceeded to the end of the 5th Chapter without any other omissions than those which I prepared the Reader to expect, and having thus given him an idea of the MS. generally, I will pursue the Collation somewhat further, noticing only the more remarkable deviations.

CHAP. VI.

Received Text.	*Codex Bezæ.*
1. τῳ ἐν τοις οὐρανοις.	τω εν ουρανοις.
4. σου ἡ ἐλεημοσυνη.	ἡ ελεημοσυνη σου.
5. ὥσπερ.	ως.
Same v. ὅτι φιλουσιν ἐν ταις γωνιαις των πλατειων ἑστωτες προσευχεσθαι.	οτι φιλουσιν στηναι εν ταις συναγωγαις και εν ταις γωνιαις των πλατειων εστωτες και προσευχομενοι. One of the Latin Verss. of Sabatier.
6. τῳ ἐν τῳ κρυπτῳ.	εν τω κρυπτω. Several MSS. chiefly those suspected of latinizing, Arm. Arr. Slav. all the old Lat. Verss. and the Vulg.
8. προ του ὑμας αἰτησαι αὐτον.	προ του υμας ανοιξε (i. e. ανοιξαι) το στομα. One of the Latin Verss. of Sabatier, the same as above, ver. 5.
10. ὡς.	deest. Three old Latin Verss. and two Latin Fathers.
14. ἀφησει και ὑμιν ὁ πατηρ.	αφησει υμιν και ὁ πατηρ.
17. ἀλειψαι.	αλειψον.
18. ὅπως.	ινα.

From vi. 20. to ix. 2. is a chasm.

CHAP. IX.

4. εἰπεν.	ειπεν αυτοις.
6. ἐξουσιαν ἐχει ὁ υἱος του ἀνθρωπου.	ὁ υιος του ανθρωπου εξουσιαν εχει. Vulg. *Filius hominis habet potestatem.*
Same v. ἐγερθεις ἀρον.	εγειραι (i. e. εγειρε) και αρον. Vulg. *surge, tolle.*
9. ὁ Ἰησους ἐκειθεν.	εκειθεν ὁ Ιησους. Vulg. *Inde Jesus.*
Same v. ἠκολουθησεν.	ηκολουθει.
10. και ἰδου.	ιδου. Vulg. *ecce.*
Same v. συνανεκειντο.	συνεκειντο.
11. και ἰδοντες.	ειδοντες (i. e. ιδοντες) δε.
Same v. μετα των τελωνων και ἁμαρτωλων ἐσθιει ὁ διδασκαλος ὑμων.	ὁ διδασκαλος υμων μετα των αμαρτωλων και τελωνων εσθιει.

APPENDIX I.

Received Text.	Codex Bezæ.
15. μη δυνανται.	μητι δυνανται.
Same v. ςυμφωνος.	νυμφιου. 1 MS. Æth. Goth. Sax. All the old Latin Verss. Vulg. Arnob. Aug.
17. ῥηγνυνται οἱ ἀσκοι.	ρησσει ὁ οινος ὁ νεος τους ασκους.
Same v. και ὁ οἰνος ἐκχειται και οἱ ἀσκοι ἀπολουνται.	και οι οινος απολλυται και οι ασκοι. Arnobius.
Same v. ἀλλα βαλλουσιν.	βαλλουσιν δε.
21. μονον ἁψωμαι.	αψωμαι μονον. Vulg. *Tetigero tantum.*
22. ὁ δε Ἰησους ἐπιστραφεις.	ὁ δε εστη στραφεις.
25. ἐκρατησε της χειρος.	εκρατησε την χειρα. Vulg. *tenuit manum.*
28. ἐλθοντι δε εἰς την οἰκιαν προσηλθον.	και ερχεται εις την οικιαν και προσηλθον. Vulg. *Cum autem venisset domum, accesserunt.*
Same v. οἱ τυφλοι.	οι δυο τυφλοι.
29. ἡψατο των ὀφθαλμων αὐτων, λεγων.	ηψατο των ομματων αυτων και ειπεν.
30. αὐτων οἱ ὀφθαλμοι.	οι οφθαλμοι αυτων. Vulg. *Oculi eorum.*
Same v. ὁ Ἰησους.	ὁ deest.
33. ἐφανη οὑτως.	ουτως εφανη.
Same v. ἐν τῳ Ἰσραηλ.	εν Ισραηλ.
34.	deest. An old Latin Version and two Latin Writers.
36. ἐκλελυμενοι.	εσκυλμενοι. A multitude of authorities.
Same v. ἐῤῥιμμενοι ωσει.	ρεριμμενοι ως. Could ρεριμμενοι have originated in the Greek?

The following variations are confined to the uses of the Article.

CHAP. X.

6. τα προβατα τα ἀπολωλοτα.	τα προβατα απολωλοτα. Contrary to the Greek idiom.
13. ἡ εἰρηνη ὑμων.	ειρηνη υμων. Against the usage: ἡ added *à secunda manu.* Kipling.
15. ἐν ἡμερᾳ κρισεως.	ἐν τῃ ἡμερα κρισεως. Contrary to the Greek idiom.

CHAP. XI.

7. ὁ Ἰησους.	Ιησους.
11. ἐν γεννητοις γυναικων.	εν τοις γεννητοις των γυναικων, à pr. manu.
12. βιασται.	οἱ βιασται. See above ad loc.

CHAP. XII.

Received Text.	Codex Bezæ.
1. τοις σαββασιν.	σαββασιν. Against the usage.
12. προβατον.	του προβατου.
35. ὁ ἀγαθος.	primò ἀγαθος. Kipling.
42. Σολομωντος.	του Σολομωνος. à pr. manu.

The circumstances to which principally I would direct the attention of the Reader, may be comprised under the following heads: 1. Synonyms. 2. Transpositions. 3. Compound for simple, and simple for compound, Verbs. 4. Wrong Moods and Tenses. 5. Alterations in the sense. 6. Questionable Greek. 7. Latinisms. 8. The uses of the Article. The point which he has to consider is, whether *all* these phenomena can be satisfactorily accounted for on any hypothesis, which does not resemble that of Matthäi: that *some* of them may be otherwise explained, is evidently insufficient. Mr. Marsh allows (Notes to Michaelis, vol. ii. p. 680.) that through the two first Chapters of Mark, which he had collated, "in most of the readings in which the Codex Bezæ differs from all the Greek MSS., it agrees with some one of the old Latin Versions published by Blanchini:" he adds, "but shall we therefore conclude that those readings were actually borrowed from a Latin Version, and translated into Greek? It is at least as possible that they might have had their origin in the Greek as in the Latin; and this very possibility is sufficient to defeat the whole of Wetstein's hypothesis." In examining the phenomena of the MS. let us keep in view this and the former remark of the same distinguished Critic.

1. *Synonyms.* The Collation furnishes at least one striking example, (see on ix. 29.) ὀμμάτων for ὀφθαλμῶν. It will hardly be contended that this was the reading of the original (or Greek Translation from the Hebrew,) for then we should expect to find it in other MSS.; which, however, does not happen: besides, ὄμμα is a word not much in use with the Writers of the N. T.: the received text has it only once, viz. Mark viii. 23: ὀφθαλμὸς is extremely common, and occurs in Matthew alone about twenty-five times. Ὀμμάτων, then, must be considered as an error: and where did it originate? in the Greek, by a slip of the Transcriber? In a single instance, this solution might be tolerated: but in the Codex Bezæ these slips are very frequent: in verse 24. of Chapter v. we have καταλλαγηθι for διαλλαγηθι: yet ΔΙ and ΚΑΤ have not, to the eye, any great resemblance: I believe, therefore, that the *oculi* of the Latin presented to the Translator of this passage two Greek words; and that, there being a right one and a wrong one, he unfortunately chose the latter. The passage has another mark which betrays its origin: instead of the reading of the MSS. ἥψατο λέγων, it has ἥψατυ καὶ εἶπε, a variety of which the Codex Bezæ furnishes probably an hundred examples: see the Collation on ix. 6. second instance. 2. *Transpositions.* I do not think that devi-

ations of this kind, especially when they affect passages of considerable length, are likely to be the mistakes of a copyist; not, at least, of one so unlearned as the Transcriber of the Codex Bezæ is commonly allowed to have been. A man to whom Greek is very familiar, may indeed catch up a sentence, and during an interval of interruption, the words which are still floating in his mind may receive a new arrangement: but this could hardly have happened to the Writer of our Codex, who at ix. 36. has formed the Preterite of $ῥίπτω$ like that of $τύπτω$, and at ii. 1. has declined Ηρώδης like Δημοσθένης. Add to this that the order of the words in the Codex Bezæ is frequently that of no existing MS., but the very same which is observable in the Vulg. or some of the old Latin Versions. 3. *Compound for simple, and simple for compound, Verbs*, are explicable in the same manner with Synonyms: and, as it appears to me, where they are *lectiones singulares*, which very frequently they are, on no other hypothesis. 4. The same may be said of the use of *wrong Moods and Tenses*: thus, ix. 9. $ἠκολούθει$ for $ἠκολούθησε$, i. 25. $ἔγνω$ for $ἐγίνωσκεν$, iv. 8. $ἔδειξεν$ for $δείκνυσιν$, may equally be made to represent *secutus est, cognoscebat, ostendit*, the last being supposed in the Latin to be not the Present, but the Preterite. 5. We come next to *Alterations of the sense*, whether by addition, omission, or substitution: thus in the Collation, v. 11. last instance, vi. 5. second instance, and vi. 8. How, for example, in the last case, could any transcriber give the reading of the *Codex Bezæ?* Was it by mere accident? but between the *words* of that reading, and that of the received text, there is not the least similitude. Is it the true reading? Then we should have expected to have found it in some other MS. besides the *Codex Bezæ;* or, at any rate, in the Syriac, Sahidic, or Coptic Versions: yet, according to Griesbach, it is found only in a single Latin Version of Sabatier, the Claromontanus. If it be asked, How came it into the Claromontanus, if not from the Codex Bezæ, I answer, that I suppose the author of that Latin translation to have expressed himself loosely, and to have been contented, as translators often are, with giving something like the sense. This supposition is very much easier than the alternative of believing that $ἀνοῖξαι\ τὸ\ στόμα$, instead of $αἰτῆσαι\ αὐτόν$, was a mere slip of the copyist, and that the error passed from the Greek into the Latin. This, I think, would be true, if the present were a solitary example: but since the Codex Bezæ contains many such, the conclusion is infinitely more strong.—There are instances also in which the reading of the Codex is not found, so far at least as appears from Griesbach, in any authority whatever: and yet even of these it can hardly be doubted that they are translations: thus John ix. 11. instead of the very natural Greek, $ἀπελθὼν\ δὲ\ καὶ\ νιψάμενος\ ἀνέβλεψα$, we have $ἀπῆλθον\ οὖν,\ καὶ\ ἐνιψάμην,\ καὶ\ ἦλθον\ βλέπων$. Can any one imagine this to have originated in the Greek, supposing the received reading to be authentic, which we are compelled to suppose, from the general consent of MSS. Versions, and Fathers?—But our Codex has also, as is well known, numerous additions, consisting of whole sentences. Thus Acts v. 29. between $αὐτὸ$ and $μήποτε$, it inserts the frigid gloss $οὔτε\ ὑμεῖς,\ οὔτε\ βασιλεῖς,\ οὔτε\ τύραννοι·\ ἀπέχεσθε\ οὖν\ ἀπὸ$

τῶν ἀνθρώπων τούτων. The authorities for this reading are, besides the Latin Version of the Codex, the Syr. Philox. *cum asterisco*, and one MS. of the Vulgate. Now of this and similar interpolations, I would not affirm that they necessarily originated in the Latin: a single MS. of the Vulg. may have been corrupted from the Greek, or rather from the Latin, of the Codex Bezæ : and as to the Philoxenian, if we may trust our great Orientalist, Professor *White*, (Philox. Vers. vol. i. p. 28.) the asterisk proves the reading to have been originally in the margin of that Version, and subsequently to have been admitted into the text by Thomas of Harkel, the editor of the Version. When we add, that there are strong reasons to believe that our very Codex was collated by Thomas for his new edition, (see *Adler Verss. Syr.* p. 130, and the evidence is stronger in the Acts than in the Gospels, which alone were collated by Adler,) the authority for the reading is reduced to that of one MS. of the Vulg. If, therefore, it was not taken from the Latin, and it betrays no marks of latinizing, then was it a mere marginal annotation written on the MS. which I suppose to have been the *basis* of the *Codex Bezæ*, and taken by the writer of the fair MS. into the text. Still, however, such interpolations, though of Greek origin, affect the integrity of the Codex, as much as if they were translated from the Latin: and this want of integrity is the point for which chiefly I contend; though I believe that the Latin was the source of the greater part of its corruption. But this leads us, 6, to *Questionable Greek*. It must be conceded to Mr. Marsh, that "the purity of a reading is no proof of its authenticity in a work, the style of which is confessedly impure :" it is obvious, however, that this concession has its limits. The language of the Evangelists, unless we must, in deference to the *Codex Bezæ*, reject the evidence of all other MSS., if it rarely be remarkable for elegance, never solecizes ; and the evidence of *all* the MSS., unless indeed in casual instances, which may be imputed to error, proves the same truth with respect to the writings of the Apostles: the Apocalypse I have already excepted. It may, therefore, be replied, that neither is the *impurity* of a reading any proof of authenticity in a work, the writers of which rarely express themselves awkwardly and unnaturally, and never ungrammatically and unintelligibly. Now he who shall examine the *Codex Bezæ*, will perceive, that in a very great number of its *lectiones singulares*, it differs from the other MSS. only in exhibiting a balder and more clumsy phraseology: I mean, to a person moderately conversant with Greek; for to any other it might appear the more obvious and natural. Its perpetual resolution of the Participle and Verb into two Verbs coupled by καί, as προσελθὼν εἶπεν (Matt. iv. 3.) into προσῆλθεν καὶ εἶπεν, falls under the present head: though very allowable Greek, it is inferior to the reading of the MSS. The same may be affirmed of the addition of the Participle of existence, v. 12. where to τοὺς πρὸ ὑμῶν of the MSS. the Codex subjoins ὑπάρχοντας: so in Mark v. 40. to τοὺς μετ' αὐτοῦ it adds ὄντας. Still more glaring is its very frequent use of ὅταν before the Indicative : see Collation v. 11 ; x. 19. 23 : though in the Greek even of the N. T. this Conjunction, if we may trust the MSS., usually prefers the Subjunctive. By the same

APPENDIX I.

writers, as well as by others, Neuters Plural are placed before Verbs Singular: but the *Codex Bezæ*, xv. 27. instead of τὰ κυνάρια ἐσθίει has τὰ κυνάρια ἐσθίουσιν: so also twice xiii. 40. In John xi. 19. for the well-known Grecism πρὸς τὰς περὶ Μάρθαν καὶ Μαρίαν, we read πρὸς Μάρθαν καὶ Μαρίαν. This, according to Griesbach, is the reading of no other MS. than D., though πρὸς τὴν Μάρθαν καὶ Μαρίαν is in B. C. L., &c. but is not adopted by Griesbach: but τὰς περί, we learn from Griesbach, is omitted *in Versionibus omnibus vel plerisque:* so I should have conjectured, for the plain reason, that probably no version was capable of expressing the Greek idiom; and thus it was wanting in the Latin or other Version whence this passage was rendered. All these are *improbable* readings, considered as having originated in the Greek: but as re-translations, they are discrepancies of precisely the same sort which are observable in the exercises of school-boys, (and for the most part of ill-taught or half-taught boys,) who re-translate into Greek what they have translated from the Latin.—But there are passages in the Codex Bezæ which are really solecisms. What, for example, are we to say of Mark xi. 12? where, instead of ἐξελθόντων αὐτῶν, the Syr. and some old Versions have in the Singular ἐξελθόντος αὐτοῦ: but D. has ἐξελθόντα ἀπὸ Βηθανίας ἐπείνασεν. On this Mr. Marsh (p. 684.) observes, that "the writer of this passage has converted ἐπείνασεν into an Impersonal Verb, and made it to govern ἐξελθόντα;" but he thinks "that the alteration may be ascribed rather to error or carelessness, than to actual design." I cannot dissemble that I am of a different opinion; ἐξελθόντα appears to be here purposely employed in the sense of a Genitive Absolute: and the following passage is similar in a degree which can hardly be imputed to accident: in Luke ix. 37. instead of the reading of the MSS. κατελθόντων αὐτῶν ἀπὸ τοῦ ὄρους, συνήντησεν αὐτῷ ὄχλος πολύς, we find ΚΑΤΕΛΘΟΝΤΑ ΑΥΤΟΝ ἀπὸ τοῦ ὄρους, συνελθεῖν αὐτῷ ὄχλον πολύν. Here the latter clause is changed into the common Latin form of the Accusative with an Infinitive Mood, in consequence of ἐγένετο preceding: but if ἐξελθόντα αὐτὸν do not mean *quum descendisset*, I can make nothing of the place. Now these appear to me to be egregious solecisms; for no Critic, I imagine, will wish to consider them as examples of the elegant Attic Accusative Absolute: he who would adopt this solution, may consult *Brunck,* Aristoph. Ran. 1437, and *Duker,* Thucyd. viii. 66. and iv. 2. These instances, perhaps, will in some measure reconcile us to the famous reading, Matt. iii. 16. τὸ πνεῦμα καταβαίνοντα. A most ingenious conjecture by *Knittel,* by which he would account for this peculiarity, has been given by Mr. Marsh, p. 683. *Mill* supposed it to be a Latinism arising from the Masculine *Spiritum:* I think that this solution is confirmed by the remainder of the reading, καταβαίνοντα ἐκ τοῦ οὐρανοῦ ὡς, which is preserved in many Latin authorities, but no where else [1]. 7. We

---

[1] Yet such a reading, if genuine, might be defended as an instance of the σχῆμα πρὸς τὸ σημαινόμενον, and would not be *very unlike* John xvi. 13. ὅταν ἔλθῃ ἐκεῖνος, τὸ πνεῦμα τῆς ἀληθείας, κ. τ. ἑ. followed by ἐκεῖνος ἐμὲ δοξάσει in the next verse: in which passage, though the gender of ἐκεῖνος might through-

next proceed to *Latinisms;* which, however, have in part been unavoidably anticipated. Of Latinisms so flagrant that they could not possibly have arisen in the Greek, the number, perhaps, is small: but it may be questioned whether the criterion be not, by such a condition, too closely restricted. If the *Codex Bezæ*, in almost every page, present us with variations from all existing MSS., and yet in Latin authorities, and most commonly in them alone, we find passages which, being closely rendered, give us the Greek of the Codex in such cases, even if that Greek be not absolutely intolerable, we may still, I think, safely infer in what quarter the variation originated. It is asked, Why, in any single instance, may not the Latin have been taken from the Greek? In *some* instances this is not impossible; but in *many*, it is highly improbable, for this reason; a transcriber, notwithstanding that he may and must sometimes err, is not liable so frequently to deviate from the text, as is the re-translator of a translation: and if we add to this, (allowing to a transcriber a much greater number of errors than experience requires us to allow,) the extreme improbability that his errors should commonly be precisely such as a re-translator, from still existing translations, might easily commit, either the inference which I would deduce is natural and reasonable, or no conclusion can safely be drawn from the doctrine of chances. I mean not to deny that the *Codex Bezæ*, like other MSS., has traces of the haste or carelessness of the Copyist: in Matt. x. there are two instances of passages being lost by the *homœoteleuton;* viz. a clause in ver. 19, and the whole of verse 37: there are examples also of a letter or a syllable being omitted, and supplied by a later hand: but these are mistakes to which all copyists in all languages are subject: to give synonyms—to alter Tenses—to transpose the words of whole clauses—and to add whole sentences, are not the faults of the most blundering copyist. We may, therefore, include under the head of Latinisms passages which, varying from all the MSS., Greek Fathers, and Oriental Versions, and being wholly inexplicable as the usual errors of copyists, are yet easily accounted for as translations from the Latin; especially if any thing of the Greek idiom be lost, and something of the Latin be introduced into its place. The following will serve as examples: In the Collation v. 40. instead of τῷ θέλοντι depending on ἄφες, we have ὁ θέλων: this has strongly the appearance of being a rendering from *qui voluerit*, by some one who did not look forward to the end of the sentence; and ἀφήσεις for ἄφες rather corroborates the suspicion. In a work of so stupendous labour as the N. T. of Griesbach, no man who knows the toil of collating, will expect that every reading of every MS. should be noticed. This reading, however, is remarkable; and Matthäi commends the *prudence* of Griesbach in passing it over: "*quis enim sanæ mentis homo Cod. D. sequatur?*" If this were prudence in his *new* edition, Griesbach is equally discreet; for of this reading οὐδὲ γρύ: however, I

out be referred to παράκλητος, I confess that the structure of the whole appears to me to furnish a strong argument for the personality of the Holy Spirit.
—J. S.

have seen it with my own eyes. That it is the mistake of a re-translator, and not of a transcriber, is pretty plain; since in iv. 16. we have its exact parallel, οἱ καθήμενοι for τοῖς καθημένοις : the former of these is the reading of six Latin Versions. In v. 42. for τὸν θέλοντα, which is right after ἀποστράφῃς, we have τῷ θέλοντι to express *volenti* of the Vulg., which is equally proper after *avertaris*. It should be observed, however, that two or three inferior MSS. have the same fault: yet it could not originate in the Greek. —Mark iv. 31. for τῶν ἐπὶ τῆς γῆς D. has ἅ εἰσιν ἐπὶ τῆς γῆς: this was very natural to a man not conversant with Greek, and who had before him the rendering of the Vulg. and of all the old Latin Versions, "*quæ sunt in terrâ.*"—Mark vi. 2. for γενομένου σαββάτου D. reads ἡμέρᾳ σαββάτων : this, in form, little resembles the Greek of the MSS., but perfectly well expresses the meaning of two old Latin Versions, *die sabbatorum*.—Mark viii. 2. instead of ὅτι ἤδη ἡμέρας (or ἡμέραι) τρεῖς προσμένουσί με, D. has ὅτι ἤδη ἡμέραι τρεῖς εἰσιν, ἀπὸ πότε ὧδέ εἰσιν; this reading has for its corresponding Latin, *triduum est, ex quo hic sunt* in five old Latin Versions; and there surely no one will doubt that it took its rise, especially if he attend to ἀπὸ πότε: the Latin is a loose rendering of the received text, and the Codex a very bad rendering of the Latin.—8. Under the eighth and last head, I must advert to the very remarkable manner in which the Cambridge MS. employs and rejects the Greek Article. Here, however, I am scarcely authorized to give an opinion. To condemn a MS. because it violates the rules, is to suppose that the rules are true; and yet the whole inquiry proceeds on the ground, that to the truth of the rules, so far as the N. T. is concerned, the evidence of this MS. is wanting. I am permitted, however, to state, that in respect to the Article, the *Codex Bezæ* averages probably, in every chapter, two or three *lectiones singulares ;* and that, consequently, if it be right, all other MSS. must be wrong. I may also remind the Reader, that many of these variations are contrary not merely to the usage, but to principles which have been demonstrated: and I may add, that on the hypothesis of re-translation, this variation is very explicable; since from whatever language those re-translations were made, especially if from the Latin, such errors, however numerous, were to be expected.

All Scholars know more or less of the famous *Velesian Readings :* but the fullest, and by far the best, account which I have seen of them, will be found in the Appendix, No. III. to Marsh's "Letters to Mr. Travis." In 1540, R. Stephens published a splendid edition of the Vulgate, and in 1550, an edition of the Greek Testament. Many readings of the latter were observed to vary from the Latin of the former: in order, therefore, to support this edition of the Vulgate against the Greek, Peter Faxard, Marquis of Velez, from whom the readings are called, took the pains of translating the Latin of the Vulgate into Greek, wherever the Greek Testament differed from the Vulgate, except, indeed, where Stephens's Greek margin supplied him with the readings which he wanted; and there he had only to transcribe. These translations purported to be a collection of various readings, and for a long time imposed upon the world: they are said to be still of some authority in the Romish Church, and are quoted as such even by Sabatier. Now Mr. Marsh has clearly demonstrated that the whole is a forgery: but I think that much of his reasoning, *mutatis mutandis*, will apply to the *Codex Bezæ*: I allude to his 3d, 11th, 12th, and 13th heads of proof. The *third* is, that "The Velesian readings agree in general with Stephens's Vulgate text of 1540." Mr. Marsh (as quoted above) admits that the readings of the *Codex Bezæ* commonly coincide with the Vulgate, and with the Latin Ante-hieronymian Versions published by Blanchini: and of this every one must be sensible, who turns over the new edition of Griesbach, where he will find D. in company with Vulg. It. (the old Italic,) or with *some* of the old Versions, Veron. Verc. Vind. Corb. Colb. Brix. Germ. &c. and the Latin Fathers continually.— His 11th proposition is, that " though upwards of 450 MSS. of the Greek Testament have been collated, yet all these Greek MSS. put together do not contain one-half of the Velesian readings." Without having made the inquiry, which, however, in a portion of the Codex I might easily make,

———————— *extremo ni jam sub fine laborum*
Vela traham, et terris festinem advertere proram,

I suspect that neither do all the collated MSS. put together contain one-half of the readings in which the *Codex Bezæ* varies from the received text.—The 12th proposition is, that " the greatest part of those Velesian readings, which have never been found in a Greek MS., evidently betray a Latin origin." Mr. Marsh then refers us to his ample lists of Velesian readings, and observes, that "many of them bear on their very forehead the certificate of their birth." He who has examined the brief specimen of the readings of the *Codex Bezæ* given above, will probably have little difficulty, in the case of some of them, in ascertaining their parentage: *their speech bewrayeth them*.—As a 13th proof, Mr. Marsh shows, that "in many of the Velesian readings, the *Greek Article* is neglected, where a native Greek would have used it." I mean not to deny, that in this respect the Marquis was a little unlucky; nor that we have here good evidence " that the translator was an inhabitant of the west of Europe, and not a native Greek;" but I cannot allow the Marquis to be condemned, and the Translator of the interpolations in the Codex to be acquitted: this would be *dare veniam corvis*. Velez has been guilty of certain omissions; but the Codex not only omits, but inserts the Article without rule or meaning, so far as I can discover, and certainly in defiance of the usage which prevails every where else.

I believe, then, that our Cambridge MS., though a most venerable remain of antiquity, is not to be considered, in a critical view, as of much authority. It is of use to the translator and to the dogmatical theologian, but not, I think, generally speaking, to the editor of the N. T., whose object it is to give a text approaching as nearly as possible to the Autographs. But here I would not be misunderstood. If we had at the present day no other Greek MS. of the Evangelists and Acts than the *Codex Bezæ*, the truth of our Religion would, indeed, be as evident as if we had only any other single MS. of the same writings, viz. either B. (the Vat. 1209) or the H. of Matthäi, supposing it to extend so far: we should still have a record of the same miracles, of the same Divine doctrines, of the same death and resurrection of Christ, and of the same miraculous gifts imparted to the first Teachers of Christianity: but in the view of criticism the case would stand very differently: almost every thing which the learned have determined respecting the style and language of the Evangelists, would be wholly unfounded; and *Hardouin's* hypothesis of a Latin original, of the Gospels and Acts at least, would not be altogether chimerical.—But not only the question which is the subject of this work makes it important to ascertain what is the degree of faith due to the readings of the *Codex Bezæ*: another consideration arises, which all readers will think of much greater moment; it respects the inviolate integrity of the Oracles of God. Now here we have no alternative, but to confess that the *Codex Bezæ* has been much corrupted; or else to prove that it alone is pure, while the rest have been tampered with by critics and transcribers: either this MS. Latinizes, or the others Grecize, i. e. have been corrected and modelled to the Greek idiom by persons who wished to mend the Sacred Text: between these opinions the Reader can have little hesitation in deciding. It is true, indeed, that our Codex is not the only one which has been suspected: some others, though, I believe, in a less degree, share the accusation. It ought, however, to be understood, that in the latinizing readings those MSS., for the most part, agree with the MS. of Beza: D. L. 1. 13. 33. 69. &c. will commonly be found together in Wetstein. But we are not by this circumstance driven to the necessity of supposing that *many* MSS. have been corrupted in the same manner with Beza's; which, of course, would proportionally weaken the probability that any had been so corrupted. The Codex D., from its very great antiquity, may be imagined to have had considerable influence on subsequent copyists; and this hypothesis will go far to account for the latinizing of some other suspected MSS., without our supposing that in so many instances they were corrupted immediately from the Vulgate. To me, indeed, it appears that the influence of this MS. has been even less than might reasonably have been expected.

As to the goodness of its readings, considered with regard to the *sense,* I have already observed, that for this fact we may in part account by the natural supposition of the great antiquity of the MS. which was the *basis* of the *Codex Bezæ*: we may add, that admitting it to latinize, we have no cause to infer that its readings, considered in the same light, are therefore faulty. Perhaps no translations come nearer to the *sense* of the Autographs than do the very ancient Latin Versions, the *Veronensis* and the *Vercellensis*. A great part of the defence which is set up in behalf of the integrity of the *Codex Bezæ*, really goes to the fidelity of the Latin Versions, which is not involved in the dispute.

The agreement of the Syriac and some other Oriental Versions with our Codex, has also been insisted on: but this too may be safely conceded by its opponents, for a reason already alleged. The Dean, indeed, to repel the charge of latinizing, observes, that we may as well affirm that the MS. *Syriacizes*, or that it is modelled to some other Oriental Version. Certainly if the same proofs can be adduced of its corruption from other sources besides the Latin, they ought not to be suppressed: I have noticed, however, that where D. agrees with Sahid. Syr. Copt. Origen, &c. we there commonly find it agreeing also with some of the old Latin Versions: to these, therefore, it may immediately be indebted. Besides, the *basis* of the MS. is a part of the hypothesis which ought to be kept in view.

I conclude with subscribing to the opinion of Matthäi, somewhat modified. I believe that no fraud was intended; but only that the critical possessor of the basis filled its margin with glosses and readings chiefly from the Latin, being a Christian of the Western Church; and that the whole collection of Latin passages was translated into Greek, and substituted in the text by some one who had a high opinion of their value, and who was, as Wetstein describes him, "καλλιγραφίας quàm vel Græcæ vel Latinæ linguæ peritior."

APPENDIX II.

(BY THE PRESENT EDITOR.)

A TABLE

SHOWING

THE USAGE OF THE VARIOUS APPELLATIONS

OF

OUR BLESSED LORD,

IN THE

FOUR EVANGELISTS, ACTS, AND ST. PAUL'S EPISTLES.

Usage of Ἰησοῦς *and* Χριστός.

I.

MATTHEW uses only (1) ὁ Ἰησοῦς, (2) ὁ Χριστός, or (3) Ἰησοῦς ὁ λεγόμενος Χριστός.

(1). I find from Schmidt and other sources the following exceptions, eighteen in all:

i. 1. 16. 18. 21. 25 ; viii. 29 ; xiv. 1 ; xvi. 20 ; xx. 30 ; xxi. 11 ; xxvi. 51, 52. 69. 71 ; xxvii. 17. 22. 37 ; xxviii. 5.

Of these, some are not real exceptions. I will mention first those which fall under certain rules. Nos. 2. 15. and 16. belong to class (3). Nos. 4. and 5. are regular, Ἰησοῦν being the Predicate. No. 6. is no exception, Ἰησοῦ being the Vocative. No. 7. is according to a well-established licence, viz. that the Article is often omitted before the Genitives of Proper Names following another Substantive. See Matt. i. 11. and 16. Luke i. 5. and Gersdorff, pp. 48. and 305. Nos. 8. 10. 13. 14. 17. and 18. as well as all class (3), belong to a given rule. Winer (Dis. III. Syntax, c. 1. § 12. 1. Obs.) says, that the Article with Proper Names is regularly omitted, when any word of particular description is added, as Δαβὶδ ὁ βασιλεύς. Nos. 11. and 12. likewise belong to a fixed rule, viz. that the Article is often omitted after a Preposition.

Thus the only exceptions not belonging to a rule are, Nos. 1 [1]. 3. and 9 ; and in Nos. 1. and 3. the reading is quite uncertain.

---

[1] In No. 1. if the common reading be right, not the omission of the Article, (which is by rule,) but the addition of Χριστοῦ forms the exception.

USAGE OF THE APPELLATIONS OF CHRIST. 487

There are 155 instances, besides these, of the occurrence of Ἰησοῦς, and in all these it has the Article.

(2). The word Χριστὸς occurs only sixteen times in St. Matthew.

The exceptions to the remark are, i. 1. 16. 18; xxvi. 68; xxvii. 17. 22. But of these Nos. 2. 5. and 6. belong to class (3). No. 4. is a Vocative, and therefore no exception. In Nos. 1. and 3. the reading is uncertain.

(3). Finally, the third form occurs as above, i. 16; xxvii. 17. 22.

II.

St. Mark uses only (1) ὁ Ἰησοῦς, (2) ὁ Χριστός.

(1). The exceptions are, (nine in all,)

i. 1. 9. 24; v. 7. 13; x. 47. (twice;) xiv. 67; xvi. 6.

Of these, Nos. 3. 4. 7. are no exception, Ἰησοῦ being the Vocative. Nos. 6. and 9. fall under the rule noticed in (1), as to the addition of a word of definition; and in some MSS. No. 8. stands, Ἰησοῦ τοῦ Ναζαρηνοῦ; in some, Ἰησοῦ is wholly omitted. In No. 1. it seems not unlikely that the words Ἰ. Χ. υ. τ. θ. are an interpolation; see Gersdorff, p. 319. In No. 2. many MSS. supply the Article.

The word occurs with the Article eighty-four times.

(2). The exceptions are, i. 1; ix. 41. Of No. 1. I have spoken above. No. 2. is wanting in one MS. The word occurs five times with the Article.

III.

St. Luke in his Gospel uses only (1) ὁ Ἰησοῦς and (2) ὁ Χριστός.

(1). The exceptions are, (fifteen in all,)

i. 31; ii. 21. 27. 43. 52; iii. 21; iv. 1. 4. 34; viii. 28; xvii. 13; xviii. 37, 38; xxiv. 3. 19.

Of these, Nos. 1. and 2. are no exceptions, Ἰησοῦν being the Predicate. Nos. 4. 12. 15. fall under the rule as to the addition of a definition. Nos. 9. 10. 11. and 13. are instances of the Vocative. In No. 14. some MSS. omit the words τοῦ Κ. Ἰ. altogether, and others omit Κ.

The word occurs with the Article eighty-three times.

(2). The exceptions are, ii. 11; xxiii. 2.

In both of these the reading is uncertain.

The word occurs eleven times with the Article.

IV.

St. John writes (1) ὁ 'Ιησοῦς usually, (2) ὁ Χριστός, and (3) 'Ιησοῦς Χριστός.

(1). The exceptions are, (twenty-six in all,)

i. 17. 46. 49. 51; iv. 1, 2. 10. 47; v. 15; vi. 15. 24; viii. 1. 14. 54. 59; ix. 11; xi. 33. 38. 54; xii. 44; xiii. 7; xviii. 4, 5. 7; xix. 19. 26; xxi. 4.

Of these, Nos. 1. 21. 22. 24. fall under the rule as to the word of definition. No. 8. is an instance of the Predicate.

The word occurs with the Article 226 times, or 225, if in xxi. 12. we adopt the reading ὁ Κύριος. We ought, in deciding, perhaps, to compare xx. 14.

(2). The exception is ix. 22.

In i. 42. many MSS. omit the Article; but others, of good authority, (though fewer,) retain it. It may be doubtful whether, even if the Article be omitted, this place forms an exception, as X. there is given expressly as the Greek rendering of an Hebrew word, and is therefore taken out of the common laws of construction.

The word occurs eighteen times with the Article.

(3). This form occurs i. 17; xvii. 3.

V.

St. Luke, in the Acts, has the following varieties:

	Times.
(1). ὁ 'Ιησοῦς occurs	16

Regular exceptions, i. e.

1. 'Ιησοῦς with words of definition, viz. ii. 22; v. 42; vi. 14; ix. 17. 34; x. 38; xxii. 8; xxvi. 9.	8
2. v. 30; ix. 5; xxvi. 15. are nearly of the same kind	3
3. Vocatives.	
4. 'Ιησοῦς with τις (a certain Jesus) xxv. 19.	1
(2). 'Ιησοῦς Χριστός occurs	7
(3). ὁ Χριστὸς 'Ιησοῦς (xvii. 3; xviii. 5. 28; xix. 4.)	4

In (1) A. D. and other MSS. omit the Article. In (2) the reading is doubtful. So in (3). In (4) A. B. E. and other MSS. omit Χριστόν.

(4). ὁ Κύριος 'Ιησοῦς (including one Vocative without the Article, vii. 59.)	13
(5). ὁ Κύριος 'Ιησοῦς Χριστός [1]	6

[1] In two of these, viz. xv. 26; xx. 21. we have Κύριος ἡμῶν 'I. X.

In xv. 11. the form is K. 'I. X.; but I suppose that the Article is left out from the word following a Preposition.

USAGE OF THE APPELLATIONS OF CHRIST. 489

Times.

(6). Ἰησοῦς ὁ Χριστὸς occurs twice, v. 42; ix. 34. See (1) 1. above.

(7). ὁ Ἰησοῦς Χριστός, viii. 37; but the reading is doubtful...... 1
In viii. 12. only *some* editions have the Article.

(8). Ἰησοῦς ὁ Ναζωραῖος... 4

(9). Ἰησοῦς with ὁ παῖς and a Pronoun, viz. τὸν παῖδα αὐτοῦ Ἰησοῦν, iii. 13. 26; iv. 27. 30.................................... 4

VI.

St. John, in his Epistles, uses

(1). Ἰησοῦς... 5
It is singular that in four of these the *form* is, Ἰησοῦς ἐστιν ὁ Χριστός, or ὁ υἱὸς τοῦ Θεοῦ. In the Gospel we have ὁ Ἰησοῦς ἐστιν ὁ Χριστός, viz. xx. 31. Ἰησοῦς ἐστιν ὁ ποιήσας, v. 15.

(2). Ἰησοῦς Χριστός [1]... 6

(3). ὁ Ἰησοῦς Χριστός (i. 4. 3.).................................... 1
But some editions omit the Article (the Compl. Plantin.)

(4). Ἰησοῦς ὁ Χριστός (i. 5. 6.).................................... 1

(5). Κύριος Ἰησοῦς Χριστός (ii. 3.)............................... 1
Where probably the Article before K. is omitted from the word following a Preposition.

(6). ὁ Χριστός (ii. 9. *bis*)... 2

VII.

St. John, in the Revelation, uses

(1). ὁ Ἰησοῦς (xix. 10. ἡ μαρτυρία τ. Ἰ.)....................... 2

(2). Ἰησοῦς... 4
Of these, however, two may perhaps be reckoned legitimate exceptions from (1), viz. xiv. 12. τὴν πίστιν Ἰησοῦ.
xvii. 6. τῶν μαρτύρων Ἰησοῦ.
xx. 4. τὴν μαρτυρίαν Ἰησοῦ.
See 'I. under (1), No. 7.

(3). Ἰησοῦς Χριστός.. 5

In these we find
{
ἡ μαρτυρία Ἰησοῦ Χριστοῦ, i. 2. and 9.
ἀπὸ Ἰ. Χ. .... i. 5.
ἀποκάλυψις Ἰ. Χ. ...... i. 1.
and
ὑπομονὴ Ἰ. Χ. .... i. 9.
}

And perhaps all these may be reckoned legitimate exceptions from the next Number, but the instance under that Number will at least show that there was no uniformity.

---

[1] These are, ὁ υἱὸς αὐτοῦ Ἰησοῦς Χριστός, 1. i. 3; iii. 23; v. 20.
Ἰησοῦς Χριστὸς ὁ υἱὸς αὐτοῦ, 1. i. 7.
Ἰησοῦς Χριστός .... 1. ii. 1; iv. 2.

490   APPENDIX II.

	Times.
(4). ὁ Ἰησοῦς Χριστός. xii. 17. ἡ μαρτυρία τοῦ Ἰησοῦ Χριστοῦ	1
(5). ὁ Κύριος Ἰησοῦς. xxii. 20. the Article being omitted in the Vocative	1
(6). ὁ Κύριος ἡμῶν Ἰησοῦς Χριστός	1
(7). ὁ Χριστός	2
(8). ὁ Χριστὸς αὐτοῦ	2

N.B. In the following Table of the places in St. Paul's Epistles, the first column shows those cases where the instance of the usage is a fair one, i. e. where it cannot be accounted for by the word being one of two Correlatives, (in which case the presence and absence of the Article may be accounted for,) or by its following a Preposition. The second column contains those cases where the word is one of two such Correlatives, the first of which *has* the Article. The third shows the cases where the word follows a Preposition; the fourth, those cases where the word is one of two Correlatives, the first of which has not the Article.

VIII.

St. *Paul* has the following forms [1]:	Real.	After words with the Article.	After Prepositions.	After words without the Article.	Total.
(1). ὁ Ἰησοῦς (occurs 4 times).					
2 Cor. iv. 10	..	1	..	..	
11	..	1	..	..	4
Eph. iv. 21	..	..	1	..	
1 Thess. iv. 14	..	..	1	..	
(2). Ἰησοῦς (occurs 9 times).					
Rom. iii. 26	..	..	..	1	
viii. 11	1	..	..	..	
1 Cor. xii. 3	1	..	..	..	
2 Cor. iv. 5	..	..	1	..	
11	..	..	1	..	
14	..	..	1	..	9
xi. 4. This, however, is no real exception to (1). The phrase is, 'To preach *another Jesus*,' where the Article is inadmissible.	1	..	..	..	
Phil. ii. 10. See No. 7. in Matt.	..	1	..	..	
1 Thess. i. 10	1	..	..	..	
(3). ὁ Χριστός (occurs 95 times).					
Rom. i. 16	..	1	..	..	
vii. 4	..	1	..	..	
viii. 11	1	..	..	..	6
35	..	1	..	..	
ix. 3	..	..	1	..	
5	1	..	..	..	

---

[1] None of them occur in the Hebrews. There I find once one form, Κύριος ἡμῶν Ἰησοῦς, (xiii. 20.) which I have not yet found in St. Paul.

USAGE OF THE APPELLATIONS OF CHRIST. 491

	Real.	After words with the Article.	After Prepositions.	After words without the Article.	Total.
(3). ὁ Χριστός. *(Continued)*.					
Rom. xiv. 10.	..	1	..	..	
xv. 3.	1	..	..	..	
7.	1	..	..	..	7
18.	1	..	..	..	
19.	..	1	..	..	13
29.	..	1	..	..	
xvi. 16.	..	1	..	..	
1 Cor. i. 3; x. 4. 9; xi. 3; xii. 12; xv. 15. 23.	7	..	..	..	
i. 6. 16; vi. 15; ix. 12. 18; x. 16. (2). On vi. 15. observe, we have μέλη Χριστοῦ and τὰ μέλη τοῦ Χριστοῦ in the same verse.	..	7	..	..	15
xv. 22.	..	..	1	..	
2 Cor. xi. 2	1	..	..	..	
i. 5. 11, 12; iv. 4; v. 10. 14; ix. 13; x. 1. 5. 14; xii. 9.	..	11	..	..	15
ii. 14; iii. 4; xi. 3.	..	..	3	..	
Gal. i. 7; v. 24; vi. 2. 12	..	4	..	..	5
v. 4.	..	..	1	..	
Eph. ii. 5; iii. 17; iv. 15. 20; v. 2. 14. 23, 24, 25; vi. 5.	10	..	..	..	
ii. 13; iii. 4. 8. 10; iv. 7. 12, 13; v. 5.	..	8	..	..	23
i. 10. 12. 20; iii. 6.	..	..	4	..	
vi. 6.	..	..	..	1	
Phil. i. 15, 16.	2	..	..	..	
ii. 30; iii. 18.	..	2	..	..	5
iii. 7.	..	..	1	..	
Col. iii. 1. (2) 4. 13.	5	..	..	..	
i. 24; ii. 2. 11. 17; iii. 16; iv. 3.	..	6	..	..	15
ii. 20; iii. 3, 4.	..	..	3	..	
i. 7.	..	..	..	1	
1 Thess. iii. 2.	..	1	..	..	1
2 Thess. ii. 2; iii. 5.	..	2	..	..	2
1 Tim. v. 11.	1	..	..	..	1
In 2 Tim., Titus, and Philemon ὁ Χριστὸς does not occur.					
(4). Χριστός (occurs 122 times).					
Rom. v. 6.	1	..	..	..	
8.	1	..	..	..	
vi. 4.	1	..	..	..	
8.	..	..	1	..	
9.	1	..	..	..	
viii. 9.	..	..	..	1	12
10.	1	..	..	..	
17.	..	..	..	1	
34.	1	..	..	..	
ix. 1.	..	..	1	..	
x. 4.	1	..	..	..	
6.	1	..	..	..	

492   APPENDIX II.

	Real.	After words with the Article.	After Prepositions.	After words without the Article.	Total.
(4). Χριστός. *(Continued.)*					
Rom. x. 7.	1	..	..	..	
xii. 5.	..	..	1	..	
xiv. 9.	1	..	..	..	
15.	1	..	..	..	9
xv. 20.	1	..	..	..	—
xvi. 5.	..	..	1	..	21
7.	..	..	1	..	
9.	..	..	1	..	
10.	..	..	1	..	
1 Cor. i. 12. 17. 23, 24; v. 7; viii. 11; ix. 21; xi. 1; xv. 3. 12, 13, 14. 16, 17. 20. 23.	16	..	..	..	
....	..	0	..	..	28
iii. 1; iv. 10. (2) 17; viii. 12; xv. 18, 19.	..	..	7	..	
ii. 16; iv. 1; vi. 16; xi. 3; xii. 27.	..	..	..	5	
2 Cor. v. 16; v. 15; x. 7. (three times); xiii. 3. (The three in x. 7. belong rather to Col. 4.)	6	..	..	..	
....	..	0	..	..	24
i. 5. 21; ii. 17; iii. 14; v. 17. 19, 20. (twice); xii. 2. 10. 19.	..	..	11	..	
ii. 10. 15; iii. 3; viii. 23; xi. 10. 13. 23.	..	..	..	7	
Gal. ii. 17. 20 (2), 21; iii. 13. 16. 27. 29. (?); iv. 19; v. 1, 2.	12	..	..	..	
....	..	0	..	..	21
i. 22; ii. 16, 17; iii. 17. 24; iv. 7.	..	..	6	..	
i. 6. 10, 11. 16.	..	..	..	3	
Eph. i. 3; ii. 12; iii. 21; iv. 32; v. 32.	..	..	5	..	5
Phil. i. 18. 20, 21. (?); iii. 8; iv. 13. (?)	5	..	..	..	
i. 27.	..	1	..	..	13
i. 13. 23. 29; ii. 1.	..	..	4	..	
i. 10; ii. 16; iii. 9.	..	..	..	3	
Col. i. 27; iii. 11.	2	..	..	..	5
i. 2; ii. 5. 8.	..	..	3	..	
1 Thess. iv. 16.	..	..	1	..	2
ii. 16.	..	..	..	1	
2 Thess. none.	..	..	..	..	0
1 Tim. ii. 7.	..	..	1	..	1
2 Tim. ii. 19.	..	1	..	..	1
Titus none.	..	..	..	..	0
Philem. 8.	..	..	1	..	1
(5) ὁ Ἰησοῦς Χριστὸς does not occur.					
(6). Ἰησοῦς ὁ Χριστός.					
1 Cor. iii. 11.	1	..	..	..	1

USAGE OF THE APPELLATIONS OF CHRIST. 493

	Real.	After words with the Article.	After Prepositions.	After words without the Article.	Total.
(7). ὁ Χριστὸς Ἰησοῦς.					
Phil. ii. 21. A great preponderance *against* this reading	1	..	..	..	
Eph. iii. 1. (? as to reading.) There is a great preponderance *against* this reading	..	1	..	..	4
Phil. iii. 12. Several of the best MSS. have not this reading	..	..	1	..	
Col. ii. 6. (ὁ Χρ. Ἰ. ὁ Κ.) D. E. have a different reading	1	..	..	..	
(8). Ἰησοῦς Χριστός (occurs thirty-nine times).					
Rom. xv. 8.	1	..	..	..	
i. 1. 6; iii. 22; xv. 16.	..	..	..	4	8
i. 8; ii. 16.	..	..	2	..	
xvi. 25.	..	1	..	..	
We have also ὁ εἷς ἄνθρωπος Ἰ. Χ. in v. 15. and ὁ εἷς Ἰ. Χ. in v. 17	..	..	..	..	2
1 Cor. ii. 2	1	..	..	..	2
i. 1	..	..	..	1	
ὁ υἱὸς αὐτοῦ Ἰ. Χ. i. 9	..	..	..	..	1
2 Cor. xiii. 5	1	..	..	..	
v. 18	..	..	1	..	3
i. 1; iv. 6	..	..	..	1	
ὁ Θεοῦ υἱὸς Ἰ. Χ. i. 19	..	..	..	..	1
Gal. iii. 1.	1	..	..	..	
i. 1	..	..	1	..	5
i. 12; ii. 16; iii. 22	..	..	..	3	
Eph. ii. 20.	1	..	..	..	
i. 5; iii. 9.	..	..	2	..	4
i. 1.	..	..	..	1	
Phil. ii. 11.	1	..	..	..	
i. 19.	..	1	..	..	6
i. 11.	..	..	1	..	
i. 1. 6. 8.	..	..	..	3	
Col. i. 1.	..	..	..	1	1
1 and 2 Thess. none.					
1 Tim. i. 16.	1	..	..	..	3
i. 1; iv. 6.	..	..	..	2	
2 Tim. ii. 8.	1	..	..	..	2
ii. 3.	..	..	..	1	
Titus i. 1.	..	..	..	1	1
Philemon 1. 9.	..	..	..	2	2
(9). Χριστὸς Ἰησοῦς (occurs 58 times, of which 54 are after Prepositions).					
Rom. iii. 24; vi. 3. 11. 23; viii. 1. 2. 39; xv. 5. 17; xvi. 3.	..	..	10	..	10
1 Cor. i. 2. 4. 30; iv. 15; xv. 31; xvi. 24	..	..	6	..	6
2 Cor. none. Χ. Ἰ. Κύριος occurs iv. 5. and only there.					
Gal. iv. 14.	1	..	..	..	1

APPENDIX II.

	Real.	After words with the Article.	After Prepositions.	After words without the Article.	Total.
(9). Χριστὸς Ἰησοῦς. *(Continued.)*					
Gal. ii. 4. 16; iii. 14. 26. 28; v. 6. 15	..	..	7	..	7
Eph. i. 1; ii. 6, 7. 10. 13; iii. 11. 21.	..	..	7	..	7
Phil. i. 1. 26; ii. 5; iii. 3. 14; iv. 7. 19. 21	..	..	8	..	} 9
iii. 8. (Χ. Ἰ. ὁ Κύρ.)	..	1	..	..	
Col. i. 4. 28	..	..	2	..	2
1 Thess. ii. 14; v. 18	..	..	2	..	2
2 Thess. none.					
1 Tim. i. 15	1	..	..	..	} 4
i. 14; iii. 13; vi. 13	..	..	3	..	
ἄνθρωπος Ἰ. Χ. occurs ii. 5.					
2 Tim. i. 9. 13; ii. 1. 10; iii. 12. 15.	..	..	7	..	7
Philem. 6. 23	..	..	2	..	} 3
1	..	..	..	1	
(10). ὁ Κύριος Ἰησοῦς.					
Romans, none.					
1 Cor. v. 5; vi. 11	..	2	..	..	
xi. 23	1	..	..	..	
2 Cor. iv. 14	..	1	..	..	
iv. 13	1	..	..	..	
Gal. vi. 17	..	1	..	..	} 10
Eph. i. 15	..	..	1	..	
1 Thess. iv. 2	..	..	1	..	
2 Thess. i. 7	..	1	..	..	
Philem. 5	..	..	1	..	
(11). Κύριος Ἰησοῦς.					
Rom. x. 9	1	..	..	..	
xiv. 14	..	..	1	..	
2 Cor. iv. 10	..	..	1	..	} 5
Col. iii. 17	..	..	..	1	
1 Thess. iv. 1	..	..	1	..	
N.B. Κύριος Χριστὸς occurs Col. iii. 24.					
(12). Ἰησοῦς ὁ Κύριος.					
Rom. iv. 24	1	..	..	..	1
(13). ὁ Κύριος Ἰησοῦς Χριστός.					
Rom. xiii. 14	1	..	..	..	
1 Cor. xvi. 22	1	..	..	..	
23	..	1	..	..	} 5
1 Tim. iv. 1	..	..	1	..	
22	1	..	..	..	
(14). Κύριος Ἰησοῦς Χριστός.					
Rom. i. 7	..	..	1	..	
1 Cor. i. 3	..	..	1	..	
2 Cor. i. 2	..	..	1	..	} 7
Eph. i. 2; vi. 23	..	..	2	..	
Phil. i. 2	..	..	1	..	
iii. 20	1	..	..	..	

USAGE OF THE APPELLATIONS OF CHRIST.

	Real.	After words with the Article.	After Prepositions.	After words without the Article.	Total.
(14). Κύριος Ἰησοῦς Χριστός. *(Continued.)*					
Col. i. 3	..	..	1	..	
1 Thess. i. 1. *bis*	..	..	2	..	
2 Thess. i. 1, 2	..	..	2	..	10
i. 12. (but?)	..	1	..	..	
1 Tim. i. 1	..	..	..	1	17
v. 21	..	..	1	..	
Titus i. 4	..	..	1	..	
Philem. 3	..	..	1	..	

I do not find ὁ Κύριος ὁ Ἰησοῦς Χριστός.
ὁ Ἰησοῦς Χριστὸς ὁ Κύριος.
Ἰησοῦς Χριστὸς ὁ Κύριος.

	Real.	After words with the Article.	After Prepositions.	After words without the Article.	Total.
(15). ὁ Χριστὸς Ἰησοῦς ὁ Κύριος.					
Col. ii. 6	..	1	..	..	1
(16). Χριστὸς Ἰησοῦς Κύριος.					
2 Cor. iv. 5	1	..	..	..	1
(17). Ἰησοῦς Χριστὸς ὁ Κύριος ἡμῶν.					
Rom. i. 4	1	..	..	..	
vi. 25	..	..	1	..	3
1 Cor. i. 9	1	..	..	..	
(18). ὁ Κύριος ἡμῶν Ἰησοῦς Χριστός.					
Rom. v. 1. 11	..	..	2	..	
xv. 6. (In this place and Col. i. 3. the expression is, ὁ Θεὸς καὶ πατήρ τ. Κ. ἡ. Ἰ. Χ.)	..	1	..	..	
xv. 30	..	..	1	..	
xvi. 20. 24	..	2	..	..	
1 Cor. i. 2. 7, 8. 10; v. 4. *(bis)*	..	6	..	..	
xv. 37	..	..	1	..	
2 Cor. i. 3	..	..	1	..	
viii. 9	..	1	..	..	
Gal. vi. 18	..	1	..	..	
Eph. vi. 24	1	..	..	..	34
Phil. iv. 23	..	1	..	..	
Col. i. 3	..	1	..	..	
1 Thess. i. 3; iii. 13; v. 28	..	3	..	..	
ii. 19; v. 9	..	..	2	..	
iii. 11	1	..	..	..	
2 Thess. i. 8. 12; ii. 1; iii. 18	..	4	..	..	
ii. 14; iii. 6. (N.B. In each case the omission of the Article in question occurs after a Preposition.)	..	..	..	2	
ii. 16	1	..	..	..	
iii. 12	..	..	1	..	
1 Tim. vi. 14	..	1	..	..	

N.B. Κύριος ἡμῶν Ἰησοῦς Χριστὸς occurs after a Preposition Gal. i. 3.

APPENDIX II.

	Real.	After words with the Article.	After Prepositions.	After words without the Article.	Total.
(19). Χριστὸς Ἰησοῦς ὁ Κύριος ἡμῶν.					
Rom. vi. 11; viii. 39	..	..	2	..	
1 Cor. xv. 31	..	..	1	..	
Eph. iii. 11	..	..	1	..	
Phil. iii. 8	..	1	..	..	8
1 Tim. i. 2	..	..	1	..	
i. 12	1	..	..	..	
2 Tim. i. 2	..	..	1	..	

Χριστὸς Ἰησοῦς Κύριος ἡμῶν occurs Rom. vi. 23. after a Preposition.

I do not find ὁ Ἰησοῦς Χριστὸς ὁ Κύριος ἡμῶν.
ὁ Κύριος ἡμῶν ὁ Ἰησοῦς Χριστός.

INDEX.

The preceding pages will be found to contain Hints on the following subjects.

A.

	PAGE
Ἀββᾶ, a familiar appellation	200
Abstract Nouns, anarthrous in Homer	90
Adler	170. 237
Æthiopic Version	317. 392. 439
ἀμφότεροι, whether it can have the Article	297
Apocalypse, perhaps written in Hebrew	464
—— Critical difficulties of	467
Apollonius	3, *et passim*
Appellations, National, take or reject the Article	85
Aquila, Version by	128
ἄρθρον, etymology of	20
Aristophanes, when he prefixes Article to Proper Names	80
—————— passage in, considered	87, 88
ἁρπαγμὸς	370
Articles, French, not used arbitrarily	1
—— English one, (THE), whence derived	4
—— Greek, defined	6
Article and Pronoun not essentially different	13
—————— difference between unknown to Homer	10
Article without its Noun pronounced vehemently	12

	PAGE
Article in cases beginning with T	14
—— its reference always anticipative	23
—— not merely a Definitive	24
—— uses of, reducible to two	25
—— arising out of one property	31
—— its inclusive sense	41
—— its hypothetical use known to Homer	ib.
—— prefixed to Proper Names	71
—— not used to distinguish Sexes	72
—— in N. T. never redundant	137. 158. 229. 261. 298
—— a remarkable use of	231
—— marked by the Aspirate	388
—— a case in which it is necessary	391
—— not used for οὗτος	410
—— importance of its position	348. 436
—— Canons respecting, neglected in the *Codex Bezæ*	471
—— Hebrew, differently used from the Greek	119
—————— an use of	461
ἀρχή, well explained	278
ἀρχιτελώνης	232

K k

INDEX.

A.

	PAGE
Assembly of Divines	396
Assumption	23. 27
Athanasian Creed	240
Attributives, what assumable	56

B.

Bacon, Lord	172
Barabbas, whether surnamed Jesus	236
Bartimæus, conjecture respecting his name	196
Basil, St., a passage from, considered	352
Βασιλεύς, though definite, may reject the Article	36. 427
Beauty of Holiness	416
Bengel	142. 202. 441
Benoni Participle without Article	159
Bentley, Conjectures by	11. 91. 418. 425
Blood of God	295
Bode	124. 367
Books, Titles of, when they take the Article	204
——— of the N. T. carefully preserved	239
——— Canonical, none probably lost	326
Brother, a Christian Appellation	322
Bruce, Mr.	229
Burder's Oriental Customs	217
Butler, Mr.	441

C.

Campbell	193, *et passim*
Canon, a Coptic one	365
Casaubon	167. 216
Caution, extreme	17
Centurion, his Confession	237. 275
Chardin	226
Children, Christ's Disciples compared to	172
Christ, expected as the Son of God	166
——— his early occupation	191
——— place of his Nativity	215
——— number of his Passovers	245
——— the Creator	374
——— the Saviour God	396
Christ, ὁ ἀπ' ἀρχῆς	439
——— called Θεός, 240. 266. 314, 367. 370. 393. 402. 432. 457. 458	
Χριστός, whether a Proper Name in N. T.	193
Clarke	394. 453
Cocks, not commonly kept in Jerusalem	186
Codex Bezæ, or D. of Wetstein, 165. 228. Appendix.	
Complutensian, a Copenhagen MS. agreeing with	221
Connumeration	452
Convertible Propositions	54
——————— with Pronouns	44
Coptic Version	413
Copula	27, &c.
Corinthians, how many Epistles to the	324
Crellius and Socinianism	259
Crown-Imperial	141
Cup of Blessing	185

D.

Dathe	256
David's, St., Bishop of	Preface.
Day of Judgment, received doctrine of	147
De Missy	450
Demosthenes, when he prefixes Article to Proper Names	84
Difference in the Greek of the two Genealogies	124
Doctors, Jewish, titles of	242
Dodson, Mr.	275
Δυνάμεις	164
Durham, Bishop of	349, 378

E and η.

Eagle, the great	465
ἐγένετο, a sense of	213
εἷς and ὁ εἷς	442
ἔκτρωμα	335
Electa, a Proper Name	454
Emendations, conjectural, of N. T. gratuitous	*passim*
ἥλιος almost a Proper Name, 35, 160	
ἥμερος and αιος, Adjectives ending in	372
ἐν τό, a name of the Deity	542

INDEX.

English Version of the N. T.,
 revision of the 229
Ephesians, a Parenthesis in the
 Epistle to the 360
ἐπὶ marking a date, its Noun
 anarthrous 189
Epistolary address, form of, in
 Greek 456
Erasmus 395, 456
εὐαγγέλιον, not used in N. T.
 to signify a Gospel 346
Evil One, in the Lord's Prayer.. 139
εὐλογητός, its place in Doxologies 316
ἐξουσία 329

F.

Faith not all-sufficient 350
Fast, the great one 299
Figs, seasons of 197

G.

Gadara, its situation 144
Gaza, Theodore 3. 19. 26
Gehenna, the Hebrew........ 181
Gospels, order of the Four.... 202
Governing Nouns anarthous on
 account of preceding Prepo-
 sitions, &c.... note on p. 49, 161
Greek spoken Westward of the
 Euphrates 116
——— the native language of
 St. Luke and St. Paul...... 117
Greeks, the, altered foreign
 names 260
Grotius.... 245. 253. 261. 395. 454

H.

Harris, Mr. 3. 9. 27. 297
Hebrew *status constructus* 123
Henley, Dr. 293
Heraclitus 169
Hermann............ 87. 113. 325
Herodotus, when he prefixes
 Article to Proper Names.... 83
Hesychius, sacred Glosses in.. 205
Heyne 7. 11. 13

Homer, whether he uses the
 Article .... 7, *et seq.*
——— whether he prefixes the
 Article to Proper Names.. 72, &c.
——— passage of, considered.. 90
Horsley, Bishop 430. 443

I.

Idiom, English, wherein differ-
 ent from the Greek 36. 163
Ἱεροσόλυμα, its gender 128
Ἰησοῦς with and without Ar-
 ticle 218
Iliad 11. 90
Inscriptions, on the Article in . 286
John, St., alludes to the Descent
 of the Holy Ghost 250
——— and St. Peter, friend-
 ship of 262
Iscariot, probably a surname.. 272
Just One, the, a name of Christ 272

K.

καί 292
καύσων 422
Kennicott.................. 272
Killala, Bishop of 322
King, Mr. 142
Kipling, Dean.............. 472
Kluit, Adrian .... Pref.
κοσμικόν, a Substantive 415
κόσμος sometimes anarthrous.. 350
Krebs and Loesner 269
κρώβυλος 429
Κύριος, how used........... 206
——— Ἰησοῦς Χριστός, a title
 of Christ 366. 458
Kypke 128

L.

Lansselius 217
Laodiceans, Epistle to the.... 352
Lardner 325
Law, the Just not objects of .. 385
Lennep 26
Lessing, a conjecture of...... 204
Lightfoot 135. 147. 248
Lincoln, Bishop of 352. 371

к к 2

500   INDEX.

	PAGE		PAGE
Loaf, one used in the Eucharist	183	Nouns, same used for Substances and Attributes	62
Loaves, two in the Passover	182	——— though definite, anarthrous after Prepositions	98
Locke	63. 316		
London, Bishop of (Porteus)	221		
Lowth, Bishop	186		

M.

O and ω.

μὰ and νή, their Nouns have the Article 81
Macknight on the Epistles
     309. 403. *et passim*
Man of the Mountain of the House 270
MS. of Kennicott, remarkable reading of............... 179
——— the Alexandrian..277. 328. 397
——— of Profane Greek Writers, variations in, respecting the Article 79
——————————— Article, how interpolated in............ ib.
——— of N. T., Uncial not always the best 297
——————— the Moscow (or Matthäi's).... 236, and Addenda
——————— their excellence
     162. 242. 262. *et passim*
Markland.. 141. 320. 369. *et passim*
Marsh, Professor Herbert
     136. 168. 204. 224. 245. 441. 472
Mary and Zacharias, Songs of, from the Hebrew......... 210
Matthäi, 224. 244. 338. 429. 467. 471
——— a conjectural Criticism of 411
Michaelis, the Father........ 124
——— John David, conjectural Emendations of .. 227. 300
——— *Anmerkungen* (Annotations) of .. 131. 311. *et passim*
Monboddo, Lord 4. 35
Moschopulus 20

N.

Nestorians 282
Newcome, Archbp... 137. *et passim*
Newton, Bishop 383
Nineveh, its situation........ 287
νομίζειν Θεούς 88
νόμος and ὁ νόμος........ 303. 305

Old Testament, double sense in 403
ὢν has only a present signification........................28, 29
— incorporated with Active Greek Participles 29
ὢν understood after the Article.. 30
Oriental Tongues, usage in the 419
Origen 240. 449
ὅς why denominated a Subjunctive Article 19

P, φ, and ψ.

Paley, Dr. 353, 354
Participle with Article for Substantive.................. 160
——— and Verb, how they differ.................. 27
Particles much used by Plato.. 118
Paul, St., his style anarthrous . 302
Pearson, Bishop 207
φάτνη 216
Philo Judæus 38. 249
Plutarch 12
πνεῦμα, its senses deduced.... 125
——— when it requires a Preposition 430
πνεύματι used Adverbially,
     313. 333. 348, 349. 430
Poetry anarthrous 78
Porson, Professor 74. 78. 444
πρᾶγμα τό, an Euphemism.... 378
προάγων 245
Prophet, the expected one 254
Proposition Assumptive...... 30
——— convertible, its various forms 54
προσευχή 221
πρωτότοκος 373
Proverbial allusions, subjects of them definite 177
Psalm viii., its import examined 403
ψεύδομαι, what Case it governs. 271
πτερύγιον 135
Punctuation of the N. T. 168

INDEX. 501

Q.

	PAGE
Qui, its reference explained	18
Quirinius, enrolment under	213

R.

	PAGE
ῥά	76
Readings, Various, in N. T. supposed ones	124
———— Velesian	482
Reference obscure	18
Reinesius	285
Reland	137. 186. 260
ῥηθὲν τό, what meant by, in Citations	178
Romans, Epistle to, its subject	303
Rosenmüller	128, 201, *et passim*
Routh, Dr.	282

S.

Schleusner	2, *et passim*
Schlictingius, a conjecture of	314
Schoettgen	186, *et passim*
Scripture, Rabbinical mode of citing	198
———— Jewish, inspiration of	391
Servetus	266
LXX. not good authority for the uses of the Article	120
———— a conjectural emendation of	189
———— how they read Ps. lviii. 9.	336
Sharp, Mr. Granville, 60. 289. 362. 372. 379. 389. 392, 393. 432. 458	
Ship, the, (τὸ πλοῖον,) what meant by	158
Socinus	29
Son of Man, how applied to Christ	247
Sons of God, who	133. 263
Sophocles, a passage of	111
Spanheim	177
Spirit, the Holy Personality of	127
Stoics, how they distinguished Articles and Pronouns	9. 13
Stoning, manner of	251
Storr	463
Style of the N. T.	115. 191. 479
Suicer's Thesaurus	139
σύν, Ellipsis of	375

	PAGE
Sunday celebrated by the first Christians	330
Surenhusius	128. 178. 220
Swearing elliptically	15
Syriac and Chaldee	119
———— status *Emphaticus*	276
———— Version, remarkable readings of	345. 409

T and θ.

Tabor, Mount	137
Temptation of Christ, the scene of the	132
Tent, how applied by the Ægyptians	342
Texts, Calvinistic	269. 418
Θεῖον τό, a Pagan name of the Deity	445
Θεός, how used	206
———— its rejection of the Article, how limited	292
———— no lower sense of in N. T.	317
Thesaurus Theol. Philol.	179. 183
Thomas, St., his Confession of Faith	265
Thunders, the Seven	462
Tindal	435
τίς, Ellipsis	253. 343
Tooke, Mr. Horne	4. 28
τόπος ἅγιος	177
του for τινὸς (Atticè) not found in the N. T.	324
———————————— Feminine as well as Masculine	ib.
Transubstantiation	184
Trees of Life	470
Trinity, the Persons of the	330
———— Jewish	164
Trinity, Platonic	444
Trypho, his Treatise on the Greek Article	3
Twining, Mr.	2

V, U, and υ.

Valckenäer	74. 79. 264. 280
Vau Conversivum	463. 469
υἱὸς ἀνθρώπου	246
υἱὸς Θεοῦ and ὁ υἱὸς τοῦ Θεοῦ	134
ὑπάρχειν	370
ὑπερείδειν, what Case it governs	287

W.

Wakefield, Mr. Gilbert, 133. 136. 163. 190. *et passim*
Wells, places of resort for the profligate 244
Wetstein .. 165. 314. 402. 432. 485
White, Professor 479
Windet 181
Wolf 7
Wolffius .... 313. *et passim*
Wordsworth, Mr..... 56. 364. 380. 389. 394. 432. 458
Writer, an unknown, 152. 193. 362. 382. 395. 433

THE END.

www.ingramcontent.com/pod-product-compliance
Lightning Source LLC
Chambersburg PA
CBHW052110010526
44111CB00036B/1614